# The Internet Guide for New Users

# The Internet Guide for New Users

Daniel P. Dern

**McGraw-Hill, Inc.**
New York St. Louis San Francisco Auckland Bogotá
Caracas Lisbon London Madrid Mexico City Milan
Montreal New Delhi San Juan Singapore
Sydney Tokyo Toronto

**Library of Congress Cataloging-in-Publication Data**

Dern, Daniel P.
The Internet guide for new users / Daniel P. Dern.
p. cm.
Includes bibliographical references and index.
ISBN 0-07-016510-6—ISBN 0-07-016511-4 (pbk.)
1. Internet (Computer network) I. Title.
TK5105.875.I57D47 1994
384.3—dc20 93-25649
CIP



8 9 0 DOC/DOC 9 9 8 7 6 5 (PBK)
6 7 8 9 0 DOC/DOC 9 9 8 7 6 5 (HC)

ISBN 0-07-016511-4 (PBK)
ISBN 0-07-016510-6 (HC)

*The sponsoring editors for this book were Neil Levine and Jeanne Glasser, the editing supervisor was Nancy Young, and the production supervisor was Pamela A. Pelton. This book was set in Century Schoolbook. It was composed by McGraw-Hill's Professional Book Group composition unit.*

*Printed and bound by R. R. Donnelley & Sons Company.*

*All original artwork by Hannah M. G. Shapero.*

*For Bobbi*

# Contents

# Foreword

For many of us, the Internet provides the information highway. Along its scenic path is a plethora of roadside stops containing electronic libraries, facts, figures, and access to interesting people around the globe. In this book, Daniel Dern gives you both a road map and a driver's manual for getting on, getting to, and getting through the Internet. He describes what's available, where to find it, and how to use it. He craftily marks points of interest along the way.

This book is written in a delightful tone without using confusing jargon or computerese. It's written for regular people like students, teachers, business people, or other individuals with an interest in what the Internet has to offer. It may well be the only book you'll need to ever read about the rules of the road and the points of interest along the information highway.

The Internet offers a world of knowledge for those who venture down its path. It may take a little getting used to, it may take a bit of learning, but once you are there, you will find volumes and vast resources of information as well as connections to people around the globe.

*The Internet Guide for New Users* unlocks the car doors, puts you in the driver's seat, and gives you directions to the vast and wonderful world of the Internet. With this book, you can take a test drive. You are bound to find information and knowledge you didn't know existed.

Enjoy this book. It may be your first trip into the new world of the information era.

*Cheryl Currid*
*June 1993*

# Preface

*"This book—this book is all I need."*
*"How to Succeed in Business (Without Really Trying)"*

*"...what a long strange trip it's been."*
*The Grateful Dead*

Welcome to *The Internet Guide for New Users*—a book intended to help you learn about, join, and use the Internet. The Internet and its marvels are available to just about anyone who has any type of computer and modem, a telephone, and budget of a dollar a day—the price of a cup of coffee and the morning newspaper. You don't have to have a high-powered Unix workstation connected to a local area network (although many Internet users do). You can be an Internet user with an Apple Powerbook and cellular modem or an Apple IIc; a 386/486 PC running Microsoft Windows or a 286 or 8088 running DOS; an Amiga, an old Commodore or VIC20 machine, even a VT100 terminal or hardcopy teletype with a 300-baud modem.

The purpose of this book is to teach you how to be a *user* on and of the Internet. It won't replace a shelf-full of manuals but has enough information to get you started. It will give you some sense of what the Internet is, how to make use of it, and, most important of all, how to "think like an Internet user"—to use the pertinent facilities so you can keep learning about new resources and capabilities on your own and make educated guesses about how something new works. You'll get a mix of basic definitions and concepts plus state-of-the-art advice, a general introduction to the world of networks and comparison with and contrast to things like BBSs, CompuServe, and Dialogue.

As the book's title indicates, it's:

- For *users*—people who make use of it. This includes private individuals; students and teachers from K–12 through college; members of library, civic, research, and government communities; and business users in companies of any size and type. It isn't intended to teach you about Internet system administration or program development or how to set up a Gopher server or WAIS database.

- For *new* users—people who may never have used a computer, Unix, a network, or a modem before, who never logged into a BBS, sent an e-mail message, or even heard of the Internet. It's also for current members of the Internet community who haven't yet had the time to pursue all the virtual nooks and crannies on their own or are interested in the background and historical information I've collected.
- A *guide*—it's a combination Driver's Ed manual and overview. It isn't a complete Internet reference manual, resource catalog, or information list. It doesn't cover advanced topics like the **r** family of commands or how to set up wide-area filing systems.
- About the *Internet*—although I've taken a broad enough definition to include some aspects about Usenet/UUCP and BITNET, how Internet users can talk to folks on other networks like MCI Mail and FidoNet, and how these folks can use some Internet services.

If this book was for automotive Driver's Ed, it would be teaching you how to drive cars in general (not every car, not tractors or tanks) and how to read road signs and maps, how to drive on local roads and highways, cope with traffic, etc. You wouldn't expect it to cover every model of every car or every road in every state—but you'd expect that after a while, you would be able to apply your experience and learn specific new areas as needed.

When you're done reading this book, you should be able to:

- Get an account for yourself to gain access to the Internet or start arranging to get your computer, network, or organization connection
- Send electronic mail to other people on the Internet and on other networks that connect to the Internet, such as CompuServe and FidoNet and tell someone your "e-mail address," so they can send you e-mail
- Select and participate in the specific-interest-group Newsgroups in Usenet, the "BBS of the Internet"
- Recognize and use "smiley-faces" like :-) and :-[ and be knowledgeable in terms of "netiquette," security, and cost
- Connect to commercial and other on-line database and information services like DELPHI, Dialogue, Dow Jones News/Retrieval, the Library of Congress, LEXIS/NEXIS, and Mead Data (You may need accounts to use these services.)
- Browse and retrieve files from hundreds of software and document archives available via the Internet
- Use existing "Internet navigator" tools such as archie, Gopher, HYTELNET, WAIS, and WorldWideWeb and know enough to quickly figure out new ones as they become available

- Join and participate in electronic mail "discussion groups" and "mailing lists"
- See how being part of the Internet, and the Internet community, can make a permanent change in your business and even personal and social life
- Get help and resolve many common problems and use Internet in a responsible way

Because many aspects of the Internet change almost daily (while others remain constant), specific facts tend to go out of date faster than books like this can be put into print. I've "datestamped" as many of the facts as I can; for example, "As of early 1993 there were...." But the basic principles remain the same—many are essentially unchanged from a decade ago.

## How to Use This Book

You can read this book straight through or skip around depending on what you already know and what you want to do. Each chapter is as self-contained as possible and has cross-references to key sections in other chapters. You may want to read the book, or parts of it, more than once; much of the information may make more sense the second time around, in the context of related chapters. This is hard, strange stuff if you haven't been exposed to it before. (You won't really appreciate how weird it is until you yourself try to explain it to someone else.)

Read the "About" sections to get an introduction to and background, tips, and other general information about a topic. Read the "Using" sections to get specifics on how to invoke and use facilities. Be sure to read the "netiquette" discussions in each chapter and the netiquette section in Chap. 11—understanding and following these guidelines will make you a better user. Once you've read the netiquette discussions and obtained Internet access, don't hesitate to try things as you go along and to chat with your fellow Internauts.

Part 1, "Ramping Up, Getting Started," covers the basics of getting access to the Internet and general things worth knowing about the Internet. If you have never used a computer or network before, be sure to read Chap. 1, "Internet History and Technology: A Brief Introduction," and Chap. 3, "Internet Naming and Addressing." If you've never used Unix before, read Chap. 4, "Enough Unix to Survive as an Internet User." If you need to get an account on the Internet, read Chap. 2, "The Internet on a Dollar a Day: How to Get a User Account and Plug In." If you already have an appropriate account on the Internet, you can skip directly to Part 2.

Part 2 explains the "four basic Internet food groups": electronic mail, which lets you create and exchange messages; the Usenet, the "Bulletin Board of the Internet"; remote login (**telnet**); and file transfer (FTP). This is a good order to learn them, too, but any order will suffice. Do read the introductory chapter in Part 2—and consider rereading it both before and after you read Part 3.

Part 3 covers the "Internet Dashboard and Navigators"—the facilities that make it much easier to use the Internet and make being on the Internet vastly more valuable. Feel free to pick and choose here; what's most important is understanding the purpose of these tools and the way to use them.

In Part 4 you learn about being an "Internet citizen"—what you can and can't do, how to be a "good user," security concerns, how to understand where and when you pay and why. You'll also learn how to locate on-line, printed, and human help resources and how to do some basic problem identification and resolution—the equivalent of "checking your tire pressure and putting in gas"—and when you *should* yell for help.

Part 5 is where all the "other stuff" can be found. By the time you reach this, you probably have become somewhat fluent in "Internet-speak"—although you can just as easily begin reading in Part 5 to get a flavor of what the Internet is all about. Part 5 talks about the range of services and resources available from file archives and news services to global interactive Go and bridge games; gives you a look at what your fellow Internauts are doing; and launches you into the Internet as someone who is no longer a completely new user.

## Terminology and Conventions

I've done my best to follow common computer industry conventions in the text and examples. The names of facilities and commands have typically been highlighted in the text in **bold** fonts; for example, **telnet**, **Gopher**.

When a command syntax (its options and switches) is given:

- The portion in **boldface** is what you should enter.
- Generic terms such as **filename** should be replaced with a specific value, (e.g., enter *my-resume* where you see **filename**).
- Square brackets mean a value or keyword is optional (e.g., [ port ]).
- Ellipses (...) mean you can repeat more instances of whatever the ... follows.

In examples:

- Text in bold computer type is what you type or enter.
- Text in lightface computer type is what the computer displays to you.
- Text in text type is explanatory text from me.

One specific note on terminology: the term "FAQ" technically stands for "Frequently Asked Questions" but has come to mean, in most cases, "A list of Frequently Asked Questions and their answers."

The names and network addresses in most of the examples are derived from *Alice in Wonderland* and *Through the Looking Glass* by Lewis Carroll, the comic operas of Gilbert and Sullivan, Jonathan Swifts's *Gulliver's Travels*, and some plays by a guy named William Shakespeare.

## A Few Notes on How This Book Was Done

This book represents probably close to a year's worth of research and writing, over an 18-month span (during which I was also busy earning a living as a free-lance writer and trying to have a life) and also reflects a lot of learning, thinking, and participating over the past decade. I've spent uncounted hours at the keyboard connected to the Internet trying things out and exploring the burrows of GopherSpace, the interstices of the WorldWideWeb, and other strange places you'll be reading about.

I didn't keep careful track but probably exchanged thousands of electronic mail messages and read tens of thousands of messages in dozens of electronic mailing lists and Usenet Newsgroups, and uncounted documents. I wrote articles about the Internet for the trade press and spoke about the Internet at general-audience workshops, which taught me the hardest lessons of all, namely how to explain the Internet to people not yet part of its community and mindset and tell them what they want to know. I even became editor of *Internet World*, a magazine about the Internet. Plus all the other aspects of making a book which, like making law or sausage, are best left unmentioned.

For those who are interested in the technical aspects, this book was written on a 286-based IBM-compatible desktop PC with TTL-monochrome screen which I bought from MicroSmart in 1988 (upgraded to a 200-MB hard disk) accompanied by a Telebit 1600 9600-bps modem and an HPIIP laser printer. For software I used QuickSoft's PC-Write word processor (and generated ASCII text files) and PC-Browse pop-up browser, and the BitCom telecom program. Access to "the net" was through my account on Software Tool & Die's World public-access Internet system. WUMB-FM (91.9) and WGBH-FM (89.7) provided music to write by and took occasional requests, alleviating the need to buy a radio station. Toward the end, coffee came by mail from Green Mountain in Vermont, brewed in one of those funny push-down metal-screen dinguses and drunk in a Dick Tracy mug until the handle broke, and then I switched to the large Interop mug.

## Thanks and Acknowledgments

This book would never have happened without the help, suggestions, encouragement, reviewing, support, insights, and patience of a great many people. So herewith, three "huzzahs" and my earnest thanks to all who have helped me directly or indirectly in this book and those efforts that exorably led up to there being an Internet to write about and to my being in a position to do so. I'd like to explicitly acknowledge the major players, as follows:

First and foremost, Bobbi Fox, who warned me this would take longer than I thought (and it did) and also made numerous helpful suggestions.

Second, the people who helped make this book project happen: Mike Melford, one of the few lawyers who also has a Grammy award; Neil "Ralph" Levine, who got too much cornstarch on his mucklucks; Hannah M. G. Shapero, artist par excellence whose techno-cartoons you'll see starting in a few pages (she's also done covers for popular science fiction books such as several in Marion Zimmer Bradley's "Darkover" series); Ray Sarch, mentor, curmudgeon, and friend; plus Jeanne Glasser, Midge Haramis, Rachel Hirschfield, Nancy Young, and all the other folks on McGraw-Hill's editorial and production staff who were part of this 2-year charivari through cyberspace.

For the knowledge of the Internet and its innerds, and for too much information about Unix, I am indebted to hundreds of members of the Internet community whom I've talked and swapped electronic mail with and whose articles, essays, and Usenet postings I've read over the past decade. You will see many of these folks quoted or talked about in the chapters you're about to read but hardly all of them. The Internet is young enough that many of these folks were there creating and shaping it; this book is in part a chronicle of their work and a testimony to their vision and dedication. They deserve credit for helping assure the accuracy of facts in this book.

In terms of this book, I would like to acknowledge and thank in particular: Peter Deutsch of Bunyip, whose taxonomic perspective helped change how I think about the Internet; the "world-class" folks at Software Tool & Die, notably Barry Shein, Mary Reindeau, Elizabeth Newman, and Joe "Spike" Illaqua, who answered many questions and rescued the occasional "lost" file; techno-fan Alex Latzko; plus John Curran (NEARnet), John Eldredge (PSI), Brian Lloyd, John "Toaster" Romkey, NNSC alumna Karen Roubicek, and the several INTEROP's worth of INTEROPnet teams, who were subjected to a lot of weird questions over the past year or so.

People who helped by reviewing pieces and chapters of the manuscript include Marian Bremer, Tim Berners-Lee, Vint Cerf, Jim Conklin, Alan Emtage, VERONICA co-inventors Steve Foster and Fred Barrie, Ed "ezf" Frankenberry, Ira Fuchs, Bernard Hayes, Jack Haverty, Brewster Kahle, Steve Kent, Peggy Leedberg, Mark McCahill and the rest of Team Gopher, Alex MacKenzie, Cindy Mills, Charlotte Mooers, Craig Partridge, Jon Postel, Jeff Shaevel, Eugene "Spaf" Spafford, John Reardon, James Revell, Ed Vielmetti, and Chug von Rospach.

Other folks who helped out included Joann Anderson, Michael Baum, Tony Bono, Glee Cady, Ross Callon, Beth Cohen, Erik Fair, Geoff Goodfellow, Ken Greenberg, Phill Gross, Simon Hackett, Diane Hendry, Jim Herman, Ron Hoffman, Mark Horton, Jon Kamens, Peter Kaminski, Kibo, Brian and Connie Lloyd, April Marine, Carl Mikkelsen, the official "Old Network Boy" himself Mike Padlipsky, John Quarterman, Rob Raisch, Joyce Reynolds, Karen Roubicek, Jeff Schiller, Peter Sevcik, Mike Silton, Einar Stefferud, Michael Stein, Cliff Stoll, Brad Templeton, James van Bokkelen, Tom Wolf, and Steve Wolff, with special thanks to Steve Dyer and Elizabeth Newman who helped me stay on the net back when it wasn't as easy as it is nowadays.

I also want to thank the collective staffs of a number of those organizations where several or even all members have been of help: ANS, Beame & Whiteside, CERFnet, CNIDR, CNRI, DELPHI, Epilogue Technologies, FARnet, FTP Software, InnoSoft International, InterCon Systems, the Internet Society, the InterNIC, the Interop Company, ISI, JvNCnet, MERIT,

NEARnet, NSF, PANIX, PSI, SRI, TGV Inc., Uunet Technologies, and former staffs of some organizations that no longer exist, namely the NSFnet National Services Center (NNSC) and SRI Network Information Center (SRI NIC). Again: my apologies to anyone I've missed, and my thanks to all—I couldn't have done it without you.

## Your Comments, Opinions, and Feedback

Comments, corrections, opinions, suggestions, and other feedback can be sent to me at "ig4nu@world.std.com" (as in "Internet Guide 4 New Users") or by SnailMail to:

Daniel P. Dern
Dern Associates
P.O. Box 309
Newton Center, MA 02159

I do want to hear from you—but please understand that the realities of being a full-time writer are such that I cannot promise to reply to any or all, even with a simple acknowledgment. In particular, I can't answer your Internet questions individually; while your one question might only involve a few minutes of my time, collectively—as any author quickly finds out—they interfere with the job of writing. So please don't take it personally if you don't hear back from me. I will do my best to acknowledge important corrections and update information. Once you've gained Internet access, as of late 1993 you can also find information about this book via the Internet itself, on the Electronic Newsstand at gopher.enews.com (this will make more sense to you after you've read this book).

In addition to information you possess if you have this book, such as the Contents, Preface, and various excerpts, the Enews area for my book will include information excerpts, updates, questions from readers like yourself and my answers, and a copy of the shellscript in Appendix D (so you can retrieve it instead of having to type it in by hand). It's also possible I'll find ways to put other related stuff elsewhere on the net, so consider periodically doing a search for "ig4nu" using Internet search tools.

*Daniel P. Dern*

# The Internet Guide for New Users

Part

# 1

# Ramping Up, Getting Started

Chapter

# 1

# Internet History and Technology: A Brief Introduction

*"All the world's a net! And all the data in it merely packets*
*Come to store-and-forward in the queues a while*
*and then are*
*Heard no more. 'Tis a network waiting to be switched!"*

VINT CERF
*Rosencrantz and Ethernet*

*"Sufficiently advanced technology is indistinguishable from magic."*

ARTHUR C. CLARKE

## Meet the Internet—A Little Net History

As an Internet user, you'll be working on a network. You don't need an in-depth knowledge of computer networking to be an end user, any more than you need to know how television broadcasting works in order to use a VCR. However, *some* knowledge of how the Internet works, and of computer networking in general, may prove helpful in being an Internet user. For example, what's happening when you "do a file transfer"? How is the Internet different from—and similar to—organizations like CompuServe or the WELL—or your local bulletin board system (BBS)?

Equally, while the Internet should appear a "seamless resource"—one big network—to its users, some understanding of its structure is helpful to choosing where you want to fit in. For example, by having a basic sense of how the Internet works, you'll have more insight into:

- Detecting and analyzing problems you may encounter (many of which won't be your fault but will affect you)
- Picking the best way to do something, like locating a source for programs that do a particular task

- Learning what else the Internet has to offer, and discovering what other ways the Internet can be put to use

In this chapter, you'll get an introduction to networking and the Internet, including a very brief discussion of basic networking concepts and terms, and the history of the Internet. (Key tools like electronic mail—*e-mail*—remote login, file transfer, and Gopher will be defined in their respective chapters or sections.) Let's start with the most basic of network basics: what a network does.

## The electronic taffy-pull

Computers take information (data) in (input), push it around (processing), hang on to it (storage), and let go of it (output). In the very earliest days of computers, all this happened within one usually large air-conditioned room. Anyone who wanted to put information in or get it out had to go to the "computer room." Over time, researchers in the computer community have come up with ways to "get out of the room"—let users work from terminals far away from where the computer is, have the computer send output to equally distant printers, and even let the computers themselves communicate.

The facilities that provide these connections are called *networks.* The act of sending computer communications across networks and of connecting computers, is called *networking, data networking, data communications,* or even *computer communications.* Information flowing over a network is often called *traffic.*

In order to send data over a network, we need something called *protocols.* This refers to a set of preagreed-on ways that our computers will use to exchange information and to exchange signals regarding what they are doing. For example, Morse code, including special abbreviations, is a protocol for sending information as a series of dots and dashes.

Your VCR and its remote control use a protocol by which, for example, the "change channel" button send a specific signal, and the VCR recognizes that signal as meaning "change the channel, buster!" (But your VCR's remote control won't work with another VCR, or with your TV—if they don't speak the same protocol.) Similarly, the computer and network communities have developed numerous protocols for transmitting computer information over networks and for how computers and networks exchange information needed to manage these transmissions. (For example, "Hey, I got an e-mail message for Joe on the Macintosh in the corner office." "This is a file for the big PostScript printer on the second floor." "Slow down, I can't take information this fast!")

## Line, links, and cables

The connection that traffic flows over is called a *link,* or *line.* The amount of information that could be sent over the connection in a given amount of time, such as in 1 second (s), is called the *bandwidth, rate,* or *speed* of the line.

Computers deal with the world in the form of *binary numbers.* The smallest piece of information that can be sent is a *bit.* The value of a given bit is either 0 or 1. Information which is expressed using a sequence of these 0 or 1 bits is said to be *digitized.* For example, the music on a compact disk is stored as a series of 0s and 1s. A string of 8 bits is commonly referred to as a *byte.* A network connection's bandwidth, or rate, is usually expessed in terms of *bits per second,* abbreviated *bps.* Bit rates are commonly given using metric prefixes, such as kilobits, or kbps—thousands of bits per second, megabits, or Mbps—millions of bits per second, and gigabits, Gbps—billions of bits per second, terabits, or Tbps—trillions of bits per second, etc.

The first links were wire cables, used to connect computers directly with printers, and then terminals. Like taffy or pizza cheese, computer users began to st-re-tchhhh these lines, pulling the ends further and further apart. Down the halls, across the large buildings of the early computer companies and of universities. They started to get so far away, in fact, that the signal traveling along the line got so faint that the equipment at the other end couldn't hear it any more. And they wanted to go further—beyond the walls of the buildings, and the boundaries of the campuses, beyond where their organization was allowed to run wires of its own.

## Dialing for data: Boop boop a doop

One answer was to use telephone lines. The telephone system had the advantage that it went just about everywhere. By dialing the appropriate number, a computer user would have a connection between the two points needed. However, computers "talk" using electrical signals, but telephones work with information in the form of sound. To let computers send information over telephone lines instead of electrical wiring, devices called *modems* were invented, which *MOdulated* the computer signals into these tones and *DEModulated* them at the other end back into their original form. New protocols were also invented which translated the computer signals into tones that the phone lines could carry well enough.

Figure 1.1 shows modems and telephones being used to allow a telephone line to serve as the connecting line. This technique worked—so well that it is still in use today. Millions of PC owners use their modems daily to dial in to

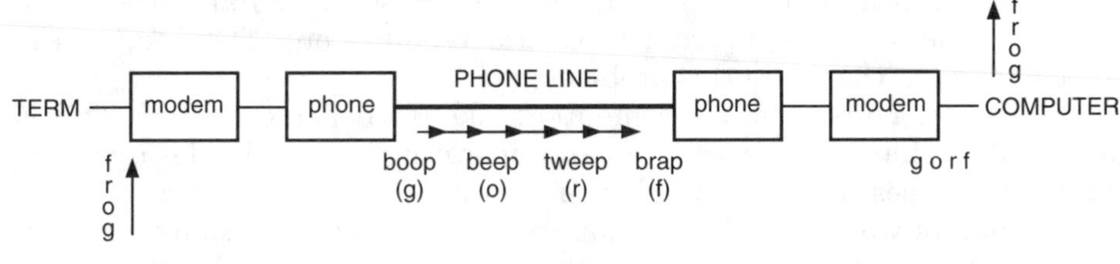


**Figure 1.1** Modems allow data to be sent over phone lines.

BBSs, electronic mail systems, the LANs at their offices, and the like. (And you may be using one to dial into the Internet, soon enough.)

### The limits of phone networking

As more people and organizations began using networking, both within their facilities and between sites, several important problems became obvious:

- Using leased telephone lines to support computer networking was expensive—particularly for the amount of phone service needed to carry the increasingly large amounts of traffic that computer users wanted to send.
- The set of telephone connections which were needed varied over time—users often wanted to connect to a different computer each time, and make use of these connections for different lengths of time.
- Users wanted to send information at faster rates, so they could get their jobs done quicker.

The answer was to first find ways to let many users, many computers, and many activities share a line and then to build networks from these shared lines that would provide the kinds of connections needed.

### Multiplexing: Time, space, and packets

There are a number of ways in which it is possible for computers to share a phone line. The first is to let computers make connections as needed by dialing up the other system, just like you call someone to talk with them. This is called *circuit-switching* because the phone network is being used to establish *circuits* between the end-points, done by switching how the lines connect. (Like those old telephone switchboard operators with their wires and jacks.)

This approach is simple—but doesn't fit the needs of computer communications very well. Only one computer at a time can use a given circuit, which isn't that efficient. Computers tend to communicate in a fashion referred to as "bursty," meaning there are periods of little or no traffic, such as a 3-minute pause while you decide what to do and then you transmit "send my database file to me," which results in "bursts" of traffic, like your database, for a while. Also, what do you do about "busy" signals, when there aren't enough incoming lines set up to a computer? As Vint Cerf, Vice-President of the Corporation for National Research Initiatives (Reston, VA) and one of the original members of the Internet community points out, "The bigger the switched network, the worse this problem gets."

Another approach is to let the computers take turns using the line. This is similar to time-sharing, where a computer operating system divides up use of computer resources among a number of users, giving each user a "slice" of time. Computers work very fast, while we tend to move—by computer standards—very slowly, wasting hundredths of seconds or more between each keystroke and entire seconds or minutes when we're thinking what to do next. To users, it appears as though each has the continuous dedicated attention of the computer.

Similarly, by using electronic devices called *multiplexors* in between a phone line and the groups of computers and users wishing to use it, it is possible to share access to this line. Several multiplexing techniques were developed. One, called *time-division multiplexing,* divided use of the line into fractions of a second, each slice given to a different user.

Time-division multiplexing improved the efficiency of the use of a line—but it meant that each user and computer was given only a fraction of the line's original speed. One advantage of this method was that each user had a guaranteed amount of bandwidth; one disadvantage was that it didn't deal with varying demands.

Other approaches are *frequency-division multiplexing* and *statistical multiplexing*. Frequency-division multiplexing works by assigning a different frequency to each connection. Radio and television use this technique—each station sends its information on a different frequency. However, the limited transmission bandwidth of the telephone lines in the late 1950s through early 1970s made this, too, inadequate.

## Packet switching

In the late 1960s, a new approach to line-sharing was proposed, called *packet-switching.* Here, instead of dividing up the line, multiplexing is done to the streams of traffic flowing between the users and computers. Each stream of data is divided into packets, much like a book can be disassembled, or separated, into a series of individual pages.

You can send a book to another destination through the post office page by page, by putting each page in an envelope, writing the destination and return address on the envelope—plus the page number, so the recipient could reassemble the pages into the original book. In terms of readability, you'd never know the book had even been taken apart. Similarly, it was proposed, computer users' streams of traffic could be split up into series of packets. Computers were able to do this for themselves, by running additional networking software. In addition to the data portion, the packet included a section called a *header,* which included information like the addresses of the origin and destination, the packet's ID number so the data portions could be reassembled in the correct order, the time the packet was created, and information to help verify that the packet's contents had been transmitted correctly. Since each packet would be labeled, you could connect up lots of lines, with a packet switch at each connection, or *node,* to form a *network.**

*The general definition of a **network** is that it is made up of **lines** and **nodes.** A line is a path along which resources (such as data) flow. A node is where lines intersect and where resources transfer to new lines. For example, rivers form networks. So do roads and so do railway lines.

Packets can be *switched* across the network—sent from one packet switch over a line to the next packet switch, which would examine the header to help it decide which line to switch, or *forward,* the packet to next. Using packet switching, many streams of data can be fed in and intermingled on a common line and sorted out back to their original form at the other end. Because of the information each packet contained, packets from one source can even flow over different *routes* and all arrive at the right destination and be reassembled. Similarly, packets from different users or programs at one computer can go to many different destinations on the network.

With enough information and calculating—exactly what computers are good at—the packet switches can *route* packets across the network, by examining the destination address, and deciding which line to send it along next. The post office does this every day, in delivering mail, if you think about it, except that they don't put things in any order. The process of sending a packet to one of many possible lines is called *switching,* like a train being directed to one of many train lines at a train yard by a train switch.

## Enter the ARPAnet

In the late 1960s, the U.S. Advanced Research Projects Agency (ARPA) launched another of its many serendipitous explorations of interesting technologies: to create computer hardware and software to do this packet-switching stuff and to build a small experimental packet-switching network to experiment with what they build. The goal was to economize on the use of "long-haul" broadband telephone lines (long-distance leased lines, which were much more expensive back then). The initial intent of the network was to connect a handful of heterogeneous computers among geographically dispersed locations. (Translation: computers from different companies, running different operating systems, too far apart to connect with electrical wires.)

The underlying purposes of this network were to help far-apart scientists work together and to research into more about how to use networks with computers. In particular, ARPA was interested in how to use one network for a broad range of types of activities, including for remote login access, exchanging files, and sharing resources such as printers. (But not electronic mail—"We didn't know that e-mail was important...," recalls Cerf. "We weren't even sure what it was at the time.")

This network became named the ARPAnet. Software for the ARPAnet was developed by Bolt Beranek and Newman, a consulting firm in Cambridge, MA, to run on computers from Honeywell. (These Packet-Switching Nodes were originally called Interface Message Processors, a.k.a. IMPs—a term rarely heard today.) ARPA also contracted a number of universities to develop the "host-to-host" protocols that let the computers use the network.

Because the packet switches were computers, the engineers were able to program them to do a number of tasks. One was to calculate the best route through the network (which changed as the traffic demand varied). Another

***The People Behind the ARPAnet and the Internet***

The ARPAnet was the result of many years of research, study, and dedicated work by people all around the world. Here are the names of a few of the major players, to give you some sense of things—but please remember that there were hundreds of people involved over the years; no disrespect is intended for those whose names aren't given here.

The notion of linking computers came from J. C. R. Licklider. Other concepts central to packet switching and the ARPAnet came from folks like Paul Baran and others at the RAND Corporation; from Leonard Kleinrock, who was writing his dissertation at M.I.T. on computer nets, which laid down the foundations for performance evaluation and design of networks; and from Kleinrock's fellow classmate Larry Roberts was experimenting with networking concepts at MIT's Lincoln Labs.

The team that built the IMPs included Robert Kahn, Licklider, Roberts, Steve Taylor, Dave Walden, Frank Heart, Alex McKenzie, and Severo Ornstein; the host-to-host protocol development was led by Steve Crocker and included a team of 40 or so graduate students including Vint Cerf, Steve Carr, Dave Crocker, Bob Metcalfe, and Jon Postel, many of whom went on to leading positions in the Internet community and network industry.

Many of these people are still actively involved in the Internet; you may well run into some of them at trade shows or see messages from them on Internet e-mail lists and Usenet Newsgroups.

was to determine whether parts of the network weren't working because of problems such as a line breaking or a packet switch crashing. The packet switches usually detected problems and recalculated routes fast enough that users rarely lost their network connection (although they sometimes noticed slower service).

On January 2, 1969, work began on software for the new network. On September 1, 1969, the Honeywell 516 minicomputer, which was the first of the network's initial four Interface Message Processors, arrived at the UCLA campus, air-shipped from Bolt Beranek and Newman in Cambridge. A few weeks later, this IMP and its three fellows located at Stanford Research Institute (SRI) in Stanford, CA, the University of California at Santa Barbara, and the University of Utah (shown in Fig. 1.2) were successfully exchanging packets with each other. And thus the ARPAnet—and the seeds of the Internet—was born.

## Networking for Success

The ARPAnet succeeded beyond anyone's wildest dreams, with the possible exception of its founders, who could see the future lurking implicit in their offspring's electronic insides. The new network grew—slowly at first, then more rapidly. And it kept growing.

For over a decade, the ARPAnet grew by an average of one new computer being connected every 20 days. The "coming-out party" for the ARPAnet was in October 1972—a public demonstration at the International Conference on Computer (ICCC) in Washington, D.C. Dr. Kahn had arranged for an ARPAnet IMP and terminal multiplexor to be on-site, demonstrating remote

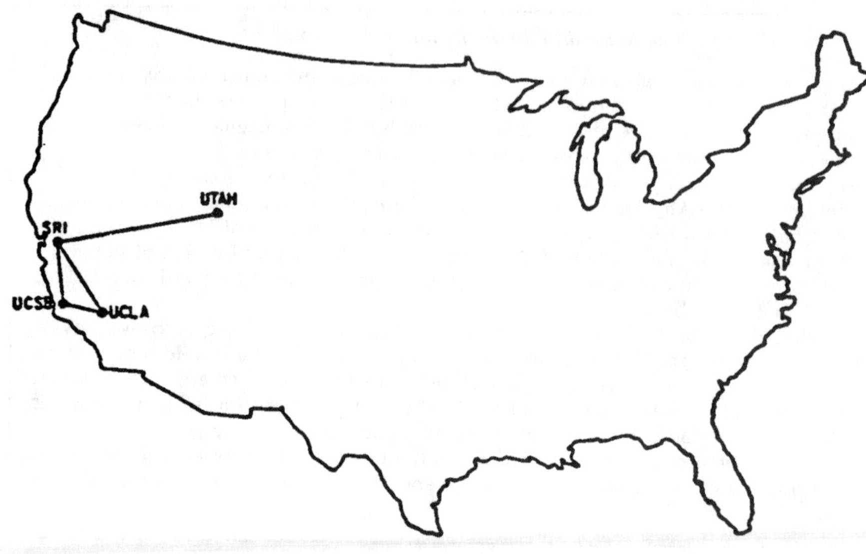


**Figure 1.2** The original ARPAnet.

connections to many of the participants' sites. "This was the first public demonstration of what packet-switching could accomplish, and made people begin to take this technology seriously," recalls Alex McKenzie, Vice President at Bolt Beranek and Newman. It was at this event that members of the global interconnected computing community began talking about the notion of a global network.

Meanwhile, the ARPAnet itself began spawning other networks, like starfish being cut up. In 1975, the ARPAnet was put under control of the Defense Communications Agency in the U.S. Department of Defense. (That's DoD DCA for you acronym collectors.) Here, ARPAnet technology became the basis of the Defense Data Network program, a.k.a. DDN.

### TCP/IP—Protocols, the next generation

The ARPAnet and the DDN originally used a protocol called *Network Control Protocol* (*NCP*). During the same period that the ARPAnet was growing, ARPA—known as DARPA, for Defense Advanced Research Projects Agency, from the mid-1980s until early 1993, when they re-renamed the agency back to ARPA—was developing satellite and radio packet networks which they wanted to connect to the ARPAnet.

NCP's design was closely tied with the then-current characteristics of the ARPAnet; to do this type of network interconnection required new ideas and new protocol capabilities. DARPA therefore sponsored development of a new protocol named *Transmission Control Protocol/Internetworking Protocol,* or *TCP/IP,* suitable for the interconnection of heterogeneous packet networks.

"The approach taken in developing TCP/IP, which was needed for projects that involved computers on different networks, like satellite networks, packet radio, and the ARPAnet all working together, represented what has become the 'Internet methodology,'" observes Jack Haverty, today Internetwork Architect at Oracle Corporation (Redwood Shores, CA), who at the time implemented the first Unix version of TCP/IP at DARPA's behest,* for the Digital Equipment Corporation PDP-11 minicomputer. The Internet methodology? "Build something because you need it, test it out in the real world, and only then generalize and standardize it."

To no one's surprise, the new protocol proved its worth over NCP. On January 1, 1983, the DCA officially changed the ARPAnet and DDN over from NCP to TCP/IP. The migration from NCP to TCP was one of the keys to the coming expansion of the Internet; this date is considered by many the official beginning of the Internet. (But not by all. Vint Cerf comments: "We had an Internet running in full swing in 1979—we just didn't insist everyone use it until 1983 when enough implementations [of TCP/IP] on different platforms were available.")

**More networks emerge.** In 1983, the ARPAnet was split, first logically and then physically as well, into two separate networks—the Milnet, DDN's unclassified operational military network, and the rest remaining known as the ARPAnet, which resumed the ARPAnet's original role as a research testbed and nonmilitary traffic highway.

Nor was the ARPAnet the only packet-switching network in town. Education and research sites whose activities fell outside the guidelines in the original ARPAnet charter formed networks of their own: CSNET (Computer + Science Network) and BITNET ("Because It's Time" or "Because It's There" Network). CSNET remained an active network until 1989, when the network was dismantled and its administrative activities merged with those of BITNET to become the Corporation for Research and Educational Networking (CREN). BITNET itself is still an active international educational network (see Chap. 17).

## From ARPAnet to Internet

One outgrowth of the ARPAnet was the concept of internetworking—the connecting of individual networks into a larger entity. During the same period, spurred by discussions at the 1972 ICCC meeting, research networks around the world began thinking about interconnecting with each other. After the

*DARPA subsequently funded a group at the University of California at Berkeley to incorporate TCP/IP into its Berkeley bsd Unix code. This strong association of Unix and TCP/IP continues to this day.

adoption of TCP/IP by ARPAnet, this began to happen, resulting in a "network of networks." The internetwork connections were made using network devices called *gateways,* in a similar way to how packet switches amalgamated individual host computers into a network.

Within the network industry, the technical term for connecting networks was *internetworking,* and for a network of networks, *internetwork* or *internet.* This new internetwork, centered around the ARPAnet, was dubbed the Internet, with a capital "I," often referred to by its users informally as "the net" (as if there were only one—which is how many Internet users feel). And it is this network which has evolved into the Internet we talk about and use today—and the network which this book is about. To quote Cerf:

> The real birth of the Internet was a combination of events and developments. There was the binding together of ARPAnet, packet radio, packet satellite, and, later, Ethernet network technologies. There was the idea of gateways, to interconnect networks into an internetwork. And encapsulating IP packets within lower-level *network* packets, which made it possible to bring up IP on virtually every type of network. The gateway concept plus encapsulation plus TCP/IP, which Bob Kahn and I designed and documented in 1973–1974, is the heart of the Internet. Many contributed to this effort and have been totally surprised, as were we, by the incredible explosion.

**The National Sciences Foundation, the NSFnet, and the NREN.** As the original Internet population climbed, and more bandwidth-intensive applications emerged, such as graphic-oriented workstations and supercomputer access, the service provided by linkages such as the ARPAnet's 56-kbps lines (once considered capacious) became woefully inadequate.

In 1987, the National Science Foundation embarked on a program to encourage the use of supercomputers, by setting up several Supercomputer Centers across the United States, and putting together a high-speed backbone network to access them, the NSFnet.

Rather than have organizations plug in directly to this new backbone, the NSF proposed a middle tier of networks between the NSFnet backbone and user organizations—"mid-level" or "regional" networks, providing (1) connections between the organizations that they served (e.g., the New England network would connect M.I.T., Harvard, various research laboratories, etc.) and (2) connections to the NSFnet backbone. For example, to connect to a computer in San Francisco, a user at M.I.T. would (1) be on the network at M.I.T., which (2) connected to the New England regional network, which (3) connected to the NSFnet backbone, (4) connecting to the San Francisco area regional network, (5) which in turn connected to the network at the remote computer's site. This may sound somewhat complicated, but the networks handled all this automatically.

A variety of for-profit and not-for-profit companies known as "network service providers" were formed to handle the actual creation and operations of many of these networks. In 1990–1991, IBM, MCI, and Merit helped form a company named Advanced Network & Services, Inc. (ANS) to provide service for the NSF's own NSFnet, first by providing a dedicated network of leased lines and network switches, later by providing service through a network ANS owned and operated that also served other communities besides NSFNET users.

At the same time, other federal agencies began building high-speed backbone networks of their own. National Aeronautics and Space Administration (NASA) created NSI, the NASA Science Internet, with two backbones: the NASA Science Network (NSN) and the Space Physics Analysis Network (SPAN). Over time, these networks have grown to serve over 100,000 users and tens of thousands of computers located all over the world.

### NREN, the U.S. "government information highway"

Many came to view NSFnet as a stepping stone and transitional program to building a high-speed U.S.-wide infrastructure of high-speed networks for use by government agencies, initially named the National Research Network. An E for Education was added later, turning the name into National Research and Education Network, or NREN.

NREN was part of the High Performance Computing Act proposed by Albert Gore, at the time Democratic Senator from Tennessee (as of 1993, Vice President of the United States). The NREN is the government program to provide next-generation networking facilities for its research and education communities, who need network access, whether at 2400 baud for electronic mail and curriculum development, T3 (45 mps) rates for high-speed scientific computing, or gigabit-to-terabits per second. NREN is a major effort by U.S. federal agencies including DARPA (renamed back to ARPA in 1993), the National Sciences Foundation (NSF), NASA, Department of Education (DOE), and Health & Human Services (HHS). The combination of the NSFnet, NSInet, and ESNET are called the Interim Interagency NREN.

Some of the uses envisioned for the NREN include:

- Enabling meteorologists on the West Coast to gather weather data from an array of instruments, send it to special analysis programs running at supercomputer facilities across the country
- Giving faculty and students remote access to hundreds of general and specialized university and public library catalogs, databases, and full text material
- Enabling researchers at different universities to share data and work together on data and computationally intensive problems such as medical imaging, materials analysis for better industrial processes, meteorological simulation, earthquake prediction, environmental analyses, and more

The technologies, speeds, and methods by which NREN service is provided to its users keep evolving. This is partly because the needs of network users keep growing and because faster network service continues to become available.

Steve Wolff, Director of Networking at the National Science Foundation, has also repeatedly stated that the goal of the NSFnet and NREN programs is to "provide network service, not build a specific network." As appropriate network service becomes available in the same fashion as utilities such as electricity and telephone service, this becomes increasingly possible. The NSFnet and NREN are rapidly turning into "virtual networks," with connections and service provided by a number of "network carriers."

As of early 1993, many aspects of the NREN program remain somewhat fuzzy, but there is no doubt that government agencies, the research and education communities, and the other myriad organizations and people who work with these groups all need Internet network service one way or another. In any case, the NSFnet and NREN are only part of the Internet within the United States—and the U.S. activity is only part, albeit a major one, of the total Internet phenomenon. This brings up one important, commonly misunderstood aspect of the Internet, namely, appropriate usage. Some discussion of this follows; for more specific information, see Chap. 11.

### Commercialization and appropriate usage: Respecting and getting around the government rules

The growing corporate membership, and corresponding increasing desire to use the Internet for business-related traffic and activities, raised one concern to a level too large to ignore—appropriate usage of government-subsidized parts of the Internet.

Back in the original days of the ARPAnet, the only organizations allowed to connect were those with needs that related to U.S. research or defense. The interpretation of these guidelines was often somewhat loose, particularly for e-mail versus other types of traffic, but even so, this was restrictive enough that "having an account on the ARPAnet" was definitely considered a privilege (and to many, a mark of status).

The original NSFnet charter was to support "educational and research" activity—and therefore only carry traffic relevant to such efforts. The occasional noneducational e-mail message or file transfer might be tolerable, similar to the occasional brief personal phone call made from work. But any significant use for inappropriate purposes was forbidden, impossible, or both.

Meanwhile, other organizations had begun an important new concept: "Commercial Internets," also called "IP Commercials." Offering a combination of backbone and regional services, organizations like Uunet Communications Services and Performance Systems International Inc. did something once unthinkable—offering connectivity into the Internet for anyone willing to pay for it, forming commercial IP networks like AlterNet (from Uunet) and PSInet.

In the same time frame, many of the "regional and mid-level" networks initiated by the NSFnet project also began accepting commercial users. Users on these individual networks soon discovered that they either couldn't or were forbidden to send certain traffic to other networks across the NSFnet backbone. There were clear definitions regarding which users or uses were okay and which weren't—but enforcing this in such a way to permit only okay traffic was not possibly by technical means. The result: many organizations, notably those connected to the "commercial" Internet portions such as AlterNet and PSI, either couldn't make connections to each other's sites (although they could other exchange e-mail) or were able to make connections via the NSFnet for uses that were contrary to the NSFnet appropriate usage policies.

In March 1991, the organizations running AlterNet, CERFnet and PSInet announced a solution: the formation of an interconnection point, named the Commercial Internet Exchange, or CIX (pronounced "kicks"), consisting of high-speed routers and links to its member neworks.

The CIX was formed so that links among the "AUP-free" (meaning free of the NSFnet AUP) would not make use of the NSFnet backbone and thus raise questions like whether a given activity met NSFnet AUP guidelines. For example, the CIX meant that "transit traffic," such as a file transfer session between sites on AlterNet and PSInet use a connection consisting of AlterNet-to-CIX and CIX-to-PSInet, rather than AlterNet-to-NSFnet and across the NSFnet to the NSFnet-to-PSInet connection.

Suddenly, pieces of the Internet with commercial intent were no longer forced to choose between being "islands" or the possibility that they might send inappropriate traffic over the NSFnet backbone. Steve Wolff offers the following reminiscence which may help you understand the importance of the CIX to Internet users (and of the Internet as a whole):

> When I was growing up, in Pennsylvania, we had two systems: Keystone Telephone Company and Bell of Pennsylvania. They didn't interconnect—so you had to have a phone and phone number from each, to be sure you could reach everyone. Similarly, without a CIX, you have only separate user communities, one for each commercial Internet carrier, and that diminishes the value of each to all their subscribers. The value grows as a power set—the total number of subsets—of the user populations.

For example, users on Internet networks connected by the CIX can perform activities such as cooperative program development, customer technical support (including remotely handled systems administration and network management), file backup, product-related e-mail and file transfer, wide-area file-serving and LAN interconnection, and distributed computing—without worrying whether a given activity is violating the NSFnet AUP.

"The CIX opened up a lot of commercial opportunities," says Cerf. "It is now a lot easier for organizations to interact with each other." Since then, other networks have also joined the CIX. This includes networks already part of the

Internet, such as NEARnet and JvNCnet, and other networks seeking to become part of the Internet, such as Sprint's SprintLink, and INFONET's InfoLAN service. (Note: CIX members are network providers, not individual users, LANs or sites.)

Meanwhile, outside the United States other major national and international backbone networks have been formed, such as CA*net in Canada, EBONE, NORDUNET in Europe, PIPEX and JANET in the United Kingdom, and WIDE in Japan.

The "topology" of the Internet and its constituent member networks is unlikely to stay the same; over time, the piece of the Internet you access may change which other networks it directly connects to. What is clear is that the ability to establish connections for commercial and unrestricted activity keeps improving—and that the Internet isn't just for research, education, and government use any more.

## The Internet Today

The Internet today is a worldwide entity whose nature cannot be easily or simply defined. From a technical definition, the Internet is the "set of all interconnected IP networks"—the collection of several thousand local, regional, and global computer networks interconnected in real time via the TCP/IP Internetworking Protocol suite—although parts of the Internet are running OSI protocols and carrying others such as Novell IPX and Appletalk and DECnet packets.

To many, the term "Internet" also includes the 1.5 million-plus computers attached to these networks, at thousands of sites in dozens of countries, belonging to thousands of business, government, research, educational, and other organizations.

And equally, for many Internet users—soon, perhaps, including you—the Internet is a global *community*—one with a very active life. The "population" of the Internet proper is several million strong—people whose computers are connected in a fashion permitting remote login, file sharing and transfer, and other real-time activities.

But the Internet also connects to many, many other networks for exchange of messages such as e-mail: on-line services such as CompuServe with its one million users, MCI Mail, GEnie, and others; networks such as BITNET, EARN, EBONE, NORDUNET, and virtual networks such as Usenet and FidoNet; and tens of thousands of companies, such as Digital Equipment Corporation and Apple Computers; and tens of thousands of BBSs.

Author and consultant John Quarterman in his book, *The Matrix: Computer Networks and Conferencing Systems Worldwide,* dubbed this superentity "Matrix," encompassing "all computers and networks able to communicate with each other." (Many call this "WorldNet" or the "Mail Internet.") This community was estimated at anywhere from 15 to 30 million as of early 1993—as big as the largest cities, larger than many countries. Quarterman first used the term "Matrix" in his article "Notable Computer Networks," *Transactions of the ACM.* The article capriciously grew into a book-sized object, *The Matrix,* from Digital Press. Because of its size and color, Quarterman's book is often referred to as "The Big Yellow Book" by many people in the Internet community. Figure 1.3 summarizes the Internet topology as of April 1993.

The Internet, and other parts of Matrix, provide the electronic home for leading-edge development, active discussions and information dissemination, and sets of relationships that span space and time and can obliterate differences in type of computer and operating system and even those of age, sex, ableness, national, and ethnic identity.

The Internet supports more "magazines" than are in the biggest newsstand, and hundreds of thousands of multiperson electronic conversations go on via e-mail every second. It offers access to information and resources beyond measure, limited only by your ability to find them (and possibly pay for their use).

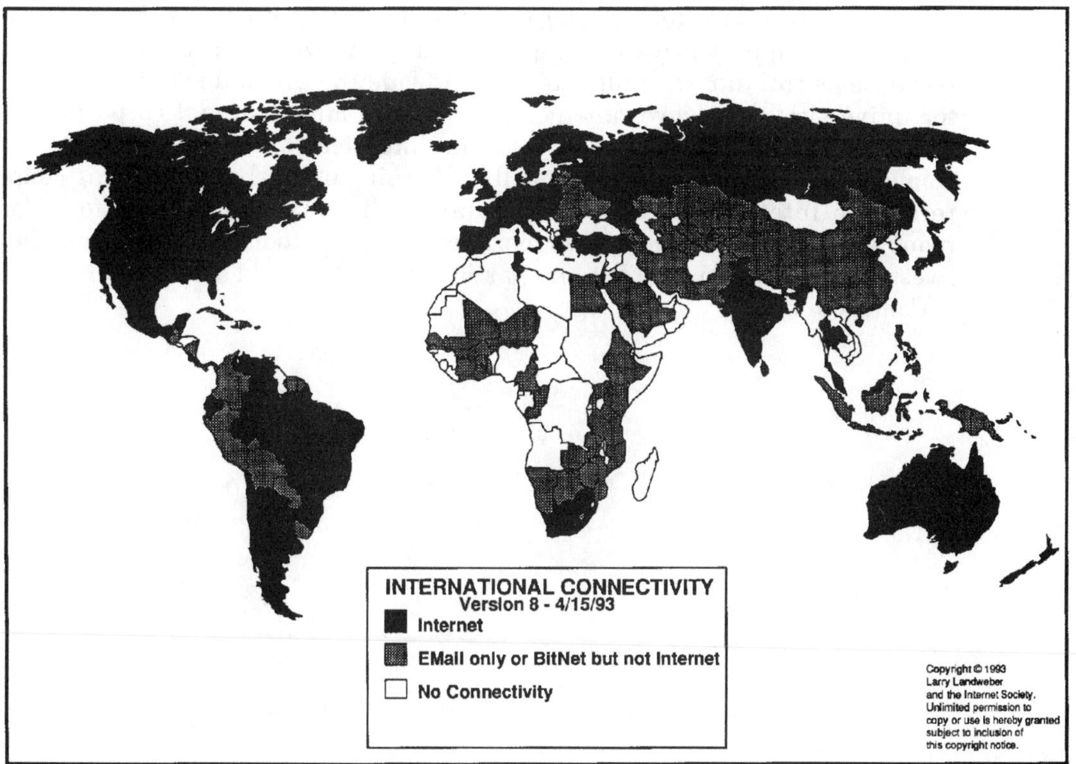


**Figure 1.3** The Internet today.

## Conclusion: The ARPAnet Legacy, the Internet Promise

The ARPAnet is often nicknamed the "grand-daddy of packet networks," and rightly so. (The more staid journals often say "progenitor.") For an experimental program, the ARPAnet was inarguably a rousing success. Twenty-plus years later, ARPA's modest experiment has yielded a legacy almost too mind-boggling to grasp.

One way or another, the ARPAnet, its direct and indirect network descendants, and its technological and cultural by-products touch a startling number of the industrialized population.

For people in the computer, research, engineering, and other technical communities, the ARPAnet's impact explicitly permeates the work we do and how we do it. Technical successes stemming from the ARPAnet programs—many of which were not on the original "shopping list"—included numerous landmark demonstrations, ranging from routing algorithms to packet radio, TCP/IP, and learning how and why networked individuals work together—and come to prefer being networked. And we learned many, many other lessons, such as the value of e-mail, how to create and be part of on-line communities and cultures—and that computer-based communication can be as real and valuable as the telephone or printed word.

Today, ARPAnet/Internet-type networks carry our credit card authorizations. They support private and public e-mail networks, BBSs, whose total populations run into the millions. They provide the communication backbone for universities, for government agencies, and multinational corporations. Application and "navigation" programs like electronic mail, the Usenet, Gopher, and WAIS, all of which you'll be learning more about in coming chapters, help Internet users create, exchange, and manage information. For many of us, being "on the net" is inextricably linked to our jobs, our personal lives, and how we think about and participate in the world around us.

Come join in.

Chapter

# 2

# The Internet on a Dollar a Day: How to Get a User Account and Plug In

*"'Come on, then!' roared the Queen, and Alice joined the procession, wondering very much what would happen next."*
*"The Queen's Croquet-Ground," Alice in Wonderland*

## So You Want to Join the Internet: What You Need, Who to Call, Where to Start

To use almost any service or facility these days, whether it's long-distance telephone calling, borrowing books from the public library, sending packages by overnight courier like Federal Express, or getting information from an on-line service like CompuServe, you need an *account.* Having an account makes it possible for the service provider to identify you as an authorized user and do billing and accounting. For many of these services, you also need some type of *equipment,* such as a telephone, terminal, or PC, and a *connection* to reach this service provider (e.g., phone line, Ethernet connection to your organization's network, etc.). Similarly, to use the Internet, you need an *account, equipment,* and a *connection.*

Today, any user can plug in quickly, easily, and affordably. If you've already got a modem and communications program, you're 95 percent of the way there. If you are part of a company or school that's already on the Internet and have a computer, an account, and a LAN connection or a modem, you're probably 98 percent there.

You'll probably need to learn at least a little Unix (see Chap. 4), but many of these systems provide on-line help tutorials. Once you've gotten your account and logged in, try typing "help" at the system prompt—and see Chap.

12 for more about how to get information and cope with some of the problems you'll inevitably encounter.

In this section, we'll take a look at how to go about taking the first steps to become an Internet user and what "an Internet account" consists of. The next several sections in this chapter then talk about how to get an account on the Internet, the related aspects of connection and equipment, how to decide what's appropriate for your needs, and how to find out who offers these types of accounts. As you'll see, these accounts run the gamut from a few services which may be adequate for your needs and only cost a few dollars per month—less than buying a daily newspaper—to accounts that give you access to the full suite of Internet services and resources, for about a dollar a day—to high-end, high-speed connections suitable for connecting an entire organization (this costs more but comes out to about the same cost per user per day).

The section "What's a Computer Account?" explains what an Internet user account is and how to get one even if you don't belong to an organization like a computer company or academic institution. (Short answer: by paying for it—and surprisingly little, as you'll see.) This section also covers other, possibly more convenient and affordable ways to make use of a limited—but quite possibly more than adequate—subset of Internet resources, services, and communities.

The section after that, "Networking-Style Connections to the Internet," covers somewhat more advanced (and usually more expensive) ways to connect to the Internet. It's not just for people with Unix workstations, either—it's just as available to people with Macintoshes, DOS or Windows PCs, and others, including notebook computers.

The information in this section may or may not be relevant to your needs and interest—or it may give you ideas about interesting possibilities you hadn't previously considered. For example, if you can't be connected regularly or for long periods of time—e.g., you have a notebook computer and want to work on planes—this may be an important solution.

The final section, "Internet Access Lists and Tips," tells you how to get current lists of Internet Access Providers and information from individual providers, brief information about the hardware and software you may need, and a few general tips. (The lists are long and the information changes frequently—so instead of getting the lists themselves, you'll learn how to find the most current information.)

### Who ya gonna call?

"How do I get an account on the Internet?" and "Who do I call to join?" are perhaps the most frequently asked questions asked in the Internet community. ("Who's in charge here, anyhow?" is another good one. It isn't asked as often, and is a *lot* harder to answer.)

Steve Wolff, the Director at the Networking Division at the National Sciences Foundation, states: "People wanting to connect to the Internet should call the InterNIC [at 1-800-444-4325]." And one network user quips:

"If you don't already know at least one person in the Internet community, you probably wouldn't be wanting access—so call that person!"

Answering these questions and gaining access may be as simple as making two phone calls or may involve several hours or days of research and decision making. The best choice will differ from person to person and place to place. I've offered some shortcuts to get immediate answers. But, like choosing a car or a long-distance carrier, if you're new to using the Internet, you may need to research and think a bit before making final choices.

If you're interested in using the Internet, hop on now, even with a dial-up terminal-style account that may involve message units or long-distance phone calls. You may want to start in with the first easy-to-find-and-use service, and reevaluate after you've racked up a few months of experience on the Internet.

"It's important to understand that you can explore the value of Internet membership for almost zero initial cost," emphasizes Barry Shein, whose organization, Software Tool & Die, runs The World, where several thousand individual end users (including me) have accounts that give us access to the Internet and its myriad resources. "You don't have to start big."

And don't worry about being locked in by what you do now; you can always get a new account. For individuals, you may have to let people know your new e-mail address. For organizations, it's actually more transparent, like switching long-haul telephone carriers. (Many organizations prefer to have connections to more than one Internet Service Provider, and many users have more than one account.)

As I said up above, this book *doesn't* include lists of Internet Access Providers (IAPs)—organizations who offer Internet accounts and access. The full list could be a book in itself. And the information changes so fast that any printed list is soon out of date. (I'll be using some IAP names as examples throughout this book—but this doesn't mean there aren't others or that anyone I don't mention is necessarily less appropriate.)

Instead, I'll identify some of the more established lists of IAPs and give you ways to get them—including via voice phone, fax, e-mail, modem—even sending a letter. If you're on the Internet, it's easy—if you know someone who is or who has e-mail access to the Internet, you may want to ask them to obtain the list(s) for you. Some of these lists are long—hundreds, even thousands of lines. By the time you read this, there may be an on-line database of IAPs you can query.

If you need to get an account, do read through this section. But if you know anyone who already has Internet access, contact them when you're ready to obtain your account—even if they don't necessarily know any more about this process than you do, they're in a position to help you by getting important information via e-mail. As you'll see, someone with an account on a system or network that can exchange e-mail with the Internet (e.g., America OnLine, CompuServe, MCI Mail, or on another network such as FidoNet) can help you.

To make things as easy as possible, I've put basic information on how to get an account as an individual early up in this section. You can always change or upgrade your type of service later, as you become more experienced and knowledgeable. Be patient. If you haven't used an on-line electronic service before, a lot here may be unfamiliar. You may, in fact, want to read through the rest of this book and then come back to this section, when you've got a better sense of what you're trying to accomplish. Or you can jump in and get that account in the next hour.

### To use the Internet, you need an account

You use the Internet by having *an account on a computer system that is connected to the Internet.* From your account on this computer, you can use programs that interact with other programs, resources, and services on one or more other computers also connected to the Internet, such as **telnet** (for remote login), **ftp** (for file transfer), front-end and navigator programs such as Gopher and the WorldWideWeb, Internet information services such as *archie*'s list of public-domain files and documents, and assorted other Internet facilities like the Internet Relay Chat. You can also create, read, and exchange e-mail with other Internet users (and programs) and read and post messages to the Usenet, the "BBS of the Internet." (These programs and services are all explained in upcoming chapters.) There are two ways to go about this:

- Get a user account on a computer with Internet access. This is discussed later in this chapter.
- Connect a computer which you have an account on to the Internet. This is discussed later in this chapter.

Before explaining how to get an account, let's take a look at what an "account" and "having an account" mean. (We'll talk about it again in Chap. 4.)

### What's a computer account?

An account on a computer represents a combination of authorization to use designated resources (programs, storage, CPU cycles, etc.) and information so the computer "knows who you are" and can properly assign, support, and account for your use of resources.

Accounts are generally found on computers whose operating systems can support more than one user. These are often called multiuser systems, or timesharing computers, and, depending on the computer and the type of users, can support hundreds, even thousands of users.

If you've got a DOS or Windows PC, or a Macintosh, by contrast, there may be no "account." Most unnetworked PCs make the assumption—quite possibly unwarranted—that only one person ever uses it or keeps files on it. Sometimes these single-user computers are set up with accounts, giving different users access to different sets of files and programs. With the advent of LANs, file servers, and other aspects of computing in the 1990s, accounts have become necessary even when using personal computers, to let many users share file servers, printers, and other resources.

Having an account on a computer system means that various resources are available to you, such as:

- Use of applications, such as text editors, word processing, spreadsheets, e-mail, software you've written, and on-line CD-ROM
- Space in the file system to create and store personal and/or work files
- Use of resources such as printers, modems, and other devices

The account definition may also include names and locations of files for your incoming e-mail, what shell (command processor) you'll be using to start with, and billing-related information. As a rule, your account will include identification information used by the computer or by the organization who owns it, such as:

- Your full name (e.g., Alice N. Wonderland). Among other things, the computer will use this in the "From" field of e-mail messages you create. On many systems, you can change the full-name value as you please.
- A user-name, or user-ID, which is unique at least to the system, probably to the entire organization. They're often no more than eight characters, particularly on Unix systems.

Your user-name is usually derived from some combination of your first name, last name, and initials; for Alice N. Wonderland, it would be:

Last name, all or up to eight letters—wonderland, wonderla

First initial plus last name—awonderland, awonder, a_wonder, a.wonder

First name plus last initial—alicew, alice_w

Initials—anw

First and last names separated by punctuation—alice_wonder, alice.wonder

Sometimes systems use combinations of letters and numbers, which may bear no relation to your name and appear completely random and meaningless, for example:

```
706302,546
abj09vm4
alice21
```

A user-ID almost never has spaces (i.e., you won't see "alice wonder"). On some systems, you may be able to request a user-name. Choose wisely; while it may be possible to change it later, this is the most important part of your "network identity," so be sure it's easy to remember.

A password is a sequence of characters, like the personal identification number (PIN) that you punch in when you're using your bank card to get money from the automatic teller machine. Passwords are typically at least six characters long. Different companies and systems have different methods for assigning passwords. Some will assign one; others will let you choose one—possibly rejecting your choice if it is too short or fails to meet other built-in rules. Guessed passwords are probably the most common method used to breach security on computer systems. For more about choosing, using, and guarding your password(s), see the discussion later in this chapter, and the section "Becoming a Secure Internet User" in Chap. 11.

On computers that use the Unix operating system, accounts also tend to include:

- Your "home" directory—The location in the file system of the directory space assigned to you, usually set as your "current," or "working," directory, when you log in.
- Default "shell"—The version of the Unix command interpreter started up for you (see Chap. 4).
- Login (and logout) file(s)—commands automatically processed when you log on to (and out of) your account.
- Default files for e-mail—One is in a directory "owned" by the system, for messages you haven't "picked up" and read yet. (We'll talk about how this is handled when your account is on "your" computer, which may not be always connected to receive incoming mail.) The other is a file known as a "savebox" or "mailbox" where messages you have read are put if you don't otherwise move or dispose of them.
- Group memberships, permissions, etc.—Which "groups" of programs and files you have permission to use.

Chapter 4 talks more about what having an account (on a Unix system) means.

## Terminal/Shell End-User Accounts—The Easy-to-Do, Inexpensive Way to Start

If you're reading this section, the odds are good that you don't yet have an account on the Internet (i.e., an account on a computer that connects to, and thereby gives you access to, the Internet). It's also possible that you *do* already have an Internet account—but want another because:

- It's through work, school, etc., and you want a separate personal account for other uses that are unrelated or inappropriate to your current account. For example, sending personal e-mail (such as job-hunting), participating in discussion groups, retrieving files unrelated to your work or school activities (such as Amiga software, genealogy research), and participating in multiuser interactive games (such as MUDs—Multiuser Dungeons—Go, Chess, or Bridge).
- It's going away soon, as you leave your current job, graduate, or move—and regaining access to the Internet is high on your priority list.

**_You May Already Be a User—Do You Already Have an Internet Account and Not Know It?_**

It is quite possible that you *do* already have an account that includes Internet access but aren't aware of it or aren't aware that your account gives you access to the Internet.

If your organization is Internet-connected and you have a workstation that is attached to your organization's network, you may already be on the Internet, and simply don't know it. If you are associated with a college, university, or other academic institution that uses computers and networks or work at a computer or engineering-related company, the odds are quite good, in fact.

Thousands of organizations around the world are currently connected to the Internet—with more joining every day. This includes the vast majority of 4-year colleges and universities within the United States, plus a startling number of community colleges and even high schools, junior high schools, and primary schools. Plus hundreds of libraries, thousands of computer and engineering and other technology vendors, plus large and small businesses, government agencies, and a surprising assortment of other organizations.

If networks and e-mail are used by your organization, you may at least be able to exchange e-mail with the Internet. If you're not sure, ask. (Try the network or computer center operations staff.)

It is quite possible that you *do* already have an Internet account but aren't aware that you have this account or aren't aware that your account gives you access to the Internet (see Box: You May Already Be a User).

In this section, you'll learn:

- The different categories of Internet Access Providers
- What kinds of organizations offer Internet accounts
- Other organizations providing limited types of access to the Internet.

### Anyone can get an Internet account

The good news for prospective Internet users in the 1990s is that *anyone* should be able to obtain some form of access to the Internet, as long as you have at least (1) a PC (or even a terminal), (2) a modem, and (3) telephone service. If you belong to an organization that is already on the Internet (e.g., a major academic institution, computer company, government agency, or any of thousands of other organizations and businesses around the world), it's likely that you can get an account as well as the associated hardware, software, and communications facilities that's paid for by your department or organization. If not, however, be of good cheer. Unlike in the 1980s, you should be able to get an Internet account with relatively little trouble—all it takes is a few phone calls or e-mail messages, making a few decisions, and being willing to pay at least between $10 to $50 per month. (How much depends on where you live and what kind of service you want.)

For people in North America near many major metropolitan areas, an hour or two a day's worth of interactive access to the Internet may be available for as little as $10 to $20 a month, or $1 to $2 per hour. That's comparable to the basic fixed-price rates at services like CompuServe and GEnie or a few hours per month of their charge-for-time services. Comparable in price, that is—

what you get for your money is use of the Internet, which may be very different in value.

If Internet access isn't a free, local telephone call for you, the cost of accessing the Internet may have to include long-distance calls as well. However, within the United States, services such as Sprint's PC-Pursuit, PSI's Global Dial-up Service, and the CompuServe Packet Network can bring long-distance calling costs down to about $30 to $50 per month or $1 to $5 per hour. (Some of these services may be after-prime-time-hours only.) That translates to full interactive Internet access for anyone in the continental United States for $2 to $5 per hour—still highly competitive with other leading on-line electronic services.

And for only $20 to $40 a month, anyone in the continental United States should be able to get an 800-reachable Internet account good for e-mail, Usenet News, and anonymous-FTP retrieving files from public archive sites through services such as PSILink. (This kind of access may also be available outside the United States, but I can't speak for how obtainable or inexpensive it will be.)

If electronic mail and access to the Usenet is all you want—and you don't require remote login, Gopher, or other Internet services that require real-time connections—you have many more options, ranging from free to dollars per month, available all over the world. In fact, depending on what you want, your current BBS and e-mail accounts (e.g., CompuServe, MCI Mail) may offer sufficient connectivity for your Internet needs.

Lastly, at the high end, Internet access is readily available to any and all organizations anywhere within the United States and to much of the rest of the world, for a cost ranging from several hundred to several thousand dollars per month. (This can work out to a few dollars or less per user per month—a bargain. More about this in the next section.)

If you feel you already know what's involved in getting and having an Internet account and simply want a list of "who's selling Internet accounts," feel free to skip ahead to the section "Internet Access Lists and Tips" at the end of this chapter. And if you belong to an Internet-connected organization, you can skip ahead to the next appropriate chapter after this one.

**Getting an account if your organization is already on the Internet.** If you belong to an organization with Internet connectivity, getting an account should be comparatively straightforward. (If you want access through your organization and they're not on the Internet, see Box: Help, My Organization Isn't on the Internet, Sigh.)

Contact your system administrator, network administrator, MIS department, or whoever it is that's in charge of computer accounts, and tell them you're looking for an account on a computer system with Internet access. As mentioned above, it is quite possible that you *do* already have an Internet account—but aren't aware that you have this account—or aren't aware that your account gives you access to the Internet. (See Box: You May Already Be a User.)

***Help, My Organization Isn't on the Internet, Sigh***

If your organization isn't on the Internet, you either have to persuade them to join and then have them give you an account—or you can seek an account somewhere else (which is most of what this chapter is about). Getting your organization onto the Internet may be oversolving the "want an account" problem—unless Internet connectivity can make a big (positive) difference to your organization and enough people want or need access.

Like getting an individual account, joining the Internet as an organization is a matter of evaluating requirements and matching them to the appropriate provider. Explaining how to do this is outside the scope of this book.

The last section in this chapter provides pointers to lists of Internet Service Providers and a short list of things your organization will need to know or think about.

If you can't get an account, for some reason, or if what you want to do isn't appropriate, see the section "Getting an Individual Account" below.

### Getting an Internet account as an individual: Public-access Internet sites, hurrah

In the 1990s, a variety of organizations have started up *public-access Internet sites,* offering "Internet accounts"—end-user accounts on computer systems that are in turn connected up to the Internet—to any individual ready to pay the quite reasonable costs and agree to the associated rules and regulations. What this means, simply, is you don't have to belong to any particular or special club, organization, or company. All you need is:

- A personal computer (or even a terminal), a modem, and maybe a software program—not even necessarily anything new or fancy. Low-power, old or used equipment costing as little as a few hundred dollars can be sufficient.
- A telephone, connected to an active telephone line, of course.
- The willingness to pay a reasonable price for the use of an account.

Rates for use of one of these Internet accounts range from $1 to $2 per hour, or fixed prices of $15 to $50 per month. Depending where you live, you might have to pay 1 to 3 times this amount for long-distance phone costs. This puts dial-up use of Internet services for an hour or two per day—more than adequate time for surprising amounts of e-mail, browsing Usenet Newsgroups, retrieving files, and noodling around at random—in the ballpark of $20 to $100 per month. That's a quite reasonable price for anyone needing access as a business resource and, at the low end, within the reach of student and personal budgets for limited, after-hours activity.

Dozens of such public-access Internet sites exist in leading metropolitan areas around the United States, from Alaska to New York, and in other countries. Every month brings announcements of public-access Internet sites in new areas and more ways to reach the existing ones affordably. The first public-access site to offer direct Internet access was The World, in the Boston area, run by Software Tool & Die. Among the other better-known public-access

Internet sites are NetCom and Portal (California), PANIX (New York City), Express Access (Washington, D.C.), Halycon (Seattle), MSEN (Southeast Michigan), Rock-CONCERT (South Carolina), and Demon and IBMPCUG (London). (I'll tell you how to get lists of these sites elsewhere in this book.)

Additionally, many of the Internet Service Providers have also begun offering individual end-user terminal-style accounts, such as CERFnet (San Francisco), JvNCnet (New Jersey), and CONCERT (North Carolina). Many of these sites also offer standard BBS-style services, such as local chat and conferencing, their own archives of downloadable files, and other services. For many users, however, the most important service is the site's connection to the Internet.

Accounts like these are the answer to many peoples' needs (including mine): an account "on the Internet" available to anyone, without the need to belong to some specific organization, or be a student or employee somewhere, that can be used freely and explicitly—and that, because we are paying for the service, we can expect a reasonably high level of system availability and reliability.

In addition to the use of any local facilities and archives, users with accounts at these sites have the ability to do standard Internet activities such as remote login and file transfer with other computers on the Internet, use Internet applications such as Gopher, WAIS, archie, WorldWideWeb, and the Internet Relay Chat (all covered in this book, of course) as well as exchange e-mail messages with other Internet users, and read and post messages to the Usenet (explained in upcoming chapters).

To use one of these accounts, you most likely will access the computer on which you buy the account as a *terminal user* or *terminal-style user* and equally likely, connecting your computer to one of these accounts via telephone and modem. For individuals who aren't part of an Internet-connected organization, this is the easiest and least expensive way to plug into the Internet. If you've already got a home computer—even an old PC or a terminal—and a modem, you've got all the equipment you need to start using the Internet.

Because this type of Internet account is the easiest—and most affordable—approach for many prospective Internet users, it makes sense to talk about this first. Then we'll talk about the more expensive and complex—but potentially more powerful—networking-style type of Internet account and connection.

### Connecting as a terminal-style user

Terminal-style connection refers to accessing a computer as if you are using a terminal, such as a Digital Equipment VT100, or even an old, slow teletype or thermal-printing "portable" terminal.

You'll need a PC (or a terminal). If you're using a computer, you'll also need a type of program called a *terminal emulator, communications program,* or *telecom program.* (Explained next, in "Terminal Emulators, or How to Turn Your Expensive PC into a Cheap Terminal.")

Unless your computer is directly connected to a local-area network or some other direct-wired network connection, you'll also need a *modem*.

If you've ever used any of the popular on-line services like CompuServe, DELPHI, GEnie, or MCI Mail, or a BBS, the combination of computer, modem, and terminal emulator program is probably what you worked with.

**Terminal emulators, or how to turn your expensive PC into a cheap terminal.** The odds are relatively high you have a PC or workstation rather than a computer terminal. *Terminal* basically means a keyboard and screen—no CPU, no RAM (random-access memory), no hard disk or floppy disks. A terminal by itself is about as useful as a telephone that isn't connected to anything or a set of stereo speakers with no stereo. A terminal can't run programs, download files, or do a spreadsheet. It needs to be connected to a computer—either by a cable or via a modem and telephone connection.

Most computer systems support remote access from terminals. A *terminal emulator* program is a program that makes your PC appear to be a terminal rather than a full-fledged computer. When you are running this program, your computer takes whatever you type at the keyboard, and passes it along nonjudgmentally through the modem, and displays whatever is sent back on your monitor's screen. As far as the computer you're accessing is concerned, you're using a terminal.

If you are going to connect via your modem, you also need a program that lets your keyboard (and mouse) input, and the computer output, be sent through the modem. These programs are often called *communications programs* or *telecommunications* programs. They typically include a terminal emulator function. Most communications programs also include functions to let you move copies of files between your PC's disk drives and the computer you've connected to. Uploading means copying from your PC; downloading means copying to your PC. You may also be able to capture a copy of your session—all input and output that occurs—to a file on your disk drive. (It often takes a few tries and some handholding by a friendly expert to get the hang of this. Pretty soon, you'll find you're uploading and downloading without much effort.)

The odds are high that one of these programs was included with your computer or modem. If not, or if you don't care for that program, others are available for $50 to $200 (and there are many excellent *freeware* and *public-domain* telecomm programs available, which won't cost you anything except possibly the cost of obtaining their files).

If you've got a multitasking PC, you may be able to use the terminal emulator in one window and do other things, like edit documents, in other windows, switching back and forth among the activities in the different windows.

So, a terminal connection means you are using a terminal emulation package (or a real terminal), connecting (probably by dial-up) to an account on a computer which is on the Internet. Figure 2.1 shows this arrangement. You open Internet connections between this computer and remote systems; to, say, download files to your PC requires a further step, such as using the

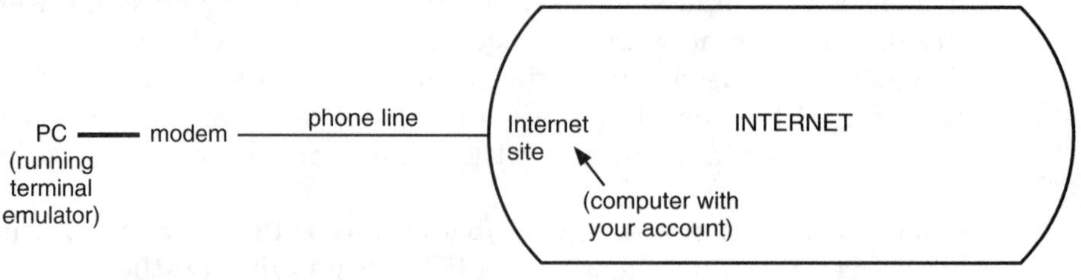


**Figure 2.1** Terminal emulation access to the Internet.

Kermit program/protocol (which can be done automatically). Also, your terminal emulation connection can only support one activity at a time (such as working with the remote system or doing file up- or downloads between your hard disk and the system your account is on.)

As a rule, a terminal-style communications program can only support one "session"—connection to a remote system over the modem line—at a time. This is easy, and the equipment is very inexpensive. Some people consider it to be limiting. (I have been using terminal-style access quite happily for several years now.)

**Modems and connect speeds.** Most Internet Access Providers have state-of-the-art high-speed modems which support the movement of data over phone lines at rates once impossible or prohibitively expensive. Up to even the late 1980s, modems that could support 2400 bps were all many users could afford, and modems only capable of 1200 bps were still common.

Today, modems offering effective speeds of 9.6 to 14.4 kbps are standard and available for as little as $200 to $300—with prices continuing to drop. And many Internet Access Providers also have arrangements with leading modem vendors to let users buy modems at near-cost prices. Most modems today include telecommunications software for your PC with terminal emulation functions.

On lines where the modems at both ends support the right matching protocols, speeds of anywhere from 14.4 to 56 kbps are possible, for certain types of activity like file transfer.

### Terminal accounts, a.k.a. shell accounts

A *terminal-style account* means you have an account on a computer, which you access from a terminal (or a computer running a terminal emulator), connected either by a wire or by a modem which you have plugged your phone line into. Terminal-style accounts are often simply referred to as *terminal accounts.* Another common term is *shell account,* referring to the fact that when you connect as a terminal on a standard Unix system, you are giving commands to the Unix shell (see Chap. 4).

Many Unix systems available to Internet users have been set up with "restricted shells" which only provide access to a subset of the computer's commands and resources. Other systems on the Internet, in particular many commercial BBSs, may have their own menuing system or graphic front end, such that you'll never see a Unix shell prompt directly or have to request it as a menu item.

### How to get a terminal or shell account

How you get a terminal account depends primarily on whether or not you belong to an "Internet-attached organization" (i.e., have an affiliation with an organization that has Internet access).

**If you belong to an Internet-attached organization.** If you work for an organization that's on the Internet, but don't have Internet access, ask your system administrator (or other appropriate authority) for an account on Internet-attached machine. You may be able to access this account over your organization's internal network; you may also be able to access it by dial-up from a computer and modem at home.

**Getting an individual terminal, or shell, account on the Internet: IAPs, PAIHs, PDIALs, and Internet BBSs, oh my.** If you don't belong to an Internet-attached organization, or any organization, the alternative is simple: get an account from an *Internet account provider,* an organization that sells individual end-user accounts to its Internet-attached computer. This kind of public access to the Internet is a relatively new—and exciting—phenomenon.

Up to the late 1980s, getting Internet access was difficult to impossible unless you were a student at an institution which was on the Internet or knew someone who could get you an account which technically you weren't entitled to have. Today, in the 1990s, things are very different. Anyone can have an account, simply by paying for it. You access this account with the same computer, modem, and communications software that you use to dial up BBSs, CompuServe, DELPHI, etc.

Barry Shein, President of Software Tool & Die, which runs The World, observes that public-access Internet sites offer the missing piece for many individual end users. "Hooking your site up to the Internet can be a big up-front investment. For some companies, the $10,000 to $15,000 in router hardware, and the work, may be more than they want to commit to. But now anyone with a terminal or PC and a modem can get login connectivity to the Internet."

Organizations offering terminal, or shell, Internet accounts go by a variety of names. Please bear in mind that these terms are far from standardized. As you read more about the Internet in other magazines and books and on-line messages, you'll see a wide variety of other terms and see these terms often used with very different meanings. In this book, the terms and definitions I'm using are as follows:

- *Internet Access Provider (IAP).* Any organization providing *access* to the Internet for users, in any fashion, including end-user terminal, or shell, accounts, networking-style (PPP/SLIP/UUCP) service, and full Internet site connections.

- *Internet user account provider (IUAP).* Any organization offering individual end-user accounts accessed as a terminal-style basis.
- *Public-access Internet host (PAIH).* A computer on the Internet with accounts available to the public, presumably run by an Internet user account provider. You won't see this term that much. *Host* generally means "a computer that is on a network."
- *Public-access Internet site (PAIS).* An organization offering public access to the Internet, generally end-user terminal-style and/or networking-style type accounts. (They have a public-access Internet host, obviously.)
- *Dial-IP provider, a.k.a. PDIAL.* A public-access Internet site—site offering Internet services that require IP connectivity to the Internet—that you can reach by dialing-up via modem. Same as public-access Internet site.
- *Free-net.* A BBS generally intended for people in the corresponding city and vicinity that offers some degree of Internet access.
- *Internet BBSs.* A BBS connected to the Internet. There are differing opinions as to whether this is a meaningful term, but many people use it, and there are some lists of "Internet BBSs."

Additionally, some of the existing conferencing network systems are beginning to offer full Internet connections to their users. DELPHI, for example, announced full Internet service for its users in December 1992. By paying an additional fee of $3 a month, DELPHI users can make use of real-time Internet facilities such as remote login (**telnet**), file transfer (**ftp**), archie, Gopher, and WAIS. Within a few months, thousands of DELPHI users had upgraded to have Internet access. (Over 20,000 had tried it for a month, according to DELPHI.)

For as little as $10 or $20 per month or $1 to $2 per hour, Internet Access Providers such as The World in the Boston area, PANIX in New York City, and Demon in London provide individual, unaffiliated users with terminal-style accounts.

From your account on one of these systems, you can make use of those Internet facilities that require real-time IP connectivity. In fact, you will be able to use the full range of Internet services and resources (subject to access and usage restrictions, and possibly needing accounts for certain services). Examples are file transfer (**ftp**), remote login (**telnet**), the Internet Relay Chat (IRC), Gopher, WAIS (Wide-Area Information Server) access to text datasets, library catalog access, multiuser interactive games like MUD and Go, and more. You can also read and write electronic mail, post to and read Usenet groups, and make use of other local programs and archives.

### How much does an Internet account cost?

The cost to access and use your Internet account can include:

- The charge(s) for use of the account itself.
- The cost of telephone service to access your account.
- Pay-for-use services. In using your account, it's possible to access and use a number of pay-for-use services on the Internet. These may either be charged to your account, or you may need separate accounts with these services. (For more about this, see Chaps. 11 and 14.)

**Does it cost to use my account, and if so, how much?** As mentioned elsewhere, hourly rates for Internet accounts range from $1 to $4 per hour; monthly rates from $10 to $50. Some public-access Internet sites charge by the hour, some charge a fixed rate for up to a certain number of hours per month, and some offer unlimited time for a fixed fee. (Usually during off-prime hours; some organizations consider "business hours"—9 a.m. to 5 p.m.—as "prime," and others may work on "programmer time," defining "prime time" as, say, 9 p.m. to 3 a.m. And some use a mixed approach.

World, for example, offers $20 for the first 20 hours per month, $1 per hour for additional hours. NetCom charges $17.50 per month. (All prices are as of early 1993.)

Some sites will also have different prices depending on whether you want to use only local services, such as e-mail and Usenet, versus services such as Gopher or **telnet** that require connecting somewhere over the Internet. Most sites will have additional charges for storing over a certain volume of files. Some, such as DELPHI, will have additional charges for transferring over a certain amount of files per month, and other fees. But it's still a bargain.

Your user fees, in turn, cover Internet-related and other operational costs such as the modems you dial into, the phone numbers, the computer, the salary time for the systems administrator(s) who manage the computer (including answering occasional user questions), service fees to the site's Internet Service Provider, Usenet feeds (possibly including special-interest groups such as the Dave Barry, Ms. Manners, and UPI newswire items from ClariNet), plus their rent, utilities, etc. (see Chap. 11).

Unlike services such as CompuServe, DELPHI, GEnie, MCI Mail, and other popular on-line services, who often "turn on the meter" when you access certain services or interest groups or send e-mail to and from other networks, these Internet Public-Access sites rarely add such charges. (But do read the contract agreement when you sign up. Some local and remote services may be available only by having an account with them or by otherwise agreeing to pay for their use.)

Some IAPs do charge more if you want to use facilities that require direct Internet usage, such as file transfer from distant systems and remote login, versus activities that involve only local resources, such as using e-mail and Usenet groups. This reflects the additional cost of sustaining the real-time link to the Internet and typically makes a difference of $5 to $10 per month on your bill.

Express Access (Baltimore, MD) and PANIX (New York City), for example, both offer accounts for users who want e-mail and Usenet and slightly more expensive accounts for users who also want real-time Internet facilities like remote login, Gopher, Internet Relay Chat, etc. As of late 1992, full Internet service cost about $15 more per month.

Much of your activity, in fact, may not involve direct use of Internet facilities. In my own case, for example, I suspect that indirect Internet facilities such as e-mail and the Usenet represent over 90 percent of my normal use of my account on the World. (I did make more direct use of the Internet while researching and writing this book, of course.) But the cost to be on and use The World is no greater than any other system I'd choose. And when I have the need, it is gratifying to be able to make use of the Internet to remotely login to other systems, or log onto The World from other Internet sites, to retrieve files and so on. One additional factor worth considering, even if you don't feel the need for real-time services: if your system is directly attached to the Internet, your e-mail messages will "hit the Internet" and get to you much faster than otherwise. Instead of delays of 30 to 60 minutes to "hit the net," your messages should get out within seconds. Depending on how fast the networks and mail systems at your recipient's site are, your message may arrive within seconds. (Or it could take days, due to delays by the mail systems at either end. Don't blame the network, though.)

**"Free" accounts: Do they exist?** As you begin using the Internet, you'll periodically run across messages from people seeking an account they can use for as little cost as possible—preferably a free one. It may be possible to locate and obtain a low- or zero-cost (to you) account. Many people have set up extra computers to offer direct or indirect Internet access. Many BBSs and Community Free-Nets similarly offer free-for-use accounts. And it's often possible to get an account through a local academic institution.But somebody's had to pay for the computers, the modems, phone numbers—if not you, someone else. The "price" you may pay for least-cost or free access is lesser service: restricted calling times or session length, limited resources, access phone numbers being busy frequently, no system administration, etc.

If your interest in using the Internet is strictly for personal, nonbusiness use, and not spending money is a priority, you may find an account that meets your needs. Your best bet may be an account on a system that isn't directly connected to the Internet, offering only e-mail, Usenet access, and other BBS features but not Gopher, **telnet**, etc. Prices here range from zero to $10 per month—and there are systems like this available as local phone calls in areas where full local-call Internet access has yet to arrive (see the discussion of *nixpubs* later in the chapter).

**The cost of the phone calls.** Unless you are on a computer network such as a LAN, or have been fortunate enough to set up a high-speed microwave link from your roof, you'll need to make a connect to your account via a phone call.

**Local calling—Do you have "unlimited" time?** If the phone number you call is local, and you're fortunate enough to have phone service that includes unlimited time to this number—an option usually available to "residential" but not "business" phone numbers—then you're in luck; the phone charges for your connect time won't cost you anything beyond the regular monthly cost of the line. Otherwise, you'll be paying something like "message units"—which can add up quickly for several hours per week of service. (Once you know where you'll want to call, check with your phone company to see if they offer an "unlimited calling" service to an area including this number.)

**Toll calls—Long-distance, 1-800 and 1-900 numbers.** If dialing up the system is a toll call, you'll pay for this, too, one way or another. Dialing directly may be the least expensive if you're only doing this occasionally. If you need to access your account as a toll call regularly, services like PSI's Global Dial Service and Sprint's PC-Pursuit offer one way to reduce your long-distance access costs.

In the section "Internet Access Lists and Tips," you'll see how to get current lists and information about Internet Access Providers. But first, let's take a look at a few other alternative ways to access some of the Internet's resources which may be more suited to your budget, location, and interests.

### If you don't need full Internet access—Other ways to access Internet accounts and services

If you don't feel the need for Internet facilities that involve being able to make real-time connections from your account to remote computers [e.g., remote login (**telnet**), file transfer (**ftp**), Gopher, WAIS, or Internet Relay Chat], you have a wider selection of additional types of accounts, and organizations offering them, available to you—and at potentially lower rates than a full Internet account. These types of organizations (for whom these is no collective term) include:

- Public-access Unix/UUCP sites (a.k.a. *nixpubs*)
- Internet e-mail/file-transfer services
- Public e-mail and conferencing services
- Other networks, conferencing systems, and BBSs
- Other methods (satellite, CD-ROM, etc.)

**Public-access Unix sites.** Public-access Unix sites are computers running the Unix operating system offering accounts to dial-up users. These sites can exchange e-mail and Usenet postings with the Internet even though they are not necessarily connected on a round-the-clock basis. (Every so often one of these sites connects to the Internet and turns into a public-access Internet site.)

These sites usually provide e-mail and Usenet Newsgroups. In addition, many of these sites offer gigabytes of popular software archives, local programs, conferences, and multiuser interactive games. There are hundreds, perhaps thousands, of such sites all over the world. Account costs range from free or donation to a dollar an hour or $10 to $20 per month. This type of site may be more accessible (and affordable) than a public-access Internet site, by being within your free (or cheaper) calling range. The advantages are that if you want primarily e-mail and Usenet Newsgroups but don't need real-time IP connection, this may be good enough. The disadvantage is that e-mail may be delayed additional minutes to hours in going between your site and the Internet. (In the section "Internet Access Lists and Tips" of this chapter, you'll learn how to get a copy of the "nixpubs" file which contains a relatively comprehensive list of public-access Unix sites.)

**Internet e-mail and file-transfer services.** Internet e-mail and file-transfer services are account offerings from Internet Access Providers designed to give specific types of service at bargain prices. Examples are e-mail and retrieving files from public-access archives—which you access via a 1-800 number for $20 to $30 a month. The advantages are that it is inexpensive and possibly 800-number accessible. If you travel or are not near a local public-access Internet site and primarily want e-mail, this type of service may be your best bet.

The disadvantage is that it has limited services and may not support English-like account user-IDs (e.g., you'll be *f062937@pml.com* instead of being *awonderland*).

**Public e-mail and conferencing services.** This category includes the several dozen big commercial public e-mail and conferencing services that can exchange e-mail with the Internet. There are dozens of organizations in this category, for example, America OnLine, AppleLink, ATT Mail, CompuServe, GEnie, and MCI Mail, to name only a few.

If you are already using one of these, you may be able to exchange e-mail with the Internet at little or no additional charge. Most services charge to send e-mail to other networks. (Some also charge to receive e-mail *from* other networks—so read the pricing information carefully—particularly before you join any electronic mailing lists or try retrieving software via e-mail.) The advantage is that these systems may be easier to use than a standard Unix shell. (Maybe not, however.) If you're already using one of these services, it may be easier, perhaps cheaper, not to have to get another account in addition. The disadvantages are that they have no Internet service except e-mail (and maybe Usenet), many e-mail-based services may not work well (e.g., long files, binary file attachments, name lists), and message-based billing may end up costing you a lot more. E-mail may be delayed minutes to hours between your account and the Internet; overall costs may end up being surprisingly high.

**Other networks and BBSs.** There are also thousands of other networks, such as BITNET (see Chap. 17), and tens of thousands of BBSs that exchange e-mail with the Internet and possibly also exchange topical messages with the Usenet, one way or another. (If you're a BBS-ophile, I recommend subscribing to Jack Rickards' *Boardwatch* magazine if you don't already. *Boardwatch* has been covering Internet news and services with increasing regularity.) The advantage is that it may be cheaper and have easier-to-use user interface. The disadvantages are possible delays in e-mail, restricted session times or time limits, or limited number of dial-up phone numbers available.

**Other ways to access Internet and Usenet services and information.** Lastly, there's an assortment of other ways to exchange e-mail or get selected types of access to the Internet and Usenet. Here's a few. Companies such as RadioMail Corporation (San Mateo, CA) provide e-mail gateways between the Internet and your company's networks, including popular LAN e-mail packages such as cc:Mail. One advantage of this approach is you can gain controlled Internet access without having to add more accounts for your individual users.

**UUCP connections.** UUCP, which stands for Unix-to-Unix Copy Program, is a protocol that lets two computers exchange messages and files over connections, including phone lines. UUCP is outside the scope of this book, but no Internet book would be complete without at least some mention of it.

Versions of UUCP are available for nearly all types of computers, including the Amiga, DOS PCs, and Macintoshes, as commercial products and through Internet archives. UUCP can include commands to modems to place a call to a specified phone number, so, for example, your computer can call another computer that supports UUCP and has "agreed" to exchange files with yours.

UUCP won't let you do any "real-time" Internet activities like Gopher or **telnet.** But it can be used to convey e-mail, files and BBS messages such as Usenet News articles. UUCP and similar protocols form the basis for worldwide e-mail and BBS-type network activity such as Usenet and FidoNet.

UUCP is not recommended for casual, nontechnical users. See the excellent books on UUCP from O'Reilly & Associates. The advantages are that it automates Internet/Usenet interaction and makes possible low-cost participation in global BBS and e-mail activity. The disadvantages are that it requires more technical knowledge and possibly more hardware and software than you've got or want to think about.

**Download software via UUCP directly from Uunet Inc.** Uunet Inc. (who also run Alternet) offers dial-in access via UUCP to its gigabytes of software for downloading at 50 cents per minute. Using your modem, call 1-900-GET-SRCS (1-800-468-7727). Login as "uucp." No password is required and it has speeds up to 19.2 kbps with PEP protocol. You'll need software to run UUCP on your computer; you may also need facilities like *uuencode, uncompress,* and/or *tar* to turn the files you retrieved back into executable binary files. The advantage is that no account is needed; it is ideal for specific needs. The disadvantages are that it does not provide on-going e-mail or other access or services. It may be more technically complicated than you want to get involved with.

**Internet printers and publishers.** Internet-based information such as Usenet postings and popular file archives are available via CD-ROM from organizations such as Walnut Creek CD-ROM (Walnut Creek, CA). Internet printers such as ZIP Press (Columbus, Ohio) will print and mail you a hardcopy of Usenet postings—or files sent to them via e-mail or file transfer.

**Nonnetwork solutions.** To send a message, sometimes picking up the telephone or sending a fax may be easier. And there may be times where sending a floppy disk or magnetic tape is easier than doing a long file transfer.

**Limited access to the Internet may suffice.** Depending on what you want to do, one of the above may meet your needs and budget. Figure 2.3 in the section "Internet Access Lists and Tips," provides a quick chart to help you match your needs to types of choices.

**When e-mail is enough.** If all you want to do is exchange e-mail with people on the Internet, you don't necessarily need a full-fledged account at an Internet site. You'll still be able to exchange e-mail with Internet users and also with users on other networks such as America OnLine, BITNET, CompuServe, FidoNet, GEnie, MCI Mail, and the thousands of individual BBSs around the world.

Don't underestimate the value of e-mail-only Internet access. Recognizing that e-mail access is much easier and more prevalent than full Internet connections, many organizations have provided e-mail-based access to their archives and services. For example, archie, the resource indexing facility created by Peter Deutsch and Alan Emtage, has an e-mail interface so you can do queries and obtain compressed listings. (This is explained fully in Chap. 10.)

Members of the Internet community have developed automatic e-mail interfaces to file servers, databases and database search tools, and many Internet information services. If you know how to use them, you can send e-mail to the right server and get back the file(s) you want—all through e-mail. (See the section on "Things You Can Do With E-Mail" in Chap. 5. You can even get, install, and set up your own e-mail-based applications.)

**Usenet access.** For many, access to the Usenet, the "BBS of the Internet," is the primary goal. (Chapter 6 explains more about Usenet and how to use it.) If that is your goal, look for a site offering Usenet (make sure it carries the Newsgroups you want). These sites usually also provide e-mail service.

**Archive access.** For access to specific public-access file archives, one of the limited-services offerings may be adequate. Many Public-Access Unix sites maintain copies of popular Internet public-domain software locally; also, popular collections of Internet public-domain software are available on CD-ROM. If you already have a CD-ROM drive, the $25 to $50 for a disk full of up to half a gigabyte of software can be a much easier solution than endless search-and-downloading.

In the next main section of this chapter, we'll talk about connecting to the Internet as a networking computer, versus as an end-user terminal-style account. You don't have to read it to understand or use the rest of this book; so if you aren't interested at the moment, consider skipping directly to the main section after that, where you'll find out how to locate the source of your new Internet account.

The last main section of this chapter, "Internet Access Lists and Tips," includes charts and lists to help you determine the best way for you to access the Internet and how to obtain information about organizations that provide appropriate services.

## Networking-Style Connections to the Internet: TCP/IP and PPP/SLIP for Dial-Up

Up to now, we've been talking about how to get access to the Internet by getting an account on a computer that is connected to the Internet—an account you obtained by either belonging to the organization that owns this computer or by paying for the account as a customer. To make use of this account, you use a terminal-emulation program on your computer—or perhaps an actual terminal—which you connect to the account-bearing computer via a telephone line and modem or a network cable.

That's one way. It's straightforward, easy, and inexpensive. It also leaves the worries of system and network administration to someone else, not you. (Other than those of being a responsible user, that is.) On the other hand, this method does have limits:

- You can only do one network-related activity—have one session—over this connection at a time, even if your computer is capable of having lots of windows and programs running at the same time.
- If you are transferring files between your computer's hard disk and some other computer on the Internet, you may have to go through additional—and possibly somewhat difficult—intermediate steps through the file system of your Internet account-bearing computer.
- If you're connected by phone, you're limited by the speed of your modem connection and the current system response time, even for reading through e-mail, Usenet News messages, and other files.
- You can't read your e-mail or Usenet messages except when you're "on-line"—connected and logged in.
- You often have to work through user interfaces that support few or none of your computer's nifty features like icons, graphics, menus, mouse-pointing, scroll bars, etc.

In this section, we'll look at another way: *networking-style,* using TCP/IP directly in your computer. You'll learn:

- What a direct networking-style connection is
- The advantages (and disadvantages) compared to a terminal-style connection
- What you need to do this

### A network connection to the Internet: IP, PPP, and SLIP service

In the previous section, we went to a great deal of effort to obtain an account on, and access to, a computer that was connected to the Internet. There's another way, however, points out Brian Lloyd, an internetworking consultant in Cameron Park, CA: "Get a computer that you already have an account on, and access to, connected to the Internet." In other words, connect *networking-style*—network your computer directly to the Internet. Basically, this means establishing a network connection between your computer—on which you have an account—to the Internet.

You connect your computer either through your organization's network which in turn connects to the Internet or directly through an Internet Access Provider that supports this type of service. Other commonly used terms for this connection method include:

- *IP connection,* because to communicate across the Internet and interact with the other attached computers, your computer must support and be running TCP/IP (more about this soon)
- *Packet access,* because your computer and the Internet are exchanging traffic in packet form

If your computer is connecting via a phone line, rather than via a network cable, it may also be called:

- PPP or SLIP service, because to establish this kind of connection over a phone line, you need to be running a *Serial Line Internet Protocol* such as *PPP,* the Point-to-Point Protocol, or *SLIP,* the Serial Line Internetworking Protocol, which will be explained soon.
- Dial-up IP service

To access the Internet in this fashion, you'll need an account of the appropriate type. Names for this type of account include IP account, PPP account, and SLIP account. Many people prefer this method of connecting to terminal-style accounts. If you belong to an organization that is on the Internet, and the computer—such as a Macintosh, Windows PC, or Unix workstation—in your office has LAN access to the Internet, this is what you'll probably have.

If you're an individual end user buying service through a public-access Internet site or other Internet Service Provider, you'll want to explore your options carefully. An IP account costs more than a terminal, or shell, account. There are cons as well as pros, including cost and possibly needing to know more about how everything works. But if this is what you want or need, it's worth it.

### Benefits of direct IP access to the Internet

By running TCP/IP directly on your computer, and establishing a network-layer connection, your computer can interact directly as a *peer* with the other computers and services on the Internet:

- You can access distant file servers and programs, download files from remote sites directly to your hard disk (and vice versa), and open windows to applications on remote systems as easily as you do to another local program.

- With a network connection to the Internet, you can have more than one connection, or session, open at the same time, and these can be from your computer to different other computers—even when your connection is over a phone line. For example, you can be remotely logged into a medical images database in one window, downloading Fortran programs in a second, running an earthquake simulation on a remote supercomputer in a third window, reading Usenet Newsgroups in a fourth, doing a client-server query to archie on a fifth, participating in an Internet Relay Chat discussion on a sixth, and so on. (Assuming your computer can support this much activity, of course.) Figure 2.2 gives you an example of this.
- Your e-mail is available directly on your computer; there is no need to download messages from a shell account. By bringing the Internet all the way to your computer, you avoid an immense amount of nuisance and message management.
- Use your native environment and user interface (e.g., Macintosh MacOS, Microsoft Windows, Unix X Windows) and have the same mouse, menuing, icons, and other features for your Internet activities that you already use for your word processor, etc.

### What you need to connect as an IP user

To establish an IP connection from your computer (or LAN) to the Internet, you'll need:

- TCP/IP software that can be installed and run on your computer. This includes the network protocol part of TCP/IP, so your computer can "speak" TCP/IP and thus communicate with the Internet. It also includes versions of the Internet-oriented software programs you want to run. Appendix A lists representative retail TCP/IP software products you can get.
- A connection to the Internet—by LAN, other network, or modem and telephone. If you are connecting via a telephone line, you'll need a modem, and PPP or SLIP serial line communications protocol software that runs on your computer. Many TCP/IP products will include software for either or both of these protocols. If you are connecting via a local network, you'll need the appropriate network interface card or other suitable connector. If you don't already have one, contact the appropriate person in your organization or your network or computer supplier.
- An IP networking account. You'll need an account for the appropriate service with an Internet Access Provider (and one or more phone numbers, if

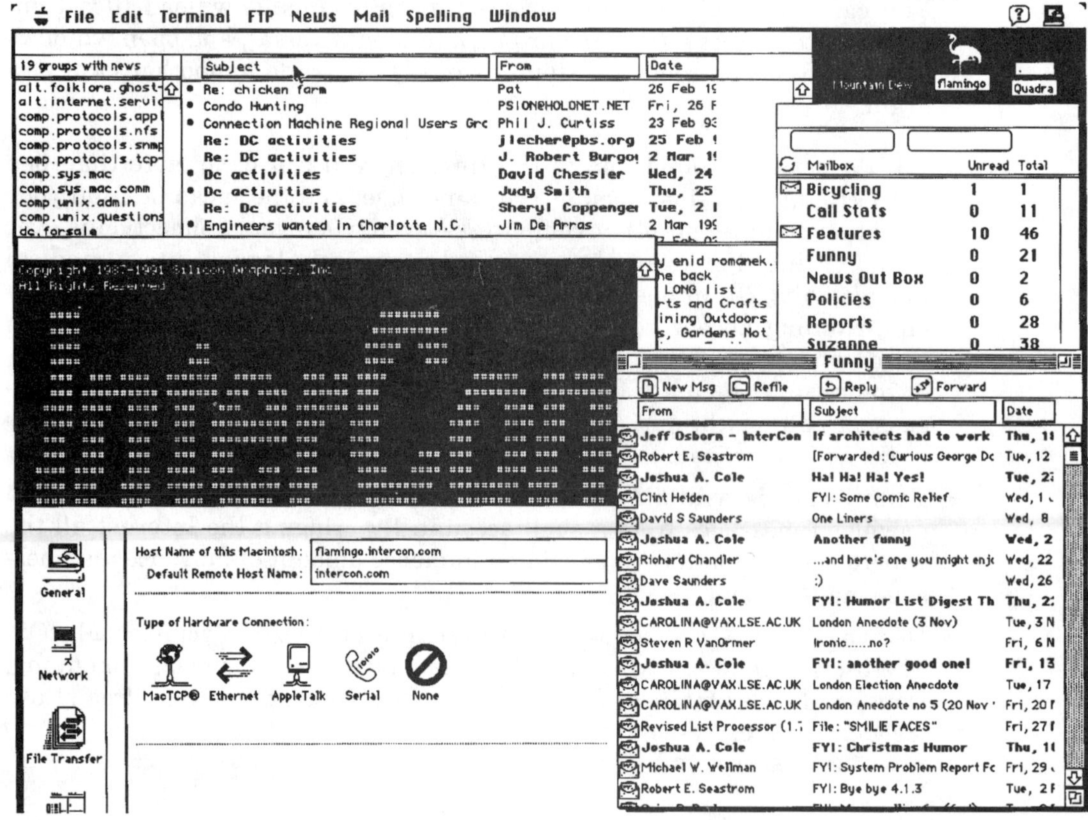


**Figure 2.2** Multiple activities over a PPP/SLIP connection.

you're dialing in) and may also have to arrange for services such as mail queuing (more about this soon), Usenet News feeds, or other information and support services. The next main section tells you how to get lists of Internet Service Providers that offer PPP and SLIP dial-up IP services.

Let's take a look at each of these steps in more detail.

**Getting TCP/IP software.** TCP/IP software is included in nearly every version of Unix and every Unix-type system (e.g., SunOS, Apple AUX, NeXt, IBM AIX, Digital Ultrix, or almost every Unix workstation). If your computer didn't come equipped with TCP/IP, you can add it. TCP/IP can be obtained for, and run on, probably almost any kind of computer you can find—even an old 8088-based IBM PC (the first model ever introduced)—and for pre-DOS personal computers running things like CP/M.

Commercial and/or free public-domain versions of TCP/IP are available for nearly every popular type of computer environment. For example, Digital, IBM, Novell, and other vendors offer TCP/IP along with their proprietary network protocols for most of their computing environments. More importantly, TCP/IP is available for most desktop computing systems including MS-DOS, Windows, MacOS, and Amiga. (See Box: TCP/IP Considerations for Windows Users.) That's right; even your Macintosh Powerbook or portable Windows notebook computer can connect as a peer computer on the Internet.

Single-user versions are available for a few hundred dollars or less; many TCP/IP-based applications include TCP/IP code bundled in, through licensing arrangements with the TCP/IP vendor. Plus there are public-domain and shareware implementations of TCP/IP available via software archives on the Internet. (Appendix A lists several TCP/IP vendors and products for personal computers. Public-domain software is available for many TCP/IP applications—see Chaps. 10 and 15.)

**A connection to the Internet.** If you belong to an organization that is already connected to the Internet, is internally networked, and you can connect your computer directly to this network (e.g., via a network interface connector), do so. (You will probably need to consult your local network or system administrator.) Otherwise, you'll need a network port you can dial into—that is, the

***TCP/IP Considerations for Windows Users***

If you use Microsoft Windows, by running TCP/IP on your PC you can have the same familiar and easier-to-use graphic-user-interface (GUI) you're used to rather than having to use character-oriented line-interfaces, and can work directly from your own computer rather than through another system. This applies to standard Internet facilities like remote login (**telnet**), file transfer (**ftp**), e-mail, Usenet newsreaders, and also possibly to tools like archie, Gopher, and WAIS.

The "innards" of TCP/IP products for Windows may not all be done the same way, however—and this may affect your ability to use your Windows PC on the Internet. Here's a few comments from Carl Beame, President of Beame & Whiteside Software, Ltd. (one vendor of a TCP/IP for Windows product):

- Is the version of TCP/IP a "True Windows Application" (TWA) or "Windows compatible"? If the latter, you may only be able to do a single activity through your TCP/IP window—and you can't switch to another application or window without closing this one (because you have to run Windows in Enhanced Mode and TCP/IP in the foreground). Being a true Windows application means it can run in protected mode, letting you switch among applications in other windows without closing or losing this one. A TWA also will let you iconify the window (create an icon to represent it) and support applications within the window that use the graphic, point-and-click Windows user interface.
- Does the TCP/IP run under DOS or directly under Windows? A version of TCP/IP written to work directly under Windows, rather than through DOS, won't let you run DOS TCP/IP applications from a DOS window or directly from DOS—and DOS programs may not recognize network drives created with a Windows TCP/IP.
- Speed—a TCP/IP written completely under Windows is not necessarily faster than one written completely under DOS. In fact, in many cases it is slower. How the Windows-TCP/IP interface is done can limit performance and other capabilities.
- Other important technical concerns include: Can you use multiple stacks (multiple copies of this or different TCP/IPs or even also other network protocols concurrently)? Does your version of TCP/IP use DLLs? Does it support the network adapter(s)? What TCP/IP utilities are included?

phone number of a modem connected to a communications port, which in turn connects to a *dial-up server*. (There are lots of types of servers, providing different types of computer and network services: *terminal server, IP server,* ***telnet*** *server, mail server, host computer*, etc.)

Don't worry—when you get your account, you should be given the appropriate phone or other contact information for the right type of server for what you'll be doing. This dial-up server may be part of your organization's network or may be run by an Internet Access Provider. Your organization may, in fact, have arrangements so you can use the dial-up services from one or more Internet Access Providers for access to the Internet when you're traveling or in a remote office.

**Modems for networking.** To use the telephone system to connect your computer to the Internet, you need a modem on your end as well (unless you have ISDN service where you live). While almost any full-duplex modem can support some form of networking connection, you'll probably want one that does it well, namely, at reasonable speeds.

Modems that support 9.6- to 14.4-kbps connections are readily available today—not only for desktop systems but even for notebook and palmtop-sized systems—for as little as $200 to $300. If your modem and/or communications software and your network access provider's modems support the same communications protocols, V.42bis, and/or compression algorithms, you may be able to get higher virtual speeds over regular dial-up phone lines, anywhere from 14.4 up to 56 kbps. (You'll see the most improvement on file, e-mail, and news transfers, the least on remote login sessions.)

**To use TCP/IP over phone lines: PPP, SLIP Serial Line Protocols.** To run a TCP/IP network-level connection over a telephone line (versus directly plugging into a LAN), your computer must also support an underlying protocol for communicating over a serial line (i.e., a phone line), in addition to TCP/IP. The serial line protocol performs functions such as packetizing, error control, and other activities to let the TCP/IP programs intercommunicate; it also renders your connection much less vulnerable to line noise and is used by the computers at each end to "handshake" on configuration settings for the session.

The serial line protocol you will use will be either PPP, the Point-to-Point Protocol, or SLIP, the Serial Line Internet Protocol. PPP is the newer of the two; it is considered more flexible and feature-laden than SLIP. (XRemote is a version of the PPP serial line protocol included with some versions of X Windows, "tuned" for use with X Windows.)

Most TCP/IP products you buy for use on PCs will include either PPP, SLIP, or both. There are also public-domain implementations available for downloading from Internet program archives (see Chaps. 10 and 15).

**An IP networking account—from your organization.** If you work for an organization that's on the Internet but don't have Internet access, ask your system administrator (or other appropriate authority) for an account on an Internet-attached machine or to attach your machine and network segment to enable Internet connectivity. You may also be able to access your organization's network by dial-up from a computer and modem at home.

**An IP networking account—for individuals.** As with individual terminal-style Internet accounts, you can obtain an account that lets you connect networking-style to the Internet through one of the growing number of Internet Access Providers that offer these services. Dial-up access servers are available in many locations (a.k.a. Points of Presence, or PoPs) across North America (and in some locations outside North America) via 1-800 and 1-900 numbers. The cost for such services ranges from $5 to $10 per hour to several hundred dollars per month.

### E-mail queuing

If you do decide to access the Internet on using your computer as a networking-style user, rather than as a terminal-style user to a user account, you will need a place where your incoming mail can be received and stored (i.e., an account on a *mail server* computer that will hold messages in its *queue* for you and a network address that causes e-mail for you to go to this mail server; see the discussion of *MX Records* in Chap. 3).

You retrieve your messages by dialing in to your IP account; your e-mail program retrieves them from the mail queue using an e-mail facility called the Post Office Protocol. Using this protocol, your e-mail program downloads any messages waiting for you from your account with the mail server, as a single *batch,* to your computer. You can then disconnect and, using your e-mail program as a local *mail reader,* read and process your downloaded messages individually. You can also create responses and new messages; when you connect to the Internet, your mail program can upload them to a mail server, which will in turn send them to their destination.

Many commercial and public-domain mail readers are available, such as Eudora, available in versions for the Macintosh and Microsoft Windows, and POPmail for the PC. Most Internet Access Providers that offer dial-up network service offer mail queuing; if not, you'll need to find a site that will act as your mail drop. Similar arrangements, protocols, and programs are available for browsing, downloading, and posting to Usenet, the global multitopic BBS structure of newsgroups that intertwines strongly with the Internet proper.

The next main section of this chapter, "Internet Access Lists and Tips," includes charts and lists to help you determine the best way for you to access the Internet and how to obtain information about organizations that provide appropriate services.

### Other ways to access the internet

In addition to terminal-style and networking-style, there are a number of other ways to access and connect to the Internet, other than as an individual user. Discussion of these methods is outside the scope of this book, but they are worth mentioning briefly:

*UUCP site.* See the discussion of using UUCP earlier in this chapter.

*X Windows.* If you've got the right software, connection (including one of the XRemote, PPP, or SLIP protocols, if you are working over a phone line), and account(s), you can open an X Window to another computer, across the Internet. (XRemote is a version of PPP for use with X.) However, you still need an account or other appropriate authorization to establish connections.

*Becoming an Internet site.* The big time—hooking up the computer(s) and LAN(s) at your organization as a site, either on a full-time or on-demand basis (i.e., your network dials up a connection to the Internet when a program needs access). The cost of Internet service can run anywhere from a few hundred to a few thousand dollars per month, depending on how much bandwidth you want (56 kbps, T1, etc.) and how much (or little) service and support. Other costs may include the telephone line(s), telephone and network equipment, and network and system administration—plus facilities, power, defining user and security policies, and the like.

Now let's take a look at how to decide which is the most appropriate way for you to access the Internet and how to get lists of organizations that offer the relevant services.

## Internet Access Lists and Tips

Now that you understand the variety of ways which you can connect to and make use of the Internet, this section will:

- Help you decide which one is most appropriate for you
- Help you get lists of current account providers for this type of Internet access and/or information about these providers
- Give you a sense of what questions to ask them (and what answers they'll need from you)
- Give you a few miscellaneous tips in arranging your Internet access

A number of factors will determine the most appropriate mode and provider for your connection into the Internet. Then once you've gotten your account and have successfully accessed it, you can begin trying the various Internet tools and services described in this book. (You can begin learning about them before you try them, of course.)

### Criteria for picking an appropriate type of account or service

Here are the key questions for you to consider in order to know what kind of Internet access will be best for you. You may want to go through this exercise again in another 3 to 6 months, and see if you're ready to "move up"—or, equally, to scale down to something less expensive.

1. *What do you want or need to do?* If all you want to do is exchange e-mail with Internet users, and access e-mail-served facilities, you have the widest range of choices. If you want to access Usenet Newsgroups, this narrows the field somewhat, but, depending where you live, you still have many choices, all in the same price range. Do you want to use services that require real-time Internet connectivity, such as remote login and file transfer, Gopher, WAIS, and other Internet navigators or the Internet Relay Chat? This shortens the list of account and service providers further and may increase the minimum cost depending on where you live—but you should still have several choices. For example, as I have mentioned elsewhere, probably 95 percent or more of my normal Internet activity consists of reading and sending e-mail and reading messages on the Usenet. Developers and programmers are more likely to also use file locating and transfer facilities extensively. Many users are hopping on the Internet for access to on-line database services and libraries. Still others are on the Internet to participate in multiuser conversations and games. Figure 2.3 provides a chart matching types of Internet services with types of accounts.

2. *What kind of computer and operating system will you be using (e.g., Unix workstation, DOS, Windows or OS/2 PC, Macintosh, Amiga, NeXt, or other system)?* This mostly relates to whether your system supports a terminal emulator and/or a TCP/IP protocol stack (and nearly every one should); otherwise, it shouldn't be a major factor. For example, for the past several years, I've been using a 286-based PC running DOS, using the communications/terminal emulator package that came with my internal modem—the same set-up system I use with MCI Mail, CompuServe, and other on-line services. Internet users have everything from Apple Powerbooks and Windows PCs to Amigas, NeXt machines, and old 8088-based IBM PCs.

3. *Will you connect by plugging directly onto a LAN, or by dialing up through a modem?* If you're connected directly to a LAN, you'll need some form of network protocol on your system (your MIS department should be responsible for this). If you're dialing up as an IP-speaking computer, you'll need TCP/IP plus a serial communication protocol such as Point-to-Point Protocol (PPP) or Serial Line Internet Protocol (SLIP) (or XRemote, the X Windows serial line protocol).

4. *If you're using a modem, what speed?* The speed (and compression protocols) your modem supports may help determine what is most sensible for you—and a faster modem will make a big difference in how you work on the Internet. Modems supporting 9.6 to 14.4 kbps are now in the $200 to $300 range.

5. *How important is the reliability and availability of your connection to the Internet?* Do you need assured 24-hour per day times 365-days per year business-grade service, or is your Internet activity likely to be for personal, non-time-critical use?

We like to think of network service and Internet system availability as

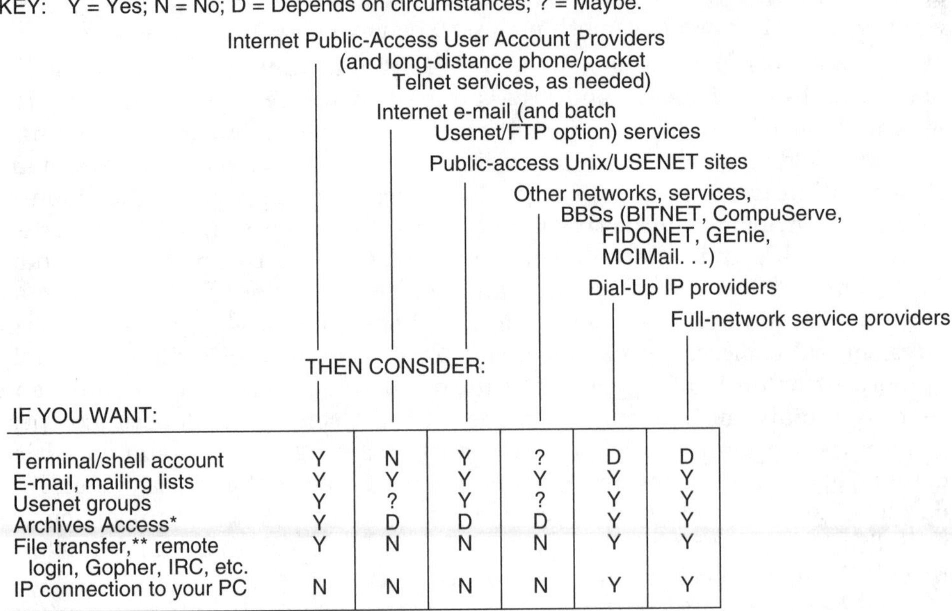

KEY: Y = Yes; N = No; D = Depends on circumstances; ? = Maybe.

THEN CONSIDER:

| IF YOU WANT: | Internet Public-Access User Account Providers (and long-distance phone/packet Telnet services, as needed) | Internet e-mail (and batch Usenet/FTP option) services | Public-access Unix/USENET sites | Other networks, services, BBSs (BITNET, CompuServe, FIDONET, GEnie, MCIMail. . .) | Dial-Up IP providers | Full-network service providers |
|---|---|---|---|---|---|---|
| Terminal/shell account | Y | N | Y | ? | D | D |
| E-mail, mailing lists | Y | Y | Y | Y | Y | Y |
| Usenet groups | Y | ? | Y | ? | Y | Y |
| Archives Access* | Y | D | D | D | Y | Y |
| File transfer,** remote login, Gopher, IRC, etc. | Y | N | N | N | Y | Y |
| IP connection to your PC | N | N | N | N | Y | Y |

*Including access via "ftp-by-e-mail" and other file/document server facilities.

**Other than via e-mail or UUCP facilities.

**Figure 2.3** The right Internet Access Provider for you.

being "utility grade," meaning that "network dial tone" is always there when you want it. The reality is, some network service providers are better than others. Many are run as part of an academic institution and may not be staffed as well or continuously as you need. How closely is the network monitored? How fast is service restored after outages? What is the ratio of dial-up ports to dial-up accounts? Unfortunately, as of early 1993, there were still no publicly available rigorous analyses of Internet Service Provider performance to help guide making choices. Equally, not all organizations running public-account Internet systems have the same degree of on-going system administration, frequent file system backups, attention to modem and computer status, etc. For example, I rely on Internet e-mail as a business resource, just as I do my MCI Mail account. I want to feel confident that the system will be up and running 99.9 percent of the time and that a modem port will be available on the first try when I dial up 99 times out of 100, and within 15 minutes otherwise. Software Tool & Die's World site has met these criteria; that's part of what I believe my fee goes to assure.

For other people whose use of the Internet is less urgent or nonbusiness, this may not be an issue—which means you can possibly use a less expensive, less formal service. (Price doesn't always equate directly to quality of service, however.)

6. *Where are you, geographically (city, state, and country), and how much does the phone call to connect cost?* Money may well be a factor in your decision, of course; different locations have different options available within local calling ranges. Also, do you expect to be calling mostly from one place, or moving around? Most—98 percent—of my access is done from my office; the rest is split evenly between being on the road, where making a long-distance call is often the easiest answer, or being at an event or organization that has Internet access, enabling me to remotely login to my account at World. Steve Roberts, the "Internet Bicycle Guy," by contrast, may be literally anywhere, as may hundreds or thousands of developers and managers who rely on Internet mail, Usenet News, and other Internet-based services on a daily basis. Thanks to wireless services like wireless data and cellular telephone networks combined with increasingly small, affordable (for some people, anyway) cellular and radio/modems, a lot of Internet users are using them to connect for e-mail and file-serving access.

7. *Are you financially able to stay connected for long (hours) or only for short (minutes) periods of time?* Connect time or phone time can be inexpensive or costly; IP connectivity usually costs several times what terminal access does.

8. *Are you circumstantially able to stay connected for long (hours) or short (minutes) periods of time?* Do you want to read e-mail and Usenet news when you're not connected (e.g., while on the plane, train, hotel room, or restaurant)? Cellular TCP/IP services can let you stay connected—but at a price. This can be a good reason to get dial-up IP service and use an "off-line" recorder.

9. *How much do or don't you plan to spend for Internet access?* The bottom line is what's your budget? $10 per month? $250 per month? $3,000 per month? Bear in mind that using the Internet, like any on-line service, can consume more time than you anticipate—and that you'll probably find more valid reasons to use the Internet as time goes on.

10. *How TCP/IP-savvy and Unix-savvy are you willing to be (e.g., what level of support do you want or need)?* As an end user, would you rather just be a terminal user and let someone else be sysadmin? If you're a company, will you dedicate a full-time person to this? Me, for example, I'm quite happy to be a terminal-style user. When I have a problem or question, I call or send e-mail to one of the system operators at The World.

### Getting list(s) of Internet Access and Service Providers

It's (finally) time to talk about how to get lists of Internet Access and Service Providers. First, there will be a summary of the types of accounts available, including:

- What types of services they offer
- Who they're appropriate for
- Advantages and disadvantages
- What kinds of organizations provide this type of account

- Representative providers
- Typical costs
- Good lists to check

Then, we'll discuss the leading lists and how to get them. This book makes no attempt to include full lists of who you can get Internet access from for several reasons. First, the information grows and changes too fast. Second, many of the lists are long—hundreds, even thousands of lines of information, almost a small book in itself—and you only need a few lines or pages of listings. Furthermore, there is no one "master list." There are a number of on-line lists of Internet Access and Service Providers put together and maintained by the Internet community, as well as printed lists, appendixes, and sections of books.

Each of these lists was created and is managed by a different organization or individual and each possibly contains different information, is organized differently, and is intended to serve a different need. Not everyone uses the same categories or tracks the same information and not everyone includes the same IAPs in their lists. Also, it's worth noting, some of the list makers are themselves selling Internet accounts and access. While no one is suggesting a given list may be biased, it is important to consider the source. So instead of including a partial or full, and inevitably out-of-date, list, I've done my best to identify what I and others consider to be the best lists offered by the members of the Internet community, and tell you how to get these lists—including ways for those of you who don't yet have an Internet account or access to the Usenet.

I've done my best to identify (or have organizations establish) ways that you can get computer access to this information if you don't yet have access to the Internet or Usenet, without having to unnecessarily consume the time of a person. In most cases, you don't need an entire list, just those entries that are appropriate—probably between zero and 20 providers that offer local-calling access in your city, area code, or state, plus another 5 or 10 that offer 1-800 or 1-900 number access.

If you have a computer and modem, you should be able to get information that's available on-line (1) if you already have an e-mail account that can reach the Internet or (2) by dialing up a system that you can query or download a list. In most cases, you'll be able to get the information you want by reading or downloading files, querying a server that has Internet Access Provider information, or sending an e-mail request to a server, which will send you back information without requiring attention from a person.

By the time you read this, one or more organizations should also have made this information available by voice mail requests for fax or hard copy response. Failing that, call a human being for information—or ask someone you know who's on the Internet for help. Once you've read through these chapters and decided what kind of service you want, you should be able to describe reasonably clearly and succinctly what you want, for example:

- Full Internet access as a dial-up terminal user during both business and evening hours, preferably a local call from San Francisco
- Inexpensive access to Usenet groups and some e-mail from Dallas, Texas, evening only OK.
- Dial-up network access with PPP any time, and I travel a lot all over the United States.
- My cousin's going to school in London, and we want to stay in touch by e-mail.

Remember that while many of the organizations mentioned will let you know who offers service, it's your responsibility to decide who's best for you.

## Summary of Internet accounts and providers by account category

The categories of Internet Access and Service Providers, and their offerings, can be grouped into several categories:

- Internet Public-Access User Accounts (terminal, or shell)
- Long-distance phone, Packet, or **telnet** connections to your account
- Internet e-mail, FTP, or Usenet accounts
- Public-Access Unix or Usenet site or BBS accounts
- Other networks, systems, and services that can exchange messages with the Internet
- Dial-up IP accounts
- Full network service (site) connections

Here's summary information on each of these categories, followed by the popular provider lists and how to get them.

### Internet Public-Access User Accounts (Terminal, or Shell)

*Services offered.* End-user accounts accessible via dial-up or remote login. Standard Unix (or other operating system) shell, or custom user interface and front-end Internet "navigator" software; Internet connectivity for real-time applications (**telnet**, **ftp**, **finger,** Gopher, WAIS, Internet Relay Chat, etc.). They typically also offer Usenet Newsgroups, selected software archives, and possibly special services, files, and activities.

*Appropriate for.* Individuals, students, and organizations who don't need full access; users who don't want to be responsible for system or network administration; mobile users who don't want to buy and carry a TCP/IP-capable notebook computer; entry-level users.

*Advantages.* Very easy to start and use; no system or network administration needed; no investment in extra hardware or software needed; inexpensive; can be obtained without impact on your network.

*Disadvantages.* Can require extra work to upload and download files and messages; is limited to one activity at a time.

*Provided by.* Public-access Internet sites, Public-access Internet hosts; some Public-access Unix hosts, Internet BBSs, FreeNets; also offered by some ISP and Dial-up IP providers.

*Representative providers.* CERFnet (San Francisco), DELPHI, Halcyon (Seattle), NetCom (San Francisco and Los Angeles), PANIX (NYC), World (Boston).

*Cost of service.* $1 to $5 per hour or $10 to $50 per month, possibly plus start-up and monthly administrative feeds.

*Listed in.* InterNIC provider lists, PDIAL list, and *The Internet: Getting Started,* by Marine, Kirkpatrick, Neou, and Ward (Prentice-Hall).

**Long-distance phone, packet, and *telnet* connections to your account—to get (cheaper) long-distance connections to your provider.** These aren't user accounts in themselves but may be helpful if access to your desired account isn't a free or low-cost call.

For many, dialing into the Internet Access Provider you want to use will be a free call. Most likely, this is the case if you're a residential user in a major metropolitan area and have "no message unit" service.

For others, however, accessing the Internet may be a toll call—possibly expensive—potentially costing as much or even more per hour than the actual connect time to your provider.

Many Internet providers offer "toll-free" 800-number service; however, this isn't necessarily cheaper; it just shifts who bills you. Peter Kaminski, author of the PDIAL list, suggests that other long-distance providers are generally cheaper.

There are several ways to reduce the costs of calling:

- Via public data networks (PDNs), such as the CompuServe Packet Network (CompuServe's network, which you can use without accessing the CompuServe system); PC Pursuit (SprintNet) ($30 for 30 off-peak hours at 2400 bps); BT Tymnet
- Via connection services from Internet Service Providers, such as PSInet's Global Dial Service. GDS provides "**telnet** servers," meaning you need a terminal emulation package and an account to login to; as of early 1993, GDS was about $40 per month for unlimited service at 2400 bps, accessible as a local phone call in major U.S. metropolitan areas.

Be sure to check with your phone company to see what services they offer; it's possible that your best bet will be to increase your calling range.

---

*Tip:* **Telnet** access from another local Internet site may be the cheapest. If your Internet Account Provider is beyond your free calling range, but you're near a Public-Access Internet Account Provider, telephone-call-cost-wise, consider getting an account with them, too, and then **telnet** (do a remote login) from there to your account. For example, if your Internet account is on Halcyon in Seattle, but you're in San Francisco, also get an account with NetCom; dial up NetCom, log in to this account, and then log in remotely over the Internet to your account on Halcyon. (Be sure the site considers this an acceptable use of their service.)

---

*Representative providers.* BT Tymnet, CompuServe packet network, PC-Pursuit, PSI Global Dial-up Service

*Typical costs.* $30 per month for 30 nonprime hours, $40 per month unlimited.

*Listed in.* InterNIC provider lists and PDIAL list

### Internet e-mail, FTP, Usenet accounts

*Offering.* Dial-up terminal accounts for sending and receiving Internet e-mail; may also support anonymous-FTP connections and access to Usenet groups.

*Appropriate for.* Users mostly seeking e-mail, maybe for anonymous-FTP or Usenet access.

*Advantages.* Often fixed-price; often bundled in with 1-800 access; systems are usually directly on the Internet, so e-mail to and from other Internet users is not subject to potential delays through e-mail gateways (e.g., versus coming from MCI Mail).

*Disadvantages.* User names often cryptic; access is as batch downloads, which may not match your needs for accessing Usenet newsgroups.

*Provided by.* Internet Service Providers, usually providers also running a network, or via cooperative marketing arrangements.

*Representative providers.* PSIlink, WorldLink

*Cost of service.* $15 to $40 per month.

*Listed in.* InterNIC provider lists and PDIAL list.

### Public-Access Unix, WAFFLE, Usenet site, and BBS accounts

*Offering.* Dial-up terminal account to Unix or custom shells, with access to Usenet, e-mail connectivity to the Internet; also typically has some Internet archives, usually also has special-interest software, conferencing, etc. Many are based on systems running Unix; WAFFLE is a program that lets X86-based PCs support Usenet and e-mail activity.

*Appropriate for.* Organizations and individuals who want e-mail or Usenet access but don't need real-time IP connectivity to the Internet.

*Advantages.* Less expensive and more accessible to users outside of mainstream locations.

*Disadvantages.* Can't do real-time Internet applications. Dial-up access may not be available when you want it.

*Provided by.* Public-access Unix systems and Unix BBSs.

*Representative providers or sites.* wariat (Cleveland), hcs (Peoria, IL), gna (Paris), scuzzy (Berlin), kralizec (Australia).

*Cost of service.* Free to a few dollars per hour or $5 to $20 per month.

*Listed in.* InterNIC provider lists and "nixpub" list (some are also "dial-up IP providers)

#### Other networks, systems, services that can exchange messages with the Internet

*Offering.* Accounts on e-mail, conferencing, forum, and SIG services that can exchange e-mail with the Internet.

*Appropriate for.* People wanting to also send e-mail to Internet users and e-mail-driven applications but not necessarily as primary or only on-line activity.

*Advantages.* Avoids the need for an additional account just for Internet access; may have easier-to-use user interface.

*Disadvantages.* Probably will cost more than Internet Account Provider. Message length may be insufficient for longer documents and programs. May not support, or may charge more for, 9600-bps access.

*Provided by.* Leading conferencing, SIG, and e-mail services.

*Representative Providers.* ATT Mail, America On-Line, CompuServe, GEnie, MCI Mail; BBSs, FidoNet, and other store-and-forward BBS networks.

*Cost of service.* Anywhere from free to hundreds of dollars per month, depending on pricing and how much you use. Many have fixed prices of $5 to $10 per month for a fixed amount or range of services.

*For information.* Call telephone directory service; most will have 800 numbers for voice sales operators.

#### Dial-up IP

*Offering.* Dial-up IP connectivity, 2400 to 56 kbps (depending on your modem), over PPP or SLIP serial protocol. Generally implies on-demand connections, either automatic (e.g., for mail polling) or explicit (e.g., to do remote login, file transfer, file serving). Service usually also includes mail queuing and may include Usenet NetNews feeds.

*Appropriate for.* Individual and mobile users, especially those who want to read or send e-mail and Usenet NetNews off-line in batch mode; smaller organizations; users with sporadic needs or who don't have the budget for leased lines; offices that can't dedicate a full-time phone line to network connectivity; small-to-medium organizations.

*Advantages.* Lower costs, fewer security and administration requirements, supports needs of traveling and home-based users, lets multiple users access the Internet through a single connection.

*Disadvantages.* Access may take noticeable time to be provided; outside world can't necessarily "find you" for remote login, file transfer, etc.; connection speeds may be limited.

*Provided by.* Internet Access Providers, Dial IP providers, a.k.a. "PDIAL" providers.

*Representative providers and services.* Alternet, NetCom, Performance Systems Inc., General Atomics/CERFnet (Dial'n'CERF), Global Enterprise Systems/JvNCnet (Dialin' TIGER)

*Cost of service.* \$2 to \$10 per hour (may include 1-800 phone access) or \$150 to \$300 per month plus the costs of phone service and possible start-up and monthly administrative fees.

*Listed in.* InterNIC and PDIAL lists.

### Full network service

*Offering.* Leased-line IP connectivity at between 56 kbps to T3 (45 Mbps). Generally implies a full-time Internet connection and that your network IDs are in the Internet Domain Name databases, enabling users to establish remote login, file transfer, and other IP connections *to* your systems without knowing your numeric IP address.

*Appropriate for.* Organizations connecting one or more LANs, workstations, etc., such as universities, corporations, and computer vendors. However, many individual Internet developers and consultants have this kind of service.

*Advantages.* The felicity of unbounded Internet connectivity. Highest possible bandwidth for connection; supports large number of users and activities concurrently; can make applications, archives, and services available to outside users.

*Disadvantages.* Requires greater commitment to network and computer administration, security, and user training; higher one-time and recurring costs.

*Provided by.* Internet Service Providers, Internet Access Providers, and network service providers. Connections are also often offered by larger universities and other users to smaller sites.

*Representative providers and networks.* Advanced Network & Services (ANS)/ANSnet; General Atomics/CERFnet; Global Enterprise Systems/ JvNCnet; NEARnet; Performance Systems International Inc. (PSI)/PSInet; Sprint/SprintLink; Uunet, Inc./AlterNet.

*Cost of service.* Anywhere from a few hundred to a few thousand dollars per month for the line and network service. Determined by some mix of connection bandwith, organization size and type, level of customer support; services such as Usenet NetNews may be extra.

*Listed in.* InterNIC lists and *The Internet: Getting Started* (A. Marine et al., Prentice-Hall).

### Internet Access and Service Provider lists and how to get them

The most useful and comprehensive lists of Internet Access and Service Providers include the "PDIAL" list, lists maintained by the InterNIC, and queriable databases. These lists are available in a variety of ways, including:

- Via Gopher access to the InterNIC or other Yellow Pages Services
- As automatic responses to e-mail messages
- As postings to Usenet groups, for reading or downloading
- Retrieved from archive directories using anonymous-FTP file transfer
- Query from on-line or via e-mail
- Downloaded by direct PC and modem dial-up
- Hard copy
- By having a friend do one of the above for you
- Call and ask

*Automatic e-mail response* means that you can get the list as an automatic reply to e-mail you send to a specified address (depending on which system, possibly requiring keywords in the message header or body text). Most of these methods assume that you at least have a PC and modem or some other facility that lets you send and receive e-mail. If you don't have this, you may not be ready to access the Internet.

Some of these methods also assume some familiarity with one or more basics of being a PC user, such as using e-mail. Others assume some experience in being an Internet user, such as performing remote login or file transfer, using an Internet navigator, or reading Usenet postings. This is part of the "chicken and egg" Catch-22 of trying to become an Internet user. How to use facilities such as these are discussed in detail later on in this book—indeed, they are what this book is all about.

Once you've figured out what you want, calling may be easiest. On the other hand, getting a copy of a list such as the PDIAL list to read over may be necessary.

**The PDIAL list: Public dial-up Internet Access list.** If you want an individual Internet account to be a terminal or shell, or network PPP/SLIP user, my recommendation is to start by getting the PDIAL list, maintained by Peter Kaminski, who among other activities runs the on-line Information Deli. PDIAL is a list of Internet Access and Service Providers that users can access by dialing up via modem, and other helpful information. Providers listed in PDIAL offer outgoing Internet access (i.e., file transfer, remote login, and other applications). Most of them provide e-mail and Usenet and other services as well. Kaminski posts a fresh version of the list roughly every month.

PDIAL does *not* list Unix or Usenet sites which do not support real-time Internet services; these can be found in other lists, such as the nixpub list (see below). The PDIAL list is available from numerous sources, including by anonymous-FTP file transfer, from several Usenet groups, and by e-mail auto-server.

- *Automatic e-mail reply.* To receive the most recently published PDIAL, send e-mail to "info-deli-server@netcom.com" with the text "Send PDIAL" in either the message subject or body. To subscribe to the electronic mailing list which receives future editions as they are published, send an e-mail message with the subject "Subscribe PDIAL" to "info-deli-server@netcom.com". To receive both the most recent and future editions, send both messages.
- *Usenet.* The PDIAL list is posted regularly to several Usenet groups, including, as of early 1993, alt.internet.access.wanted; news.answers; alt.bbs.lists; and ba.internet. (If you cannot find the group in question, query your system administrator, since the names and hierarchy of Usenet groups may have changed. If you can find the group, but PDIAL isn't posted, send e-mail.)
- *FTP archive sites.* The PDIAL list should be available by anonymous-FTP from sites and archives including the InterNIC.

**The InterNIC Provider List(s).** Among its other responsibilities, the Internet Network Information Center, or InterNIC, maintains and provides access to lists of Internet Access and Service Providers, including the various commercial, academic, and agency regional, mid-level, and backbone networks, for North America and outside North America.

These lists should be the most complete and impartial ones available, at least within North America. (International information may be less complete.) These lists incorporate and replace the ones previously maintained by the NSFnet Network Services Center (NNSC). The InterNIC is also likely to have copies of other popular lists, such as the PDIAL list, available.

The InterNIC makes its information available via the fullest-possible range of access methods, including Gopher, anonymous-FTP, e-mail servers, and people answering telephone calls. For information on how to get information from the InterNIC, see Chap. 12 and App. C.

***The Internet: Getting Started* and other books about Internet providers.** Lists and information about Internet Service Providers has begun to emerge in book form. The first and most well known is *The Internet: Getting Started,* by April Marine, Susan Kirkpatrick, Vivan Neou, and Carol Ward; it includes comprehensive information about many of the leading Internet Access and Service Providers. Originally published by SRI International, the book is now available from Prentice-Hall. Like any book of resource lists, the information in here won't be completely up to date; however, the book contains a wealth of other useful information and may be more accessible—for example, you don't need to have a computer and modem to obtain a copy.

**The nixpub list of public-access Unix sites.** The nixpub list is a frequently updated list of public-access Unix systems—Unix-based BBSs usually carrying Usenet news, supporting e-mail connectivity to the Internet, and having some mix of local archives, multiuser games, etc.; it is maintained by Phil Escallier. The full nixpub list is long (over 1000 lines); there is also a shorter version, nixpub.short, with less information about each of the sites.

As a courtesy, many of the public access sites have made the nixpub (and other documents) available through e-mail servers. To get a current copy of nixpub as an automatic e-mail reply, you can send a message to:

- "nixpub@digex.com" (no subject or message text needed)
- "mail-server@bts.com" with one of the following message bodies: get PUB nixpub *or* get PUB nixpub.short.
- "archive-server@cs.widener.edu" with one of these messages: send nixpub long, send nixpub short, send nixpub long short, *or* index nixpub.

On the Usenet, the nixpub lists are regularly posted to groups including, comp.misc, comp.bbs.misc, and alt.bbs.

By anonymous-FTP, the nixpub lists are available from GVL.Unisys.COM [128.126.220.104] under /pub/nixpub/{long,short}.

**Other sources of provider lists and information.** The Usenet Newsgroup alt.internet.access.wanted is one place to ask about Internet access. This is a far from efficient way to look for this type of information; if possible, avoid asking your question here until you've looked through the above lists and perhaps made a phone call or two. If you do decide to post your query here, first read the FAQ (Frequently Asked Questions and their answers) document for the group—it may answer your question, or help you ask it in the best way. The FAQ file for this Usenet Newsgroup may also be found in the Usenet Newsgroups: news.answers and alt.bbs.internet.

**FARnet.** If your Internet involvement is related to academia or research, consider contacting FARnet, the Federation of American Research Networks. A relatively small umbrella organization, FARnet provides a focal point for roughly 20 of the U.S. regional and mid-level networks serving academic and

**Check the Internet "Yellow Pages," and Other New Ways to Locate an Account or Service Provider**

By the time you read this, there will probably be one or more additional ways to get account or service provider listings. For example, the first Internet "Yellow Pages" may be up and running, on an archie server—the long-awaited and overdue Internet equivalent of the telephone directory of business services, indexed by type and category as well as by name. Most likely, this will be a free-access resource on the Internet, which you will be able to query by a e-mail, a local program, or remote login (see Chap. 10); it will contain short and long listings of services offered by organizations on the Internet, such as public-access accounts, on-line databases, special-purpose software archives, supercomputers, games, classified ads, mailing lists, SIG discussion, and much more.

Other possibilities are:

- A definitive FAQ and/or FYI (For Your Information) document on Internet Account or Service Providers from the User Services Group of the Internet Engineering Task Force (IETF).
- Other list servers that you can send an electronic message to containing keywords such as your state, country, area code, and class of service wanted.

research sites. *Warning:* The FARnet providers list may not include all the commercial-only network service providers. However, FARnet's funding is more stable than many of the government contract-funded network information and service centers; so the odds are high they will still be around 6 months or more after this book goes to press. You can reach FARnet as follows:

FARNET
114 Waltham Street, Suite 12
Lexington, MA 02173
800-723-2763
617-860-9445
FAX: 617-860-9345
Laura Breeden, Executive Director
breeden@farnet.org

On-line information is available by anonymous-FTP from: farnet.org: in directory farnet/farnet_info.

## Tips for getting connected

### Phone lines tips for dial-up users

Q: Now my phone's busy all the time and no one can reach me for voice calls or faxes. What do I do?

A: Get an additional phone line. If you find yourself using your phone line frequently for on-line activity, you may want to add an additional phone line. Depending on how much time you spend on-line versus sending and receiving faxes, you may share this line between your modem and fax machine—or you may want a separate line for each. If you want to be connected to the Internet almost continuously, price a leased line. You might also see if ISDN service is available from your office or residence; if it is, you may decide it's worth trying. (You'll need ISDN equipment in addition to or instead of your current analog phone equipment. Be sure everything works as promised.)

Q: That *&$%@! Call Waiting keeps killing my connection when I'm halfway through reading my e-mail! What do I do?

A: If the phone line you use for your modem connection has Call-Waiting service, be sure you know how to deactivate Call Waiting before making a call to access the Internet. On most telephone systems, you do this by dialing *70 before dialing the number you want to call. This deactivates Call Waiting for the duration of the call (i.e., if anyone calls, they'll get a busy signal). When you hang up, Call Waiting reactivates automatically.

### Modem tips

Q: What do I set my modem to?

A: The standard telecommunications setting for dialing up Internet terminal accounts is: 8 bits, 1 stop bit, no parity. Most Internet dial-up terminal accounts support access at rates of 300 to 9600 bps. Depending on the features your modem supports, such as V.32*bis* for compression, you may get higher virtual rates, particularly on file transfer (it is least noticeable for interactive login activity). Access numbers for some sites may only go up to 2400 bps. (And remember that if you're experiencing unusual amounts of line noise, try setting your rate down to 2400, 1200, or even 300 bps.)

Q: What modem should I get?

A: Any modem should be able to work with any Internet dial-up phone number. On the other hand, some modems will support higher speeds and more protocols, and offer more features, than others. Also, there are several brands and models of modems used by many Internet and Usenet sites and by many users. Your Internet Access Provider may have some recommendations—they may also have arrangements with modem vendors or distributors that make them available to you as a user at good prices. (You may currently have only a 1200- or 2400-bps modem and be interested in a 9600-bps modem, for example.) There may also be other users at your site offering used modems for sale.

### Getting accounts, selecting providers

Q: What if I want to change to a different Internet Access Provider?

A: Getting a new account is easy, easier than getting your first one in fact because once you're on the Internet, you have better access to lists of access providers, and by then you should be more experienced in locating Internet information. So don't worry about making a wrong choice. Reasons to change can include:

- A new provider becomes available that offers new services your current provider doesn't or better prices or more affordable phone access where calls are in your free calling area or are less expensive.
- Dissatisfaction with current service and support.
- Phone numbers are busy too often.

If you get a new e-mail address, just be sure to tell people, and send "change of address" messages to any mailing lists you're on (be sure you're writing to the list administrator, not the entire list).

## Conclusion

If you've made it this far, you should be able to get an Internet account. Now it's time to get that account, login, and start taking the Internet out for a spin.

Chapter

# 3

# Internet Naming and Addressing

*"...And how odd the directions will look!*
*Alice's Right Foot, Esq.,*
*Hearthrug,*
*near the Fender.*
*(with Alice's love)."*
*"The Pool of Tears," Alice in Wonderland*

*"'Must a name mean something?' Alice asked doubtfully. 'Of course it must,' Humpty Dumpty said with a short laugh."*
*"Humpty Dumpty," Alice in Wonderland*

Everyone and everything on the Internet has some unique way to identify who and/or where it is. As a user with an account on a computer on the Internet, you have (or will have, if you don't already) a user-name and Internet address which uniquely identifies you among all the millions of other people, computers, and organizations on the Internet.

Chapter 4 talks about how every user and program has a unique name and how every file has a name that is unique, either absolutely unique from all other files in its file system or at minimum unique when you include its full address path from the top of the file system. Similarly, every person, program, file, computer, and organization you interact with on the Internet can be uniquely identified, whether it's the computer on your desk, someone using a computer on the other side of the world, an on-line library catalog, or one file among thousands at an archive site. This is done by using a combination of Internet *names* and *addresses*.

In this chapter, we'll take a look at what make up Internet names and addresses, how to use them, and how to find them out. You'll learn enough about Internet names and addresses to:

- Figure out "who" and "where" you are—your "Internet address"

- Know the right questions to ask when asking people what their "net addresses" are
- Be familiar with IP and Internet naming and addressing conventions

## Is This More Information About Naming Than You Really Need?

You may feel this chapter goes into more detail about Internet naming and addressing than you'll need. It's quite possible—but don't be too sure. Many of the newer Internet facilities handle names and addresses for you automatically. But not all of them will—and there will be occasions when you won't have these helpful tools at hand. Perhaps the support services that make these tools work will be out of order or you'll be at a site that doesn't have them or you will be trying to explain a procedure to someone who doesn't have the same helpful facilities.

By analogy, if you only use speed-dialing on your telephone and don't know the actual phone number, you can't place these calls from another phone or location, particularly if the phone number isn't available through Information. At times like these, a basic knowledge of Internet naming concepts, syntax, and conventions may prove necessary—and Murphy's Law (If something can go wrong, it will) virtually guarantees that at least one of these occasions will be important to your work. This is the same reason that this book includes a good-sized chunk of introductory information about Unix—you're bound to need it sooner or later. (The box, "For More Information about Internet Names and Naming," suggests further reading about these topics for the curious.)

So let's spend some time on the general concepts of names and addresses.

### For More Information about Internet Names and Naming

There are entire books on the subject of Internet and TCP/IP naming and addressing that discuss technical and other aspects of these topics. However, don't worry—if you're simply planning to be an Internet user, you don't have to read them. (You can, if you're curious, of course.) These books are relevant to application developers, system and network administrators, network providers, and Internet planners.

There are also articles and books on electronic mail addressing within and to and from the Internet—how to find someone's name, how to specify it correctly, and the like.

See the Bibliography for information about relevant books and other Internet informational and directory books. Depending on what you are doing and who you are communicating with, you may want to have one or more of these books close at hand.

Lastly, there are numerous directory-type books, listing the many electronic mailing lists, library catalogs, file archives, and other resources available on and through the Internet. Any organization serious about being part of the Internet should have a copy of most of these books in their library, possibly even one for each Internet-using department or workgroup.

Once you've been using the Internet, you may want to buy or borrow these books, and browse through them. (About half the contents are reference lists.) System administrators, network operators, and developers may also want their own copies. However, for the most part, you as an individual average user don't need personal copies of these books near at hand. (I use mine a few times each a year, other than when I'm writing books like this.)

## Names Are Important

In the world of computers and networks, names are important—even magical. The importance of names and naming has literary and mythological antecedents. Names and naming play a particularly large role in many works of fantasy and science fiction. One familiar example is the fairy tale *Rumpelstiltskin,* where, by discovering the name of the strange intruder who was spinning hay into gold, the princess retained her firstborn son who she'd promised as payment. (Reneging on her deal in the process, admittedly.) Similarly, in Ursula K. LeGuin's Wizard of Earthsea series and many other works about magic and magicians, to know the true name of a magician was to hold absolute power over him or her. In Vernor Vinge's science fiction novella *True Names,* arguably the first book about cyberspace and virtual realities, knowledge of a user's "true name" (i.e., who they were in the "real world" versus within the shared-space computer networks) gave the name-holder major leverage over the holdee's activities in the "other world" of cyberspace.

In the world of computers and networks, every user has a user-name (also referred to as "user-ID"). Equally, every program, file, computer, resource, service, and organization has a name of one form or another. Without user-names, your computer wouldn't know who you are and therefore wouldn't know which files to allow you to work with, which programs to use, which e-mail messages are for you. (More precisely, giving a user-name tells the computer who you claim you are. To authenticate yourself—prove you are who you say you are—you usually must give a password, insert an electronic key of some sort, or match some other authenticating record like retina or voice-print matching. As you can probably appreciate—particularly if you've watched enough high-tech spy movies like *Sneakers*—ensuring that "you're really you" can become a big-time challenge.)

Without names, your computer wouldn't "know" it was itself, as opposed to some other computer (e.g., to accept e-mail and other incoming traffic and to "namestamp" outgoing traffic). Without addresses, networks wouldn't work at all—your Ethernet interface wouldn't know whether a stream of packets was for you, bridges wouldn't know if traffic should be forwarded, routers wouldn't be able to determine which path to pass traffic along, etc.

## Internet Names Must Be Unique

To be useful within the Internet, every name within a group of names must be unique—different from every other name in use. (This discussion is about naming within the Internet and TCP/IP technologies. Other types of computer and network technologies, such as Novell NetWare, IBM SNA networks, and DECnet networks may work very differently.) One way to have unique names is to have all names be different. However, at some point, doing this while keeping the current naming method can become too complicated. Or perhaps your group gets involved with another group that has some similar or identical names, so you have, say, two "Jonathons" or "Flying Aces" and you can't agree who should change their names and who gets to keep theirs.

One common way to solve this is to add more information, for example, "Bill with the long gray beard," "Jack, son of Joe," "Nancy, the computer fixer," etc. In the Internet world, one common way to make a name absolutely unique is to include its *address* as part of the name.

## Addresses: They're Important, Too—They Help You Locate Things and Differentiate Among Similarly Named Things

A *name* usually refers to entity, like you, a file, your computer, or your organization, for example, "alice," "my-resume," or "spacetronics." (It may also refer to a service, like "printer.")

An *address* is the location of that entity (e.g., your mailing address, an office number, or a path in your file system), for example, "221B Baker Street, London," or "in the Resumes directory on my hard drive." Addresses help organize users, files, computers, organizations, and the like so they can be easily found. Like names, addresses are important. In fact, they're essential to the use of computers and networks.

To talk with someone on the telephone, you need to know their telephone number. To send someone a letter, you need to know their name and their mailing address. Within the Internet, names and addresses are needed for activities such as:

- Identifying who you are so people (and programs) can send you e-mail and who they are so you can send them e-mail
- Identifying other people, and groups of people, so you can send e-mail to them
- Accessing programs, files, computers, and other resources, such as on-line library catalogs, special databases, interactive multiuser programs, programs to retrieve, etc.

Thus, every *user* with an account on an Internet-connected system has a user-name and an e-mail address. When you get an account on an Internet-attached computer, you have a user-name and an Internet address. Every *computer* directly attached to the Internet has an Internet name and address. Your computer—the one you log onto—has an Internet name and address. Every *resource*—library catalog program, database, program archive site, commercial information service—reachable through the Internet—has an Internet name and address. Every network port on each computer can be identified and reached by an address.

This includes everything from the computer you use when connected to the Internet to those big supercomputers in the National Science Foundation Supercomputing Centers. It includes the parts of the U.S. Library of Congress and commercial "pay-for-view" information services like Dialog, Mead Data, Lexis, and Nexis. It even includes a motley assortment of soda and vending machines at various colleges and even a few toasters, CD players, elevators, boats, and bicycles.

Depending on what you do on the Internet, you may use hundreds of names and addresses—or only a few. But don't start worrying about having to remember them all. (At least not yet.) Over the past two decades, the steerers, developers, vendors, users, administrators, and gadflies in the Internet community have made on-going efforts to help ensure that naming and addressing within the Internet works and that it works as "automagically"* as much as possible.

Furthermore, the programs you'll be using to work on the Internet are getting more sophisticated and user friendly. Many of the programs you'll be using include features that let you create and save lists of names and addresses, in a way that is similar to how the speed-dial feature on many telephones and the phone-book feature in many telecommunications and e-mail programs work. Even better, many of the new Internet "front-end and navigator" tools which you'll be learning to use, such as Gopher, Hytelnet, and WAIS, minimize or almost entirely do away with the need to learn and remember Internet names and addresses. Lastly, as you get more familiar with the various Internet tools, and (possibly) with Unix, you may also see additional ways you can save and recall this information.

## Is Something a Name or an Address?

Often, things that look like addresses turn out to really be names. A postal address, for example, is an address—it indicates where in the physical world you can be reached. A telephone number, on the other hand, is actually a type of name, not an address, if you think about it. When you dial a phone number, the telephone system determines where the location of that number is—where the area code is and so on—and makes the appropriate connection. One sign that phone numbers are a type of name is that you can often keep the same phone number when you move your office within a building or your home within a town—even though your mail address changes. That's the sign that it's a name, albeit one made from numbers rather than letters—not an address.

Yet phone numbers are used and act as addresses. My fax machine is connected to my second phone line; effectively, its address is that phone number. If I move the fax machine, it gets a new "address." On the other hand, while my fax machine "knows" it's a fax machine, it doesn't know it's "my" fax machine. If I put another fax machine on this phone line, it would work just as well; if I moved my fax machine elsewhere, it would act as someone else's fax. (Machines have no loyalty.) My answering machine, by contrast, "knows" when I call—because I give it the several-digit code that lets me playback the messages it's recorded.

---

*A portmanteau of "magic" and "automatically" (i.e., magic that works automatically). Televisions, for example, let you select a channel by number (e.g., Channel 7) without needing to know or enter the frequency. Radio, by contrast, wants you to find a station by tuning to its frequency.

The notion that we may move around over time is reflected by the difference between names and addresses. As a rule, we keep our names but may change our addresses. A name that refers to you, or your computer, is unlikely to refer to someone else, or someone else's computer (although you may replace your computer with another, which gets the old one's name)—but, over time, someone or some other computer may be located at your address. Your department or entire organization may move locations, even state or country. You'd like to keep the same network address, so you don't have to update all the people and computers' directories. On the other hand, if you change companies, you will get a new network address. We'll look at how the Internet simplifies keeping track of this shortly.

## Uniqueness in Addresses

The uniqueness of network names and addresses is similar to file-naming conventions on your computer. As mentioned earlier, using names that include addressing information can make them unique. The addressing information must point to a single, unique location; however, there can be many users, files, etc., at this location, as long as each has a name that is locally unique.

As you probably know, within your computer's file system, every file and directory must be uniquely specifiable by an absolute path. For example, the file containing this chapter was located in: /usr1/dern/Projects/Internet/Chapters/naming.txt. Within a given subdirectory, every filename must be different. If you specify a filename that already exists, the operating system assumes that's the file you mean, not some new one with an identical name. On the other hand, files can have identical names if they are in different places within the file system (i.e., have different addresses). For example, you may have many files all named "README":

/usr1/dern/Projects/Internet/Chapters/README

/usr1/dern/Projects/Internet/Examples/README

/usr1/dern/Projects/Internet/README

/usr1/dern/README

Similarly, within the Internet environment, names may be unique locally within your computer, site, or organization. For example, you may be the only "alice" or "dormouse" in your organization, but there may be 23 or 2300 other "alice"s or "dormouse"s around the world. There may even be "alice" accounts on different computers that don't all belong to you. (Although one would hope that your system administrators would catch this.) There are some valid uses for commonly used naming methods like this. For example, every Internet site should have an account named "postmaster" as a name that other sites can use for sending e-mail to. This convention ensures that you can send a message to a site without knowing a specific person or e-mail name and that this name will remain constant even if specific employees leave.

Equally, you may have accounts named "sherlock" on several systems or accounts on different systems, under different user-names (sherlock, sherlock_h, s_holmes, sholmes) and even several accounts on the same system, with different user-names.

Similarly, computers at different sites on the Internet may have identical names. For example, there's no reason there couldn't be trios of computers "named" *mikado, pinafore,* and *pirate* each at a hundred different sites. But you don't want several machines named *pinafore* at one site. To sum up:

- Everyone and everything in the Internet has a name, address, or both.
- Everyone and everything in the Internet can be identified by a unique name and/or address.

Now, let's talk about Internet names and addresses.

## Internet Names and Addresses: Domain Names and IP Addresses

Within the Internet, there are two major identification systems:

- The Domain Name system, which is relatively English-like, and specifies address-like things which are actually names
- IP addresses, which are numeric-based names that act as logical addresses

Each has its uses. You'll be using Domain Names more. However, to explain Domain Names well, it's easier to start with IP addresses.

### IP Addresses: Address-like naming

When the technology for the Internet was being invented, its developers were aware that some mechanism would be needed to tell the network equipment where traffic was coming from and going to, and for each computer to determine whether traffic was for it, rather than its neighbor or another computer halfway around the world. This led to the creation of IP addressing—defining network addresses used by computers and networks based on the TCP/IP protocol suite.

IP stands for Internetworking Protocol, which is part of TCP/IP (Chap. 1 contains a brief explanation of TCP/IP). An IP Address identifies a location within an IP network—that is, within a network of computers that are using the TCP/IP IP protocol to communicate. (All computer networks have and use addresses, by the way, including AppleTalk networks, IBM SNA networks, Novell NetWare and Banyan VINES LANs.)

An IP address contains two pieces of information: the *network* portion, known as the *IP network address*; and the *local* portion, known as the *local address.* Each IP address identifies a specific location within the Internet, specifically, to a network interface on a given network or subnetwork. A computer that's on a network is often also referred to as a *host computer,* or *host*; the IP address corresponding to where the computer is connected is also often called its *host address.*

Every packet of user network traffic traveling the Internet includes the IP network address of its *source*—the computer that it came from—and for its *destination*—the computer it is going to. These addresses are examined by various network equipment in order to route your packets to their destination.

IP addresses are actually names, not addresses, points out Jack Haverty, Internetwork Architect at Oracle:

> When an IP address comes into a LAN, some lookup mechanism has to translate the IP address into the LAN's address, such as an Ethernet 48-bit address, in order to actually deliver the data. The real principle is the "one level's address is another level's name" until you get right down to the hardware.

**IP network addresses must be unique.** Each IP network address in the Internet must be different and unique, just as every organization must have a unique telephone number. Similarly, each local IP address within an organization must be unique. If your organization has more than one IP network address, there can be identical local IP addresses, because the corresponding full IP network addresses will still be different. (See Box: Where Your IP Network Address Comes From.)

Deep inside Internet computers and network equipment, IP addresses, like everything else, consist of strings of 0s and 1s, of course. For the convenience of the Internet's human users and administrators, however, the Internet IP addresses are expressed using our familiar base 10 decimal notation (i.e., using the full set of digits from 0 through 9). In the familiar decimal notation, an Internet IP address consists of a set of four numbers, also called *parts* or *fields.* When writing and using Internet addresses, such as when giving them in commands, or saving them in ASCII text files and program source code, these fields are separated by periods. Examples are 128.40.5.1, 2.31.0.42, and 192.33.33.12.

The network portion of the address starts on the left; the local portion of it ends on the right. (Which portion the middle fields belong to will vary, depending on what *Class* the address is. But if your involvement with the Internet is just as a user, rather than as network administrator or network developer, you don't need to know anything about address Classes, or what Classes there are.)

### Telling someone an Internet IP address

When giving an Internet IP address, for example, over the phone, the period is usually pronounced "dot" (less commonly, as "period" or "point") or a pause is left between each field. The numbers may be either said as the full number or one by one. For example, you might say 128.40.5.1 as "one hundred twenty eight dot forty dot five dot one" or "one hundred twenty eight (pause) forty (pause) five (pause) one" or "one two eight (pause) four zero (pause) five (pause) one" and so on.

### Where Your IP Network Address Comes From

If each IP network address used in the Internet must be unique, who's in charge and how does an organization get its Internet IP network address(es)? A central addressing authority, the Internet Assigned Numbers Authority (IANA) is in charge of managing the IP network addresses used in the Internet, among its other responsibilities. The IANA is at USC Information Sciences Institute (USC-ISI), Marina del Rey, CA. The actual requesting, issuing, and registration of Internet identifiers and distribution of the lists is done by the InterNIC and the DDN Network Information Center (DDN NIC). The IANA has delegated the day-to-day work of assigning the IP addresses to the Internet Registry (IR), which is operated by the InterNIC Registration Service, run by Network Solutions Inc. (Herdon, VA). The Internet Registry has in turn delegated the IP address assignment duties to regional registries, such as the RIPE NIC in Europe.

End users don't need to be involved in obtaining or registering IP addresses; if you are, you've probably "changed hats" when you weren't looking. As part of connecting its computers, LANs, and sites to the Internet, an organization has to obtain network identifiers which are unique and assigned to it. Obtaining and registering these names, numbers, and other identifiers is usually handled by the Internet Service Provider as part of the process of obtaining a connection to the Internet.

By the way, you don't need to have an Internet IP network address of your own if you're accessing the Internet by dialing up as a terminal user to an account on an Internet computer (but this computer will have an Internet IP address). If you are connecting via a dial-up network connection (using PPP or SLIP), you'll need an IP address, but this address may be one automatically assigned by the system you dial into, for the duration of the session. (And the next time you dial in, you may get a different IP address.) Only computers that are intended to be continually connected to the Internet need permanent IP addresses of their own.

It's also worth noting that an organization can get a set of IP network addresses assigned for use in its networks even though it may not necessarily expect to hook up to the Internet. Peter Sevcik, a Principal at Northeast Consulting (Boston, MA), advises all organizations with internal internetworks, not just those planning Internet connections, to register their domain names with the NIC and get a network address. "Even if you aren't connected to the Internet today, you may well need to be in the future. This way, you're already set up, with a unique name and the appropriate subnet addressing. You want to do this right. I know one organization where two departments went to the NIC, and they now have two separate schemes to be resolved."

## Domain Names: Something more convenient than numbers

With any communication system that requires identifying the "other end"—telephones, the post office, intercoms—it's essential that you be able to determine and specify a user or computer's address quickly and easily. Imagine, for example, if you wanted to call or write to someone and knew their name—but not their address. (Indeed, lack of good, comprehensive network address directories is one of the biggest obstacles to internetworking.)

The numeric IP addresses which we've just discussed meet the Internet's need for an addressing scheme that identifies things uniquely. But it does have a few drawbacks:

- *Inconvenient and difficult to remember numbers.* Numeric IP addresses can be difficult to remember, particularly if you're using a lot of them.

It's not obvious whether you've typed the right number or a wrong number. Quick: is the main public-access WAIS site you access located at [this number] or [that number]? Is your home computer's address [NUMBER] or [NUMBER]? What was the address of the ERIC Clearinghouse's archive of retrievable documents? You get the idea. (Some people do feel that Internet names can be just as hard to remember as IP addresses.)

- *Volatility; things change.* IP addresses refer to specific locations within specific networks. Moving something—a resource, computer, or even organization—may mean (1) getting a new IP address and (2) making sure that this new information is made available throughout the Internet.
- *Errors are hard to spot.* Like phone numbers and other IDs, it's very hard to tell if an Internet IP address is wrong, except when it doesn't work—and even then, you can't be sure that was the problem.
- *Addresses are impossible to guess.* If you don't know a given address, you have to be able to look it up. There's no way to deduce an IP address by knowing, say, an organization's name and type.

So, any naming and addressing system for use in the Internet needs to do more than simply identify—it also needs to strike a balance between precision and convenience. Fortunately, associating and converting information is one thing computers are very good at. For convenience, users in the Internet community began assigning English-like names to their computer systems, such as "nisc.sri.com" and "ut-sally." Programs that used IP addresses were written or modified to be able to automatically do lookups when a name was encountered and replace it with the appropriate IP address.

To simplify the task of identifying and using Internet addresses, the Domain Name System (DNS) was developed by Paul Mockapetris back in 1984 to identify networks, organizations, and individual computer systems and other entities within them.*

The Domain Name System lets us create and use alphanumeric names (I'd say English-like, but the Internet is becoming too globally oriented for this to be accurate) for the computers and sites on the Internet and provides a well-defined way to organize and categorize these names.

Under the Domain Naming System, all names are organized into a hierarchical tree-like structure, similar to the directories, subdirectories, and file hierarchy within a computer filing system. (Folders and subfolders for graphic-interface-oriented readers.) The top level of the Domain Naming System

---

*The Domain Name System replaced a previous system, where every computer kept a copy of the full list of names of computers on the Internet and their IP addresses, periodically downloading a new copy of the list from a central location. This worked well when there were only a few hundred computers on the entire network. (Now, even a medium-size company may have that many.) But as the Internet grew, it became too cumbersome; the Domain Name System replaced it.

consists of the *Domains*. Every computer, and every Domain Name, must belong to an existing Domain.

As with the network portion of IP addresses, the IANA is in charge of the names of the Domains. Each Domain usually has its own Domain Administrator, responsible for approving and managing the registration of names within a particular Domain.

Jon Postel of ISI notes, "The administrators of the DNS are the same as for IP addresses—the IANA has the overall responsibility, the day-to-day operations is delegated to the Internet Registry, and there are further delegations to the regional registries. (The process of registering domain names is usually handled by your organization's Internet Service Provider.)"

### The structure of Domain Names

A Domain Name consists of two or more alphanumeric fields, separated by a period (usually pronounced "dot"). Each field consists of some combination of the letters A through Z (in either upper- or lowercase), the digits 0 through 9, and the hyphen (-). No other characters may be used in the elements of a Domain Name; however, certain of these forbidden characters may be used in constructing Internet addresses, notably **.**, **@**, **%**, and **!**.

Like IP addresses, the components of a Domain Name are separated by periods; examples are world.std.com, ftp.uunet.net, osf.org, cs.umass.edu, dragon.cs.umass.edu, and researchco.reston.va.us.

Domain Names are case-insensitive; that is, it shouldn't matter whether letters are upper- or lowercase or any combination. For example, the following are considered to be identical: cs.umass.edu, CS.UMass.EDU, Cs.Umass.Edu, and CS.UMASS.EDU.

The field on the right is the name of the *top-level domain* the name-owner belongs to. The other fields may specify one or more levels of subdomain, and the computer and/or organization name. An example is:

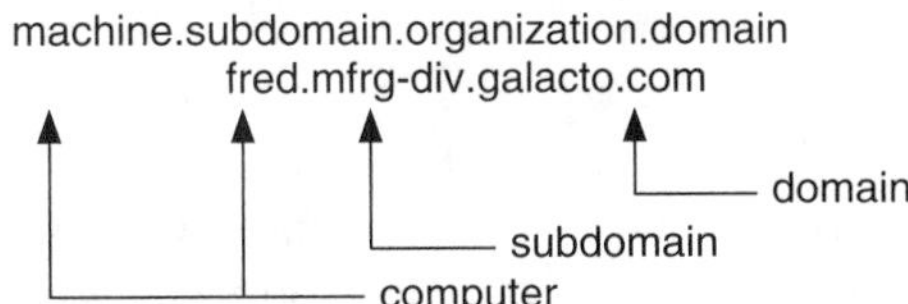


A small organization may only need its own name, for example, laputa.org. A large organization may have its names divided across several layers of subdomains, for example, jabber.wock.com, cs.laputa.edu, or flack.cs.laputa.edu. world.std.com, cs.mit.edu, and platypus.cs.mit.edu are other examples.

### Top-level Domains

The top-level Domains are types of organization and countries. Back when the Domain Name System was created, the top-level domains were according to types of organization; since that time, top-level domains based on countries have been added as well. As you will see, organization-type domains can have geographic subdomains, and vice-versa.

**Organization Domains.** The main organization-oriented, nongeographical domains are:

*COM (pronounced "comm").* Commercial organizations. Most of these belong to companies, such as Apple Computer, Digital Equipment, Texas Internet Consulting, etc.

*EDU (pronounced either "ed-you" or "ee-dee-you").* Education and academic organizations. For example, M.I.T., Harvard University, and the University of Saskatchewan are all in the EDU domain.

*INT (pronounced "int").* Special international organizations.

*MIL (pronounced "mill").* Networks and organizations that are part of the Milnet, a network run by the U.S. Department of Defense.

*GOV (pronounced "guv").* Networks and organizations that are part of the U.S. government, for example, the U.S. Treasury, Library of Congress, Internal Revenue Service, Smithsonian, NASA.

*NET (pronounced "net").* Networks and organizations running networks that are part of the Internet; also, many of the network operations, information, and services centers. Examples are the backbone, regional and commercial networks such as AlterNet, ANSnet, BARRnet, CERFnet, NEARnet, PSInet; networks run by government agencies, such as ESnet and NSFnet; and the NSFnet Network Services Center. However, many network organizations are in the ".com" domain.

*ORG (pronounced "org").* Organizations that don't easily fit into any of the other types, such as research and not-for-profit organizations. Examples are Electronic Frontier Foundation (eff.org) and Open Software Foundation (osf.org).

**Geographic Domains.** There is also a geography-oriented set of Internet domains, using a format developed by ISO, the International Organization for Standardization. The top-level domains are country-oriented, with the countries as two-letter names. For example:

CA = Canada

IL = Israel

UK = United Kingdom

US = United States

Each country establishes its own naming structure for the subdomain naming. Some countries use organization-type structures such as "ac" for academic and "co" for commercial. Others use a geographical structure. The "us" (United States) domain, for example, is divided in states and cities (e.g., sf.ca.us for San Francisco, CA, and well.sf.ca.us are Fully Qualified Domain Names).

Domain names can also have a mix of organization-type and geographic components, such as dims.demon.co.uk. As another example, many schools have names including both geographic and organizational information, such as north-high.menlo.k12.ca.us or central.sussex.ac.uk.

In the United Kingdom and some other countries, the fields in domain names are in the reverse order (e.g., gulliver@uk.ac.strathclyde.flack instead of gulliver@flack.strathclyde.ac.uk).

### Domain Names are unique

As with IP network addresses, filenames, and the like, parts of domain names may be similar, just as there is a city named Springfield in nearly every state and a Main Street in what seems like every city and town. However, within the Domain Name System, every name is unique. Thus, every organization within the Internet has a unique Domain Name and so does every computer attached to the Internet. Examples are ftp.uunet.net and ftp.psi.net.

### Other things you should know regarding Domain Names

As an Internet user, there are a few other things you should know on the subject of Domain Names in order to work with them properly and understand what is going on in some cases. (As opposed to if you are a system or network administrator or network software developer, in which case there may be a lot more you may need to learn.)

**Fully Qualified Domain Names.** A Fully Qualified Domain Name (FQDN) is an Internet address that all the higher-level fields, including a top-level domain, such as ".com" or ".us", need to uniquely identify something. When writing documents and using Internet applications internally within an organization, it's often possible to use only a part of an address and have that be understood and used. For example, you might refer to a document as "plan-draft@marketing2," send e-mail to "joe@marketing2," or give "telnet eng-3" as a command. Depending on how your organization has set up its network, these may well work—internally within your organization.

However, if you try using addresses like these, which are not Fully Qualified Domain Names, for Internet-related activity, such as to send electronic mail or remote login to another computer, it may not work. If you refer to such an address in an electronic-mail message, you will be supplying unusable information to your readers.

**What happens when you use a Domain Name—turning Domain Names into IP addresses.** Every time you use an Internet application and it encounters a Domain Name instead of an Internet IP address (you type it in, it finds it in a file or list, etc.), the application program automatically invokes a facility called a *Domain Name Service,* or *DNS,* which translate the Domain Name into the corresponding Internet IP address.

This happens automatically, usually so fast you won't even be aware of the delay, as long as the facilities providing name service are working. Occasionally, there may be a delay or problem (we'll shortly talk about some of these and what to do when this happens). As a rule, DNS service should be highly reliable; if you feel you are experiencing problems more than once every few months, send a message to your network operator.

There are also a number of Internet commands and facilities for displaying the IP address for a given Domain Name (i.e., you want the answer instead of having it be used by a program at this point).

**MX Records.** The Domain Name System also supports a special type of address called Mail eXchanger, or MX, Records. MX Records are used for computers and networks that wish to exchange electronic mail with the Internet but aren't connected appropriately and don't have IP addresses.

The MX Record contains the name of a non-Internet computer and, instead of its IP address, the name of a computer that has "agreed" to accept electronic mail on its behalf. The most important benefit of MX Records is that they allow e-mail to be addressed to a domain address which isn't connected directly to the Internet, but the e-mail gets reliably forwarded. This includes addresses on networks such as BITNET and FidoNet which can only connect with the Internet for e-mail and e-mail-like traffic.

It also includes addresses for users who access the Internet with a network-style connection (e.g., dialing up from a desktop PC or Macintosh Powerbook running TCP/IP plus the PPP or SLIP serial line protocol). Since these computers aren't connected full-time, any e-mail destined for them has to "pile up" somewhere. Usually, these users arrange for some other, always-connected Internet computer to act as their *mail host* and provide a service called *mail queuing.* If these users have their own Domain Names as their e-mail addresses, the MX Record lets these Domain Names cause e-mail to go to the mail host.

**Telling someone a Domain Name.** When saying a Domain Name, the period is pronounced either as "dot" or "period" and any ambiguous subnames may be spelled out, or even letter-named. For example, to tell someone "world.std.com" I might say: "That's World, double-you, oh, are, ell, dee, dot, ess as in Sam, T as in Tom, D as in David, dot, Com, that's cee as in Charley, oh, m as in Mary." It's often advisable to have the other party repeat this back to you.

#### Other points to remember

1. Domain Names are not case-sensitive. Upper- and lowercase letters will be treated identically, so FooBAR, FOOBAR, fooBar, and foobar are all the same—as parts of a Domain Name.
2. There are no spaces in Domain Names.

3. Be careful to distinguish between a hyphen (-) and underbar (_)—the Internet treats these as different characters.

## Your Internet Name, Address, and Other Essential Information

To use the Internet, there are several pieces of identifying information you'll want to learn and remember:

- Your user-ID (and password) for your "home" account. If you have an account on a multiuser system, this is the name assigned to you, and its authenticating password, for the account from which you read your electronic mail and do most of your other Internet-related activity.
- The Domain Name and IP address for the main computer(s) you login to and work on—particularly the one(s) you read e-mail on. You may not need these for everyday activity—but if you're ever away from your organization, you'll need to know this information to do remote login (**telnet**). For example, my main account is presently on The World, run by Software Tool & Die; World's Fully Qualified Domain Name is "world.std.com" and "192.74.137.5" is its IP address.

  Why you want to learn your IP address will be explained very soon. (You can determine your IP address—and other people's—using common TCP/IP commands like **finger, whois, hostname,** and **nslookup**—and commands such as **telnet** and **ftp** tend to display your local IP address. "Steps to Determine Your Internet E-Mail Address" in Chap. 5 talks more about determining your Internet address information.)
- Your Internet e-mail address. This is probably the single most important piece of information to learn and remember. It's what you tell people as an answer to the question, "What's your (Internet) e-mail address?" (Other ways this question may be asked include: "Are you on the 'net?" or "Who are you on the Internet?" or "Where are you on the Internet?" or "What's your 'net address?") Give them your user-name and a Fully Qualified Domain Name, such as alice@jabber.wock.com, lemuel@cs.lilliput.edu, ralph_r@topdeck.pinafore.nav.uk, or fred@bigfoot.kimball.ma.us.

Depending on how your organization has set up its networks and its e-mail system, you may have more than one valid e-mail address that delivers mail to your account. For example, your computer may have more than one name, resulting in lemuel@cs.lilliput.edu, lemuel@endian.lilliput.edu, and lemuel@laputa.cs.lilliput.edu. Your organization may also have set up matters such that there's a general address for e-mail, such as "lilliput.edu," which forwards all mail appropriately. In a case like this, you could simply use lemuel@lilliput.edu.

In general, when someone asks you "What's your Internet address?" the answer is the account you receive your e-mail at and the corresponding Domain Name for this system, for example, ddern@world.std.com.

### Why you may want to know your IP address and a few other key IP addresses

In general, the Domain Name System, and the name services supporting it, mean you don't need to know IP addresses, only the Domain Names that get translated to them. But for the most important computers you use, notably the one you read your e-mail from, it's worth finding out and writing down the numeric IP address as well. Here's a few reasons why:

- You're on a network that doesn't have name serving. This is common at the banks of "e-mail terminals" at trade shows—and if you don't know your IP address, you can't log in to read your e-mail.
- The network connection between you and the name services may be out of service, even though you can establish a network connection to your target.
- The name services your system accesses may not be able to "resolve" the domain address you enter (i.e., it is not in the name services your system is permitted to access). If this is the case, it's also quite possible that you are requesting a network connection not permitted by your Internet Service Provider or by the set of providers between you and your target.
- The systems providing name services are reachable—but the load on them is so great they are taking an unacceptable amount of time to send back the IP address. (If they take too long, your application may decide to "time out" and quit.)
- The systems providing the name service for the Domain Name you entered are out of service, although the name service systems are network-reachable.

By knowing the IP address for your target system, you can enter the numeric address, instead of the Domain Name. Often, this will do the trick, and you will get connected. Problems like those listed above may occur, for example, when you're using a temporary extension to the Internet, such as electronic mail stations at a trade show or convention whose network has been hooked up to the Internet—or at a relatively new Internet site that hasn't gotten everything working perfectly yet.

Consider writing down the IP address for the systems you have accounts on and use and carrying this information around in your wallet. Don't worry; this is not a security breach. IP addresses are *not* secret. Of course, you don't write down your password.

---

*Tip: How to get your IP address at a show.* If you don't know your Internet IP Address, but someone else has been able to login—ask if they will help you determine your IP address. Several possible methods:

- Have them try the "host" or "nslookup" commands.
- If you can **telnet** from their host, using your Domain Name, see what your number is once you connect.

---

### Other things worth knowing about Internet names and addresses

- It's possible, and common, for a computer or site to have multiple names, all assigned to the same IP address (i.e., a computer can have several very different names, such as spqr.papa-bear.com, papa.bear.com, and spqr.big-bear.bearhaven.com).
- Internet addresses that use geographic domain naming aren't necessarily where you think they are. Most likely, when something is assigned a geographic Domain Name, such as bedlam.sf.ca.us, its true geographic location is likely to correspond to the address; in the example, it would be San Francisco, CA, in the United States. But it doesn't have to be that way or stay that way. Remember, the Internet is converting these alphabetic names into numeric IP addresses in any case, and these aren't organized geographically. Suppose "bedlam" relocates to New York or Florida or from one network to another. It would get a new *IP address*—but there's no reason it would need to change its Domain Name. The Internet name-server system would handle this with no difficulty.
- Changing an IP address can be done "transparently" to users. Similarly, if a computer has to be moved to a different network—or even an entire organization switched from one Internet Service Provider to another—the names can stay the same. Only the IP numbers have to be changed.
- An Internet Domain Name or IP address may not always be working. A Domain Name assumes that the information has been put into the appropriate Internet databases; an IP address assumes that the computer at the designated address is the correct one—and that all relevant computers and networks are configured properly and working at the time. In other words, something may be broken or set wrong. This is similar to the reality that the telephone company occasionally connects the wrong phone number to your home or gives Directory Information misinformation or your phone line may be broken; things can also go wrong with the Internet names-server facilities. If you're having problems, consult your local system or network administrator.

## Summary and Conclusion

Every user, computer, and organization on the Internet has a uniquely specifiable name, which contains a Fully Qualified Domain Name. Domain Names are hierarchical; the right-most part is called the "top-level domain."

Every location on the Internet where a computer can be attached has a unique numeric IP address. You have a user-ID for every computer account you have. One of these computers, the one you read your e-mail from, is most likely your "main" computer, and this user-ID should be the one you tell people. You should learn and remember this user-ID, and the Fully Qualified Domain Name and numeric IP address of this computer.

You have an Internet electronic-mail address which people should use in sending e-mail to you and which is what you should supply when asked for your e-mail address. The Fully Qualified Domain Name in this address may or may not be identical to that of your "main" computer.

Chapter

# 4

# Enough Unix to Survive as an Internet User

*"You are in a maze of twisty little directories, all alike."*
*Message from the Adventure-shell*

*"Here's a pretty how-de-do."*
*Yum-Yum, Nanki-Poo, Ko-Ko, The Mikado*
GILBERT & SULLIVAN

## Why You (Should) Care About Unix

Although the Internet can be considered to be made up of both networks and computers, when you make use of the Internet, what you interact with are the computers—more precisely, with the software programs running on your computer and on remote computers and information on these computers.

The networks that constitute the Internet are essential. Without them, you couldn't talk to any remote computers, and you couldn't access any of the plethora of Internet-based services and resources, such as remote login, file transfer, Gopher, or WAIS. But you don't talk directly to, or work with, any of these networks. Their existence and what they do should be "transparent" to your activities as a user, just as you aren't directly aware of the radio waves in the air or the electricity going to the wires of your stereo speakers. You're most likely only aware of the networks when they *aren't* working. Even then, it's often hard to be sure if problems are related to the network, your computer, or a remote system you're accessing.

When using the Internet, the program(s) you run on your computer, such as **telnet, ftp,** and Gopher, interact with other Internet programs, services, and resources which are running on other computers elsewhere on the Internet. To work with your computer, and to use the services and software programs on the other Internet-attached computers and exchange files, you need to "speak their language."

This includes becoming familiar with the basics of their user interface—

how you give commands—and other aspects of the environment, such as how files are named and organized. You need to learn this for any on-line services—CompuServe, Dialog, Dow Jones News/Retrieval, GEnie, MCI Mail, etc. Just like the many different word processors, graphics programs, and other programs, each of these services typically has its own user interface, commands, and naming conventions.

The Internet as a network doesn't have a user interface or an operating system. You as a user work with a computer at your end and, using the Internet, connect to and interact with programs and resources on other computers. The operating system most commonly used by computers on the Internet are versions of Unix, an operating system developed by AT&T Bell Labs. The most common user interfaces you will encounter on the Internet are character-based command-line or menu-choice interfaces to Unix systems. If you use the Internet, sooner or later you'll probably need to know something about Unix. Unix knowledge and skills worth knowing include:

- How to log in
- Directory and file naming concepts and conventions, including (for DOS users) how they differ from DOS conventions
- How to navigate—specify and change directories—in Unix file systems
- How to issue Unix commands, including how to correct or recover from typing errors
- How to display files on-screen, including how to make then "scroll"—pause at the end of each screenful
- How to search for text in your files
- How to display messages to your screen and how to send files to printers
- How to move, copy, and rename files
- How to change your password
- How to determine, set, and change permissions on your files and directories
- How to exit from text editors frequently found on Unix systems (see App. B) and how to use at least one of them
- Being aware of the programming capabilities—available directly from the Unix prompt level—and learning how to create your own *shellscript* command files
- How to find (and "yell for") help—and who and where to ask

In this chapter you'll get a crash course on the basics of what Unix is, how to use it, and common errors made by new Unix users.

## Why do I need to know Unix?

There is a good chance you may end up never needing to know much, even any, Unix. It depends on what type of computer you use, what software has been installed, and what other Internet resources and services you use. Here's some reasons you might *not* need to know any Unix:

- Increasingly, systems and services on the Internet are offering graphical, mouse-and-menu, point-and-click user interfaces which are "intuitive," meaning you should be able to use them without too much effort to figure them out. Most systems also provide a self-explanatory "help" feature.
- Many of the Public-Access Internet Account Providers are providing Internet "front end" programs, and there are many other such products becoming available. (There is a free Internet front end program you can customize in App. D.)
- Many new versions of TCP/IP software offer graphic, icon-oriented interfaces at the Unix level and for services like remote login (**telnet**), file transfer (**ftp**), electronic mail, and Usenet News.
- Many of the resources and services available on the Internet will have their own user interface so that you don't need to know much Unix to use them. For example, a few simple commands is all you need to know to use Gopher, WAIS, and World-Wide-Web (WWW).

However, you can't always count on any or all of the above being the case. Many Internet resources are accessible via a Unix system, which you'll have to log in to as a user before you can invoke the resource you want. Moreover, in order to access many of these resources, you have to first use a command such as **telnet** or **ftp.** Programs to do **telnet** and FTP are available today for Unix and non-Unix systems—but in most cases, the syntax for their commands will be Unix-like.

And when you're not at your home system, you may have to start or work from a command-line-oriented, nongraphic user interface. By knowing some basic Unix commands and concepts, you dramatically increase your chances of being able to use the many services, computers, and programs available through the Internet. So it's a good idea to know something about Unix.

If the computer you're using runs Unix, you've probably already had to learn something about Unix. Most computers that are classified as workstations are running a flavor of Unix, for example. (In this case, you may feel you already know everything in this chapter and can skip ahead.) However, if you're using a PC which is running DOS or OS/2, a Macintosh running MacOS, a Digital VAX running VMS, or some other non-Unix system, you may not know any Unix. Also, if your system has a graphic user interface (GUI, pronounced "gooey") like X Windows or Motif, you may be working on a Unix-based system yet have not had to learn much about Unix.

Let's start at the beginning, with some basic definitions of computer terms and concepts.

## What's an operating system?

If you've never used a computer before, or have used primarily a personal computer such as a PC, Mac, or Amiga, you may not be familiar with the concept and term *operating system* (OS). A computer's operating system is what's between you—the user—and the hardware. The operating system makes it possible for you to "operate the system"—to use the computer without having to know, remember, and tell it exactly what to do. For example, instead of entering a command that means "Find the program located at so-and-so, a location on my hard disk, and use it on the file stored in the following blocks elsewhere on the disk," you can simply say, "edit proj-news.txt"—or click your mouse on the appropriate icons for word processing and the file you want.

Operating systems make it much, much easier for most of us to be computer users and to run application programs like word processors, spreadsheets, e-mail—and Internet-oriented activities like remote login and file transfer. Other well-known computer operating systems besides Unix include DOS, which runs on IBM PCs (and compatible systems, a.k.a. "PC clones"), MacOS for the Apple Macintosh family, OS/2 from IBM, and VMS for Digital's VAX series of computers. (Products like Novell NetWare, Banyan Vines, and Microsoft Windows for Workgroups, are *network operating systems* (NOSs). A NOS lets one or more PCs, which were designed to be self-contained computers, to share access via a network—usually a local area network (LAN)—to files, printers, and other resources.)

The operating system does a lot of things so that it's easier to use your computer:

- It provides the *user interface,* which is responsible for translating your keyboard and mouse input into commands meaningful to the computer, and presents the results of your commands to your screen. This includes the *command language,* which means the "words" it recognizes, and the *syntax* of how you can specify commands. These functions are often provided by a program called a *shell*; some operating systems, such as DOS and Unix, have a variety of different shells available for them, offering different features and ways to give commands.
- It manages the *file system*—access and storage of the files and directories on your storage drives (hard and floppy disks, CD-ROM, tape, etc.) so you can identify them by filenames rather than needing to know physical locations on the disk.
- It initiates and supervises the actual running of your programs in the CPU, possibly enabling other programs to run simultaneously.

Without a sophisticated operating system, only one task could run on the computer at a time. Early versions of DOS and MacOS were not multitasking; products like Microsoft Windows and Apple's MultiFinder have addressed this limitation.

### What is Unix?

Unix is a multitasking, multiuser computer operating system originally developed in 1969 by two researchers at Bell Laboratories in Murray Hill, NJ, named Dennis Ritchie and Ken Thompson.*

---

*First described in "The Unix Time-Sharing System," K. Thompson and D. M. Ritchie, *Communications of the ACM,* vol. 17, no. 7, July 1974, pp. 365–375. For a good historical and technical overview on the origins of Unix, see "The Evolution of the Unix Time-Sharing System," D. M. Ritchie, and other essays, reprinted in the *AT&T Bell Laboratories Technical Journal,* October 1984, vol. 63, no. 2, part 2, a special issue dedicated to Unix.

*Multitasking* means the ability to do several things together, a step or piece at a time. For example, you could be cooking breakfast, making lunch, brewing coffee, and reading the morning paper in the same time period, shifting every few seconds from one task to the next. For a computer, this means doing tasks such as sending a file to the printer, letting you do word processing, checking periodically for new e-mail messages, and running other programs.

*Multiuser* means that several people can share use of the same computer, at the same time. Most DOS PCs, for example, don't include the concept of "a specific user." Whoever turns it on becomes the sole user. There is no mechanism built into DOS to automatically identify you versus someone else. Many PCs can only support one "user" at a time, unless a fair amount of modifications are done to the software and hardware. (Network operating systems were developed to link personal computers onto LANs, helping to remove the one-user/one-machine limitations of the original DOS.)

Unix, like other multiuser operating systems, can handle dozens, hundreds, or even thousands of individual users, each with personal user-name, password, and sets of files.

The name Unix is a mild pun on MULTICS, which stands for MultiUser Interactive Computer System. Project Multics began at M.I.T. in the mid-1960s, several years before the beginning of the ARPAnet project.

Legally, UNIX is the trademark for the operating system owned by Unix System Laboratories, Inc., or USL. (USL was spun off from AT&T Bell Labs and then purchased by Novell in the early 1990s.) Over the years, many other computer companies have developed their own versions of Unix, usually marketed and sold under their own names. Some of these names look or sound something like "Unix," while others don't. Sun Microsystems, for example, has products such as SunOS and Solaris for its workstations. Digital Equipment has Ultrix. Apple Computers has AUX for the Macintosh. IBM has AIX, and so on. "Nonsoundalikes" include OSF/1 from the Open Software Foundation, Coherent, and bsd/386. However, the term Unix is commonly used as shorthand to generically refer to any and all of these operating systems.

Unix was developed to be an operating system for more than one type of computer. Prior to the creation of Unix, each computer company made not only its own hardware but also its own *proprietary* operating system—meaning one which belonged to the company and was only useful on its machines or on "clones" (referred to as "plug-compatibles") of these machines from other companies. Each proprietary operating system had its own commands, syntax, and rules.

Unix was intended, among other things, to define an operating system standard that could be implemented by any and all computer vendors. This way, programmers who learned one OS—Unix—could develop software that would run on many different types of computers (or at least have fewer differences for the version of a program for each different type of computer). It also meant that users familiar with a single-user interface and shell could use different computers more readily. It hasn't worked out quite this well, but Unix is still a near-standard for computers above the level of DOS and MacOS size.

### Why Unix is popular

In addition to being available on systems from a wide range of computer vendors, Unix is also popular for Internet-type uses because of its multitasking, multiuser design, which makes it well suited to supporting lots of people and running in a network environment. Being on a network calls for a computer that can do many things at once—"watch" for e-mail, turn output from program activity into network traffic, receive network traffic and convert it into input to programs, and so on.

On Unix systems, a program that is running is often referred to as a *process*. Some of these processes run automatically and don't belong to a human user (i.e., to no particular individual) but instead belong to the operating system itself. These processes have been termed *daemons** (from the Greek *daimon*), retroactively acronymized by some to stand for "Disk And Execution MONitor." These daemon processes are often referred to as "demons," such as the "mail demon," "print spooler demon," "network demon," etc. (They are also often referred to as "background processes," because they are running on the computer without requiring input from a user.)

### Unix and networking

While DOS and Macintosh computers can be made to participate on a network, Unix was designed early on to work well on networks. Unix is also highly network-oriented, that is, designed to "talk to" and make use of networks. It's the rare version of Unix that doesn't include facilities to "speak" TCP/IP; most versions of Unix also include a number of programs intended for use over networks, such as **telnet** for remote login, **ftp** for file transfer, and a program to create and read electronic-mail messages. (**telnet, ftp,** and electronic mail will be discussed in upcoming chapters.) Unix emerged as the standard operating system for workstations; when many of the first workstations were being invented, they were based on Unix and used TCP/IP to communicate with their file and print servers. With the growth in the use of computer workstations, the use and importance of Unix and TCP/IP have grown as well.

That's why you'll find a lot of Unix across the Internet—because it can support many users as well as the background processes needed by networking, and it provides a "common language" on the many disparate types of computers connected to the Internet.

## Basic Unix Concepts

Let's take a look at some of the key concepts of Unix. If you're familiar with DOS, VAX/VMS, or other operating systems, you'll see some similarities (and

---

*So if you get an e-mail message from "somebody" named Daemon or Demon, don't panic. It's a message generated automatically by a program on your or some other computer. These messages are often sent to let you know that your e-mail couldn't be delivered, you've used up your allotment of file space, etc.

differences). We'll start by looking at files and directories and how they're organized under Unix.

### File systems: Putting information in its place

Your computer works by manipulating information: executing programs, such as a word processor, and manipulating data, such as your resume. When not in use, this information—data and programs—has to be stored somewhere. Physically, all this information is kept on *storage media:* hard disks, floppy disks, optical disks, CD-ROMs, cassette tapes, DAT tapes, etc.

Part of the job of any operating system is to organize and provide access to this stored information. It does this by having a *file system.*

The information in your office could, in theory, be stored as a long, continuous roll of paper—perhaps a very thin roll, one character wide, on which you type one very long line, with no carriage returns. But no matter how the information is formatted and organized in its stored form, you use it as a number of individual documents. Even if you used one single, immensely long roll of paper, you'd soon be making marks and attaching paper clips and scraps of paper to say, "Tax returns start here," "Resume, Old," "Resume, New," and the like. You might end up with half of one document in feet 56 through 62 and the rest in feet 397 through 516.

Programs and data exist on your computer's storage media as series of 1s and 0s. It's not uncommon for a given file to actually be split into a series of strings of bits. The operating system includes a function called a *file system,* which let you define blocks of these 0s and 1s as *files.* Most operating systems include ways to let you refer to these files by English-like names, called *filenames*; some also let you create graphic icons to represent them.

### Files: Where the data is (and programs are)

A file is the smallest amount of stored data that can be accessed by the operating system, and it is what any program must first access in order to get access to the contained data. A file contains information. Most files contain text, programs, databases, and the like. Examples are:

- Your word processing program
- The text to this chapter
- A spreadsheet for a department's yearly budget
- Your database of contact phone numbers and addresses
- An x-ray of your foot, in digitized form
- The Grateful Dead singing "Sugar Magnolia"

### Directories: Putting files in their places

If your office files consisted of 3000 folders all arranged in a row, that would be some improvement over that one long roll of paper, but not much. Most of

| mystuff (a directory) | to-bearco (file) |
|---|---|
| resume.txt | Dear Mr. Bear, |
| resume.old | |
| pubslist.txt | I'm writing to apply for the |
| letters (directory) | position of consumer product |
| recipes (directory) | tester at BearCo as advertised in |
| banjo-jokes | the Sunday, July 24, 1993 Bear |
| to-do-list | Facts. I feel that my many years of |
| addresses (directory) | experience in assessing "too hot, |
| work-files (directory) | too cold, just right..." make me |

**Figure 4.1** A directory is a file containing filenames.

us prefer not only to put a label on our folders, but to put related folders into a hanging folder, put related hanging folders in the same file drawer, keep related file drawers adjacent in the same file cabinet, etc. Most file systems make your life easier in a similar fashion, by allowing you to organize these files into a file-drawer–like hierarchy, defining *directories,* which can contain files. (Not everyone takes advantage of this capability.)

A directory is basically a special type of file, whose contents are files, just as your file drawer can be considered a very large file folder that contains smaller folders (technically, a directory contains a list of names of files, rather than the actual files). Figure 4.1 illustrates this.

### Directory listings: What's in a directory

Just as you can look at, or display, the contents of a file, you can also look at—display—the contents of a directory. Since the contents of a directory is a list, this is usually called a *directory listing*; on most command-line-oriented operating systems, the command to obtain such a listing is usually **dir** (for directory) or **ls** (for list directory).

Often you'll be looking for specific files within a directory. Most operating systems include ways to specify filenames or lists of filenames to be displayed, such as "all the files beginning with resume" or "all files ending in .Z." or (on some systems) "all files created or changed since June 1, 1993." (See the discussion of wildcard characters and regular expressions later in this chapter.)

### Directories and subdirectories

Just as a file cabinet contains drawers, and each drawer may contain folders, which in turn have subfolders, a directory may also contain other directories. And these directories may themselves in turn contain directories, as well as files. A directory which is part of a larger directory can be called a *subdirectory.* A directory can contain any combination of files and subdirectories, as shown in Figure 4.2. Notice that there can be directories and files in a directory. The directory that contains a file or subdirectory is called its *parent*; files and subdirectories within a directory are called its *children.*

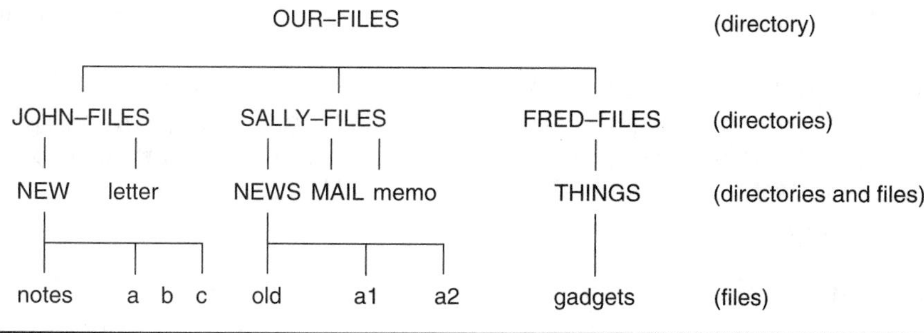


**Figure 4.2** Directories, subdirectories, and files.

In Unix, the conventions ., .., and ~ are often used for filenaming shorthand. . means "the current directory," .. means "the parent directory of the current directory." For example, in Fig. 4.2 if THINGS is the current directory, .. references FRED and ../.. references OUR-FILES, and you could reference SALLY-FILES as ../../SALLY-FILES. ~ means "your HOME directory," as in ~/mybin, ~/Projects/BigDig.

Figure 4.3 shows these relationships. Notice that there can be directories and files in a directory.

## Directories and the directory tree: Organizing files into a hierarchical structure

The use of directories and subdirectories provides organization for your files. By organizing your files within a hierarchy of directories and subdirectories, it's possible to manage dozens, hundreds, even thousands of files so they can be found readily. (One sign of a novice computer user is that they have hundreds of files under the topmost directory in their account and have almost no subdirectories.) The majority of the work you do involves using files—making files, reading files, adding to files, changing the contents of a file, printing out files, executing program files, etc. Not all these files are contained in the

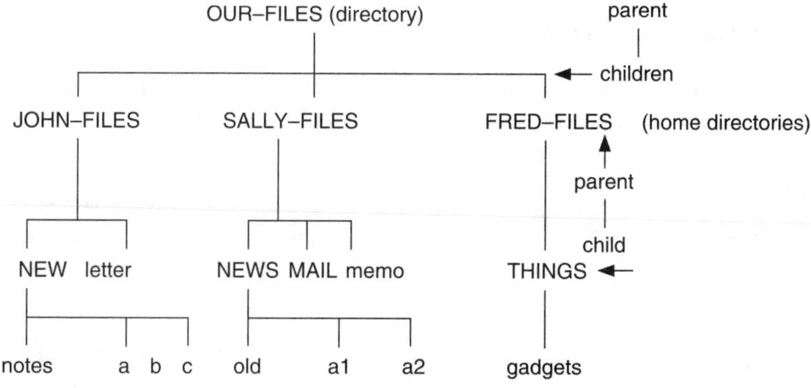


**Figure 4.3** Home, parent, and child directories.

same directory. So you need to be able to specify what file you want, and/or what directory you want.

All the files and directories in Unix's file system fall into place in a definable arrangement. Directories in Unix are organized like a giant, upside-down drawing of a tree. The specific details of this "tree" will vary as people create and modify their individual directories and files, but the underlying principles remain constant.

### The "root" of a Unix filesystem

The Unix file system, like a real tree, begins at its root. The *root* of the Unix file system is a directory known simply as / (the forward slash character). This top directory is, not surprisingly, called *root*. Root is the "big daddy" directory. It contains *everything* in a Unix file system—all files, all directories, all subdirectories—everything is filed within /. For example:

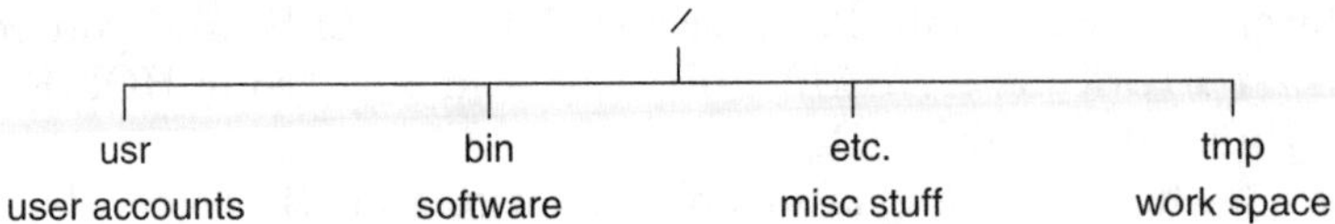


### Filename and pathname

Each file on a Unix system has a unique location within the file system on its computer. If you look at the Unix file structure, you'll see that you can identify where any file or directory is, by starting at root and listing the names of directories and subdirectories you traverse to get there.

The location consists of "directions" of how to get to the directory or file in the tree structure—the *path*. Just as the filename is the name of a file and identifies it, a *pathname* identifies a route, path, or location of a specified file or directory. A pathname consists of a string of directory names, each separated by a /, with the topmost (closest to root) name at the left and the lower (furthest from root) name at the left.* For example:

```
/usr/ddern/book/chapters/unix.txt
```

Note: / is usually referred to as "root" when you mean the top-level directory; when you're talking about a pathname, it's usually said as "slash."

### Current directory, working directory

The pathname of a file or directory starting from / is called its *absolute pathname*. Absolute pathnames can get long; remembering "where you are" and retyping

*MS-DOS systems use the backslash character (\) instead. If you work on a DOS-based PC and access a Unix computer for your Internet activity, it's easy to forget which system you're giving a command to and use the wrong slash character.

these strings can be great sources of opportunity to make errors, especially if you have similarly named directories. For example, imagine having to retype:

```
/usr/lgulliver/Workfiles/BigDig/Progreports/Prg-july.99
```

all the time. To avoid this, Unix (also DOS and most operating systems) provides a feature known as *current,* or *working* directory.

The operating system assumes that any filename (which can be a directoryname) you give that does *not* begin with / (root) is found in your current directory. For example, if your current directory is:

```
/usr/lgulliver/Workfiles/BigDig/Progreports
```

and you specify the file "Prg-july.99" in a command, Unix assumes that this file can be found in your current directory; by combining the name of your current directory (which Unix keeps track of in a "blackboard" piece of its memory called your *environment,* as something called an *environment variable*) and the filename it gets the file's full name:

```
/usr/lgulliver/Workfiles/BigDig/Progreports/Prg-july.99
```

Any directory in the file system that you have the appropriate permissions for (read and execute) can be your current directory. The file of system information that contains information about your Unix account includes an entry specifying what your current directory is to be set to initially every time you log in. This directory is usually your "home" directory. Unix also has several commands that let you "change your working or current directory" and several features to simplify the number of keystrokes (and amount of memorization) to let you move around your directory structure with the least amount of effort.

### Relative pathname

Because your computer always knows what your current directory is, there is another way you can refer to a file or directory that is not directly in the current directory, other than giving its absolute pathname. You can indicate files and directories in relation to it and let the computer do some of the work of converting these to absolute pathnames. This kind of pathname is a *relative pathname.* As mentioned above, if a pathname does not start with /, Unix assumes the path starts from the current directory. For example:

```
Workfiles/BigDig/Progreports/Prg-july.99
BigDig
Prg-july.99
```

are all relative pathnames.

You can use the .. convention to indicate relative pathnames that are above, or not directly under, your current directory. For example:

```
../BigDig/OldDig/TunnelInfo
../Laputa/EnvImpact/Reports
../../alice/MarchHare/glove-sizes
```

### Setting and resetting the current directory

You can change your current directory as often as you want during a computer session. Your computer will set the current directory for you every time you log on (or for PCs, start up). On a single-user computer, the initial current directory is usually the root of the file system, unless your start-up file (such as AUTOEXEC.BAT on an MS-DOS system) includes a "change directory" command.

The Unix command to change directory is **cd** (change directory). (We'll be talking more about giving Unix commands in a minute.) You can give an absolute or relative pathname with the **cd** command (indeed, with all Unix commands), including use of ... If you don't specify a new current directory, Unix returns you to the directory specified by the current value of your HOME environment variable. For example:

```
cd /usr/spool/news/comp/protocols/tcp-ip
cd
cd ../../Projects/BigDig
cd ../Resume
cd .
```

Note that the second of these commands takes you (back) to your home directory—and that the final one "does nothing"—leaves you where you are.

In some Unix shells (discussed shortly), you can use a feature called *aliases* to make shorthand commands to reset your current directory. Some versions of Unix let you set a list of directories to jump among directories or to go back and forth between a pair of directories.

### Multiple current directories

When you're connecting to another computer via the Internet, you're often working on two or more computers at once—the one you're at (which may be your PC, Mac, or workstation), and the one(s) you're connected to. For example, if you are going to transfer files, you need to be working on two computers at the same time: the one you're transferring files from and the one you're transferring them to. This means you may be working in several different file systems at the same time. So you may have current directories on each system. In cases like this, it is possible to have a current directory on each, and you may be able to change both of these, independently, from within the same program.

Usually, the current directory on your computer is called the *local current directory* and the one on the remote computer is called the *current directory* or *working directory*. Some Internet facilities, such as FTP, let you change these independently and have clearly designated commands to reset your current directory on each computer.

### Rules for Unix filenames

You create and specify filenames using a very clear set of rules. Every operating system has its own set of rules for creating and specifying filenames. Here's a summary of the rules for Unix:

- A filename can consist of as few as one character or up to a certain number of characters. Many older versions supported only up to 14-character filenames; many newer versions of Unix support longer filenames, up to 32 or 64 characters.
- A filename can use any of the following characters in any combination: the letters A through Z and a through z, the digits 0 through 9, and other characters including period (.), hyphen (-), plus (+), underline (_), percent (%), and tilde (~). For example:

```
Myfiles
hytelnet9.3
README
```

  Unix systems are case-sensitive; they consider upper- and lowercase letters in file and directory names as different (i.e., MAIL, Mail, and mail are considered different filenames).

- A filename may *not* contain the <return> character.
- There are several permissible characters whose use is *not* recommended in filenames since they have special meanings or consequences when entered at the Unix command prompt. If you don't know that these characters often have special behaviors—or know how to prevent their interpretation other than as literal characters—you'll get frustratingly unexpected and odd responses. Characters whose use is permitted in a filename but *not* recommended include <SPACE>, *, \, !, @, $, &, (, ), >, <, [, ], {, }, and "nonprinting characters."

Other rules relating to filenames:

- Avoid beginning filenames with a hyphen. For many Unix commands, the – character at the beginning of a word indicates it's a parameter, often making it difficult to specify it to begin a file, or it can lead to problems and errors. There are ways to enter such filenames, but it's best to avoid creating potential problems.
- Unlike DOS and some other operating systems, Unix does not divide up filenames into a "name" and "extension" (e.g., autoexec.bat, readme.Z). The . is simply considered a character in the filename. Names like "autoexec.bat" are legal within Unix; they're simply considered one continuous string.
- Some Unix commands do make assumptions about the ending of a filename, and there are associated conventions. The **make** command, for example, has C files end in "**.c**" and it's common practice to end files created by the **tar** command with **.Z.**

- Directory names end with the / (slash) character. However, the final / can be omitted if it is not essential, and it will not always be displayed by Unix.

There's no way you can distinguish between files and directories simply by looking at their names. There are some Unix commands which help you determine whether something is a file or a directory. For clarity, however, many people adopt a particular naming convention for their directories, such as using initial capitals or all uppercase letters for directory names—Projects or PROJECTS—and beginning filenames with lowercase letters—Projects/intro.txt or PROJECTS/readme-1. (Remember, unlike DOS, Unix distinguishes between upper- and lowercase letters [e.g., you can have two separate files named "README" and "readme"].)

Filenames that begin with the . character, such as .login and .mailrc, won't be displayed in most directory-listing commands unless you give the appropriate parameters (discussed later in this chapter, under the heading, "Those dot Files").

### The root of the UNIX file system and its major branches

Many of the files and directories on Unix systems are usually named and organized in a similar way. This includes the programs, utilities, and libraries used by the system and by users—and also many of the directories where publicly available files are kept. By knowing these conventions, and a few basic Unix commands, you can usually find and recognize directories you're looking for on remote systems within a few minutes. (Often, the systems are set up to make this even easier—and the Internet community is continually developing and providing new facilities, such as archie, Gopher, and VERONICA which make finding things even easier and more automatic.)

### Naming conventions in the Unix world

The Unix community has evolved a number of conventions for naming and organizing files and directories. These directory-naming conventions include:

- Directories with names such as /usr1, /usr2 (pronounced "you-zer, you-zer-one"), /home usually contain the home directories for users (e.g., /usr1/alice, /usr2/lgulliver, /home/ralph_r). Note that there is no e in usr.
- pub (pronounced "pub" as in "grub") is usually a "public" directory, containing files intended to be publicly sharable, configured so that they can be accessed by anonymous-FTP for file transfer.
- news—Usenet Newsgroups usually are found within this directory.
- Directories with names like lib (pronounced "libe") usually contain files and subdirectories with "libraries" of files used by a program, such as libraries of programming interfaces, math subroutines, data files, printer definitions, compiler routines, etc.
- Directories with names like /local usually contain files with programs or information specific to this system

- Directories named man (pronounced "man" for "manual") usually contain text for on-line documentation; in particular, for the Unix commands, called *manpages,* or *manual pages.* (More about this soon.)
- Directories named etc (pronounced "et-cee" or "etcetera") often contain things that configure the system on startup, and various utilities and daemons run by the system.
- Directories with names like /tmp usually contain temporary files created and used by software. This is a "workspace" area. Sometimes interim system copies of files you're working on, such as editing, can be found here, if you feel you have lost important work in progress. (Don't count on it, however. Also, don't count on any file(s) you put there staying there—system administrators and automatic daemons can randomly delete these files for "housekeeping" or to reclaim file space.)
- dev (pronounced "dev" not "deev") relates to *devices* such as printers, terminals, tape-drives, CD-ROM drives, etc.
- Files with names beginning with tty (pronounced "tee-tee-why") are used by Unix to exchange input and output with terminal communication ports. For example, whenever you log in, you are assigned a tty number for the duration of the session.

Commonly used filenames and conventions on Unix systems include:

- /dev/null—a "black hole/garbage can file." This is a file "with no bottom or contents," which anyone can write to (send output to), but it has no contents. /dev/null is useful for sending program output to if you only want to see its diagnostic and error messages (or vice versa). Think of it like the "memory hole" in George Orwell's *1984,* or a wastebasket with a papershredder in it—don't send any information here you expect to retrieve. /dev/null is often used conversationally, as in "Send all complaints to /dev/null."
- Filename endings often indicate a file's nature or use, for example:

  filename~ is a backup file created by a text editor.

  .bak is a backup file created by a program.

  .PS is a PostScript output file.

  .Z is created using the **tar** (tape archive) Unix command or the ZIP compression function.

  .n, .nr, and .nro are for document source text including **nroff** formatting commands.

  .t, .tr, and .tro are for document source text including **troff** (typeset nroff) formatting commands.

  .P is an Nroff output file.

  .T is a Troff output file.

### Those "dot" files

Many Unix and Internet programs you'll be using allow you to personalize and customize their operations: how certain features will behave, lists of abbreviations they'll accept, and the like. This information can be saved in files in your account, called *initialization files*; the program will automatically check for this file each time when you start it up and will perform the commands in the file before executing your command or giving you its prompt.

How does the program know where to look? How do you know which file is being used, in case you want to inspect, create, or modify it? As a rule, Unix programmers employ the following conventions in defining the name of the initialization file(s):

- It is located in your home directory so you know where to look, and your initialization files don't get mixed up with anyone else's.
- Begin with . so that you don't have to see the list of initialization files every time you do a directory listing of your home directory. (There can easily be 10, 20, or 30 such files.)
- End with "rc"; historically, "rc" stood for "run commands." This term is no longer necessarily accurate and applicable, but the naming convention remains in common use.

Unix and Internet tools that may have "dot" files include:

csh (.cshrc).

.login (executed when you log in).

mail (.mailrc).

Usenet news (.newsrc).

Gopher (.gopherrc)—any "bookmarks" you create will also be saved here.

Xwindows (.Xdefaults, .Xinit, .Xstart, .xinitrc, .xsession, and others); initialization and configuration files for using X Windows.

**System-level dot files.** In addition to your own personal initialization files, many Unix and Internet facilities can have initialization files that apply to everyone on your computer system, setting parameters and configuration specifics that relate to your computer system as a whole. For example, **csh** (the C shell) and **sh** (the Bourne shell) all accept system-level initialization files. These files typically use the same names but are kept in a part of the file system "owned" by the operating system. Generally, a program will first process the system-level initialization file, then, if you have one, your own.

**Other "dot" files you should know about: .signature and .plan.** In addition to the "dot-rc" files, there are a few other dot files you should know about, notably your .signature file and .plan file.

**.signature.** When you post a message to a Usenet Newsgroup or send an e-mail message, your name and e-mail address are usually in the message, but you may want to "sign" the message with standard information about who you are: your name, title, organization, phone, fax, one or more other e-mail addresses, and perhaps a one-line comment and your Public-Key encryption code. By convention, this information is kept in a "signature" file, which on Unix systems is named .signature (pronounced "dot signature") and located in your home directory. (Remember, Unix **ls** and **dir** directory listing commands don't display filenames beginning with . unless you explicitly tell them to.) For brevity, this file is often referred to as ".sig" (pronounced "dot sig" as in "your dot sig file").

When you create a posting to a Usenet group, for example, the Usenet software will automatically look for this signature file and include it at the end of your message automatically. E-mail software won't necessarily include it automatically, but it will be easier to insert this file than retype it all, and your program may have a special command which inserts this file.

You should try to keep your .signature file to four lines or less. Some programs won't handle longer ones; overlong .signature files are also considered contrary to *netiquette* (network etiquette). For example:

```
Alice Liddell alice@hearthrug.wonderland.com
Voice: 617-666-5555 FAX: 617-666-5559
SnailMail: Wonderland Software, 42 Jabberwork Way, Vorpal MA
02199
Wonderland Software: "You won't think you're in Kansas anymore"
```

("SnailMail," by the way, means your post office address for physical mail. The term is considered to often imply the greater speed and convenience of e-mail over paper mail.)

The .signature file is frequently referred to in electronic and spoken discussion as "dot-signature file," "dot-sig," ".sig file," "sig file." A person's .signature file is a common place to put a short general message, a humorous remark, or a disclaimer.

Here's what Mark Horton and Eugene Spafford have to say about .signature files in their introductory message in their "Rules for Posting to Usenet," which you can find in the Usenet news.announce.newusers Newsgroup (explained in Chap. 6).

> Please keep your signatures concise, as people do not appreciate seeing lengthy signatures, nor paying the phone bills to repeatedly transmit them. 2 or 3 lines are usually plenty. Sometimes it is also appropriate to add another line or two for addresses on other major networks where you can be reached (e.g., Internet, Bitnet). Long signatures are definitely frowned upon. DO NOT include drawings, pictures, maps, or other graphics in your signature—it is not the appropriate place for such material and is viewed as rude by other readers.

**.plan, .project.** Your .plan or .project file is a well-known place to put information about yourself that you want to be readily available to anyone else on the network, such as your name, title, phone number, what you may be working on. You can inspect the contents of anyone else's .plan or .project file, using the **finger** command. (This command finds and takes information from these files; you don't have to specify any filenames.)

Similarly, other people can read your .plan or .project file via **finger.** This is a convenient way to let people determine where to send you physical mail or get your phone number. *Caution:* Remember that this information is very publicly available. Don't include information like your password or the fact that you're away on vacation for a month.

Now that you know something about the Unix file system, it's time to learn how to use—formulate and issue commands to—Unix.

## Using Unix

In this section, you'll learn some of the basics of how to issue Unix commands and some essential Unix commands and tips. You work with Unix the same way as with any other computer program: You give it commands, and Unix executes—does—them. Some of these commands will invoke or involve Internet services and resources or may lead to other Internet-oriented activity. Others may not. Depending on how your computers, software, and networks are set up, you may not be able to tell ahead of time, or the same software may do both Internet and non-Internet activities.

Some of these commands will invoke programs to do activities like editing text and document files, creating and reading electronic mail, and reading Internet bulletin boards. Others may connect you to Internet resources and services on distant computers. Examples are:

| | |
|---|---|
| `% emacs my-resume` | (Edit this file, using the emacs editor.) |
| `% mail` | (Read e-mail.) |
| `% finger alice@jabber.wock.com` | (Get information about this user from their system.) |
| `% telnet jabber.wock.com` | (Remote login to this system.) |

### Giving commands to Unix

As a rule, you will work with Unix as an *interactive user*—you give a command, and Unix responds by doing its best to perform this command; Unix lets you know it is ready for another command, usually by displaying another command prompt. You tell Unix what to do—give it commands—in one of two ways, depending on the type of user interface you've got: (1) by typing commands and keywords and stuff at the *command line,* when you see a *command prompt,* or (2) by selecting menu choices or icons with your mouse or other pointing device. (In some cases, you'll choose menu items and then supply other pieces of information by typing them in.)

Some of the programs, facilities, and services you use will similarly be interactive, offering you a prompt (such as an e-mail program), or "being there" (such as a visual word processor) until you *quit* or *exit,* at which point you return to the Unix command prompt.

Other programs will be *noninteractive*; once you give the command, the program begins executing; when it can take a new command, Unix displays a new command prompt. (Some programs display intermediate messages to let you know they are currently active, possibly even how far along they are.)

### Talking with Unix: You and the shell

Rather than talking with their users directly, most operating systems interact through a type of program usually called a *shell* or *command interpreter.* Unix starts up a shell for each user when you log in, automatically. (To be precise, it executes a copy of the shell program, resulting in a *process.*) This is referred to as your *login shell.* If you are using a windowing system, such as X Windows, each window has its own shell. In addition, because Unix is a multitasking operating system, other shells can be running at the same time to start up you, other users, or programs run by you or other users or even by Unix itself.

Your additional shells can "subordinate" to, or run "below," your "main" shell. Such additional shells are called *subshells*; the process, or executing software, is called a *child process.* You can also have *parallel* subshells, such as in separate windows or running in the background. It is possible to have a lot of subshells and parallel shells and windows running.

**A choice of shells.** The shell program for use on DOS PCs is usually called *command.com*. There are a number of different versions of this program available from companies who sell DOS; in addition, there are other shell programs available from other software developers which offer different interfaces and features. Similarly, there are a number of different shells available on most Unix systems. Some are considered a standard part of a full Unix product; several additional shells have been developed over the years by members of the Unix community. (You generally select one shell to be your default shell, meaning the one you get every time you log in; it's very easy to invoke a different shell for part or all of a session on the computer and equally easy to change your choice of default shell.)

The standard shells available for UNIX are **sh** and **csh,** the *c-shell:*

- **sh** (pronounced "ess-aitch"), also known as the Bourne shell (after S. R. Bourne, its creator), is the most common and most standardized shell. It doesn't have as many features as other, newer shells, but it has the important virtue of being available on every Unix system. If you know **sh,** you can count on knowing how to use any Unix system; if you write Unix shellscripts (batch files of Unix commands), using **sh**'s commands means they'll work anywhere.
- **csh** (pronounced "see-ess-aitch"), the c-shell, is the second most prevalent Unix shell. **Csh**, according to the Unix manual, is "a shell (command interpreter) with C-like syntax" (as in C, the programming language). The csh offers some features not available in Bourne shell, such as *history* and *aliasing* (explained shortly).

Over the years, Unix developers have created additional shells with other features, such as:

- **ksh** (the Korn shell), a public-domain extension to the Bourne shell (**sh**), initially written by David Korn.
- **bash** (Bourne-again **sh**), a version of the Bourne shell (**sh**), written primarily by Brian Fox of the Free Software Foundation, that incorporates **csh** features such as aliasing, plus the ability to scroll through your "history" of previous command lines and to edit the current command line as if with a one-line word processor. (I've been using **sh** and **csh** for years; I just recently discovered **bash** and tend to use it instead.)
- **tcsh**, an enhanced version of the C-shell (**csh**) with a number of additional features, including command-line editing and filename completion.

**Shells have commands and features.** Most of the Unix shells are themselves highly sophisticated programs. They have several dozen subcommands of their own and many features you commonly expect from a programming language, such as parameters and substitution, environment variables, conditional programming constructions such as **do, for,** and **if,** logical and numerical evaluation, error and exit codes, and much, much more. With a little reading and practice, you'll discover you can do remarkably sophisticated "shell programming" in Unix—and that even a one-line Unix shellscript can be a potent tool. You'll find a few sample shellscripts in this chapter and in App. D.

**What the shell does.** The shell is responsible for:

- Displaying the "ready for another command" prompt. Many users like to have the prompt include the system name (which is helpful if you have multiple windows on your screen), their own name, the current directory, and even the date and time. Common default prompts are $ and %.
- Checking your input (from the command line or mouse or menu choices) for syntax errors (i.e., did you enter a "grammatically understandable" command?).
- Looking for the program(s) you're requesting, and finding (or creating) files for input or output.
- Translating any wildcard descriptors for files, special characters, redirection of input or output, etc., into their full meaning.
- Once it has finished accepting your command, the shell "asks" the operating system to do it (e.g., invoke your word processing program, start up e-mail, or access an Internet service). When you're done using the program, you are generally returned to the shell (get back the command prompt).
- Making sure that output from programs you use gets properly displayed at your screen, sent to files, etc.

### Input, output

Activity between you and the computer—and between two computer programs—consists of *input* and *output*. What you type at your keyboard is input. So are the mouse clicks. What the computer program reports back to you in response to your commands is output. By default, output goes to your screen. You can also capture output to a file. Unix also lets you use the output from one program as input into another and use the contents of a file as input.

Now let's talk about giving commands to your Unix shell.

### Command lines and syntax

You tell your Unix shell what to do by giving it commands. [For the moment, let's assume you're using a Command-Line User Interface (CLUI) rather than a mouse or menu-oriented Graphic User Interface (GUI).] A Unix command consists of a *program name,* a.k.a. *command,* and command line arguments—information as needed. Much of your Unix activity may consist of simply entering one or two word command lines. For example:

| | |
|---|---|
| ***telnet*** | (invoke remote login facility) |
| ***telnet quake.think.com*** | (do remote login to Thinking Machine's WAIS server) |
| ***ftp*** | (invoke file transfer facility) |
| ***mail*** | (invoke e-mail facility on unread mail) |
| ***mail -f mbox*** | (invoke e-mail facility on read mail) |
| ***gopher*** | (invoke Internet Gopher) |
| ***archie eudora*** | (have archie identify sites which have Eudora software available for retrieval) |
| ***archie -m10 -t -s hytel *.ca.us / more*** | (have archie identify up to 10 sites, sorted by date, with software whose name contains "hytel," in sites in the California domain and display this output scrolled by screenful) |

The "other information" can consist of:

- Filenames to take information from (input) or put results (output) into. For example, you can specify a file, such as *my-resume*:

  ***more my-resume***

- Parameters and switches—specify settings to the command, such as keywords or patterns to search for, what order to sort or list things in, or how to behave. For example, grep's **l** switch causes grep to only list the files containing the pattern but not the specific lines.

  ***grep -l kludges lab-report***

- Operations indicators that specify how to parse the command line, use files for input or output, or how to execute the command. For example:

```
ps | grep $USER | wc -l > top-processes
```

Sound complicated? It can be. Unix has a lot of "power"—which means there is a lot you can learn. What's important at this stage is to learn enough of the "rules of the command line" to "speak basic Unix."

When you are entering a Unix command, rules to know and follow include:

- Remember that Unix is case-sensitive. An uppercase letter and a lowercase letter never have the same meaning.
- Parts of a command line are separated by one or more spaces or tabs. In some cases, where the shell can unambiguously interpret what you're entering, you can omit the spaces.

**Wildcard characters and regular expressions.** You can specify patterns, such as to match words, or filenames, with *wildcard characters* such as ? and * and *regular expressions.* Whenever your shell encounters any of these constructs, say, to specify a set of files in a command line, it looks to see which of the possible names of files or directories satisfy the pattern, and *replaces* the pattern expression with the names of these matching files and/or directories and then executes the command using the full list. A ? matches any *one* character. For example, **mac?** will match macA, macP, mac+—but not macII, macOS, or mac2e. **mac??** will match macII, macOS, etc., and **m?c** will match mac, m1c, m+c.

A * matches a filename, even one of zero-length—except filenames that begin with a **.** character. For example, **hytel*** will match hytelnet, hyteln601, hyteln601.Z, and hytel; **go*r** will match gopher, gor, gomer, and googler.

Unlike MS-DOS, if there are other characters after the * in your pattern, Unix will take them into account. For example, DOS will consider **go*r** to match goph, gotta, and goph.Z as well as gopher. This is not true in Unix; **autoe*.bat** will match autoexec.bat—but autoe*yz.bat won't.

? is often used in combination with * to help limit what matches (e.g., **???*** will match only files with at least three characters).

**Regular expressions.** Wildcard characters, like the name implies, match *any* nonspecial characters. Sometimes you want to limit the match to a select set or range of characters, however. Unix also lets you do this, with its regular expressions feature. A regular expression defines a list of characters; if any of these characters occur at a corresponding location in the filenames or other objects being matched against, that part is considered a match.

You indicate a regular expression by enclosing it between the left square bracket ([) and right square bracket (]) characters. If you give a list (e.g., [abcglz145]), if any of these characters is used in the corresponding position of the item being matched against, it will be considered a match.

For example, **foo[bdtny]** would match foob, food, foot, foon, and fooy, but not foo, fooa, fooc, or foobar.

A regular expression can also contain *ranges* of characters, such as [a-cl-p2-6] (which is equivalent to saying [abclmnop23456]). Unix interprets ranges based on the ASCII character sequence. (So, for example, [m-b] is a meaningless range; [b-m] is a meaningful range.)

You can mix and match lists and ranges, such as [a-cA-Cdegh-m02-3]. You can also use several regular expressions in a given specifier, such as [abc][abrnz][159].Z. You can also mix and match wildcards and regular expressions, such as .[ckb]sh*, gopher*[ZPT], and hytel[5-7n]*Z. To look at all the files with "new" in their names, you could specify ***new***.

It's worth investing an hour or so just learning how to use regular expressions in Unix. Check your on-line Unix and other help information—and various Unix manuals—for more information on regular expressions. And when you have access to the right facilities, experiment until you feel comfortable using at least basic wildcards.

Knowing how to use these features will come in very handy, particularly if you become interested in searching for and retrieving files—and many Unix-oriented write-ups use wildcards and regular expressions in their text; for example, "See the hytel*Z files in the /pub/hytel* directories."

**Characters with special meaning to Unix shells.** Certain characters have special meanings to the shell (and not always the same meaning in both **sh** and **csh**, etc.). Some of these characters have their special meaning if used as the first character of a word; others have it anywhere.

**|**, the "pipe" symbol, sends output from one command to become input for the next command on the command line. Most shell commands have been written as small, specific-function utilities. "Piping" lets you use them together, in plumbing fashion, sending the output from one to be input for the next. For example, **cat | etc | termcap | more.** Here, **cat** outputs the contents of the file | etc. | termcap; this command line "pipes" them through the **more** command, so if you have more than a screenful of information, it doesn't whiz by too fast.

Suppose you want to check for new mail from a specific person whose e-mail name you know (e.g., alice@jabber.wock.com). By using Unix's pipe facility, you can send the output of the **msgs** command to **grep,** a command which searches its input for matching text strings:

**msgs | grep alice@jab**

By using this simple ad hoc command sequence, you can do something without having to write a complicated program or go into e-mail, read through new-message headers, etc.

**$** is the first character for a parameter or environment variable and means that a value is to be substituted in these expressions (e.g., $HOME, $1, $MAIL). For example, **echo $USER** displays the current value of your USER variable. (This is useful if you forget your user-name.)

> (right-angle-bracket) filename sends output to the filename immediately following. For example, **man grep > grep.txt** sends the manual page for **grep,** as displayed by the **man** command, to a file named grep.txt, so you can read it or print it out at your convenience.

Be careful using the > character. If you already have a file with this name, > first deletes it and then creates a new file with this name. >> causes output to be *appended to* filename if filename already exists; if filename doesn't yet exist, it is created and input sent to it. For example:

```
% ls -l grep.txt
grep.txt not found
% man grep > grep.txt
% ls -l grep.txt
-rw------- 1 aliddell    14402 Apr 01 12:17 grep.txt
% man sh > grep.txt
% ls -l grep text
-rw------- 1 aliddell    44589 Apr 01 12:17 grep.txt
% man grep >> grep.txt
% ls -l grep.txt
-rw------- 1 aliddell    58991 Apr 01 12:17 grep.txt
```

**<** (left angle bracket) takes input from the filename immediately following it. For example, **more < grep.txt.more grep.txt** is sufficient, but this works too.

**;** (semicolon) means the end of this command; the next word begins a new command. It lets you put multiple commands on a single line. For example:

```
% cd; echo $USER; pwd   Change directory back to home directory, then echo
                        username, then display current directory
alice
/usr/alice
%
```

**** (back slash) causes the next character to be interpreted literally, "deactivating" any special meaning it normally has. For example:

```
%echo \$USER
$USER
% echo \*
*
%
```

**Correcting erroneous commands.** If you make a typing error, or change your mind in issuing a command to Unix (and to most other facilities you'll be using), you can use:

- The Delete-character to erase characters, from left to right. On most systems, there is a key labeled <DELETE>. On some keyboards, you can also use <CONTROL-BACKSPACE> or <CONTROL-H>.
- The Delete-word character to delete the right-most word (characters from the end up to the first space on the left). On most Unix systems, this is set to <CONTROL-W>. (You can change this setting.)
- The Delete-line character to delete the entire line back up to the cursor. On most systems, this is set to <CONTROL-U>. (You can change this setting.)

**Ending a command line.** To end a Unix command line, and tell your shell to begin processing it, press the <RETURN> key; this tells Unix to read what you've typed and act on it.

**Stopping a command: Interrupting versus pausing.** To stop a command you have started:

- The Interrupt character will kill most noninteractive programs and return you to the shell prompt. On most systems, this is set to <CONTROL-C>.
- The Flow-control-stop character will "pause" output until you hit the Flow-control-start character. On most systems, these are <CONTROL-S> and <CONTROL-Q>, respectively; on some, the <PAUSE> key will have the same effect.
- If you are running a Unix shell with *job control* (such as **csh** or **tcsh** but not **sh**), entering <CONTROL-Z> at the beginning of a line will *stop* the program you have started and return you to the Unix command prompt. You can run other commands and return to the stopped job, by entering **fg,** the "foreground" command, at the Unix prompt.
- The End-of-file character will quit you out of many interactive programs. On most systems, this is set to <CONTROL-D>. If you enter <CONTROL-D> to your login shell, it will usually log you out.

Again, consider reading through the Unix manual or a Unix textbook to learn more about this.

### Environment and environment variables

When you log in, in addition to starting up a shell to serve you, Unix sets up a "scratch pad" area, called your *environment space,* where it (and you) can make temporary notes regarding your session, called your *environment.* Your environment includes information such as what shell you're using, where your home directory is, what text editor you want to use from the e-mail program, and so on. In fact, every shell and every program that you use gets its own environment—some of which is "inherited" from any parent shell.

Each piece of information is stored in an *environment variable,* which has a name, such as $HOME (your home directory) or $USER (your user-name). Both you and the programs you use read and use these variables and their values. You can also change some (but not all) of them.

The most important environment variable to know about is PATH. When you give a command, PATH is the list of directories the shell searches through to find this command and the order to search in. If the appropriate directory isn't in your PATH, the command won't be found or executed. PATH is usually defined in your .login file. As you create commands of your own, and put them in a directory such as your own *mybin,* you'll want to add *mybin* to your PATH definition. Also, if there are utilities you want to use frequently, such as X Windows, Internet navigators, math libraries, or games, you may want to add their directory to your PATH.

## A Dozen Useful Unix Commands

There are over a hundred standard Unix utilities available to users; in addition, each shell (**sh, csh,** etc.) has dozens of "internal" commands and programming capabilities. Here's a quick overview of about a dozen Unix and shell commands. Some of these you'll use very often; some you'll use far less frequently, but I consider them essential for you to know about.

I want to point out that I'm deliberately *not* giving you even a fraction of the available switches or parameters here. When you feel ready, read the full descriptions and discussions of these commands in the Unix manual pages (more about this soon)—there's a wealth of powerful features lurking inside these often apparently simple commands!

**The *more* command.** To read files and output easily:

```
more [filename(s)]
```

It displays output or files one screenful at a time, pausing until you tell it to go on to the next screen. For example:

```
% more myresume joe-resume
```

Scroll through these two files.

```
% more *resume
```

Scroll through all files whose names end in "resume"

```
% grep MUMPS *resume | more
```

Find all uses of "MUMPS" (a programming language) in "resume" files and keep them from zooming across the screen.

**The *cat* command.** To display files, output continuously:

```
cat [filename(s)]
```

Displays file(s) or output continuously. Useful for downloading ASCII files to your PC. First set up a local "capture" file, and then tell the Unix system to "cat" the file.

**The *grep* command.** To search files, output for text strings:

```
grep -keys text-string [filename(s)]
```

Given a specified text string, look through files or other input and find all lines that match the string. The *keys* determine what **grep** does when it finds matches (e.g., display lines, display nonmatching lines, just indicate files with a match in them, etc. **grep** has been said to stand for "get regular expression and print," "global regular expression pattern-matching," among other things). **grep** can be a tremendously useful tool; it's worth reading the manual page and playing with it a while.

**The *echo* command.** To display a text string or message:

```
echo text
```

Displays specified text, including values of variables. Useful for checking current variable values and for putting in display comments in Unix batch files (shellscripts). For example:

```
% echo "Hello, World."
Hello, World.
% echo $USER
/usr/alice
% echo "Hello from $USER"
Hello from /usr/alice
```

**The *cd* command.** To change current directory:

```
cd [directoryname]
```

Make "directoryname" your new current directory. (If you enter just **cd,** you will be returned to the $HOME directory.)

**The *pwd* command.** To display current directory:

```
pwd
```

Displays the full pathname of the current directory.

**The *man* command.** To see the manual page for a Unix command:

```
man command-name
```

Displays the on-line manual page (manpage) for the specified Unix command. Many Internet utilities have a manpage, such as archie and Gopher. (For more about the **man** command and the information it supplies, see Chap. 12.)

**The *mv* command.** Move a file to a new place or name:

```
mv filename target
```

Moves the specified file to another place in your file system. If you specify a directoryname as the target, the file is moved with its current name; if you specify a filename as the target, the moved file gets this new name; **mv** can therefore also be used to rename files within the same directory. For example:

```
mv dig-notes MEETINGS
mv dig-notes ~/MEETINGS/dignotes.92
mv dig-notes dignotes.92
```

**The *chmod* command.** Modify file read, write, or execute permissions for files and directories:

```
chmod filename(s)
```

Unix lets you define the read, write, and execute privileges for every file and directory in your account. The default permission settings are often defined in one of your login files.

The **chmod** command changes the read, write, and execute permissions for files and directories for any of three categories of user: you, users in your group, and anybody. The permissions on your account's directories should be properly set by your system administrator. The most common use you're likely to have is to make a shellscript (Unix command batch file) executable so that you can use the filename as a command name and for making files available to other programs and users. For example:

```
chmod +x mybin/budget
```

**The *cp* command.** Copy file(s):

```
cp filename(s) target
```

Makes a copy of the specified file or files. If "target" is a filename, the copy gets this name; if "target" is a directoryname, the copies have the same name as the originals and are in the specified directory.

**The lpr or *print* command.** Send files to a printer:

```
lpr filename(s)
```

Send file(s) to a printer. You'll need to find out what printers are available, what the default printer is, and how to select among them.

**The *clear* command.** Clear the screen:

```
clear
```

Clear the screen and reset the visual display. Useful to get rid of "garbage" characters and display formatting errors.

**The *logout* command.** End session and log out:

```
logout, exit, <CONTROL-D>
```

End the session and log out. Some systems and shells let you set up "logout" files, similar to "login" files, of commands that get executed when you leave in this orderly fashion.

## Getting On-Line Help: Manpages and Other Facilities

Most Unix systems contain a good deal of on-line information on the commands and other key concepts. You can display this text on your screen or send it to a printer. There are a number of commands and methods available to access this information and to help determine what you want to ask for, notably:

- The **man** command, which displays on-line manual pages (manpages) for Unix commands (and some keywords and files)
- The **apropos** command, which displays command summaries that contain matches to specified keywords

Many Unix commands will display their syntax if you give the appropriate parameter; there are also numerous other on-line help and information facilities built into most Unix systems. For more information about on-line Unix help, see Chap. 12.

## Ten (or So) Common Mistakes That Unix Users Make

Unix users who praise the "power of Unix" often lose sight of the fact that, as the late Isaac Asimov noted, "It's a poor atom blaster that can't point both ways." That is, the power of Unix can just as well be employed by users to make bigger, harder-to-undo errors as it can to provide working environment platforms. Not just catastrophic errors, of course; Unix also lets you make small, niggling, persistent errors that makes things that *should* work appear "broken." But it all adds up to less results for more effort. And more confusion and frustration, which also tend to discourage the timorous new user.

Errors fall into categories by source. Some are typical of new-to-computer users or those coming from the MS-DOS world. But even experienced "power" users who know the manpages by heart commit occasional mistakes. Even if you don't make errors or mistakes, it's helpful to understand what may happen to others around you. Especially if you're a system administrator or are mentoring Unix novices.

Here's a double handful of "popular" Unix user errors, based on observation, personal experience, and some programmers and system administrators of my acquaintance. In some cases, I've noted reasons or solutions. (A special thank-you here goes to Ed Frankenberry, who helped review and advise me on most of these, and who helped me learn much of what I know about Unix.)

Disclaimers: The list of problems, symptoms, and solutions here is not exhaustive or necessarily meaningful for all versions of Unix. And some of these mistakes are for Unix commands, features, or aspects this chapter hasn't otherwise discussed.

### Spacing out and other digital dexterity

Minor typing errors, such as an unintentional space, in a Unix command line can result in serious consequences. Nowhere is the "power of Unix" more evident than in the ability of a user to cause great, sweeping, potentially irrevocable damage in a single command. Flakey keyboards and noisy lines can also add to the input error problem—but most of the danger is where your fingertips hit the keys. For example, one careless space in an **rm** (remove file) command that also contains an asterisk, issued within the wrong directory, can ruin your whole day (and it's a rare novice who doesn't do this at least once). Don't use the **rm** command until you have read more about it, either; the odds of getting your file back may be low to nonexistent, depending on how your system is run. Other typing errors can be equally disastrous, such as typing > instead of >>, which will wipe out the existing file instead of appending to it.

### Just say yes—error messages and responses

When something has gone very wrong, some Unix applications offer diagnostic messages rivaling those of many computer games in terms of their mixture of ominous portent and lack of useful information, like "Warning! All buffers corrupted!", "No more space available!", or "There is a dwarf with an axe at the i-node table!" Read these warnings carefully. It's very easy to say "Yes" when you should have said "No," or vice versa. When in doubt, remove hands from keyboard and phone your system administrator for help.

### Environmental impact and other strange behavior

Perhaps it seems that the Character-Erase and Line Kill characters don't work or your variable's setting isn't staying. More often than not, Unix is working fine, and the problem is that you, the user, misunderstand what's going on.

If you don't understand the concepts of "shell," "environment," "parent/child/sibling processes," and the "dot" (.login, .newsrc, etc.) files, it's easy to feel like Nancy Drew wandering down the back staircase with a dim candle in hand, about to be clobbered. Other examples of "not-doing-what-you-expect" behavior are:

- **csh** refuses to overwrite files (you're set to "noclobber").
- **more** disappears episodically (because on your system, it's an alias and therefore not available when you drop to a Bourne shell (**sh**).
- Shellscripts to change your current directory don't work, to DOS users' dismay. (Changes to the environment of a child process environments are not inherited by the parent.)

Learning how and why all these things are happening is part of the "joy" of Unix—if you like figuring this stuff out.

### Trading options

Misunderstanding how options and switches in various Unix commands work, or not knowing which ones are set, is another source of potential trouble, particularly for users who don't know enough to inspect their environment.

The **mv** (move) and **cp** (copy) commands, for example, often have a **-f** (force) switch, which lets an existing file be overwritten, even if they are write-protected. If you don't know that you're using, say, an alias or shellscript for **mv** preceding the regular executable, you'll feel like your shell is refusing orders. This often accounts for believing something serious has broken. When in doubt, read the documentation. Consult the on-line manual page or a reference manual, if you can find one nearby.

### Accounts

Depending on how attentive and methodical your system administrator is, the standard account created for you as a new user may contain any manner of errors and historical irrelevancies in its "dot" files, particularly the startup files for logging in (.profile for **sh**; .login for **csh**) and for your shell (.cshrc for **csh**). Read through these files and then clean out or customize them, after checking with your system administrator. You'll learn a lot about Unix in fixing the mistakes you make in the process. I sure have (and still do).

### Double, double: The wages of syntax

Shell syntax—how you enter commands for **sh, csh,** etc.—is potent but very, very finicky. And there are syntactical differences among the various shells.

Make sure you've used and matched up those single, double, and back-quotes (', ", \`), parens, brackets, and braces, ( (), [], and {}) and whatnot accurately; correctly used single > and < characters, or double >> and << characters, and inserted those "make-next-character-literal" backslashes (\) in the right places and quantities.

### It ain't the computer, it's the network

What many naive users perceive as Unix problems often really are legitimate behaviors because you're on a network or are network troubles. Sometimes the other computer is running slowly or the network in between you gets congested. Or you may inadvertently give a reserved or escape character.

Remember, networked computing involves a lot of computer resources all working together; there's a lot that can go wrong. The name servers may be unavailable; network daemons may run amok; someone may be running CPU-grabbing processes or sending big files down the network. Don't blame the computer all the time.

### The PATH not taken

Can't find certain programs? Getting the wrong version? Maybe your PATH is missing essential directories, like the current directory (.) and any personal bins, or maybe the PATH sequence is ordered wrong. Check your dot files (.profile, .cshrc., .login); display your PATH via **echo $PATH**.

### Blowing away files

Overall, the most common mistake is deleting lots of files by accident or changing your mind—a microsecond too late. The general remedy is to set up a nondestructive "move unwanted file(s) to a trash directory" command (and *don't* call it **rm**). Use an **rm** shellscript on the trash—after a backup has been done. After-the-fact utilities may help. But prevention is better than recovery.

### Running out of environment space

Your "environment" is the scratchpad space the shell uses in its memory to keep track of variables and other information during your session. A certain amount of space is available per user.

It's possible to do something that requires more space than you've got available. While this is harder to do in Unix than DOS, it can be done. Usually, you'll see an error message like "Run out of environment space."

### Potpourri

- Exiting the shell, job controllers, or window manager through one CTRL-D or CTRL-Z too many. (Csh users, set "ignoreeof" in your .cshrc file.)
- Recursive shellscripts
- Using **test, test1, test2**... as program names. You'll forget what they are—and sysadmins will delete them.
- Not documenting your shellscripts.
- Using **chown** (change ownership) at the directory level.

This list is clearly not exhaustive—but with any luck, you'll discover or invent new, frustrating Unix user errors, instead of repeating these.

## Programming in Unix: Shellscripts

As mentioned, you can write Unix programs consisting of a series of shell and Unix commands. You can enter them at the command line; more commonly, people put these into files, called *shellscripts.* (DOS users call the DOS equivalent *batch files.*) You'll need to test and "debug" them to make sure they work, which can be time-consuming, frustrating, and educational.

Once a shellscript works, however, you'll most likely appreciate having it—and soon, you'll start "thinking in Unix" and getting ideas of how and where other shellscripts can make your life as a Unix user easier. Recommended practice is to include "comments" so you and other people can tell easily what the purpose of a shellscript is (e.g., your name, the date written, and purpose, and anything tricky or important to know).

### Some simple unix shellscripts

Here's a few one or few-line shellscripts that I've written over the years, which I find make my use of Unix much easier. You're welcome to use them or to consider them examples of what you can do. Also see App. D for a basic 10- to 20-line shellscript you can copy and modify for your own use to simplify using the Internet.

***add,* append to a file reliably.** One great use for the **cat** command is to add lines to a file—if you know how and are careful. Here's one of my long-time favorite shellscripts, which always appends to the file, instead of possibly deleting the existing one because I've accidentally used **>** instead of **>>.** Note the internal documentation and the use of **echo** commands to always remind you what you're doing:

```
#!/bin/sh
# add filename - a simple shellscript to append to a file
# without worrying about getting the >> syntax right
# If filename is new, creates file; if exists, appends
echo Appending text to file ${1?"No file specified"}
echo Type CONTROL-D at beginning of new line to end. . .
cat >> ${1}
echo Done!
```

***puppies,* make use of your *add* shellscripts.** Once you've got a shellscript that does something useful, the next step is to use it in other shellscripts. Here's a simple shellscript that invokes **add** to always append to a predefined file, **puppies**. Notice how Unix lets the filename be grabbed by both the **add** shellscript and the **echo** command in **add** so you are reminded what file is being appended to.

```
# puppies
# add another name to people wanting our new puppies
echo "Adding new person to 'want-puppies' list"
add ~/want-puppies
```

***flense,* create output-cleaning filters.** Here's a simple use of the Unix **tr** (translate) command to get rid of specific unwanted character sequences. Formatted text files I want to download, such as manpages, often have <BACKSPACE><UNDERLINE> sequences. Getting rid of them from the word processor on my PC is a nuisance; using this shellscript as a filter when I download gets rid of the problem.

```
#!/bin/sh
# flense - remove BACKSPACE-UNDERLINE sequences from piped output
# Use for downloading to PC, e.g. cat filename | flense
# text (convert them to null character)
tr -d <BACKSPACE><UNDERLINE>
```

***ngrep,* Make a version of the grep command with the desired options.** The command **grep** has options that reverse its actions—identifying lines that *don't* match the pattern, versus those that do. But I'm always forgetting the right option. Now I just remember I've got a personalized command, **ngrep.**

```
#!/bin/sh
# ngrep - grep NON-matching lines [ -v option ]
# D Dern, Aug 1991, use as filter to remove lines
grep -v ${*}
```

***rot13*, Rotate (encrypt/decrypt) text.** By popular convention, Internet and Usenet members "rotate" potentially offensive text so that someone can't read it by accident. Thirteen characters is the standard; the process is called "rot13" ("rot-thirteen"). Most Usenet Newsreader programs include a rot13 function you can invoke with one or two keystrokes. Here's one of several ways to use the **tr** command to make a rot13 filter:

```
#!/bin/sh
# rot13 - rotate input 13 characters to encrypt or decrypt
tr [a-mA-Mn-zN-Z] [n-zN-Za-mA-M]
```

Depending on the version of Unix you're using, this may not necessarily work. If it doesn't (and it will be obvious when you try it), here's some other ways that may work on your system:

```
tr [a-z][A-Z]  [n-z][a-m][N-Z][A-M]
tr A-Za-z N-ZA-Mn-za-m
tr "[a-m][n-z][A-M][N-Z]" "[n-z][a-m][N-Z][A-M]"
```

Some versions of Unix don't require the [] in the **tr** command. In fact, some systems will get upset if you use them in an unquoted manner. The following should work for everyone but may be shortened on some systems:

```
tr '[a-m][n-z][A-M][N-Z]' '[n-z][a-m][N-Z][A-M]'
```

Don't forget the single quotes.

The following is an example of how this may be used:

```
rot13 < hidden-joke > readable-joke
cat hidden-joke | rot13 | more
```

For more about rot13, see the section "Rot13: The Secret Decoder Ring of the Internet" in Chap. 11.

This brings us to the end of "Enough Unix to Survive." As you can probably tell, we've hardly scratched the surface of what there is to learn, know about, and be able to do with Unix, even as a nonprogrammer end user. Other Unix capabilities and features you may want to learn include:

- How to remove files
- How to check what programs you've got running
- How to stop, start, and change jobs
- How to create "aliases" for commands

- How to create shellscripts
- How to change directories efficiently
- How to do simple shell programming, such as **if, for, do,** and **case** statements
- How to use parameters in shellscripts

The Usenet is a good source for on-going Unix information and answers to your Unix questions. Good Newsgroups to read include: news.answers (for monthly reposting of Unix FAQs) and comp.unix, which includes over 20 subgroups, including:

| | |
|---|---|
| comp.unix.questions | FAQs and other questions. |
| comp.unix.shell | Using and programming any Unix shell. |
| comp.unix.aux | Unix for Apple Macintosh II computers. |
| comp.unix.bsd | Discussions relating to BSD Unix. |
| comp.unix.large | Unix on mainframes and in large networks. |
| comp.unix.misc | Various topics that don't fit other groups. |
| comp.unix.msdos | MS-DOS running under Unix by whatever means. |
| comp.unix.programmer | Q&A for people programming under Unix. |

And now that you know enough Unix, let's go learn something about using the Internet.

Part

# 2

# Electronic Mail, Usenet, Remote Login, and File Transfer: The Four Basic Internet Food Groups

In the chapters in this part of the book, you'll learn about the "Big Four" activities you're likely to do on the Internet and the main tools you'll use to work with them: *Electronic Mail,* a.k.a. *e-mail*; *Usenet,* the "BBS of the Internet"; *remote login,* using **telnet**; and *file transfer,* or transferring files, with FTP. For most users, in terms of the actual time you spend using these facilities, and the frequency you use them, e-mail and Usenet will probably account for the majority of time spent as an Internet user, so I will cover them first. We'll then explore remote login and file transfer.

In these chapters, you'll be learning about the "raw" facilities themselves: what they are, how they work, and how to use them. Many versions of these tools have menu-oriented graphic interfaces and other features which make them much easier to use. You may also end up using them through Internet "front-ends" and "navigators" such as *Gopher, Hytelnet,* and *WorldWideWeb* (see Part 3). Tools like these can vastly simplify the use of remote login and file transfer facilities—so much so, in fact, that you may not even be aware they were invoked. But even if you get an "automatic transmission and pilot" for zooming around the Internet, it's helpful to understand some of what is going on—and if you can't, for whatever reason, use your favorite Internet front-end or navigator, you'll be glad you learned how to "drive a manual transmission" version of the basic tools.

## General Things to Know About Internet Tools

Before we plunge into specific Internet facilities, a few words are in order about some basic issues and aspects that apply generally to most Internet tools, including these and also others you'll learn about in other parts of this book. I recommend that you should read this section now and then come back to it again, especially the parts about finding clients and servers, after you've read the rest of Part 2 and Part 3; at that point, the tips and suggestions will be more useful (and you'll probably understand them better).

### Ensuring interoperability: Similarities and differences among different versions of TCP/IP, *telnet,* FTP, etc.

One common concern that potential Internet users who have some experience in using computers have is, "Will whatever programs I'm using on my computer work with their counterparts on other Internet computers? For example, will my FTP work with the FTP on the computers where all those Apple and Amiga files I want are?" A related and equally good question is: "If there are lots of versions of these programs, how close will the information in this book be to how my particular program works? Are the command names, menus, and icons all the same?"

The answer to the first question is: It's most likely that the different versions of Internet-using programs like **telnet,** FTP, archie, Gopher, and WAIS will work with each other. As for the second question, that's admittedly a bit harder. There will be more variation at this level. But the different programs should *do* the same things, subject to new versions and features since this book was written. Because of concern about this question, I spent some time talking with a number of TCP/IP and Unix software developers and other Internet experts (and went back to a few articles I've written). You can skip the following explanation if you want, but in case you're curious or concerned, here's what I found.

Because two computers you're connecting via **telnet**, FTP, etc. are as likely as not to have dissimilar hardware, operating systems, and versions of TCP/IP, the Internet community has gone to great lengths to ensure that versions of TCP/IP applications such as **telnet** and FTP, and the underlying networking, will be "highly interoperable" (i.e., will work together properly).

This means that the **telnet** package running brand new TCP/IP software on your new NeXt workstation, Macintosh PowerBook, or DOS'n'Windows desktop PC should be able to connect with the 10-year-old **telnet** code on a Honeywell minicomputer, an old Digital PDP-10, or PDP-11, etc.

In particular, **telnet** and FTP are probably *the* most standardized facilities used across the Internet. They need to be in order to work with their counterparts on other systems; also, users don't want to be learning new commands all the time. Developers in the Internet community, the main source of these facilities, have gone to extreme efforts to define and follow standards for TCP/IP applications,* focusing on standardization and interoperability.

Standardization means supporting a common command set so that you can use **telnet** and FTP at any computer you are using at the time without having to figure it out or learn a new version. Interoperability means ensuring that these multiple versions of **telnet,** FTP, etc., can all work with each other.

The second question is a reasonable and very important one. The following answers are based on phone and e-mail conversations with a number of leading software developers and consultants—some of whom were instrumental in making TCP/IP what it is today.

According to several leading Unix and TCP/IP consultants and developers, from the user perspective, FTP and **telnet** are highly similar across different versions of Unix and, to a slightly lesser degree, across non-Unix TCP/IP products (e.g., VAX/VMS or DOS). Some TCP/IPs may offer additional "aliases" for commands or use slightly different names, but the underlying functions remain the same. According to Barry Shein, President of Software Tool & Die (Brookline, MA):

---

*An Internet standard for the application of the TCP/IP protocols to host systems can be found in the Internet Host Requirements Documents, issued in 1989 as RFC-1122 and RFC-1123. These documents are intended to serve as the official specification of how TCP/IP protocol specifications are to be applied in computers used on the Internet to help ensure they do the proper tasks and interoperate (work with each other). According to IETF member Bob Braden at Information Sciences Institute, who was technical editor for the Host Requirements Documents, "These two RFCs reflect extensions, clarifications, and corrections to many of the older documents and provide a home for our collective 'folk wisdom' about TCP/IP design and implementation issues. They also define the requirements for TCP/IP so that vendors will produce products which meet a fairly uniformly high standard of interoperability. There are a number of areas where interoperability was the key issue."

> Most versions of **telnet** and FTP are derived from the ones in the Berkeley bsd implementation of Unix. Some vendor versions may have new features and commands—but as a rule, they all contain the same basic core set of commands or convenience and compatibility.

According to John Romkey (romkey@elf.com), a partner at ELF Communications (Cambridge, MA), who was one of the original developers of TCP/IP for MS-DOS (and inventor of the Internet Toaster):

> Most versions of **telnet** and FTP that use a Command Line User Interface [CLUI, also known as CUI, for Character-Oriented User Interface] where you type in a command plus some filenames or parameters and hit <RETURN> are similar or come from common "software ancestors," so they will be very similar to the Berkeley bsd version of TCP/IP.

Most of the differences in line-oriented versions of **telnet** and FTP, suggests Steve Knowles, of FTP Software (Andover, MA), will be additions, such as support for other terminal types beyond the standard Digital VT100 "dumb" terminal. For example, they may support Digital VT220, or IBM 3270. DOS versions may also support the function keys common to DOS keyboards.

In GUI (Graphic User Interface) mouse-and-menu-oriented systems, such as Motif, Macintosh, and Microsoft Windows, implementations are likely to reflect their particular GUI's style and conventions, and additional keys and functions available. This is done to make the user interface seem more familiar (i.e., like other Apple Macintosh, Microsoft Windows, or X Window/MOTIF applications). PC-oriented versions of **telnet** may support the PC keyboard's function keys. In these, there will be more variation—but again, the functions they provide will be the same.

Differences in terms of the terminal types supported by your local computer versus the remote system are more likely to be important. L. Stuart Vance, Vice President of Engineering of TGV, Inc. (Santa Cruz, CA), points out:

> Suppose you want to **telnet** from a VMS computer system, on which you are emulating a VT100-type terminal, to an IBM MVS or VM system which needs to be accessed by a 3270-type terminal. Your local system will likely have software for regular terminal-style **telnet** clients, as well as a tn3270 client, which layers an IBM 3270 terminal data stream on top of a **telnet** session. The **telnet** client program in some vendors' versions of TCP/IP will be able to automatically negotiate with the remote system and detect which terminal emulation is needed. Others may only support tn3270 as a separate command. In this case, you will have to know in advance the type of system to which you are trying to **telnet,** and specify the appropriate command. And not all TCP/IP products will support (have) tn3270.

### Client-server: The front and back ends of tools

Most tools tend to have two ends—a front end and a back end. The front end is usually the one you work with—the handle on a screwdriver or power drill, the control panel of your VCR, the dashboard of your car, etc. The back end is the part that does the work—the VCR tuning and recording mechanism, etc.

An increasing number of computing facilities use this approach of dividing up the work into front and back ends. In computerese, it's often called "client-server computing"; the programs are called "client-server programs."

In client-server programs, the software is developed as a set of programs, including two pieces: a *client,* and a *server.* (There can easily be other parts.) The client programs are the ones that you, the user, give commands to. The client programs, in turn, interact with one or more server programs; you as a user never interact directly with a server program; you always work through a client program. FTP, **telnet,** archie, Gopher, and WAIS, for example, all consist of the client programs, which you interact with, and their corresponding server programs and databases, which their clients work with. When you work with electronic mail or the Usenet, you use a client program to read and create messages; server programs are responsible for moving these messages among sites and users.

The client and server programs "talk"—exchange messages—using a *protocol* created or selected by the program's developers. **telnet** and FTP each have their own protocol, for example; so does Gopher. WAIS was based largely on an existing standard protocol, Z39.50, used by library scientists.

**Client programs are what you use.** The client program is usually responsible for:

- Providing the user interface, such as a prompt, a menu screen, or icons, and support for cursor movement, mouse and menu control, and possible function keys such as the <F1> through <F12> keys common to most PC-type keyboards
- Taking your commands and turning them into messages to convey to a server program (using the corresponding protocol for this facility, such as the FTP protocol, Gopher protocol, etc.)
- Opening and maintaining connection(s) to the appropriate server programs, which may be located on the same system or anywhere else at your site or on the Internet
- Passing your commands to the server
- Receiving messages and information from the server and displaying the appropriate output at your screen, saving files within your account, etc.

Client programs may also provide other functions such as built-in help, command completion and error-checking, and offering "bookmarks" and other aids to help you save and recall frequently used activities. They may perform some preprocessing on your commands before passing them along, do some processing on the information returned by servers, "handshake" with servers to agree on what types of data your system can display (e.g., audio, different levels of graphics, etc.), and perform certain conversion tasks automatically as part of a file transfer.

**Server programs: Doing what the client says.** The server program does the corresponding activities, as specified by your client program in response to your commands, sending the output of any of these commands back to the client program, which in turn displays them to you. For example, suppose you are remotely logged into another computer, using the **telnet** program. When you enter the command to obtain a directory listing, this command is passed by **telnet** to the operating system on the remote system, and its response is conveyed back to you, by **telnet,** and displayed on your screen.

**Benefits of the client-server approach.** Using client programs as the front ends of Internet facilities can reduce the load on a computer that is providing an Internet service or resource by handling aspects of the processing of your commands which are not directly related to the resources accessed by the server. For example, a client program can support a sophisticated graphic-oriented mouse-and-menu-driven presentation and contain numerous help files. If the server's computer has to support this kind of activity for each user, it will not be able to support as many users and commands at a time. By enabling each user's computer to share its piece of the load, the server can serve more users. This is the same reason that many PC-based LANs are turning to client-server computing approaches.

Among other tasks, part of the role of most client programs is to minimize the amount of network and server resources consumed by a user's command. More likely than not, the server and client programs will be running on different computers. If more of the overall load can be passed back to the computers on which the clients are running, the server will be able to support more users and give them better service. And if there is more than one server available for a given tool, separating the tool into client and server pieces makes it easier to select and switch from server to server within one session of using the client program. For example, when you access Gopher, you can easily switch among over a dozen different Gopher servers with as many minutes, but you do this all from one single Gopher client.

By early 1993, for example, there were well over a thousand publicly accessible Gopher servers around the world on the Internet, well over a dozen archie servers, and several hundred WAIS servers, plus thousands of anonymous-FTP servers. (Part 3 talks about how to find out about, select, and use these resources.)

**Where the clients are.** To use an Internet tool, you need to run the appropriate client program. This can be one which is installed on your system or on another system which you access through the Internet. Typically, when a new Internet tool becomes available, a client program is provided which can be accessed by remote login over the Internet so interested parties can try it without having to obtain and install new software on their own systems.

One next step that typically happens, depending on the type of program, is the propagation of client programs across the Internet, in the form of local and public-access clients.

**Local clients.** A local client is one installed on the system you use, such as the workstation on your desk, the public-access Internet site you have an account on, or a portable like a Macintosh Powerbook running TCP/IP and the PPP or SLIP serial protocol.

For popular tools, the Internet community tends to develop versions of client programs for the various types of computers they use. Typically, one or more versions of client programs become available for Unix (line-oriented and GUIs), MacOS, DOS, Microsoft Windows, NeXTStep, and VMS, often also OS/2 and VM, and possibly others.

Good ways to locate copies of these clients and related information include: checking for the appropriate FAQ (Frequently Asked Questions and their Answers) documents (see Chap. 12), reading articles in the corresponding Usenet Newsgroup (see Chap. 6), and doing an *archie* search (see Chap. 10). (If your computer is on your organization's network, be sure to check with your system administrator before installing new client software.)

**Public-access and other "proxy" clients.** If you can't run a client on your computer, the alternative is to find a "proxy" client program elsewhere, and access it. If you access the Internet by dialing up using a PC, modem, and terminal-emulator program to an account on another computer, this is basically what you're doing.

There may be a client program for the tool you want on the system your account is on. Try it and see: type the tool's name (e.g., archie, Gopher, or HYTELNET followed by <RETURN>). If that doesn't work, you may want to ask your system administrator; the program may be installed, but the appropriate entry may not be in your PATH configuration, for example.

If the system where your account is has no local client, you may remote login to another system where a client is available. For example, suppose there is no Gopher client on your home machine, but you know there is one available on another system which you can access via remote login—you connect to that second computer, where you run the local Gopher client and then have access to Gopher servers.

As such programs grow in popularity, a number of Internet sites often provide "public-access clients"—a copy of the client programs for various Internet tools. These clients are available to all Internet users (subject to usage restrictions). These are, in effect, "proxy" accounts for Internet users who don't have direct access to an appropriate client program on their own computers. These public-access accounts are therefore often referred to as "public-access clients," "public-access sites," or simply "public clients."

The publicly accessible on-line files and databases maintained by the InterNIC, for example, are accessible via servers for standard Internet facilities such as anonymous-FTP, e-mail, archie, Gopher, and WAIS. You can access these servers directly by running a local client—but the InterNIC also provides corresponding client programs at its system, which users can access by remote login to the InterNIC (see App. C for more information).

Public-access clients don't always have as many features or versions you can run on your own computer, and using them consumes more Internet resources—but it is a convenient way to gain occasional access to useful Internet services when they aren't available on your own computer elsewhere in your organization.

Good ways to locate public-access clients and popular servers include: checking for the appropriate FAQ documents (see Chap. 12), reading articles in the corresponding Usenet Newsgroup (see Chap. 6), and doing an archie search (see Chap. 10).

Members of the Internet also accumulate lists of resources, which are usually available via the Usenet, e-mail, or local help and Gopher files. In particular, the list "Special Internet Connections" compiled by Scott Yanoff (see Chap. 18) provides an excellent summary of publicly accessible Internet services.

**Think globally, look for clients locally: Why you do (or don't) want to use a local client.** Throughout most discussions of Internet tools in this book and in other documents, you'll see frequent reminders to find and use a "local client" for a tool whenever possible—even to find and get one installed, if you're going to use it frequently. There are a number of good reasons for this:

- *Familiar user interface which takes full advantage of your system's capabilities.* Internet developers can—and do—write versions of clients geared to each system, which can use windowing, graphic, and other user interface features. New tools often begin with client versions for the Macintosh or X Windows, plus a "dumb" version compatible with standard VT100 terminal-emulation suitable for remote login (**telnet**) access. Within months, one or more versions of clients typically become available for most other popular user platforms. These local clients often have more features than the versions of clients for "VT100 terminals" accessed by dial-up terminal emulators or **telnet** remote login. The TurboGopher client for the Macintosh, for example, makes use of the same features as other Macintosh programs, like use of the mouse, pull-down menus, scroll-bars, etc. Versions of WorldWideWeb clients for the Macintosh and for X Windows provide "hypertext" linking.
- *Maximum availability.* Public-access clients aren't always available when you want them. They often will permit only a limited number of users at a time or are available only during certain times. Because they are running at someone else's site, you have no control over their reliability or performance; if other users place a heavy load on the system or the network goes down, your work may suffer.
- *Work locally with your files.* A client program running on your system can incorporate files from your account more readily and can place retrieved files into your account.
- *Be sparing of network resources.* The last, but equally important, reason to run a local client is that this places the load on *your* system, versus someone else's, and avoids the network load (admittedly often minimal) on the connection between your system and the client program.

The standard advice is: try a public-access version of the client; if you like the tool, obtain (or ask your system administrator to get) the appropriate local client.

***Client-Server Aids Internet Tool Development: The Story of Sigmung***

Separating a tool into client and server pieces also makes it easier for Internet developers to make versions for several different types of computer systems; examples are MS-DOS, Microsoft Windows, MacOS, and Unix command-line and GUI interfaces. Only the client portion need be changed; all can access the same server. In turn, this makes it much, much easier to make a new tool available to a greater number of Internet users. Let's take an example that was hypothetical at the time I wrote it—but by now something like it is probably available:

Suppose you created a program which would identify possible Internet resources of interest, based on keyword matches against the lists of electronic mailing lists, Usenet Newsgroups, file archives, library catalogs, Gopher "burrows," and more, based on a user specifying a few keywords, perhaps also date, type of data (image, sound, etc.), and cost if any. Your program can send queries to archie, VERONICA, WAIS, and other databases. Perhaps you'd name it *Sigmung,* because it locates resources based on SIG, or special-interest group, relevance. (And the "mung" for the process of chomping through the info to find pay dirt. In computer jargon, *mung* is a recursive acronym which stands for "mung until no good.")

Let's say you had a spare 386-based PC, or an old Digital PDP-11 not being used, so you used this as your development computer. So you make the first version of your Sigmung server program to run on this. You also have to develop a client program for Sigmung; your first client runs on this computer, and users are forced to remote login via **telnet**, emulating character-oriented ASCII terminals. You announce the availability of Sigmung, by posting e-mail to several electronic mailing lists and Usenet Newsgroups.

Within hours, hundreds of users all over the world are attempting to remote login via **telnet** to the Sigmung client on your machine. Twenty-four hours later, over 100 sites make Gopher entries for Sigmung, and you can almost see the smoke pouring from your computer. Plus someone from your organization's network center calls to ask what you're doing that is threatening to swamp their Internet connection.

The next day, someone you've been exchanging e-mail with offers to "port" your client to the Macintosh—make a version that runs on the Macintosh, using the Mac's mouse, icon, and other features. Someone else ports your Sigmung client to a Unix character-oriented client, perhaps using Clifford Neuman's Prospero, similar to how the archie client was done. Two weeks later, Sigmung clients are available not only for Unix and Macintosh systems, but also for NeXt, VAX/VMS, DOS, Atari, and Microsoft Windows as free-for-use software and have been installed in over 1000 sites around the world.

Similarly, as new tools are developed, programmers can modify existing clients to work with new servers. To continue the previous scenario, as the request load continues to grow, several other sites offer to run Sigmung servers. They port the Sigmung server code to run on, say, a Thinking Machines' Connection Machine, or a Sun workstation, or an old Macintosh—and all the copies of the different Sigmung clients can access and work with the new Sigmung servers without needing any modification.

By this time, you've been ordered to stop running Sigmung within your organization because it's interfering with everyone else's activities. Two dozen Internet sites and service providers around the world have assumed responsibility for providing public-access Sigmung servers. Six companies contact you expressing interest in Sigmung for internal and pay-for-use applications; you pack up your office and set up shop as a consultant. Do you succeed? Some do, some don't. (Don't quit your day job too hastily.)

Again, this is an imaginary story—but it's hardly unlikely. See the "origin stories" of archie, Gopher, and VERONICA in Part 3.

**Where the tools are: Rules of thumb and other tips.** In general, the way to locate public-access clients and servers is to "do your homework": Read through the FAQs or other documents, watch the Usenet, or check lists such as Yanoff's "Special Internet Connections." Finding a client program for a tool is the first step. The second is to find servers to access. Some Internet tools, such as

Gopher and WAIS, will automatically connect you with a server when you begin your session. Others, such as HYTELNET, will present you with lists of resources they can access. However, this isn't true for all Internet tools, and you may not see the site you're looking for. It may not yet be "registered" in the master list; even though it's available, a new server may be "invisible" to your client unless you can tell it where to look.

One useful fact to know, then, is that the Internet community uses a few relatively standardized naming conventions for many of the publicly accessible clients and servers. By knowing these conventions, you can often find and access a tool within one or two educated guesses.

**Accessing local and remote clients and servers.** The general rule is:

- To use a local client, try the client name; for example:

```
telnet<RETURN>
archie<RETURN>
gopher<RETURN>
```

- To reach a remote client, use the remote login (**telnet**) facility (see the discussion of names which follows). For example:

```
telnet internic.net<RETURN>
telnet gopher.internic.net<RETURN>
telnet quake.think.com<RETURN>
telnet archie.sura.net<RETURN>
```

- To reach a server, use the appropriate client. For example:

```
ftp ftp.uu.net<RETURN>
gopher internic.net<RETURN>
gopher gopher.internic.net<RETURN>
```

**Popular address conventions to try.** If you don't know an address for a client or server, you may be able to find one by making educated guesses:

- First try using the Domain Name of the organization as a Fully Qualified Domain Name for a target server (e.g., internic.net, cnidr.org, or uu.net). For example:

```
gopher internic.nic<RETURN>
```

- If this doesn't work, preappend the name of the type of server and a separating period. For example:

```
ftp ftp.uu.net<RETURN>
gopher gopher.internic.net<RETURN>
ftp ftp.cnidr.org<RETURN>
ftp ftp.apple.com<RETURN>
gopher gopher.panix.com<RETURN>
```

In many cases, especially with anonymous-FTP file transfer, if you've guessed a name that does belong to the correct organization, but not for the appropriate service, you may get a message giving the appropriate Internet address to use. For example, Apple's "apple.com" will do this.

Because anonymous-FTP archive sites have been in existence longer, there are a few more possibilities to try, basically representing other terms meaning "archive." For example:

| | |
|---|---|
| **archive.umich.edu** | (U Michigan) |
| **net-dist.mit.edu** | (MIT) |

And now it's time to start learning about the first of the four main tools and activities you'll employ as an Internet user: electronic mail.

Chapter

# 5

# Electronic Mail—How to Exchange Messages with Other Internet Users and Other Exciting Things You Can Do

*"You have new mail."*
*System message*

*"A daemon will reply."*
*Another system message*

In this chapter, you're going to learn about what is for most members of the Internet community the most frequently used facility: electronic mail, a.k.a. e-mail.* Electronic mail deserves this much space because it may be the first Internet service you make use of—and may remain the one you use most frequently (Usenet being the other).

## Electronic Mail: What It's All About

Electronic mail is the glue of the Internet and the Internet community. It's also the glue between Internet and the rest of the on-line world that interconnects to the Internet. You don't have to be on the Internet to use e-mail,

*Reading and posting articles to Newsgroups in Usenet—the "BBS of the Internet"—is usually considered the other leading reason; retrieving files from public-access archives is third. Many define *net access* as a combination of being able to read and post to the Usenet and to send and get e-mail—and consider them equally important. Usually, however, if your system has Usenet access, it also supports e-mail. It's also true that technically the Usenet is not necessarily an Internet service. On the other hand, as you'll see, talking with other Internet users by e-mail doesn't require direct connection to the Internet, either.

either (although you do need at least e-mail access to the Internet to exchange e-mail with its users, of course.) Thousands of companies who never have heard of the Internet, TCP/IP, or Unix use e-mail. Tens of millions of people use electronic mail in the course of their everyday professional and personal activities. If you have ever belonged to and used one of the conferencing systems, such as America On-Line, CompuServe, DELPHI, or GEnie, or a local BBS (electronic Bulletin Board System) or MCI Mail, you probably know what I'm talking about.

Entire companies such as Apple, Borland, Digital Equipment, Lotus, Microsoft, and Sun Microsystems literally run on electronic mail, as do many universities. Businesses, graduate theses, science fiction anthologies, friendships, and even marriages have emerged through electronic mail. Personally, I've written entire articles, conducted interviews, and done the editorial contents of a newsletter almost exclusively through electronic mail. I typically spend half an hour to an hour a day reading, answering, and creating electronic mail; it has replaced much of my former paper correspondence, as well as many other information exchanges I might otherwise do via telephone or fax or by sending floppy disks through the mail. This saves me an immense amount of time, money, and effort.

Much of the research and reviewing that went into this book was done via electronic mail, in fact. I didn't keep count, but I'm sure there were hundreds of messages from many sites and states, and probably a dozen countries as well, back and forth between me and my various sources, experts, people quoted, and reviewers, not to mention the many people who contributed their thoughts, suggestions, and questions.

Other than through electronic mail, I've never spoken with or met many of these people in person. In many cases, I don't even know someone's "real name," only their "e-mail handle." This last may sound odd, but I assure you it's quite common in the Internet-oriented on-line worlds. One of the benefits of going to Interop and other trade shows and events is getting to meet people you've only previously interacted with by e-mail. (To help recognition, we often add our e-mail name and address to the badge.)

More and more of the world is coming on-line at least for electronic mail. The Internet carries e-mail from 10 million people in over 54 countries, according to John Quarterman in the March 1993 issue of his *Matrix News* newsletter; the total world e-mail community is estimated at 20 to 30 million people in 130 countries and seven continents.

### What is e-mail?

Electronic mail, simply, is a way for computer users to exchange messages, including between different, distant computers, as long as there are networks such as the Internet connecting them. You may be on the same local area network, even on the same multiuser timesharing computer. Or you may be in a completely different office, location, organization, city, country, even continent. (Or even planet—at least one U.S. space shuttle swapped e-mail with users back here on Planet Earth.)

For many users, electronic mail, or e-mail, which is how I'll also refer to it, is their first real exposure to, and use of, networks. (I don't consider sending files to the printer or having files stored on a fileserver, while involving the use of a network, as a deliberate use of networking.)

I may only do a remote login (**telnet**) or file transfer (FTP) a few times a month (although I did a *lot* more while researching and testing information for this book). But I check for, read, and send e-mail typically several times a day. And it's quite likely that some non-e-mail activities are related to using e-mail, such as trying to determine someone's electronic mail address or looking for something which I then forward to them.

Back when the ARPAnet was first being conceived and deployed, although e-mail was already popular with users on timesharing computers and local networks, its creators assumed that it would mostly be used for remote login and file sharing. To the surprise of the network's creators, e-mail turned out to be equally popular. In fact, the ARPAnet didn't support e-mail initially; the ARPAnet began operation in 1969, but the first known ARPAnet e-mail message wasn't sent until the early 1970s. Today, in terms of the volume of traffic that flows over the Internet, e-mail typically accounts for about 6 percent of traffic on the NSFnet (it's the fifth highest activity, just after Usenet)—but in terms of number of times that people are making use of Internet facilities, e-mail probably accounts for a substantially larger percentage.

For many—myself, for one, and I suspect millions of others—e-mail remains *the* most important aspect of the Internet in terms of day-to-day use. Other activities and services like remote login and file transfer are far less essential, as a rule—but e-mail is as much a part of our work and lives as the telephone, radio, fax, and newspaper.

## What can you use e-mail for?

The communications systems we use today are surprisingly versatile. The postal system can be used for more than carrying letters; everything from bills (and checks) to magazines and newspapers, bulk advertisements, books, records, presents, food, photographs, and products can be sent—even such odd things as newborn chickens and cartons of live bees (with proper packaging, of course). We can use the phone system to check our bank balances and pay our bills; in some cities, you can get current stock exchange prices through a gadget on an FM radio.

E-mail is equally versatile in what it can carry and how it can be used. For example, you can use e-mail to:

- Send messages to a specific individual
- Send a message to many individuals
- Send a message to a predefined list of users
- Send text files
- Send binary objects such as programs, graphics, "rich text" (word processed, fonted, etc.), spreadsheets, even audio and video attachments

- Distribute "electronic magazines"
- Broadcast announcements
- Get alarm messages from network management systems or other computer monitoring programs.

You can even use electronic mail as a way to use distant computer programs and services, such as to retrieve files and documents, and query databases. (We'll do this later in the book.)

With all this, it's no wonder that e-mail has become the CB radio, party line, water cooler, and bulletin board of the computer networking world. Let's look at a typical morning's worth of new Internet e-mail messages in my Internet "mailbox." (Figure 5.1 shows one screen's worth of message headers.) They are:

- A broadcast newsletter from a PR person and two press releases from companies I'm interested in. (I had requested they put me on their e-mailing lists.)
- A text copy of a document relating to an article I'm working on and several related messages, including review comments, a scheduling note, and phone numbers of more contacts
- Notification of upcoming meetings of the Internet Engineering Task Force, including the registration form and the agenda
- A copy of a job-offered notice from a Usenet news group, forwarded by a friend who wasn't sure I'd seen it originally
- Half a dozen messages from on-line discussion groups I'm a member of, including about the Internet Gopher, Internet commercialization, and new Internet services (you can see a trend)
- Two personal responses to questions in a message I posted to a Usenet Newsgroup
- The latest schedule from the Tech Squares, the MIT square dance club
- A note from someone I used to work with who saw an article of mine in a magazine recently

```
Mail version SMI 4.0 Thu Oct 11 12:59:09 PDT 1990 Type ? for help.
"/usr/spool/mail/ddern": 35 messages 7 new 35 unread
 U 21 rcapulet              Thu May  6 13:55 397/19593 Now here's my plan
 U 22 ddern                 Thu May 13 11:03  44/1684  A.M. weather FYI
 U 23 nankipoo@radiomail.com Fri May 14 00:49 51/1788 Tell me where dwell
 U 24 a.noble@titipu.org   Fri May 14 01:14 38/1831 Who are you who asks
 U 25 lgulliver@laputa.org Fri May 14 01:16 20/1002 GPS positioning info?
 U 26 ddern                 Fri May 14 02:41 39/1821 Meeting time, place
>N 27 aliddell@jabber.wock.com Fri May 14 02:44 83/3886 Re: Resizing windows
 N 28 ddern                 Fri May 14 07:34 19/435 Please add me to NIT mail
 N 29 rcapulet              Thu May  6 15:24 21/482 May be out tomorrow
```

**Figure 5.1** A typical screenful of e-mail messages.

- A brief "hi, how are you" note from a former coworker, mostly to let me know he's "back on the net again" and give me his new Internet address and new work phone number
- A query from someone in California asking how to subscribe to the newsletter I'm editing
- Three messages from someone who read an article I wrote for *Byte*—one about 20 miles from me, one in Washington, D.C., and one in Brazil—asking where they can get more information, and two from people I mentioned in my article
- Mail from Steve "Pedalling through Cyberspace" Roberts, sent from his high-tech bicycle while pedalling in Maine
- Two files I sent to myself from other systems
- An automatically generated message telling me that the computer was unable to "deliver" my message, and why
- "Carbon copies" of four messages I sent to other people.

In the 15 or 20 minutes it took me to process these messages (open, read mail, and respond), I read and probably deleted a third of the messages without replying, filed another third, downloaded several to my PC's hard disk, and responded to maybe half with acknowledgments, comments, or other remarks. During the same session, I probably also created and sent an equal amount of "outgoing" mail, such as:

- A request for information to someone whose comments I'd seen in a message on one of the mailing lists
- Article text to one of my editors and for my newsletter
- Questions to one of my expert sources regarding something I'm writing about
- A "head's-up" message to about a dozen people mentioned in an article I'd been working on advising them that the issue had appeared on the newsstands
- A joke forwarded from the Usenet *rec.humor.funny* Newsgroup
- A message to the World system administrator requesting an increase to my on-line storage allotment
- To someone who posted a question in a Usenet group, a direct message with information

### E-mail can save time and money

This may seem like a substantial amount of activity—and it is. However, as you can see, I performed the equivalent of making and receiving perhaps one or two dozen phone calls, sending an equal amount of letters, faxes, or floppy disks, and reading perhaps half a dozen newsletters. "Electronic mail is efficient and cost-effective," states Craig Partridge, Research Scientist at BBN

Systems and Technologies (Cambridge, MA). "It saves time, effort, money, paper, and resources."

In most cases, the messages I sent probably arrived within seconds to minutes after I sent them, even to people across the country or around the world. It's quite likely that one or two reply messages arrived while I was still reading and creating the initial handful of messages; I may have had several exchanges of messages with people during the session. And I did all this without leaving my desk, using or discarding a single piece of paper, making any long-distance telephone or fax calls, using any overnight delivery services—for a total cost of less than a dollar (for the time I was connected to The World—if I used a tool to batch download messages and later upload my responses, I'd probably reduce these times and costs by 75 percent.)

As you can see, e-mail can be quite useful. Once you get the hang of it, and begin using e-mail to communicate with people for work and other activities, you'll find yourself using it as naturally as you do the telephone or fax. And you'll know you're a serious e-mail user when your first question is no longer "What's your phone number" or "What's your fax number?" but "What's your e-mail address" or "Are you on the Internet?"

## How E-Mail Works

E-mail is provided by the activities of two main types of programs: the e-mail *user agent,* a.k.a. *mail reader,* which you use to create, read, and manage your e-mail messages, and the *mail delivery agents,* the programs that act as the local "post office," taking messages created by your and other users' e-mail programs, receiving messages and making them available to you, and handling the movement of messages among computers and networks.

### Your e-mail user agent program

The e-mail program you use, in all likelihood, acts as the equivalent of secretary, filing clerk, and local messenger between itself and the "post office" program on your computer, LAN, or site. This program, often called an *e-mail client* or *mail reader,* provides and manages the functions you need to read, write, and manage e-mail messages. (Generally, a *client* is a program that you use, which in turn interacts with a corresponding *server* program—except in the X Windows system, which uses the terms *client* and *server* in the opposite senses.)

Popular e-mail client programs include: **mail**, **sendmail**, **pine**, and **elm** for Unix systems and Eudora for PCs and Macintoshs. These programs also may manage lists of e-mail addresses, enabling you to create nicknames and lists. Some of the more sophisticated e-mail programs may also have features like "rules" to file or sort incoming mail automatically, "autoreply" mode for when you plan to be away. (While a useful feature, automatic-replying mail programs can lead to "mail storms" and other problems. For example, suppose two such programs keep replying to each other's "Sorry, I am away for a week" messages. It's possible they'll keep playing "mail tag" until they fill up the file system or otherwise overload a critical computer resource.)

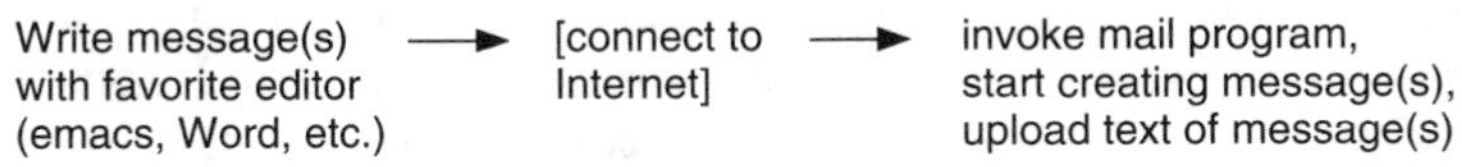


**Figure 5.2** Using your text editor to create e-mail messages.

Most e-mail programs offer a simple "typewriter-mode" editor for the text of messages you create and also will let you invoke your favorite text editor (**emacs, vi,** or whatever) explicitly or automatically when you give a command to create a message. Some text editors (notably **emacs**) and other programs will do the converse, letting you invoke your e-mail program from within them. (If you get stuck in an unfamiliar editor, see App. B.)

You may also use a text editor to create your messages, either to write your message as a file before you invoke the e-mail program or launched from within your e-mail program, as shown in Fig. 5.2. If your Internet connection is dial-up or otherwise billed by the hour, and you have specific messages in mind to send, consider writing messages before you connect. This will be gone into in more detail in "Creating and Sending Messages" later in the chapter.

---

*Tip:* When uploading files from your PC into an e-mail message, consider setting up a special directory (e.g., on a DOS computer, \UP.TMP, and putting a copy of the intended file[s] here). Edit these temporary copies as needed (e.g., to remove non-ASCII characters) and then upload. This helps minimize the chance of overwriting the master version of the file. Similarly, set up a directory like \DOWN.TMP and download to here and then copy across to the appropriate directory later.

---

## The mail delivery agent: The electronic post office

The other program involved in e-mail is the *mail delivery agent,* also known as the *e-mail server.* This is the post office program that your e-mail client sends your outgoing messages to. The post office program queues them up (puts them in a "pile"); periodically, it does the equivalent of sending out mail trucks—except that, being a computer program, it can give each message individual attention. The post office does its best to determine where to send your message. Figure 5.3 shows the relationship of the mail user agent and delivery agent programs.

| User agent | Delivery agent |
|---|---|
| Read messages<br>Create messages<br>File messages | Receive messages from users and programs on your and other systems<br>Take messages from your user agent; deliver them to other users on your system or to delivery agents on other systems |

**Figure 5.3** Mail user agent and delivery agent programs.

The post office program also receives messages sent to it from other e-mail systems, on your or other networks—which may be elsewhere on the Internet or even from some other computer or network that can exchange e-mail with the Internet (e.g., CompuServe or MCI Mail). When incoming mail is received, it puts it in a "queue" for your e-mail client to "pick up." Also, it may receive e-mail destined for some other system; if so, it does its best to forward it along to the appropriate "next stop."

### E-mail: It works by store and forward

E-mail is called a *store-and-forward* technology. This means that when a mail server receives a message, it makes a copy (stores it) and then does its best to pass it along (forward it). (The stored copy is deleted after the receiving computer confirms receipt.) A server will try its best to forward a message and shouldn't delete its copy until the next server has acknowledged successfully receiving the forwarded message.

Store-and-forward activities like e-mail are considered "non-real-time" or "noninteractive" applications, meaning the traffic you generate doesn't have to get to its destination and be responded to in any particular hurry. Examples of other activities you do that don't require real-time, interactive service include: sending a letter, making a copy of your vacation videotape and sending it to a friend, playing chess by mail, and using a voice-mail-forwarding system.

By contrast, other things you typically may do on the Internet are considered to be real-time, interactive activities, meaning you are having an interactive "conversation" with the computer across the Internet where the server program is running and need responses in "real-time" (e.g., within a few seconds of giving a command). Examples of real-time Internet activities include remote login (**telnet**), file-transfer (FTP), querying an archie, Gopher, or WAIS server from a local client program, and the Internet Relay Chat.

Within the Internet, there are lots of highly useful non-real-time services. The two most popular are e-mail and the Usenet, which acts as the BBS for the Internet community. But there are many more. Many, in fact, use e-mail; because e-mail is a widely available, well-understood, well-working service, application developers have put together programs called "e-mail-enabled applications" where you send a message to a computer program rather than to another person.

An increasing number of Internet information facilities have e-mail front ends that let you query them by e-mail, in fact. For example:

- Information and document servers at most of the Internet account and service providers. Typically, sending a message to "info" at the organization's address will cause the system to send you back the starter information file. (Each information server's rules and commands may be different, but this is a good start.) For example, sending e-mail to info@world.std.com or info@panix.com should get you starter information on the World and PANIX Public-Access Internet Account Providers.
- archie resource index servers can be queried by e-mail.

- Many popular information files put out by Internet services (and individuals) can be gotten automatically, by sending e-mail messages to servers they've set up. (In fact, you, too, can set up your own e-mail-server. For a list of public-domain e-mail server software, including short comments on each program's pros and cons, see the appropriate FAQ in the Usenet Newsgroup news.answers.) For example, you can get a current copy of Peter Kaminski's popular PDIAL list of organizations offering dial-up Internet accounts, by sending e-mail to info-deli-server@netcom.com with "Send PDIAL" in either the message subject or body. (This is explained shortly.) You can send queries to the archie resource directory service and receive replies the same way—without ever "talking" to a human being.
- BITNET e-mail lists and information-providing are largely managed by programs responding automatically to e-mail from users. For example, the LISTSERV facility manages subscribing and unsubscribing to most BITNET e-mail lists. (The difference between how traditional Internet e-mail lists and LISTSERV-based lists work is an on-going source of unintended traffic to all readers on a list.)
- "FTP-by-mail" servers let users who may not have direct FTP access to desired archives retrieve files by sending an e-mail request; typically, the FTP-mail server sends back an automatic response very quickly which acknowledges your request and tells you when to expect the file or how many requests are ahead of you, followed on schedule by the file. (See "Internet Services Based on E-Mail: Access to Archives, Documents, Programs, and More" later in this chapter and see also Chap. 10.)

**Interesting consequences of e-mail's store-and-forward nature.** The store-and-forward nature of e-mail has several very important implications.

**E-mail can go "beyond the Internet."** E-mail is the glue between the Internet and the rest of the Matrix. If you remember, one definition of the Internet is "networks connected in *real-time* (i.e., letting you establish a real-time connection between two points)." Other networks such as BITNET and organizations such as CompuServe aren't considered part of the Internet for this reason. (If they become able to, they will be.) Since e-mail doesn't need this kind of connection, e-mail can go across the Internet boundary into other parts of the Matrix.

Through e-mail gateways, Internet users can exchange e-mail with users on other networks such as: America On-Line, ATT Mail, BITNET, CompuServe, DELPHI, FidoNet, MCI Mail, and UUCP-based networks; with users on internal corporate networks, such as Apple, Digital Equipment, Lotus, MicroSoft, Oracle, and Sun; with users in universities, government agencies, research labs; with users on the many public-access Internet sites, like Digital Express, NetCom, PANIX, Portal, WELL, and The World; and uncountable others—tens of millions of people worldwide.

**E-mail can be forwarded by phone, in "hops."** Most of the networks listed above are permanently, continuously connected. Many networks, sites, and BBSs, however, "reach out and touch" only part-time. For example, an e-mail system can be programmed to periodically dial-up other computers (that is, make a call to modems attached to them, just like you would call CompuServe or a BBS) and, once connected, query the other system to see if there's any mail in the other's queue for it and upload outgoing mail destined to go to—or through—this other system.

The e-mail system may be set to place outgoing calls every 10 minutes—when there are messages to be sent out—to any of several dozen systems. And it can be set to check four of these, say, every half-hour, for "incoming" mail. With enough computer systems equipped with modems, the right software, and a way to do addressing, you could set up a "mail relay system" capable of forwarding messages literally around the world. In fact, this is exactly how things like FidoMail and the Usenet work: cooperating computer systems automatically store and forward mail (and other types of messages). It may take several days for a message to get from start to finish, but it works.

## Fifty ways to get your e-mail

E-mail can even go by nonnetwork methods—lots of them. E-mail, like files, can even travel off the network and get back on. There's no reason that e-mail messages can't be loaded onto tape cartridges, floppy disks, CD-ROMs—even IBM (Hollerith) cards or paper tape—carried by hand (a.k.a. "SneakerNet"), and then loaded back into a computer and put back into the network.

Originally e-mail users retrieved messages the same way they sent them—as on-line ASCII text, logged in by network or phone. But, particularly in the business world, not everyone has a terminal, connection, or e-mail account; even those who do often lack easy access when away from their office. MCI Mail was one of the first public mail network services to recognize the business value of gatewaying e-mail into other worldwide communications infrastructures. CompuServe, ATT Mail, and others rapidly followed suit.

Today, Internet mail flows among and from all types of non-ASCII, noncomputer devices. In most cases, this is done through e-mail gateways which send messages to appropriate devices in your organization's network or to accounts with services such as MCI Mail or RadioMail, which handle the conversion and delivery. This costs extra, but users obviously feel it's worth it. As a result, anyone with a PC, modem, and accounts with the appropriate services can send e-mail messages and get them delivered to almost anyone, almost anywhere in the world, in one or more ways, for often negligible per-message costs.

If your intended recipient doesn't have an e-mail account, services such as ATT Mail, CompuServe, and MCI Mail offer a comprehensive roster of alternative delivery options. Your e-mail messages can be delivered as faxes, Telexs, or TWXs; sent to wireless pagers (usually just the first few lines); "read" by voice-synthesizing computers to you by phone; or printed and given to the local post office, an overnight courier, or (in major metropolitan areas) a taxi delivery service. Businesses like ZIP Press (Columbus, OH) will print your messages, even turn them into custom-printed, bound books.

These services and other delivery options aren't free—but if you are trying to communicate for business purposes, this is part of the cost of doing business, and it's bound to be far faster, easier, and cheaper than any other method. Fax modems have done away with some of the need for e-mail-to-fax but not all.

**Have messages "read" aloud over the phone.** ATT Mail was one of the first to offer voice pick-up—you could call ATT Mail from any touch-tone phone and enter the appropriate codes and ATT Mail's voice synthesis software would read your messages to you, slowly, and making all sorts of "errors" of pronunciation, but as a way to check your mail without a computer or modem, it couldn't be beat. The VoxMail option from VoxLink Corporation (Nashville, TN) adds text-to-speech telephone retrieval to e-mail, letting you check your voice and e-mail in a single system.

With the advent of cheap speech recognition, we can expect more voice options to keep appearing.

**Wireless e-mail to pagers and pocket PCs.** In addition to wireless pagers and cellular telephones, we now have wireless e-mail for people with pagers and pocket-sized PCs. RadioMail Corp. (San Mateo, CA) was one of the first companies to offer e-mail-to-pager messaging, under the name RadioMail. RadioMail connects public and private e-mail networks, including the Internet, with wireless data services, including numeric and alphanumeric pagers and portable and pocket PCs equipped with radio modems such as Ericsson GE's Mobidem. From one of these devices, small enough to almost fit in a pocket, you can send and receive e-mail without a phone or wire connection.

According to Geoffrey S. Goodfellow, President and CEO of RadioMail, "RadioMail users can send and receive messages from local and wide area e-mail networks such as ATTMail, CompuServe, the Internet, UUCP/Usenet, nationwide 'packet' data-radio network such as ARDIS, and the RAM Mobile Data Network."

Today, companies like RadioMail, PSI, and RAM Mobile Data have made wireless one- and two-way e-mail available to anyone who wants it. (It's a little pricey for personal use, admittedly.) Who wants wireless e-mail? Network managers who want to get alerts quickly (network management systems can use e-mail to send alarm messages, after all), and managers who want to be able to check messages quickly, without having to find a phone. Steve Roberts, as he pedals across the backroads on BEHEMOTH, his recumbent Internet bicycle, or paddles down the river in his Sea Moss Microship (a pun on CMOS integrated circuits), stays in touch with the world this way.

Robert Jesse, Senior Director for Desktop Development, Oracle, has his Oracle*Mail e-mail selectively forwarded to his account with RadioMail. (A program determines which to send by checking a file of sender names and other criteria.) "RadioMail has turned me into a 24-hour manager," says Jesse. "It increases my business effectiveness by decreasing my response time to messages." Jesse's pager captures and stores the first several hundred characters of the most recent 20 messages—enough information to let him decide whether he needs to get to a phone or terminal for further action. "I carry my RadioMail receiver with me almost everywhere."

Novell Netware administrators at companies like Price Waterhouse, Deloite Touche, and Chase Manhattan are also keeping in touch and receiving alert and alarm messages from their sites' Novell NetWare servers, relayed to e-mail pagers by the Frye Utilities for Networks' NetWare Early Warning Systems from Frye Computer Systems Inc. (Boston, MA).

What's next? Perhaps downloading to your TV or to a microdot and carrier pigeon. Meanwhile, now that you've got a basic idea of what e-mail is, and why people use it, let's look at the basic types of commands and functions you will want to learn for your e-mail programs.

## A Few Other Thoughts Regarding E-Mail

Before moving into the nitty and gritty of how to use e-mail, let's take a brief Cook's tour through some of the many organizational, cultural, and other aspects of e-mail that are worth being aware of.

### Information overload, underload: Automating and organizing your e-mail

As science fiction/fact writers like Arthur C. Clarke and Isaac Asimov have observed, survival in the Information Age requires a happy medium between *finding* the information we do want and *filtering* out the information we don't. E-mail is ripe for solutions. Users in active networks report anywhere from dozens to hundreds of messages per day. I've heard several people talk about going away for even a few days—and returning to over a thousand new messages to wade through.

One potential helper is "smart" e-mail programs that can sort, filter, and perhaps even react or respond to messages. Many new e-mail programs let each user define "rules" such as setting priorities, automatic responses, sorting into separate files, etc. (At some point, human secretarial help becomes a necessary part of the solution, acting as the first-pass read and sort on received mail.) Attempts to automate e-mail aren't without risk. Systems and entire networks have been brought to their knees by overeager autoanswer programs swamping the disk with replies to replies to replies.

Dealing with e-mail once it's arrived and you've read it is yet another challenge. One answer is to use search programs that can munch through weeks or years of saved messages (see Chap. 10). Another may be e-mail programs that provide better filing features, such as "description" fields and database-like indexing.

### Using e-mail doesn't necessarily mean you're using the Internet

Just because you're using e-mail doesn't necessarily mean you're involving the Internet. This can also be true for activities like remote login (**telnet**) or file transfer (FTP), but it's even more likely when in regards to e-mail. For example, you may be exchanging messages with someone else who has an account on the same computer (there are a dozen or more people who also have accounts on The World who I periodically swap messages with). Or, if you're a student or employee at an organization that uses e-mail, you may be exchanging messages with people on your organization's e-mail network.

The fact that someone is elsewhere on the Internet, or sending you e-mail through the Internet, doesn't change the basics of what you're doing. It may affect the name and/or address you have to supply and change the time it takes your message to be delivered, but, in general, the fact that someone is within your system, site, or organization versus elsewhere on the Internet or elsewhere on Matrix is immaterial.

## Legal aspects of e-mail

For most people, e-mail is probably the computer resource most likely to be abused, whether deliberately or accidentally—and equally likely to generate legal consequences. 1991 and 1992 saw a number of e-mail-related lawsuits, ranging from accusations of invasion of privacy to misuse of company resources.

It's therefore essential that you be aware of e-mail's trouble-making potential—and take care in using e-mail to avoid getting yourself into any. One common theme in privacy-related disputes is a lack of policies and a lack of employee education by employers.

"Do managers—or system administrators—have the right to look at your stored e-mail or e-mail as you send it?" asks Mike Godwin, Legal Services Counsel at the Electronic Frontier Foundation (Washington, D.C.). "Are your e-mail files and messages personal property—or do they belong to your organization? It's important to find out what your company's policy is." (For information on how to set up an organizational e-mail policy, consider getting a copy of: "Access to and Use and Disclosure of Electronic Mail on Company Computer Systems: A Toolkit for Formulating Your Company's Policy," a 36-page document put together by two Washington, D.C., lawyers, John Podesta of Podesta & Associates, and David Johnson of Wilmer Cutler & Pickering. Copies of the document are available for $45 [prepaid] from the Electronic Mail Association, 1555 Wilson Boulevard, Suite 300, Arlington, VA 22209.)

Misunderstandings over issues like these can lead to litigation. Some of the legal cases have been a result of user assumptions differing from those of their employers.

## Can companies do business by e-mail?

Conducting business via e-mail and other computer-based mechanisms raises another whole realm of issues, according to Michael Baum, a Cambridge, MA-based consultant specializing in legal and security aspects of electronic commerce, messaging, and EDI. "In what cases are legally enforceable commitments created electronically, such as in e-mail messages?" asks Baum. "To what extent do e-mail messages satisfy conventional legal requirements for documents being legally 'signed,' 'in writing,' and of 'sufficient evidentiary value'?"

Additionally, notes Baum, the use of e-mail raises legal factors that should be resolved. "Timing on contract bids is one immediate concern," he says. "If contract bids are submitted by e-mail, when are they legally considered dispatched, communicated, or 'received'? When should or are such messages considered as having reached the intended recipient's corporate e-mail system? Is it when it gets to the Sales or Contracts host? Or when they're read? Or when they are acknowledged? What determines order of arrival?"

Many of these and other questions actually can be resolved today, notes Baum, by the use of trading partner agreements, which are executed between the prospective trading partners. Such agreements can deal with and provide confidence in the resolution of communications issues affecting the binding nature of electronic contracts. "These trading partner agreements are, in many instances, only a short-term solution," cautions Baum. "We'll need law reform and the establishment of clear industry practices, guidelines, and conventions to further define and support transactional certainty."

## Using Your E-Mail Program(s)

Now that you've got a sense of what e-mail can be used for, let's take a look at using your e-mail program. In this section, we'll take a look at:

- Software for working with e-mail
- Mail messages and files: Mail queue and "savebox"
- Components of an e-mail message
- Important files for e-mail users: configuration file, mailbox file(s), .signature file, and "dead letters"
- The commands, features, and facilities in e-mail programs
- E-mail "netiquette"

Then, in the rest of this chapter, we'll cover other things you should know about e-mail and show you some of the main uses for it.

### Software for working with e-mail: Many choices available

Unlike the "Using" sections in this book for Internet facilities such as FTP, **telnet,** archie, Gopher, and WAIS, this "Using" section will be comparatively general rather than focusing on one or even several e-mail programs. You'll learn essential commands for **mail**, a prevalent mail program on Unix computers, and for its "typewriter-mode" message editor. However, for any further specifics, you will be referred to on-line and printed documentation that came with your account and computer(s).

The reason is that just as there are lots of different text editors and word processors that can be used (e.g., **emacs**, Microsoft Word, and PC-Write), there are many popular e-mail programs available—certainly dozens, probably hundreds—and there's no way to know which one you'll end up using. In fact, there are e-mail programs available for almost every type of hardware and software platforms—MS-DOS, Microsoft Windows, Apple MacOS, Unix, VAX/VMS, IBM MVS, and so on. Different products support different features, different command styles and syntax, and so on.

Unix systems often include several different e-mail programs available for users. If you're using an account on a public-access Internet site, you have a number of mail programs available, such as:

**mail**

**elm**

**pine** (which originally stood for "Pine Is Not Elm")

**sendmail**

**mm** ("Columbia Mail Manager"), a mail manager program written by Chris Maio, based on the TOPS-20 MM program running on Digital Equipment Corporation DEC20 systems.

**mh,** RAND Message Handling system

**mailx**

Plus, if you're connecting from a personal computer, you have the option of using e-mail management programs that run on your computer, like Eudora or TechMail.

Some e-mail programs are commercial products (including shareware programs, which are commercial products with a different distribution mechanism—and shareware programs are often as good as or better than conventionally marketed products), public-domain and other freeware programs. Many products include e-mail as one of their functions; examples are Digital Equipment's All-in-One, Lotus NOTES, IBM's PROFS, and the **gnu-emacs** editor.

No one e-mail program is necessarily better or worse than another. Which one you choose and use will be largely a matter of what program your organization has standardized on, what you're used to—or what's available on the system you're using. And if you access your system in both GUI and line-oriented modes, have accounts on several different systems, or use both a direct-attached workstation and a dial-up terminal or network-style computer, you may be using several different e-mail programs in your everyday activity.

While these programs all have to use standards to speak to each other, each e-mail program may have different ways of creating, reading, and managing e-mail messages—different command names, syntax, and functions. Some may use abbreviations, some may use cursor or mouse control. Work by the creators of these programs and members of the Internet Engineering Task Force groups helps ensure that these different mail programs can exchange messages and be able to read them.

The point is: Since there is no one standard Internet e-mail program all Internet users will employ in common, I can't predict which e-mail program you'll be using and teach you how to use it. Instead, let's talk about what you can and want to do using your e-mail system. We'll look at the essential and most commonly used functions—these should be relatively constant across almost all mail systems—along with tips, gotchas, netiquette, and where to go for more information.

### Your e-mail curriculum

As you and your organization become more e-mail-intensive, you'll be using e-mail more frequently and in more ways, so learn how your e-mail system works. You don't have to master everything, but it's worth going through the manual once and trying key features. Set aside a few hours during the first day or so after you've gotten your account. At minimum, you want to be able to:

- Check to see if you have mail
- Read new messages, "scrolling" a screen at a time
- Scan new and existing messages by header and sender
- Save, file, delete, forward, and print messages
- Reply to messages
- Create and send messages
- Include a file or existing message in a message you're creating
- Quit with and without making messages you just read "go away"

On most systems, once a message has been sent, you *can't* reach out and stop it. If it seems too easy to send a message accidentally, learn how to compose messages with an editor and then load those files in. Also learn whether and how you can undelete messages you've deleted by mistake (e.g., can you simply type "undelete" at the mail system prompt, or is it instantly gone forever? Can your system administrator or postmaster recover it?). On some systems, recent messages can be retrieved. On others, only messages saved by system backups are recoverable.

Don't rely on e-mail for time-critical messages, especially outside of core business hours, unless you're sure that e-mail connectivity is working at that moment and that your recipient (1) is at their workstation, (2) is logged in, and (3) checks mail frequently (i.e., if it's 4:30 in the afternoon, and you want to send someone a message about a meeting for the next morning, pick up the phone).

Here's what we'll talk about:

- Mail messages and files
- The components of an e-mail message
- Typical e-mail functions/capabilities: reading and managing mail messages and creating and sending mail messages

### Mail messages and files

E-mail systems work by exchanging messages created and read by users like you (and sometimes by message-making/reading programs). As mentioned earlier, you use a client e-mail program, often called a mail reader or user agent, to create, read, and manage your messages. Your incoming and outgoing e-mail will be received and forwarded by one or more mail agent server e-mail programs.

These are the programs that take care of sending the messages you create to their recipients and of receiving messages "addressed" to you, including storing them until you take them; they also perform other post office tasks.

As a rule, your e-mail program won't actually communicate directly with these mail server programs; instead, it will put your outgoing messages in a file checked periodically by the mail server and similarly will check one or more other files for messages to you.

As explained earlier, e-mail works with messages, which are stored in files. E-mail messages are treated as strings of data, which can be stored in files, often called *mail files* or *mailbox files.* Some e-mail systems must use a separate file for each message. However, most of today's e-mail programs let you put many messages into a single file and move messages back and forth among these files. (In fact, you can have more than one file containing e-mail messages, as you'll see later on.)

These e-mail programs use a predefined format* to structure your e-mail messages, in particular, to put together the "header" that contains addressing and other information. This format is how your e-mail program can tell where in a mail file one message stops and the next begins—essential if you want to work with your e-mail as individual messages.

Client e-mail programs include editing facilities that "understand" this format and manipulate the contents of files of e-mail messages as a series of messages (i.e., you can look at the first message, the fifth message, messages three through seven, or the last message). This is similar to how database management systems "understand" the format of the records and how spreadsheet programs "understand" how a spreadsheet is stored.

As a rule, *don't* use a text editor to edit a file of messages, if you ever intend to access it again using an e-mail program. It's very easy to damage the mail-specific formatting. For example, each message includes an indicator of how many bytes long the message is (see Fig. 5.4). If you edit the message such that this number is no longer accurate, or remove other critical information, your e-mail program may no longer be able to deal with the file as a series of messages.

Your e-mail program should allow you to move messages to new files, which you can then edit with your text editor. Similarly, you will be able to edit the contents of a message you are creating, which can include the contents of files or other messages which you've inserted into your new message.

**Where mail you haven't "picked up" yet is.** On most computer systems, e-mail which has been received for you that you have not retrieved is held in a file (usually called a mail queue, just as files waiting to be printed are in a print queue). On some systems, your mail queue is in a directory "belonging to" the

---

*Within the Internet, e-mail systems make use of a standard format. This common format lets Internet users with different types of e-mail systems exchange messages. It is specified in a Internet RFC (Request for Comments) document, RFC 822. Unless you're a software developer or system administrator, you don't need to know anything more, or even this much, about e-mail formats.

```
From mikado@mikado.gov Tue May 4 11:00:44 1993
Return-Path: <mikado@mikado.gov>
Received: from MIKADO.GOV by world.std.com (5.65c/Spike-2.0)
        id AA12382; Tue, 4 May 1993 11:00:40 -0400
Received: from mikado.gov by MIKADO.GOV id aa02679; 4 May 93 10:30 EDT
Received: from dinlaw.mikado.gov by MIKADO.GOV id aa02675; 4 May 93 10:29 EDT
Date: Tue, 1 May 93 10:27:36 EDT
From: mikado@mikado.gov
To: mikado-list@mikado.gov
Message-Id: <23380563@mikado.gov>
X-Mts-Userid: W080
Subject: PFtC update meeting reminder; integrating "Little List"
Status: R

The Lord High Exec in Titipu is ready to submit an official Working
Draft of his "Little List." We are looking to integrate it with PFtC
which currently is done in our homegrown ALL-subLime object-oriented
language. Let's see if WAIS can use LL entries as PFtC queries!

T. Mikado

---Emacs: meeting-msg.1 11:32am Mail (Fundamental)--Top--------
Loading time...done
```

**Figure 5.4** Looking at an e-mail file through a text editor.

operating system or e-mail server program; on others, it may be in your home directory.

**What happens to mail you have picked up.** Once you have "read" a message (displayed at least some of its contents), failing other activities, most e-mail programs will move this message from the mail queue to the file which is your personal mailbox. The name and location of this file is usually specified as part of the definition of your account; typically, it is a file in your account's home directory and is called something like "mbox," "mailbox," "mail," or "savebox." (This file can easily get very large over time; you should plan to periodically use your e-mail program on this file to examine what's in it.)

Your mail reader program should also let you put these messages into other files. If you don't use a text editor on these (or do so carefully), you can use your mail reader program to read and manage the messages in these files as well. (The program you use to read Usenet Newsgroup postings may be able to save copies of Usenet postings for you as mail messages to these or other files.)

### The components of an e-mail message

Every message consists of a header, a body, and an end of message marker.

**The message header—The e-mail "envelope."** Message *headers* are the equivalent of the envelopes your paper mail comes in, including destination and return addresses and "cancellation" postmarks (but no stamps). The message

***Warning—Don't Assume Suspicious E-Mail Messages Are Real***

One important note: Don't trust what you read in a message header or contents absolutely. Some fields can be changed by the sender easily. Others may be harder to change but not impossible, given enough knowledge and system privileges. And once a message has been received, it's possible to edit significant changes in. Making the message appear valid—contain the appropriate checksums and other indicia—may be easy, difficult, or impossible. Just remember: Messages *can* be forged. Especially if they're coming from across another network.

Tools and techniques are being made available to make it possible to authenticate message sender, recipient, and contents, such as the Kerberos system developed at M.I.T. and the Privacy-Enhanced Mail system developed by the Internet Engineering Task Force, using RSA public-key cryptography. If you deal in sensitive messages, a little paranoia is always in order.

header includes a variety of information, some of which was created by the person (or program) sending you the message; the rest, by the various e-mail programs on the various computers that forwarded the message from the sender to you and by the program that "received" the message on your behalf.

If you look at a file of e-mail messages by simply displaying a stored message (e.g., with the Unix **cat** or **more** command, or using a regular text editor, such as **emacs** or **vi**), you'll see the message as your mail program sees it. (Unless you saved the messages without the headers, of course.) Try this at some point, and you'll see. (You may want to use a read-only command, such as **more,** rather than an editor, to avoid inadvertently altering the contents of a mail file.) Some of this information, discussed below, relates to the message itself and may be relevant or of interest to you as the recipient.

**The "To:" field—who the message has been sent to.** If you're creating a message, you put one or more names here, separated by commas, (e.g., alice@jabber.wock.com, lgulliver@laputa.org, help-desk@laputa.org). These names can be:

- Individuals (e.g., alice@jabber.wock.com, lemuel@laputa.edu)
- Programs that accept e-mail (e.g., archie@sura.net)
- Abbreviations (a.k.a. "aliases") that you have previously created to avoid having to remember or type the full name (e.g., "al" instead of "alice@jabber.wock.com")
- Names of mailing lists (e.g., com-priv@psi.com, risks@sri.org)
- Abbreviations for mailing list names (e.g., "chess" instead of "chess-club-reminders@laputa.org")
- Names of files which have names in them, if your e-mail system supports this feature

**The "Subject:" field—what the sender decided the message is about.** If you're creating a message, choose subject text that summarizes what the message is about or otherwise conveys the important information. Bear in mind that:

- Your recipients may decide how urgent reading your message is, whether in fact to read it at all, based on the subject.

- Often, readers may only see the first 20 to 40 characters when looking at a summary of received messages.

Here's some "good" Subject lines:

Subject: Urgent! Today's 10 AM mktg meeting resched' to 9 AM

Subject: FYI: What they're saying about our new product

Subject: Oct 95 monthly report, note Recommendations at end

Subject: Help! Shuttle filled with tribbles!

Subject: Wanna join us for lunch today (Tuesday)?

And here are some "bad" subject lines:

Subject: News update

Subject: Here's what Joe had to say at the meeting

Subject: FYI

Subject: Meeting

Subject: Trouble

**The "From:" field—who sent it, probably including their "real name" and user-address.** Your e-mail system handles putting in this information for you automatically. An example is:

```
From: ralph@topsl.pinafore.nav.uk (Ralph Rackstraw)
```

You can choose your "real name" when you get your account and probably change it at will. (See Chap. 3.) On a Unix system, try using the **chfn** command. (It's possible to spoof the from-user-name field, but a bit harder.) Given this, you can understand why you are advised not to trust the real name field, as most users can change what gets inserted at will.

**The "Date:" field—when the message was created.** The information here is based on time as kept by the sender's computer.

The sender can't change this information casually, but again, it can be done by someone who knows how. Keep in mind that the computer where a message originates may be in a different time zone, may be using Greenwich Mean Time, or may have its "clock" misconfigured.

**The "Cc:" field—who else the message has been sent to.** Like a Cc: line on a paper letter or memo, the Cc: field includes names of other recipients. For example:

```
Cc: captain@pinafore.nav.uk, sir-jos@ruler.nav.uk
```

If you are creating a message from within your e-mail program and want to keep a copy, be sure to include yourself in the Cc: field. This is usually the best way to ensure you'll have a copy, particularly if you tend to compose letters from within your mail system (rather than create a file with an editor, then invoke the mail system and insert the completed file to a message).

---

*Tip:* Many e-mail programs let you configure your account to automatically include you in the Cc: field; for example, if you use the *mail* program, include:

```
set askcc
```

in your .mailrc file. Check your e-mail documentation for more on this (try looking for things like "environment variables," "configuration," or "initialization files"). If keeping a copy of a given message is particularly important, consider creating the message first as a separate file, using your text editor, and then inserting the finished file into the message. (We'll talk about how to do this shortly.)

---

**The "Bcc:" field—who's been sent "blind carbon copies."** Again mimicking hard-copy letter conventions, the Bcc: field lets you include names of people you want a copy of the message to go to, without letting any of the To: or Cc: names being aware of it. Your mail program should omit the Bcc: field from the copies of the message that go to the To: and Cc: names. (You may want to test this out before trying it on a potentially job-damaging message.)

**The "Reply-to:" field—where answers should be addressed to.** The Reply-to: field contains the e-mail address you should send any replies to, which may be different from the address in the From field. (Often, for example, what's in the From: field isn't the sender, but some other entry, such as the name of an electronic mailing list.) The "answer/reply to a message" command in most e-mail programs usually uses this field automatically.

**Other message header fields.** An e-mail message header may also include fields such as message-ID:, Received:, and Resent-from:. This information is created by e-mail programs as your message is created and passed around. It's mostly useful when looking at network problems or figuring out what route and how long a message to go from sender to receiver.

**Sample message headers.** Here's some sample message headers. The header of a message I created:

```
From ddern Fri May 14 07:34:29 1993
Return-Path: <ddern>
Received: by world.std.com (5.65c/Spike-2.0)
    id AA00638; Fri, 14 May 1993 07:34:28 -0400
Date: Fri, 14 May 1993 07:34:28 -0400
From: ddern (Daniel P Dern)
Message-Id: <199305141134.AA00638@world.std.com>
To: hronir-request@ulibrary.org
Subject: Please add me to HRONIR mailing list
Cc: ddern
Status: RO
```

The header of a message I received from a person:

```
Message 32:
From Flack@laputa.org Fri May 14 15:01:46 1993
Return-Path: <Flack@laputa.org>
Received: by world.std.com (5.65c/Spike-2.0)
    id AA16706; Fri, 14 May 1993 15:01:45 -0400
Received: from spool.uu.net (via LOCALHOST) by relay2.UU.NET
with SMTP
    (5.61/UUNET-internet-primary) id AA14886; Fri, 14 May 93
13:10:54 -0400
Received: from laputa.UUCP by spool.uu.net with UUCP/RMAIL
    (queueing-rmail) id 130844.18729; Fri, 14 May 1993 13:08:44
EDT
Received: by laputa.org (1.64/waf)
     via UUCP; Fri, 14 May 93 12:16:10 EDT
     for ddern@world.std.com
To: ddern@world.std.com
From: flack@laputa.org (Media Relations Office)
Message-Id: <vxqo5zw164w@laputa.org>
Date: Fri, 14 May 93 12:16:10 EDT
Organization: City in Flight, Laputa
Status: R
```

**Message body.** The message body is your message—the equivalent of the sheets of paper and whatever else you've put into the "envelope." To maximize the chances that other people will be able to read your e-mail, and you theirs, most e-mail programs have been created to follow certain standards for physical and data format.

**Width.** The physical format in terms of width is straightforward: Message lines of no more than 80 characters. The reasons are simple:

1. This is what most of our monitor screens are designed to handle.
2. Many text editors won't take lines longer than this.
3. Some e-mail systems can't handle lines longer than this.

If you create a message that has lines 120 characters wide, your addressee may be able to receive it—but to read it, they'll have to somehow reformat it or go through other time-consuming and annoying gyrations. This is inconsiderate. It also decreases the odds of this person bothering to read your next message—or they may only read what is easily viewed on their screen without reformatting and miss important information.

If you're creating messages from a text editor or word processor, you shouldn't have to worry about this too much. Most text editors will automatically keep you to within this limit, for the same reason—your screen is bound to display the same length lines. However, if you're creating messages using the local text editor on some of the on-line e-mail services or uploading files to be message text, you can easily create lines that are too long.

What happens to these too-long lines? Some e-mail systems will truncate lines longer than a certain number of characters (i.e., simply not get those characters beyond a certain length). Some may tell you your lines are too long. Some systems may get "confused" if your input text line is too long. Moral: Keep your line length under 80 characters.

**Length.** Most of the e-mail messages you create and send will most likely be anywhere from 10 to 100 lines long—but some may be longer. If you're sending documents, lists, text files, or the like, messages with several thousand lines are quite common. All e-mail systems have some limit on how long a file they can handle as a single message. The e-mail gateways that relay e-mail from one network to another, such as between the Internet and CompuServe or MCI Mail, may also have length limits.

Many can handle very large files—long enough to send the entire manuscript of a book—or huge image files. Others are restricted to about 63,000 characters. CompuServe, for example, used to have a size limit of about 63,000 bytes for an e-mail message—more than enough for most text messages but often too short for programs and other binary files being sent by e-mail.

Each mail program or gateway may behave differently when it gets a message longer than it can handle. It may send only as much of the message as it can handle, automatically split it up into pieces, or refuse to send your message and reply to you with a warning message.

---

*Tip:* To send a too-long message, such as a book-sized document:

1. Use a compression program on your message, such as the Unix **compress** command or ZIP. Be sure that the person on the other end has the program needed to uncompress the message, however, and knows how to do it.
2. Break the file up into smaller parts. Some systems will have commands to do this, with names like **split.**
3. Consider using file-transfer, such as FTP.

---

## What types of data can go into an e-mail message?

As discussed earlier, until a few years ago, most e-mail consisted of ASCII text. Today, the messages you create and receive may have anything from audio annotations to weather maps and spreadsheets. One reason is the use of e-mail as a delivery method for programs, images, and other types of files; another is the growing use of multimedia e-mail. (See Box: "Multimedia E-Mail Ain't So New," and its discussion of MIME, in the section "Useful Things to Know About E-Mail.")

---

*Tip: Keep the ASCII bitstreams flying.* When in doubt, send your messages in text consisting of plain old ASCII characters. This ensures that anyone and everyone who gets your messages will be able to read them.

---

### Important Files for e-mail users: configuration file, mailbox file(s), .signature file, "dead letter"

Your e-mail program makes use of a number of different files in addition to the ones where your new or unprocessed, processed, and saved messages are. The most important one is the configuration file.

**E-mail configuration file.** As with many other programs you may run on your computer, most e-mail systems have a file containing configuration information, stored by default in your home directory, whose contents you create, edit, and maintain. On Unix systems, these files commonly have names consisting of an initial . plus the name of the command plus the characters **rc**. For example, the configuration file for **mail** is usually .mailrc. When you invoke your e-mail program, it should process the contents of this file before accepting any input from you. It may contain things like:

- Parameter definitions, such as "set crt=24" to define how many lines of information any "paged" display should present
- Aliases—abbreviations for e-mail addresses and list of addresses, such as alias aw alice@jabber.wock.com

**"Signature" file: "Dot sig," your .signature file.** When you're nearly done composing an e-mail, you may want to include standard information such as your full name, title, organization, and contact information such as e-mail, phone, fax and postal addresses, etc. You could type it in fresh each time—but computers make this unnecessary.

Many e-mail programs used on the Internet will have a command to insert your "signature" file (named ".signature" on Unix systems) automatically at the end of a message, or prompt you as to whether you want it inserted. All e-mail programs also should let you insert a file by name. For more information about signature files, see the discussions about .dot files in Chaps. 4 and 6.

**The dead letter file.** Often, when you're creating a mesage, something happens that interferes—the phone connection disappears, you quit by hitting a few <CONTROL-C>s, etc. Many e-mail programs will do their best to save your message in progress, in a file with a standardized name, such as dead.letter in your home directory. You can't count on messages-in-progress being there, but it's worth looking before you start to retype from the beginning.

### Invoking your e-mail program

Like most Internet services, you invoke your e-mail program by giving the appropriate command name or selecting the appropriate command or icon with your cursor, mouse, etc. Most e-mail programs have two modes: "read-messages" mode and "create-a-message" mode. In read-messages mode, your e-mail program will let you examine and manage mail messages in one or more files. In create-a-message mode, your e-mail program will let you create a new message, optionally including existing messages and files.

---

*Tip: To use e-mail, use it.* Remember that e-mail, like voice mail or any other facility, only works if you use it. Be sure to check regularly for messages—at least first thing in the morning, before and after lunch, and before you go home. Read important messages and respond to them. The odds are good that you, too, will soon be a frequent e-mailer, and won't know how you ever got along without it.

---

**To enter read-messages mode.** Read-messages mode usually includes a command to enter create-a-message mode, so you can create and send e-mail as you are processing your e-mail without having to be continually exiting and restarting your e-mail program.

As a rule, to read new and unprocessed e-mail, if you want to enter read-messages mode to check for and read new and unprocessed messages, you can simply give the command, without any parameters such as filenames. For example:

```
% mail
% elm
```

Your e-mail program will get your messages from the mail queue for your unprocessed messages. There may be a standard place on the system where this file is located, or it may be specified in your account information.

**To read already-processed and filed mail.** Your e-mail program can work with messages you have already processed and filed, in your "savebox" and other files. Most e-mail programs allow you to give a filename as a parameter to the command (among other options). For example:

```
% mail -f mbox
% mail -f MAIL/fanmail
```

Your e-mail program should also include one or more ways to change what mail file you're working on within your session; however, you may want to hold off trying this until you've mastered the basics of using your e-mail program.

**To enter create-a-message mode.** You may also be able to select which mode you enter when you invoke your e-mail program, based on the parameters. Most e-mail programs, for example, enter create-a-message mode automatically if you give an e-mail address as an argument on the command line; for example:

```
% mail lemuel@lilliput.org
```

There may also be a separate command that starts up your e-mail program in create-a-message mode. When you exit create-a-message mode, you are returned to wherever you were when you invoked this mode. If you were in read-messages mode of your e-mail program, you're back there. If you were at the operating system prompt or using some other facility, such as **ftp,** Gopher, reading Usenet articles, etc., you are returned to the same place you left off.

### What you see when your e-mail program starts up

Typically, when an e-mail program starts up, it shows you information about your new and unprocessed messages, such as displaying a series of one-line summaries, called *headers* or *message headers.* Each header line contains some or all of the sender's name, the date the messages were created, and as much of the Subject: field as fits within this one-line summary. Some e-mail programs will have separate commands for selecting headers based on different fields; others will let you do this by giving the appropriate keywords and values in their "headers" command.

You may be able to modify various aspects of this display by making the appropriate changes to the configuration files associated with your e-mail program. (On Unix systems, the names of these files commonly consist of an initial ., the name of the program, and the characters rc (.mailrc, .elmrc, and so on.)

Now that you have started up your e-mail program, let's take a look at typical functions, capabilities, and commands you can expect from your e-mail program.

### Typical e-mail functions, capabilities, and commands

Since I can't predict which e-mail program you will use or expect any recommendations I make to be best for you, it's nearly impossible for this book to instruct you in how to use your e-mail program. However, all e-mail programs share a basic set of functions in common:

- Inspect and read new, unexamined, examined, and filed messages
- File, forward, delete messages
- Create a message
- Respond to messages

For character-oriented systems, single-keystroke commands may be sufficient for many common operations, either as one-character abbreviations or as single-keystroke menu choices. (Or, for programs with mouse and icon-oriented user interfaces, a single click.)

**Common e-mail commands.** Common keystrokes and their associated functions for e-mail programs include:

| | |
|---|---|
| **<RETURN>** | Display next unread message |
| **t** | Display current or specified message(s) |
| **h** | Display headers for a screenful of messages |
| **?** | Display help information |

| | |
|---|---|
| **d** | Delete current or specified message(s) |
| **r** | Reply to current or specified message |
| **q** | Exit mail program, applying any changes you've made to the current message file |
| **x** | Exit mail program leaving current message file as when you started |

**Specifying message(s).** Your e-mail program should let you specify sequences and groups of messages based on their numeric position in the mail file, or other information. These numbers are not in the actual file; they are assigned by the mail program for the duration of the session. Examples are:

```
42
1-9
10,11,12
from ralph@topsl.pinafore.nav.mil
to alice@jabber.wock.com
```

Some e-mail systems also have a way for you to refer to messages, such as "the last group of messages I specified" or "the final message in the file."

**Message status.** Many e-mail programs will indicate the current status of messages as you progress through a session; in character-oriented programs, usually by changing the character at the beginning of the header line.

### Examine, read, file, forward, delete, etc.: Common e-mail management tasks

As mentioned earlier, the variety of e-mail systems available makes it difficult to advise you on what commands you'll give to your e-mail system. (If

***You Have New Mail***

There is an easy way to know whether you have new messages, without starting up your e-mail program. Many of the shells such as the Unix **sh** and **csh** include a useful "watch the mail file" feature. (**nethack,** a screen-oriented computer game in the tradition of Adventure, Zork, and Rogue, created by a number of Internet programmers, often delivers "a scroll of mail" to your character, which you can read and then come back to your place in the game.)

A part of the program takes a look at your mail queue file (or any other specified file) periodically; if any new messages have been added since the last time you checked, it displays a "new mail" message on your screen as soon as you do something that generates another command prompt. For example:

```
% cp resume.txt resume1.txt
You have new mail.
```

Many systems will let you change or specify a different message. This is usually done as an entry in one of your "dot" files, such as .login or .cshrc. Some shells will also have a message such as "You have mail." This message is a reminder that you have still-unprocessed mail in the system's mail queue. You'll often see it when you open a subshell (pop "down" to a shell below your current executing program).

they aren't reasonable, obvious, intuitive, or well marked, you may want to get another e-mail program.) However, what people do with e-mail remains relatively constant. The most common things to do with e-mail messages in read-messages mode include:

- Examining message headers
- Reading message(s)
- Replying to a message
- Filing message(s)
- Forwarding message(s)
- Deleting message(s)

**Examining messages headers.** Every mail system should include one or more commands that let you inspect headers—the one line summaries usually including the sender's name and some or all of the subject—for some or all messages. **h** is commonly used for the "examine-message-headers" command.

Many e-mail programs will let you select message headers by specifying a set or range of message numbers (e.g., 20-39), the name of the sender (e.g., alice@jabber.wock.com—you'll probably have to give the full e-mail address), subject, etc. Some e-mail programs will have separate commands for selecting headers based on different fields; others will let you do this by giving the appropriate keywords and values in their "headers" command.

**Reading messages.** The most important function in e-mail is to display one or more messages at your screen, so you can read it or them. There may be one or several message-reading commands. On character-oriented e-mail programs, <RETURN> typically means "read the next message."

There should also be a "read the current message" command—**t** (for type) is commonly used for this. You should be able to specify one or more messages to read in a way that is similar to how you specified headers. Typically, giving the message number(s) without any command means "display these messages."

**Scrolling or paging messages a screen at a time.** Since messages can easily be more than a screenful long, you want a way to read through a message a screen at a time and may also want other capabilities, like being able to search through a message to the next occurrence of a word, move backward, etc. Your e-mail program should include a "pager" function to let you do this. As with the newsreader program you may use to read articles in Usenet Newsgroups, your e-mail's pager function may look very similar to the Unix **more** command. Quite possibly, it, in fact, is using the **more** facility on your computer.

You should also be able to specify how many lines you want your pager to display (e.g., 24, 50, 80). This is commonly done in the configuration file for your e-mail program. For example, if you use **mail** and have a 25-line screen, you want to include **set crt=24** in your .mailrc file.

**Deleting messages.** You won't want to save or file all the e-mail you receive. Every e-mail program should include a "mark-message(s)-for-deletion" command, more commonly referred to as "delete-message." For example, **mail**'s "delete-message" command is **del** or simply **d.** When you give this command, most e-mail programs will mark the appropriate message as "to be deleted upon exiting." Messages so marked may or may not be displayed by the "show-headers" command later on in the session, depending on your e-mail program.

**Quitting your mail program and performing deletions to your message queue.** If you quit your e-mail program with its standard exit command (e.g., **q,** or **quit**), at this point, the program should update the file of mail messages you were working with and actually erase those messages marked for deletion. Until you quit, you should be able to "undelete" these messages—remove the "to-be-deleted" mark.

**Quitting your mail program without performing deletions on your message queue.** Most e-mail programs should also have another command or way to quit which leaves the mail file unchanged, including without performing any deletion of messages (or moving of "examined" messages from your queue to your "saved-mail" file). **x** is commonly used as this command. You should find, learn, and practice using your e-mail program's "quit-without-updating-mail-file" command; it can come in very helpful. If you believe you have inadvertently marked an important message for deletion, and can't find it by using "undelete," exiting in this fashion should solve the problem.

Delete acts on current or specified message(s). In most e-mail systems, if you don't specify one or more messages, the "delete-message" command acts on the current message. However, what your e-mail program considers to be the current message may not always be the same one that you believe is, if

**_Be Careful When Deleting Messages_**

Exercise caution when using your e-mail program's "delete-messages" function. Unlike most text editors and word processors, few e-mail programs make a backup copy of a file before applying changes such as deleting messages. If you quit your e-mail program in the standard fashion such that it deleted appropriately marked messages, they are gone, and your e-mail program is unlikely to be able to recover them. However, it may be possible to recover these messages:

- Contact your system administrator *immediately.* Explain what happened. A copy of the file containing the message may have been saved in a recent backup. Well-run systems commonly make frequent "saves"—backup copies—of mail queue files. It *may* be possible to find and recover your message using an UNDELETE utility such as in PC-TOOLS, Norton Utilities, etc. However, if your files are kept on a disk shared by other users, or if you're running an operating system such as Unix, the storage area occupied by this message may already have been "grabbed" and reused.
- Contact someone else you believe received a copy of the message (e.g., whoever you sent it to or sent it to you, or someone else on the distribution list). Ask them to forward you another copy of the message, if they still have it. (And if you'd previously contacted your system administrator, let them know you've been able to recover, so they don't keep looking on your behalf.)

you've been reading new or unprocessed messages. When in doubt, inspect (display) the current message before you give the "delete-message" command, or check the message header afterward. You are advised to experiment with this (using messages you can afford to have deleted).

**Filing messages.** Your e-mail program should include a facility to let you move copies of messages into other files. The standard procedure for e-mail programs, when you exit normally from reading your new or unprocessed messages, is to move all messages you read (or at least started to read) from your mail queue to the file it uses to save "read/processed" messages to. (That's the "savebox," commonly named "mailbox" or "mbox.")

Your e-mail program should also include a facility to "save" copies of messages in the current mail file to any other file, in one or more ways, such as:

- Append message(s), in message format, to the specified file (create a new file if it doesn't already exist)
- Append message(s) or create a file but without the "header" portion

Many e-mail programs, such as **elm** and **pine** include mail-filing features such as "folders" to help you better organize your e-mail messages as you save them. Your e-mail program should let you specify both which message(s) you want to save copies of and what file you want them saved to. The filename can be a pathname (absolute or relative) (e.g., you can save a message to ~/MAIL/PROJECTS/warp-drives).

Make sure you understand how the information you give is handled; **mail**, for example, if you give message number(s) but no filename, assumes the number(s) are the name of the file you want to save to, and it moves a copy of the current message to this file (e.g., if you say

```
mail> s 13-15,
```

you'll get a copy of the current message, in a file named "13-15").

### Creating and sending messages: New, replies, forwarding

Creating a message means what it says—putting together a message to be sent to one or more electronic mail addresses, which may be individuals, groups (distribution-lists), or even computer programs that take commands via e-mail and causing it to be sent. The two primary ways to create messages are to:

- Create a new message
- Reply to an existing message

The process of creating a message can be divided into two parts: the header for the message and the body. Your e-mail program should have a number of commands and facilities for working with each of these, for creating, replying to, and forwarding e-mail. All involve entering create-a-message mode; there may be different commands and options, depending on whether you want to create a new message or reply to or forward existing messages.

**Creating a new message.** As indicated above, your e-mail system probably offers two ways to enter create-a-message mode to create a new message: a command within your e-mail program and one given at any command prompt, such as to the Unix shell, from within a subshell under **more,** etc. When you are creating a new message, you need to provide some information for the message header and the body text.

**Header information.** As you saw earlier, the message header contains the information needed by e-mail reader programs to let you manage messages and by e-mail server programs to exchange messages with their fellow programs across the Internet. Parts of the header are created and changed only by the e-mail programs themselves, not by you. Some are determined by settings you make in your various configuration files and by the information defining your account. You must provide, at minimum, at least one e-mail address for the message, in the To:, Cc:, or Bcc: field. (Otherwise the message can't be sent anywhere.) You can (and should) specify the Subject:, and there may be one or more other header fields you can specify. Your e-mail program may also let you set it to automatically include your name in the Cc: field.

**Address(es).** An address can belong to an individual, an electronic mailing list, a computer program, etc. Your e-mail program may prompt you for one or all of these fields. (See the discussion of "Replying to a message," below.)

**Subject.** For the Subject field, as discussed earlier, enter informative text, rather than something vague like "FYI" or "Message re lunch." You should be able to configure your e-mail program to automatically prompt for Subject text.

**Editing the header fields.** Most e-mail programs should also let you revise and edit the contents of header fields before you send the message. (For an example of how one e-mail program, **mail,** does it, see Box: Some Useful Escape (Tilde) Commands for **mail**'s Built-In New-Message Editor.)

**Entering message body contents.** You can put text (and other information) into your message body in a number of ways. One is by entering it using an editor, such as **emacs, vi,** one provided by your e-mail program, etc. Your e-mail program may include a "standard dumb editor" for entering the text of simple messages. This editor typically assumes you're entering text but don't need to revise any but the current, last line of text. **mail**, for example, comes with one of these facilities; you can edit the current line, typically with:

```
<DELETE>      delete last character on line
<CONTROL-W>   delete last word on line
<CONTROL-U>   delete entire line
```

Even these editors, however, usually offer a number of other facilities which you can invoke. **mail,** for example, lets you do this via its Escape (Tilde) commands. (See Box: Some Useful Escape (Tilde) Commands for **mail**'s Built-In New-Message Editor.)

**Some Useful Escape (Tilde) Commands for *mail*'s Built-In New-Message Editor**

When composing a message in **mail**'s built-in new-message editor, you may want to do other things besides simply enter new text. You enter commands to the editor by starting a line with its Escape character, followed by the commandname—usually a single character—and any other parameters needed. For example, you can edit header fields, review the current message, invoke a screen editor, and include messages and files.

Unless you have set it to something else, the default Escape character is usually the tilde (~) character; these commands are therefore often known as the "mail tilde commands." Here's a list of the more useful "tilde" commands in **mail**'s built-in new-message editor. (For a complete list—if you use **mail**—check the on-line manual page.)

**~?** Display a summary of tilde escapes.

**~e** Invoke the editor to edit the message. (You can specify which editor via a parameter in your mail configuration file.)

**~f [message-list]** Include the current message or listed message(s). Assumes you're currently reading a mail file, of course.

**~h** Prompt for the message header lines: Subject, To, Cc, and Bcc. You can revise existing text in these lines by backspacing and then retyping.

**~m [message-list]** Insert the text from current or specified messages, putting at the front of each line the string value of the variable "indendprefix" (which can be set in your mail configuration file), for example, **>, YOU SAID>.**

**~p** Display the current header and text.

**~r [filename]** Include filename in message.

Even if you don't plan to use common Unix text editors like **emacs, vi,** or **ed,** it's worth knowing a little about them—specifically, how to exit them. (See App. B.)

You can also put text into your messages as follows:

- By inserting the contents of one or more files, using your mail program's appropriate command(s).
- By inserting the contents of the current or other messages—assuming you're in the middle of reading a mail file. This is a common way (and for some e-mail programs, the only way) to *forward* messages.
- By inserting the response to a command, such as a directory listing, into your message. Many e-mail programs will include a way to do this.

**Sending your created message.** Once you have finished creating your message, your next step is to send it—that is, tell your e-mail program to pass it to the e-mail server program on your system, which in turn forwards it to the appropriate destination(s) on your computer or elsewhere within your site or across the Internet. Unlike systems such as MCI Mail, which distinguish between finishing a message's text and dispatching it, many e-mail programs used in the Internet consider exiting the message-editor to be the "I'm done, send this for me, please" command (e.g., giving the <CONTROL-D> command to **mail**'s built-in new-message editor. (However, if you had invoked another editor, such as **emacs** or **vi,** from this editor, leaving that invoked editor would simply return you to the previous one.)

Remember—once you've sent an e-mail message, you can't "get it back." It's on its way, and that's that.

**Replying to a message.** In addition to creating a new message, you can enter create-new-message mode, from within your e-mail program, by "replying" to an existing message. Typically, your e-mail program will inspect the (current or specified) message, do its best to figure out the appropriate e-mail address to send the reply to, and also set the Subject: field to be "Re: " plus the subject of the message you're replying to.

This is a very convenient way to handle mail, including avoiding typing of the To: address. However, be careful. If you're replying to a message sent to a mailing list, you may be replying "to the list" instead of to the person who originally sent that message. *Always* be sure to inspect the header of your new message.

Also, the return address information in the message may be such that your e-mail program can't figure out the correct "return path." Don't blame your program—this is a complicated task, and it's amazing how well e-mail programs can do it. In these cases, look through the message you're replying to or other information you've got for another viable address and insert the correct address manually. You can also edit the Subject: field, if you wish.

At this point, your e-mail program should enter create-a-message mode, and let you enter the message body, which is the same as creating a new message.

**Forwarding message(s).** Many—but not all—e-mail programs include one or more commands to create a message by *forwarding* one or more messages in a mail file. This is the same as creating a new message and then including specified message(s), as discussed just above.

### A quick e-mail self-test checklist

To see if you've mastered some basics of your e-mail program, see if you can:

- Send a message to yourself by putting your own address in the To:, Cc:, or Bcc: fields
- Edit the address and Subject: header fields in a message you're creating
- Include a file in a message you're creating
- Save a message as a file
- Temporarily escape to a shell, without quitting
- Quit your mail system with and without changing the status of messages in your new/unprocessed queue

If you can find and master these functions in your e-mail program, you know enough to manage, create, and send e-mail. Once you grow more proficient, you should see what other commands are available and consider learning them. If you're having trouble with your e-mail program, you may want to consider trying a different or easier one for now—ask your local system administrator for suggestions.

Now that you've learned enough about how to use your e-mail program, it's time to start learning more about what you can do with it and more of what you should know as an e-mail user on the Internet (or anywhere, for that mat-

### *Confirming that the E-Mail Goes Through*

E-mail, like voice mail or any other messaging system, is only useful if people use it and only as reliable as the people and systems involved. I worked with someone who, in the 2 years he was at a very e-mail-oriented company, never once logged in and never read his messages. Someone else I ran into hadn't figured out how to scroll long messages one screenful at a time—so she assumed that anything important was in the final screenful.

[Hint: Include the line **set crt=<n>** in your .mailrc file, or a similar command in your mail program's configuration file. <n> is the number of lines you want to pause after (e.g., "set crt=24"). Check your mail program's manual page for things like "Paging" or "Scrolling."]

Just because you send someone a message doesn't mean they got and read it. The only way you can be 100 percent certain is if you receive a confirming e-mail message or phone call, or by another event. If you are sending e-mail about something that must happen at a specific time or otherwise is important, like meeting for lunch or asking them to bring an essential book with them, confirm with a "handshaking" message. Your intended e-mail recipients must:

- Have accounts that can receive Internet e-mail
- Check for and read their e-mail regularly (every few minutes to few days, depending on how they work)

And a lot of things can go wrong in the process of sending an e-mail message. Communicating successfully via electronic mail involves a number of parties, ranging from e-mail programs to computers and networks, all being connected and working in the right order—and also requires the human beings at each end to be *using* e-mail and not making certain types of mistakes.

"Never assume that an e-mail message you've sent arrives AND HAS BEEN READ unless you have direct evidence—such as an electronic or voice reply that relates to your message," states Wes Morgan <morgan@engr.uky.edu>, Systems Administrator for the University of Kentucky Engineering Computing Center (Lexington, KY). In his "Introduction to E-mail" lecture for engineering students, Morgan highlights the components necessary for successful "delivery" of e-mail and estimates what percentage of "undelivered" e-mail each such problem or error accounts for (see the list below). Note that some of the things that go wrong come from user errors—but hardly all.

- The sender must specify a proper address. "Erroneous addressing accounts for 90 percent of our undeliverable mail."
- The sending system must "know" the receiving system. "This accounts for less than 1 percent of our undeliverable mail."
- The sending system must be able to connect to the receiving system. "About 4 percent of our undeliverable mail."
- The receiving system must have a place to deposit the mail (a mail queue or other file). "About 5 percent."

And, lastly, "The recipient must READ the mail and reply to your message to confirm it was received and read." In many cases, Morgan notes, sites could receive mail but not reply for technical reasons—a frustrating circumstance.

If you are having problems sending e-mail to or from a particular site, send a message to "postmaster" at that site (e.g., postmaster@laputa.org). All Internet sites should receive mail to this address and deliver it to the person(s) in charge of e-mail administration. Don't ask the postmaster for help determining other peoples' e-mail names or addresses (unless it's work-related and urgent). But do call or send messages if you have other problems.

ter). In the section "How to Determine E-Mail Addresses," you'll learn how to determine e-mail addresses (including your own). The section "Other Useful Things to Know About and Do with E-Mail" contains information about some things you can *do* using your e-mail program, other than simply reading your mail and sending messages to other individual users, such as how to get files by e-mail instead of using anonymous-FTP file transfer, how to send mail to users on other networks, plus e-mail tips and netiquette. In Chap. 16 you'll learn what e-mail lists are and how to join and participate in them.

Now that you've learned what e-mail is, and how to use it, let's take a look at some of the things you need to know, or may want to know, to use e-mail on the Internet.

## How to Determine E-Mail Addresses

*"Gentlemen, I pray you tell me*
*Where a gentle maiden dwelleth*
*Named Yum-Yum, the ward of Ko-Ko?*
*In pity speak—oh, speak, I pray you!"*

*Nanki-Poo, The Mikado (Act I, Scene 1)*
—GILBERT & SULLIVAN

Knowing e-mail addresses—your own and those of the people you're corresponding with—is the key to using e-mail. Like phone numbers and addresses, you won't always know someone's e-mail address. You'll want to become familiar with how to get "Internet directory information" services and databases via which you'll obtain e-mail addresses for people and services on the Internet. In this section, you'll learn about the various tools and methods available for determining e-mail addresses. Let's start by looking at the easier question: determining your own e-mail address.

### Determining your e-mail address

As an Internet user, unless you are sharing an account with a group of people, you should have an e-mail address uniquely your own. (Although there may be more than one way to state this address.) This is the identifier other people and programs should use to send e-mail to you and the one you include in e-mail messages, on your business card and stationery, and in your "signature" file.

As explained in Chap. 3, your Internet e-mail address consists of your username (a.k.a. user-ID) plus a Fully Qualified Domain Name, joined by an @ sign, for example:

```
alice@jabber.wock.com
lgulliver@flapper.laputa.org
```

Within your company's network, your e-mail address may be as simple as your login-ID (e.g., lgulliver or your name plus a system/network name, like lgulliver@laputa) but to participate in the Internet e-mail community, you'll need an e-mail address that includes a Fully Qualified Domain Name, like the above examples.

If your organization is connected to networks of trading and business partners, to the Internet or is gatewayed to public e-mail networks such as CompuServe, MCI Mail, or AT&T Mail, learn your network address (e.g., rcapulet@mcimail.com, jmontague@delphi.com).

**Steps to determine your Internet e-mail address.** Here's how to find out your own (and help other people find out theirs—possibly your first chance to be the expert instead of beginner). One way to determine your Internet e-mail address is to ask your system administrator—and then try it out by having someone else, outside your organization, send a message to this address. Another way is by using one or more of the commands and facilities on the computer that your Internet account is on. You can also use this process to help other people determine their Internet e-mail addresses by talking them through the steps over the phone or faxing or mailing the suggestions to them.

**Step 1: Get your user-name.** Your user-name, or user-ID, on the computer your account is on, should be available in one of several ways (aside from being told). For example, on a Unix system:

- Inspect the value of the $USER variable. This is an environment variable used by other programs and normally contains your user-name. On a Unix system, you can inspect its value this way:

```
% echo $USER
lgulliver
%
```

- Check the /etc/passwd file. On many Unix systems, user-names and other nonsecret information for user accounts is stored, one line per user, in a file named /etc/passwd. If the value displayed doesn't look right, you may want to double-check by checking the entry for this name in the /etc/passwd file, as follows:

```
% grep $USER /etc/passwd
rrackstr:##rrackstr:1084:1084:Ralph
Rackstraw:/users/rrackstr:/bin/csh
```

- Check the name of your home directory, which is usually your user-name. Your home directory in your user account is usually the same as your user-name, so you can check this, too. On a Unix system, for example, you can change the directory back to your home directory by giving the **cd** command with no arguments and can display the full pathname of the working directory name with the **pwd** as follows:

```
% cd
% pwd
/usr/lgulliver
%
```

- Try the "who" command with the arguments "am i" (On many systems, this means "give information about current user"), for example,

```
% who am i
```

If you're not directly on the Internet, but on a network that can exchange e-mail with the Internet, get your user-ID and then see "Exchanging E-Mail with People Outside the Internet" later in the chapter.

**Step 2: Get your computer's name, and Fully Qualified Domain Name.** Next, you want to get the Fully Qualified Domain Name for your computer (e.g., jabber.wock.com, bedlam.sf.ca.us, world.std.com, etc.). Commands to try include **host** and **hostname.** Depending on what version of Unix or other TCP/IP commands are installed on your computer, you may be able to do this in one step, or it may take two steps. You may have to use one command to get the local name of your computer (i.e., the **host**), which is not a Fully Qualified Domain Name and then use this command's results with another command to get the full name. For example, I tried this on World, currently a Solbourne computer and had to use two commands: (Notice how when I tried **host** with no parameters, I got an error message.)

```
% host
Usage: host [-l] [-w] [-v] [-r] [-d] [-t querytype] [-a] [-s
server] host ... -l for a complete listing of a domain (zone
transfer) [ rest of error message deleted - DPD ]
% hostname
world
% host world
world.std.com has address 192.74.137.5
world.std.com has address 192.203.74.1
world.std.com mail is handled by world.std.com
world.std.com mail is handled by relay1.UU.NET
world.std.com mail is handled by relay2.UU.NET
%
```

On my guest account at another Unix-based Internet system, there was no **host** command—and **hostname** automatically displayed a Fully Qualified Domain Name:

```
% host
host: Command not found.
%
% hostname
den.bear.com
%
```

**Step 3: Put user-name and full computer name together for Internet address.** Now simply join the user-name and Fully Qualified Domain Name, using an @ to give the full Internet address:

```
ddern@world.std.com
ddern@den.bear.com
alicel@jabber.wock.com
```

Again, if you're not directly on the Internet, but on a network that can exchange e-mail with the Internet, get your user-ID and then see "Exchanging E-Mail with People Outside the Internet" later in this chapter.

**Step 4: Verify your Internet address.** Before telling anyone this Internet address, or including it on your business card or stationery, verify it. "Have someone send you a message to this address and confirm that you get it," advises Craig Partridge (craig@bbn.com), Research Scientist at BBN Systems & Technologies. "Don't believe people when they tell you what your e-mail address is. Give it out only after you've proven it's right."

You may also want to use the **finger** and/or **whois** TCP/IP commands, if possible, giving your Internet e-mail address, to see what they report.

---

*Tip: Giving out your Internet e-mail address.* When telling someone your Internet e-mail address, be sure to dictate it slowly. If someone is not familiar with the conventions of Internet addressing, do your best to be extra clear and careful:

- First "pronounce" it.
- Then spell it out, using "A as in Able, D as in Dog," etc.
- Emphasize the correct spelling for the Domain, especially for .com addresses, that it's "M as in Mary, not N as in Nancy, and only one, not two m's.
- Point out that there are no spaces, that the "at" portion is the @ character and the "dot"s are **.**'s.

When including e-mail addresses on business cards and stationery, common practice is to place it after telephone and fax numbers, with a note about which network the address is for. (Be sure that company policy allows including your e-mail address.) For example,

**Alice Liddell**
Senior Programmer

**Brown Bread Computing, Inc.**
318 First Street
Belfast, Maine 04915
207/555-6896
207/555-3071 (FAX)
Internet: alicel@jabber.wock.com
MCImail: aliddell@mcimail.com
Compuserve: 12345.678@compuserve.com

(These would be different accounts and different mailboxes.)

---

### Locating other network users

Just like you need to know someone's phone number to call them or mailing address to send them a birthday card, in order to send e-mail messages, you need to know e-mail addresses. In this section, you'll get a sense of why trying to determine someone's Internet e-mail address is not necessarily a simple question nor necessarily easily answered and will learn about a range of methods and tools to obtain the Internet e-mail addresses you're looking for (and possibly telephone, fax, or mailing information as well).

**Why getting e-mail addresses isn't necessarily easy.** People unfamiliar with the Internet tend to assume there's a big on-line directory containing the names and addresses of all Internet users, readily accessible by all users. That's because people who aren't familiar with the Internet tend to think of its users as belonging to a single entity, like to a company or like members of CompuServe. Therefore, finding someone—getting their e-mail address—should be easy. Right? Wrong. But the Internet isn't a single entity, in this sense. It's like expecting there to be one giant phone book with the names and extensions of everyone at every company and organization in the world. It's like asking the telephone company or post office, "I'm looking for someone's business phone and extension, but I'm not sure where they work." "I'm looking for Joe's address and home phone—and I think he lives on the East Coast." Do you begin to see the problem?

Every Internet user, in terms of an account and e-mail address, belongs to a specific organization, whether it's a public-access Internet site such as NetCom, an educational institution like Rutgers University or a company such as Sun Microsystems, etc. So when you ask, or someone asks you, about finding someone on the Internet, and getting their e-mail address, you're really saying, "Let's look through all the 'e-mail phone books' for all the possible organizations this person might be in."

One way to do this is to keep guessing which organization to check, checking that organization's e-mail phone book, and keep going until you strike pay dirt. Another would be to invoke some software tool that would help you choose these target sites and do the looking up for you. Still another possibility would be to launch "software probes" ahead of time to bring back copies of lots of e-mail phone books and bundle them together, so you could search them all in one shot. And, in fact, the Internet toolkit includes facilities for all these approaches, plus a few more.

Many of these methods and facilities are, admittedly, "kludges" thought up by various members of the Internet community as partial solutions to a big problem. The Internet community continues to get closer to good global solutions (see "**Whois**++—A 'Next-Generation' Network Address Finger"—by the time you read this, finding someone when you don't have the right pieces of information may no longer be an impossible task).

**Methods to try to locate someone's e-mail address.** As with any Internet activity, you want to start with the solutions that use the least amount of other people's network and computer resources—and the least amount of other people's time and attention. Let's start with the easiest methods.

**See if you already have their e-mail address.** You may already have the information on hand, in any of several forms:

*E-mail messages.* Have you received e-mail from this person? Have you received e-mail which included this person in the To: or Cc: field? Or any messages which mention this person and included their e-mail address? And if so, did you save at least one of these messages? Here's where your skills with file-searching commands, such as the Unix **grep** command, come in handy. For example, if you use a Unix computer, keep all your e-mail messages in the directory ~/MAIL, and are looking for a message from or mentioning Lemuel Gulliver, you can try:

```
% grep Gulliver ~/MAIL/* | more
```

And then examine any files that contain matches.

*Business card or stationery.* Internet and network users commonly include their e-mail address along with their voice phone, fax phone, and postal mailing address information. Do you have a card?

*Conference program, magazine, newsletter, or book citations.* If you recall reading anything by or about this person recently, particularly in regard to networking, the odds are good that an e-mail address was included. If the article was Internet or Unix-related (e.g., in the Interop Company's ConneXions newsletter), the odds are *quite* good.

*Internet and other organization phone books.* You may want to check printed phone/address directories, such as the NSFnet Network Services Center's *Internet Network Managers Phone Book* or listings in Internet Resource and Service Guides.

**Call this person and ask.** There's no substitute for direct action. If you know the phone number, pick up the phone, call, and ask "What's your Internet e-mail address?" If they know it, write it down (carefully), repeat it if there's any doubt, and then try it at your first opportunity.

It's possible they don't know their own e-mail address. (After all, you don't have to know it to send or receive e-mail messages; your e-mail program and site's post office programs take care of that automatically.) In this case, you can offer to help them determine their own e-mail address—which they're going to need, if people like you want to send them e-mail messages. Here's several ways:

- Tell them *your* Internet e-mail address—being sure to spell it out letter for letter and be clear about the @ sign, the .s, and "no spaces between pieces"—and have them send you e-mail, if they can figure out how. Get their e-mail addresses from their messages' headers, verify the addresses work by sending them messages (and having them confirm that they were received).
- Have them check to see if they have any e-mail and have them look at the To: and Cc: fields in a message.
- See if they can determine their e-mail address using local commands or give you enough information to do the look-up from your end. (See "Determining Your Electronic Mail Address" earlier in this chapter.)

If you can't reach someone by phone and know what organization he or she works with or are otherwise affiliated with, try someone else in his or her department or group or the operator/message center, if there is one. Organizations increasingly are keeping central track of e-mail addresses along with phone numbes. (But don't be surprised if they don't know or don't even know what e-mail is.)

**Use Internet tools, starting locally.** If the above methods don't work, it's time to start using the Internet. You have several categories of tools and methods; which you use next is up to you:

- Internet on-line user information services
- Checking through network "footprints"
- Sending "broadcast" queries to Usenet Newsgroups and other outlets

**Internet on-line user information services.** Over the years, the Internet community has invented a sizable number of user information directory services. (One implication is that we haven't gotten it right quite yet.) This includes a variety of commands and intraorganization and cross-organization databases. Many of these were intended for a particular organization or type of organization. User information systems and databases currently in use in the Internet include:

- **finger** servers
- **whois** servers (being run by 100 to 200 organizations)
- CSO "phone books" (being run by several dozen organizations)
- "White Pages" and X.500 projects (experimental)

User information databases, in addition to those maintained by specific organizations about their own users, include:

- DISA NIC Whois (a.k.a. DDN NIC)
- Usenet posters database
- College/University E-Mail Directory

**User information front ends and navigators.** In addition, there are a number of front end and navigator tools to make finding people somewhat easier, in terms of locating and searching through lots of organizations' user directory information. General-purpose Internet front ends and navigators that help identify and access user information services include Gopher, TechInfo, and HYTELNET.

User-information navigator tools, like the front end and navigator tools for the Internet itself, and for other pools of Internet information, fall into two categories (and some belong in both):

- Front ends to access any of a list (built-in or otherwise automatically generated) of user information databases and services. Examples: **netaddress**

(KIS), **whois++,** and **netfind**; also Gopher, TechInfo, Hytelnet, etc. This reduces the challenge of identifying and accessing user information services, to "look at the list and select a service."

- Front ends that can search many user information services together, in response to one user query. Examples: **netaddress** (KIS), **netfind,** and **whois++.**

However, most of these front ends still leave you with the same problems: you need to know which organization(s)'s information you want to search, and you have to do each search separately. This is similar to the problem faced by users looking for files among the Internet's many public-access anonymous-FTP archive sites and looking for resources among the growing number of Gopher sites.

There are a number of projects to try and solve this "locate and search many phone books" challenge; notably the **whois++** project (discussed later in this chapter). As you'll see, each offers some unique capabilities—and none is yet a definitive Internet phone book service.

To give you an idea of the wide range of Internet directory services projects going on, here's a list generated by Peter Scott's HYTELNET front end on World in December 1992. Notice how many different types of systems there seem to be:

```
           Whois / White Pages / Directory Services

<DIR001> Australian White Pages Pilot Project
<DIR002> British Telecom's "Electronic Yellow Pages"
Service
<DIR015> CSO Nameservers
<DIR003> DDN Network Information Center (NIC)
<DIR004> Knowbot Information Service at nri.reston.va.us
<DIR017> Legal Information Institute Directory Server
<DIR005> Lund University Information System
<DIR006> Ohio State University WHOIS Service
<DIR007> PARADISE Directory Service
<DIR008> PARADISE Directory Service (United Kingdom)
<DIR009> PSI White Pages Pilot Project
<DIR010> Swiss Electronic Phone Book
<DIR011> University of California at Berkeley Network
Information Server
<DIR012> University of Colorado Netfind server
<DIR013> University of Maryland Umail
<DIR016> USENET contributor e-mail addresses
<DIR014> WHOIS searches

See also the Campus-Wide Information Systems and Directory
Services

<CWC000> Canada
<CWG000> Germany
```

Through these tools and databases, information about an estimated three to five million network users at over 5000 organizations and sites is available. (At present, it's only fair to point out that this assumes you know enough to select the right tool and give it enough starting information.) Which tool and/or database should you choose? That depends on what information you know, such as:

- User-name
- Full name
- Organization
- Domain address
- Affiliation or activities (e.g., works with Internet Engineering Task Force, has posted to Usenet).

To know which tool to use, it's helpful to understand what information is available, where it's stored, and which tools can access it. (Ideally, you shouldn't need to know this; simply use a tool—but for now, this is how it works.) User information is located in a variety of places, which can be accessed and searched by different tools:

- Your personal information (e.g., in your .plan or .project files). These are files you create, in your home directory; they may contain your phone number, Internet e-mail address, mailing address, perhaps a humorous comment or two. Since this information is created and maintained by hand, it may have errors (e.g., typos, unupdated phone numbers). These files can be accessed by **finger** and **whois** programs, which in turn can also be accessed by programs such as **netaddress, netfind,** and **whois++** (subject to restrictions by your organization or site).
- System-wide information. This includes information in the files about all users on the system, such as /etc/passwd, and includes your user-name, for use in sending and receiving e-mail. It may also include real-time information regarding who's logged in, how long they've been logged in, and the like. This information is by definition correct, since it reflects how the computer will work, and what it's doing. These files can be accessed by **finger** programs, which in turn can also be accessed by programs such as **netaddress, netfind,** and **whois++** (subject to restrictions by your organization or site).
- Databases created by your organization. This includes phone books and other information directories. This information, like your .plan file, may not be complete or accurate. These often require a specific software program to access them, such as CSO or X.500; these programs may be usable through **netaddress** and **netfind** (not as of late 1992, but possibly in 1993).
- Cross-organization databases. These are databases put together by individuals or organizations containing people and information from more than one organization. Examples are the DISA NIC Whois database and the "Usenet Posters" database. These may be accessed by specific tools

**_Who's Listed, What Does It Mean_**

The e-mail addresses contained in the various Internet information services and databases don't necessarily represent all the Internet users:

- Listings may not be just individuals. Other possibilities: groups of people, "job functions" (such as postmaster, the -request list administrators, sales), automatic e-mail servers (info-servers, etc.), and other programs, plus services—"Yellow Pages" type of listings for organizations and offerings ranging from library catalogs and on-line databases to commercial pay-for-use services.
- Not everyone who can be reached by e-mail within and from the Internet is necessarily listed in the various information directory services. "Because most of the CSO and whois server databases are based on university faculty/staff/student directories, they are not necessarily white pages of Internet *users,*" notes J. Q. Johnson (jqj@ns.uoregon.edu), Director of Network Services, University Computing, University of Oregon (Eugene, OR). "For example, although every faculty and staff member at my institution is reachable by Internet e-mail, probably only one third of them actually read e-mail regularly; nearly half of them receive any e-mail in hardcopy format through campus mail and would be unable to reply to it."
- Don't forget the users on all the other networks and systems you can't directly get user information for—hundreds of companies who don't make their user directory information publicly accessible, the Unix and other sites running UUCP and FidoNet communications, CompuServe and America On-Line, etc.

such as **netaddress,** and other Internet tools you've learned about elsewhere in this book (e.g., **telnet,** e-mail, WAIS, FTP).

#### Programs and databases

***finger.*** **finger** is a TCP/IP program that lets you examine on-line and current status information about Internet users and the computers they are working on. (On some computers, **finger** will also be available under the command name **whois**; on others, they may be slightly different programs and give different 'slices' of information.)

**finger** gets its on-line information from individual user files in their home directories (on Unix systems, typically named .plan or .project) and system-level files, such as /etc/passwd. Status information comes from the operating system. For example:

```
% finger ralph_r@topdeck.pinafore.nav.uk
[topdeck.pinafore.nav.uk]
Trying 192.55.43.7
topdeck—Pinafore—Waterproofed Workstations OS v1.1
  10:34am up 9 days, 19:49, 8 users, load average: 8.14, 9.08, 9.43
ralph_r . Ralph ("Rafe") Rackstraw s8 hms-annex.nav.uk
(Virtual Terminal)
  ralph_r has new mail as of Thu 6-May-93 10:23AM
  last read Thu 6-May-93 10:19AM

Plan: (last modified Wed 5-May 93 11:56PM)
  Ralph ("Rafe") Rackstraw ralph_r@topdeck.pinafore.nav.uk
  Able seaman, H.M.S. Pinafore—Currently off Portsmouth
    "I'm a remarkably fine fellow."
  Plan: To marry Josephine and whistle all the airs from
    that infernal nonsense Penzance :-)
    %
```

Because **finger** is a TCP/IP command, it gets this information not only from the computer it's being run on but also from other computers in the Internet. **finger,** like **telnet** and FTP, can establish connections to remote systems across the Internet and work with its counterpart program—the "**finger** daemon"—on these computers. [Assuming, of course, that (1) your computer can establish a connection to the requested system, (2) the **finger** daemon is running on them, (3) the remote system permits these types of queries, and (4) the users in question have put this information into their files.]

To use **finger** to get information about users outside of your computer or site, you will need a Fully Qualified Domain Name for their site.

It's worth learning how to use **finger**—it's easy to use and can be a quick way to identify or verify user information, if you know the organizational address. If you're using a Unix computer, you may want to use other Unix commands to help you capture and examine results of **finger** queries, for example, pipe output through **more** for screen-scrolling:

```
% finger @laputa.org | more
```

Or save output to a file, to inspect via **more** or a text editor:

```
% finger alice@jabber.wock.com > alice-info
```

For more information about **finger** and **whois,** consult the on-line manual pages on your computer or your command reference manual.

***whois.*** The original **whois** was written for a specific database maintained by the Defense Data Network's Network Information Center (DDN NIC), known, not surprisingly, as the DDN NIC Whois Database (discussed shortly). The DDN NIC was recently renamed the DISA NIC. The DISA NIC Whois database runs on a server and can be accessed via several means.

Other organizations on the Internet have now created their own "**whois**" databases, available through their own "whois" servers, accessible through **whois** or other commands. This includes many of the Network Information Centers (NICs) and organizations such as universities and companies.

Where **finger** tends to access information for users of a given computer, **whois** information tends to be organizationwide—although, as noted above, sometimes **whois** will be the same facility as **finger. whois** information often comes from "template" forms filled out by users, rather than on-line and status information.

*CSO phone books, PSI White Pages, X.500, and other database and services projects.* These are information directories, and services to get them, using a variety of formats, including:

- CSO, a "phone book" protocol popular at many universities
- The White Pages pilot project being run by Performance Systems International
- X.500, information services based on the OSI standard (in use at a number of companies but not widely deployed within the Internet to date)

CSO servers are useful if your party is at a university—and you believe you know which one. As for the other projects, they are largely experimental; there's no predicting whether someone's in their databases or not.

As a rule, you access these facilities through a front end, such as Gopher or the **netaddress** Knowbot. The PSI "White Pages" can also be reached via remote login, by:

```
% telnet wp.psi.com
```

Login as "fred"; no password is necessary. For more information, send a message to WP-INFO@PSI.COM.

*The DISA NIC Whois database.* The DISA NIC Whois, started up many years ago, is a database primarily for developers, managers, and other key players in the Defense Data Network and Internet operations, research, and development. It includes many people who worked on the original ARPAnet and on the current NSFnet and other network projects funded by the U.S. government.

You can access DISA NIS Whois database directly via remote login (**telnet**) and also via **netaddress** (which includes querying by e-mail), and via Gopher. To access the DISA NIC Whois database via remote login:

```
% telnet nic.ddn.mil whois
```

Simply type the name of the person, host, domain, network, or mailbox-address you're looking for, and the Whois program will do its best to identify matches. If you put a period (.) at the end of a name (e.g., gulli.), the Whois program will list all entries that start with this string. For more information, when logged in to the DISA NIC Whois, enter **?** or **help** or **man** (for manual page).

*The database of people who have posted to Usenet.* Another useful database is "usenet-addresses," a database of e-mail names and addresses of people who have posted to the Usenet, stored in a WAIS (Wide-Area Information System) database. The resources necessary to make this service available are provided by M.I.T. The M.I.T. database can be queried via e-mail and from a WAIS client; there may also be other copies of the database available via WAIS.

According to Jonathan Kamens (jik@gza.COM), who runs the service, addresses are taken from Usenet articles that are received by the Usenet feed at M.I.T., which includes all the main Newsgroup hierarchies and several dozen of the specialized and regional hierarchies.

Roughly every 10 days, according to Kamens, the Usenet articles currently on-line at M.I.T. are scanned for addresses in the Reply To or From fields, which are entered into the database along with the entry date (with duplicate entries being removed). Kamens estimated that as of late 1992, the master database at M.I.T. held over 415,000 addresses, gathered over the previous year, with 60,000 previously gathered addresses stored in compressed form. This database is only helpful if the user you're looking for has posted a message to one of the Usenet Newsgroups, of course. On the other hand, it has a number of significant advantages:

- The list spans organizational and geographic boundaries—including users who have e-mail-only access to the Internet.
- The list includes individuals who may not be registered or findable via any other of the means in this chapter.
- You don't necessarily have to know a person's organization, full Domain Name, or even user-name. Queries are done as simple case-insensitive word matches, using whatever information you have.
- Because the Usenet Newsgroups include many Internet, BITNET, FidoNet, and other e-mailing lists and discussions, the database actually represented may be "more than just Usenet posters."
- The query syntax is very simple, and you can query via e-mail.

Given that there are several thousand topical Newsgroups within the Usenet, there's a strong chance that the person you're looking for may have contributed to one or more of them within the time period that the database covers.

One or more copies of the usenet-addresses database are located elsewhere in the Internet—for example, the one currently listed in the WAIS "Directory of Servers" is run by CICNet (Ann Arbor, MI). However, notes Kamens, there is no guarantee that their information is current relative to the master database (i.e., querying different sites may give different results).

One way to query the "Usenet posters" database is to send an e-mail message. The M.I.T. mail-server will automatically turn your message into a WAIS query; you'll get back the results by e-mail. Send the e-mail message to:

```
mail-server@pit-manager.mit.edu
```

with the message body (the Subject: contents are ignored) consisting of one or more lines (one per search) in the format:

```
send usenet-addresses/<search-word(s)>
```

"search-word(s)" consists of one or more words to search the database for, separated by one or more spaces, in any order. The search is case-insensitive—that is, it doesn't matter whether you use upper- or lowercase letters. For example, "ALICE," "Alice," and "alice" are all treated the same.

The search words can be things like the user's first or last name, the user-name, one or more fields of the site's Fully Qualified Domain Name (e.g., world, world.std, but *not* part of a word, like "worl"), etc. The WAIS searching program will do "fuzzy matching"—trying to find the addresses that best match all the search words you've given.

Giving "help" as the search-word will get you back a short help message including specific help information on using the usenet-address database, how to get other related files, and how to use the mail-server. For e-mail queries, the program will give you up to 40 matches; listing the best match first. If you get 40 matches and don't see one that appears to be the one you want, you may want to try again, with slightly different search keywords.

You'll get back a separate e-mail message with the results for each line in your message. For example:

```
% mail mail-server@pit-manager.mit.edu
Subject: Looking for a friend
send usenet-addresses/alice jabber

% mail mail-server@pit-manager.mit.edu
Subject:
send usenet-addresses/gulliver
send usenet-addresses/rackstraw
send usenet-addresses/Ralph_R
send usenet-addresses/@jabber.wock.com
<CONTROL-D>
```

You'll get back results of the search via e-mail. If you include more than one request in your message, each request's results will be put in a separate message. Notice that you can look for any search string, including part or all of a computer or site name.

You can also access a WAIS client via the Internet and select and search a copy of the usenet-addresses database. If you can access the WAIS databases (e.g., via a WAIS or Gopher client, or other Internet front end navigator—for more information, see Chap. 10), select "usenet_address," and do your search. If you cannot locate the usenet-addresses database in the "Directory of Servers," or the copies you locate don't have what you're looking for, you may want to query the master database at M.I.T. directly, at port 210 of **pit-manager.mit.edu.**

**Front ends: Accessing information services.** As mentioned earlier, front end tools can offer a number of benefits when you're looking for a given user or users and aren't sure where the information is to be found. They:

- Provide a list of available information services and databases
- May provide a single front end to these services and databases
- May let you search many services and databases with a single query

In late 1992, the most popular front ends for user-finding were the **netaddress** Knowbot Information Service and **netfind.**

*The* **netaddress** *Knowbot Information Service (KIS).* Knowbots, short for "knowledge robots," are another of the many information-gathering technologies being explored by various members of the Internet community. The Knowbot project is being done by the Corporation for National Research Initiatives (where Internet movers and shakers such as Vint Cerf and Robert Kahn, among others, work). A Knowbot is a program that "takes your command, goes out (across the Internet) and gets information for you, and then tells you what it found."

**netaddress,** also known as the Knowbot Information Service (abbreviated as KIS), is a Knowbot intended for locating information about network users. **netaddress** is available in a number of ways, including:

- Via remote login or local client. **netaddress** offers a number of front end interfaces for **netaddress,** including ones for simple VT100-style terminals and X Windowing systems. The VT100 line interface is sometimes referred to as "fred." (You may encounter fred as front end to other information services, too, by the way.) KIS can be reached for interactive queries via remote login (**telnet**), at nri.reston.va.us 185. For example:

```
[19] world% telnet nri.reston.va.us 185
Trying 132.151.1.1...
Connected to cnri.reston.va.us.
Escape character is '^]'.
Knowbot Information Service (V1.0). Copyright CNRI 1990. All
Rights Reserved.
Try ? or man for help.
```

- **via e-mail.** You can also query KIS via e-mail, by sending e-mail messages to:

  **netaddress@nri.reston.va.us**
  **netaddress@sol.buckness.edu**

  **netaddress** will process the contents of your message body as commands, and e-mail results back to the message's "return address"
- As a menu choice on Gopher and other general Internet navigators. Like many of the "people-finder front ends," one goal of KIS is to offer a uniform front end through which you can get information about users on a variety of networks—even search a number of remote networks' user information services with a single query—and get your results back in a uniform format.

The **netaddress** on-line manual page says the following:

> **netaddress** is an information service that provides a uniform user interface to heterogeneous remote information services. By submitting a single query to **netaddress** a user can search a set of remote information services and see the results of the search in a uniform format.

**netaddress** can query a number of Internet and non-Internet information services and databases, including the DDN NIC Whois database, **finger** daemons, and the PSI White Pages pilot project, among others. One of KIS's more important features is that it can query the information services for several other networks besides the Internet; an example is MCI Mail.

To query KIS, you give commands and user-names. If a line begins with a KIS command word, KIS treats it as a qualifier for the next search. If a line doesn't begin with a KIS command word, KIS assumes it is a user-name and performs a new search for network addresses, using all the current qualifier information. If you only give one word as the user-name, KIS assumes it is the last name; if you give two, KIS assumes the first word is the first name, and the second word is the last name.

When accessing KIS interactively, you enter your commands and search words on each line in response to the KIS prompt (usually >). When querying

KIS via e-mail, simply enter your commands one per line. To get help information, type **?** or **help.** To get the on-line manual page, type **man.** (You may find **netaddress** a bit difficult to use until you get used to it. However, it's worth learning, if nothing else, for access to the MCI Mail user directory.)

***Netfind.*** **netfind** is a program written by Mike Schwartz (schwartz@cs.colorado.edu) to help you find another Internet user's e-mail address when you aren't sure where they are in terms of their organization but have enough clues to possibly narrow the possibilities down from "on the Internet" to a few dozen. As of late 1992, Schwartz's **netfind** was capable of locating an estimated five and half million users located at over 5000 Internet sites.

**netfind** has its own database, plus it accesses **finger, whois,** and other information on remote Internet computers. **netfind**'s database contains a list of names of computers, organizations, and Domains in the Internet. When you access **netfind,** the first step you go through is giving it enough information to try to identify possible Internet computers or sites to search. For example, if you know your target is in the computer science department, at a university, and in the state of Florida, you might give **netfind** your target's name (e.g., "gulliver" plus keywords like "cs" (for computer science), "fl" (for Florida), and "edu."

By looking through its internal database, **netfind** sees which, if any, are the best potential matches for these keywords and then proceeds to use other TCP/IP facilities, such as **finger,** to these sites to look for an appropriate possible user-name match. If **netfind** has more than a handful of possible sites to search, it will display them to you and ask you to choose which should be searched.

As of late 1992, **netfind** is not yet the definitive "Internet people finder." Among its problems and limits:

- A lot of output is generated before "pay dirt."
- It can be difficult to give the right number of keywords, and the best ones, to narrow the search.
- **netfind** doesn't "talk to" all the types of computers and user-information services currently running.

Because the "lookup" limits the number of sites actually queried, **netfind** consumes relatively little network or computer resources (other than the Netfind server).

As of late 1992, about half a dozen organizations, throughout the United States and the rest of the world, have also made **netfind** servers available, in addition to Schwartz's original one. The **netfind** "to do" list includes a number of features which should make the facility both far easier to use, and more powerful. More information about **netfind,** and copies of **netfind** software are available; for more information, contact netfind@xcaret.com.

***Uwho**—Another people-finding front end.* **uwho** (pronounced "you-who") is another people-finding front end program that was created by Daniel Kegel (dank@alumni.caltech.edu) "because **whois** seemed difficult to use—you had to know what the hostname of the **whois** server was, which is a detail that users shouldn't have to know."

According to Kegel,

> **uwho** is a front end to several white pages services (currently, **whois, ph,** and KIS). It accepts a name and partial organization name, does a search for matching organizations, runs **whois, ph,** or KIS queries (as appropriate) in parallel, then shows the user the results. It is powerful simply because it accesses a continually updated list of white pages servers [i.e., it searches current information, not its "own list of users"], so its power will grow as more [user-information] servers come online.

The latest version is available from punisher.caltech.edu in directory pub/dank/uwho. It is written in C and runs under Unix, VMS, NT, and should soon run under Windows and MS-DOS.

***whois++**—a "next-generation" network address finder.* As of early 1993, none of the Internet "address locator" tools currently in use are adequate for networkwide searches. Their limits range from requiring you to know some or all of the network portion of your target's address, only querying a subset of the Internet's "phone books," or otherwise being difficult to use. One tool under development holds promise of a comprehensive, general-purpose, easy-to-use solution. Its current name is **whois++** (implying it's more than just the old **whois**), although it's likely to get some other name when made generally available. The **whois++** program was begun, like many famous scientific and engineering projects, on the back of paper napkins, by Peter Deutsch and a few other Internet developers during the summer 1992 meeting of the Internet Engineering Task Force in Cambridge, MA.

The goal of **whois++** is to make available information not only for White Pages directory information about Internet users but for Internet services and other types of information, such as descriptions of software programs. Rather than try to accumulate and maintain complete information about all Internet users, services, etc., **whois++** uses the "data harvesting and indexing" concepts employed in Internet tools such as archie and VERONICA. The **whois++** database holds summary records of the information found in Internet organizations' **whois,** CSO, and other information directories.

A **whois++** record includes text information such as your full name and Internet e-mail address, an identifier for the **whois** or other service that contains your full information, plus a few other pieces of information used by **whois++.** A search of the **whois++** database will show all known matches and where these records are located, so you can query them directly. Just as archie lets you search for files without knowing their full name or archive location, **whois++** will let you search for people—or services or other Internet resources—without necessarily knowing the full name or specific site information.

As of early 1993, it's too soon to know just when **whois++** will be generally available with a comprehensive database, what features will be supported, or its ultimate name. Check around, though—this could answer a lot of common Internet user needs.

**Other methods and resources to try.** In addition to the methods listed above, there are a variety of other resources and facilities for locating user e-mail addresses you can try.

*The college/university e-mail directory.* The file "Student_Email_Addresses" (maintained by Mark Kantrowitz <mkant@cs.cmu.edu>) tells how to get e-mail addresses for many of the universities and colleges on the Internet, including what user-finding services are available (e.g., support for **finger, whois,** etc.), the account and e-mail address policies, how to query for user-names, and general contact information. This file is available:

- As a WAIS database.
- Via file transfer using anonymous-FTP file, from pit-manager.mit.edu (18.72.1.58) in directory /pub/usenet/soc.college/Student_Email_Addresses*Z (you'll need to uncompress them).
- Via e-mail, by sending a message to "mail-server@pit-manager.mit.edu" with the subject: send usenet/soc.college/Student_Email_Addresses*.

**Merit Network NetMail database.** Given part of the address, this database may be able to find the appropriate Internet, BITNET, or UUCP address, if it's in the database. To access: do **telnet hermes.merit.edu**; at the "Which Host?" prompt, type **netmailsites.**

*Check recent Usenet postings.* If queries to the "usenet-addresses" database fail, but you recall seeing a message from this person recently and remember in what Newsgroup, or at least the hierarchy (e.g., comp., alt.) you might be able to locate it—assuming you have access to the Usenet, and can use the appropriate file-searching commands (e.g., for Unix users, **grep** and possibly also **find**) well enough.

*Search WAIS archives of Usenet and e-mail postings.* Many of the popular electronic mailing lists and Usenet Newsgroups are "archived"—all messages saved and, increasingly, made searchable via a WAIS server. If you believe you know an electronic mailing list or Usenet Newsgroup that the person you're looking for has contributed to, and it is available as a WAIS database—and you can access an Internet WAIS client (directly, through Gopher, etc.)—do a text search for their name. For example, if you have a vague recollection that you saw something from this person in the RISKS mailing list within the past year, search the RISK archives. I've used this method myself. Not often—perhaps once every 3 or 4 months—but it's worth knowing about.

*Inter-Network Mail Guide.* If you know which network or service the person you want to reach has an account on (e.g., ATT Mail, GEnie, FidoNet) and some or all of the user-ID, you may be able to get some helpful hints in the "Inter-Network Mail Guide," posted regularly to the Usenet in comp.mail.misc Newsgroup. (Note: It isn't always working. That's one problem with unofficial tools.)

*Usenet's soc.net-people: The next to last resort.* The Usenet's soc.net-people Newsgroup is for users who are trying to find a particular person. Posting to Usenet puts your query out to lots of people (who subscribe to and read this group) at lots of locations. On the other hand, this method consumes a substantial amount of network and computer resources, just to try to get a single question answered. Before you use this method, try as many other methods as possible; also read through the document "Tips on using soc.net-people," available:

- As a recent posting to this Usenet Newsgroup
- Via anonymous-FTP from pit-manager.mit.edu (18.72.1.58) in the file /pub/usenet/soc.net-people/Tips_on_using_soc.net-people
- Via e-mail from mail-server@pit-manager.mit.edu by sending a message with a message in the body: send usenet/soc.net-people/Tips_on_using_soc.net-people.

**And if all else fails.** If one or more of these methods don't work, pick up the phone again and either try calling this person again or someone who you think will know how to reach him or her. Or send them a fax or a letter.

**Saving and collecting e-mail addresses.** You'll also want to start saving other people's e-mail addresses. Many e-mail systems include some form of directory facility, helping you do lookups. Some let you save e-mail "aliases," (so when you use the address "dejah," it gets expanded automatically to "dejah.thoris"). Some company paper directories include e-mail IDs.

For more information on finding people's Internet e-mail addresses, try the following:

- "FAQ: How to find people's E-mail addresses" maintained by Jonathan I. Kamens <jik@mit.edu>, available:
  - On the Usenet, as a regular posting to the Usenet Newsgroups news.answers and comp.mail.misc
  - Via file transfer using anonymous-FTP, from pit-manager.mit.edu (18.72.1.58) in the file /pub/usenet/news.answers/finding-addresses
  - Via e-mail, by sending a message to "mail-server@pit-manager.mit.edu" with a line in the message body: send usenet/news.answers/finding-addresses.
- "Strategies for Finding People on Networks," by John S. Quarterman, *Matrix News,* vol. 1, no. 6, p. 3, Matrix Information and Directory Services, Austin, TX, September 1991.

## Other Useful Things to Know About and Do with E-Mail

To conclude this chapter on electronic mail, let's take a look at some of the other useful things there are to *know* about electronic mail:

- Netiquette and other tips for e-mail users
- Exchanging e-mail with people outside the Internet
- Message data format: 7-bit/8-bit, multimedia, encoding, and other message content issues

and some of the things you can *do* with electronic mail:

- Internet services based on e-mail: Access to archives, documents, programs, and more
- E-mail enabled applications

This is far from a complete list of what you can do with e-mail—new uses for e-mail are appearing regularly—but these are considered to be the most popular and essential categories. (Some of this information is also covered or touched on in other chapters that discuss specific other Internet tools and services and other networks, such as the chapters on mailing lists, archives, the archie tool, and BITNET.)

## Netiquette and other tips for e-mail users

**E-mail netiquette—how to be a good e-mail user.** To use e-mail effectively, users need to know the basics of how it works and, even more essential, your company's rules and some of the cultural conventions, or netiquette, that have arisen around e-mail use. Because e-mail lacks contextual cues like facial expressions or tones of voice, e-mail users have taken to inserting indicators like <GRIN>, or "emoticons," commonly referred to as "smiley faces" in their messages. The most common emoticon is **:-)**—the smiley-face (look at it sideways, left-side up). For more information and a short list of smiley-faces, see the Glossary.

The most important pointer: Remember that any e-mail message you send has the potential to become a public document. So:

- Don't send anything you wouldn't say to the receiver in person, or be willing to see in tomorrow's newspaper or posted on the front bulletin board. Label confidential messages as such, ideally in the "subject/header" line and at the start of text.
- Write clear messages. Identify them with a comprehensible subject/header line, like "Feedback on 2/15 Project Meeting." State the point of the message in the first paragraph. Spellcheck important messages. Keep a copy of important messages. Wait 24 hours before sending emotional replies.
- Keep copies of important messages you're sending—like those CYA memos.
- Avoid silly user-names, like "fuzzybunny" or "Arnie over by the water cooler" on work-related messages.
- Keep messages to a reasonable length. If you do need to send something long, especially if the recipient will have to print it out anyway, send a "heads up" message first—and consider sending the physical document through interoffice mail.

- If you're sending personal messages, remember that e-mail is not inherently secure. Be careful about sensitive information. Also determine what your company's policies are regarding the privacy of e-mail messages, personal use of e-mail (nonwork messages), and files "belonging" to you. If management reserves the right to read and monitor, think twice before writing and sending erotic love notes or insulting remarks about your boss.

**The three most common mistakes in sending e-mail.** The three most frequently made mistakes in sending a message via e-mail are:

1. Making spelling or typing errors on addresses, causing your messages to not be delivered. Good mail systems will inform you if a message can't be delivered.
2. Replying to a mailing list when you meant to reply to one person. You'd be surprised how easy it is to unintentionally broadcast a personal, possibly private message, to a few thousand other people.
3. Sending messages to a mailing list rather than to its moderator/administrator. One convention, common in the Internet, is that, for a mailing list named, say, "cobol," administrative messages go to "cobol-request" or "cobol-requests." While less embarrassing than the previous error, it shows you're still an "e-mail newbie."

**Cleaning house—getting rid of old e-mail.** Mail piles up. It's not uncommon to get mail messages several hundred, even several thousand lines long. Each one is consuming on-line storage space in your account. Pretty soon, you can be over your quota or otherwise contributing to overfilling the system's hard disks, and you get administrative messages—first, polite ones automatically generated by system daemons and then, less polite ones from the system administrator, suggesting that you prune things down before they do it for you.

Someone is paying for the cost to keep these messages on-line. If you have an individual account, that someone is you. Start cleaning house as follows:

- Check to see if you have made multiple copies of longer messages.
- If you're dialing in from a PC to a shell account, start downloading files and directories to your own system, possibly to floppies. Perhaps your sysadmin can do some of this for you locally.
- See if you can have your files archived to tape, if they're large and important.
- Get rid of messages and files you don't want. (Be careful in deleting. And if you do accidentally delete something you want to keep, contact your system administrator immediately. If the file is more than a day old, there's probably a copy on a backup tape.)
- Make compressed versions of inactive files, using Unix facilities like **cmp** and **tar.** (Practice, and be careful.)

And if all else fails, add more storage or get your account quota increased.

### Exchanging e-mail with people outside the Internet

The Internet itself is vast—but, as you've probably begun to appreciate, is only one part of the many electronic computer networks in the world. There's the private networks operated by companies such as Digital Equipment Corporation and IBM; public e-mail and conferencing services such as America On-Line, ATT Mail, CompuServe, MCI Mail, GEnie; plus tens of thousands of Unix systems and electronic BBSs, linked by UUCP, FidoNet, and other methods. And increasingly, they are interconnected to the Internet via *gateways* capable of exchanging messages, such as e-mail, Usenet Newsgroup postings, and other files.

This doesn't permit non-Internet users real-time use of Internet applications, such as remote login (**telnet**), direct file transfer (**ftp**), or such navigators as Gopher. But for many, sending e-mail to Internet users is what counts—and for Internet users, it means it's possible to send messages to non-Internet users as well as to fellow members of the Internet. The number of people outside the Internet who are reachable by e-mail is larger, in fact, than the "population" of the Internet itself.

**What you need to know to send e-mail to someone on another network.** To send e-mail to someone on another network who can be reached from the Internet, you need to know:

- The network address. For example, an MCI Mail user's name, "nickname" (short address) or user-ID number or a CompuServe user's numeric ID (e.g., 1234567,8901)
- The Internet Fully Qualified Domain Name for the other network (e.g., aol.com, mcimail.com, compuserve.com, or genie.com)
- How to express this address in a format that will be understood by the e-mail programs within the Internet. For example, Internet e-mail programs don't accept the comma (,) character, so the comma in a CompuServe address gets replaced by a period (.) (e.g., 1234567.8901@compuserve.com). Most e-mail addresses at Digital Equipment Corporation use the format COMPUTER::NAME (e.g., PATIENCE::MAYBUD)—to send a message to this person from the Internet, you have to know that in "Internet-ese" this address may become either maybud@patience.dec.com or maybud@patience.enet.dec.com.

You may also need to know the address of a gateway between the Internet and your target's network (e.g., one of the several Internet-BITNET gateways).

There is no one simple rule. Instead, there are some general guidelines, specific conventions for specific networks, and a variety of services and documents summarizing this information. Similarly, there are guidelines for sending e-mail *to* Internet users *from* non-Internet sites, organizations, and networks. (If you have an account on one, try looking for help information by trying commands such as "help internet" or "help mail internet.") If you are talking or otherwise in communication with someone, tell them *your* Internet e-mail address and ask to have a message sent to you.

***Gateway Syntax for Sending E-Mail to Other Networks***

Many other networks besides the Internet use Domain Names as part of their internal e-mail addressing conventions. Digital Equipment DECnet networks, for example, often use e-mail addresses in the form hostname::user-name, for example, pequod::ishmael. To send e-mail from the Internet to someone on one of these networks, you not only have to include a Fully Qualified Domain Name that can reach this network but also the Domain Name within this other network.

Some of these networks will let you supply the remote network's Domain Name as part of the Fully Qualified Domain Name, for example, ishmael@pequod.enet.dec.com. Not all networks may support this, however.

An older convention is *gateway syntax*, where you give your destination's full address as the user-name, using the % character to separate the user-ID from the internal computer or domain and, as the address, one for a gateway system that connects the Internet and the remote network. For example, ishmael%pequod@decwrl.dec.com, where "decwrl.dec.com" is a computer attached to both the Internet and Digital Equipment's internal network.

Similarly, to send e-mail from the Internet to someone on BITNET, who does not have an Internet address, you use gateway syntax to include the BITNET address in the user-name field, and send the message to a BITNET gateway. For example, jwelling%myst.bitnet@cunyvm.cuny.edu. If there is more than one gateway between the Internet and your target network, it shouldn't matter which gateway you specify.

**Suggestions for sending e-mail to other networks.** General guidelines and things to try include:

- Make an educated guess about your target's user-name and a network address consisting of the organization or network name and either ".net" or ".com". For example, rmaybud@mcimail.com. Of course, the user-naming conventions may be very different, making it much harder to guess. When in doubt, try calling or using other Internet address-locating facilities.
- Respond to a message from this person, if you've got one.
- Look for messages from other users on this non-Internet system (in Usenet Newsgroup postings, and other sources).
- Find someone with an account on this system and ask them how to reach them from the Internet—or ask them to have an e-mail message sent to *you*.

Issues to bear in mind when exchanging e-mail with users on other networks are:

- Limits such as maximum message length (32 to 60 kbytes per message limits are common).
- Appropriate usage policies and other potential restrictions (e.g., commercial messages).
- Are non-Internet users charged for sending or receiving Internet e-mail?

**E-mail addressing conventions and formats for other networks.** Here's a summary of some of the leading networks and services that can exchange e-mail with the Internet and how to address Internet e-mail to them. (Some of this information was taken from the "Inter-Network Mail Guide," put together by John J. Chew <poslfit@utcs.utoronto.ca>, who in turn was working from contributions by numerous participants of the Usenet comp.misc.mail Newsgroup. Information on how to get this guide is at the end of this section.)

- America Online (on-line consumer service including e-mail). **username@aol.com**
- AppleLink (run by Apple Computer). **username@applelink.apple.com.**
- AT&T Mail (public e-mail service). **username@attmail.com.**
- BITNET. Many BITNET users can be addressed straightforwardly, as **username@bitnet-host.bitnet**. Otherwise, you'll have to send your message via any of the Internet-BITNET gateways (i.e., **username%site.BITNET@bitnet-gateway**, that is, gsmith%emoryu1.BITNET@cunyvm.cuny.edu). Any BITNET-Internet gateway can be used. For more information on this, and several of these gateways, see Chap. 17.
- BIX (Byte Information eXchange); (originally owned by Byte Magazine, now owned by the organization that also runs DELPHI). **username@bix.com.**
- BMUG, the Berkeley Macintosh Users Group BBS. **username@bmug.fidonet.org**; for example, **John.Smith@bmug.fidonet.org.**
- CompuServe (consumer on-line service including e-mail). **user.id@compuserve.com**; for example, **123456.789@compuserve.com.** Note: Be sure to replace the comma in the CompuServe userid with a period.
- DELPHI (consumer on-line service including e-mail). **user-name@delphi.com.**
- Digital Equipment Corporation's EasyNet internal network. **username@computer.ENET.DEC.COM.** Note: DEC addresses are expressed internally as COMPUTER::USER-NAME.
- FidoNet (store-and-forward BBS network). FidoNet addresses consist of a person's name plus the address of the FidoNet node. FidoNet node addresses are in the format: **zone#:net#/fidonet-node#.point#** (e.g., 1:103/419.0). The Internet format for FidoNet addresses is: **firstname.lastname@p<p#>.f<fn#>.n<net#>.z<zone#>.fidonet.org** (e.g., **alice.liddell@p0.f419.n103.z1.fidonet.org**). The default point value is 0; if the address you're using has point 0, this field (.p<p#>) can be omitted in the Internet address. **net#** refers to the number of the FidoNet Network, also known as the FidoNet Region.
- GEnie. **user-name@genie.geis.com.**
- MCI Mail (public e-mail service). MCI Mail users have a full name, user-number, and possibly a "nickname." The user-ID is guaranteed to be unique, the other identifiers may not be. **user-number@mcimail.com**; for example, **1234567@mcimail.com** or **123-4567@mcimail.com** (the

hyphen will be ignored, but can be included): **nickname@mcimail.com**; examples are **jgull@mcimail.com, full_name@mcimail.com,** and **lemuel_gulliver@mcimail.com** (the "_" is required).

**UUCP users.** There are many ways to send to UUCP users (users on systems connected to the Internet via UUCP store-and-forward messaging), including:

- *MX record Domain Name.* If the site has registered its Domain Name, and there's an MX record for it, you can give what looks like a regular Internet Domain Name address.
- *Let the system do it.* Many of the Internet mail systems today can find and deliver UUCP e-mail quite well if you simply identify the target as a UUCP site (e.g., **username@sitename.uucp**). You may need to identify a UUCP/Internet gateway (e.g., **user%host.UUCP@uunet.uu.net** or **user%domain@uunet.uu.net.**
- *Explicit (bang) address.* If you have an explicit UUCP path, (host1!host2!host3!username) you can use that. (Each **!** means "forward this message to the next host computer on this list." For example, earth! mcmurdo! penguin! rent;s.

  Remember that **!** is a reserved character in Unix; if you're entering these addresses on the Unix command line, you'll need to precede each **!** with a **** to "treat next character as literal," e.g., **foo\!bar\!baz**).

You can obtain the Inter-Network Mail Guide as follows:

- Via Usenet. It is posted monthly to Usenet Newsgroups including comp.mail.misc and alt.internet.services.
- Via e-mail. Send a message to mail-server@pit-manager.mit.edu with "send inter-network-mail-guide" in the message body.
- Via anonymous-FTP. Check a number of sites (do an archie query).

**Remember, Exchanging Internet E-Mail With Non-Internet Users May Be Costly**

Within the Internet, the cost of sending and receiving electronic mail messages is typically included in the overall charge for your account. It is rare to find a site or organization that charges you for sending or receiving messages. Outside the Internet, however, it's often the other way around, especially for the commercial consumer services. Depending on the nature of your account, services such as ATT Mail, CompuServe, DELPHI, and MCI Mail may charge for each message sent. And sending a message to a user on another network (e.g., from CompuServe to MCI Mail or MCI Mail to the Internet) costs more than sending to fellow users on a service (e.g., to another MCI Mail user). (This charge helps cover the cost of the electronic mail gateway connection.) Some networks may even charge for *receiving* messages from certain other networks. In 1992, for example, CompuServe users were charged not only for sending messages to Internet users but also for *receiving* messages from the Internet.

If you intend to subscribe to one or more electronic mailing lists from any organizations that charge for incoming Internet messages or expect to get a lot of e-mail that comes from the Internet, choose your account-providing organization and read your user agreement carefully.

### Message data format: 7-bit/8-bit, multimedia, encoding, and other message content issues

Until recently, most e-mail messages consisted of text, in 7-bit ASCII (or EBCDIC) characters. In other words, alphanumeric characters (A through Z, a through z, 0 through 9, and punctuation)—no special fonts, formatting, graphics, dingbats, widgits, icons, or other obfuscatory ornamentation. There are two reasons for this:

- 7-bits is the most common denominator for computer networks.
- ASCII is the most common denominator for computer users.

However, e-mail isn't just for ASCII anymore. People want to send information that doesn't consist of ASCII characters—Microsoft Word documents, spreadsheets, graphic images, programs, and more. And they often want to send it over networks and through systems that want e-mail message contents to consist of 7-bit characters.

In addition, people often want to send many files in a single message and people are sending longer things in messages—long enough to seek ways to reduce the amount of network resources consumed by sending them. These are related but not identical issues. The Internet and other communities have come up with a number of solutions. Let's look at them separately. First, however, in case you are someone uncertain what "7-bit" means, and why there appears to be an obsession with it and with ASCII, here's a little background.

**Seven-bit characters go everywhere.** The term "7-bit" refers to how many bits (0s or 1s) are used by an e-mail system for a given character. Seven bits equals 255 characters. This is enough to represent all the printing characters in the ASCII. Many computer networks and telecommunications programs use 7-bit characters. Try to send 8-bit characters through and like the Batmobile trying to fit between two narrow buildings in the second Batman movie, only some may get through. So ideally, all your e-mail will be in ASCII because that can be reliably sent through most of the e-mail networks and gateways your messages may want to traverse.

**Everyone uses ASCII.** E-mail is the most likely of all computer communications to be exchanged by highly different computers and programs. ASCII text is considered the lowest-common-denominator data, created, understood, and editable by nearly every computer, operating system, and e-mail system around. If you're used to using a word processor such as Microsoft Word or Word Perfect, you're probably used to writing even everyday letters and memos in "rich text," meaning you may use several types and sizes of fonts in a single document. However—as you may have already discovered—the odds are good that other people you want to communicate with use a different word processing program than you do—different enough that you can't casually exchange document files. In today's graphic, desktop-publishing-oriented world, even using the same word processing program may not guarantee this—you may need to have the same version of the program and the same fonts loaded in. We're not that far away from an on-line Tower of Babel.

Many word processors include a function to convert documents to ASCII, by stripping out formatting, font commands, etc. However, the days of ASCII, or just ASCII, are rapidly ending. More and more users, especially those with DOS, Windows, or Macintosh computers, are using word processors rather than ASCII text editors, and they often want to send these documents through e-mail. Moreover, the global perspective of networking is pushing the limits of ASCII and of 7 bits. The new international character sets require more than 7 bits; indeed, some want two 8-bit words to specify a single character. (Think about wanting to create and send e-mail in Cyrillic, Greek, Hebrew, or Japanese. Even French and Spanish require non-ASCII characters.)

There are also a lot of nondocument types of files that users want to send via e-mail: spreadsheets; graphic and image files, in formats like .TIF and .GIF; databases; program source and executable code; and multimedia, from MIDI sound samplings to "sound bites," graphics, photo and x-ray images, 3D animations, color images—anything that can be created and stored in digital form. All of these data types use binary format, not ASCII.*

**Encoding: Stuffing non-ASCII contents into ASCII.** Unlike FTP, the TCP/IP facility for transferring files, most e-mail programs don't have a "mode" setting to select ASCII, binary, or other formats. It's not possible since you can't predict whether your messages will only traverse appropriate gateways for 8-bit characters and be received by e-mail programs that can read them.

One answer to the ASCII/binary, 7-bit/8-bit problem is *encoding*—using ASCII characters to represent the contents of binary files. It could be as straightforward as converting the nonprinting characters that indicate font changes and formatting positions—or as comprehensive as representing a medical x-ray. After all, all ASCII and binary files ultimately consist of 0s and 1s. The challenge is to be able to convert a given type of non-ASCII file into ASCII—and back again.

This is not a new requirement. Unix users have had a facility to do this for some time; it is called *uuencode* and is used for things like sending executable programs via e-mail. Programmers posting software to BBSs and to on-line forums such as CompuServe, PC MagNet, and ZiffNet have had to create and use similar facilities. Some word processing programs offer features to convert "high-bit" codes into ASCII codes (and back again). Until late 1992, MCI Mail used 7-bit format; to send things like Macintosh documents and Lotus spreadsheets required use of programs like Lotus Express, which performed the necessary translations on each end.

**Making e-mail multimedia.** Internet e-mail developers are expanding what can be sent, "stuffing the envelope" with nontraditional, non-ASCII contents, better known as multimedia. Multimedia e-mail refers to e-mail messages containing files, documents, and applications that may have "rich" formatted and

*If a Star Trek transporter datastream could be captured and stored, we'd want to be able to send that by e-mail too. (Yum, pizza by e-mail.)

fonted text (e.g., Microsoft Word), bitmapped graphics, and files representing other types of data objects, such as spreadsheets, presentation graphics, video images and motion, audio, databases, and executable programs.

Multimedia e-mail systems have been around for a while. Slate, for example, from BBN Software Products (Cambridge, MA) is a Unix-based multimedia document management system, which can be used variously as for e-mail and real-time document "blackboard" conferencing. Slate is not the only entrant in the multimedia e-mail fray. Lotus Notes lets its users mix word processing files and images. Notework supports attached files containing voice messages, spreadsheets, etc.

What will we use this for? Although trade show demos tend to hawk video and audio "because they're the most interesting to run," the most immediate use for multimedia e-mail is "to send complex unprintable nontext, spreadsheets, and other data models as part of a message," suggests Kevin Carosso, a vice president at Innosoft International, Inc. (Claremont, CA), a VAX/VMS-based multimedia e-mail developer. "Images and sound are further along in the future."

Rensselaer Polytechnic Institute (Troy, NY) has a 500-station license for Slate and 6000 user accounts, running on Sun and IBM RS/600 workstations. RPI freshmen use Slate for e-mailing in assignments, which can include attachments such as computer programs, and teachers send back assignments with grades and comments, according to Adelaide Lane, Senior Graphics Applications Programmer. "It's easy to use, and means there's only one interface to learn for many packages."

By now, you've probably figured out that capabilities like this are only of real use if there's a standard. After all, if my e-mail program uses one method to indicate "spreadsheet start/stop" and yours uses another, we haven't really gained the ability to send spreadsheets.

### *MultiMedia E-Mail Ain't So New*

In 1992, Internet Engineering Task Force (IETF) members came up with MIME, the Multipurpose Internet Mail Extensions, a standard set of definitions for non-ASCII e-mail. The MIME standard specifies a way to include binary data as attachments to Internet e-mail messages and a way to encode binary data into 7-bit form using ASCII characters and to convert back at the other end. The MIME standard supports word processing documents, PostScript, graphic, binary files, video, voice messages, and other message types.

Obviously, not all e-mail systems will be able to display all these content types; we'll also need e-mail programs that can determine what capabilities your PC or workstation has and alert you if there's something in the message that it can't show you. We may also begin including multiple versions, such as plain text and PostScript, and let the receiving program display the "highest-level" version it's capable of.

According to the manual page for the PINE e-mail program, "MIME allows for alternative representations of the same data. For example, there can be an attachment in text form followed by one containing bitmap page images of the same information."

MIME-capable mail software is not yet widely deployed, but MIME support is growing rapidly. If you need to send binary data to colleagues at institutions not yet supporting MIME, the PINE manual also suggests "encourage them to talk to their system administrators about installing MIME tools. MIME software, compatible with many different mail programs, is freely available."

### Internet services based on e-mail: Access to archives, documents, programs, and more

Don't underestimate the value of having e-mail-only access to the Internet. You'd be amazed at how much you can do even through this one facility. Recognizing that e-mail access is much easier and more prevalent than full Internet connections, many organizations have provided e-mail-based access to their services. For example, you can get files from Internet public-access archives, help documents, answers to database queries, and FAQs (Frequently Asked Questions and their answers documents). You may even be able to send queries to Usenet Newsgroups and receive Newsgroup postings.

You can do all these activities from any network account that can exchange e-mail messages with the Internet (subject to possible concerns such as cost, and constraints such as maximum message length). For example, you can use Internet e-mail-based services from an Internet e-mail-only/mostly service as PSILink or WorldLink; a Unix computer connecting to the Internet via UUCP; other networks, such as BITNET; public on-line services such as MCI Mail or CompuServe; and tens of thousands of BBSs communicating via FidoNet or other protocols to the Internet. (For more information on what types of accounts and organizations offer e-mail access to the Internet, see Chap. 16.)

You can even set up your *own* e-mail-based Internet service, using your own computer or "renting" time and storage space from public-access Internet and Unix sites such as MSEN, NetCom, PANIX, and World. Peter Kaminski, for example, distributes his "PDIAL List" from his "Info-Deli" run from NetCom. There's even a number of public-domain e-mail server software programs available. Here's some of what you can do with Internet services and resources via e-mail:

- Query databases of Internet resource and service listings (such as the archie public-access "anonymous-FTP" file archives; see Chap. 10).
- Retrieve (and get directory listings for) programs, documents, graphic images, and other types of files from many of the Internet's 1500+ public-access archives. The e-mail server retrieves the requested files or information from its location via anonymous-FTP and then e-mails the results back to you (see Chap. 15).
- Query and retrieve records, files, and other information from Internet document servers, such as FAQ, FYI, and RFC documents (see Chaps. 2, 12, and 17).
- Access help and other information about Internet organizations, Internet access and server providers, and Internet resources and services (see Chaps. 2, 12, and 16).
- Get e-mail names and addresses for Internet and other network users.
- Get information from Internet resources and services; examples are NASA and related space files, from archive-server@ames.arc. (See Box: Almanac Offers Information by E-Mail as one example.)

***Almanac Offers Information by E-Mail***

Almanac, one of the many e-mail-based information programs available, is in use at half a dozen university sites across the United States. These Almanac servers make available information collections such as Sustainable Agriculture, Water Quality Information Management Database, Food Market News, Family Economics News, Disaster Factsheets, National Agricultural Market News, and Satellite Teleconference Calendar.

Almanac commands must be in lowercase only; no subject line is required. To get a site's catalog, put in your message: **send catalog.** To get a short user guide, put in your message: **send guide.** Almanac sites (each has different information) include:

| | |
|---|---|
| Extension Service-USDA | almanac@esusda.gov |
| North Carolina State University | almanac@ces.ncsu.edu |
| Oregon State University | almanac@oes.orst.edu |
| Purdue University | almanac@ecn.purdue.edu |
| University of California | almanac@silo.ucdavis.edu |

### E-mail-enabled applications

E-mail-enabled applications, a.k.a. mail-enabled applications, refer to computer programs that use e-mail as a way to exchange messages. These programs may be anything from the document and file servers we've already talked about to facilities that accept "forms" and add information to a database, do a lookup and return information to you, help route forms and documents, etc.

Many developers and users are turning to e-mail as the delivery mechanism to fax, pagers, for carrying non-ASCII, and to move messages among application programs among LANs and networks and across company boundaries. "Electronic mail offers the right mix of features these other applications also need, like store-and-forward message queuing, and addressing and directory services," points out RadioMail's Goodfellow. "Plus e-mail has the 'home team' advantage—it's a mature technology already widely accepted, installed, and in use. It's the same reason that fax machines use the phone system—it's a ubiquitous resource."

By building on e-mail, Goodfellow observes, "Users can gain access to many new capabilities on a 'no change to existing systems' basis." The RadioMail gateway, for example, can be accessed as a cc:Mail address by other corporate cc:Mail systems.

Other reasons for e-mail's growing popularity for delivery and embedded messaging service include:

- E-mail is highly interoperable and transparent—it works well across administrative boundaries (e.g., between companies), different operating systems, and network protocols.
- E-mail systems support file importing and exporting. For example, Cc:Mail's Import/Export feature makes it a popular choice for messaging services.
- E-mail systems offer Application Programming Interfaces (APIs) which make them easy-to-use tools for independent software vendors (ISVs) and

MIS. As of March 1993, there were three major APIs for programmers who want their software to make use of e-mail: VIM, the Vendor-Independent Messaging Specification, a joint venture of Lotus, Novell, Apple and Borland, which can be used with products such as Lotus's cc:MAIL; MAPI, Microsoft's Messaging Applications Programmers Interfaces; and SMF from Novell, for use with Novell's Message Handling System.

Now that you've got a sense of what electronic mail is and what you can do with it, let's move on to another type of message-exchange—the Usenet, the "Bulletin Board System" of the Internet.

Chapter

# 6

# Usenet—The Bulletin Board of the Internet

*"For everything, trn, trn, trn*
*There is a Newsgroup, trn, trn, trn*
*And a thread for every subject under heaven*
*A thread to be born, a thread to die*
*A thread for excess, a thread for control-X*
*A thread to kill, a thread to read*
*A thread for a laugh, a thread for a weep*
*A thread to follow up, a thread to fork off*
*A thread to advance, a thread to scoff*
*A thread to cast away .sigs*
*A thread to gather .sigs together"*

*From "trn, trn, trn, or,*
*For Everything There Is a Newsgroup,"*
*posted to rec.humor.funny, March 1993*
MARK MAIMONE (MARK.MAIMONE@A.GP.CS.CMU.EDU)

If e-mail is the telephone and CB radio of the Internet, the Usenet is its bulletin board, its supermarket tabloid, classified ads, cable TV, magazine rack, giant wall of Post-It notes, and collective unconscious. Usenet, along with electronic mail, probably accounts for the majority of net-related time spent by most Internet users. Once you learn what the Usenet is and how to work with it, this will probably be true for you, too. If you've ever used an on-line service such as America On-Line, CompuServe, DELPHI or GEnie or a BBS, you'll find strong similarities between their forums and Special-Interest Groups, and the Usenet's Newsgroups. (However, as you'll see, there are a number of significant differences as well.)

The purpose of the Usenet chapter in this book is to provide you with an overview of what the Usenet is and how you work with it and to help you get started participating in Usenet (if you want to) either as a reader or also as a contributor. The Usenet can be a valuable professional resource for your job; equally, it can be a source of recreational information and a way to "meet" and interact with people all over the country and the world.

It's possible you'll spend only a few minutes per day or week reading and posting to the Usenet. As you learn more about what's there—and possibly follow more discussions via Usenet than through electronic mailing lists—this can easily grow to half an hour or an hour per day (or night) (see "Many Ways to Participate in Usenet"). In extreme cases, reading and participating in Usenet can become a major "time sink." It's surprisingly easy to follow more and more Newsgroups and become involved in on-going discussions. (Some people appear to post so much, and to so many Newsgroups, that one might wonder if they do anything else.)

This book is not the place for a complete discussion of Usenet and the program(s) you use to access Usenet, anymore than it can include a complete tutorial on Unix or on text editors and e-mail systems. You can get by with a reasonably small amount of basics. The Usenet, and the programs you use, contain more than enough help information, which you will be able to access soon enough. And if you want more information, there are a number of books available about the Usenet. In this chapter, you'll learn:

- What Usenet is; how it relates to the Internet, BITNET, FidoNet, and other networks
- The origins of Usenet
- How a global BBS such as Usenet makes information available
- What kinds of information are available in Usenet—categories of Newsgroups
- How to access and use the Usenet, including what software you'll need
- Required and recommended reading within Usenet Newsgroups
- Usenet netiquette

There will also be some other suggestions and advice for getting started with Usenet.

## What Is Usenet?

Even more so than the Internet, defining the Usenet is both simple and difficult. So, rather than attempt yet another definition, here's a number of defining facts about Usenet:

- Usenet is a worldwide community of electronic BBSs that is closely associated with the Internet and with the Internet community.
- The messages in Usenet are organized into thousands of topical groups, or "Newsgroups"—over 3500 as of mid-1993. Many of these are the messages that constitute electronic mailing lists on the Internet, BITNET, and other networks; many of these groups are also linked to similar groups on other BBSs and networks.
- As a Usenet user, you read and contribute ("post") to your local Usenet site. Each Usenet site distributes its users' postings to other Usenet sites,

based on various implicit and explicit configuration settings, and in turn receives postings from other sites. Usenet traffic typically consists of as much as 30 to 50 Mbytes of messages per day.*

- Usenet is read and contributed to on a daily basis by a total population of millions of people. (However, many contribute infrequently or never. To how many of the magazines to which you subscribe do you submit articles or letters to the editor?)
- There is no specific network that is the Usenet. Usenet traffic flows over a wide range of networks, including the Internet and dial-up phone links. Messages can even be conveyed by cassette tapes traveling by air or ship and "injected" back into the network at the other end of their journey.

According to Ed Vielmetti, Vice-President for Research at MSEN, Ann Arbor, MI:

> The first thing to understand about Usenet is that it is *big,* really big. Netnews (and Netnews-like things) have percolated into many more places than are even known about by people who track such things. There is no grand unified list of everything that's out there, no way to know beforehand who is going to read what you post, and no history books to guide you that would let you know even a small piece of any of the 'in' jokes that pop up in most Newsgroups.

### Some definitions of what Usenet is

"Usenet is fair, cocktail party, town meeting, notes of a secret cabal, chatter in the hallway at a conference, Friday night fish fry, conversations overhead on an airplane, and a bunch of other things," Vielmetti remarked in an e-mail message. "Usenet is in part about people. There are people who are 'on the net,' who read rec.humor.funny every so often, who know the same jokes you do, who tell you stories about funny or stupid things they've seen. Usenet is the set of people who know what Usenet is."

Through Usenet, millions of computer users around the world share information, pose and answer questions, conduct multipeople discussions, and the like. You may be familiar with other, similar services, such as BBSs and conferencing systems, from organizations like America On-Line, CompuServe, DELPHI, GEnie, Prodigy, and the Well. Your own organization may even have internal BBSs, possibly BBS software, or a product like Lotus Notes or VAXnotes.

"While a good portion of the Usenet is devoted to recreational and nonprofessional issues, the availability of information on computing systems and

---

*How much traffic flows through Usenet? Here's a snapshot, taken from the regularly posted statistics provided by the folks at Uunet, Inc. (I've rounded numbers off a tad.) On November 9, 1992, during the previous 2-week period, the total Usenet traffic as seen flowing through Uunet (the hub of most Usenet traffic) consisted of 319,446 articles, totaling 589 Mbytes (753 Mbytes including headers), averaging 42 Mbytes (54 including headers) per day. These messages were submitted from 27,699 different Usenet sites, from 75,906 different users, and were posted to 4526 different Newsgroups.

applications is unmatched anywhere," points out Joel Snyder, Senior Partner at Opus One, a network consulting firm in Tucson, AZ. "The level of discussions and quality of advice is substantially better than local bulletin boards, and the access to problem-solving abilities is unmatched."

Usenet has a number of important defining characteristics, some of which it shares in common with other BBSs, and some of which are unique to Usenet:

- Information consists of individual messages, each of which can be read and shared by many users.
- Messages are organized into topical *groups,* usually referred to as *Newsgroups.*
- There are special software packages for being a Usenet user (reading, posting) and for being a Usenet site.
- Usenet comprises lots of computers, at many different organizations and sites. Copies of messages are distributed to multiple sites, based on various criteria.
- There is strong overlap between Usenet groups and electronic mailing lists on other networks.
- Specific individuals may be in charge of specific topical groups, or specific Usenet sites, but (like the Internet), no one person or organization is "in charge" of Usenet.

We'll talk more about these characteristics later in this chapter.

"It is almost impossible to generalize over all Usenet sites in any nontrivial way," states Chip Salzenberg (chip@tct.com) in the periodic informational Usenet posting, "What is Usenet?" "Usenet encompasses government agencies, large universities, high schools, businesses of all sizes, home computers of all descriptions, etc., etc."

### And some definitions of what Usenet is not

Equally important for you to understand is what Usenet is not. Salzenberg stresses:

> Usenet is not an organization. No person or group has authority over Usenet as a whole. No one controls who gets a news feed, which articles are propagated where, who can post articles, or anything else. There is no "Usenet Incorporated," nor is there a "Usenet User's Group." You're on your own...
>
> Usenet is not a public utility. Some Usenet sites are publicly funded or subsidized. Most of them, by plain count, are not. There is no government monopoly on Usenet, and little or no government control.
>
> Usenet is not an academic network. It is no surprise that many Usenet sites are universities, research labs, or other academic institutions. Usenet originated with a link between two universities, and the exchange of ideas and information is what such institutions are all about. But the passage of years has changed Usenet's character. Today, by plain count, most Usenet sites are commercial entities.

## The Many Ways to Participate in Usenet

What can you do as a Usenet user? There is a wide range of ways you can be a Usenet user. How you participate in each group you read is up to you. Here are some ideas:

- *Read lots, contribute little or none.* How many of the newspapers and magazines that you read do you write letters to or articles for? Probably only a few, if any. Similarly, don't feel obligated to post messages to every Usenet Newsgroup you want to follow. True, as you'll quickly notice, some individuals contribute frequently to one or more Newsgroups. But simply being a reader—often referred to as "lurker"—is appropriate.
- *Ask questions.* One strong use of Usenet is to pose questions to a large group, namely, those reading the Newsgroup, in the hopes that someone out there knows the answer. Often, you'll get answers within hours from experienced fellow users or even from people who were involved in creating whatever it is you're asking about. (If you haven't been following a Newsgroup recently, be sure to check its FAQ before posting any queries to it.) If someone else has asked a question whose answer you're also interested in, you can e-mail them a request to share their findings with you. (Remember, send them personal e-mail—*don't* post the request to the Newsgroup.)
- *Answer questions.* You may know some or all of the answer to a question and want to share your information. When in doubt, reply via e-mail to the poster. Your newsreader should include a command to do this; see its on-line help command summaries (and the discussion of the difference between "follow-up" and "reply" to a Usenet article later in this chapter).
- *Participate in discussions.* Many Usenet Newsgroups have spirited ongoing discussions; if you enjoy this, and have something to contribute, you may want to participate. (Before you do, however, be sure to review Usenet guidelines and netiquette—see the various "Periodic Postings" about Usenet netiquette and the netiquette section later in this chapter.)
- *Post information.* Newsgroups are a good place to make information available—just be sure you learn and follow guidelines regarding the specific intent of the Newsgroup and overall Usenet guidelines regarding announcements, commercial messages, etc.
- *Learn things.* Usenet Newsgroup postings offer a wealth of information about many topics; you'll probably learn a lot.
- *Retrieve, or download, information, programs, etc.* The Usenet provides a home for a multitude of documents, as well as program sources, graphic images, etc., available for downloading or retrieving. (Be sure to respect copyright, shareware feeds, and other author rights.) See the discussion of Usenet sources in Chap. 15.
- *Find out about other resources.* Many Usenet Newsgroup postings offer pointers to other resources, ranging from on-line services and things elsewhere on the Internet to books, magazines, events, etc.

- *Become responsible for an FAQ or another document, archive, Newsgroup, etc.* You may decide to become an active participant to the point where you create, or take over maintaining, an FAQ, list, or other document; be in charge of maintaining an archive; or even create or moderate a Newsgroup.

## The Origins of Usenet

The origins of Usenet aren't shrouded in any mystery. Like so much else on the Internet, it was started because a few computer users wanted to do something, and it kind of grew from there until it became global in scope and an essential resource for millions of users in their daily activities—a phenomenon we'll encounter again when we talk about Internet facilities such as archie, Gopher, and VERONICA. The following "origin story" is based on the message "USENET Software: History and Sources," by Gene Spafford (spaf@cs.purdue.edu), which is periodically reposted to the Usenet news.announce.newusers Newsgroup.

Usenet came into being in late 1979, when Tom Truscott and Jim Ellis, two graduate students at Duke University in North Carolina, thought of hooking computers together to exchange information with the Unix community, making use of the UUCP (Unix-to-Unix-copy) facilities that had just been added to a new version of Unix. Steve Bellovin, then a grad student at the University of North Carolina, wrote software to manage the exchange of messages, which was installed on computers at the Duke and UNC campuses. The service was named "News," the set of sites carrying News became known as "Usenet," more or less for a network of Unix users.

Over the next few years, these and other members of the Unix community including Steve Daniel, Mark Horton, Matt Glickman, and Rick Adams wrote new versions of the "News" software for reading, posting, and distributing News messages across the ever-expanding Usenet. By the mid-1980s, Usenet had spread to Unix systems at thousands of universities and computer-making and computer-using organizations. Conventions evolved for coordinating "joining" Usenet, starting new News groups, and social rules. By the late 1980s, Usenet had established itself as a major resource for technical discussions and development within the Unix, TCP/IP, and Internet communities and as a community within its own right.

As of the early 1990s, Usenet is available on all seven continents, including Antarctica, according to Vielmetti. In late 1992, for example, "A recent analysis of the top 1000 Usenet sites showed about 58 percent as U.S. sites, 15 percent unknown, 8 percent in Germany, 6 percent in Canada, 2 to 3 percent each in the United Kingdom, Japan, and Australia, and the rest mostly scattered around Europe. The state of California is the center of the Usenet, with about 14 percent of the mapped top sites there."

Today, everything from research and product development to friendships culminating in marriage take place within the Usenet; entire companies, such as UUNET Technologies and ClariNet, have been formed whose major functions include providing information via Usenet News groups. For many people, losing their access to the Usenet (typically when they leave a university or job or move) is as traumatic as losing one's electronic mail account. Fortunately, it's increasingly easy for anyone to (re)gain Usenet access.

There are lots of ways for an organization to get a Usenet feed, at costs ranging from free to several hundred dollars per month—and commensurate differences in speed, Newsgroups provided, feed-only versus allowing users to post messages, etc. Usenet "feeds" of Newsgroup articles to sites are available through Internet Service Providers and other Internet-related organizations, such as ANS, RadioMail Corp., MSEN, PSI, and UUNET Technologies.

Pagesat Inc. (Palo Alto, CA) provides Usenet feeds via satellite, as a side effort to their commercial data broadcasts, letting you get 50 Mbytes of Usenet News every day using some relatively inexpensive equipment—(about $1800 for hardware and software. The "feed" is free for 2 years, then about $30 per month. For more information, send e-mail to "pagesat@pagesat.com" or call 415-424-0384.) Usenet Newsgroup postings are even available in non-network outlets. Organizations like Walnut Creek CD-ROM (Walnut Creek, CA) provide Usenet postings on regularly issued CD-ROMs; ZIP Press (Columbus, OH) will deliver hardcopy of requested Usenet groups and postings. (Obviously, these are read-only access methods; you'll need access to a Usenet site to post messages.) As an end user, however, Usenet is probably available through your Internet account.

## Basic Concepts of Usenet and BBSs

If you've never used Usenet or any other BBS or conferencing system, it's worth taking a look at the general concept of electronic, networked bulletin boards and how Usenet is similar and different from other BBS systems and services.

### Electronic bulletin boards: An effective way to share information

If you've read Chap. 5, you can see how networks and electronic mail make it possible to exchange messages and information, carry on "conversations," and communicate in a very powerful way. Through "mailing lists" it's possible to have remarkably sophisticated and on-going discussions and even have electronic "magazines." However, electronic mail can have several limitations as a way to share information among a community of people:

- You have to be "sent" messages; someone has to be administrator of a mailing list.
- You have to manage messages—decide whether to save or delete them and where to file them.
- Important person-to-person e-mail can easily be swamped by large volumes of mailing-list messages.
- As more people get copies of each message, the amount of computer and network resources required—network bandwidth to transmit, computer

storage to save, and CPU cycles to manage—for essentially the same information goes up remarkably fast.

BBSs were created to help solve these problems. In electronic mail, each message goes to a specific "electronic mailbox" file owned by a specific computer user. In a BBS, unlike personal electronic mail, information is organized as a communally shared pool in directories that don't belong to any one user. Messages go to areas "owned" by the bulletin board software; like a shared newspaper or a notice posted on the wall by the water fountain, many people can all read the same copy, using software programs designed to organize and read the many messages. Instead of sending a message to one person, you send, or "post," it to a group in the BBS.

In one form or another, this method is used by the tens of thousands of electronic BBSs around the world, including CompuServe, DELPHI, and GEnie and the many special-purpose and noncommercial BBSs.

### Newsgroups: Organizing articles into topical groups

Just as you probably organize your various on-line files into directories and subdirectories, most BBSs organize messages into topical groups, also referred to as special-interest groups (SIGs) or forums. As the number of groups grows, they usually get put into some form of hierarchy, such as Business, Professional, Recreation, Education, Programs. On Usenet, News messages are organized into groups, also known as Newsgroups. Over time, a group may be divided, new groups may be added, groups may be renamed, reorganized, subdivided, or even terminated if there's lack of interest. The naming for Usenet Newsgroups follows a number of conventions:

- All group names are in lowercase, for example, tcp-ip, wais, infosystems.
- Group and subgroup names are separated by a period (.). The left-most name is the top-level hierarchy, for example, *comp.infosystems.gopher* refers to the gopher subgroup in the infosystems group in the comp hierarchy. When using Usenet group names in spoken conversation, the . is either pronounced "dot" or as a pause. So, for example, "Did you see the latest collection of one-liners in rec humor funny?" or "Be sure to read the messages in new dot newusers before posting your first message."
- The subgroup name d indicates discussions of certain issues related to the group itself, for example, comp.sources.d.

Within each Newsgroup, each message is stored as an individual file, whose name is a number. The number is assigned based on the order the message is received (e.g., the current messages in comp.infosystems.gopher may be 150, 151, 152, 153, and so on).

### Unmoderated, moderated, digest

Like electronic mailing lists (see Chap. 16), every Usenet Newsgroup is either unmoderated or moderated, and moderated Newsgroups may be in digest or single-message format:

- *Unmoderated* means that when someone creates a message for a given Newsgroup, copies of the message are distributed to all appropriate sites, without any inspection or intervention by people. An example is: alt.internet.services.
- *Moderated* means that only one person (or e-mail address)—the moderator—is able to post messages to a given Newsgroup. When someone creates a message for a given Newsgroup, it is mailed to the moderator, who decides whether and when to let it be distributed. An example is rec.humor.funny.
- *Digest* format means that the moderator accumulates messages and periodically (daily, weekly, monthly—depending on how many messages there are and how time-critical getting them out is) posts these messages in one message, called a digest. An example is comp.risks.

## Threads: Organizing articles within Newsgroups into discussions

The Usenet, as you're probably beginning to see, holds a vast torrent of articles. You aren't going to want to read them all. Sorting the thousands of articles posted daily to Usenet into appropriate Newsgroups helps you identify which messages you want to consider reading. But even this may not be adequate; a high-volume Newsgroup may easily have dozens, even hundreds, of postings arriving daily.

One method that has evolved over the years, within Usenet as well as among other Internet and BBS users, is the concept of "threads" and "threading." A thread, in BBS slang, is a topic, and a series of messages about this topic. In electronic mail discussions and some on-line forums, thread simply means an on-going topic. (Some people have begun using this term informally, in e-mail and even conversationally, as in "Going back to our previous thread.")

Increasingly, "threading" also means that your article-creating software is capable of incorporating thread information into message headers, such as identifying the previous article you are commenting on (i.e., creating or continuing a thread). "Threaded" newsreaders, in turn, are able to use this information to sort articles into threads and organize articles within a thread based on their relationships—which ones are commenting on which.

According to the manual page for **trn,** "Being threaded means that the articles are interconnected in reply order. Each discussion thread is a tree of articles, where all the reply (child) articles branch off from their respective originating (parent) articles."

The topic of an article is defined as the contents of its Subject: field. (This makes it possible to use a new Subject: in your article so it relates to your own message; the newsreader will still recognize your message as belonging to an existing thread, and which one.)

Most BBSs and conferencing systems (e.g., CompuServe, DELPHI, and GEnie) today support threading in their forums and SIGs. Remember that in the Usenet, instead of all users accessing one giant system, each site has its own set of copies of the articles—which may have been received in a different time order. It's therefore possible—most likely, in fact—that newsreaders at different sites will present a thread's articles in a slightly different order. (Usenet software takes this into account, of course, and handles the identification of messages within threads properly, so you don't have to worry about it.) It should also be possible to disable (turn off) threading and simply examine and read articles in the order they arrived to your site.

### Expiration, archiving, and periodic posting: No message lives forever everywhere

BBS-style conferencing may help reduce the consumption of disk storage for messages, but even so, Usenet information adds up over time to a considerable volume—more than most sites can or are willing to maintain. (Imagine trying to tape and save every show from every cable TV channel.) Some BBS systems, such as GEnie, try to keep every message ever posted saved on-line, but for most, this is not practical. Many sites support Usenet with spare, noncritical resources; many Usenet sites are run as an after-hours, labor-of-love activity on scavenged systems. At 40+ Mbytes of new messages every day, the Usenet can easily overwhelm the available storage of almost any site, within a few months. As a result, several conventions and procedures have evolved:

- *Message aging and expiration.* Each Usenet site decides how long it will keep messages around, on a per-group basis, and periodically will purge all messages older than these thresholds. How long can depend on the amount of traffic in a given group, how important the system owners feel a group is, and how much storage capacity is available. For example, at a company specializing in computer security, "issues" of the RISKS forum in comp.risks may be saved for 6 months, while postings to the Mac or PC groups may be purged after 2 weeks.

  Sites providing Usenet access for pay-for-access users, such as PANIX or World, are more likely to retain Usenet postings for longer. Also, messages may include an "expiration" date, after which the system can automatically delete them. Your site *may* include Usenet postings in its regular backup tapes (assuming they do backups). However, finding the one you want may be nontrivial—remember, you're talking about files whose names are numbers, with no relation their contents.
- *Archiving by Newsgroup.* Certain individuals or sites will decide to act as the permanent archive for one or more Usenet Newsgroups. These archives may be searched or queried via anonymous-FTP, WAIS indexing, or other mechanisms.
- *Back issues.* Companies like Uunet make archive tapes of Usenet postings, which can be retrieved. To the extent they are available, the CD-ROM versions of Usenet may contain postings you're looking for.
- *Periodically updated and posted messages.* Postings of on-going interest to the Usenet community such as the FAQs (Frequently Asked Questions

and their answers) and postings intended for new Usenet users ("Primer," "Dear Emily PostNews") are reposted regularly, as the old versions expire and are deleted or if there is new information. Usually, one or more people have assumed responsibility for a given message.

## How Usenet Works, at the Cosmic Level

Most BBSs, whether they're a small BBS run by a high-school student on an old PC, or a million-user enterprise like CompuServe, have one thing in common: Their goal is to let people share messages in a group forum, including everything from announcements and questions to discussions, documents, and programs. BBSs and other on-line consumer services like CompuServe, DELPHI, and GEnie basically consist of a large computer system, and some arrangement of computer networks to let you access them. CompuServe, for example, uses four dozen or so mainframe IBM computers located in Ohio. CompuServe has over a million users; typically, according to CompuServe, 20,000 of them are logged in at any one time. The "network," in these cases, is simply acting as a possibly less expensive and less error-prone telephone system—a relatively expensive way to give users access to information.

Usenet, by contrast, uses networks and networking to distribute copies of messages to lots of computers; users in turn seek to access a site with Usenet messages that's as close (inexpensive as a phone call) as possible, perhaps even within their organization and attached to their organization's own network. Usenet messages travel by any and all means, from their initial UUCP approach, where participating computers make modem-to-modem phone calls and pass along copies of all appropriate messages, to flowing over the Internet and even via radio, floppy disk, backup tape, and CD-ROM. This approach is not unique to Usenet; it's also used by FidoNet and other cooperating BBSs where minimizing the cost of sending and access messages is more important than messages being seen within seconds to minutes. Usenet takes the philosophy of "think locally, distribute globally" to a mind-boggling extreme. An estimated two million people read one or more of the Usenet Newsgroups, on nearly 70,000 computers in over 50 countries.

## What Usenet Newsgroups Are There?

As of early 1993, there are at least 3500 Newsgroups within the Usenet hierarchy. Your site may carry all or nearly all. Like the variety of offerings from cable TV or your local newsstand, the range of topics covered by Usenet Newsgroups is vast. The odds are good that there will be some of interest to you. The odds are equally good that most won't be of interest to you. And there will be some you're interested in only parts of or only some of the time. (Don't worry—the Usenet community has evolved good software programs to help you select and read what you want from this info-torrent.)

Here's an overview of the top-level groups and examples of the groups in them. (See the section "Required, Recommended, and Suggested Usenet

Groups to Follow" later in this chapter for a list of recommended groups all new Usenet readers should be reading.)

### The seven basic Usenet groups

Seven top-level Newsgroups, a.k.a. "hierarchies," have been around the longest (admittedly with some changes and structuring over the years) and can be considered to constitute the "core" of the Usenet. These are comp., misc., news., rec., sci., soc., and talk; these are also the groups you are most likely to find at all Usenet sites. A quick overview of these seven groups follows.

**comp.** Contains computer, network, and information sciences, including hardware, software, product and vendor-specific issues, topical discussions, and software source code for a wide variety of operating systems. For many Internet and Usenet users, access to and participation in this group alone justifies their use of Usenet and the Internet. "Have a question about your Oracle database?" suggests network consultant and author Joel Snyder:

> Check comp.databases.oracle. Working on a particularly knotty Postscript problem? See comp.lang.postscript. Want to know about the latest developments in massively parallel systems? Comp.parallel. Have to check a rumor about security problems in Novell? Comp.sys.novell.
>
> The 300+ "comp" groups, aimed at computer professionals and hobbyists, cover every major and minor application package, networking technology, and topic of interest to system managers and users. To find out the latest before it appears in *PC Week* or to get in direct touch with users and programmers the world over, IBM PC aficionados will want to explore the 30+ different groups which distribute advice for DOS and Windows users and programmers, freeware and shareware.

Examples are:

comp.benchmarks
comp.fonts
comp.infosystems.gopher
comp.mac
comp.protocols.tcp-ip
comp.lang.forth.mac
comp.multimedia
comp.robotics

**misc.** This is where the several dozen groups that don't fit clearly into any other top-level Newsgroups hierarchy go, including investing and taxes, legal issues, and job postings. (Many regional hierarchies also have local job Newsgroups.) Examples are:

misc.books
misc.handicap
misc.forsale

misc.jobs.offered

misc.jobs.resumes

misc.taxes

**news.** The news. hierarchy is where you find Newsgroups about the Usenet, including administrative issues, announcements, general information, questions, and answers. Examples are:

news.announce.important

news.announce.newusers

news.answers

news.newusers.questions

news.lists

**rec.** rec. is short for "recreation." The 200+ groups in the rec. hierarchy offer information and discussion on interests from antique, audio, comics, and cooking through science fiction, television, and travel. In addition to the general-topic groups, there are lots of dedicated subgroups for specific interests, such as *Dr. Who, Mystery Science Theater 3000,* the Grateful Dead, and *Star Trek* (old and new). Examples are:

rec.antiques

rec.bicycles

rec.gardens

rec.juggling

rec.scouting

rec.skiing

**sci.** The sci. hierarchy holds Newsgroups about science, research, and engineering other than computer sciences (which is in comp.), and includes over four dozen groups such as astronomy, cryptography, economics and electronics, medicine, and space. Examples are:

sci.aeronautics

sci.archaeology

sci.bio

sci.fractals

sci.nanotech

**soc.** The 100+ soc. groups include a wide range of social issues, politics, culture, and socializing; soc.motss, for example, has been a global BBS forum for the gay community for nearly a decade. They tend to be mostly for discussions to explore their topics; users seeking to debate, preach, or convert are generally expected to go to the appropriate talk. group. Examples are:

soc.college

soc.penpals

soc.motss

soc.culture

**talk.** These groups are closer to debates than discussion on the more controversial topics (e.g., religion). Examples are:

talk.bizarre

talk.environment

talk.philosophy

talk.rumors

### Alternative Newsgroups: Alt and others

In addition to the seven main groups, Usenet has grown to include "alternative" News groups, notably:

- The alt. hierarchy
- ClariNet clari.*, MSEN msen.*, and other commercial groups
- BITNET, K12, DDN, and other "gatewayed" and relayed groups
- Regional hierarchies
- Other specialized and commercial hierarchies

Here's a summary of some of them. (For a current overview and list, see the multipart "Periodic Postings" summarizing Usenet Newsgroups in news.announce.newusers.)

**The alt. hierarchy.** alt. is where many Newsgroups get created that don't clearly belong elsewhere. There are no restrictions on what these Newsgroups can be (and no guarantee that your site will subscribe to them). At present there are hundreds of on-going Newsgroups in alt., including:

alt.cyberspace

alt.fan.mike-jittlov

alt.fan.monty-python

alt.folklore.computers

(1993 has also seen a rash of new groups in the alt.* hierarchy with strange names and on very esoteric, bizarre topics.)

**ClariNet, MSEN: The clari.*, msen.* Newsgroups.** Interested in UPI feeds—or keeping up with your favorite print newspaper columnists like Ms. Manners, Dave Barry, or Mike Royko? Perhaps your site should subscribe to ClariNet.

***Representative ClariNet Newsgroups***

| | |
|---|---|
| clari.news | ClariNet UPI general news wiregroups |
| clari.news.hot | Temporary groups for hot news stories |
| clari.biz | ClariNet UPI business news wiregroups |
| clari.sports | ClariNet UPI sports wiregroups |
| clari.feature.davebarry | Columns of humorist Dave Barry |
| clari.feature.mikeroyko | Chicago Opinion Columnist Mike Royko |
| clari.feature.missmanners | Judith Martin's Humorous Etiquette Advice |
| clari.tw.health.aids | AIDS stories, research, political issues |
| clari.biz.market.amex | American Stock Exchange reports & news |
| clari.biz.market.dow | Dow Jones NYSE reports |
| clari.biz.market.otc | NASDAQ reports |
| clari.news.arts | Stage, drama, & other fine arts |
| clari.news.gov.corrupt | Government corruption, kickbacks, etc. |
| clari.news.law.supreme | U.S. Supreme court rulings & news (moderated) |
| clari.sports.baseball | Baseball scores, stories, games, stats |

Need information from the Reuters newswire? Get it hot off the net from MSEN, Inc. The clari. groups represent an "electronic newspaper" published via the Usenet by ClariNet Communications (Cupertino, CA), offering over 200 Newsgroups to sites (including dial-up BBSs) or users for a regular fixed-price subscription fee.

MSEN, similarly, offers Reuters articles, available as a dozen or more Usenet Newsgroups; Counterpoint Publishing offers daily issues of the U.S. government Federal Register and Commerce Business Daily publications—delivered to your site as Usenet Newsgroup articles; and many other organizations are rapidly turning to the Usenet Newsgroup hierarchies as a highly effective way to distribute information. (Many of these can be browsed and searched via Gopher and WAIS as well as via Usenet newsreaders; some of these services make the information available through their own Gopher or WAIS servers. See Chap. 14 for more information about ClariNet, MSEN and other commercial, pay-to-get information.)

### BITNET, K12, DDN, and other gatewayed and relayed groups

Many of the Usenet Newsgroups are or include messages from Internet and non-Internet mailing lists and from groups and forums on other networks. For more about this, see Chaps. 16 and 17.

**bit.—Mailing lists from BITNET.** The Usenet bit. hierarchy provides a Usenet home for BITNET e-mail LISTSERV discussions, appearing here in the form of Usenet groups. Over 1000 such groups may be available. (Your site may not carry them all; ask your system administrator if there's one you want; also see Chap. 17.)

**k12.—Education Newsgroups.** The K12 groups that originated on FidoNet are for discussions among students, faculty, and curriculum developers in grades

Kindergarten through 12. For example, there's "k12.chat.elementary" for an informal discussion among elementary students, grades K–5. (See Chap. 13 for more discussion about K12 Usenet Newsgroups.)

**ddn. and other Internet e-mail lists.** These Usenet hierarchies carry messages sent to various Internet e-mail lists, appearing here in the form of Usenet Newsgroups to minimize network bandwidth and storage and to make it easier for users to browse, read, and participate in these discussions. ddn refers to the Defense Data Network; there also used to be fa, referring to "From the ARPAnet". Examples are:

```
dnn.mgt-bulletin, ddn.newsletter
```

### Regional hierarchies

Regional top-level hierarchies are dedicated to a regional area, which may be a city, state, group of states, country, continent, or language. Examples are, ba. (Bay Area), dc (Washington, D.C.), ne. (New England), au. (Australia). These hierarchies make it easier to have discussions with strong regional concerns, such as restaurant reviews, buy/sell/job ads (e.g., ne.jobs), etc. But don't be misled by the names; your site may easily carry Newsgroups from the other side of the country or world and many may be of interest to you.

### Other specialized and commercial hierarchies

Increasingly, other organizations and commercial information providers are taking advantage of the Usenet as a way to disseminate information, as Usenet Newsgroup hierarchies. For example:

**ieee.** The Institute of Electrical and Electronics Engineers (IEEE) has its own Usenet hierarchy, ieee.; its groups include ieee.announce, announcements of general nature to IEEE community.

**biz.** Two dozen or so Newsgroups with business product information, product announcements, demo software, bug fixes, etc., can be found here. Not surprisingly, most of the postings are about computer-related products and services.

**Language-oriented hierarchies.** Most of what's posted to Usenet is in English—but not all. There are hierarchies in other languages, such as de. (German), fj. (Japanese), relcom. (Russian), etc. Usenet postings are created using 7-bit ASCII characters—which includes all the letters needed for English but not necessarily for other alphabets or character sets. To solve this, non-ASCII characters are encoded into sequences of 7-bit ASCII characters for transmission and storage. This is similar to how binary programs, sounds, spreadsheets, and other non-ASCII information can be represented by encoding their contents into sequences of commonly used ASCII characters, for example, send non-ASCII files via e-mail. (See the discussion of MIME and of encoding in Chap. 5.) To convert these 7-bit ASCII character sequences into something you can read, and in reverse to post messages to these Usenet groups, you'll need special programs, which run on your computer.

"Software for creating and reading non-English Usenet postings is readily available from a variety of commercial and public-domain sources," assures Mary Riendeau (mer@world.std.com), Vice President of Information Services for Software Tool & Die (Brookline, MA), who has been studying Japanese and regularly reads the Japanese Newsgroups on ST&D's World. For users seeking Japanese-related software, "crl.nmsu.edu [128.123.1.14] appears to be the best archive site to use," recommends Riendeau. "They also keep a list of other ftp sites for Japanese software and utilities. And the Newsgroup sci.lang.japan talks a great deal about Japanese software as well as about the Japanese language and electronic Japanese dictionaries."

Similarly, the alt.chinese.text Newsgroup, read by over 28,000 people around the world, carries Chinese text encoded using one of two protocols. (See the Newsgroup's FAQ for more information.) In general, to see if there are any Newsgroups available in a language you're interested in, check the Periodic Posting lists of Newsgroups, then check the FAQ and other intro/answer documents for information about the protocols and software used to read and post to these Newsgroups.

## Using Usenet

Now that you've got a basic sense of what the Usenet is, it's time to learn how to access and use the Usenet. In the following sections of this chapter, you'll learn:

- How to access the Usenet
- What software is available
- Important files for Usenet users: .newsrc, .signature, "kill files," "dead.article"
- Required reading for new Usenet users
- Using your Usenet Newsreader program; joining, selecting, reading, posting, etc.
- Required, recommended, and suggested Usenet groups to follow
- Basic Usenet netiquette and vocabulary
- Tips, advice, and suggestions for new Usenet users
- Where to go for more information.

### How to access the Usenet

To access the Usenet, you need an account with an organization that is a Usenet site—that is, one that receives Usenet Newsgroup postings (also known as a "News feed") and is able to send user postings to other Usenet sites.

If you belong to an organization that is a Usenet site and have an account on a computer on the organization's network, you should be able to get Usenet access—check with your local system administrator if this is not the

### *Reading Usenet via Unix*

While the Usenet newsreader program you use makes it easier to read and reply to messages in the Usenet Newsgroups, it's worth understanding how the Newsgroups and messages are actually organized on most Unix systems. As a rule, the entire Usenet Newsgroup hierarchy is stored somewhere within the file system of one or more computers in your organization. For example, on Software Tool & Die's World, they are located within the subdirectory "spool/news" (owned by "user" **usenet.**). Within this "news" directory, there is a subdirectory corresponding to each Usenet top-level Newsgroup. And within each of these subdirectories, there are further levels of subdirectories, again corresponding to the Usenet Newsgroup hierarchy. For example:

news/comp/protocols/tcp-ip
news/comp/lang/sys/mac
news/newusers/questions
news/clari
news/rec/humor/funny
news/alt/internet/services
news/alt/magic
misc/jobs/offered
ba/internet

Within each Newsgroup, each message is stored as a file, with a number as its filename. As each new message arrives, it is assigned the next number in sequence. For example:

```
% cd /spool/news/comp/risks
% ls
167 168 169 170
% cd comp/infosystems/gopher
% ls
...
4367    4386    4405    4424    4443    4462
4368    4387    4406    4425    4444
4369    4388    4407    4426    4445
```

It's possible to treat the Usenet directories and files as any other Unix files (which they are). You can search through and read Usenet messages via the Unix commands you learned in Chap. 4. For example, you can search through these files with **grep** or read them with **more.** (You *can't* edit them or create new files in these directories; as a user you don't have the appropriate privileges. Only the Usenet software can do that.) For example:

```
% grep -l clipper*
169 170
% more 169
```

Most of the time, you'll be using your Usenet newsreader software, but there may be occasions where you need to do things you haven't yet figured out how to do via your newsreader software, which you know how to do via Unix commands—or you may be accessing the Usenet on someone else's system, which doesn't have the newsreader programs you're familiar with.

case. Alternatively, you have access to the Usenet if you have an account with a public-access Internet site, Unix site, Internet Access Provider, or dial-up e-mail/Usenet service that offers Usenet service. If you believe that Usenet access is one of the services offered, and you are unable to find it, contact the appropriate customer support representative. Lastly, it's possible to set up your own computer to be a Usenet site in its own right. (This is outside the scope of this book; there are informational postings about how to do this in the Usenet news.answers Newsgroups, as well as books, and commercial and public-domain software.) If you do not currently have Usenet access, see Chap. 16.

Remember, Usenet access does not require "full Internet service." There are hundreds, possibly thousands, of Usenet sites that do not have real-time TCP/IP connections to the Internet, only periodic connections for the exchange of e-mail, Usenet News, and other messages and files. For read-only access to the Usenet, you can even obtain Usenet Newsgroup postings on CD-ROM, issued every few weeks from Walnut Creek-CD-ROM.

### Software for being a Usenet user: What's available

Just as you use e-mail programs to read, create, and manage your electronic mail and word processors to work with your documents, you read and post to Usenet via special programs, called *newsreaders* (more on this soon). These newsreader programs, developed over the past decade by the Usenet community expressly for this purpose, hide the way the Usenet Newsgroups and messages are actually stored on-line and make it easier for you to select, scan, read, and reply to the messages.

If you intend to read and follow more than a handful of low-traffic Usenet Newsgroups, you'll probably find that a good newsreader program is invaluable. (But see Box: Reading Usenet via Unix.)

### Typical Usenet Newsreader software

There are many Usenet newsreader programs available for different types of computers to take advantage of the various graphic user interfaces and other computer-specific features. Many of these programs are available at no cost via Internet file-retrieval services (anonymous-FTP, e-mail, Gopher, etc.). Others are sold commercially or are included as part of TCP/IP products. There is an entire Usenet Newsgroup dedicated to newsreader software, news.software.readers, and another dedicated to off-line newsreaders, alt.usenet.offline-readers.

**Popular features for newsreader programs.** Popular features in newer Usenet newsreader software include:

- *Thread tracking.* Many of the newer Usenet newsreader programs are threaded, meaning they can examine, sort, select, and present articles within a Newsgroup sorted into subject threads. This makes it much easier to find and follow the articles you're interested in—and to skip the ones you aren't interested in.
- *Kill files.* These are files created and managed by your newsreader which keep a per-Newsgroup list of people you *don't* want to read postings from and topics you *don't* want to read postings about. Some newsreaders even let you specify things like a time-period for which you want a given kill command to remain active.

- *Follow-up formatting.* In making comments about previous messages, you often want to include some of that message, marked in some way to indicate it's not yours, and its source. This feature inserts the desired message, usually indented and with a character such as > in the left margin of each line, plus a line above the message indicating who it was from and when posted.

**Popular Usenet newsreader programs for Unix users.** Popular Usenet newsreaders found on most Unix-based sites include:

- ***rn*** *(ReadNews).* An older Usenet newsreader, replacing the even older **readnews** program, **rn** has been revised and updated over the years; it is available at probably every Usenet site and is used by many people. **rn** was created by Larry Wall <lwall@jpl-devvax.jpl.nasa.gov> and is now under the direction of Stan Barber <sob@bcm.tmc.edu>.
- ***nn*** *(No News is Good News).* A popular alternative to **rn**, **nn** offers point-and-shoot menu-oriented operation, presenting menus of article subject and sendername lines; it helps you read and navigate Newsgroups and available articles faster by keeping a database of article headers on-line. **nn**, developed by Kim F. Storm of Texas Instruments A/S, Denmark, was released in 1989 and is now generally available at most Usenet sites.
- ***trn*** *(Threaded ReadNews).* This extended version of **rn**, written by Wayne Davison (davison@borland.com), displays messages sorted by subject lines, a.k.a. threads. I discovered **trn** in early 1992 and have been very pleased with it. I have been using it ever since. The up side of using a threaded newsreader like **trn** is that I can scan through and avoid reading far more messages and Newsgroups. The down side is it encourages me to subscribe to and read from far more Newsgroups.
- ***tin.*** Another thread-oriented full-screen newsreader but with a different way of organizing and presenting article and thread headers. **tin** is based on the **tass** newsreader and was developed by Rich Skrenta in March 1991. According to the **tin** manual page, **tass** was itself heavily influenced by Plato NOTES, an early computer-based conferencing system developed at the University of Illinois by Ray Essick and Rob Kolstad in 1982. (For those interested in computer software genealogy; both Lotus' NOTES and Digital Equipment Corporation's VAX Notes programs are derived from, or otherwise related to, Plato NOTES.)
- ***xrn.*** A Usenet newsreader for use on workstations running the X Windows system, written by Rick Spickelmier and Ellen Sentovich (UC Berkeley).
- *The Gnus and Gnews macros packages.* These let you read, reply, and post to Usenet Newsgroups while using the GNU Emacs text editor.

Your site may also have other Usenet newsreader programs available. The newsreader programs mentioned above should be easily available from Internet public-access file archives. If the one you want isn't installed, ask your local system administrator.

**NNTP-based newsreaders: Using Usenet from your personal computer.** The above Usenet newsreader software must all be used directly on a computer that has access to its site's Usenet files. If you're accessing the Internet via an account on another computer (e.g., dialing in from your PC, running a terminal emulator), you must have file access to the Usenet Newsgroups. However, if your computer is running TCP/IP (see Chap. 2), you can access and browse the Usenet from your computer without having to have an end-user account on a Usenet system. Examples are an Apple Powerbook or a notebook computer running Microsoft Windows.

In addition to TCP/IP—and PPP or SLIP if you're accessing the Internet over a phone line—you'll need a protocol called NNTP, the Network News Transfer Protocol, plus a Usenet newsreader that supports NNTP. Most TCP/IP products will include NNTP; they may include an NNTP newsreader, or you may want a different one. You'll also need an account that supports NNTP Usenet access. Usenet newsreader packages that support NNTP can read and post news from computers that don't have Usenet software or Newsgroups directly installed. This makes it possible, among other things, for users to browse and read Usenet Newsgroups from their PC or workstation while connected to the Usenet system without having to download the entire article or Newsgroup. Also, similar to e-mail packages like Eudora for computers running TCP/IP, NNTP-based Usenet newsreaders let you:

- Retrieve selected Usenet articles for off-line reading (e.g., while on an airline, in a hotel room, or otherwise able to use your computer but not maintain a connection to the Usenet)
- Create Usenet and e-mail responses to these articles, which will be posted or e-mailed the next time you establish a TCP/IP connection to the Internet from your computer

There are also a number of Usenet NNTP-based newsreader programs for use on DOS, Windows, Apple Macintosh, Amiga, and other personal computers. xrn and the GNU packages can run in NNTP mode. For example, Macintosh users can use TCP/ConnectII, from InterCon Systems Corporation, or Bill Cramer's TheNews shareware package; MS-DOS users can use PC/TCP from FTP Software; Microsoft Windows users can use commercial products such as PC/TCP, or BW/TCP from Beame & Whiteside to name but a few of the available packages. (See Appendix A for more information on Usenet newsreader software.) WorldLink-Basic ($29.95 per month) gives you a real-time connection to the Internet to send/receive mail and transfer files, plus a Network newsreader for Usenet.

### Important files for Usenet users

The newsreader program(s) you use to read and post messages to the Usenet make use of one or more special files in your account, as do many other of the programs you use to work with Internet-related programs. (For example, **mail** uses **.mailrc** and Gopher creates and uses **.gopherrc**.)

**.newsrc—Keeping track of Newsgroups you follow and messages you've read.** The most important of these files is the file used by your newsreader program to keep track of what Newsgroups you do and don't want to read and which messages you have read. Most Usenet newsreader programs call this file ".newsrc" ("news" being the name of an older Usenet program and "rc" being the standard filename ending for a file of configuration information). As a rule, this file is in your home directory. (Remember that the Unix **ls** and **dir** directory-listing commands do not list files with the initial . in their filename unless you have given the appropriate command switches or filename specifications.) For purposes of this discussion, this book will use ".newsrc" as the name of the file used for this purpose by your Usenet newsreader program; be sure to check the name of the file your newsreader program uses.

Your .newsrc file contains a one-line entry for each Newsgroup you currently wish to follow, in the default order you want to check Newsgroups for new messages. This entry consists of:

- The name of the Newsgroup, starting with its top-level hierarchy, using the Usenet "dot" naming convention (e.g., comp.infosystems.gopher)
- A colon character (:) if you currently are following this Newsgroup or an exclamation point (!), indicating you currently do *not* want to follow this Newsgroup

It possibly also includes a list of message numbers and number ranges, representing messages you have read or have indicated should be "marked as read" even though you may not have read them. For example, here's an entry for a Newsgroup you have just subscribed to, so there are no message numbers:

```
rec.humor.funny:
```

Here's an entry for a Newsgroup you've been following for a while and are completely "caught up" with:

```
alt.internet.services:1-350
```

Here's an entry for a Newsgroup you're following that you haven't read or "marked as read" all current articles:

```
misc.jobs.offered: 1-22409,22412,22414-22496,22538-22560
```

Here's an entry for Newsgroup you don't subscribe to:

```
bit.listserv.pc-ip!
```

And here's an entry for a Newsgroup you were following that you told your Newsreader you wanted to "unsubscribe" to:

```
tamu.gopher! 1-27,31,34,40-58
```

Depending on how your computer is set up, if an entry is longer than a line on your screen, when examining this file with a Unix command such as **more,** or editing it with a text editor, the entry may either linewrap—making it look like it's actually several lines—or run off the screen. Figure 6.1 shows

```
news.announce.important: 1-24
comp.risks: 1-418
rec.humor.funny: 1-2799,2801,2804
alt.internet.services: 1-2434
alt.internet.access.wanted: 1-1243
news.answers: 1-4854,4858,4863,4868,4874,4877
news.newusers.questions: 1-11199,11201
ne.jobs: 1-2043
misc.jobs.contract: 1-7840,7843
misc.jobs.offered: 1-24362,24365
biz.jobs.offered: 1-586
comp.archives.admin: 1-936
comp.archives.msdos.announce: 1-162,167-170
bit.listserv.pc-ip:
rec.arts.comics.strips: 1-3272
```

**Figure 6.1** Sample .newsrc file.

part of a sample .newrc file. As you can see, once you understand the names, :, !, and number conventions, this is a very efficient way to keep track of what Newsgroups you want to follow and which articles you've read or otherwise decided not to read.

Your newsreader program should include commands to let you subscribe and unsubscribe to Usenet Newsgroups, modify the list of which articles have been read, and rearrange the default order in which you want to read Newsgroups. You can also edit this file directly, using a text editor. One reason for working with your .newsrc file this way is to remove the entries for Newsgroups you don't want to subscribe to.

Many newsreader programs create a line for *every* Newsgroup—which can result in a .newsrc file of several thousand lines, even though you're only following a dozen or so. If you're paying for your own storage, this can be annoying; it also makes the file harder for you to inspect and edit (see Box: Learn How to Edit Your ".newsrc" or Other Newsgroup File).

**"Dot sig"—Your .signature file.** As you begin to read the articles in Usenet Newsgroups, you'll see that almost everyone's message ends with a signature—a few lines of information about them (so do many, but not all, e-mail messages). This information usually includes the person's full name, Internet e-mail address, and possibly other contact information such as phone and fax numbers, mailing address, and possibly a quote or two. This information is commonly referred to as your "signature" and can be kept in a file in your home directory so that instead of retyping it every time, the file can be inserted into your posting to Usenet. When you're creating a message to post to a Usenet Newsgroup, most Usenet programs will ask if you want to include your .signature file or even do so automatically.

For many, the .signature file has become a minor art form (or obsession). Many users will change their quotes or disclaimers on a regular basis. Some have different .signature files for use in postings to different Newsgroups—or

***Learn How to Edit Your ".newsrc" or Other Newsgroup File***

Before you edit your .newsrc file, it's always a good idea to make a backup copy, just in case you make a mistake. For example, on a Unix system, you could say:

```
% cp .newsrc .newsrc.old
```

Then, to restore a copy of your original file, you can simply say:

```
% cp .newsrc.old .newsrc
```

This overwrites the edited version of .newsrc (and still leaves you with a backup copy, which isn't a bad idea in any case).

If you are accessing Usenet as a terminal-style user from a PC, and haven't mastered a text editor on the system you're accessing the Usenet from, you may want to download a copy of your .newsrc file to your PC, edit it with your own text editor, and upload a fresh copy. (You'll need to know how to download and upload files, of course.) If you've made a formatting error in editing this file, most newsreader programs will attempt to fix it up, but they can't always unscramble your mistakes. Also, in editing, you might accidentally wipe out the list of groups you *do* want to follow and which messages you've seen to date—another good reason to always make a backup copy first.

To stop following a Newsgroup but leave its name in, to make it easier to rejoin, change the : to !, for example, change:

```
comp.risks: 1-433
tamu.gopher:
```

to:

```
comp.risks! 1-433
tamu.gopher!
```

For Newsgroups you don't expect to follow, you can edit their entries out altogether. For example, change:

```
comp.archives.msdos.announce: 1-162,167-170
comp.risks!
kw.news.stats!
tamu.gopher:
sci.virtual-worlds.apps: 1-1
alt.philosophy.objectivism!
misc.jobs.offered: 1-24362,24365
```

to:

```
comp.archives.msdos.announce: 1-162,167-170
comp.risks!
misc.jobs.offered: 1-24362,24365
```

You can also add and reorganize Newsgroups, of course.

Consider checking and editing your .newsrc file every week or so. You may find that your newsreader has been adding "don't watch" entries for Newsgroups without telling you.

even have programs to change the quote after each posting.

See "Other 'Dot' Files You Should Know About: .signature and .plan" in Chap. 4 for more information about signature files.

**"Kill files."** Many Usenet newsreader programs also let you specify users and topics you don't want to see any more articles about, on various levels, such as "all Newsgroups" or on a per-Newsgroup basis. Your newsreader program manages this information by creating one or more special directories and files in your account.

> ***Each Newsreader May Have Its Own Files***
>
> Keep in mind that different newsreader programs may each create their own files and directories, in particular their "kill file" files and directories. So if you use more than one newsreader, they may each present you with different lists. On Unix systems, the directory-names will typically begin with ., so you won't see them when you give **ls** or **dir** commands unless you give the appropriate switches or file-specifiers.

The phrase "kill file" is usually used generically to refer to your "I don't want to read these people or topics" information, even though it may be contained in more than one file or directory.

**Other files: Saved and dead articles.** Most Usenet newsreaders include the ability to save a copy of articles as files in your account. You can usually specify a name; if you don't, the article will probably be saved under your account with a pathname similar to that of its Newsgroup, for example:

```
/user1/aliddell/News/news/answers  (nn)
/user1/aliddell/News/news.answers  (trn)
```

When you are creating an article to post to a Usenet Newsgroup, if you decide to not post it, depending on what stage you are in of the article-creating process, your message may be placed in a file in your account, with a name such as "dead.article."

### Required reading for new Usenet users: "Periodic postings"

In addition to the Usenet information in this book, there are several articles written by members of the Usenet community that are considered to be "required reading" for all new Usenet members. There may be printed copies where you are; in any case, these articles are available from the Usenet, as well as via e-mail and anonymous-FTP file transfer. You should begin reading them as soon as possible once you have gained access to Usenet; you should definitely have read them *before* you post (write a message and send it to a group) to any Usenet Newsgroup.

These articles have been written by leading members of the Internet and Usenet communities; their advice reflects over a decade of experience in Usenet activity. Some of their key points will be reiterated in this chapter—but you are strongly advised to find and read the full articles. They aren't included in this book because they're readily available from the Usenet—and to include them in this book would be at the expense of some other information not universally available. And until you have gotten access to the Usenet, you don't need to read them.

As Gene Spafford, of Purdue University's Department of Computer Sciences (W. Lafayette, IN), points out in the "Introduction to news.announce" posting:

> If you aren't familiar with the netnews guidelines in news.announce.newusers, please read them carefully. Your understanding of these rules will assure that

you don't annoy the more than 1 million members of the net community (estimated) by unintentionally abusing the net and will help you get more value from the net.

You should read them relatively soon after you gain Usenet access in any case, since they will also help you better understand the Usenet and figure out what groups are available to you and which ones you want to subscribe to. Also, if you don't read these articles, and then proceed to ask questions or make mistakes discussed in these articles, don't expect to get much help or sympathy any more than you can expect to avoid a speeding ticket by claiming you'd never learned about speed limits.

You may want to go back and reread some or all of these articles again after a few weeks of exploring the Usenet—you'll find they make a lot more sense at this point, and you may discover a lot more information that you didn't see the first time around because you didn't really understand what they were talking about.

These messages are called "Periodic Postings," meaning they are posted to their respective Usenet Newsgroups on a regular basis, updated as necessary. For 12 years starting in 1981, Gene Spafford (now an associate professor at Purdue University), developed, edited, maintained, and published these periodic lists. In April of 1993, citing workload, disillusionment, and the changing nature of the Usenet, he passed the continued maintenance and posting of the lists to David Lawrence and Mark Moraes. Lawrence is maintaining the list-oriented postings, such as the list of Newsgroups, list of moderators, et al. Moraes is maintaining the informational postings for new users.

The important articles for new Usenet users to read will be placed in the Usenet Newsgroup news.announce.newusers, according to Spafford. "This makes it safe for experienced users who have already read these messages to unsubscribe to news.announce.newusers without missing anything new..." Articles that should be seen by *all* people reading the Usenet, regardless of whether they are new or long-time users, appear in a separate Newsgroup, news.announce.important, which all users should always subscribe to.

Most of these articles of interest to new users can also be found in the news.answers Newsgroup. "Periodic Posting" Usenet articles you should read include:

What is Usenet?

A Primer on How to Work With the Usenet Community

Rules for posting to Usenet

Answers to Frequently Asked Questions

Emily Postnews Answers Your Questions on Netiquette

Hints on writing style for Usenet

Introduction to the news.answers Newsgroup

Once you've read these, depending on what you're interested in, see "Further Periodic Usenet Articles Worth Reading." These articles include things like lists of Usenet Newsgroups with one-line explanations, lists of mailing lists available via e-mail, etc.

Here's a little information about each of the above articles to help you understand what they're about and why you should be reading them. (You probably don't want to read any of these messages in their entirety—but it's worth becoming familiar with them and the types of information they offer. Then, at later dates, when you're looking for information about Usenet Groups, mailing lists, etc., you'll remember to go locate current versions of these messages and read/search through them.)

**What is Usenet?** This posting, originally done by Chip Salzenberg and then edited by Gene Spafford, offers some definitions of the Usenet and key background information (e.g., "The first thing to understand about Usenet is that it is widely misunderstood. Every day on Usenet, the 'blind men and the elephant' phenomenon is evident, in spades").

**A Primer on How to Work With the Usenet Community.** This was originally written by Chuq Von Rospach (chuq@apple.com), Technical Support Engineer, Apple Computer, Inc. (Cupertino, CA).

> This message describes the Usenet culture and customs that have developed over time. All new users should read this message to find out how Usenet works. *** (Old users could read it, too, to refresh their memories.) ***
>
> This document is not intended to teach you how to use Usenet. Instead, it is a guide to using it politely, effectively, and efficiently. Communication by computer is new to almost everybody, and there are certain aspects that can make it a frustrating experience until you get used to them. This document should help you avoid the worst traps.

**Rules for posting to Usenet.** Originally written by Mark Horton (mark@stargate.com). This message describes some of the "rules of conduct" on Usenet. The rules vary depending on the Newsgroup.

**Answers to Frequently Asked Questions about Usenet.** Originally written by Jerry Schwarz:

> This document discusses some questions and topics that occur repeatedly on Usenet. They frequently are submitted by new users, and result in many followups, sometimes swamping groups for weeks. The purpose of this note is to head off these annoying events by answering some questions and warning about the inevitable consequence of asking others.

Sample questions answered in this article are:

1. What does Unix stand for?
2. What is the derivation of "foo" as a filler word?
5. What does :-) mean?

6. How do I decrypt jokes in rec.humor?
9. rec.games.*: Where can I get the source for empire or rogue?
10. comp.unix.questions: How do I remove files with non-ascii characters in their names?
17. Why do some people put funny lines ("bug killers") at the beginning of their articles?
20. How do I get from BITNET to UUCP, Internet to BITNET, JANET, etc., etc.?
25. What is "anonymous ftp"?

**Emily Postnews Answers Your Questions on Netiquette.** Written by Brad Templeton (brad@looking.on.ca), this is a satirical posting. As it says in the message's beginning:

> **NOTE: this is intended to be satirical. If you do not recognize it as such, consult a doctor or professional comedian. The recommendations in this article should be recognized for what they are—admonitions about what NOT to do.

**Hints on writing style for Usenet.** This is a summary of writing tips in general, specifically geared to writing for an electronic medium that will be viewed on a computer screen.

**Introduction to the news.answers Newsgroup.** According to this article:

> This is the monthly introductory article for the moderated Newsgroups alt.answers, comp.answers, misc.answers, news.answers, rec.answers, sci.answers, soc.answers, and talk.answers (hereafter collectively referred to as "*.answers"). It explains the purpose of the Newsgroups, what kinds of articles should be submitted to them, how to submit, how to participate in the mailing list for periodic posting maintainers, and where to find archives of *.answers postings.

**Further periodic Usenet messages worth reading.** Here's a list of "Periodic Postings" worth looking at and becoming familiar with. As you can see from their subjects, these messages contain the definitive lists of what's available in Usenet Newsgroups and Internet mailing lists. Become familiar with Usenet. You're unlikely to read most of these all the way through—but when you want information about Newsgroups and mailing lists, these messages should be one of the first resources you turn to. (Suggestion: Try searching via whatever Internet navigator you use. This information may be available via WAIS, Gopher, or other Internet tools in a more readily searchable form than reading through these very long text files.)

A Guide to Social Newsgroups and Mailing Lists

Alternative Newsgroup Hierarchies, Part I

Alternative Newsgroup Hierarchies, Part II

How to Get Information about Networks

Introduction to news.announce

List of Active Newsgroups

List of Moderators

List of Periodic Informational Postings

Publicly Accessible Mailing Lists, Part I

Publicly Accessible Mailing Lists, Part II

Publicly Accessible Mailing Lists, Part III

Regional Newsgroup Hierarchies, Part I

Regional Newsgroup Hierarchies, Part II

Regional Newsgroup Hierarchies, Part III

USENET Software: History and Sources

### Using your Usenet newsreader program: Joining, selecting, reading, posting, etc.

This section discusses the basic types of activities you'll do as a Usenet user. As mentioned earlier, the range of Usenet newsreader programs available is too great to cover each, so instead, we'll look at the activities in a general way and include a few examples from some of the more popular Newsreader programs. The section "What You'll Want to Learn to Do as a Usenet User" later in this chapter lists the basic Usenet activities you'll want to be able to do.

**Newsreader levels and modes.** Most newsreaders have several levels, also called modes, of operation:

- Newsgroup selection
- Thread selection
- Article selection
- Article paging, a.k.a. reading mode

Activities done in the Newsgroup selection level include selecting a current Newsgroup from your .newsrc list, adding new Newsgroups to this list, and subscribing or unsubscribing against this list. At the Thread selection level (assuming your newsreader program supports threading), you can move among and read articles in the selected Newsgroup as groups based on their

**_Learn by Observing_**

"The easiest way to learn how to use Usenet is to watch how others use it. Start reading the news and try to figure out what people are doing and why. After a couple of weeks you will start understanding why certain things are done and what things shouldn't be done." —From "Primer on How to Work with the Usenet Community," Chuq von Rospach.

common subject threads. At the Article selection level, you can select and read articles within the current Newsgroup or thread. At the Article paging level, also often called *reading mode,* you browse and read through individual articles in the current Newsgroup. If you use the Unix **more** program on your computer, your newsreader's text-reading commands and activities will probably be very similar.

**Short, easy commands.** Like most other Internet facilities, navigators, and other tools, most newsreaders use one- or two-keystroke commands for the bulk of their features. A small number of one- and two-keystroke commands should be sufficient for a lot of your Usenet Newsgroup selection and reading, such as <SPACE>, <RETURN>, -, +, =, >, <, ?, h, y, n, and q. The bulk of these commands don't require <RETURN> and are executed as soon as you press the appropriate key or keys.

**<SPACE>, the first frontier.** To make using newsreaders even easier, at most prompts, if you want to do the most common operation, you can simply hit the SPACEBAR. Usually, you'll know you can enter <SPACE> because the prompt consists of a short list of command letters, such as +ynq or [y]n?. If one of the options is in [square brackets], that's the one that <SPACE> will do.

**Press h or ? for help.** At each level, there should be one to three screens of help information, consisting of a summary of commands available at that level. You should be able to enter a help command any time you're at a prompt.

---

*Tip: Jump in and experiment with the Usenet.* Don't be shy about just jumping right in and muddling about to begin the process of learning to use your Usenet newsreader program and becoming familiar with the Usenet. Most of what you do as a Usenet user is examine and read information that should reside locally on your system in such a way that you can't accidentally change or delete it. So as long as you aren't writing messages to be posted, you are only consuming local resources and probably not too much of these.

You'll probably soon discover that with only a few commands, using an equally small number of keys and keystrokes, you can navigate and read Usenet Newsgroups and articles remarkably quickly and easily. Then, as you become more familiar, and get a better sense of what else you want to do, you can determine and master more and more of your newsreader program's commands.

---

## What You'll Want to Learn to Do as a Usenet User

### Beginner's activities

- Start up newsreader
- Edit .newsrc file manually
- Add (subscribe to) new Newsgroups to follow
- Select next, previous Newsgroup

- Select thread(s), article(s) to read
- Read thread(s), article(s)
- Save a message as a file
- Quit (exit) newsreader
- Quit (exit) newsreader, restoring .newsrc to its state at startup

#### Intermediate

- Go to specified Newsgroup (by name, searching)
- Mark messages and threads as having been read, with and without actually reading (or finishing) them
- "Catch up"—mark all unread articles in this Newsgroup as having been read
- Create and post a follow-up article, with and without excerpts from original message
- Reply to an article via personal e-mail, with and without including excerpts from original message
- Post a message on a new topic
- Unsubscribe and resubscribe to Newsgroups
- Read message "rot13"-encrypted

### Start Your Newsreader Program

First, of course, you start up your Usenet newsreader program by giving the name of the appropriate command and selecting the menu item or icon, etc. (Most of the newsreader programs will let you include any of a variety of optional switches or parameters, such as additional Newsgroups you want to examine—but as a beginning user, you don't need to be concerned with this.)

Most newsreader programs, when you start them, will begin looking at your .newsrc file. **trn,** for example, indicates how many unread articles are in the first six Newsgroups listed in your .newsrc file, like so:

```
% trn
Unread news in alt.internet.services              1 article
Unread news in ne.jobs                            1 article
Unread news in misc.jobs.contract                 3 articles
Unread news in misc.jobs.offered                  2 articles
Unread news in news.newusers.questions            3 articles
etc.

******** 1 unread article in alt.internet.services—read
now? [+ynq]
```

And **tin** starts up like so:

```
% tin
tin 1.1 PL3 (c) Copyright 1991-92 Iain Lea.
Reading active file...              h=help

Group Selection (41)          1 comp.risks
       2      rec.humor.funny
       3      alt.internet.services
       4      alt.internet.access.wanted
       6      comp.archives.admin
       7      alt.magic                          2
       8      ne.jobs                            5
       9      news.answers                       80
      10      misc.jobs.contract                 3
      11      misc.jobs.offered                  71
      13      bit.listserv.pc-ip
      14      news.newusers.questions            13
      15      comp.infosystems.wais
                        .
                        .
                        .
```

And one of the GUI newsreaders looks like this:

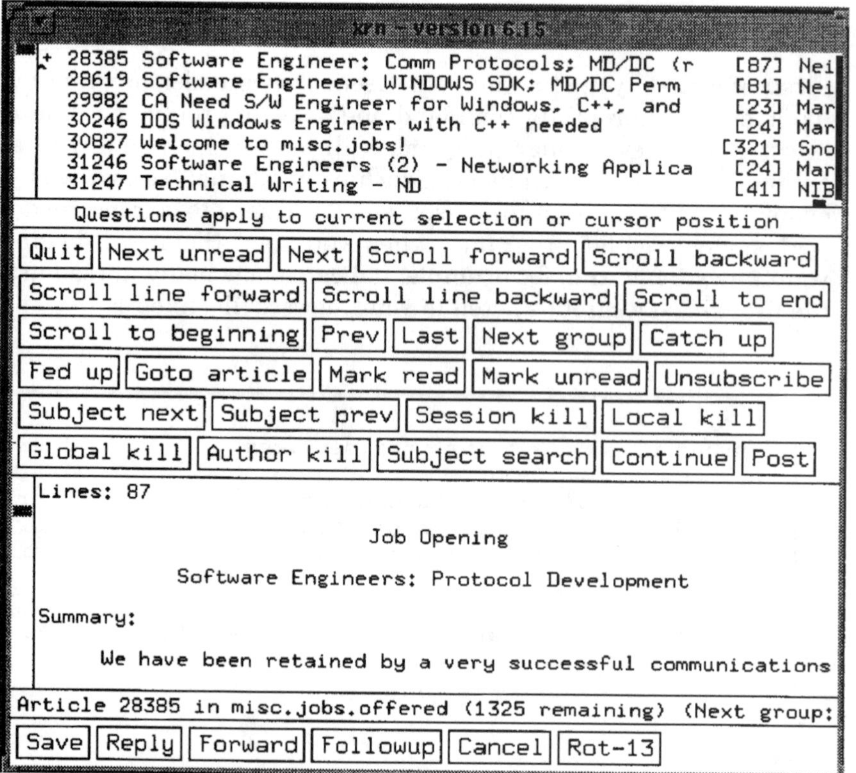

At this point, your newsreader is probably at Newsgroup level, with the first Newsgroup in your .newrc file as the current Newsgroup.

### Newsgroup level

At Newsgroup level, most newsreaders let you do things like:

- Select the next current Newsgroup
- Subscribe and unsubscribe to Newsgroups in your .newsrc file
- Add new Newsgroups to your .newsrc file and subscribe to them
- Catch up—mark all the articles in the current Newsgroup as "having been read"

### Selecting the next current Newsgroup

Selecting a Newsgroup means defining it as the one whose articles you want to examine. The "current" Newsgroup is the one whose articles will be selected by the thread and article-level commands and read by the pager commands. By default, your newsreader program selects the next current Newsgroup based on the order of entries in your .newsrc file.

Most newsreaders should also allow you to:

- Go to the previous Newsgroup listed in your .newsrc file
- Give the name of the Newsgroup you want, and if it isn't one you already subscribe to, change or add the appropriate entry to your .newsrc file
- Search forward or backward in your .newsrc file for a Newsgroup whose name matches a text string (e.g., "skiing" or "goph")
- In graphic/GUI newsreaders, select the next Newsgroup with your mouse or cursor-moving commands

Here's **trn**'s Newsgroup-level Help menu:

```
******** 3 unread articles in rec.humor.funny—read now?
[+ynq] ? *h* Newsgroup Selection commands:

 y,SP     Do this Newsgroup now.
 .cmd     Do this Newsgroup, executing cmd as first command.
 +   Enter this Newsgroup through the thread selector (like
     typing .+<CR>)
 =   Start this Newsgroup, but list subjects before reading
     articles.
 U   Enter this Newsgroup by way of the "Set unread?"
     prompt.
 u   Unsubscribe from this Newsgroup.
 c   Catch up (mark this Newsgroup all read).
 A   Abandon read/unread changes to this Newsgroup since you
     started trn.
 n   Go to the next Newsgroup with unread news.
 N   Go to the next Newsgroup.
 p   Go to the previous Newsgroup with unread news.
 P   Go to the previous Newsgroup.
 -   Go to the previously displayed Newsgroup.
 1   Go to the first Newsgroup.
 ^   Go to the first Newsgroup with unread news.
 $   Go to the last Newsgroup.
 g name   Go to the named Newsgroup. Subscribe to new
          Newsgroups this way
 /pat     Search forward for Newsgroup matching pattern.
 ?pat     Search backward for Newsgroup matching pattern.
     (Use * and ? style patterns. Append r to include read
     Newsgroups.)
 l   pat List unsubscribed Newsgroups containing pattern.
 m name   Move named Newsgroup elsewhere (no name moves cur-
          rent Newsgroup).
 o pat    Only display Newsgroups matching pattern. Omit pat
          to unrestricted.
 a pat    Like o, but also scans for unsubscribed Newsgroups
          matching pattern.
 L   List current .newsrc.
 &   Print current command-line switch settings.
 &switch {switch}
     Set (or unset) more command-line switches.
 &&  Print current macro definitions.
 &&def    Define a new macro.
 !cmd     Shell escape.
 q   Quit trn.
 x   Quit, restoring .newsrc to its state at startup of trn.
 ^K  Edit the global KILL file. Use commands like /pattern/j
     to suppress pattern in every Newsgroup.
 v   Print version.
 Macros:
 ,   =
 .   cy
 /   cy=
```

The **tin** Newsgroup-level help looks like this:

```
Group Selection Commands (page 1 of 2)4$     Select group 4
                                              ($=select)
^D^U       Down (^U=up) a page
^L         Redraw page
^KZ        Delete (Z=undelete) group from .newsrc
^R         Reset .newsrc
<CR>       Read current group
n<TAB>     Goto next group with unread news and enter it
b<SPACE>   Back (<SPACE>=forward) a page
B          Mail bug/comment to
           iain%anl433.uucp@Germany.EU.net
cC         Mark group read (C=and goto next unread group)
g          Choose a new group by name
jk         Down (k=up) a line
h          Command help
I          Toggle inverse video
l          List & select another spooldir
m          Move current group within group selection list
M          Menu of configurable options
N          Goto next group with unread news
qQ         Quit
su         Subscribe (u=unsubscribe) to current group
PgDn,End,<SPACE>,^D - page down.
PgUp,Home,b,^U - page up.
<CR>,q - quit
```

At this point, you can begin examining unread articles in this Newsgroup or select another Newsgroup.

### Thread and article levels

Once you've selected a current Newsgroup, the next step is to select articles—tell your newsreader program which of the articles, or groups—threads—of articles you want to read. (Unthreaded newsreaders, such as **rn,** will simply go directly from Newsgroup level to article paging level.)

### Thread selection level

At this level, your newsreader presents you with a list of the available thread subjects, the number of related unread articles, and possibly per-article information such as author full/e-mail name and (if they vary) individual article subjects. Usually, there is also a letter or number displayed on the screen to help you select which threads to read. Some newsreaders may let you pick from a choice of display formats, offering different information and in different presentations. For example,

```
news.newusers.questions              3 articles
a Alice Liddell        2 problems using Gopher
  Lemuel Gulliver
b Frederick        1 accessing archives for comp.sources.unix
– Select threads—All [Z>] –
```

As the **trn** manual page points out, “Most people who don’t have all day to read Usenet News news will want to enter a Newsgroup by way of the thread selector.” Most threaded newsreaders should include a way to set this as the standard way they start up.

### Article selection level

At this level, your newsreader will probably display one-line article summaries, similarly allowing you to choose articles for reading. By default, your newsreader will look only at “unread” articles, meaning those (1) whose numbers aren’t in your .newsrc file, (2) haven’t been read during the current session, and (3) aren’t ruled out by information in your “Kill” files. Most newsreaders should also let you “toggle”—switch back and forth—between examining “unread” and “read” articles in the current Newsgroup. An unthreaded newsreader, by contrast, may display article headers—but organized simply in the order they were received, leaving you to determine which ones, if any, are follow-ups to earlier messages. Here’s an example using **nn**:

```
********  10 unread articles in bit.listserv.help-net—read
now? [ynq]
 2012 Re: IBM mail
 2013 Re: Newsreaders
 2014 OCR Software Search
 2015 Bitnet Countries
 2016 Re: OCR Software Search
 2017 Penguin on multimedia workstation
 2018 LISTSERV list
 2019 Programming the LOGIN.COM
 2020 Un-DIGESTing
 2021 Re: Un-DIGESTing
What next? [npq]
```

In these levels, you select articles, and possibly threads, you want to examine. If you’re being presented with a list of article or thread topics, you should be able to move among these lists either a line at a time or a screenful at a time. You can also begin deselecting articles and threads. Graphic-oriented newsreaders will update the display as you make changes to message status (selected or unselected). Here is an example using **trn:**

```
bit.listserv.help-net            10 articles

a+Rafe Rackstraw     1   >IBM mail
b R. Montague        1   >Newsreaders
d+Lil Buttercup      2   OCR Software Search
  M. Hernani
f+Alice Liddell      1   Bitnet Countries
g+Calvin Rentis          Penguins on multimedia
i J Wellington Wel   1   LISTSERV list
j R. Montague        1   Programming the LOGIN.COM
l+Mark Turtle        3   Un-DIGESTing
  T. Gryphon

— Select threads — All [Z>] —
```

At any point, you can start reading articles; by default, your newsreader will probably start displaying articles when your selection process reaches the end of the article list. Other newsreaders, such as **rn,** go directly from Newsgroup selection to displaying article contents, in article pager level. Here's part of **trn**'s thread-level Help menu:

```
Thread selection commands:
a-z,0-9 Select/deselect the discussion thread by its letter
or number.
By default the letters h, k, m, n, p, q and y are omitted.
SP   Perform the default command (usually > or Z).
CR   Start reading. Selects the current thread if none are
     selected.
Z,TAB     Start reading. If no articles are selected, read
          everything.
y, `.'    Toggle the current thread's selection.
k, `,'    Mark the current thread as killed.
m, \      Unmark the current thread.
-    Set a range, as in 2 - 5. Repeats the last marking
     action.
@    Toggle all visible thread selections.
n, ]      Move down to the next thread.
p, [      Move up to the previous thread.
<, >      Go to previous/next page.
^, $      Go to first/last page.
X    Mark all unselected articles as read and start reading.
D    Mark unselected articles on the current page as read.
     Start reading if articles were selected, else go to
     next page.
J    Junk all selected articles (mark them as read).
^K   Edit local KILL file (the one for this Newsgroup).
:cmd      Perform a command on all the selected articles.
/pattern/modifiers
```

**trn**'s article-selection level help looks like this:

```
End of article 2338 (of 2339)—what next? [npq]
Article Selection commands:

n,SP      Find next unread article (follows discussion-tree
          in threaded group).
N    Go to next article.
^N   Scan forward for next unread article with same subject.
p,P,^P    Same as n,N,^N, only going backwards.
-    Go to previously displayed article.
<,>  Browse the previous/next selected thread. If no threads
     are selected, all threads that had unread news upon
     entry to the group are considered selected for brows-
     ing. Entering an empty group browses all threads.
[,]  Go to article's parent/child.
{,}  Go to tree's root/leaf.
t    Display the entire article tree and all its subjects.
number    Go to specified article.
range{,range}:command{:command}
     Apply one or more commands to one or more ranges of
     articles. Ranges are of the form: number | number-num-
     ber. You may use . for the current article, and $ for
     the last article. Valid commands are: e, j, m, M, s, S,
     t, T, |, +, and -.
:cmd      Perform a command on all the selected articles.
/pattern/modifiers
     Scan forward for article containing pattern in the sub-
     ject line. (Use ?pat? to scan backwards; append h to
     scan headers, a to scan entire articles, r to scan read
     articles, c to make case sensitive.)
/pattern/modifiers:command{:command}
     Apply one or more commands to the set of articles
     matching pattern. Use a K modifier to save entire com-
     mand to the KILL file for this Newsgroup. Commands m
     and M, if first, imply an r modifier. Valid commands
     are the same as for the range command.
f,F  Submit a followup article (F = include this article).
r,R  Reply through net mail (R = include this article).
e dir{|command}
     Extract to directory using /bin/sh, uudecode, unship,
     or command.
s ...     Save to file or pipe via sh.
S ...     Save via preferred shell.
w,W  Like s and S but save without the header.
| ...     Same as s|...
C    Cancel this article, if yours.
^R,v      Restart article (v=verbose).
^X   Restart article, rot13 mode.
c    Catch up (mark all articles as read).
b    Back up one page.
```

```
^L   Refresh the screen. You can get back to the pager with
     this.
X    Refresh screen in rot13 mode.
^    Go to first unread article. Disables subject search
     mode.
$    Go to end of Newsgroup. Disables subject search mode.
#         Print last article number.
&    Print current values of command-line switches.
&switch {switch}
     Set or unset more switches.
&&   Print current macro definitions.
&&def     Define a new macro.
j    Junk this article (mark it read). Stays at end of arti-
     cle.
m    Mark article as still unread.
M    Mark article as still unread upon exiting Newsgroup or
     Y command.
Y    Yank back articles marked temporarily read via M.
k    Kill current subject (mark articles as read).
,    Mark current article and its replies as read.
J    Junk entire thread (mark all subjects as read in this
     thread).
T    Trash current thread (like `J'), and save command in
     KILL file.
K    Mark current subject as read, and save command in KILL
     file.
^K   Edit local KILL file (the one for this Newsgroup).
=    List subjects of unread articles.
+    Enter thread selection mode.
U    Unread some news—prompts for thread, subthread, all, or
     select.
u    Unsubscribe from this Newsgroup.
q    Quit this Newsgroup for now.
Q    Quit Newsgroup, staying at current Newsgroup.
End of article 2338 (of 2339)—what next? [npq]
```

## Article pager level

At the article pager level, you are reading, creating, and working with individual articles. The "pager" is the facility that "pages through," or displays, article contents, on a screen-at-a-time basis, along with providing other article-level functions. Article-level activities include:

- READ the current article. Your newsreader should display messages in such a fashion that if a message contains more lines than are available on your screen or in your newsreader window, it will scroll, a.k.a., page—automatically pause when you have been presented with a screen or windowful of data, to allow you to read it. The scrolling facility is probably using, or is similar, to the standard **more** command from your computer;

in this case, for example, <SPACE> should advance to the next screen, <RETURN> should advance one line's worth, **b** should move you back one screenful.

As with selecting Newsgroups, you can move back and forth among articles in the current Newsgroup, or can move to a specific article. If an article has been encrypted using "rot13", determine and give the command to "decrypt and display article contents (excluding the header)." Most Usenet newsreaders include a rot13 command; like other pager commands, you should be able to give it the command while in the middle of reading an encrypted message. Assuming that parts of the article have indeed been "rot13"ed—encrypted using "rot13"—this will convert the encrypted portions of the text into something readable. (And the rest of the message, which had been readable, into unreadable, rot13ed text; see the discussion of *rot13* in Chap. 4 and in the "Appropriate Use" section of Chap. 11.)

- STOP READING the current article, marking it as "having been read."
- MARK all articles with the same subject as the current article as "having been read."
- CREATE A FOLLOW-UP MESSAGE for submission to the same Usenet Newsgroup, possibly including (some of) the message yours is a follow-up to (usually with something like **>** in the left margin of each line of the message you're commenting on).
- REPLY PERSONALLY via electronic mail to the person who posted the current article, versus posting a follow-up message to the Usenet, possibly including some or all of the message being replied to (usually with something like **>** in the left margin of each line of the message you're replying to).
- CREATE AND POST AN ARTICLE about a new Subject rather than one that's a follow-up to a current Subject.
- UNSUBSCRIBE to the current Newsgroup.
- SAVE the current article, either saving a copy to a file or piping a copy through one of the commands on your computer (e.g., a Unix command). For example, save a copy in your account, mail a copy to a friend or pipe through **grep** to find specific lines. If you are saving a copy of the article as a file, if you don't specify a file pathname, your newsreader should save it under your home directory with a pathname similar to the current Newsgroup name, in "mail format" (if this file already exists, it should append the new article).

Here's some of **trn**'s paging-level help information:

```
Paging commands:
SP       Display the next page.
x        Display the next page decrypted (rot13).
d        Display half a page more.
CR       Display one more line.
^R,v,^X  Restart the current article (v=verbose header,
         ^X=rot13).
b        Back up one page.
^L,X     Refresh the screen (X=rot13).
t        Display the entire article tree and all its sub-
         jects.
g pat    Go to (search forward within article for) pattern.
G        Search again for current pattern within article.
^G       Search for next line beginning with "Subject:".
TAB      Search for next line beginning with a different
         character.
q        Quit the pager, go to end of article. Leave arti-
         cle read or unread.
j        Junk this article (mark it read). Goes to end of
         article.

The following commands skip the rest of the current article,
then behave just as if typed to the 'What next?' prompt at
the end of the article:

n        Scan forward for next unread article.
N        Go to next article.
^N       Scan forward for next unread article with same
         title.
p,P,^P   Same as n,N,^N, only going backwards.
-        Go to previously displayed article.
<,>      Browse the previous/next selected thread. If no
         threads are selected, all threads that had unread
         news upon entry to the group are considered
         selected for browsing. Entering an empty group
         browses all threads.
[,],{,}  Go to parent/child/root/leaf in thread.
```

### Posting (submitting) articles to Usenet

There are two major ways you can post an article to the Usenet. One, you can do it using the appropriate command in your newsreader program (e.g., the **f** or **F** common in **rn** and **trn**). Alternatively, the computer your Internet account is on may have one or more additional commands, such as **Pnews, Pn,** or **postnews,** which create and post an article to the Usenet—just as you may have a command which lets you create and send an e-mail message without first opening one of your files of e-mail messages. Your article may be a FOLLOW-UP to an existing article, or it may be an article on a new subject.

***Formatting Your Messages to Be Usenet Articles***

Eugene Spafford and Mark Horton, in their periodic informational posting "Rules for Posting to Usenet," advise, "In preparing an article, be aware that other people's machines are not the same as yours." The following is a list of things to keep in mind:

- Except for source, keep your lines under 80 characters, and under 72 if possible (most editors have a "fill" or "format" mode that will do this for you automatically).
- Right-justified text may look "prettier" in some sense, but it is almost always harder to read than leaving ragged right margins. Don't right-justify your article text.
- Most special control characters will not work for most newsreaders.

Even <TAB>s aren't always the same from machine to machine and should be avoided. Many mail agents will strip or remap control characters. In fact, the <SPACE> character is about the only one you can be sure will work consistently—and some systems may strip off "trailing" spaces (space characters at the end of a line). Other things to keep in mind are:

- Pictures and diagrams should not use embedded tabs.
- Refer to articles by Message-ID and never by article number.
- What you think is the previous article is unlikely to be so elsewhere.
- Submissions in a single case (all upper or all lower) are difficult to read.

If it's a follow-up, it may include some or all (preferably some, only what's necessary) of the article(s) you're following up.

You may already have some or all of your message prepared, as file for inclusion or uploading. If you are charged for Usenet/Internet access based on connection time, it may make sense to go off-line (disconnect from your account) while you compose, format, and revise your message. You may post your article only to one Newsgroup—or you may "cross-post" it to several Newsgroups. (Cross-posting is frowned upon, unless you have good reason to, since it consumes yet more network and computer resources than posting to only one Newsgroup.)

There are numerous guidelines regarding creating and submitting articles to Usenet. These guidelines deal with everything from message-formatting recommendations (see Box: Formatting Your Messages to Be Usenet Articles) to why, when, and where (which Newsgroups) to—and *not to*—post your articles to Usenet (see the "Summary of Points to Remember as a Usenet User" and "Tips, Advice, and Suggestions for New Usenet Users" sections in this chapter).

### Canceling articles

Once you have told your Usenet software to post an article you've created, you may be able to stop it, recall it, cancel it, or whatever, but probably not, or not 100 percent. Remember, unlike CompuServe, DELPHI, etc., your message may easily be en route to hundreds or thousands of sites, just like an e-mail message to a mailing list. Some Usenet newsreader programs have a "Cancel" feature that sends out "cancel request" messages following your original message, but you can't be sure that:

- These cancel request messages will go to *all* the sites your original message did

- No one will read your message before it's canceled—if it's canceled
- People who have read your message don't quote, reference, or otherwise talk about it, even after the message itself is canceled
- No one has saved, forwarded, or reposted a copy of your message before the article was canceled at their site.

In other words, don't assume you can call back a message, or erase it, once you've posted. If the computer or site from which you are running your Usenet newsreader (or other posting program) isn't directly connected to the Internet, you *may* be able to kill a message before it gets relayed to at least one other Usenet site (e.g., from your notebook PC running TCP/IP and NNTP or a public-access Unix site linked via dial-up). But you must assume that once it leaves your system, it's beyond your control. So think before posting; compose and edit with a text editor.

## Required, Recommended, and Suggested Usenet Groups to Follow

As you've probably gathered by now, you won't follow all the Usenet Newsgroups available to you—or even a fraction of them. Here's a list of Usenet Newsgroups you *must* (well, ought to) subscribe to and follow and also suggestions for some that you should *consider* subscribing to and following.

### Required Newsgroups for new users

*news.announce.newusers.* Here's where you'll find the basic information, as periodic repostings. As a new Usenet user, you should subscribe to and read through the postings in this group, say, for about a month or until you feel familiar with what's there.

*news.newusers.questions.* This group is worth watching, even though most of these questions won't be of interest to you. You may learn about things you didn't know about and get answers to questions you weren't ready to ask.

### Required Newsgroups for all users

*Every* Usenet user should subscribe to—*news.announce.important*—for important announcements. There are very few postings to this group—perhaps a few per month or year—but subscribing to this group ensures that you'll be alerted to any important general Usenet news.

### Recommended Newsgroups

Newsgroups worth subscribing to in general include:

*news.answers.* A good way to get an "overview" of what's in many of the Usenet groups

*comp.risks.* Helps gain an appreciation for the challenges and problems of technology; one of the Internet's longest-running "magazines," moderated by Peter Neumann *alt.internet.services.* Questions and some answers regarding what's available on the Internet

*rec.humor.funny.* A few topical and other jokes per day; moderated

*clari.feature.davebarry, .missmanners, and .mikeroyko.* Columns by leading syndicated humorists and commentators

## Usenet Netiquette: Usenet Dos and Don'ts

Usenet netiquette begins with the same advice and warnings given for electronic mail, both person-to-person and mailing list. Over the years, the Usenet community has evolved a number of additional conventions and guidelines, reflecting the differences between Usenet and e-mail. Because Usenet is by definition a public medium, it's *essential* that you familiarize yourself with the dos and don'ts that make up the Usenet community's conventions and guidelines. Remember:

- Anything you post may be seen locally and around the world.
- Your postings may easily be quoted or reposted by other people, to other Newsgroups, even other networks and BBSs besides Usenet, without your permission or knowledge. Your postings may also become archived to tape, hardcopy, or CD-ROM, where they may be found and read weeks, months, or years later.
- Just because people *shouldn't* repost or forward something you have sent to Usenet doesn't mean they can't or won't.

It's also important to remember that creating, sending, receiving, and reading Usenet Newsgroup articles involves a substantial amount of computer and network resources. Even though you may not be directly paying for your use of Usenet, it still costs money, and that money is coming from somewhere. If you abuse your privileges as a Usenet participant, you may lose them. Worse, your site may lose some or all of its ability to participate in the Usenet, which can directly affect hundreds or thousands of people. Or your activities can have even graver consequences to entire groups and organizations.

### Summary of points to remember as a Usenet user

Here's a summary of netiquette-oriented points to remember as a Usenet user, taken from Chuq von Rospach's periodically reposted informational message, "A Primer on How to Work with the Usenet Community":

Never forget that the person on the other side is human

Don't blame system admins for their users' behavior

Be careful what you say about others

Be brief

Your postings reflect upon you; be proud of them

Use descriptive titles [in your articles' Subject: lines]
Think about your audience
Be careful with humor and sarcasm
Only post a message once
Please rotate material with questionable content
Summarize what you are following up
Use mail, don't post a follow-up
Read all follow-ups and don't repeat what has already been said
Double-check follow-up Newsgroups and distributions
Be careful about copyrights and licenses
Cite appropriate references
When summarizing, summarize
Mark or rotate answers or spoilers
Spelling flames considered harmful
Don't overdo signatures
Limit line length and avoid control characters

### Some other Usenet netiquette and appropriate-usage issues

Here's some other common questions, concerns, and things to know about Usenet netiquette and appropriate usage:

- *Can I advertise on Usenet?* "Announcement of professional products or services on Usenet is allowed; however, since someone else is paying the phone bills for this, it is important that it be of overall benefit to Usenet." (From "Rules for Posting to Usenet," Mark Horton and Eugene Spafford) A few Newsgroups explicitly allow advertising; elsewhere, stay within the guidelines of your site and the specific Newsgroup.
- *Ownership, privacy, copyright.* "It is generally considered rude to post private e-mail correspondence without the permission of the author of that mail. Furthermore, under copyright statutes, the author of the e-mail possesses a copyright on mail that he or she wrote; posting it to the net or mailing it on to others without permission of the author is likely a violation of that copyright as well as being rude." (From "Rules for Posting to Usenet," Eugene Spafford and Mark Horton)
- *Your opinion is yours, not your company's.* "All opinions or statements made in messages posted to Usenet should be taken as the opinions of the person who wrote the message. They do not necessarily represent the opinions of the employer of that person, the owner of the computer from which the message was posted, or anyone involved with Usenet or the underlying networks of which Usenet is made up. All responsibility for

statements made in Usenet messages rests with the individual posting the message." (From "Rules for Posting to Usenet," Eugene Spafford and Mark Horton)

- *Post responsibly.* "Posting of information on Usenet is to be viewed as similar to publication. Because of this, do not post instructions for how to do some illegal act (such as jamming radar or obtaining cable TV service illegally); also do not ask how to do illegal acts by posting to the net." (From "Rules for Posting to Usenet," Eugene Spafford and Mark Horton)
- *My site doesn't carry a certain Newsgroup.* Individual sites can decide whether or not to carry a given Newsgroup. If you learn about one you want that isn't carried, ask the system or network administrator in charge of the Usenet activity at your site. If your site won't or can't get a particular group you want, you have several options, including:
  - See if you can get access to another Usenet site that *does* carry the group(s) you want. This may involve obtaining another account.
  - See if the Newsgroups you're interested in are available as e-mail lists or via other Internet facilities (e.g., Gopher).
  - Arrange for someone to e-mail you copies of the Newsgroup articles.
  - Become a Usenet site.
- *Use the "distribution" feature, pick appropriate regional hierarchies, to control where your postings go.* If your article is only relevant to users in a certain geographical area, it's inappropriate to send them to the entire continent or the whole planet. Therefore, use the "distribution" feature to restrict distribution to your local area and look for regional hierarchies and groups within them [e.g., "ne.jobs" (New England)].
- *Be considerate with your use of network resources.* "Your individual usage may not seem like much compared to the net as a whole, but in aggregate, small savings in disk or CPU add up to a great deal," notes the "Rules for Posting to Usenet" posting originated by Mark Horton. "For instance, messages offering thanks, jibes, or congratulations will only need to be seen by the interested parties—send these by mail rather than posting them. The same goes for simple questions and especially for any form of 'me-too' posting."

## Rules from a Usenet Site: The Ways of the World

So far, the advice and guidelines you've been reading have come from experienced users and major Usenet honchoes. Granted, the points are all reasonable and consistent. But so far, they're advisories, not mandates. Are there any rules you're obligated to obey? Yes—those set forth by the organization that you have your account with, which you have presumably agreed to obey, as part of the contractual agreement between you and them.

The World, the public-access Internet site run by Software Tool & Die, offers Usenet access to its thousand-plus users, who range from private individuals (such as myself) to staffs of various organizations. For many of the World's users, this is the first time on Usenet or the Internet. Here's text from the World's "Usenet Netiquette and Rules" on-line information (used with permission):

**Some Rules (We Have to Ask You to Honor!)**

Almost no USENET groups allow ANY commercial messages. For example, you can't brag about the great prices at your brother-in-law's hardware store or try to sell anything.

If the topic comes up in a general discussion (for example, in the cooking group people are always asking for recommendations of kitchen knives) it's usually all right to recommend a product you were personally happy with if you have no financial interest in the recommendation.

Similarly, you can gripe about a product you were unhappy with as long as you don't have any financial interest, just personal experience. However, don't be shocked if you get a call from the company the next day, there are more people on these newslists than you might think! When in doubt it's usually better to just let it go by.

There are several groups with names like ne.forsale (ne is New England) where it's ok to sell personal items like your car or dining room set but it's not ok to sell commercial products. For example, if you sell Avon or Tupperware products as a company representative DO NOT pitch these on those groups.

Why not? Well, there are several reasons.

First, because it's been mutually agreed to by everyone on the network. It's part of the deal. There's a general fear that if people were allowed to advertise the network would soon become nothing but advertisements.

Second, a lot of this traffic is carried by corporate and government network and it costs them money to send out these messages. They have no interest in paying to have advertising for someone else's product pass through their computers. In the case of the government they are forbidden from doing this because it would be considered an unapproved government subsidy of those companies doing the advertising.

Finally, it's because if other sites find that commercial messages are coming from this computer they can cut us off the network entirely. That's how it's enforced. We won't allow that to happen so to maintain our connection we will instead have to cut off the individual's access, if we receive legitimate complaints. We would have no choice.

**NO COMMERCIAL MESSAGES ON THE USENET OR ELECTRONIC MAIL NETWORKS!**

Locally, on this machine we can provide plenty of places for you to sell goods and services if that's what you want to do, just ask.

On the other hand, we will not let people bother others by trying to sell them things. It will always be VOLUNTARY whether anyone is exposed to such messages or not.

The only major exception on the USENET is the biz.whatever groups. They are a commercial area and only carried voluntarily by organizations who don't mind this. A lot of places carry these so this might be the place to go if you have a horn to blow.

**Obscenity, Arguing, Illegal, or Obnoxious Behavior...**

In the first place, if you think you're playing a clever prank on someone, a computer or the network, don't.

It's all been done before and almost always just makes people angry. In many cases it may even be illegal, even if your intents were only humorous.

Software Tool & Die, as an Enhanced Services Provider, must cooperate with all investigations of illegal behavior and must do what it can to correct any such situation.

We do not and will not edit posted material actively as a corporate policy. We have no control over lewd or otherwise questionable text people type in unless it is strictly illegal or being complained about as breaking agreed-upon rules of network behavior.

Another area to be careful about is typing in copyrighted materials. The copyright holders can go after you, legally.

As a general rule just keep in mind that you are speaking in public.

## Tips, Advice, and Suggestions for New Usenet Users

An assortment of pointers taken from experienced Usenet participants and other sources follows.

### Bobbi Fox's Rules for Sensible Usenet Use: One User's Advice

Based on half a dozen years of reading and selectively contributing to Usenet and to internal company BBSs, Bobbi Fox (fox@cadse.enet.dec.com) offers the following advice and reminders to newcomers to Usenet:

1. *Think twice about posting. Then wait 48 hours.* Unless you are The Acknowledged Expert in the Field, you are not the only one with the answer. Somebody else will usually respond with what you are going to say, frequently more eloquently.
2. *When you post, Remember Your Audience.* Check your posting for spelling, grammar, and clarity—not only will you get your point across more effectively, but you will also spare yourself tiresome spelling and grammar flames.

2*a*. *Be tolerant, and flame infrequently.* Not all people who post have been blessed with your ability to write coherently without errors in grammar and spelling. Some of them may even be writing in what to them is a second, third, or fourth language. Try to take this into account before flaming. Reread the posting to make sure you understand the point. Remember that newbies forget to add smilies, and may be writing ironically or sarcastically.

3. *Remember Your Audience, Take 2.* Most Newsgroups have *thousands* of "lurkers"—people who read, but never post. You never know who may be among the thousands—ex-lovers, creditors, potential employers, co-workers—and sometimes your boss!
4. *Never write anything you wouldn't want attached to your resume.* See Rule 3.

5. *Take it to E-mail.* If you find yourself repeating your points more than once, try sending E-mail to your "adversary." You will look less foolish, and the rest of us will be grateful!

5*a*. *You are not obliged to respond to E-mail from people you don't know [unless it's part of your job].* Conversely, if you send E-mail to someone, they do not have to respond to you. In fact, they may call it "harassment"—especially if you have flamed them to a crisp, repeatedly E-mail them, or continue to E-mail after they've told you to stop. Many companies and universities have strict policies about E-mail harassment, and you may find yourself without an account.

5*b*. *Posting someone's E-mail to you (without permission) is Not Nice. Don't do it!* It may get you sued. In almost all circumstances, it will incline the rest of the Usenet audience to be sympathetic with the other side.

6. *Remember that the verb "to summarize" has a different meaning on Usenet.* When people ask for E-mailed replies to an issue, and promise that they will summarize, what they mean is that, basically, they concatenate all the mail received together. If you are replying, keep it brief, and with Rules 3 and 4 in mind.

7. *Beware the "September Onslaught," and don't be part of the problem.* Every September, thousands of new college students get their first Internet accounts, and exuberantly flood Usenet with ill-considered postings. DON'T post a reply pointing out their flaws; if you must, send them E-mail—but rest assured that if *you* don't, someone else will.

## Before you post! Read the FAQs and other advice

Before you post to a Usenet Newsgroup, you should "do your homework." For questions:

- Make sure you aren't asking a basic or common question whose answer is already readily available.
- See if the answer's available—Check the FAQs. In particular, check for and read the Newsgroups FAQs or other regular informational posting. Many Usenet Newsgroups have their own FAQ periodically reposted within the group and possibly also to the news.answers Newsgroup. If your question is a general Usenet question, check general Usenet FAQ and other new user postings; also check recent postings to the Usenet news.newusers.questions Newsgroup.

In general, before posting an announcement, follow-up to a discussion, new topic, etc.:

- Make sure your posting is appropriate. Some Newsgroups are for discussion but not announcements, etc. Few other than in the talk. hierarchy are for challenging the basic premises—(e.g., don't complain about why you hate classical music in the classical music group).
- Read the Newsgroup before posting a question. If your question pertains to

a specific Newsgroup, and you know which Newsgroup that is, subscribe to or otherwise read other user's messages before posting one of your own.

- Pick your Newsgroup(s) and distribution carefully. The worldwide, replicated-broadcast copy nature of the Usenet means that each message posted consumes a nontrivial amount of network and computer resources. So try not to send your message to more than one Newsgroup or to a wider distribution area than necessary. For postings of geographically limited interest, see if there's an appropriate hierarchy [e.g., ba. (Bay Area) and ne. (New England), etc.].
- Avoid "agreement" messages. Messages like "I agree with what <so and so> just said," "Me too," "Good for you!," and the like aren't adding any value to discussions; don't waste resources with them.
- Don't post personal messages; use e-mail. If you want to send a reply or message to an individual, use e-mail rather than posting your message to the entire group of people following the Newsgroup.

Read frequently; Post infrequently: In general, as a new user, you should plan to participate in the Usenet primarily as a *reader*. As you'll see in all advisory postings, new users are discouraged from posting for at least their first month; all users are discouraged from posting frivolously and encouraged to check out other resources before posting queries. Each Usenet posting, as you'll be continually reminded, has the potential to consume resources on hundreds, even thousands of computers around the world, along with the network resources to get the article copies there. The resources involved for a single message may not necessarily be much—but it adds up. Given that much of the computer and network resources are volunteer, low-priority, or individually funded, it's important that you *not* "help run up the bill" without good reason.

## Basic Usenet Vocabulary

Usenet users and postings make use of a number of "Usenet-isms"—terms, phrases, expressions, and abbreviations peculiar to the Usenet, as well as many also in use elsewhere in the Internet e-mail activity and on other BBSs. Here's a short list of common Usenet-isms included in the Glossary:

article

/dev/null

dot sig, sig file, .signature

flame

feed, Newsfeed

join

kill file

line eater

net.gods

net.police

Newsgroup

newsreader

NNTP

post, posting

rot13

smileys, smileyfaces, emoticons

spoilers, spoiler warnings

string

subscribe

summarize to the list

thread

Popular abbreviations and their meanings, such as BTW, IMHO, IMNSHO, WRT, and YA are also included.

## For More Information about Usenet, Usenet Software, etc.

The best place to start for Usenet information is within the Usenet itself. Check the FAQs and other periodic postings in the news.newusers.announce Newsgroup; also consider trying the news.newuser.questions and alt.internet.services Newsgroups. If you don't have Usenet access, or the postings you're looking for aren't currently available, they should be available via anonymous-FTP file transfer or e-mail from one or more sources—also perhaps via Gopher or WAIS.

One good source for the Usenet periodical postings is pitmanager.mit.edu, via anonymous-FTP in /pub/usenet/news.answers or by e-mail. To get started, send e-mail to mail-server@pit-manager.mit.edu with the following in the message body:

```
send usenet/news.answers/news-newusers-intro
help
```

For more information about your newsreader program, check for the online manual page (enter **man <your-program-name>**). These documents should provide comprehensive, if somewhat terse, information and may also include pointers to other useful documents. Also see if other documentation is available.

You can also check the on-line help and information files and facilities on your computer and at your site.

Chapter

# 7

# Remote Login with *telnet*

*"How can you be in two places at once when you're not anywhere at all?"*

*"If you lived here, you'd be home by now."*
*The Firesign Theatre*

This chapter talks about one of the major uses of the Internet—*remote login* (**telnet**), the Internet facility you use to do remote login. In this chapter you'll learn:

- What remote login is
- Why it's useful
- How to use the Internet **telnet** remote login facility, including about half a dozen of its most useful commands
- Several popular uses for **telnet**
- Netiquette regarding the use of remote login

## Astral Projection for Computers

Remote login is a lot like astral projection for computers, as illustrated in Figure 7.1. In astral projection, you visualize some distant person and suddenly, Boom, instead of being in your own body, it seems as if you're in some other, distant body.* You "see" what their eyes see, and when you "give your body a command" like "pick up that glass up milk," you're commanding this

*For example, the DC Comics character DeadMan, the still-Earthbound spirit of circus acrobat Boston Brand, would routinely possess people's bodies to interact with the real world. Over at Marvel Comics, Dr. Strange often seemed to send his astral self out as casually as you'd walk out to get a quart of milk.

Figure 7.1 Remote login is a lot like astral projection.

remote body to move. Similarly, as a computer user, you often want to use computers that aren't where you are. Remote login is a way to become a user of a computer other than the one you're directly connected to, using your computer as a terminal.

## Remote Login: Getting There from Here

The odds are good that there are programs you want to use and files you want to access that aren't on your computer but are available—on other computers. One way to do this would be to get a copy of that program and run it on your computer. (We'll look at how to get copies of things in Chap. 15.) But suppose that isn't possible. Perhaps the program can't be run on your computer, or you aren't allowed to make a copy. Maybe your computer is far too slow, the program takes up more storage than you have available, your computer cannot understand the program, or you need access to data that also is stored on the other computer.

Another way to solve your problem would be to go to where these other computers are. If the other computer is down the hall, or elsewhere in the building, you can get there by a few minutes' walk. If the other computer is, say, at the Cornell Supercomputer Center, in upstate New York, and you're located in Springfield, Iowa, or in Edinburgh, Scotland, you can't go from where you are to that other computer's location quite that easily. You could travel there. But this would take a lot of time. For a month-long project, it might be justifiable—although think of the nuisance. You'd have to leave your office, be away from the rest of your office, information, and equipment—and disrupt your personal life. For only a few minutes' or hours' worth of access—or you don't have time and budget to travel—you want to get access some other way. (Plus you might have to wait in line to use the system or find it not working.)

Computer networking was invented to solve problems like this. In fact, if you started programming before the early 1970s, chances are you didn't even have direct terminal access to the computer—you wrote your programs out by hand, keypunched them onto decks of Hollerith cards, which were fed into the computer, and got back reams of printout. At best, you were able to work at a console located a few feet from the computer.

As you read in Chap. 1, terminals and terminal access networking were invented to "stretch the wire" between offices and these computers. Telecommunications, using modems, in turn allowed computer traffic to be sent over telephone lines, enabling you to be even further away from your computer. If you have a PC at home, it probably isn't connected to a network; when you want to access another computer, you need to establish a connection through a modem and a phone line. If you use any computer BBSs or any of the popular on-line services like America On-Line, CompuServe, DELPHI, or GEnie, you've had experience doing this. The same is true if you've accessed computers at your workplace or school this way. However, as mentioned elsewhere, connections like this require having modems at both ends, are usually relatively slow—2400 to 9600 bps—and the cost is often directly related to how much time you spend with this connection open—even if you spend 95 percent of it sitting in front of the keyboard thinking and reading output from the remote system.

Most computers within organizations, however, *are* on a network. The network can be used to provide connections between your computer and authorized remote systems. This means that if your computer is connected to the Internet, directly or through your organization's LANs, you can connect via the Internet to remote systems and, where appropriate and allowed, do a remote login.

Remember, the Internet consists of thousands of interconnected networks and hundreds of thousands of computers connected to these networks. As an Internet user, you're at a computer which is connected. Since your computer already has a network connection, you can take advantage of this and log in to these remote computers by having your computer establish a network connection and emulate a terminal that is connected to this remote system.

The original ARPAnet was created partly to let researchers do exactly this—log in to remote computers—in a way that let them share the expenses and resources of the network in common. Today, users continue to use the Internet for remote login, from terminals, PCs, and workstations to systems supporting library catalogs, on-line databases, special applications, and a growing number of pay-for-use services like Dialog, Mead Data, and more.

## To Connect, Emulate a Terminal

Most user access to computers is done from terminals. You may be connected to your computer by a terminal, or you may be on a PC or workstation all your own. In any case, to access the desired remote computer, you need to find a way to "pretend" to be a terminal. One interesting thing most computers can do is "emulate" a terminal, which in turn then talks to other computers. This is done by having your computer run a type of program usually called a *communications* package or a *terminal emulator*.

Your computer is already doing whatever is involved in taking input from your keyboard and sending output to your screen, so it isn't much of a stretch to have it "pass through" your terminal input and output to some other computer. The commands you type or mouse at your keyboard are executed by that remote system; the system output that would be directed there shows up on your screen. From the perspective of any other users on this system, you appear to be simply another user (i.e., you haven't "gained control" of this remote computer) in a technological equivalent of astral projection (or demonic possession, if you prefer). For science fiction fans, it's a lot like establishing a Waldo connection via the network—or a very limited form of virtual reality. This is what nearly all "communications programs" for personal computers (such as ProComm, CrossTalk, MicroPhone, and PC-Talk) do to let you dial up BBSs, CompuServe, and other remote systems.

## What Remote Login Lets You Do

The Internet's remote login facilities, combined with the connectivity provided by the Internet, gives you access to an ever-growing universe of information and systems. For example:

- On-line library systems and their catalogs and databases
- Supercomputers (assuming you have an account and authorization to use them)
- Weather, geographic, and other information, from on-line databases or near-real-time information from live instruments
- Soda and candy machines, to see what's in stock

Remote login via the Internet also lets you connect to your own hosts, over the network, from elsewhere. You may be visiting another organization connected to the Internet or at an event, such as the Interop Conference or at a user's group meeting, where workstations are available, from which you can **telnet** to your home host, across the Internet, and log in. To other users on that system, you simply appear as another user who has logged in (although they can easily determine that you've accessed the computer via remote login). The Hanover Hackers caught by Cliff Stoll used the Internet's **telnet** facility as their primary mechanism to "hop" from computer to computer around the Internet.

Basically, what's going on is called "remote login." When you run **telnet,** your local system:

- Opens a connection to the specified remote system
- "Pretends" to this remote systems that it is a terminal, rather than a computer
- Acts to you as a terminal
- Forwards your input as *its* output to the remote system, which it takes as terminal input
- Forwards the remote system's output back to you

Interactive login connections typically generate small amounts of traffic, particularly from you to the computer, plus, often, a fair amount of "dead air." In most cases, user input consists of short command lines, often containing a single word or letter. The computer returns anywhere from a few lines to many screenfuls of information. And we tend to spend seconds to minutes reading this, thinking, or considering what we're doing next. With a dedicated connection, such as dialing up from a terminal and modem, this means most of the line's bandwidth is being wasted.

## telnet: Remote Login for TCP/IP Users on the Internet

Over the years, various computer manufacturers have invented facilities which allow their users to log in remotely from one computer to another. For example, Digital's VAX/VMS operating system uses one called SET HOST. Some old IBM computers called this facility "pass through." In the OSI open protocol specification, this function is called VTAM, for Virtual Access Terminal Method. Within the Internet, the most commonly used method is a facility called **telnet,*** which is the name of the TCP/IP protocol used to support remote login sessions and also the name of the TCP/IP remote login program. The **telnet** protocol defines how local and remote computers "talk" to each other to support a remote login session, for example, what EndofRecord terminator will be used. The **telnet** command is the software you invoke, by issuing (or selecting) the **telnet** command.

Like FTP (the TCP/IP file transfer protocol used on the Internet), **telnet** runs over TCP/IP and assumes that TCP/IP protocols are taking care of network-level activities such as error correction and ensuring that packets get routed between your computer and the remote one properly. Because TCP/IP is strongly associated with Unix, it is often thought of as a Unix command; if you have a system running a version of Unix, or a Unix-like system, TCP/IP functions such as **telnet** are mostly included. However, **telnet** is a TCP/IP command. You don't have to be running Unix or a Unix-like operating system to support **telnet.** As indicated in Chap. 2, versions of **telnet** and other TCP/IP functions are available for nearly every popular computer hardware

*That's *telnet,* not *Telenet.* Telenet was one of the first public packet-switching networks, started up by Bolt Beranek and Newman in the 1970s. BBN subsequently sold Telenet to GTE. As of early 1992, Telenet had been bought most recently by Sprint, who promptly renamed it SprintNet, although you still see the Telenet name in places.

and operating system, including shareware and free public domain software (see App. A). **telnet** and other TCP/IP software can be run on everything from supercomputers and mainframes to personal computers and even notebook portables, running everything from VAX/VMS to DOS, Microsoft Windows (as a "True Windows Application"), MacOs, and others.

You invoke the **telnet** facility via the **telnet** command. You may often see **telnet** used as a verb in discussions (e.g., "First, **telnet** to demo.laputa.org and login as..."). Other TCP/IP commands can be used to perform remote login, notably the **rlogin** command (remote login), or you can open an X Window. Also, many facilities will perform remote login implicitly. Many of the new "Internet navigators" will perform the remote login sequence automatically (just like many telecomm programs and on-line service navigators can be "scripted").

## How telnet works

**telnet,** like many other Internet facilities, is a "client-server" type of service (see the discussion of "Clients and Servers: How Many Internet Tools Work" at the beginning of this part of the book). To log in to a remote computer, **telnet** facilities must be on your system and on the remote system; these two programs work together to enable your input to be passed along to other facilities on the remote system. When you do a remote login from your computer, you work with the *client* portion of the **telnet** program on your computer; the **telnet** client in turn interacts with the **telnet** *server* program on the remote system.

The **telnet** client program, running at the "originating" side of a **telnet** session, is responsible for:

- Taking your commands
- Processing and performing them
- Sending the appropriate information to the **telnet** server program on the remote system
- Receiving and displaying output from server commands on your screen

The *server* program does the corresponding activities, receiving your commands from client for execution and sending the output of any of these commands back to the *client* program, which in turn displays them to you. When using **telnet,** once you have established a connection, most of what you do is with the facilities on the remote system, and **telnet** itself becomes "transparent" to your activities. For example, if you request a directory listing on the remote system, instead of the command being executed on your system, listing files from your local computer's file system, the command is passed to the remote system you're logged into and executed by that system. In turn, instead of the output from that command being sent to a screen that is directly attached to a workstation on that system, the **telnet** server program receives the output and passes it along the network to your **telnet** client, which then displays it on your screen.

### Do you need to learn every system's version of telnet?

You may encounter different versions of **telnet** if:

- You **telnet** from one of the remote systems you've accessed (see the discussion of "**telnet**-through" here and in Chap. 8)
- You have accounts on multiple systems with different versions of TCP/IP
- You've got a workstation and a portable computer
- You're borrowing a friend's system (e.g., to log in over the Internet to your home system to check your e-mail)

For **telnet,** what's most important is to learn how to use the version of **telnet** on systems that you are telnetting *from*; since you don't interact directly with the **telnet** server on the other systems. [On Unix systems, you can "detect" the presence of the server, as an executing process invoked by you, by issuing the Unix **ps** (show processes) command, if you're curious.]

Differences among versions of FTP may be more important. If you are more familiar with the FTP version on the "other end," you may want to **telnet** across and do your FTP from the other side of the connection. (Differences among versions of **telnet** tend to be less important, as most people invoke it and connect directly, rarely giving any commands directly to **telnet.**)

## Using telnet

Now that you've got a sense of what the **telnet** remote login facility is all about, it's time to learn the basics of how to use it. Using **telnet** is very easy and straightforward—so much so that you'll usually forget you're connected via **telnet** versus directly.

### Things you'll need to know to use telnet

To use **telnet,** you'll need to know:

1. What system you want to connect to. If you are using a traditional version of **telnet,** this means knowing the target system's Internet name (e.g., jabber.wock.com) or IP address (e.g., 123.45.678.90). Many of the new versions of **telnet,** and many Internet "navigators," let you save and select system addresses as entries from a list, as names (e.g., BORIS) or as icons.
2. A user-ID, password, and account on the target system. Just as you need an account on your own system and a user-ID and password to log in, you need one on most remote systems. For many systems, however, you may need different account information—or none. If the remote system is one you work on, you probably have an account established—and if you don't, you'll need one.

You should apply the same standards of security and "user etiquette" for using this account as you do your own. Don't waste computer time or storage;

guard your password carefully and report strange or problematic events to your system manager. As with system names and addresses, some **telnet** and Internet navigator facilities may supply your user-ID and password automatically to the remote system.

Many systems and programs are available to the general public for reasonable use. Commonly, you access systems like this by using a standard user-ID, such as "guest," and either no password (just enter <RETURN>) or by providing your Internet address as the password, to enable the system manager to track who's using what. Often, the appropriate user-IDs and password (if any) will be posted or displayed in the "banner" when you establish a connection.

Many systems that offer pay-for-use access, such as The World, NetCom, and Express Access Public-Access Internet Account Providers and on-line service providers such as DELPHI, let you request an account or get basic information, by log in as "new" with no password. Once you are logged in to this remote system, you may access programs such as:

- A Unix shell, either character-oriented or GUI
- A menuing shell which gives you a set of specific options
- A specific application, such as Gopher, HYTELNET, WAIS, archie, or a Free-Net.

---

*Tip: If you have problems using* **telnet.** Here are some common problems you may experience when telnetting to another computer over the Internet and some things you can try to resolve them:

- *Response seems slow.* **telnet** is a reasonably fast, efficient program. If it seems to be running slowly, the problem is more likely due to network or computer problems, such as (1) your network connection being inherently low-bandwidth, or local conditions are slowing it down, (2) the computer you've accessed is heavily loaded (too many users running programs), (3) network-related services may be overloaded (often causing file-serving and name-serving to slow down).
- *How to abort a session.* Use the **telnet** escape character and then close the session by entering "close" at the **telnet** prompt.
- *How to get back to your system without aborting.* Use an escape character.

---

### Invoking telnet

Like most computer programs and utilities, you invoke **telnet** by either entering the program name at the command prompt or clicking your mouse on the appropriate icon or menu choice. You can give the name (or number) of the target system—the one you're going to log in to—along with the command or give the name (or number) to **telnet** once it's started up.

**telnet** is an interactive utility, like the Unix shell and TCP/IP utilities such as FTP, meaning that the **telnet** program displays a prompt (usually

**telnet>**), you enter a command at the prompt, and hit <RETURN> or click your mouse or whatever; **telnet** executes this command and then displays a prompt to indicate it's ready for your next command; when you're done, you quit, and get back the system prompt.

**telnet**'s interactive nature may not be obvious if you include the target system name when you enter the **telnet** command. Here, **telnet** skips offering you its **telnet>** prompt and attempts to establish the requested connection; depending on how you exit from **telnet,** you may get the **telnet>** prompt or may be returned to the system prompt or menu. Here's a nontechnical summary of what happens when you invoke **telnet** and open a connection to another computer over the network:

1. The client **telnet** program running on your computer the network tries to establish a connection to the specified system, for example:

```
% telnet dormouse.treacle.wonderla.com
Trying 158.100.4.3
```

2. At the target system, a corresponding **telnet** server program is started up.
3. The server invokes the appropriate program on its system, usually an operating system shell which asks for a user-ID, possibly displaying your network name and address as who it believes you are; in most cases, you'll need to give a user-name and password before you can do anything else.

```
% telnet dormouse.treacle.wonderla.com
Trying 158.100.4.3
Connected to dormouse.treacle.wonderla.com
Escape character is '^]'.

UNIX System V Release 3.2 (dormouse.treacle.wonderla.com) (ttyp1)

login: aliddell
Password:
```

4. Once logged in and accepted as a user, the **telnet** server program passes along your input sent by your **telnet** client and sends back output, done transparently. When **telnet** is awaiting commands from the user, it displays the prompt **telnet>.**

```
% telnet
telnet> set esc CONTROL-Y
escape character is '^Y'.
telnet> open dormouse.treacle.wonderla.com
Trying 158.100.4.3
   ...
   (Telnet escape character issued during session
telnet> close
telnet> Connection closed.
telnet> quit
%
```

### telnet command synopsis

The general synopsis for the **telnet** command is:

```
telnet [ remote-system [port-number] ]
```

If you include the hostname, **telnet** attempts to open a connection.* For example:

```
telnet jabber.wock.com
```

If you also include the port-number, **telnet** attempts to open a connection specifically to the numbered port. In most cases, this is unnecessary; port-numbers are needed only for specific applications, such as opening an X-window. If you omit the hostname, **telnet** gives you its prompt; to open a connection, you must then give the **open** command and the hostname. For example:

```
% telnet
telnet> open jabber.wock.com
```

**telnet input mode.** Once you have successfully opened a connection to the remote computer, **telnet** enters input mode. In input mode, all text you enter to the keyboard, and possibly all mouse or cursor activity, is sent to the remote computer—all characters and activity, that is, except those recognized by other programs and computers between your fingers and the remote computer. For example, **telnet** won't pass along:

- The **telnet** Escape character (explained shortly)
- If you are connected from a PC:
  - Any TSR (terminate-and-stay-resident) and task-switching programs such as Pop-Up Browsers, DesqView, Windows, etc.
  - Functions from your telecommunications program (e.g., ProComm, for uploading, downloading, invoking a transfer protocol, etc.)

As a rule, your input will be sent by **telnet** every time you enter a character or there is mouse or cursor action. This is called "character at a time" input mode. In some cases (which you may never encounter), your **telnet** connection will use "line by line" input mode. Here, text you enter is echoed (displayed at the screen) by your local system; when you complete a line (usually by entering <RETURN> or clicking on your mouse), the entire line is sent to the remote computer.

**telnet command mode.** In **telnet** command mode, your keyboard and mouse input go to **telnet**; you can give any **telnet** commands (including commands to be passed back to your shell). Unlike most versions of Unix and DOS, in

---

*There are other parameters and switches you can enter at the command line, but you don't need to know any of them as a beginning user, and they will vary from system to system. When you are ready—or simply curious—consult the on-line manual page or your reference manual.

entering **telnet** commands, you only need to type enough letters for **telnet** to uniquely determine what command you are specifying. For example, to give the **telnet** "close" command, any of the following will do: **cl, clo, clos.**

**Returning to telnet input mode.** While you are connected to the remote computer, you can return to **telnet** command mode to issue commands to your **telnet** client program by entering the **telnet** Escape character. Most versions of **telnet** use the character Control-] (Control-Right-Bracket) as their Escape character; however, the default value can be reset by your system administrator or often by commands in your local software configuration files.

As a rule, **telnet** displays the initial Escape character just before opening a connection. You can display and change the Escape character during a **telnet** session using the **telnet** "set" command (see below). When you're in **telnet**'s command mode, your regular command-line editing features should work (e.g., delete-character, delete-previous-word, delete-entire-line).

## Essential telnet Commands to Know

**telnet** has about a dozen and a half commands (also called subcommands). The names for these commands are highly standardized across the many implementations of **telnet** in use on systems across the Internet, helping ensure you'll be able to use **telnet** on new computers with a minimum of difficulty.*

It's helpful to essential to know about half a dozen of **telnet**'s commands to use **telnet** as a beginning user:

| | |
|---|---|
| **!** | Invoke a subshell |
| **close** | Close current connection |
| **display** | Display current values of **telnet** parameters |
| **help, ?** | Display summary information about all or specified commands |
| **open** | Connect to a site |
| **quit** | Close **telnet** connection and exit **telnet** |
| **set** | Set new value for specified operating parameter(s) |
| **status** | Display status information |
| **Z (CONTROL-Z)** | Suspend action; return to current Unix shell |

These should be all you need for most common remote login activity—and there's no point in learning more until you've learned and mastered all these. (You can, in fact, do remote login with **telnet** without knowing *any* of **telnet**'s commands by using just the **telnet** command itself and being able to quit from the remote system. However, knowing these **telnet** commands gives you basic information and control over your remote login activity.)

*Various versions of **telnet** may not support all the same names for **telnet** commands. You should be able to locate the functions you want by reading through **telnet**'s on-line help text displayed in response to the **telnet help** or **?** command or the on-line manual page for **telnet** on your system.

**open remote-system [ port ]**

This command opens a **telnet** connection to the specified remote system, identified by either its Internet network name or address. To connect to certain applications, such as Gopher servers, MUDs (Multi-User Dungeons), or graphic-oriented WAIS servers, you may need to give a port-number:

```
telnet> mud.jabber.wock.com 105
```

**close**

This closes the current **telnet** session (logs you out from the remote system, if necessary, and closes the connection) and returns to **telnet** command mode (as opposed to exiting **telnet** as well).

**quit**

This closes any open **telnet** session and exits **telnet.** Entering an End-of-File (EOF) character (usually Control-D), when you're in **telnet**'s command mode is the same as entering **quit.**

```
telnet> <Control-D>
%
```

**Z, Control-Z**

If you invoked **telnet** from a Unix shell that supports *job control,* such as the c-shell (**csh**), entering Control-Z suspends the current **telnet** session ("freezing" it and putting it in the background) and brings your keyboard and display to your local system's Unix shell. It shouldn't matter what you were doing on the remote system at the time you entered Control-Z. (Or you can enter the **telnet** escape character; at the **telnet** prompt, enter **z.**) This feature lets you give other commands to your computer such as to check or send mail without shutting down your current **telnet** session. You return to the current session by entering the Unix **fg** command at the beginning of the line. **z** or Control-Z works only if you're using a Unix shell that supports job control, such as the C-shell (**csh**).

**display [ telnet-variable ]**

This displays the current value of specified or all **telnet** variables.

**? [ help command ]**

This command displays **telnet**'s one-line summary of the command; if you don't specify a command, **telnet** prints a list of its commands and one-line help information.

**Set *telnet*-variable value**

This sets the specified **telnet** variable to the given value; if you use "off" as the value, the function is turned off for the duration of the session (or until you give it a value again). For example:

```
telnet> set escape X
```

sets the **telnet** Escape character to X.

### Other telnet commands

The nine or ten **telnet** commands just discussed should be all you need for most common remote login activity—and there's no point in learning more until you've learned and mastered all these. It is worth knowing that **telnet** does have other commands and capabilities and what they are. Once you've mastered these basic **telnet** commands, you may want to locate on-line or printed documentation for the version of **telnet** you have available, especially if you are a programmer and software developer.

Other commands commonly found in **telnet** include:

logout

mode

status

send

slc

toggle

type

unset

## Popular Uses for telnet

Several specific uses of **telnet** are worth discussing since you may need to know about them at some point; they are phoning home, anonymous-**telnet,** telnetting to public-access accounts for services and systems, and **telnet**-through.

### Using telnet to phone home to read e-mail, etc.

One of the most popular uses of the **telnet** remote login facility is to phone home and check for e-mail messages—to connect across the Internet to your account on your main computer, log in, and check for, read, answer, and send e-mail. Increasingly, meetings for Internet-related activities will often have facilities set up for this purpose. Since 1988, for example, the INTEROP show typically has several e-mail terminal rooms or areas in its primary exhibition halls and hotels. Here, dozens of terminals (often including color X Window terminals) are lined up—all connected up to the Internet. I've also seen similar facilities at meetings of the Internet Engineering Task Force, NEARnet user meetings, and even some vendor presentations and press conferences.

At any hour, you'll see people sitting there checking their e-mail, staying in touch with their workmates (and often family). In addition to checking e-mail, they may be writing, running, or debugging programs, transferring files, reading Usenet News, and doing other urgent work-related activities. This is a great convenience—and added testimony to the degree that many people (including me) have come to use and rely on the Internet for purposes of work and communication.

---

*Tip:* Be sure you remember or have written down the full "name" of the computer your Internet account is on (e.g., world.std.com, jabber.wock.com, laputa.org) as well as your user-ID. (And remember your password.) If possible, also write down and bring along the IP address number for your computer (e.g., 142.29.83.77). Sometimes, the network connections at these events will not be able to reliably access a "name server" which converts your Internet address into the numerical IP address. By having this information at hand, you can use it to log in and read your mail. Lastly, if you get the chance, try this out before you go on the road. There may be other passwords you need to know, or you may discover you can't access your system through the Internet, for security or other reasons.

---

If you are having trouble accessing the appropriate prompt or otherwise connecting, ask the people around you. There is often something very simple you need to do which no one has bothered to write down in an obvious place, like at every station or on the wall. Also, at some events, notably Internet-oriented conferences and the INTEROP shows, some computers at booths on the show floor may be connected to the Internet. If you ask politely, you may be able to use them to quickly check for urgent e-mail. (Tell them you're testing to see if their claim to Internet connectivity is true—and don't get in the way of people trying to get their job of selling done.)

### Anonymous-telnet

Anonymous-**telnet** refers to systems offering remote login access with a shared account-name. Many Internet resources are available by remote **telnet** login to anyone who can reach them (i.e., anyone who can establish a **telnet** connection). Examples are the on-line information provided by the InterNIC, archie servers, the public-access WAIS system at Thinking Machines, and many user directory and information services. (Be sure to read the Netiquette section for anonymous-**telnet.**)

Accounts have been created with a login name—usually a generic one such as *anonymous* or *guest* or the name of the service, such as *archie* or *gopher.* This access is often referred to as anonymous-**telnet.** Some of these systems don't require any password or simply instruct you to hit <RETURN> at the password prompt. Others require a password, which may be used for some combination of validation and accounting. If you are asked to provide a password, Internet etiquette is to provide your Internet electronic mail name and address. (Remember: even if you don't enter your information, the remote system will know "who you are" and where you're accessing it from—see the section "Electronic Privacy: The Trail of Virtual Breadcrumbs" in Chap. 11.) Often, the login prompt will tell you what to do for user-ID and password. For example, here's a remote login to a system that offers the **netfind** service:

```
% telnet bruno.cs.colorado.edu
Trying 128.138.243.151...
Connected to bruno.cs.colorado.edu.
Escape character is '^]'.

SunOS UNIX (bruno)
Login as 'netfind' to access netfind server
Login as 'da' to access CU Boulder directory assistance

login: netfind
```

Typically, these systems have been set up to provide carefully restricted access to files, directories, and programs; often, when you **telnet** to such systems, you get the login prompt from the application itself rather than from the operating system.

### Using telnet to reach public-access accounts for Internet services

One common use for **telnet** is to access Internet services and resources you want to make use of that aren't available directly from your site. Examples are the Usenet multiuser facilities such as the Internet Relay Chat and Internet navigator and information-finding tools such as archie, Gopher, WAIS, and WorldWideWeb. This is often the case for relatively new and experimental Internet services. If your Internet access is through an organization, your network managers may not want to support these facilities locally. (Universities and public-access Internet sites are most likely to have the fullest set of Internet services.)

To make access to these facilities available, there are usually one or more *public-access accounts* that can be reached via remote login, offering access to a copy of the program or the client portion of the program. These public-access accounts are therefore often referred to as "public-access clients," "public-access sites," or simply "public clients." For example, as of early 1993, there were dozens of public-access Gopher clients and several public-access WAIS clients, two or three public-access clients for WorldWideWeb, and a number of public-access sites for reading Usenet and participating in the Internet Relay Chat and in MUD (Multi-User Dungeon) interactive games. The various portions of the InterNIC, in addition to running Gopher, archie, WAIS, and anonymous-FTP servers to make their information available, have Gopher, archie, and WAIS client programs, which can be accessed by telnetting to the InterNIC sites.

If you have software for the Internet service in question (e.g., archie, Gopher, WAIS), you can simply access it from your own account. If you don't, but you know the Internet address for a public-access client, you can do remote login to that site and account using **telnet** and use the facility as if you had it locally on your computer.

Public-access clients don't always have as many features as versions you can run on your own computer, and using them consumes more Internet resources—but it is a convenient way to gain occasional access to useful Internet services when they aren't available on your own computer elsewhere in your organization.

### telnet-through: doing multiple telnets

**telnet**-through is my term, analogous to IBM's mainframe "pass-through," and refers to the fact that once you've telnetted to a remote system, you can in turn **telnet** from that system to another one. This isn't as silly or useless as it may sound, as you'll see in a minute. Let's say we've started on jabber.wock.com and have successfully telnetted to laputa.org. To then reach topdeck.pinafore.nav.uk, simply give the **telnet** command:

```
telnet topdeck.pinafore.nav.uk
```

and laputa.org will establish a connection, giving the illusion that your keyboard and screen at jabber.wock.com are attached to topdeck.pinafore.nav.uk, like so:

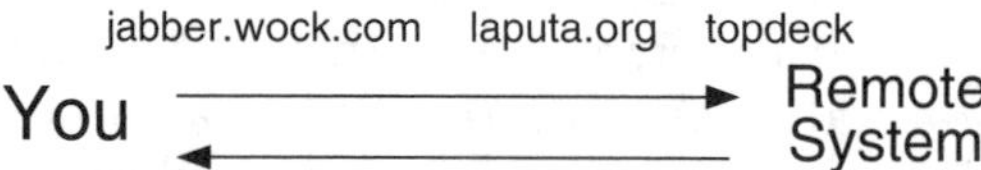


**How this can happen.** It's easy to do this sort of arrangement by accident. Perhaps you've been connected to laputa.org long enough during the session to have forgotten that you had started from jabber.wock.com. Perhaps someone else came along and is borrowing your workstation and wasn't aware that laputa.org was accessed via **telnet** rather than via a more direct connection (e.g., from a terminal server to laputa.org, versus from terminal server to jabber.wock.com and then from jabber.wock.com to laputa.org).

Using laputa.org as an intermediary system is consuming some degree of CPU cycles for the processing and to maintain the connections. So, if you're done with your current **telnet** session, close it out (which you've learned at least three possible ways to do, above) and return to your home host; then **telnet** out again.

**Why you may want to telnet-through.** There is at least one common circumstance under which you may want to **telnet**-through—when you can't reach your target system through a direct **telnet** connection. The most common obstacle will be that your target system lies on the other end of a network that your Internet provider isn't authorized to provide **telnet** or FTP-type connections through. For example, suppose NED, the NASA Extragalactic Database, is connected through one of the NASA networks, which in turn connects to the NSFnet backbone and that your account is on a computer at a site, say, lilliput.org, that does not have the right privileges to make **telnet** connections involving the NSFnet. But suppose you also have an account on a system, big.bear.com, which is connected to NEARnet, and you know (through previous activity) that you can reach NED from big.bear.com. So, once you log in to your account on lilliput.org, you then do a remote login to big.bear.com and from there you do a remote login to NED.

There may be any number of reasons that you didn't just log in directly to big.bear.com, versus telnetting. One, you might be directly connected to laputa.org and all outgoing connections would go through it. Two, you might be connected to laputa.org from home, using a PC and modem, and big.bear.com might not have any dial-in modems attached to it. Three, perhaps big.bear.com has dial-up modems, but their modems might be much slower, say, 2400 baud versus 9600 baud at laputa.org. This wouldn't make any difference in the **telnet** connections. It's the basic limit of how fast your PC screen will fill. Four, perhaps big.bear.com's dial-up modems are already in use. And five, perhaps big.bear.com is a significant geographic distance away, making it an expensive phone call, whereas the **telnet** connection over the Internet is part of the use of service which your laputa.org account fees and laputa.org's payments to its Internet Service Provider cover. Six, you're also doing other activities on your workstation and don't want to shut that all down just to make the most direct connection to big.bear.com.

**Using the telnet escape in telnet-through's.** When you enter the **telnet** Escape character, **telnet** "sees" it and immediately suspends (pauses) this session. But what happens when you enter the **telnet** Escape character if you are telnetted through a series of systems? For example, if you're telnetted from A to B and from B to C and Control-] is the Escape character for **telnet** sessions at A, B, and C, what happens when you enter Control-]? I tried doing just that; in the tests I performed, the Escape character was, as far as I could tell, passed through the closer systems and acted upon by the furthest system (i.e., C). Giving it again "escaped" me increasingly closer to A.

The **telnet** command, **set escape <char>,** lets you define a different Escape character. If you for some reason will be doing a complex multitelnet session, you may want to set a different escape character for each hop (e.g., set A's to Control-}, B's to Control-[, and then leave C's as the default).

## Netiquette for Using Remote Login (telnet)

When you remote login via **telnet** to a remote system, you should always remember that you're using that system's CPU, storage, and other resources as well as network resources. As with any Internet activity, it's therefore important to be aware of the various aspects of your activity: how your remote login **telnet** connection is consuming resources, such as logon time, network bandwidth, remote CPU cycles, and storage, etc.

One reason for this is netiquette—being considerate of the owners of these other resources and other users. Another is cost charges, which may be billed directly to you or to your system's owner, your department budget, etc. Lastly, using network and computer capacity unnecessarily can give planners and managers an inaccurate sense of the demand for services and force them to overbuy. In particular, the network and computer resources that **telnet** usage can affect are discussed below.

### Tieing up the computer resources required for a TCP/IP connection (for too long)

Maintaining a TCP/IP connection for an Internet activity such as **telnet** ties up some degree of resources (buffer space, control resources in the operating system kernal, etc.) on the computer at each end. When you are maintaining a **telnet** connection, for example, you are tying up resources on both your local system and the remote system, even if you aren't doing anything over this connection. The resources are still "assigned" to your activity, and no one else can use them until you free it up by closing the connection.

Most systems have only a limited amount of resources; for this reason, it's considered good manners to close your connection if you aren't using it actively (e.g., expect not to be sending or receiving traffic for 15 minutes or more). (This doesn't necessarily mean you have to stay connected the whole time a program is running or wait until the evening when demand for system resources may be slower. Many Unix systems will let you "detach" using a facility called "nohup." You can launch a process and reconnect to it later or have the output sent to a file—even have the output or job status sent to you automatically by e-mail.) Leaving an open **telnet** connection can also be a potential security breach.

---

*Tip:* Increasingly, many Internet utilities are moving from **telnet**-based access to having a local client for the program on user machines. For example, to query the archie resource locator system, on many systems you can simply type **archie** (or **xarchie**). This invokes a local archie *client,* which then talks over the network to the archie server. (The archie client—and many others—are based on the Prospero system developed by Clifford Neuman of ISI.) These clients and servers are designed to be much more sparing of network and system resources; use them instead of regular **telnet** whenever possible.

---

### Network bandwidth

This can include local bandwidth within your organization, bandwidth on the connection between your computer's site to its access point within the Internet, and the Internet backbone or other networks between your site and the remote system. **telnet** connections tend to use relatively low amounts of network bandwidth, relative to other activities such as doing file transfer via FTP and relative to the bandwidth of most links in the Internet.

If you think about it, this makes a lot of sense—other than the network overhead to maintain the connection itself, you're sending the equivalent of typing at your keyboard, or clicking the mouse, and getting back what's shown on your screen. However, it's something to be aware of. Especially outside the United States there are still many links that are 56 and even 9.6 kbps; here, every bit and byte counts.

### CPU cycles and storage on the remote system

Most likely, you're one of many people on this remote system—and you may be a guest, versus a "regular resident." Just as you would think twice before taking a long hot shower or bath when staying at a friend's house—you'd want to make sure no one else needed to use the bathroom in a hurry, that there was enough hot water, towels, etc. (i.e., if you've **telnet**ted to someone else's system, your work could easily interfere with somebody else's).

CPU cycles are something to be particularly aware of because many computer processes and applications, including simple Unix commands, can be "resource pigs." Jack Haverty, a long-time Internet developer, currently Chief Architect at Oracle Corporation, observes, "When I run Unix **cmp** (compress) command on my workstation, everything else slows down."

Also, Unix lets users start up several activities concurrently, running in the background or in multiple windows. This makes it even easier to overload a remote system. Most Unix systems include a number of facilities which you can use to minimize the "antisocial" nature of your activities. For example:

- *Slow down your background applications.* The Unix **nice** command (not available on all systems) makes a command run slower by taking smaller "timeslices." If you aren't in a hurry, **nice** can therefore reduce the effective load.
- *Defer execution until later, when the demand for the system will be less.* The Unix **at** command lets you effectively submit a command as a batch job to be executed at the specified day and time. **at** is useful for things like starting up long, intensive computing, printing huge documents (to avoid tying up printers during core working hours), or simply doing major processing that you don't need immediately. **at** includes options to notify you by e-mail when the job has been done, even send you the results by e-mail.

On-line storage is a limited resource, especially when you're a guest. Try to keep storage consumption on these accounts to a minimum. Some ways to accomplish this are:

- Transfer files to your home system (via the **ftp** facility, explained in Chap. 8 or by e-mailing files to yourself, as explained in Chap. 5)
- Store files in compressed form, using local compression facilities such as the Unix **compress** and **tar** commands, versions of ZIP, etc.
- Move files to off-line storage such as tape, if available (consult the local system administrator)
- Delete what you don't need or can easily regenerate

If you are strongly concerned that the contents of some files may be lost permanently, ask the local system administrator about their file backup and archiving procedures; once files have been saved to backup, you should be able to get them restored even if you delete them, just as on your local system.

### Netiquette for anonymous-telnet

Anonymous-**telnet** usually means you are accessing a resource provided by somebody else, at their expense. There may be a limited number of access ports available so don't stay on any longer than you have to—somebody else may need access. Also be sensitive to whether you are creating requests that may consume a disproportionate amount of CPU time. *Note:* Not all "anonymous" accounts are meant to be open for general public usage. The facility was created as a way to make computer resources available to a group of people—but the fact that an "anonymous" or "guest" account has been set up does *not* mean it is open to use by the general public.

### Warnings regarding privacy and remote login

The name "anonymous"-**telnet** is somewhat misleading. "Guest" is more accurate. Although you are accessing a system that does not require you to have an authorized account, the fact of your access, and what you do while connected, is not privileged information. The system can easily be keeping track of where connections are being established from (i.e., the system you **telnet** from) and keep a log of your commands, even your entire session's worth of what you type and what is sent back to your system. Equally, system operators can legitimately monitor your activities—after all, you're visiting their property. (Also see the section "Electronic Privacy: The Trail of Virtual Breadcrumbs" in Chap. 11.)

## Summary

**telnet** is the TCP/IP program for remote terminal login used with the Internet community. (TCP/IP includes support for packetization and reliable assured transmission.)

To use **telnet** you:

1. Need to know the target computer's Internet name (e.g., world.std.com) or IP address (e.g., 192.74.137.5 is its IP address)
2. Need to be connected to the Internet.

   At the system prompt, give the command name and target address as follows:

```
% telnet world.std.com
```

or

```
% telnet 192.74.137.5
```

To quit **telnet** while **telnet** is still trying to establish a connection, enter CONTROL-C. To quit once you have established a remote login connection do the following:

- End the remote session and return to **telnet.** Typical commands that will do this include Control-D, logout, quit, and bye.
- Return to **telnet** by typing the current **telnet** Escape character (usually Control-]) and at the **telnet** prompt, enter **close<RETURN>** to terminate the remote session while staying in **telnet** or **quit<RETURN>** to stop using **telnet**

To "pop back" to your computer without closing your **telnet** connection, type the current **telnet** Escape character (usually Control-]) and at the **telnet** prompt, enter **z<RETURN>** or **Control-Z** to put your **telnet** session into the background. When you want to resume your **telnet** session, type **fg<RETURN>** (foreground).

Chapter

# 8

# Transferring Files with FTP

This chapter talks about one of the major uses of the Internet—to transfer files between computers in different locations—and about FTP, the Internet facility you use to do file transfer. FTP stands for *both* File Transfer Program and File Transfer Protocol. [FTP was also used in the name for a company, FTP Software (North Andover, MA), a software company that sells TCP/IP products for PCs—including programs for doing file transfer, not surprisingly.] Transferring files over the Internet, and using FTP, is very easy and straightforward. So is driving along a four-lane highway at 65 miles per hour, when there isn't much traffic and the weather is good and there's enough gas in your tank. However, there are many "gotchas" and often-not-obvious tips for doing file transfers, which can't be covered in a page or two. One reason is that you're often contacting very different computer systems and trying to wend your way through filenames and directory structures organized by someone else—and quite possibly reorganized such that the Readme files or electronic mail postings no longer accurately describe what's where. So it's worth understanding what is going on when you transfer files, and how to use the tools. In this chapter, you'll learn:

- What file transfer means
- How file transfer is done over the Internet
- How to use the **ftp** command
- Important techniques and "gotchas" in using FTP
- Facilities available to locate desired files
- Alternative ways to get the files you want

If you're interest in file transfer is to obtain copies of public-domain and/or shareware programs and other files from other sites on the Internet, you'll also want to read the sections on retrieving files by electronic mail in Chap. 5, the discussions of archie and Gopher in Chap. 10, and Chap. 15.

## Introduction: Why Transfer or Share Files?

File transfer, the moving of files from one computer to another over the network, was one of the original reasons why the ARPAnet was developed and is one of the leading uses of the ARPAnet's "most successful offspring," the Internet.

The use of fileservers, network filing systems, and personal computers has changed, but far from eliminated, the need for file transfer. By using a fileserver—shared-access high-capacity hard disks and other storage devices managed by a more or less dedicated computer—many users can keep their files on one disk and share files with other users. The fileserver approach tends to be cheaper and easier to manage than giving every user big hard disk drives on their own PC. (The definition of "big" changes every few months—a 200- or 300-Mbyte hard disk used to serve dozens of users, where today you can find notebook computers with that much storage and desktop PCs with a gigabyte or more of dedicated hard disk space. But the principle remains the same.)

Equally, network filing systems have eliminated much of the need to explicitly upload and download files between one's own hard disk and the network fileserver, instead making a user's files stored on the server appear to be "local"—directly accessible as if they are on your own hard disk. And for many organizations and activities, the Internet and other networks make possible "wide-area filing systems"—network filing systems accessed by users in different parts of the country and world—and "distributed file systems," which keep users from needing to know that given files and directories are scattered across different computers, locations, and even types of computers. But the need and desire to do file transfer remains and will remain for some time to come.

## The Importance of File Transfer

For many organizations, in fact, the need to move files from one computer, LAN, site, or organization to another is the initial reason they join the Internet. For example, engineers at a development center in upstate New York could transfer files via the Internet to and from another of their company's sites, say, in California, simply by issuing direct commands. Equally, developers at cooperating companies use the Internet to send files back and forth. This would let researchers in California send results of an experiment to fellow researchers in Chicago and Florida (assuming they are all on the network in common). Equally, if our California researchers travel to New York, they could "bring" files along, via the network. (Much less nuisance than carrying around bulky magtapes, hoping the airline security or other machinery didn't muck with the bits, and that there was a compatible tape drive at the other end of the journey. See Box: Argonne Photon Source Sees the Light for an example of this.)

For many of the Internet's millions of users, file transfer to retrieve goodies from the Internet's archives of downloadable on-line files is their first reason

**_Argonne Photon Source Sees the Light_**

The 7-GeV (billion electron-volts) Advanced Photon Source (APS) being constructed at the Argonne National Laboratory in Argonne, Illinois (near Chicago), and scheduled to start up in 1995, will rely heavily on file transfer and other uses of Internet to support its many users. The APS is a high-energy x-ray source, delivering a beam up to 10,000 times brighter than current devices. This will "permit studies of materials as complex as modern alloys, events as fast as chemical reactions, and biological systems as vital as the beating human heart," according to the CICNet DS-3 Working Group Report.

About 3500 scientists and engineers from industry, national laboratories, and medical and educational institutions comprise the research community for the APS. As of May 1993, 15 proposals requesting 19 sectors in the Experiment Hall have been approved. (Because only 16 of a possible 34 sectors will have been funded for construction when APS operations begin in 1996, the facility is already oversubscribed.) Sectors will be managed by Collaborative Access Teams whose membership will range from 10 to 40 researchers from associations of between 2 to 40 institutions each.

Each experiment—materials to be x-rayed and equipment to collect the data—is set up in one of the APS beamlines. The x-ray images captured for one such experiment can easily be about 16 Gbytes per day—and the APS will initially provide 32 beamlines, with up to 69 experimentation beamlines by 1998. In this way, data can be analyzed much more rapidly, decreasing the time between research and application, and experiment scheduling isn't driven by people's travel schedules.

to seek Internet access. Just like services such as CompuServe, GEnie, and DELPHI (not to mention the thousands of BBSs, little and large, around the world) offer their users thousands of program and text files that can be downloaded, the Internet provides a home for, and access to, millions of files, at thousands of sites around the world (see the section on "Anonymous-FTP" in Chap. 15 for more about this).

These archives contain literally millions of files, for use in MS-DOS, UNIX, C, ADA, Apple, Mac, Amiga, VAX, CP/M, and other types of systems. Much of the code is shareware, "freeware," or public-domain software. Many companies are also using the Internet as part of their distribution channel; Apple, for example, makes certain software for the Macintosh available for retrieval via the Internet.

Now that we've seen some of the ways file transfer is used, let's take a look at what file transfer is and how it works, before getting into how to do file transfer on the Internet.

## What Is File Transfer?

If remote login is like astral projection, then transferring files can be considered to be a computer equivalent of mind reading, as Fig. 8.1 shows. First of all, the word "transfer" is somewhat misleading. "File transfer" doesn't really *transfer* a file, anymore than a fax machine transmits the paper you feed into it or copying a videotape transmits the original image.

FTP transfers a *copy* of the file. In file transfer, very simply, you are having one computer "read" the contents of a file over the network and having another computer "listen," putting what it "hears" into a file, as opposed to displaying it on your screen. With network file transfer, you are using the network

**Figure 8.1** File transfer is a lot like mind reading.

to, in effect, carry the file contents, copy the file to a floppy disk (magnetic tape, DAT tape, etc.), convey the physical copy by walking it over ("sneaker-net"), or using car or air couriers for longer distances, and then loading the floppy into the other system. The network (i.e., the Internet) ensures that no noise or errors muck up the packets carrying the file contents across and that the packetized portions get reassembled properly (i.e., you're not "beaming it aboard," *Star Trek* style.)* The same is true when you upload or download a file between your PC and a BBS, CompuServe, or MCI Mail—you're copying the file, not actually moving it. So, for example, using FTP to get a copy of PowerBook_Guide_2nd_ed.hqx from Apple Computer's archives on ftp.apple.com doesn't make it unavailable to other people.

## Why Use File Transfer?

Today, for many businesses, physical delivery of hardcopy has gone the way of the Pony Express—too slow. (See Box: "A Very Short History of File Transfer.") Most businesses and many individuals have turned to the fax machine to speed images of paper, using the phone network; it is faster and cheaper than postal and delivery services can deliver the paper, tapes, and floppy disks.

*Is the Star Trek transporter really transporting you? Or is it sending the information needed to make a copy of you at the other end? The question of whether the transporters in Star Trek are transmitting the original (e.g., Dr. McCoy) or "information on how to build a Dr. McCoy," remains an on-going debate, and the show's "continuity cops" have been inconsistent on this point. A number of excellent science fiction novels have been written on this topic, including: *A for Anything* by Damon Knight, *Rogue Moon* by Algis Budrys, *Ginnaugap* by Michael Swanwyck.

**_A Very Short History of File Transfer_**

The use of networking as a replacement for physical delivery is not new. Back in the beginning of the twentieth century, a candle-making company in the midwest was using couriers on horseback to carry orders from its central office in town to its plant a few miles away. A "bright young man" on staff suggested that a new invention called the telegraph might get the orders there faster.

The company, Procter & Gamble, decided to stick with its existing process. The eager technology champion was none other than Tom Edison, who was instrumental in the subsequent successful mass production of incandescent light bulbs. This dealt a death blow to P&G's candle industry; they turned to another product based on tallow, namely, soap. Moral: Be careful whose ideas you turn down.

Faxing has proven popular to deliver information quickly because it makes use of an existing network that nearly everyone has and knows how to use—the phone system. However, the process of faxing has one serious limitation: it delivers the information in a manner that is hard to reuse and much harder to edit. True, you can often optical-scan text and documents back in, but this process isn't 100 percent accurate, and it can be time-consuming.

For information which is already available in on-line digitized form (i.e., stored in files and directories), a better way to move files from computer A to computer B is via a network. Using networks to do file transfer can be much quicker and easier than transporting physical copies—if:

- The network connection is fast enough, relative to the size of the files you want to transfer, and not too full with other traffic. (There's an old saying, "Never underestimate the bandwidth of a truck," referring to a truck filled with computer tapes or disks. For example, a station wagon delivering data on 1/4-inch DAT tapes to a site 200 miles away may offer effective bandwidth of about a gigabyte per second.) Spending $25 for a CD-ROM holding half a gigabyte of software may be easier than downloading all night long—and Internet software and documents are increasingly available in CD-ROM form.
- The price is right
- The network goes between you and where you want to go.

As with faxing, the phone system offers a nearly ubiquitous network reaching almost everyone who wants to transfer information to and from a computer. However, relative to the high-speed, low-error requirements of computer file transmission, many telephone systems—and most home connections—aren't good enough. In offices and organizations, workstations tend to be connected these days to LANs.

As with remote login and e-mail, the Internet offers an increasingly convenient tool for file transfer. From your access to the Internet, which you have directly through your organization's network or by dialing one phone number, you can move files to any number of other systems and retrieve files from hundreds of archive sites. To do this, you use the FTP command.

## File Transfer Programs and Protocols

FTP, like **telnet,** Gopher, and other Internet facilities you'll use, is a client-server facility. (See the discussion of "clients and servers" at the beginning of Part 2.) To send or receive files between a pair of computers, you need a file transfer program running on each: the FTP program on your system, often referred to as the *client,* and the FTP program running on the remote computer, called the *server.* The FTP client program is responsible for:

- Taking your commands
- Telling the FTP server what to do
- Displaying output from FTP server commands on your screen
- Reading specified files that are in your file system (hard or floppy disk, usually) and sending them via the network to the FTP server or receiving files sent by the FTP server and writing them as files on your computer's file system. (Some versions of FTP can actually control transfers between a second and third system.)

The FTP *server* program does the corresponding activities, receiving the results of your commands from the FTP client and executing these commands from your FTP server, such as creating files based on what you send and sending files based on what you request.

The two programs doing the file transfer must have, and "agree on," a *file transfer protocol.* Protocols define how computer programs talk with each other; a file transfer protocol includes the commands each must understand, the signals they send like "read to send," "file will be ASCII," "here comes the name of the file," and in what format the bits and bytes are being sent. If you've ever uploaded or downloaded files from a BBS or one of the conferencing services like CompuServe or between computers at your office, you've probably run into file transfer programs and protocols, such as Kermit, X-Modem, Y-Modem, or Z-Modem.

### Error correction and reliability

File transfer protocols such as Kermit, X-Modem, and MNP typically include features like error-correction and compression:

*Error correction,* which ensures that file contents are received accurately—particularly essential when you're sending databases and executable programs—was important because these PC-oriented programs were designed to support uploading and downloading across potentially noisy connections (such as your home phone line).

*Compression* features use a variety of techniques (such as looking for repeated characters and phrases) to make the files being sent appear shorter.

Compression reduces the amount of time it takes to transfer a file; when the BBS you're downloading from charges by the minute, every opportunity to reduce costs makes a difference. (Of course, many users choose to spend the same amount of time and money but get more.) Increasingly, archived files will already have been compressed, which also reduces their on-line storage requirements.

## What Is FTP?

As noted at the beginning of the chapter, FTP stands for (1) File Transfer Program, the program in the TCP/IP protocol suite used by computers on the Internet to perform file transfers and (2) file transfer protocol, which is the protocol used by FTP programs to talk to each other.

The TCP/IP File Transfer Protocol lets you establish a network connection to another computer—using an FTP program such as the one that comes with a Unix system or is bought as part of a TCP/IP product for a PC or Mac—and then transfer files, groups of files, and even entire directories between them. The transfer can be in either direction: from your system to the remote system and from the remote system to your system. In a given session of FTP use, you may do some of each. (Some versions of FTP even let you perform file transfers between two *other* computers—as long as they're on the network, and support FTP, of course—giving the commands from yours.)

Again, to transfer files, you need FTP running on both your computer and the remote computer. The FTP program that you invoke on your computer, when you succeed in opening a connection to the remote computer, causes the FTP facility on this computer to run. When you give commands to FTP on your computer, it passes them along to FTP on the remote computer, relays any responses, such as a request for a directory listing, back to you; the two FTPs also manage the reading and writing of files between their respective computers' file systems.

FTP doesn't include error correction. It doesn't need to, because FTP runs over TCP/IP, and TCP/IP was designed to support highly reliable network service, including error detection and correction. TCP/IP networking also provides another level of reliable service. As you read earlier, TCP/IP moves traffic across the Internet *routing* them—determining the appropriate path to use and then sending your packets along this path. The routing method used by TCP/IP is "dynamically adaptive." This means that if there is a problem in a portion of the path currently being used, such as a link going out of service, a router failing, or congestion from other traffic surges, the network will, most likely, seek out the next best available alternate path. You may see little or no delay due to this.

This aspect of reliability is certainly valuable when you're moving large files. With older networks and protocols, even a brief minor problem such as a burst of line noise could kill a multihour file transfer that was nearly done—and it would have to be started up all over again. Protocols like TCP/IP have done much to eliminate this kind of hair-tearing problem. (Compression programs, like **tar,** ZIP, BinHex, and StuffIt, deal with related issues of reducing file size, packaging, and encoding. More about this soon.)

So as you can see, a network such as the Internet, because it runs on a robust protocol like TCP/IP, inherently provides the essential features to assure that the contents of your files (and all other traffic) are transferred accurately, through the Network and Data Link portions of its network protocols. However, you still need a program to help specify and transfer files. On the Internet, that facility is FTP.

## Starting Up an FTP Session

Very simply, you start an FTP session by:

- Starting the FTP program
- Identifying the computer you want to connect with. You do this by giving its Internet address (a Fully Qualified Domain Name or its IP address). This information is usually done as part of the command to start up FTP. (Your version of FTP may let you store addresses as nicknames and see them as a menu list or graphic icons.) At this point, the FTP program on your computer—the **ftp** *client* program—attempts to *open a connection.* This consists of contacting the specified remote computer and, if this can be done, attempting to "talk" to the **ftp** *server* program on it. Your FTP program will do these steps automatically; if it cannot connect, it will give you an error message, such as one indicating it can't find a remote computer using the address you specified or that its request to connect has been refused.
- Logging in. The fact that you can connect to a computer over the Internet doesn't mean you necessarily can use it. You have to log in—give your account name and possibly a password. This authenticates you to the **ftp** server program as an authorized user, in turn letting it determine the privileges you have—for example, which directories and files you may have access to and whether you can create, change, or delete files on the remote system or only copy files from it.

  Most **ftp** server programs support a type of account restricting access to "read-only" types of activities, such as getting listings of directories and files, copying files from the specified directories in the remote system, and possibly having a very restricted ability to transfer files to it. Originally designed to help groups of users share information easily, this feature—known as *anonymous-FTP*—is now commonly used to let people make files generally available to Internet users (see the discussion of anonymous-FTP in Chap. 15).
- Specifying the name(s) of the file(s) or directory(s) you want to copy across. You may also want to give the copies new names. FTP also includes commands that lets you set the current directory (the working directory) on the local system and on the remote system and obtain directory listings on the remote system.

## What Kind of Files Can FTP Be Used to Transfer?

FTP can transfer any kind of file. If it's a file and it can be stored on a computer system, it can be transferred. This includes:

- Programs, in source or executable form, from other systems you have accounts on, from public archives, etc. Source code will need to be compiled, of course; and executables will need to be compatible with the new system, may require libraries, relinking, etc. (Bear in mind that just because you can retrieve a program using FTP doesn't mean you'll be able to run it on your computer. FTP can't help you run the transferred program on a type of computer other than the one it was written for; for example, FTP can't help you run a DOS program on a Mac.)
- ASCII files, such as messages, documents, lists, mail files, Readme files, Usenet postings you've squirreled away, bibliographic references from library databases, NROFF/TROFF source, PostScript output.
- Graphic images, including .TIF or .GIF format.
- **tar** (tape archive) files, which can include whole directories.
- Data in proprietary formats.
- Spreadsheets and databases.
- Audio, video, and multimedia.

Transferred files may even contain combinations of any and all of the above—it's the responsibility of your programs to be able to handle the different types of data and make use of the files you transfer.

Most versions of FTP will let you specify multiple files, using wildcard naming, which lets you use a single command to transfer several files. You can also specify a directoryname, which will copy all the files in that directory.

## Using FTP

Now that you've got a sense of what the FTP file-transfer facility is all about, it's time to learn the basics of how to use it.

### Things you'll need to know to use FTP

**What system you want to connect to.** If you are using a traditional version of FTP, this means knowing the target system's Internet name (e.g., jabber.wock.com) or IP address (e.g., 123.45.678.90). Many of the new versions of FTP and many Internet "navigators" let you save and select system addresses as entries from a list, as names (e.g., "mac-turtle") or as icons. (If you don't know where a file you're looking for is located, an Internet navigator such as Gopher and search tools like archie can help you determine what's available and from where—see Chaps. 10 and 15 about these issues.)

**Account and user-ID and password on the target system.** You'll also need an account on the target system and must know the appropriate user-ID and password. (Later we'll be talking about systems which have an account set up for general use, using a facility called anonymous-FTP, and how to use these accounts.) Your software may be able to supply your user-ID and password automatically to the remote system. Having accounts on more than one computer and at more than one organization is a common and reasonable occurrence. For example, you may have accounts on computers in the computer science and the math departments, at M.I.T. and Jet Propulsion Laboratories, and on PANIX in NYC and DELPHI. Here's some typical reasons for having multiple accounts:

- You're involved in multiple projects, which require working on different computer systems.
- Your projects involve people at several organizations (e.g., from departments at six different universities).
- You've been moving around a lot; you're transitioning from having a "guest account" on a friend's machine to a public-access account.
- You like to have multiple accounts.
- These are shared accounts used by you and other people on a project or accounts you're given temporary access to in order to retrieve files (i.e., they told you the login-ID and password—probably first changing the password and changing it again after you're done).

**Names and locations of files and directories to be transferred.** Again, many of the newer Internet tools will take care of much of this information for you—and if you don't know the name of a file, or where it can be found, tools like archie and Gopher can help you see if it exists and where it can be found. You're also about to learn to use FTP commands to display file and directory names.

**Other things worth knowing to use FTP.** It's also often helpful to know some or all of the following:

**What type of file this is (ASCII, binary, or other format)?** FTP can be set to transfer files that are in any of several formats, notably

- ASCII, a.k.a. text
- Binary, a.k.a. image
- Other, such as TENEX, for old Digital Equipment systems

Most files are either ASCII or binary. FTP can transfer files in any of these modes, corresponding to the format of the file. It is essential the correct file type be specified; using the wrong format can cause some files to be transferred imperfectly, causing programs not to run, documents to be munged, etc. Some versions of FTP will automatically detect the type, check to see if that's what they're currently set to handle, even either tell you or change to the correct type automatically. But don't count on it.

*ASCII.* ASCII means a file contains text, which is defined as only the printable characters (A through Z, a through z, 0 through 9, and assorted punctuation and other characters) of the ASCII character set. ASCII characters can be represented using only 7-bit words, where other types of data, such as Word Perfect files, spreadsheets, and programs may use many characters that need 8-bit words. Some e-mail systems only handle 7-bit characters—MCI Mail, for example. (Many programs support encoding of 8-bit characters into a form that can be sent over 7-bit networks.)

*Binary.* Binary format, also referred to as *image,* is the format used by most programs and also spreadsheet models, images, databases, word-processed documents, and other non-ASCII files. Some versions of FTP also support other file types, such as TENEX (referring to files created under TOPS-10, the operating system for Digital Equipment Corporation's PDP-10 minicomputers).

FTP's default transfer type is **text.** You must be sure that FTP has been set to use binary before transferring any non-ASCII files—otherwise the transfer will happen, but the resulting file will be unusable. (See the following discussion of the FTP **ascii**, **binary, image,** and **type** commands.)

**Where you want to put it on your system.** When you bring a copy of a file to your system, it's got to go somewhere: onto your hard disk, onto a floppy disk, into your organization's shared file system—somewhere. You may want to bring files first into a "temporary workspace" area and then move them to their final location (for example, first to a hard disk and then copies to a floppy). There are several ways to do this:

- By changing to the desired directory before invoking FTP, for example:

```
% pwd
/user/ralph_r
% cd Downloads/Morestuff
% pwd
/user/ralph_r/Downloads/Morestuff
% ftp archives.utopia.org
% ftp ftp.apple.com
Connected to bric-a-brac.apple.com
220 bric-a-brac.apple.com FTP server (IG Version 5.91 (from BU,
from UUNET 5.51)
Fri Nov 8 17:06:51 PST 1991) ready.
Name (ftp.apple.com:jcapulet): anonymous
331 Guest login ok, send ident as password.
Password:
230 Guest login ok, access restrictions apply.
Remote system type is UNIX.
Using binary mode to transfer files.
ftp> cd pub
ftp> ls
```

- By setting the FTP local working directory, using FTP's **lcd** command (explained later in this chapter)
- By using pathnames (absolute or relative) for the target files. For example:

```
% pwd
/user/ralph_r
% ftp archives.utopia.org
ftp> get buttercup.tar.Z ~/Downloads/Morestuff
```

**How much data you're going to copy over, relative to available storage on your system, and the network speed.** This helps you figure out whether you want to do the transfers now or later. Before retrieving files, you can use FTP's **dir** command to see how big they are. Some FTP's display a graphic bar showing amount or percent sent and coming. (See the discussion of the FTP **hash** command for an easy way to get a "kilobytes transferred" display even on character-oriented nongraphic systems.)

FTP itself is a reasonably fast, efficient program. If FTP seems to be running slowly, the problem is more likely due to your network connection being inherently low-bandwidth, or local conditions slowing it down.

As with **telnet**—and *all* other uses of Internet services and resources—you should apply the same standards of security and "user etiquette" for using this account as you do your own. Don't waste computer time or storage, guard your password carefully, and report strange or problematic events to your system manager.

## Invoking FTP

Like most computer programs and utilities, you invoke FTP by either entering the program name at the command prompt or clicking your mouse on the appropriate icon or menu choice. You can give the name of the target system—the one you're going to transfer files to or from—along with the command, or to FTP once it's started up.

Like the Unix shell, FTP is an interactive utility, meaning that the FTP program displays a prompt, you enter a command at the prompt and hit <RETURN> or click your mouse or whatever; FTP executes this command, and then FTP displays a prompt to indicate it's ready for your next command; when you're done, you quit, and get back the system prompt.

Here's a nontechnical summary of what happens when you invoke FTP and open a connection to another computer over the network:

1. The client FTP program running on your computer attempts to establish a connection to the specified system.
2. At the target system, a corresponding server FTP program is started up.
3. The server may ask your client for an ID and password, possibly displaying your network name and address as who it believes you are; in most cases, you'll need to give a user-name and password, using the FTP **user** command before you can do anything else.
4. Once you are logged in and accepted as a user, the server FTP program accepts commands passed along from your client FTP program; the two

FTP programs perform file transfers and execute your other commands, until you quit and close out the session.

When FTP is awaiting commands from the user, it displays the prompt ftp>.

### FTP command synopsis

The general synopsis for the **ftp** command is:

```
ftp [ hostname ]
```

If you include the hostname, FTP attempts to open a connection. (There are other parameters and switches you can enter at the command line, but you don't need to know any of them as a beginning user, and they will vary from system to system. When you are ready—or simply curious—consult the on-line manual page, or your reference manual.) An example is:

```
% ftp archives.utopia.org
ftp >
```

If you omit the hostname, FTP gives you its prompt; to open a connection, you must then give the **open** command and the hostname, for example:

```
% ftp
ftp> open archives.utopia.org
```

### FTP's commands: You don't need to know them all

FTP has several dozen commands (also called subcommands). Many of these are similar or identical in name and use to Unix commands (for example, **cd** for Change Directory, **ls** for List files, **pwd** for Print-Working-Directory). The names for these commands are highly standardized across the many implementations of FTP in use on systems across the Internet, helping ensure you'll be able to use FTP on new computers with a minimum of difficulty.

Some FTP functions have several different names (i.e., there are several commands that do the same function). For example, **bye, close, exit, quit,** and Control-D all do the same thing, namely, close out your FTP session; **binary** and **image** both set the type to binary.

Not every vendor's version of FTP may support all the same names for FTP commands. You should be able to locate the functions you want by reading through FTP's on-line help text displayed in response to the FTP **help** or **?** command or the on-line manual page for FTP on your system. Although FTP has several dozen subcommands, you only need to know about a dozen to access, navigate, and transfer files to/from remote systems:

| | |
|---|---|
| **!** | Run a command on your local system |
| **ascii, text** | Set transfer type to ASCII files |
| **binary, image** | Set transfer type to binary files |
| **bye, close, exit** | Quit, <EOF>, such as Control-D, end FTP session |
| **cd** | Change working directory on remote system |
| **dir, ls** | List directory on remote system |

| | |
|---|---|
| **get** | Transfer copy of file from remote system |
| **help, ?** | Show FTP on-line help |
| **lcd** | Change working directory on local (your) system |
| **mget** | Transfer copies of files from remote system |
| **mput** | Transfer copies of files to remote system |
| **open** | Open connection to specified remote system |
| **put** | Transfer copy of file to remote system |
| **pwd** | Display working directory on remote system |
| **user** | Specify username to remote system |

These should be all you need for most common file transfer activity—and there's no point in learning more until you've learned and mastered all these.

It is worth knowing that FTP does have other commands and capabilities and what they are. Once you've mastered these basic FTP commands, you may want to locate on-line or printed documentation for the version of FTP you have available, especially if you're a programmer or software developer.

### Specifying filenames to FTP

The most commonly used type of information you'll include in FTP commands is file- and directorynames. Depending on what FTP command you give, file specifications will be processed by your FTP client program or the FTP server program on the remote system. For example, if you give the "multiple get" command (retrieve all files matching what you specify).

```
mget astro*
```

the "astro*" is processed by the remote system, using the conventions corresponding to its operating system. If you give the "multiple put" (send copies of all matching files to the remote system),

```
mput astro*
```

the "astro*" will be processed by your computer, using its conventions.

The majority of the publicly accessible FTP sites on the Internet run Unix. Therefore, even if you don't use Unix directly on your computer, you may run into a lot of Unix-style systems in using the Internet. However, not all computer operating systems support Unix-style filenames. (Hundreds of the public-access anonymous-FTP sites on the Internet use Digital Equipment VAXes running the VMS operating system—you may encounter many other types of computers and operating systems in use, including some that are no longer made.)

There are also potentially important differences you should be aware of, for example, if you are using FTP directly between a DOS PC and a Unix system. DOS, for example, uses filenames with up to eight characters in the main filename and up to three characters in the extension, separated by a literal . and does not distinguish between upper- and lowercase letters. These differences become very important in specifying the names of files to be transferred and the names the new copies are created under.

Consultant David Shute (dks@world.std.com) points out:

> You can encounter problems in transferring files with long filenames to a DOS version of TCP/IP that doesn't support names that long. Some DOS TCP/IP versions may truncate the filename—only use as many letters as it can—others won't. This can result in overwriting existing files of apparently identical names; for example, FTPing a file named "hytel6.01.tar.Z" without specifying a local name might be received as "hytelne.Z"—and if you're also retrieving a file named "hytelnet-readme.Z" your first file may be overwritten.

Some TCP/IP versions may refuse to do the potentially overwriting transfer or may prompt you for a name, according to Shute. Also, Shute notes

> Unix and other such machines often don't have the concept of A:, B:, C: drives like you do on DOS machines. Some TCP/IP software will permit users to include and change drive specifications along with file and pathnames. Having this feature becomes useful when you are pulling files to a disk, critical to making boot copies.

Also, some DOS-oriented versions of FTP will recognize "hidden files" in DOS (e.g., ibm.bio and ibm.dos, the two hidden files that your DOS PC boot) on one or both sides of the connection and may recognize file types Local and Tenex as well as ASCII and Binary.

## Basic FTP Commands You Should Know

Now let's take a look at the basic FTP commands which you are likely to need:

### ! [command]

Run **command** as a shell command on your computer; you are returned to FTP when it's done. **Command** can be any command on your local computer (e.g., any command, batch file or alias). For example:

```
ftp> !echo $USER
ralph_r
ftp> !pwd
/user/ralph_r/Downloads
ftp>
```

If you don't include a **command** and just enter **!<RETURN>,** you get an interactive Unix shell*; to return to FTP, you'll need to exit explicitly (usually by entering Control-D). For example:

```
ftp> !
% echo $USER
ralph_r
```

---

*On some Unix systems, you may also be able to return to "shell" level by entering a Control-Z, which invokes the job control facility and puts your FTP session in the background. When you do this, you return to your FTP session by entering the Unix **fg** (foreground) command to make the stopped session in the background the current, foreground job again.

```
% pwd
/usr/ralph_r/Downloads
% <Control-D>
ftp>
```

**ascii**

Set the representation type (i.e., how the system sees and transfers files) to network ASCII. On most systems, ASCII is the default type (i.e., what it's initially set to when you start up FTP). On many systems, FTP has a **text** command in addition or instead. For example:

```
ftp> ascii
ftp>
```

This command can also be given as:

```
type ascii
```

**binary, image**

Set the representation type to Binary, a.k.a., Image. Use for binary-type transferring programs, spreadsheets, and other non-ASCII objects.

**bye, close, exit, quit, and <EOF>, such as Control-D**

End the current FTP session and return to the shell; if you had an open connection to a remote server, tell it to close out the connection from its end also. For example:

```
[ message from ftp ]
ftp> bye
[ message from ftp]
%
```

**cd remote directory**

Change the working directory on the remote machine to the specified remote directory. (If you can't remember which directory you want, use the **ls** command.) For example:

```
ftp> cd pub
ftp>
```

**dir [ remote-directory ] [ local-file ]**

List contents of the specified remote directory; by default, it is the current remote directory. If you specify a local file, put the directory listing into this file on your local system instead of displaying it on your screen. For example:

```
ftp> dir hytel* hytel-list
```

**get remote-file [ local-file ]**

Transfer a copy of the specified file from the remote system to your local system. If you don't specify a local filename, the new file will be given the same

***A Tip for Easier Examination of Directory Listings and Readme Files***

Examining directory information and file contents on remote sites using FTP can be frustrating. For long directory listings, you want to be able to scroll through a screenful at a time. Before retrieving longish text files or reading a Readme file, you may want to examine them—but not necessarily bring a copy into your file system.

Some Internet navigators, and some newer versions of FTP, include ways to browse remote files a screenful at a time. However, even if all you have is "plain old FTP," here's an easy solution: If you can give a filename as the last parameter in an FTP command, for example, "get remote-filename [local-filename]" or "dir file-spec [filename]," use the Unix "pipe" (|) character as the first character of the final filename. This causes FTP to interpret the rest of the characters as a (Unix) shell command name rather than as a filename—and sends (pipes) the output of the FTP command to this command. For example:

```
ftp> dir *.txt |more
```

will pipe the list of remote files ending in ".txt" through **more** on your screen.

```
ftp> get Readme |more
```

will display Readme at your screen instead of copying it to a file.

To include any Space characters in the shell command, you have to put the entire item in quotes, for example:

```
ftp> get Readme "| grep From"
```

name it had on the remote machine (subject to alterations based on how FTP is set; for information on how the resulting filenames will be processed, see the discussions of **case, ntrans,** and **nmap** in your on-line or hardcopy Unix documentation).

```
ftp> get PBTools_1.2 PBtool
```

**hash**

Some of the new GUI-based versions of FTP include a "percent-transferred meter" showing how much of the file has been transferred. The **hash** command gives users on character-oriented systems a way to be aware of how fast FTP is copying data across. **hash** is a "toggle" type of function; entering **hash** turns the function on if it was previously off and off if it was previously on. (When you enter **hash,** FTP also tells you how the function is not set.) For example:

```
ftp> hash
Hash mark printing on (1024 bytes/hash mark).
ftp> hash
Hash mark printing off.
```

When **hash** is on, FTP will display a hash character (#) for each kilobyte transferred, like so:

```
ftp> get adventure.7.Z
200 PORT command successful.
150 Opening BINARY mode data connection for adventure.7.Z (24183
bytes).
########################
```

```
226 Transfer complete.
24183 bytes received in 2.5 seconds (9.5 Kbytes/s)
ftp>
```

You may want to determine how big the file is, before transferring it, using FTP's **dir** or **ls** command, so you know about how many #s to expect.

**help [ command ]**

Print one-line summary of command; if you don't specify a **command,** FTP prints a list of its commands.

**lcd [ directory ]**

Change the working directory on the local machine; if no directory is specified, the change is to your home directory. For example:

```
% pwd
/user/ralph_r
% ftp archives.utopia.org
ftp> lcd Downloads/Morestuff
ftp> !pwd
/user/ralph_r/Downloads/Morestuff
```

**ls [ remote-directory ] [ local-file ]**

See the explanation for the FTP **dir** command above.

**mget remote-files**

Transfer copies of the specified files from the remote system to the current directory on your local system.

(**mget** and **mput** don't take directories as an argument. To transfer a directory subtree of files and directories, use the Unix **tar** command to create a "tape archive" file and use FTP to transfer the "tar file," as TYPE BINARY.)

You can use Unix filenaming and wildcard conventions in remote files, as shown below. (For information on how FTP will do filename expansion, see the discussion of **glob** in your on-line or hardcopy Unix documentation; for information on how the resulting filenames will be processed, see the discussions of **case, ntrans,** and **nmap.** You're unlikely to ever need any of these.)

```
ftp> mget advent*
ftp> mget adventure.[1-4].Z
```

**mput local-files**

Transfer a copy of each file specified by local-files (after expanding any wildcards in the filenames) to the current directory on your local system. [For information on how FTP will do filename expansion, see the discussion of **glob** (for "global") in your on-line or hardcopy Unix documentation; for information on how the resulting filenames will be processed, see the discussions of **ntrans** and **nmap** in FTP documentation.)]

**open remote system**

Open an FTP connection to the specified remote system for transferring files, using either its Internet Domain Name or IP address.

```
ftp> open ftp.apple.com
```

or

```
ftp> open 130.43.2.3
```

**put local-file [ remote-file]**

Transfer a copy of the specified file from your local system to the remote system. If you don't specify a remote filename, the new file will be given the same name it had on the local system (subject to alterations based on how FTP is set; for information on how the resulting filenames will be processed, see the discussions of **ntrans** and **nmap** in your on-line or hardcopy Unix documentation). For example:

```
ftp> put little-list mg-list
```

**pwd**

Display the pathname of the current working directory on the remote system. For example:

```
ftp> pwd
257 "/pub/powerbook" is current directory.
ftp>
```

**quit**

A synonym for **bye**; see the explanation of the FTP **bye** command above.

**type [ type-name ]**

Set the representation type to type-name; if type-name is omitted, display the current type. Valid typenames are **ascii** for network ASCII, **binary** or **image** for binary, and **tenex** for local byte size of 8 (used to transfer files to and from computers running Digital Equipment Corporation's Tenex operating system, most likely to be old DEC PDP-10s and PDP-20s, and LISP machines). The default type is network ASCII.

**? [ help command ]**

A synonym for help; see the explanation for the FTP **help** command above.

**Other FTP commands you may want to learn about**

As mentioned earlier, FTP has many other commands besides the ones just explained; examples are **append,** which appends the transferred file to a specified existing file, and **cr,** which toggles <RETURN> stripping during network ASCII type. Once you're comfortable using the essential FTP commands, you should at least read through the list and descriptions of the other FTP commands that are available. That way, when the need or use for one of these other functions arises in the future, you may recall that FTP can do it, or at least have the niggling suspicion, and then go back to the FTP documentation. Remember, the people who developed FTP probably had similar needs to many of yours, so there is a strong likelihood that the features you want are there.

## Aborting a File Transfer

To abort a file transfer—to stop the transfer rather than let it finish—use the terminal's Interrupt key (usually Control-C). You may need to wait a few seconds before the system responds with a new prompt. Reasons to abort a file transfer include:

- It's taking too long.
- You've decided you don't want the file.
- You realize you've set the Type wrong and are transferring a binary file in ASCII mode.
- You mistakenly gave the wrong filename.
- You're overflowing your local storage.
- It's time to go to lunch and you don't want to leave the computer running with an Internet connection open.

## FTP Gotcha's and Tips

Here's a handful of tips and gotcha's relating to transferring files with FTP:

### Beware of using existing filenames when copying

If you're transferring a file named, say, foo.txt, and you already have a file by that name in your target directory, most versions of FTP will cheerfully overwrite your original foo.txt file, so:

1. Pay attention to your current (home) and (remote) working directories. If you are really paranoid about inadvertently overwriting key files, create a special subdirectory to transfer into (e.g., Tmp_In); and when you've finished transferring, rename the files and move them to their final directory—being careful not to blow away files at this stage, of course.
2. Pay attention to filenames. In some cases, you may have trouble giving target names which are different from the source names, especially if you are doing a multiple "get." See the previous hint.

### telnet-through for FTP access

A good reason to **telnet**-through (see discussion in Chap. 7) is to gain FTP access to hosts which are inaccessible from your home host. For example, to get files on kremvax.hq.demos.su, I would

1. **telnet** from World to Bigbear. As a precaution against accidentally overwriting other files, I would probably create a new subdirectory, such as temp, and change directories to make this my current directory.

2. FTP copies of the desired files from Kremvax to Bigbear.
3. Close the FTP connection to Kremvax.
4. If I don't already have a subdirectory on World to FTP these files to, I might create one, to minimize the chance of overwriting existing files.
5. FTP copies of the files now on Bigbear to my account on World, either by staying telnetted to Bigbear and FTPing from Bigbear to World or by closing my **telnet** connection from World to Bigbear and FTPing copies of the files from Bigbear to World.
6. Once I was satisfied that all files had been copied to my account on World, deleting the copies of the files from Bigbear to avoid consuming filespace unnecessarily.

*Warning:* If you are not used to the file-delete command on your intermediate system, be sure to exercise caution, so you don't accidentally delete your or other people's files. This is why I went to the effort of creating a new subdirectory in Step 1. When I've deleted all the files I'd transferred, I'd probably also remove the subdirectory.

## File Transfer Netiquette

If you're going to do file transfers over the Internet, it's essential to be aware of and follow netiquette because FTP consumes network resources—on a per-session basis, probably more than telnetting or e-mail. Think about it: Suppose you're about to retrieve a dozen debugging programs or send over 2 months' worth of metal x-ray data. You may be contributing to overloading a link in the network or overloading the CPU of the computer being used to provide anonymous-FTP service. The Internet is designed to handle these surges in traffic as fairly and robustly as possible—but observing netiquette is essential.

Before casually transferring large files from sites outside your organization, try to determine if there is a copy within your organization on one of the hosts nearest to you. "Nearest" is admittedly a fuzzy term when it comes to networking. A host halfway across the country, but linked via a T3-speed connection, may be considered closer, in terms of transfer speeds, than one across town that you have to access via a 9600-baud connection. On the other hand, if your organization is paying on a usage basis, that crosstown link may be far cheaper.

Another reason to seek nearest sources is that too many FTP requests can easily bring a network host to a grinding halt, even crash it. This typically occurs when someone posts an announcement that they have made a PostScript version of a document available by FTP; frequently, within a few hours, that message is followed by a plea to hold off. When in doubt:

1. Contact your system administrator, etc.
2. Query to the local mailing list
3. E-mail (or heck, call) someone

The reverse is also true: If you're planning to make a file available by FTP, consider making it available via the FTP archive sites and including a suggestion to high-traffic sites that they grab a copy and that users check with their local guru.

File transfer can put a noticeable burden on the networks, as well as on the host you're connecting to. So, if you're planning to move a lot of data around, consider doing it at an off-peak time. Also, bear in mind that although you may not be directly paying for Internet bandwidth you're consuming for your **telnet** and FTP activities, or the CPU cycles on the remote systems, they aren't free. Be considerate in terms of the times of day you establish connections, the amount of data transferred, how long you maintain connections, and how heavily you use resources.

## Getting Help, Resources, and For More Information

This chapter in no way represents all the information available on FTP and how to do file transfers. FTP has two dozen or more commands not discussed here. You may have a new, old, or homegrown version of FTP with special features. Your local system administrators and developers may have configured FTP differently or added things. Plus, there's no telling what other versions of FTP you'll access on the remote systems you end up transferring files to and from. Here's where to go for more information about FTP, specifically in relation to your home system, and in general:

- On-line help information for FTP may be available on your system in any of several places: built-in to your version of FTP, in the on-line Unix manual entries, and in other help files provided by your organization or system administrators. See the discussion of how to locate and obtain on-line help information in Chap. 12.
- For a good document of more information about the procedures involved in file transfer of Macintosh files, read ftp-primer.txt on sumex-aim.stanford.edu in /info-mac/reports. For user-level questions, read Usenet FAQs such as the ones on FTP and watch Usenet "help-oriented" Newsgroups such as news.newusers.questions.
- The definitive network resource for technical discussions of FTP and related services is the Usenet comp.protocols.tcp-ip discussion group, where developers, users, and consultants in the TCP/IP community (and some crossovers) discuss everything from sources wanted to bugs (and fixes) in specific products.

Now that you have been introduced to the four major types of Internet activity—e-mail, the Usenet, remote login, and file transfer—let's look at some of the new facilities that can help you use these basic tools to navigate the Internet.

Part

3

# Navigating the Internet

Chapter

# 9

# The Internet Dashboard: Navigating the Internet Rapids

*"First star on the left..."*

*Peter Pan*
J. M. BARRIE

*"No matter where you go, there you are."*
BUCKAROO BANZAI;
also, BRUCE "U.UTAH" PHILLIPS

Imagine you've suddenly landed in a strange city, in an unfamiliar car. There are no labels on the dashboard to tell you whether you're in forward, reverse, or park and no way to tell how fast you're going or how much gas you've got. You look up and notice that the windows are painted black, making it impossible to see. You roll the window down, you don't recognize anything, and almost all the street signs are in a language you don't know. Not too encouraging, is it?

Perhaps you'd prefer this scenario: You find yourself in a strange car with a trackball and an assortment of colored buttons on the steering wheel. You touch the large Pushme button near the middle of the steering wheel and a reassuring computerized voice begins to speak: "Welcome to the town of Utopia. At any point, for help information, push the yellow button on the left. To mute this map and information and have direct control of the car, press the yellow button twice and insert your Safe Driver ID in the slot." Suddenly the windshield appears overlaid with translucent multicolored map arrows, with markers like "<-FOOD" "PHONES/RESTROOMS," and "SPACE MUSEUM." A list also appears on the dashboard, and the voice says, "To move to a destination, move the center trackball or use buttons around it. To select a destination, push the red button. To have this car drive there automatically, push the red and blue buttons together. To move to a new choice, push the blue button. To move up a menu, push both buttons."

Welcome to the next challenge of computers and networking: getting around. The first scenario represents the typical user experience: stumbling around in the dark with no information and no help. The second scenario represents where environments like the Internet had better be headed, if we expect the general public to be able to use them: systems with better user interface front ends that make the Internet services easier to use and navigation tools that make it easier to locate Internet-based services and information within these services. Smart user front ends like this are becoming increasingly popular for the Internet to serve a number of types of needs, notably, ease of use, navigation, "resource discovery," and personalization.

For many people today, gaining access to the Internet often feels like getting cable TV without a channel guide or program listing, or a telephone with no dialing instructions or directory. You know there's a lot out there, but what? And where? How do you "tune" to the right channel, and where are the daily program listings?

Much of the Apple Macintosh's success with the general public has been attributed to its use of the mouse, menus, and graphic icons for controlling the computer and the programs being used. Other graphic user interfaces (GUIs, or "gooeys"), such as DesqView, Microsoft Windows, and the X Window system, as well as most user programs, have also adapted these conventions and methods. Similarly, if you use any of the popular BBS conferencing systems, such as America On-Line, CompuServe, or GEnie, you've probably found software products to help, such as C.I.M. (CompuServe Information Manager) and TAPCIS for CompuServe or Aladdin for GEnie.

Not surprisingly, the Internet community has begun offering tools, products, and services, and entire organizations have begun to emerge to meet users' growing needs for something easier to use than "an automobile with black tape over all the dashboard and windows." In this chapter you'll:

- Get an overview of the categories of Internet tools and what's what.
- Learn basic commands that should be useful for almost any of these tools.

In the next chapter, you'll learn about and how to use some of the leading Internet tools and services, such as Gopher, archie, WAIS, and WorldWideWeb. Appendix D contains a simple Unix shellscript you can use as your own front end to Internet tools.

## Tools for Internet Users: What's What

Using any system, whether it's the radio, telephone, or Internet, requires a set of related tools and services (plus some sense of what you want to do). You've already learned about some of these tools, such as **telnet** and FTP, and about programs for using e-mail and the Usenet. You may have already heard about or tried things like Gopher, archie, or WAIS. Each of these has a different purpose and place in the Internet user toolkit.

Peter Deutch of Bunyip Systems, cocreator of the archie resource locating system, offers the following categorization as one way to view the various tools available to Internet users:

- Basic user tools—**telnet,** FTP, e-mail programs, and Usenet newsreaders
- User-interface front ends—Gopher, TechInfo, WAIS, WorldWideWeb, InterSuite, X Windows/Motif, Prospero
- Navigators—Gopher, Techinfo, WAIS, WorldWideWeb, Compass
- Internet navigator servers and their data—Gopher, TechInfo, archie, VERONICA, WAIS, WorldWideWeb, **ftp**, **telnet**, Usenet

As you can see, several tools, such as Gopher and WAIS, fall into more than one category. In fact, you can easily make use of different parts of different tools, such as doing a WAIS search of the archie anonymous-FTP file archive list from Gopher.

You've already learned about the basic Internet user tools—**telnet** (remote login), FTP (file transfer), electronic mail, and the Usenet and how to use them. These programs represent basic activities you can do that can involve potentially almost any other user, file, computer, or site on the Internet (subject to authorization, of course). Many of the other Internet tools make use of these basics. They may make it easier to do a file transfer, perhaps even save you the need to give the **ftp** command, enter a target system name, or check transfer mode.

New programs for electronic mail, remote login (**telnet**), and file transfer (**ftp**) save you memorization and steps by doing things like displaying menu choices or icons for a target, such as "connect to ftp.nnsc.net for file transfer," so you don't have to remember and enter the network name. Some of these products even automatically perform a sequence of commands to "get you there." However, while not to be sneezed at as productivity aids and stress reducers, these facilities are usually oriented to your local system and activities—whereas you're interested in reaching out to and across the Internet and its vast pool of choices to choose from.

In the rest of this chapter, we'll look at the different categories of Internet user navigation tools, how they can relate to each other, and summarize the commands being used in common by many of these tools. Then we'll look at many of these tools and how to use them.

Specific-function information-finders search for and locate information in specific files or types of files. They are often used via an Internet navigator or front end (e.g., Gopher) and are mostly used as "peoplefinders" for e-mail and other address information at present. Examples are **finger, whois, netfind, whois++,** and **fred** (KnowBot search).

Resource and service databases contain information about Internet resources and services, are managed by servers, and are accessed using clients. Examples are archie anonymous-FTP archive database, VERONICA Gopher-menu database, Internet White Pages, WAIS directory-of-servers, and other databases.

The following shows this information in table form.

| | Front end | Navigator | Server | Database |
|---|---|---|---|---|
| Gopher | Y | Y | Y | Y |
| TechInfo | Y | Y | Y | Y |
| archie | M* | N | Y | Y |
| VERONICA | M* | Y | Y | Y |
| WAIS | Y | Y | Y | Y |
| WWW | Y | Y | Y | Y |

*M = may have a custom interface or use others as available.

### User interface front ends: Making the Internet easy(er) to use

The doohickey that is in between you and any device is the *user interface,* or *front end.* Everything has one: your VCR, your microwave oven, a guitar, your telephone, your computer keyboard. A really good one is so easy to use that you stop noticing it. (That doesn't mean it's easy to learn. Many consider "easy to learn"—a.k.a. "intuitive"—as a sign of being easy to use.) Ease of use through better user-interface front ends addresses a long-standing reality: the user interfaces on most computers on the Internet (or anywhere else) are not meant to be used by normal people, that is, people who haven't had several courses in using the specific computer operating system. Many of these Internet-attached computers (but not all) are undoubtedly running Unix.*

In the past few years, techniques like mice, menus, graphics, icons, and color have helped make many computers much easier to use, whether it's starting one and selecting an application, or using that application. Now, Internet users are looking for the same ease of use: a front end that doesn't require remembering a seemingly infinite amount of facts about what's what, how it's spelled, what the options are, and what the heck is available at any point. In other words, something that isn't harder to figure out or use than the menuing system on their word processing program, Windows PC, or Macintosh.

Graphic, mouse-and-menu, point-and-click front ends, such as the X Windows system and Motif for Unix users, Microsoft Windows for DOS users, and MacOs for Macintosh users, offer the next increment in ease of use, minimizing the amount of command options and syntax you need to remember, avoiding "opportunities" for spelling or typing errors, even checking for syntax and permissible command options.

Many new versions of Unix and TCP/IP applications in fact provide this kind of help. For starters, alternative Unix shells like **bash** (Bourne-again shell) and **tsch** offer features like arrow-key scrolling through your previous

*A few years back, an article in *Forbes* referred to the Internet's "savage interface." While the author missed the point—the Internet proper doesn't have a user interface, the computers do—the Unix user interface to which the author was undoubtedly referring does, indeed, have a savage, user-unfriendly interface obscure, difficult, and cantankerous enough to send even the most patient person away screaming.

commands and command-line editing. There are menu-driven Unix front ends, too, including some that help you create and "grammar-check" multiline shellscripts.

Many of the products for use in TCP/IP networks, such as for remote login (**telnet**), file transfer (**ftp**), e-mail, and Usenet reading/posting programs, are adding these types of ease-of-use features as well. Many of the front ends being developed are used in a way such that you as a user don't necessarily see them. The local archie client, for example, makes use of the Prospero distributed filing system (developed by Cliff Neuman). But you don't say "prospero," or "prospero archie"; you say "archie." Other tools in this category include the Andrew File System, Alex, and FSP. (One might argue that something like Prospero is a "near-front-end"—a tool used by a front-end user interface but not the full tool itself.) Programs, products, and features like these are a big help for novice—and experienced—Internet users. But it's only a start, not the whole solution.

### Internet navigators: Discovering and getting to services and resources

The next tool many Internet users want is a navigator—a tool to help discover, locate, and move about among the many systems, services, and resources located across the Internet. The navigator may be getting its information regarding what choices you are presented with from any of a number of types of sources, such as:

- A list built into the navigator (not very flexible).
- A local list created by your system administrator (probably specific to your group, site, or organization—and not too useful if the available resources change faster than the list gets updated).
- Lists collected by hand or automatically ("harvested") by a separate program. New information may be distributed by e-mail in a form which can be automatically added to existing lists (HYTELNET) or maintained at one or more servers and accessed at time of request (archie, Gopher, WAIS, WorldWideWeb).
- Ad-hoc lists based on user query against a master database of choices (Gopher/VERONICA, WAIS, archie).

Like the user interface, a navigator should work in a fashion that doesn't require knowing too much about how to use the user interface or tools at our end.

The difference between a navigator and a front end is that a navigator tells you what choices are available. The front end is how it's presented. (Navigators are also more likely to be client programs, designed to work with a server program. For example, with Gopher, you use a Gopher client, which talks to Gopher servers—and possibly to non-Gopher servers. A Gopher server may in turn talk to a WAIS server, etc.) Many Internet navigators, as you'll see, have their own front end. Some can be accessed through other front ends, including those of other navigators. Equally, some navigators have their own database or lists they query; others have been designed to navigate other databases and information structures. Table 9.1 (on p. 302) shows this information in tabular form.

There's a strong overlap between navigators and front ends. A front end may not necessarily tell you what you can do—but a good navigator better make it easier for you to use it or it's not making your job any easier. Front ends and navigators are not only useful for the Internet. Whether you've got an account on a public-access Internet site or are one of thousands of users in a large university or corporation, your local environment is undoubtedly big enough that help in navigating would be welcome. Gopher and TechInfo, for example, as you'll see, each began as a CWIS ("kwiss")—Campus-Wide Information System—to serve their own organization's needs. The purpose of a CWIS is to let people within an organization, such as a university campus or a corporation, find and add information, such as:

- Meeting schedules
- Policies and procedures information
- Daily and weekly internal newspapers and magazines
- Classified ads
- Course catalogs and product information
- Help and support documents

Increasingly, information like this exists on-line; the purpose of CWISs is to make it available to users, findable without having to ask someone else.

It should be no surprise that navigator tools, such as Gopher and TechInfo that can be—and are being—put to use within the Internet, are relevant to Internet users. The Internet can be viewed as an extension to your local or campus network—larger in scale, farther away, and not under your organization's control, admittedly (or as a *very* big campus network). CWISs have been designed to also work over wide area network links as well as over local and campus-area networks and to let users navigate not only within one server but among a set of servers become WWISs—World-Wide Information Systems.

Many organizations themselves are dispersed across more than a single campus. State universities, government agencies, and corporations can easily have sites in a number of cities, states, and even countries. As CWISs evolve into WWISs, you not only can navigate within an organization's local information and resources but also across organizations. Or, from a single site, such as a public-access Internet site (Express Access, Halcyon, NetCom, PANIX, or World), a CWIS/WWIS can be your Internet Navigator.

With a CWIS/WWIS, as with Gopher or TechInfo, you can get to and explore publicly available free-for-use (and perhaps pay-for-use) information and services across much of the Internet from one facility, with the same commands and principles, accessing remote information as well as local. In fact, involving the Internet makes these navigator tools even more important—because, as you may have already discovered, you can't always count on other peoples' systems having interfaces and front ends you know how to use. Gopher, TechInfo, etc., let you get at distant data without having to learn (and remember) additional programs. The best known Internet navigators in 1992 included Gopher, HYTELNET (especially by librarians), WAIS, and WorldWideWeb.

### Internet navigator servers and their data: What Gopher, WAIS, and other front ends do

To navigate the Internet, a good front end is only part of the solution. Successful navigation also requires "back ends"—information that your navigator navigates through—and tools—servers—that handle your navigator client program's requests.

Gopher, TechInfo, WAIS, and WorldWideWeb, for example, all have client programs, which you use, and server programs, which your client programs communicate with. Many, such as HYTELNET, directly access their own lists. Some, such as archie, can be accessed by a number of types of client programs, such as the one based on Prospero, a **telnet**-accessed client, and via e-mail. Increasing numbers of Internet resources can be accessed via e-mail, including some file-transfer-by-mail e-mail FTP servers, archie, and the LISTSERV List Server on BITNET (see the section on "Internet Services Based on E-Mail" in Chap. 5).

These server tools access files, directories, and databases, which may be general "info-pools" or relating to a specific topic or discipline, such as lists of archive sites, "Internet White Pages" addresses and descriptions, lists of on-line library catalogues, or documents (such as a canonical list of smiley faces). Some of these information bases are in a format intended for use through a specific tool, such as archie, VERONICA, or WAIS; others are "just regular old files and directories," which can be "pointed to" by Gopher, TechInfo, and other navigator tools. (Some of the information bases are accessed by having a server act as a translator. For instance, a Gopher server may allow Gopher clients to access archie or WAIS by translating a Gopher request into WAIS "dialect" and then forwarding the WAIS-format request to a WAIS server. These sorts of protocol gateways make it possible for the Gopher system, for example, to access information resident on other systems.)

### Single-purpose information-finding tools: People-locators, mostly

Lastly, there is a somewhat diverse group of programs whose main purpose to date has been to find people—get their e-mail address or other information—examples are **finger, whois, netfind,** and X.500 and CSO phone-book lookups (see the section on "What's Your E-Mail Address?" in Chap. 5).

In subsequent chapters, we'll take a look at some of the most popular Internet navigators, navigator servers, and databases, including archie, Gopher, and WAIS, plus overviews of other popular tools such as TechInfo,

HYTELNET, and WorldWideWeb. Also, in App. D, I've provided a short Unix shellscript that you can use to help you remember and launch your Internet (and other) activities. As you'll see, you can even personalize and customize this so it reflects your own needs and interests in terms of using the Internet. The program is very simple and short enough to keyboard in within a few minutes.

### That's not all, folks!

Don't assume these front ends, navigators, and related tools are the only ones available to you or necessarily the right one(s) for you. There are numerous others available. There's the LIBS library front end, Panda (based on Gopher), Columbus, the CERFnet COMPASS.... In fact, nobody knows how many Internet front ends, navigators, CWISs, WWISs, and other tools are available or under development, but it's bound to be somewhere between a few dozen to a hundred.

### Customizing: Building your personal view of the Internet

Each user needs a way to *customize* his or her use of the Internet, just like we like to tune preset buttons on our radios and VCRs. There's so much to remember. While front ends and navigators can help you, they still are unlikely to itemize exactly that set of resources, services, and activities that *you* want to do.

## Using Internet Navigators: A Generic Overview

As you've just seen, there are lots and lots of programs available to make using the Internet easier: Gopher, HYTELNET, WAIS, Compass—lots. And many of these are available in multiple versions for use on different computers and operating systems, such as Unix, MS-DOS, Apple Macintosh, OS/2, and VAX/VMS, possibly in both command-line and graphic/icon form. More are becoming available every day, and new features keep getting added to the existing ones just as fast.

Telling you how to use each and every one of these is clearly difficult—impossible, in fact. However, most of these programs are likely to have some similarities in how you use them. Many of the developers are in contact with each other, after all, and also take into account existing semistandards. (Also, many use commands and conventions similar to those in popular Unix text editors, e-mail, and Usenet programs.)

In this section, you'll learn some of these commands and conventions. Armed with a short list of keystroke commands, you should be able to use and navigate your way through most of these Internet navigators and to know how to dig out further information on each. You'll also learn the general ways to access Internet tools, since they can easily be available in any—but not necessarily all—of several ways.

### Navigators tend to be made of a client and a server

Like **telnet** and FTP, the standard TCP/IP applications for remote login and file transfer, many of the Internet navigators and tools discussed in this section consist of client and server components. Gopher, archie, and WAIS, for example, all consist of the client programs, which you interact with, and their corresponding server programs and databases, which the client programs work with. The client and server are likely to be running on different computers; the servers run on the systems and sites where the information they manage "lives." In the course of a given session using Gopher, you may make use of Gopher servers all over the country or world. In early 1993, for example, there were over a thousand Gopher servers around the world, not to mention over a dozen archie servers and several hundred WAIS servers.

One purpose of these tools is to let you access information and services at different sites easily from a single familiar program. The user interface in the client program stays the same no matter how many different sites and servers you access; similarly, if you access other client programs at other locations, they should be familiar. If you've ever tried to use services from several on-line services (e.g., CompuServe, MCI Mail, Dialog, or Dow Jones), you know how frustrating it can be to have to know a new front end for each.

### Think globally, look for clients locally

Throughout this and other chapters—and in most discussions of Internet tools here and in other documents—you'll see frequent reminders to find and use a "local client" for a tool whenever possible—even to find and get one installed if you're going to use it frequently. As the section "Client-Server: The Front and Back Ends of Internet Tools" at the beginning of Part 2 indicates, there are usually compelling advantages to work via a local client wherever possible. These local clients often have more features than the versions of clients for "VT100 terminals" accessed by dial-up terminal emulators or **telnet** remote login. The TurboGopher client for the Macintosh, for example, makes use of the same features as other Macintosh programs, like use of the mouse, pull-down menus, scroll-bars, etc. Versions of WorldWideWeb clients for the Macintosh and for X Windows provide "hypertext" linking. The other reason is that running a local client also places the load on *your* system versus someone else's, without requiring a network connection between your computer and the client program. The standard advice is to try a public-access version of the client; if you like the tool, obtain (or ask your system administrator to get) the appropriate local client.

### Common commands for Internet navigators and front ends

What all these front ends and navigators have in common is a strong "ease of use" factor: with just the arrow keys, <RETURN>, and maybe two or three other commands and "clicking on the mouse," you can do 90 percent of your navigating. In general, your current choice is indicated by one of the following:

- Cursor positioned at this line (e.g., Gopher)
- Item highlighted or blinking (e.g., WorldWideWeb)
- Prompt on screen waiting for input (e.g., keywords)

Table 9.1 gives you a summary of standard functions and keystrokes likely to do them.

**TABLE 9.1 Standard Navigator Functions and Keys***

| Function | Keys to try |
|---|---|
| Select current item | <RETURN>, <RIGHT-ARROW>, <space>, l, mouse |
| Return to previous menu (Up one level) | <LEFT-ARROW>, h |
| Return to main menu or screen | m |
| Move cursor to new item: | |
| Move cursor up menu | <UP-ARROW>, u, k, Control-P |
| Move cursor down menu | <DOWN-ARROW>, d, j, Control-N |
| Move cursor to specified position | Move cursor with mouse, enter item number<RETURN> |
| Scroll menu to new page or screenful: | |
| Scroll to next page or screen | >, +, <space>, <PageDown> J, Control-V, Control-D |
| Scroll to previous page or screen | <, -, b, <PageUp> K, <ESCAPE>, v, Control-U |
| Move within current document: | |
| Go to next page/screenful | <RETURN> |
| Go to last page of document | BO |
| Quit document, return to menu | q |
| Misc. operations: | |
| Display built-in help text | ?, h |
| Quit with yes/no prompt | q |
| Quit unconditionally (no prompt) | Q |
| Search for an item in menu | / |
| Show current options | O, o |
| Refresh screen | Control-L |
| To abort current activity | Control-C |
| Other Unix, TCP/IP tricks to remember: | |
| To return from **telnet** connection | **telnet** escape, usually Control-] |
| To suspend current activity ("job") and return to your system prompt (works only if you're running a shell with job control, such as **csh**) | Control-Z |
| To return to activity suspended by Control-Z | fg<RETURN> |
| To abort current activity | Control-C |
| To escape from telnetted connections | Control-] (or whatever the **telnet** escape character is set to) |

*h, j, k, l and ^b, ^f, ^p, ^n are the cursor motion keys used, respectively, in **vi** and **emacs,** two common Unix interactive visual editors.

## Accessing Internet Navigators

To paraphrase an old proverb, the journey of a thousand Internet resources begins with a single command. The trick, of course, is to find that first command. There are several basic ways a given Internet tool may be available. Determining factors will include its nature, what versions have been implemented by its developers or other members of the Internet community, and what, if any, appropriate programs have been installed and configured on your system. These basic access methods include:

- As a locally installed program (local client)
- As a selection from some other Internet navigator
- As a public-access copy of the tool on remote system, which you access by remote login (**telnet**)
- E-mail to a copy of the program that has an e-mail interface

If you're not sure whether a given access method is available, or supports the features you want, *try* it. Keep in mind that new software, versions, and features (and bug fixes) can become available faster than books, on-line manual pages, or built-in help text can be updated. Always bear in mind that not every version and method of accessing a given tool may support the same sets of features. These may determine which method you use.

### Accessing a locally installed program

With any Internet tool, start by seeing if a copy of the program is available on your local system. For example, if you want to use Gopher, type

```
% gopher<RETURN>
```

If you want to use archie, type

```
% archie<RETURN>
```

If this doesn't work, try giving the command with an *x* (as in X Window) or *s* in front, in case the version installed has a slightly different name. For example:

```
% xarchie
```

or

```
% swais
```

Versions of Internet navigator tools typically become quickly available for systems and environments including Unix (both terminal-style ASCII and X Window/Motif graphic user interfaces), Macintosh, NeXTStep, VAX/VMS, Microsoft Windows, and OS/2. If you get an error message indicating no such command can be found, there are several possibilities:

- The tool in question isn't installed on your system.
- The tool in question *is* installed, but the setting of your Path environment

variable (or its equivalent on your computer) doesn't include the directory the program is in.

- The tool is installed, but you don't know what name it's installed as. For example, there's no reason that Gopher couldn't have been installed as *goph, gofer,* or even *platypus.*

To determine what the status of the tool's availability is, contact your system administrator.

### Try other Internet navigators

If you can't find the tool directly, see if you can access it through any of the other Internet navigation or front-end facilities currently installed in your site. Try Gopher, TechInfo, or whatever else is available. (A Gopher menu may, for example, include a gateway to WAIS and to archie. TechInfo tends to include a Gopher entry; WorldWideWeb can take you to Gopher and TechInfo.)

Also, once you've accessed one of these other navigators, you may be able to find the tool you are really looking for by making use of its indexing and query facilities; for example, within Gopher, you can give the tool's name as a search keyword to the VERONICA Gopher-searching facility.

### Find a public-access copy of the program you can access via remote login

If you can't find the tool on your computer or in the menus of other tools, your next option is to find a publicly accessible copy of the program which you can access via the **telnet** remote login facility (as described in Chap. 7). This is similar to anonymous-FTP and guest **telnet** access: one or more sites have set up accounts on one of their computer systems that are intended to be available to the Internet community as a whole. As a rule, these accounts offer access to one and only one thing: the specified Internet tool. If the tool is built-in client-server fashion, the access is to a client program on that computer.

Typically, Internet navigators are most likely to offer public-access in this fashion. For example, there are sites with publicly accessible guest accounts for archie (the **telnet** client), Gopher, HYTELNET, WAIS, and WorldWideWeb. Front ends are less likely, except for demo purposes, to let users try them out and see if they want to buy the program or purchase an account that offers this front end.

One reason for providing these public-access tool sites is to help promote use of the tools, by making it possible for you to try a new tool. Often, users may be interested in trying a new tool but not willing or able to get and install the software first. To access such a site, typically you'll have to first do a remote login to the site, using the **telnet** command; then, log in. The login name you'll need to use is usually specified in the same place you found the program's sitename; typically, it's the name of the tool. For example:

```
% telnet quake.think.com
Trying 192.31.181.1…
Connected to quake.think.com.
Escape character is '^]'.

SunOS UNIX (quake)

login: wais
Last login: Fri May 28 11:39:07 from world.std.com
SunOS Release 4.1.1 (QUAKE) #3: Tue Jul 7 11:09:01 PDT 1992

Welcome to swais.
Please type user identifier (optional, i.e user@host):
[your e-mail address here]
TERM = (vt100)<RETURN>
Starting swais (this may take a little while)…
```

Like anonymous-FTP, most public-access guest accounts for Internet tools don't require a password; however, Internet netiquette says that, if you are prompted for a password, you should supply your e-mail name and address (e.g., alice@jabber.wock.com) for purposes of resource tracking. (And always remember the site can probably determine this information even if you don't enter it—don't assume you're really "anonymous.") For some public-access accounts, you won't even need to log in; the name and address you gave to **telnet** will connect you to this account automatically.

Lists of many publicly available guest accounts for Internet tools can often be found in:

- The FAQ document in the Usenet news.answers Newsgroup, and the tool's own Newsgroup, if one exists
- The "info" file for the tool, if one exists, is often available from one or more automatic e-mail info-servers
- Internet resource and service on-line summaries, such as Scott Yenoff's "Special Internet Connections" list, periodically reposted to the Usenet alt.news.answers and alt.internet.services groups, and in Internet resource and service guides
- The information retrieved by the **finger** command to the site
- Internet White Pages listings, if available

When using public-access guest accounts, once you've succeeded in logging in, remember to keep your sessions relatively brief, and if you feel the tool is worth having, look into getting it installed on your own computer or at your own site.

#### Try finding and using an e-mail interface

Many Internet tools accept queries and commands by e-mail, sending back acknowledgments, results, even entire documents and files. Typically, the programs that accept commands by e-mail are those that don't require *interactive* sessions; archie, for example, can be queried via e-mail (although it may take you several exchanges to finish your search). It's less likely that you'll find e-mail access to a navigator such as Gopher or TechInfo. In fact, some information services, such as ListServ, the program used by BITNET and elsewhere to manage electronic mailing lists and document distribution, can *only* be accessed by e-mail. The archie anonymous-FTP file archive index, for example, can be queried by e-mail (see the section on archie in the next chapter, and the section on "Internet Services Based on E-Mail" in Chap. 5). Most e-mail server interfaces will have a summary list of their commands and other help information and possibly a list of sites to query.

In general, to access Internet tools via e-mail send the message to the tool at a specific site address (e.g., mail archie@sura.net). Start by sending a message with "help" in the subject and the body, and nothing else. (If this isn't the appropriate command to get you the starter help file, it may generate an error message which tells you how to get the help file.)

Here's some general guidelines for sending commands to Internet tools via e-mail:

- Put each command on a line of its own.
- Start each command in the first column of the line.
- Treat the Subject: line as part of the message body; when in doubt, leave the Subject: line blank.
- Don't put in messages intended for a human operator; generally, these will only "confuse" the server.

## Internet Navigation Tool Netiquette

Here's a short summary of netiquette regarding use of Internet navigators:

- Always try to use a version of the program on your own computer or at your own site, to make the least demands on the Internet and on other involved computers.
- If the tool has a client and server, always try to use a client version of the user software rather than a simple terminal-style remote login program.
- For non-work-related activity, try to use these tools in nonpeak hours.

## To Learn More About and Try Internet Tools

Information, code, clients, and servers for most Internet tools are available in a range of ways. Free public-domain versions of most Internet tools are, or are becoming, available for the leading computer hardware and software environments. Check with your system administrator if you have one. Alternatively, look for the appropriate files via Gopher or the archie archive index. If you are able to access the tool currently, check the information in its basic Help file. To learn more:

- See if any information is available on your local computer, by entering **man toolname** and *help toolname.*

  See if there are any related Usenet Newsgroups or electronic mailing lists. These usually contain discussions and announcements oriented to developers and systems managers, such as about on-going developments, new clients, new versions, installation and operations problems and solutions, and new service offerings.

- If you have access to the Usenet, see if there are any relevant Usenet Newsgroups. They are most likely to be either in the comp.infosystems.* or alt.* hierarchies. Also look for a FAQ document in news.answers.
- If you have e-mail access to the Internet, locate and subscribe to related mailing lists.
- If you have Internet anonymous-FTP access and have located a site with software and documentation, retrieve and read the documentation files.

Other good sources for information on Internet tools and navigators include:

- The ConneXions newsletter from the Interop Company
- On-line information maintained by the Clearinghouse for Networked Information Discovery and Retrieval (CNIDR) (See Chap. 12.)

Now that you've got a good general idea of how to access and use Internet navigator tools, let's take a look at some of the more popular ones.

Chapter

# 10

# Meet the Navigators: Gopher, archie, WAIS, and Others

*"Would you tell me, please, which way I ought to go from here?"*
*"That depends a good deal on where you want to get to," said the Cat.*
*"I don't much care where—" said Alice.*
*"Then it doesn't matter which way you go," said the Cat.*
*"—so long as I get* somewhere.*"*
*"Oh, you're sure to do that," said the Cat, "if you only walk long enough."*

*"Pigs and Pepper," Alice in Wonderland*

In the previous chapter, you got a general introduction to Internet navigator tools. Here, you'll "meet" some of them, including the more well-known ones and a few of their less-known, but equally useful, fellow navigators. As you'll see, many of the Internet navigators have become quite popular and widely used, not only within the Internet but also by a growing number of organizations within their own networks. (In Chap. 14 you'll see examples of companies using Internet navigator tools as ways to offer and access free-for-access and pay-for-access information services.)

There are many different Internet navigators, different versions for the different types of computers available, and many ways to use them—and new developments occur almost daily. The purpose of this chapter is to give you a sense of what's available and how to use whatever navigator tools you may find.

## Gopher: Living on Burrowed Time

Gopher, a.k.a. the Internet Gopher or "everyone's favorite rodent," is probably the best-known of the Internet navigators—a single tool that can act as a front end to literally the entire Internet's worth of tools and resources. Gopher condenses what would otherwise be using a series of separate tools such as archie, FTP, and **telnet**—quite possibly involving scribbling notes in between each step—into a sequence of Gopher commands, where each command's results become the choices in a new Gopher menu. Finding and retrieving a file via archie and FTP becomes a straightforward walk through Gopherspace—Gopher is even "smart" enough to convert retrieved files into the correct format. For example, Fig. 10.1 shows how a Gopher can find, retrieve, and display a current satellite weather map.

"We like to think of Gopher as 'duct tape' for the Internet," says Mark P. McCahill <mpm@boombox.micro.umn.edu>, Manager of Applications Systems & Programming in Computer & Information Services at U of Minnesota and the project leader of "Team Gopher" (the group of developers who created the Gopher concept and wrote the initial Gopher software). Gopher began in April 1991, as a project done at the Microcomputer, Workstation and Networks Center at the University of Minnesota to help the computer-using members on campus find and get answers to computer-related questions.

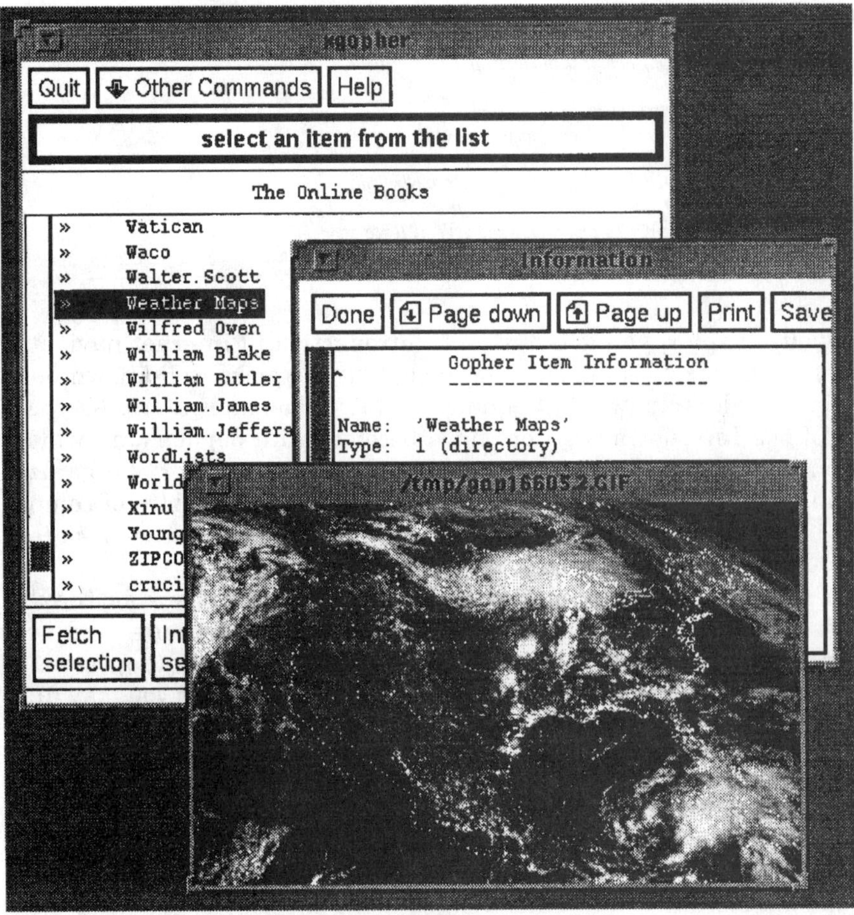


**Figure 10.1** Gopher in action.

At the time, the computer center staff had accumulated answers to literally thousands of questions by computer users regarding PCs, Macintoshes, software, and the like—and were looking for an easy way to deliver this information to thousands of students, faculty, and staff. Given that these people had computers and network access, creating a network-based information delivery system made sense; part of the goal was to automate as much as possible of the activity, freeing up the already-precious time of the network and computer support staffs. The answer was Gopher, a software system named after the official animal of the state of Minnesota (the Gopher state).* The name is also, obviously, a pun on "gofer," the nickname for people assigned to "go for" things—get coffee, sandwiches, the mail, packages, go run errands, etc. Being a "gofer" is a common job for new volunteers and staff.

Gopher was initially created to deliver, distribute, and provide access to local campus information at the University of Minnesota. The nature of Internet technology, however, makes it just as easy for users to access sites and information at other locations anywhere in the world (if they're on the Internet, of course). It didn't take long, however, before members of the Internet community began to use it as a World-Wide Information System, or WWIS (the jury is still out on how this acronym is pronounced). Within two years of its creation, Gopher has become one of the three most well-known and widely used navigator tools throughout the Internet community (archie and WAIS being the others).

In December 1991, the Gopher protocol was the 199th most "popular protocol" used on the NSFnet backbone based on relative numbers of packets generated by different applications which have individual protocols (e.g., **telnet,** FTP, e-mail, WAIS). A year later, "We were 14th, and in January 1993 we were 13th," states McCahill. "Between December 1991 to December 1992, Gopher traffic across the NSFnet backbone grew about 4000-fold, while the total NSFnet traffic grew 2.5-fold."

The term "Gopher server" or simply "Gopher" has come to refer to a computer running a copy of Gopher server software, plus whatever files, directories, and other objects are accessible through this Gopher server. As of early 1993, "GopherSpace" on the Internet included over 1100 Gopher servers, which in turn gave Gopher users access to over a million files, 100,000 directories, and 50,000 other resources and services.

## Duct tape for the Internet

"Gopher is a simple and extensible way of presenting a variety of Internet services to novice/naive users," says McCahill. "Right now [mid-1992] you can use Gopher to access archie, WAIS, FTP, Usenet, and a lot of other information and services, including other Gopher and non-Gopher servers—without [having to endure] a steep training curve.... It's the kind of system you would design if you had to do user support for around 45,000 students like we do."

---

*The gopher is also the University of Minnesota mascot and the athletic teams at the University are the "Golden Gophers."

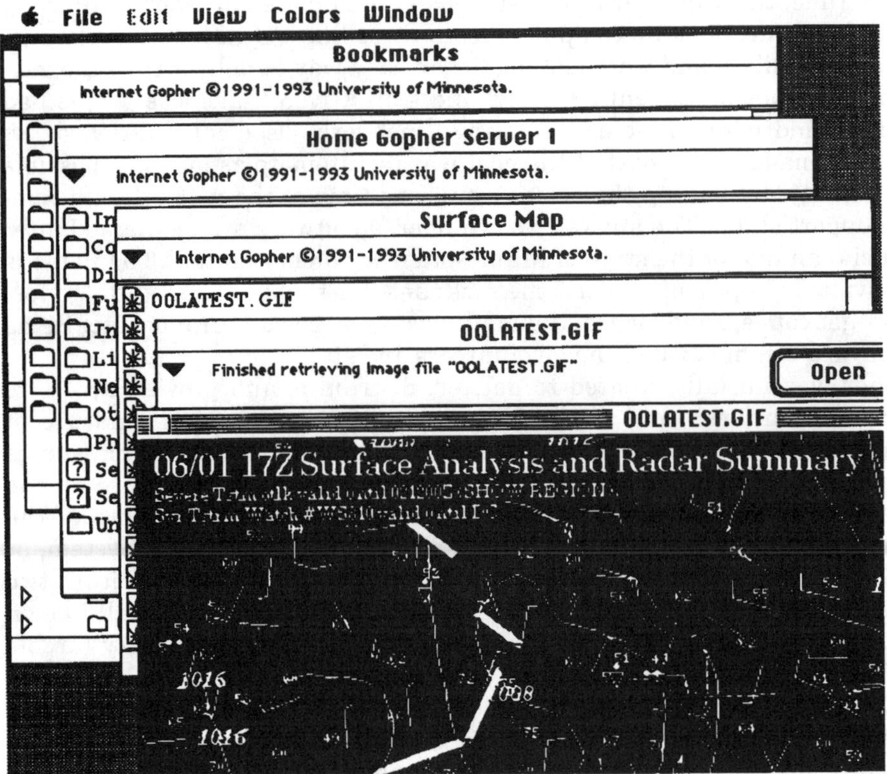


**Figure 10.2** TurboGopher on the Mac.

Like most Internet tools, the Gopher system consists of client and server software. You, as a user, run the Gopher client program (usually by entering "gopher"—see the upcoming section on "Using Gopher"). Figure 10.2 shows the TurboGopher client written for the Macintosh. Because of Gopher's ability to let users navigate not only within a server's local hierarchy but also among other Gophers and other resources, Peter Deutsch, cocreator of the archie resource locating system, sees Gopher as "a distributed information browsing and access system that combines many of the features of electronic bulletin board services such as Usenet, campus-wide information services such as PNN, and distributed directory services such as X.500."

"Gopher may be the most important new Internet service to be introduced in the last decade," suggested J. Q. Johnson, Director of Network Services at the University of Oregon (Eugene, OR). Like many other projects within the Internet, numerous people contributed time and effort to working on Gopher software and services and to making Gopher available. In fact, by mid-1992, interest in Gopher was large enough to lead to a mini-conference dedicated to Gopher. GopherCon 92 was sponsored by CICnet and held in Ann Arbor,

MI. (Attendance was intentionally limited to 50 people to keep the logistics manageable.)*

Gopher client programs talk to Gopher server programs, a.k.a. Gopher servers. Each Gopher server is set up with a pyramid of menus, whose choices are "information objects." Just as a file in a (Unix) system may contain data or be a directory pointing to other files and directories, Gopher's information objects may be specific resources (files, services, etc.), or submenus.

A Gopher server may be loaded with some site-specific information, such as University of Minnesota's help and calendar files, information and help files for your Internet public-access site, files, etc. "A Gopher menu may also 'point' to information objects which reside on a different server," notes McCahill. A Gopher client can take "pointer" information from one Gopher server and use it to automatically access other Gopher servers on the systems where the desired information resides.

It doesn't even matter what Gopher server you "start" from. The Gopher client you use can take information from, and connect to, any Gopher server on the Internet (subject to possible access restrictions). Thus, from whatever Gopher server you start from, you can navigate not only the information and resources on this Gopher server but any other reachable Gopher servers.

Another popular use for Gopher is as a focal point to "people-finding" services. Through Gopher you can access several dozen "CSO" on-line phone books (mostly for major educational institutions), a hundred or so institutions' **whois** servers, plus other popular Internet people-locater services such as **netfind,** the Usenet address server (a list of frequent contributors to Usenet groups), and an X.500 directory service. (For more about these people-finder facilities, see "'What's Your E-Mail Address?'—Locating Other Network Users" in Chap. 5.)

Gopher is based on several concepts:

- An easy-to-use user interface, with hierarchical menus that users can move around by simply using the "arrow" and <RETURN> keys, or a mouse, plus a few other simple one-letter commands
- Information objects organized into menus
- GopherSpace that "burrows" or "tunnels" through the Internet

Gopher connects your client program not only to Gopher servers on your computer or local network; it can establish connections to other resources anywhere in the Internet that you are allowed to make connections to. It is this automatic-connecting plus the hiding of different front ends that makes Gopher so popular and useful.

A Gopher server provides access to files and services, and organizes these into the menu hierarchy. Some of these choices may be other Gopher servers; some choices may turn up in several different menus. When you specify a

---

*A trip report about GopherCon, by Prentiss Riddle (riddle@is.rice.edu), was published in the on-line MSEN Internet Review (vol. 2, no. 3) and is available via Gopher, on the MSEN Gopher server. (To locate it, try a VERONICA search for **GopherCon.**)

menu choice that's a directory, your Gopher client program retrieves the list that comprises this directory from whichever Gopher server is handling this directory.

A Gopher information object can be any of a constantly growing variety of types, including:

- A file, including a BinHexed Macintosh file, a DOS binary archive, or a Unix uuencoded file.
- A directory (i.e., another menu, which may be on the same Gopher server or at another Gopher server)
- A VERONICA server—an archie-like database of the menu text lines from many (hundreds or more) Gopher servers, which can be searched for keyword matches (see Box: Indexing GopherSpace).
- A pointer to a text-based remote login (**telnet** or tn3270) connection.
- A pointer to a software gateway to other Internet services and facilities, such as file transfer (FTP) from public-access archive sites, Usenet News groups, etc.
- An alternative Index-Search server (e.g., archie, WAIS). Gopher has its own full-text search features but also lets you forward queries to non-Gopher search tools. Here, Gopher acts as the front end, accepting and passing along a search query to another service, such as archie, WAIS, **netfind,** the Usenet, **whois** or X.500 directory searches, or even other Internet navigators.
- A CSO phone-book server, sometimes also called "ph" (for phone), a server for a phone-book directory service developed by the University of Illinois Urbana/Champaign Computing and Communications Services Office.

The Gopher/Internet community continues to add new types of data and objects that Gopher servers can deliver. Experimental object types as of late 1992 included sound (with the data stream as a *mulaw* sound)*, the GIF (Graphic Interchange File) graphic standard, MIME multimedia object (using the Multipurpose Internet Mail Extension standard), and *html*, the HyperText Markup Language used by WorldWideWeb.

For many Gopher choices, when you select a resource that you'd normally have to invoke through several additional steps, such as remote login (**telnet**), file transfer (FTP), or queries to other services such as archie or WAIS, Gopher automatically performs the relevant commands or passes your commands along. In some cases, Gopher will have to "pass you along" to the client program for this new service (usually telling you first), such as for a **telnet** connection.

Conveniently, for many Gopher-accessed services, the Gopher client program will "remain in the loop," acting as the front end to this new resource.

---

*Mulaw is an encoding scheme for digitized sounds. Some Gopher clients and servers support playing 8-bit mulaw-encoded sounds, which can be played through the internal speakers on NeXt and Sun workstations.

### *Indexing GopherSpace: VERONICA, the "archie companion" for Gopher*

Until late 1992, one of the limiting aspects of Gopher was the lack of a global "index to GopherSpace." Many sites had put together searchable indexes of the objects available through their own Gopher server(s), but there was no master list of what was in all the Gopher servers. Short of finding and reading each index, plus exploring each unindexed Gopher's connecting to each one and exploring each menu, one by one, level by level, there was no way to determine what was available in the various Gopher servers.

Two years previously, frustration over similar difficulties in determining what files were available from public archives for retrieval via anonymous-FTP had led to the creation of the archie resource locator, which rapidly became one of the best-known and most widely-used Internet user services. The name "archie" was derived from "archive with no v." In November 1992, a similar solution appeared for GopherSpace: VERONICA, the "Very Easy Rodent-Oriented Net-wide Index to Computerized Archives." Developed at the University of Nevada, Reno, by Steve Foster and Fred Barrie, VERONICA has joined archie and WAIS as an essential tool for novice and experienced, occasional and regular Internet users alike.

According to Foster and Barrie,

> VERONICA was designed as a response to the problem of resource discovery in the rapidly expanding GopherSpace. Frustrated comments in Usenet Newsgroups [had] reflected the need for such a service. Additional motivation came from the comments of naive Gopher users, several of whom assumed that a simple-to-use service would provide a means to find resources "without having to know where they are."

VERONICA combines the "harvesting" and indexing resources at lots of servers into a single database, like that done by archie servers, with the "hypertext-launch" of tools such as WorldWideWeb and HYTELNET. Once you've selected VERONICA itself from a Gopher menu, you give search criteria, such as one or more keywords. VERONICA searches through all the Gopher menu entries in its database, such as "smiley" to find possible lists of smiley faces available through Gopher servers, "gophercon" to find Gopher conference write-ups, or searching for GIF files of weather via "gif" (locating GIF files) and "weather." For example, here's the results of a query based on "smiley" as the search keyword:

```
              Internet Gopher Information Client v1.1
         Search gopherspace by veronica at CNIDR: smiley

--> 1. Smiley Faces in the news (Thu, 11 Oct 90/Gene Spafford
       <spaf>).
    2. smiley-face.hqx <HQX>
    3. smiley-face.hqx <HQX>
    4. smiley.faces.
    5. Smiley_faces_and_internet_acronyms.
    6. List of Smiley Faces for E-mail.
    7. smiley.1.
    8. smiley.c.
    9. smiley.h.
    10. Unofficial Smiley Dictionary :-).
    11. smiley.txt.
    12. OFFICIAL_SMILEY_DICTIONARY..
    13. OFFICIAL_SMILEY_DICTIONARY..

    Press ? for Help, q to Quit, u to go up a menu
                                                      Page: 1/1
```

*(Continued)*

Once you find resources available through GopherSpace using VERONICA, Gopher will connect you right to them. The results, which can be Gopher links to anything from files to directories to other types of services, such as a WAIS database—are delivered as a Gopher menu—so you can choose and access any of them as another Gopher selection. (Consider saving the results, or specific found items, as Gopher "bookmarks.")

In mid-November 1992, at the time of VERONICA's first announcement, the VERONICA database contained menu entries for over half of 500 Gopher servers the developers had located. By February 1993, VERONICA was indexing over 1100 Gopher servers. "We hope that VERONICA will encourage Gopher administrators to use very descriptive titles on their menus," VERONICA's creators point out. "Notice that [VERONICA is not doing] full-text searches of data at Gopher-server sites, just as archie does not index the *contents* of anonymous-FTP sites but only the names of files at those sites. VERONICA indexes the *titles* on all levels of the menus, for most Gopher sites in the Internet."

Predictably, the demand for VERONICA service proved so great that, like the early archie service, it "melted the wire" to the initial site, overloading available computer and network resources. Other Internet sites such as CNIDR (see Chap. 12) have begun supporting VERONICA servers to help share the load from user queries.

To try VERONICA, select it from a Gopher menu (try selecting and looking in a menu item like "Other Gophers" if a VERONICA entry isn't immediately obvious). It's impossible to predict what additional features will have been added to VERONICA, so I recommend you simply go try it. For example, see if there's a WAIS database of FAQs or try locating files such as lists of smiley faces or Internet and other computer jargon. (If you have any comments or feedback, check the "About VERONICA" entry in its Gopher menu for appropriate e-mail addresses.)

In this way, when you access a program or service through Gopher such as archie, WAIS, or FTP, Gopher may be able to hide the fact that these may be different types of systems, with normally different front ends. In other words, by simply knowing a little about how to use Gopher, you may be able to also search archie, WAIS, and other databases; locate files and other resources; or retrieve files by anonymous-FTP, etc., because everything looks like Gopher. (Similarly, in reverse, other Internet navigators and tools, such as WorldWideWeb, may also query Gopher servers, transparently to their users.)

Edward Vielmetti <emv@msen.com>, Vice President of Research at MSEN (Ann Arbor, MI) offers several examples of how Gopher has succeeded in helping Internet users:

> For many users, Gopher is becoming the preferred way to retrieve files rather than directly using FTP. It's much easier for users—and it reduces the load on the computers that the files are retrieved from. Even more important, Gopher is allowing people and systems in different locations to cooperate and share resources more easily and flexibly than the traditional anonymous-FTP site approach. Gopher is being used in the biology and human genome community to "stitch together" access to various servers, as talked about in the Usenet bionet.general newsgroup.

Vielmetti also reports commercial, non-Internet uses of Gopher technology. "I've had mail from a few commercial sites who are using Gopher in-house to organize their access to resources outside the Internet." Gopher has become a standard method for Internet-connected organizations to make information available; it's not uncommon to see announcements for several new Gopher servers, and their associated information pools, per week. While there's no easy way to determine how many people are using Gopher in general, McCahill offers one awe-inspiring statistic: the U. Minn Gopher server received over a million requests from users at 35,000 computers in the 1-month period from November 2 to December 7, 1992. And that's just for one Gopher server (admittedly the most well-known one) out of hundreds.

### Using Gopher

Gopher is *very* easy to use. To use it, you first need to find a Gopher client program you can access. One may be available on your computer or through one of the Internet front ends or navigators available to you. Otherwise, you'll have to locate and do a remote login to a Gopher client at a public-access Gopher site, using the TCP/IP **telnet** command (which is what the front end or navigator may be doing, anyway). For more information about finding local and remote clients for Internet tools, see "Where the Clients Are" at the beginning of Part 2, and "Think Globally, Look for Clients Locally" in Chap. 9.

As a rule, the command to access a local Gopher client is simply:

```
gopher<RETURN>
```

To access most public-access Gopher sites, you open a remote login connection, using the TCP/IP **telnet** command; typically, you give *gopher* as the login name, and your Internet e-mail address in response to the Password prompt (if it's given). For example:

```
% telnet ux1.cso.uiuc.edu
Trying 128.174.5.59...
Connected to ux1.cso.uiuc.edu.
Escape character is '^]'.

UofI CCSO - Sequent S81 (ux1.cso.uiuc.edu - ttytz)
4.2+ BSD/5.3 UNIX - Dynix 3.1.2

login: gopher
Last login: Fri May 14 13:52:35 from world.std.com
```

or

```
% telnet is.internic.nic
   ...
login: gopher
```

See Box: Gopher Tips to learn how to get a current list of public-access Gopher sites.

If you are running the Gopher client program on your computer, it will check for your Gopher configuration file (on Unix systems, .gopherrc in your home directory). If the file doesn't exist, it may create it. This file contains configuration information. In particular, Gopher can save locations of particular information objects you have found, as bookmarks, in this file; you can look at and specify these bookmarks in future Gopher sessions.

### *Gopher Tips: To Find a Gopher*

If your Internet site doesn't have a local Gopher client, and you don't know of one, here's several ways to find one:

- The section "To Learn More About and Try Gopher" at the end of this chapter lists some of the public-access Gopher clients you can do a remote login (**telnet**) to over the Internet, as of late 1992.
- If you have access to the Usenet, look in these newsgroups:
  - news.answers or comp.infosystems.gopher for the Gopher FAQ
  - alt.internet.services for a recent posting of Scott Yanoff's Special Internet Connections list
  - Ask your system administrator.
  - Try "help gopher" and see what happens.
  - If you have any other Internet navigator, such as HYTELNET or TechInfo, see if one of these will connect you to a Gopher client or at least give you the address for a Gopher client.

In looking for an available Gopher client to access, try to find the one nearest to you on the Internet, in terms of connectivity; always bear in mind that you will be consuming network bandwidth when you are retrieving objects and Gopher menus (i.e., if you're in the United States, start at a Gopher in the States rather than one of the ones in Europe or Australia). (You may need to start with whatever Gopher you find first; once you've "entered GopherSpace," you should be able to see if there's a more appropriate site to work from.)

If you decide you like using Gopher, you'll probably want to get and install a copy of the appropriate client software locally at your site or system. "A client uses the custom features of the local machine (mouse, scroll bars, etc.)," the Gopher developers point out; also, a local client is likely to give you faster response.

The first act of your Gopher client, unless you give the "bookmark" option, is to retrieve the top-level, or "main" menu of your home Gopher server. You see this as a menu of choices:

```
           Internet Gopher Information Client v1.1

              Root gopher server: is.internic.net

      1. Information About the InterNIC.
 -->  2. InterNIC Information Services (General Atomics)/
      3. InterNIC Registration Services (NSI)/
      4. InterNIC Directory and Database Services (AT&T)/

 Press ? for Help, q to Quit, u to go up a menu
                                                  Page: 1/1
```

On Gopher menus, a / at the end of an item name (e.g., "InterNIC Registration Services") indicates that it is a directory. A **<?>** at the end of an item-name (e.g., "1: Search InfoSource by providing keyword <?>") indicates that the item is a "search engine." If you are using a local Gopher client on your own system, you can make Gopher begin on your "page of bookmarks" by including the **-b** (for "bookmark") option, like so:

```
% gopher -b
```

```
                    Quick Gopher Help
Moving around Gopherspace
-------------------------
Press return to view a document

Use the Arrow Keys or vi/emacs equivalent to move around

Up .................:  Move to previous line.
Down ...............:  Move to next line.
Right Return .......:  "Enter"/Display current item.
Left, u ............:  "Exit" current item/Go up a level.

>, +, Pgdwn, space ..:  View next page.
<, -, Pgup, b .......:  View previous page.

0-9 ................:  Go to a specific line.
m ..................:  Go back to the main menu.

Bookmarks
---------
a :     Add current item to the bookmark list.
A :     Add current directory/search to bookmark list.
v :     View bookmark list.
d :     Delete a bookmark/directory entry.

Other commands
--------------
q :     Quit with prompt.
Q :     Quit unconditionally.
= :     Display Technical information about current item.
O :     Change options.
/ :     Search for an item in the menu.
n :     Find next search item.

Press <RETURN> to continue, <m> to mail, <s> to save, or <p> to print.
```

**Figure 10.3** Instant gopher: The help screen from the ASCII Gopher client.

## Basic Gopher commands

Once you are "in" a Gopher client, you can give commands to move around the menus and menu choices, retrieve and view information, set or go to "bookmarks," initiate queries, and do whatever other choices are available. When reading a retrieved document, you can have Gopher save it to a local file or e-mail it to you or to someone else.

For most of your Gophering, all you have to do is use the Arrow and <RETURN> keys, or a mouse. (Some Gopher commands can be given by any of a choice of keys; for example, both the Left-arrow and *u* keys move you *up* one level of menu.) Here's a summary of essential Gopher commands; Fig. 10.3 shows you the Help text from the ASCII/VT100 Gopher client.

- To *move up* to the *previous* choice (up one) on the current menu, hit the *Up-arrow* key (not the caret (^) key).

- To *move down* to the *next* choice (down one) on the current menu, hit the *Down-arrow* key.
- To *select the current menu choice,* hit either the *Right-arrow* key or the <RETURN> key. (When you select a menu choice, on many Gopher clients, particularly VT100-style ASCII versions, you may see the message "Retrieving Directory..." or "Retrieving Information..." in one corner, plus a a blinking or changing character, whose motion assures you that information is being retrieved.)
- To *return to the previous menu,* hit either the *Left-arrow* key or the *u* key.
- To *quit* Gopher, hit the *q* key.

Once you've mastered these Gopher commands, if the current menu is more than one "page" (screenful), also try:

- To move forward to the next page of choices, hit >, +, <PageDown>, or <SPACE>.
- To move back to the previous page of choices, hit <, -, <PageUp>, or *b*.
- To *add a bookmark,* hit the *a* key (you'll be prompted for a nickname); to *view your bookmarks,* hit the *v* key.

When you're done browsing a retrieved document, Gopher will offer to save it for you in a file in your account, or to e-mail it to you or anyone else you specify.

Using Gopher is remarkably easy. Many of the Gopher clients are "smart" enough to "know" when you've located a file that requires special "handling" to retrieve, such as a BinHexed file for the Macintosh—and to perform associated tasks such as decoding the BinHex file for you.

Gopher can be fun to use and GopherSpace can be fun to explore. There are some frustrating aspects to using Gopher, as far as I'm concerned, as of the time this chapter was being wrapped up (although I expect most of these to be fixed over time and other nice features added as well):

1. At present, some versions of Gopher clients require you to fetch a complete document before you can examine it. This can be very frustrating when the fetch process takes more than a few seconds—is it worth waiting, or do you terminate the transaction without ever seeing the document? More advanced clients do not have this limitation. "The Macintosh TurboGopher client lets you read as the Fetch proceeds in the background," McCahill notes. "You can terminate a transaction without grabbing all the item's information."
2. There's currently no way to "leap" through menus, other than via your preset bookmarks or do a VERONICA search.
3. What's available via a given Gopher is largely dependent on what the people in charge of the server have decided to load in; new resources and services may easily have become available—but not yet made known to GopherSpace.

The addition of the VERONICA tool, providing archie-like searches of a database of Gopher menus, has resolved one of the most pressing concerns: being able to look for and find resources in GopherSpace when you aren't sure if they exist or where they are. (See Box: Indexing GopherSpace: VERONICA The "archie companion" for Gopher.)

VERONICA shares the same limitation as archie, WAIS, and all other content-driven searches, of course: if the right keywords aren't in the indexed text, you won't find certain entries. For example, searches for "smileys" [those things like :-) and :-( ] may not find entries containing "smiley"—and won't find lists labeled "emoticons" (a more official name for smiley faces).

Future releases and other versions of Gopher subsequent to the time of this writing may easily resolve any and all of these limits, for example, integrating WAIS searching of the archie database and having that result become a spontaneous, perhaps savable menu. Other Internet navigators lack some of these problems (TechInfo, described below, for example, can do the "taste before retrieving the whole" function) but may be missing other features you want.

### To learn more and try Gopher

If you have access to a Gopher client, connect to the University of Minnesota Gopher and look in the "Information about Gopher" directory. As of mid-1993, public-access remote login Gopher clients are available at nearly two dozen sites around the world.

If you are interested in news about new Gopher servers and software and have Usenet access, read the Usenet comp.infosystems.gopher Newsgroup. If you do not have Usenet access, or would rather receive this newsgroup as e-mail messages, you can subscribe to the gopher-news mailing list by sending e-mail to gopher-news-request@boombox.micro.umn.edu with a message such as "Please add me to this list" in the message Subject or body.

The Gopher FAQ "gopher-faq" is posted to the Usenet Newsgroups comp.infosystems.gopher and news.answers roughly every 2 weeks. The most recent version of the Gopher FAQ can be gotten through gopher or via anonymous-FTP from pit-manager.mit.edu:/pub/usenet/news.answers/gopher-faq.

To get a copy of Gopher FAQ by e-mail, send a message to mail-server@rtfm.mit.edu with "send usenet/news.answers/finding-sources" in the body to find out how to do FTP by e-mail (also see "Internet Services Based on E-Mail" in Chap. 5).

Public Gopher software is available via anonymous-FTP from boombox.micro.umn.edu in the directory /pub/gopher. (Gopher software copyrighted by the University of Minnesota is available free for nonprofit use but not necessarily free if used in for-profit activity. There's also Gopher software developed at other locations, which may have different stipulations.)

Clients are available for systems including Unix, X Window, Macintosh Hypercard, Macintosh Application, DOS (with the Clarkson Driver), NeXtStep, VM/CMS, and VMS. Other Gopher software available is listed in the Gopher FAQ. To contact the folks who did much of the Gopher software, send e-mail to gopher@boombox.micro.umn.edu, or write to them c/o:

Internet Gopher Developers
100 Union St. SE #190
Minneapolis, MN 55455

To read more about Gopher, see:

"The Internet Gopher," *ConneXions,* July 1992, Interop

"Exploring Internet GopherSpace," *The Internet Society News,* v1n2 1992

"The Internet Gopher Protocol," *Proceedings of the Twenty-Third IETF,* CNRI, sec. 5.3

"The Internet Gopher," *INTERNET: Getting Started,* SRI International, sec. 10.5.5

## TechInfo: The M.I.T. CWIS for Its Public Information

You'd expect M.I.T. to be highly networked. And you'd be right. Nearly every building, office, and computer at M.I.T. is connected to the campus network; the university as a whole is connected into the Internet; nearly all students, faculty, and staff has or can have an account that lets them make use of the M.I.T. network and access the Internet.

Like any university, M.I.T. has lots of information which its community wants regular access to. In July 1989, the TechInfo project was started up to develop a Campus-Wide Information System (CWIS) to meet these needs; a year later, the system was up and running and has been in use ever since. According to Steve Neitermen (wade@mit.edu), a programmer/analyst on the TechInfo team at M.I.T.:

> At M.I.T., TechInfo is used to make information available to students, faculty, and staff. We're trying to provide a central repository for official M.I.T. info, e.g., the schedule for the Athletic Pool, faculty rules and reg, campus movie schedules, campus newspapers, class schedules, course catalog (great for prospective students!), visitor information, and more.
>
> Anyone in M.I.T.—or on the Internet—can access the TechInfo system at M.I.T. to read information. We exercise control by restricting who can "write" information into TechInfo, so that not just anyone can update the weather, for example.
>
> TechInfo makes it possible for any user to "publish" a document, through the user interface, like Usenet or e-mail, except it's a different front end. It's a distributed publishing environment, unlike Gopher, WWW, etc.
>
> Like Gopher and other CWISs, TechInfo offers users hierarchical menus of documents and submenus. However, there are differences.
>
> Because the list of documents available through TechInfo is in a centralized database, as opposed to the, say, Gopher, users can query and make use of the database structure as well as the documents themselves, for example:
>
> - An "outline" feature to expand a folder to multiple levels
> - A "What's New" function, enabling a user to ask for documents changed since a specific date
> - A "path" command, where a user may have a list of documents returned from a "full text search—new in the next release" and ask the system where this item is in the hierarchy

- The ability to add information such as descriptive keywords, contact information, and "date of last modification" for each document

How successful/useful is TechInfo? Over the past 2 years, usage—both from the local M.I.T. community and elsewhere across the Internet—has trebled, according to Neiterman, and, even with no publicity or big push, TechInfo servers have sprung up around the world. New releases should support graphics, such as weather maps, full-text searching using WAIS. Versions are available for use on Unix systems—command-line and X Window/Motif GUI—as well as for Macintosh, DOS, Microsoft Windows, and VM/CMS systems (as long as it's running TCP/IP). TechInfo supports access via remote login (**telnet**) and dial-up.

TechInfo isn't just for M.I.T. At least half a dozen other sites besides M.I.T. are running TechInfo. The source code is freely available, by anonymous-FTP. For more info on TechInfo:

- To try TechInfo, use **telnet techinfo.mit.edu**
- For TechInfo code, Mac and DOS binaries, documents are available by anonymous-FTP. Try net-dist.mit.edu in /pub/techinfo/—or do an archie query to see if there's a "closer" source
- To be added to the "techinfo" electronic mailing list, send a message to "techinfo-request@mit.edu" with "Please add me to this list" in the message subject or body

## WorldWideWeb: A Hypertext View of the Internet

WorldWideWeb (a.k.a. WWW or W3*) is one of the contenders in the "be the front Internet navigator-and-front-end sweepstakes," that is, to be *the* tool through which Internet users access other Internet front ends, navigators, information, services, and resources.

WorldWideWeb was started up by Tim Berners-Lee and others at CERN, the European Particle Physics Laboratory in Geneva, Switzerland, as a way to organize information for the researchers.

WorldWideWeb uses the hypertext, or hypermedia, concept, where references within a document or list become the jumping-off points to other documents, lists, resources, or actions. Individual documents and pools of information become joined with a cosmic Chutes and Ladders (or teleportation points), letting you follow references by selecting highlighted keywords and items. According to Berners-Lee, "WorldWideWeb is a wide-area hypermedia information retrieval initiative aiming to give universal access to a large universe of documents. The project merges the techniques of information retrieval and hypertext to make an easy but powerful global information system."

---

*The "WWW" abbreviation tends to be used in print and "W3" used when in speaking. As archie cocreator Peter Deutsch likes to point out, "WWW" is one of those rare acronyms that takes longer to say than the term it stands for. But then again, so does W3.

Originally developed for the High Energy Physics community (such as the users of CERN), WWW's use has been spreading to other communities, attracting interest in particular from "the user support, resource discovery and collaborative work areas."

"Most users treat WorldWideWeb initially as an Internet navigator, as they do Gopher or other tools," observes Berners-Lee.

> As they explore the 'web,' they feel they are exploring information which is structured—but each person may perceive a different structure, reflecting the information and resources they're looking for and using.
>
> The cool thing about WWW is that if the user has an interface which supports hypertext, such as one of the ones for the Macintosh or X11 (X Window/Motif), it can be used to seamlessly represent and link anything which is out there—Gopher menu items, WAIS databases, FTP directories, Usenet News articles or newsgroups...all these things just look like hypertext.

As you may suspect, WorldWideWeb developers and users tend to be biased in favor of WWW (and correctly so, they will tell you). Like Gopher, WAIS, and other emerging client-server-based Internet tools, one of WWW's goals is to let you, as a user, search, traverse, and use many types of information, at many sites, in many forms, all from one user interface, rather than having to know and access a series of different programs directly.

Also, WWW, like Gopher, WAIS, and other systems, is intended to help people make information, resources, and services available to the widest possible community of users with a single "connection." It's like making it possible for you to, say, make an article available to people who have telephones, fax machines, Apple Macintoshes, DOS PCs, and Windows PCs, from a single version in one place.

WWW presents you with *documents* and *links.* A link leads you to another document, which in turn may have other links; you can easily never take the same path through the Web twice. If a document is itself a hypertext document, you may be catapulted to a specific place within the next document. Some documents are indexes, which you search rather than read. The results of your search give you links to other documents.

Like Gopher, TechInfo, and others, WWW uses clients and servers, allowing the user to start at one part of the Internet's mesh (or "web") of information and resources, and zip around. Using WorldWideWeb is relatively straightforward (although it can be frustrating). One of its good points is that it takes you directly to other places of interest. However, like all the other tools, someone has to decide on and enter link information; WWW can't "find" anything for you except those resources and pointers it knows about. The search mechanisms help, but they too run up against the ultimate limit: You can't find things if you don't know what you're looking for or that haven't been indexed appropriately. (This is why we have library sciences experts.)

To use WorldWideWeb, as with Gopher, WAIS, TechInfo, and other navigator tools, you access a client. (You can also make documents and services available to and via WWW, but that's outside the scope of this book.) Start by seeing if you have a WWW client available locally, by entering **www<RETURN>** (also try **worldwideweb<RETURN>**). Check with your system administrator to see if a WWW client is available but you're not getting it for some reason; ask to have one installed.

WWW clients include graphic-oriented versions for the Macintosh, NeXt, and half a dozen for X.11 (X Windows/Motif) systems. There are also line-mode browser versions for Unix systems to support VT100/ASCII terminal and **telnet** sessions, and for DOS PCs. Berners-Lee points out:

> The reason for installing the software locally is that you will get better functionality. With the X Windows or Mac browsers you will have point-and-click jumping and other hypertext and graphic-based features. Even with a client that only provides the line-mode interface, you will be able to print, save, copy, and jump to **telnet** sites—which is prohibited for security reasons if you have already telnetted to info.cern.ch. Also, you'll avoid adding another **telnet** session to our system load at CERN.

You can also connect via remote login (**telnet**) to one of the public-access WorldWideWeb sites over the Internet. As of early 1993, Scott Yarnoff's "Special Internet Connections" list (see Chap. 18) included five public WWW clients worldwide.

Some sites won't require any user-name or password; likely user-names to try include "www" or "web," as well as the standard "guest" or "anonymous." If you connect to a public-access WWW site, you'll be accessing one of the simple VT100/ASCII line-mode browsers. Like most Internet navigator tools, the main functions within WWW are easy to use and reasonably obvious—- <RETURN> or <MOUSE-CLICK> to select, h or ? for help, and so on.

Graphic WWW clients show links via highlighting. Line-mode browsers let you find information by following references or using keywords. When you see a reference—a number in brackets, such as reference[23]—you simply type the number and <RETURN>. Some documents are indexes; for these, you enter the WWW **find** command plus one or more keywords. Here's a line-browser example of WWW:

```
Example 1:    Cross-references to more WWW information: see
              also command line syntax[2], shortcuts[3],
              installation[4], customization[5], deeper
              details[6]. Pursuing these links will tell you
              more about WWW. The next gives you some sense
              of the information that WWW can transport you
              to quickly and easily.

Example 2.    Information all across the Internet made
              accessible via WWW:

Literature    Project Gutenberg[20] : two classic books a
              month, available by FTP. See their explana-
              tions[21], the index and newsletter[22], books
              published in 1991[23], 1992[24], and reserved
              for the USA[25].
Humanities    Discussion[26] , Poetry[27] , Scifi
              reviews[28].
```

and here's an example of one of the many GUI front ends:

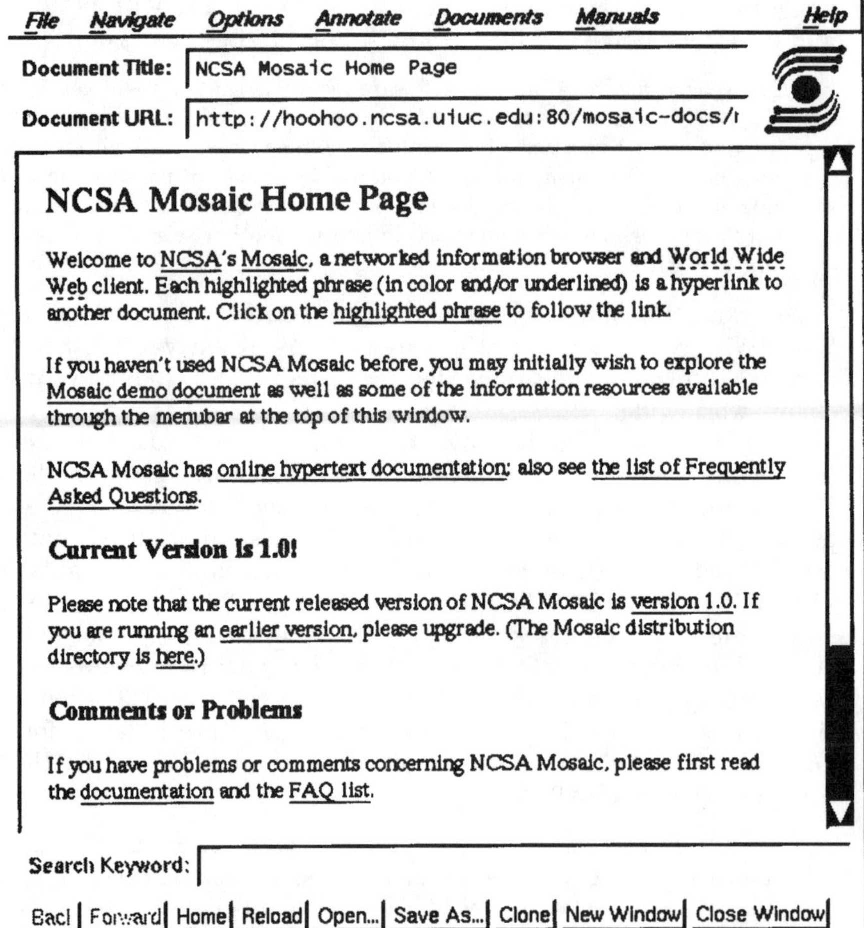

File Navigate Options Annotate Documents Manuals Help
Document Title: NCSA Mosaic Home Page
Document URL: http://hoohoo.ncsa.uiuc.edu:80/mosaic-docs/
NCSA Mosaic Home Page
Welcome to NCSA's Mosaic, a networked information browser and World Wide Web client. Each highlighted phrase (in color and/or underlined) is a hyperlink to another document. Click on the highlighted phrase to follow the link.
If you haven't used NCSA Mosaic before, you may initially wish to explore the Mosaic demo document as well as some of the information resources available through the menubar at the top of this window.
NCSA Mosaic has online hypertext documentation; also see the list of Frequently Asked Questions.
Current Version Is 1.0!
Please note that the current released version of NCSA Mosaic is version 1.0. If you are running an earlier version, please upgrade. (The Mosaic distribution directory is here.)
Comments or Problems
If you have problems or comments concerning NCSA Mosaic, please first read the documentation and the FAQ list.
Search Keyword:
Back Forward Home Reload Open... Save As... Clone New Window Close Window


If you expect to use WWW more than occasionally, install a local WWW client on your own computer (ask your system administrator if you are on a public-access site or shared facility).

Public-domain software, documentation, and installation instructions for WWW are available via anonymous-FTP file transfer from locations including CNIDR, or info.cern.ch in the directory /pub/www/src. (You may want to query the archie archives database to see if there is a "closer" copy of the file[s] you want.)

To learn more about WorldWideWeb, read:

"A Summary of the WorldWideWeb System," by T. J. Berners-Lee, *ConneXions,* July 1992.

"World-Wide Web: The Information Universe," T. J. Berners-Lee, R. Cailliau, J-F. Groff, B. Pollermann, CERN, *Electronic Networking: Research, Applications and Policy,* vol. 2, no. 1, pp. 52–58, Spring 1992, Meckler Publishing, Westport, CT.

You can also join Usenet comp.infosystems.www Newsgroup.

## Other Front Ends, Navigators, CWISs, and WWISs, etc.

As mentioned earlier, Gopher, TechInfo, and WorldWideWeb are far from the only Internet navigators and front ends available. Here's brief information about a few more.

### HYTELNET

HYTELNET is an acronym for "HYpertext browser for TELNET-accessible sites"—but since its inception has become far more than that. HYTELNET is a program developed beginning in late 1990 by Peter Scott <SCOTT@sklib.usask.ca>, Manager of Small Systems at the University of Saskatchewan in Canada, to help librarians and other Internet users find and connect to Internet sites and resources. Based on a hypertext utility Scott had previously developed to help people use an e-mail program, HYTELNET lets users browse and select from lists of Internet resources.

"HYTELNET was designed with one goal in mind," according to Scott, who has written-on-paper lists of Internet-accessible libraries, "to make access to Internet resources as easy as possible for both new and experienced networkers, and to ensure that the information being presented was timely, accurate, and understandable. It was the first software package for personal-computer users, which attempted to bring some order to the chaos of remote Internet login."

HYTELNET assists Internet-connected users in connecting to the Internet-accessible sites and resources such as "library catalogs, Free-Nets, CWISs, BBSs, Gophers, WAIS, full-text databases, 'electronic' books, network information centers, and many other useful services scattered around the globe that can be reached via remote login (**telnet**)," according to Scott. "The program also includes a glossary of Internet terms, and a file containing instructions on the use of the **telnet** program itself."

HYTELNET works from a site list that is periodically updated by Scott, currently via e-mail, and includes tools to let the updates be automatically incorporated into the HYTELNET resource list. Versions of HYTELNET are available for IBM PC, Unix, VMS, and Macintosh computers. The DOS version runs as a TSR (Terminate-and-Stay-Resident) program.

If you simply want to try HYTELNET, a public-access copy of the Unix version [written by Earl Fogel (fogel@jester.usask.ca) in Computing Services at the University of Saskatchewan] is available via remote login (**telnet**) to access.usask.ca, (login as "hytelnet"), according to Scott.

To use HYTELNET, type **hytelnet<RETURN>** on your system to see if the facility is currently installed. If not, check with your system administrator; then go retrieve the appropriate files. According to Scott, the "official" anonymous-FTP site for HYTELNET files is access.usask.ca, in directory pub/hytelnet. HYTELNET software may also be available from numerous sites; do a query to the archie archive database. (Search for the strings "hytenl" and "HYTELN"—the filenames include version numbers, such as HYTELN60.ZIP.)

### LIBS, Columbus, COMPASS, and more

There are only a few of the Internet Navigators available. For another library-oriented Internet navigator, there's also LIBS. NetCom, the public-access Internet site and service provider in California, has an easy-to-use front end for users. So do account providers DELPHI and PANIX. CERFnet offers COMPASS, yet another front end. Over in Waltham, MA, Prospect Innovation Center developers are working on a navigator; likewise, so are the folks at Harrison & Troxteth; it is nicknamed Columbus. Boston University has a custom graphic-oriented user interface for their campus network; by extension, it's also an Internet navigator. And at least half a dozen people I know of are working on their own Internet navigator products.

## Resource Discovery and Indexing: Finding Files, Resources, Services, People, and Other Things on the Internet

Knowing how to dial a telephone number isn't much use if you don't know who you can call or what their numbers are. Imagine trying to make a hotel reservation or check movie times without knowing where hotels or movie theaters are located or their phone numbers. Or trying to watch television without any program time and description listings—perhaps not even a list of available channels. How much time and effort would you be willing to spend trying to find something by guesswork? Imagine how time-consuming and frustrating it would be to call each hotel, theater, or television station individually versus looking information up in the newspaper or calling Information.

Until the early 1990s, this was an all-too-good description of the Internet's information directories (used for finding such things as information about users or the location and accessibility of services). In the 1980s, this was not as big a problem as you might think. The Internet used to consist of a few hundred organizations, and users were reasonably familiar with their tools and were connecting for specific motivations. Within each community, it was reasonably well known what files and resources were available and where they were. If someone wrote a new program and made it available for remote login (**telnet**) or retrieval by public-access file transfer (anonymous-FTP), you'd probably find out soon enough through word of mouth. And it was usually possible to query leading people in the field directly by e-mail if you had a question.

Today, however, that's a lot less likely. As of the early 1990s, tens of thousands of organizations are attached to the Internet, and there are millions of new users—many of whom use Internet facilities only infrequently and have little or no idea of how to use them properly. Also, the reasons people join the Internet in the 1990s are no longer so predefined or limited as in the past. And both the number and range of available resources on the Internet have been growing explosively—for starters, there are over 1500 publicly accessible anonymous-FTP archive sites, 1100+ Gopher servers, and hundreds of public and university library on-line catalogs.

One part of the answer may be the new point-and-shoot, graphic-oriented user interfaces, such as Gopher, Hytelnet, TechInfo, WorldWideWeb, and the front ends offered by various developers and public-access Internet sites. Another important part of the answer to the question of how to find out what's available is *resource discovery and indexing services.* The premiere example of this type of service in the Internet is *archie,* the Internet resource-locating system. Peter Deutsch, cocreator of archie (which I'll get to in a few paragraphs) points out, "Before a user can effectively exploit any of the services offered by the Internet community, they must be aware of both the *existence* of the service and the resource through which it is available. Adequately addressing this "resource discovery problem" is a central challenge for both providers of user services and for those users wishing to take fuller advantage of the Internet."

As one example, for many Internet users, particularly programmers and engineers, the main reason to have access to the Internet is software archives—shareware and freeware source code, and associated documents—which they can retrieve by file transfer (anonymous-FTP), e-mail servers, and other approaches.

Your reason for using the Internet may be seeking access to commercial pay-for-use on-line databases or joining international educational role-playing simulations or finding all the libraries, newsletters, and research groups studying the reestablishment of colonies of puffins along the coasts of Maine, Nova Scotia, and Scotland.* Maybe you simply want to find one program, like a copy of the Eudora e-mail program for your Macintosh Powerbook or Windows notebook PC. Perhaps you're enjoying playing Go with someone via the Internet Go Server and you're wondering if there's an Internet Duplicate Bridge Server, or you're about to move across the country and want to find the nearest public-access Internet site, so you can rejoin the Internet when you get there.

---

*And figuring out how a puffin can hold a dozen herring tails in its beak, particularly grabbing the last one or two without dropping the first ten. If you know or find out, send me e-mail, would you?

Or perhaps you've discovered Gopher, the Internet navigator tool developed at the University of Minnesota and described earlier in this chapter. GopherSpace provides access to over a million things at over a thousand sites. But how can you find what's there, and locate the one you want, without having to investigate "every burrow and tunnel"?

Resource discovery and indexing—enabling users to determine what resources are available, in a relatively easy fashion—is one of the many challenges facing Internet developers and service providers for the 1990s. Fortunately, 1991 and 1992 were landmark years in terms of new Internet resource discovery and indexing tools and services; with the wide availability of tools like archie, VERONICA, and **whois++,** the task of finding resources, files, services, and even people on the Internet is becoming something even novice users can do relatively quickly and effectively.

Let's take a look at archie, the first and most well known of the Internet resource indexers which has successfully addressed the discovery aspect of the question.

## Indexing the Internet: Go Ask archie

For many people and organizations, access to public-domain programs, documents, and other files is sufficient reason to plug into the Internet. Even for this one category of Internet resources, the number of archive sites, and the number and breadth of their offerings, have gone beyond the scope of most individuals to keep track of.

How can you, a user, determine what's out there that meets your needs, such as programs you can run on an old CP/M-based personal computer? And even once you find out, say, that there's an archive of CP/M programs, how do you figure out where it is, network-wise? Answer: You can't.

With so many different archives, it can be hard to figure out in which archive(s) that you can access the items you want can be found, and where, network name and address-wise, these archives are. And if you don't know what you want, beyond, say, "compilers" or "CP/M stuff," it's even more overwhelming.

### archie: Born to collect and catalog

archie is one of the Horatio Alger stories of the Internet. It begins with the creation of a relatively modest enterprise, done without any expectation that it would soon become one of the four most-mentioned Internet tools (the others being Gopher, WAIS, and WorldWideWeb) and arguably one of the two most popular and widely used such tools (the other being Gopher). The archie service began in late 1989, as a "skunk-works" project by staff and students at the School of Computer Science at McGill University, Quebec, Canada, to help keep track of free software available from anonymous-FTP archive sites on the Internet. (See Box: The Origin of archie.)

*The Origin of archie Recounted by Peter Deutsch*

It all started [in late 1989], when I was systems manager for the McGill School of Computer Science, with Alan [Emtage] working for me as a graduate student systems staff. One of Alan's responsibilities was to keep track of public-domain software available for free from anonymous-FTP archive sites, since, like any underfunded university, we had a strong aversion to spending money when we could get something for free.

To understand our mindset, you need to know that Luc Boulianne, who was another one of my staff (and now has my old job as systems manager) defined computer science as "the art of minimizing keystrokes."

At this time, there were maybe 50 to 100 archive sites that we knew about. Alan used to periodically connect [by anonymous-FTP] to each one and get listings of directory contents, to see what had been added. After doing this long enough for it to become boring, Alan wrote some Unix shellscripts to automate this process, putting all the listings into files. Then, to find filenames on demand, he would simply do Unix **grep** commands on these listings files.

At first I thought he was pretty darned clever because he was answering our requests so fast. One day I discovered the set of files and realized how he could locate things *so* fast. I started doing my own **greps** and the world was good.

The final piece of the puzzle involves, of all things, cryptography, the National Security Agency and U.S. government policy of restricted export of software, since there is a ban on export of the DES (Digital Encryption Standard) code outside the United States.

I happened to be reading one of the Usenet security newsgroups and saw a posting from someone asking for "a copy of DES from a site outside of the United States." I did a quick **grep** to Alan's files and found DES programs at about twenty suitable sites! I posted the results, along with a comment to the effect that we had a nifty little tool to gather the listings and could search them at will.

Well, by the end of the next day I'd received about thirty requests for additional searches (although, strange to say, no one asked for the listings files, nor the shellscript). I, too, decided to do some computer science: I directed the gang, including Alan and also Bill Heelan, another member of my support staff, to write a front-end program for accessing the listings files. This would let anyone [everyone?] do their own searches, including users elsewhere in the Internet, leaving me in peace so I could go back to reading Usenet News.

The rest, as they say, is history.

[The server at McGill has been out of service since 1992, Deutsch notes. quiche.cs.mcgill.ca, the borrowed machine on which the original archie ran for so long, closed down after hardware failure and was never replaced.]

## What archie consists of

The archie system consists of several components, which are discussed in the following sections.

**Data gathering.** The data gathering, or "harvesting," component consists of the programs that gather information from the many locations on the Internet, process it, and insert the results of it into a database. Examples are obtaining a directory listing of a public anonymous-FTP site's file archives and from this, generating index entries that include the site ID and the date the information was harvested. According to Peter Deutsch:

> In addition to actually gathering in information from hosts across the Internet, this component also makes it possible for information providers to register new

> sites with archie as they come on-line. This in turn means users have access to new information as it becomes available.
>
> The archie servers automatically update their listing information from indexed sites periodically. The update policy is set by the server's administrator, and can be arbitrarily complex.
>
> For example, the archie server in Australia updates all Australian sites each night, but only fetches updates from across the Pacific for each site once a month. This ensures users that the information they receive is reasonably timely, without imposing an undue load on the archive sites or network bandwidth.

(It also means that there may be items available that a given archie server doesn't—yet—know about.)

**Database server component.** This part of archie includes the programs that manage the databases, the databases themselves, and the User Access programs that receive and respond to user queries. These programs are the intermediary between whatever program you use to query archie and the database server; they accept your query and get the results back to you. The archie User Access programs make it possible to query archie in real-time from your computer or by e-mail.

Because the archie programs have been designed to share and coordinate information-gathering, it's possible to have several archie servers at various locations on the Internet, each with a full copy of the archie databases. It shouldn't matter which archie a user queries, enabling the network and processing load to be shared (and keeping a given location from becoming overloaded). For example, in February, 1993, there were 21 licensed public-access and internal-use-only archie servers on the Internet, supporting access to copies of the same database.

**User clients.** There are also the archie *user clients,* which are the programs you use from your own PC or workstation to access the archie databases. (As of early 1993 there was no Macintosh user client for archie.) It's also possible to query archie using basic Internet services, such as **telnet** and e-mail, as well more modern services such as Gopher, WorldWideWeb, or WAIS.

## Another grass roots Internet success story

archie also offers an excellent example of the community, grassroots nature of the Internet. Where else could a random group of people decide to invent something, proceed to do it on an electronic shoestring, and have it become a "big hit" in a year? Equally, dozens of individuals, including leading computer researchers and software engineers, have contributed large amounts of time to creating or modifying other software to work with archie; a dozen or more sites have provided computer cycles and storage to in turn make archie services available to more Internet users.

When archie was first implemented, during 1989 and 1990, many researchers working on Internet services "scoffed at the idea of archie and claimed that it would neither scale nor be able to handle the entire set of anonymous-FTP archives," recalls Deutsch. But, to paraphrase Stan Lee from the first issue of Marvel's Spiderman comics: "Great responsibility can come with relatively small power."

By late 1991, archie's database cataloged the holdings of over 800 anonymous-FTP sites, all of which were Unix-based systems (in terms of type of computer offering the archive, versus what types of computers the programs could be used on), and five to ten new sites were adding themselves to the archie database each week. A year later, in late 1992, the archie archive database listed over 1500 archive-bearing sites at companies, universities, government agencies, BBSs, and other organizations around the world, all connected to the Internet and available to Internet users via file transfer. The contents of these sites as listed with archie total in excess of $2^1/_2$ million files totalling in at 230+ Gbytes (230,000,000,000 bytes)—close to a quarter of a terabyte.

In these archives' millions of files are programs for use in MS-DOS, Unix, C, ADA, Apple, Mac, Amiga, VAX, CP/M, and other types of systems. Much of the code is shareware, freeware, or public-domain software. Other of the code comes from companies using the Internet as part of their distribution channel (in very legitimate ways, please note). Apple, for example, makes certain software for the Macintosh available for downloading via the Internet.

"These archive sites hold more than just programs," adds Deutsch. "There are abstracts, copies of papers and technical reports for many universities, databases such as weather satellite images, prerecorded sounds, scanned images of many types, and lots more." If you tried to put this all on 1.4-Mbyte, 3.5-inch floppy disks, the pile of disks would measure about 5 cubic yards, or a half-mile-high pancake-style stack (or 500 CD-ROMs, which you could try carrying. Even walking at 3 miles per hour, you'd have an effective bandwidth still faster than an Ethernet—almost 80 Gbytes per hour [$1^1/_3$-Gbytes per minute, or 20-Mbytes per second]).

The meaningful total may be somewhat less, since "some of these files can be considered redundant in that copies of some programs are stored in dozens of sites," points out archie cocreator Alan Emtage. "Also, this reflects versions of the same program for use on different types of computers and 'old' versions of a program which lie around for many years—but these may contain techniques useful to other people."

On the other hand, Peter Deutsch points out:

> This does not necessarily reflect the total number of sites and files on the entire Internet, just what we keep track of in the archie database. And, of course, more sites and files continue to be added daily, as more people come onto the Internet, bringing more information with them. For all of its failings, anonymous-FTP is still one of the easiest and most popular methods for sharing information with the entire Internet community.

### Tens of millions of user queries answered

The success of archie can be measured in many ways: the number of archie servers made available by Internet providers and sites, the growing number of software clients developed by the Internet community to access the archie servers, integration of archie with other Internet navigator and front-end tools, and, most definitively, the steadily growing number of user requests to archie to locate software. What is clear is that the number of queries, and users making these queries, has been growing steadily. By November 1990, the archie server at McGill was receiving about thirty logins per day. Soon after the archie group announced the dedicated-database version of archie in that month, "the popularity of the program grew by leaps and bounds," said Deutsch in an e-mail message some months later. "We are now averaging over 500 per day, with our all-time high coming in at 700 for a single day." By September, 1991, login, file transfer, and e-mail queries to the archie server at the McGill site were averaging well over 2600 per day. A year later, the archie servers around the Internet were getting an estimated 30,000 queries per day—from users on five continents and in all known countries on the Internet, reported Emtage, including Poland, Taiwan, Singapore, Iceland, South Africa, Russia, Estonia, Latvia, and other countries of the former Soviet Union.

By late 1992, there were over 20 public-access archie servers across the Internet everywhere from the United States to Australia, Austria, Finland, Korea, Switzerland, and Sweden, and several commercial network service providers are about to announce additional archie servers.

(According to Deutsch, as of early 1993, "There is a French language archie at "archie.uqam.ca" and translations into other languages is expected with the next release of the **telnet** client, which can serve 8-bit characters and thus additional character sets. Korea has already translated much of the online docs and we expect many of the European archies to follow suit.")

To minimize Internet traffic over the Internet's often-congested or lower-bandwidth transoceanic links, a number of the archie servers are configured as "satellite" servers. Satellite archies are intended to support queries from their local community, according to Deutsch. "A satellite archie server contains the entire database but is set to gather only local information. Any new information a satellite gathers is fed back to the master database, so all archie servers will 'become aware of' all new archive contents."

## From toy to tools: The business of Internet services

Over the course of its first 2 years, what began as a "way to save keystrokes" grew into a major Internet resource, namely archie. The deployment of more 3.0 archie servers across the Internet helped lighten the load on the overburdened computer, and Internet connection at McGill never intended to support that degree of load. What soon emerged as the limits to archie's growth was the limited availability of time, budget, and other resources for archie's developers to keep expanding archie's capabilities.

In 1992, Deutsch and Emtage formed a software company, Bunyip Information Systems, whose goals include developing services—including archie—for the Internet and other enterprise interworking environments, which they may either run themselves, or sell to Internet providers, sites, and other organizations.

Fall 1992 marked the official release of archie Version 3.0 from Bunyip. According to Emtage,

> archie 3.0 is a commercially supported version of the archie system and is available to Internet service providers wishing to build, maintain, and offer collections of useful information to an Internet community. This does *not* mean you will necessarily be charged for accessing archie Internet databases. What we are selling is archie server software—*not* access to archie servers themselves.

As of late 1992, Emtage reports, "all Internet sites running archie servers that we have been in contact with have agreed to purchase the new release and want to continue to provide general 'free' access to the service. The only change the average Internet user will see is the new databases and features provided."

"Commercial releases of archie software, notably server software, will include more features plus the documentation, technical support, and other services that commercial products require—plus enabling the archie gang to make a living (we can but hope) doing this," according to Deutsch.

Furthermore, each new release of archie incorporates many exciting features—features that would never have been feasible to do (or sell) as labor-of-love work. With the early-1993 release, for example, archie has been expanded from just tracking archive site holdings into a generalized information gathering and distributed database maintenance tool. Public-domain software for the archie clients will also remain available for free," adds Deutsch.

### archie's next jobs

archie was originally created to track the contents of anonymous-FTP archive sites—clearly a much needed service, but far from the only use to which archie can—and is likely to—be put. By 1991, a second database was added to archie, the "whatis" Software Description Database. This database is similar to the set of descriptions in the Unix command reference manual which the Unix **man** command uses when you do a keyword search (with the Unix **man** command's **-k** option).

In 1992, interactive-login archie users gained the ability to search the **whatis** description database, a collection of descriptions that includes the name and a brief synopsis for over 3500 public-domain (PD) software packages, datasets, and informational documents located on the Internet. The database currently contains about 3500 entries that the archie team gleaned from various sources, such as the Usenet comp.sources. and alt.sources groups and the indices to the RFC (Request for Comment) document series. (To report new documents to be added to the archie **whatis** database, send e-mail to archie-maint@bunyip.com.) The format is basically the name of a PD program, document, or software package followed by a short description of said object.

Starting in 1993, look for any of a range of new Internet databases available based on archie technology, from Internet service providers. It's impossible to predict what databases will become available via archie or when, but likely candidates include a list of Internet resources that people commonly ask "What's available for..." such as:

- Lists of public-access Internet and Usenet sites (as in "Who's offering accounts in Chicago or area-code 312?")
- Lists of Internet and BITNET mailing lists and Usenet forums
- Popular Internet and Usenet documents such as FAQs and RFCs

Meanwhile, other Internet tools have integrated their facilities with archie. Gateways to the archie system and archie databases have been built for other popular Internet navigators, including the Internet Gopher, WAIS (the Wide-Area Information Server system), and the WorldWideWeb (W3). At least one site, for example, has brought up the archie "name" and **whatis** information as a WAISed database (see the section, "WAIS: Finding Information Needles in Network Haystacks," elsewhere in this chapter), making it easier for archie users to identify the appropriate programs more readily.

Several of the Gopher servers include access to archie, either as a regular archie client, or to the WAISed archie server (thus tying together the use of archie, Gopher, and WAIS into a single combined activity). And who knows—by the time you read this, someone may have created an archie tool that finds the "best" site to retrieve from, offers to schedule the download to an off-peak time, and even automatically does associated chores like uncompressing, decoding, and virus-scanning the transferred files. Perhaps, if this hasn't been done, you'll decide to be the one to do it.

### Not just for Internet uses or users

archie, like WAIS, Gopher, TechInfo (and indeed, TCP/IP in general), is not limited to handling Internet information or databases on the Internet. "Using archie, you can build an up-to-date, accurate directory of Internet services, or define new databases and gather entries from across the network," Emtage explains. "archie will update your information collections as often as needed."

Expect to see archie-based free-access, pay-for-listing, and pay-for-use services popping up on the Internet over the next year, perhaps coupled with WAIS indexing, other front-end interfaces, and other Internet services. Some possibilities: Internet "classified ads," the automated Internet "answer-person," the Internet "store catalog" for for-sale products—perhaps even Internet job and personal ads. Don't feel you have to be on the Internet to put archie to work. Like WAIS, Gopher, and TechMail, tools like archie may be applicable

***List Your Internet Services and Resources with archie***

If you've got an Internet service or resource, such as a file archive, public-access account site, or on-line database, the archie group encourages you to send them enough details about your offerings so that the server tracking software can be configured to automatically perform updates when your site information changes. To register with archie, send electronic mail to: info-archie@bunyip.com.

to other network information management needs on BBSs and networks not linked to the Internet.

### How to use archie

The following is an overall discussion of how to use archie. Like Gopher, HYTELNET, WAIS, and other Internet facilities, there are many different versions of archie client software for the different types of computers and access methods—and I am quite sure there have been major new updates released and features added since this book went to press. Therefore, I'll focus on the essentials; once you master these, you should be able to pursue the more advanced and version-specific features on your own.

**Get access to archie.** There are a number of different methods for accessing archie, spanning literally every type of access to the Internet, reflecting the desire of the archie developer team to make archie services as usable and accessible to as wide and general a user population as possible. archie access methods include:

- *From a local archie client on your computer.* As with any Internet tool, start by seeing if an archie client is available on your local system by typing **archie<RETURN>** (also try **xarchie<RETURN>**), and your system will find and forward your queries to an archie server. This is bound to be the most resource-sparing method of doing a real-time query, so try it first. archie command-line-oriented clients are noninteractive; you give your command as a line or set of menu choices and get a response. The archie GUI (Graphic User Interface—mouse'n'menu'click) clients are interactive to a certain extent: you can enter searches, click on the results, repeat, etc.

  Client software for archie is available for Unix systems, including terminal-style and X Window graphic user interfaces. archie client software is also available for NeXtStep and MS-DOS systems.
- *From an "Internet navigator" such as Gopher or TechInfo.* archie is usually available as a choice from one or more menus. Here's an example of archie as a Gopher menu item.

  ```
  --> 3. Search FTP sites (archie)/
  ```

  If you don't see it immediately, look for menu choices such as **FTP/, Archive Sites/** or **Software/.**
- *By* **telnet** *remote login to an archie site.* Open a remote login connection (using **telnet**) to one of the sites offering a publicly accessible interactive archie server, and login as **archie.** Like most public-access guest accounts, you shouldn't need a password to access an archie, but if you do, as the prompt will most likely remind you, remember that Internet nettiquette is to enter your Internet e-mail address here. For example,

  ```
  % telnet archie.sura.net
  ```

  This method has the benefit of supporting the most archie features and giving you the most control over your session. The remote login archie client is interactive, meaning archie gives you a prompt, such as "archie>"; you enter archie commands until done. This client includes a command to have the results sent to you by e-mail instead of displayed to your screen. "First-time users should try the **help** command to get started," recommends Peter Deutsch. See the archie Tips section for how to get a current list of archie servers and determine which one is "closest."

- *By e-mail.* Because it's basically answering specific questions, archie can also take and answer your queries by e-mail. This makes archie very accessible; like other e-mail-driven information servers, you can use archie even if you only have e-mail access to the Internet, such as from CompuServe, MCI Mail, or a nixpub public-access Unix/Usenet site.

You can send e-mail to any archie server (e.g., archie@sura.net or archie@rutgers.edu) and the archie server will automatically return the answers by electronic mail. You give commands to the archie e-mail interface as follows:

- Put each one on a line of its own.
- Start each command in the first column of the line.

The archie e-mail interface will:

- Treat the Subject: line as part of the message body.
- Ignore all lines that don't match valid commands.
- Consider any message to be a "request for Help information" if it contains the command **help** or doesn't contain any valid commands or is an "empty" message (no Subject, no body). If you give the **help** command, archie ignores all other commands in this message, and only returns help text consisting of a message explaining how to use the e-mail interface to the archie server, including a list of valid commands.

The archie e-mail interface includes commands that allow for potential message content and length limitations of e-mail systems and gateways. You can tell archie to compress results, encode the compressed results into 7-bit ASCII, and if need be, split the compressed, encoded file into pieces under a certain size. The message from archie will begin with information regarding what it did and how to reverse the process.

Peter Deutsch notes, "If the generated output from archie is greater than 45 kbytes, it will automatically be split into as many parts as required to get it to you in chunks this size or less. This is so as to interact well with certain mail systems which don't handle messages larger than 50 kbytes."

In choosing the way you query archie, remember that not every version and method of accessing archie may support the same sets of features—and not all of the user client programs have been created by archie's creators at Bunyip or are supported by Bunyip. (For more information about finding local and remote clients for archie and other Internet tools, see "Where the

Clients Are" at the beginning of Part 2 and "Think Globally, Look for Clients Locally" in Chap. 9.)

**Giving commands to archie.** Although the various archie clients may support some different features, they all basically do the same thing—compose and submit queries to the archie database. As of early 1993, the syntax for the archie line-oriented Unix client is:

```
% archie
Usage: archie [-acelorstvLV] [-m hits] [-N level] string
          -a : list matches as Alex filenames
          -c : case sensitive substring search
          -e : exact string match (default)
          -r : regular expression search
          -s : case insensitive substring search
          -l : list one match per line
          -t : sort inverted by date
     -m hits : specifies maximum number of hits to return
               (default 95)
 -o filename : specifies file to store results in
     -h host : specifies server host
          -L : list known servers and current default
    -N level : specifies query niceness level (0-35765)
%
```

If you aren't used to reading Unix command synopses, this looks like a mouthful, but it really isn't that bad. You can simply enter **archie searchstring** and archie will look for exact matches of program names. You can request "substring" matches, meaning the program name contains your searchstring (e.g., "uuc" is a substring of "uucp").

You can also request different databases other than the FTP archives; for example, Yellow Pages or **whatis.** You can also restrict searches to sites matching a Domain-Name expression; for example, ***.au** will restrict your searches to sites in the Australia domain, ***.org** to those in the Organization domain and ***.apple.com** to those within Apple Computer's domain.

The **-s** option makes the search insensitive to case differences (i.e., the search string "Ab" matches against "abfoo" "ABfoo" "Abfoo" and "aBfoo"). The **c** option makes searching case-sensitive, so only "Abfoo" matches. You can specify the maximum number of "hits" (although you can't preselect to indicate "nearness" to your site in terms of Internet connectivity).

The **-t** option gives you hits sorted by date—an easy way to locate the most recent versions. "Niceness level" means how much priority you're willing to give up in acknowledgment that you're using the service as a guest.

You may find access archie via Gopher to be easier. Here's an example of archie as a Gopher menu item.

```
-> 3. Search FTP sites (archie)/
```

When I chose this, I then got:

```
                    Search FTP sites (archie)
-> 1. Exact search of archive sites on the internet <?>
-> 2. Substring search of archive sites on the internet <?>
```

Here, I chose 1 and asked for a search of "ka9q" (the name of a popular public-domain implementation of TCP/IP with versions for PCs and other common home computers) and got results that looked like this:

```
           Internet Gopher Information Client v1.03

       Exact search of archive sites on the internet: ka9q

-> 1.  wuarchive.wustl.edu:/mirrors4/ka9q//
   2.  sun.soe.clarkson.edu:/pub/ka9q//
   3.  mcsun.eu.net:/network/ka9q//
   4.  mcsun.eu.net:/comp/ibmpc/ka9q//
   5.  m2xenix.psg.com:/pub/ip-for-pc/ka9q//
   6.  nic.funet.fi:/pub/ham/packet/ka9q//
   7.  ariadne.csi.forth.gr:/pc/comm/ka9q//
   8.  luga.latrobe.edu.au:/pub/network/ka9q//
   9.  nisc.jvnc.net:/nicol/pub/msdos/ka9q//
   10. wuarchive.wustl.edu:/mirrors4/ka9q/ka9q//
```

and so on. Selecting 1 gave:

```
This is the ka9q SLIP software. To use it you will need the
following files:

net.exe        The actual executable program
autoexec.net   You will need to edit this file. See the com-
               ments in file
userref.xxx    Text and NROFF version of the user manual

Press <RETURN> to continue, <m> to mail, <s> to save, or
<p> to print:
```

One benefit of Gopher-driven access to archie is that Gopher may also invoke file transfer for some of the files you locate, saving you several additional steps you'd otherwise have to perform for yourself.

### Things to know about using archie: Searching, sorting, scrolling, stopping

In addition to the commands for the type of archie client you use, there are several general things worth knowing to use archie, including:

- Defining what will match: *search* methods available
- Defining how archie will *sort* results
- How to get the results of your search: Capturing output from archie
- How to interrupt an archie search

**Defining what will match: *search methods available.*** archie can search its database using any of a number of methods:

- *The default method.* If you don't specify a different one, the default is for your search string to be treated as a "regular expression" (as defined by the Unix **ed** facility; see the section on "Wildcard Characters and Regular Expressions" in Chap. 4: This is one of the reasons I said you might want to learn some Unix even if you aren't using a Unix system). For example, suppose you are using a Windows-based PC running TCP/IP and want a *mailreader* program. Someone mentioned that there is now a version of **eudora,** which was originally written for use with Macintoshes. By giving the pattern **eudora** to archie, all filenames that match this will be gotten; for example:

```
$ archie -sl -m10 eudor

Host brolga.cc.uq.oz.au

    Location: /netmac
          FILE -rw-r—r— 314695 Apr 28 05:59 Eudora.sit.hqx

Host aix1.segi.ulg.ac.be

    Location: /pub/mac/tcpip
          FILE -rw-r—r—  714699 Feb 19 11:52
                                Eudora1.3man.pm.sea.hqx
          FILE -rw-r—r— 1504149 Feb 19 11:55
                                Eudora1.3man.ps.sea.hqx
          FILE -rw-r—r—  250675 Feb 25 10:40
                                Eudora_1.3.sea.hqx
    Location: /pub/mac/tcpip/old
          FILE -rw-r—r—  506244 Sep 11 1992
                                Eudora_1.2.doc.hqx

Host aun.uninett.no

    Location: /pub/mac

    .
    .
    .
```

- *Exact match.* Your searchstring has to exactly match (including case) the string in the database. For example, "eudora," or "xlock.tar.Z." This is the most efficient search to request and is worth using when you know the exact name of the file in question and simply want to locate where it is. However, bear in mind that different and compressed versions of a program often have extensions (e.g., versions of HYTELNET might include hyteln6.5.Z, hyteln7.2.tar, etc.).
- *Case-sensitive substring matching.* A match occurs if the file (or directory) name in the database contains the user-given substring, matching letter-case as well as letter-sequences. For example, "hyteln7.2.Z" will be a match against the pattern "hyteln* " but not against "Hyteln*."
- *Case-insensitive substring matching.* A match occurs if the file (or directory) name in the database contains the user-given substring, treating upper- and lowercase letters as matching each other. For example, "hyteln7.2.Z" will be a match for either the pattern "hyteln*" or the pattern "HYTELN*."

The default search method in the **telnet** client for archie version 3.0 is substring matches; according to Deutsch, this is more efficient than regular expression searches.

**Defining how archie will sort results.** archie lets you choose how it sorts the database entries that match your search request. You can select a sort method by using archie's **set** command to change the value of the "sortby" variable. Putting the letter **r** in front of the variable value causes the sort to be done in reverse order. Your options for sort order are:

- *Hostname.* Sorts hits based on the name of the computer the resource is located on, in alphabetical order (use **rhostname** to sort in reverse alphabetical order).
- *Time.* Sorts hits based on the "modification time" listed for the file or directory. The most recently modified ones will be listed first, on the assumption that these are the most current versions (use **rtime** to get oldest first).
- *Size.* Sorts hits based on the size of the found files or directories, largest first (use **rsize** to get smallest first).
- *Filename.* Sorts hits based on the filename, in alphabetical order.
- *None.* As they occur in the database, the default.

If you don't specify a sort or search method—archie will use the default methods of ASCII order, sort by *none.*

**How to get the results of your search: Capturing output from archie.** archie's response to your query consists of one or more lines of information for each hit, meaning for each instance of a matching file in the archie database. These lines include the name and address of the system and the directory the file is in. If your query generates in more than a few hits, the resulting output is bound to be more than a single screenful on your system. Fifty or so hits can mean several screenfuls—and if you gave a rather general search-expression or didn't restrict the query otherwise, you can easily get hundreds of hits.

Here's several ways you can either keep the output from flowing by too fast or capture this information to a file so you can inspect it later with a text editor or other facility, based on what kind of computer you're using and how you are accessing archie. (If you're querying by e-mail, this issue is moot.)

- *Invoke Unix* **script** *command before starting archie.* If you're working from Unix system, use the Unix **script** command, which sends a copy of all your input and output to a file that you can look at afterward. This will apply to everything you do until you terminate the **script** activity.

  **script** works by copying your input and output to the file and then creating a subshell to which you give your commands. To quit **scripting,** enter **Control-D** at the beginning of the line after a command prompt. On most systems, if you don't give a filename, Unix will automatically assign one, like script1. (See the Unix manual page for script for more information.)

- For noninteractive archie clients, *pipe or redirect archie output* through a Unix facility such as **more** or to a file. For example:

  ```
  % archie eudora |more        (Pipe through more for screenful scrolling)
  % archie eudora > eudora_hits        (Send output directly to a file)
  % archie eudora | tee eudora_hits |more
     (Send output both to  a file and piped through more)
  ```

- *Use the archie Mailto option.* You can have archie e-mail you the results of a search, even when you are working interactively; after a search whose results you want, enter the archie **mail** command. This causes archie to send the results of the last search to the specified address—very convenient if you aren't sure until after the search is done that you want its results. You can specify your (or another) e-mail address by giving the archie **mailto** command before giving the **mail** command; if no address has been specified when you give the **mail** command, archie will prompt you for one. The **mail** command is also a good way to send query results to friends directly, instead of having to forward them from your account. You may want to first view results and then rerun a query with this option, or you won't know what you're sending.

  archie doesn't wait until it's done sending your results before offering you the archie prompt again and will display a message to let you know when your results have been put into the e-mail.

- *"Pager" variable.* The archie remote login client has a "pager" variable which will let you scroll through output in screenfuls (see archie Help documentation for more information).

- *Flow control.* Use the flow-control keys on your keyboard to stop and restart output to your screen. On most systems, Control-S halts output, and

Control-Q causes output to resume flowing. (On some keyboards, the <PAUSE> key acts alternately to stop and start flow control. Because your commands are going through one or more computers and networks, there may be a delay between when you hit Control-S and when the screen freezes. Also, this doesn't capture output, it just "stops the music."

- On PCs, *use your terminal emulator's features* such as:
  - Print current screen to file (after using Control-S to freeze it)
  - Session capture to a file (possibly available in several ways, such as *session logging* or *capture/download to file.*

  Before issuing the archie query, tell your terminal emulator to capture the session to a file.

- *Terminal emulator/user interface features.* On some systems, you may be able to scroll back and forth through the active session.

There are bound to also be other ways on your computer that you can capture archie output. Check it out.

**How to interrupt an archie search.** To stop an archie search, enter the keyboard-interrupt character (for most Unix users, this is Control-C). This causes archie to stop searching or sorting (depending at what point archie received the "stop" signal), and output results as of that point. Reasons to stop a search include:

- You see you've already got enough information.
- You realize you made a typo or other mistake.

### archie netiquette

The archie servers handling Internet databases such as file archives, **whatis,** and Yellow Pages resource listings are to a large extent run and made available by various Internet Service Providers, sites, and other organizations on a free-for-use basis, as a community service. To ensure this remains viable, use archie (and all other Internet resources) as considerately as possible:

- Find the most local archie server for your queries. In particular, whenever possible, please avoid the use of transoceanic links (e.g., if you're in Brazil, don't unnecessarily query the archie server in Australia), since these links tend to have limited bandwidth and are already heavily congested. Get a list of archie servers (and find out which Internet Service Provider your organization or site is connected through). For example, if you're on AlterNet, BARRnet, NEARnet, or PSInet, an archie on the ANS network or SURAnet will be relatively "close"—one in Finland or Australia will not be.
- Do queries in off-peak hours. (Off-peak in terms of the site running the archie server, which isn't necessarily the same as where you are. Many

computer and network people have very different schedules from this; also, you may be querying an archie server several time zones away.)

- Restrict your query to a reasonable number of hits, your best guess of the appropriate domain(s) to search, etc.
- For long requests, use the "Niceness" option to deprioritize your request.

### To learn more about and try archie

archie information, code, clients, and servers are available in a range of ways:

- If you have e-mail access to the Internet, *subscribe* to the mailing list archie-people. This list is for people interested in developments and progress of the archie project and is open to all who wish to subscribe. To subscribe, send e-mail to "archie-people-request@bunyip.com" with the text: add <your-email-address> archie-people in the body.
- If you have access to the Usenet, *read* the Usenet Netnews group comp.archives.admin. "This group is read by lots of people interested in Internet archiving," notes Peter Deutsch.
- archie code is available from a number of Internet sites, including from most sites running archie servers.

Using anonymous-FTP, Gopher, or other Internet file retrieval tools, you can retrieve:

- Freeware release of client code from the archie gang and other Internet developers.
- Software for the stand-alone archie clients.

A number of freely redistributable third-party software packages utilizing the archie system are available on the Internet. Clients for the Internet archives database already exist for the X Window system, NeXtStep, VMS, and stand-alone versions for UNIX and MS-DOS. The most recent versions of each are generally available for anonymous-FTP from most archie servers (e.g., **ftp** to archie.sura.net).

archie documentation includes an extensive Unix-like manual page, an overview, and documentation for each client and is available by anonymous-FPT from most archie servers, under the directory "pub/archie/docs".

Please send comments, suggestions, and bug reports to "archie-group@bunyip.com"—this reaches the implementors of archie. "It was your comments which led to many improvements," Deutsch, Emtage, and Heelan said in an e-mail message. "We'd like to keep hearing from you."

For more information on the Prospero protocol and its use, write to info-prospero@isi.edu. For more information on regular expressions, see discussions of **ed, regex,** and "regular expressions" in the Unix manual pages or in other Unix manuals. And for more information on archie, contact:

Bunyip Information Systems
310 St-Catherine St West, Suite 202
Montreal, Quebec H2X 2A1
Voice: (514) 875-8611
Fax: (514) 875-8134
General e-mail: info@bunyip.com

## WAIS: Finding Information Needles In Network Haystacks

Earlier, you've learned how Internet tools like archie and VERONICA can help you locate Internet resources such as archived files and Gopher menu items by searching through "harvested" lists which contain short descriptions of what's available. But suppose no such descriptions are available—or you're not sure that the appropriate keywords have been entered into the descriptions? Or suppose you have a very large pile of information of a form that neither archie nor VERONICA can handle, such as all the articles in the *Wall Street Journal* and *New York Times* from the past year—or the Congressional Record—or all the e-mail you've created and received in the past 5 years?

For many Internet users and Internet information store-houses, there is a new way to find things: WAIS. WAIS (pronounced "ways" or "wase"), the Wide-Area Information Server system, offers a solution to a problem common to any large pool of on-line information, namely, finding something, particularly when you're not sure where it is or exactly what you're looking for—which is about as precise a description of the distribution of information across the Internet as you can get.

One of the best features of on-line information is that you can use the computer that's storing it as a tool to look through it—something my file cabinet won't do. In fact, if you have the right tool, and know how to work it, you can crank up the command and let the computer do the work. (I wish I had a magic spell that would do this for all the paper on my desk and in my file cabinets—don't you?)

On small local file systems, where you've only got a few tens of megabytes, Unix's **grep** command, Mac utilities like ON Location, and DOS terminate-and-stay-resident (TSR) file-browser commands can be adequate. On my 286-based IBM-compatible PC, for example, my copy of QuickSoft's PC-Browse TSR file-browser program seems to be able to browse through a megabyte of files in a few seconds. On my account on The World, which uses a reasonably powerful multiprocessor Solbourne computer running a version of Unix, a Unix **grep** command will search quite rapidly through hundreds and thousands of files for lines that match my search pattern.

And for larger amounts of well-structured data, database management systems like Paradox, Oracle, and Progress let users search through millions of records—but only if you're comfortable with the query language for that product and with boolean logic operators (AND, OR, etc.) and only if the information's been put into the appropriate database format. On-line database services and catalogs like Dialog and the Research Library Group's RLIN (Research Library Information Network) offer their own tools to let you search through pools of information they've collected. But to use these effectively takes expertise. And again, the data you want to search must be available in the right format.

On the Internet, it's even more complicated. The information can be in any number of locations, within your computer's hard disk, your organization's shared file servers, or on any of thousands of other sites on the Internet which offer free-for-access or pay-for-access resources. The information may be tucked away in your personal files, such as a series of e-mail messages from 4 years ago. It may be in directories owned by your organization (e.g., 5 years' worth of your projects reports and memos or in a Human Resources Policies and Procedures manual). Or it may be elsewhere on the Internet, such as in a biology research group's archive of 3 years' of data, 10 years' archives of RISKS e-mail digests, or the archive of FAQ documents for all Usenet Newsgroups. Or the information you want may be in a combination of personal, organizational, and other locations' files. What's more, the computers involved may be different types of systems, created by different programs, and perhaps of different data types and formats. This includes the format used by Usenet News postings, e-mail messages, and others peculiar to the Internet.

The problem of finding a needle in a haystack has suddenly become the problem of also knowing where all the haystacks are and determining which one or ones you want to search through. To do this, you need a tool that can munch its way across networks and into disparate data formats. Or you can use WAIS.

## WAIS: Developed for super-searching

The WAIS project was begun January 1990 by developers at supercomputer vendor Thinking Machines Corporation (TMC) (Menlo Park, CA) under the leadership of Brewster Kahle (brewster@wais.com), working with Apple Computer, Dow Jones/News Retrieval, and KPMG Peat Marwick as a "corporate test subject." According to Kahle,

> Our goal was to see if we were able to deliver the computing system we'd been promising for 2 decades, namely, to bring the library to end users' desks, and make it possible for people to access large quantities of text in a user-friendly manner.
>
> You can view WAIS as a dynamic hypertext system—a tool that establishes connections among similar items in a given document, and among many documents and other pieces of information or as a corporate memory that allows you to access personal and corporate information and wide area information through one common interface—something that's never been done before. And you can use WAIS as a huge worldwide "find file" system.
>
> The information you want is probably out there; WAIS is a way to find it, a way to navigate across databases and the computers that house them, and search through them.

### Designed for use on networks: WAIS is a client-server tool

WAIS is designed to be used on networks—such as the Internet—where users and pools of data may be located in different locations. WAIS software uses the client-server approach we've talked about at the beginning of Part 2 and in other chapters. The client program makes it as easy as possible for users to select appropriate WAIS databases, create queries, and view results. The server programs take your queries and apply them to the data they're presiding over. In fact, not only does this mean you can access any of hundreds of WAIS servers at different sites, but WAIS lets you look through several databases with one query, even though these databases may be located thousands of miles apart.

You can use a client program on your Unix workstation, PC, or Macintosh to create queries that select which collection of information to search, enter commands and keywords, etc. WAIS client programs are available for most popular types of systems, including Macintosh, Unix (line-oriented and GUI), DOS, and NeXt.

Each WAIS server takes care of indexing of the collections of data it's handling, and the searching/retrieval activities, in response to queries by users. Indexing may be redone periodically as information is added, changed, or deleted. The server(s) you have specified applies your query to the data collections you have selected.

The first response to your search is a "list of headlines" identifying a list of what items in the data collections have matched your query, sorted in the order of how well they match. You can then select one of these items. In this case, the server transmits the item to your client, which displays it to you. The item may be a text document, a photograph, a moving image, sound, etc. (Obviously, you'll need a workstation capable of handling the types of items you're working with.)

Alternatively, you can continue searching. You can refine your search, narrowing it down or having other items added. Or you can start a brand new search, on the same or new datasets. Some WAIS clients will let you save queries, so you can ask them again another time (when new information may be available).

### Natural language and relevance feedback: Now you're querying

To phrase your query, many database systems force you to use a "query language" that is as hard to learn, master, and remember as computer programming languages. WAIS uses natural language as its query language, such as English or French; for commands, a relatively small set of keystrokes or menu choices are enough to invoke most WAIS features. Kahle recalls:

> When we went to Peat Marwick, their CIO said "No algebra"—a beautiful way of putting it. "These partners are not going to learn another query language." We

said, "no problem." All they do is say what they're interested in (e.g., say "contracts about IBM and Motorola.").

Once you give one or more keywords, WAIS searches through the specified databases, identifies which items contain them, and gives you a list, ranking these items based on how many of the keywords they contain and on other rules. You get back a list of matches. If you feel that some of these are particularly of interest, you can even say, "find me more like that one."

### Find me more like this: Relevance feedback querying

Traditional database queries use boolean methods, where you define your query as a set of keywords and other qualifiers, organized with things like GREATER THAN, LESS THAN, OR, NOT, AND, CONTAINS, and so on. A boolean-type search may find you a number of items you are interested in—but using only boolean-type queries, you can't narrow these down in a way that corresponds to only the item or items you liked best. WAIS can—by using another search technique, called *relevance feedback.*

Previously pioneered in the 1960s and 1970s, and commercialized in the Dow Jones DowQuest system, relevance feedback means you can feed back the results from one search to become the query for the next search—in other words, you can say, "find me more like these."

"The most relevant documents, regardless of size, can be sent back to the server in their entirety to further refine your search," says Kahle. "Using this technique, we've gotten end users to locate what they want from within gigabytes of information," states Kahle. "Boolean queries can't provide this; they're only useful for the trained and tolerant, and generally work on fairly small full text databases."

The Internet abounds with large databases. The archie database of files available from public-access archive sites had over 2.1 million entries by mid-1992. Many of the Internet mailing lists and Usenet Newsgroups have been around for 10 or more years, some with dozens of entries per day. Library catalogs and user directory databases likewise run into the million-or-more record sizes. For the high end of the type of information WAIS is intended to handle, the information bases being searched can be large enough to demand speed of the hundreds to thousands of processors in a Thinking Machines' Connection Machine.*

---

*This should come as no surprise—why else would Thinking Machines have decided this was an interesting project to pursue?

Thinking Machines' Connection Machines are *massively parallel parallel-processing* computers. "Parallel-processing" means that the Connection Machine has lots of CPUs, and each can compute away on a piece of a problem at the same time as the others. "Massively parallel" means a Connection Machine can have anywhere from 32 to 16,000 CPUs—enough to search through 100 years' of *Wall Street Journals* in less than a second. As Kahle noted at one point, "think of a football stadium full of people, where each person takes a page or record and everybody starts searching their page when you say 'Go!'" On the other hand, WAIS server software is available for "smaller" machines, such as Unix workstations, which turn out to be adequate for many of the databases being "WAISed."

Once done, most of the WAIS clients let you save your search and even repeat it automatically, sending you an alert as new information matching the search is found (e.g., new newspaper articles detected). Intriguingly, the server doesn't have to fully "understand" your query; natural languages can be used. To date, Kahle reports, "We have used English, French, Italian, and German!"

Most WAIS servers currently available can index documents in existing formats and make them available for WAIS searching. WAIS currently supports data formats and types including text, formatted documents, pictures, spreadsheets, graphics, sound, and video on a variety of computer platforms.

Your WAIS client obtains a current list of available WAIS servers from the "Directory of Servers" list (on the Internet, maintained by Thinking Machines). Each selected WAIS server reads your question and, based on its words, searches the full text of the database for the most relevant documents (i.e., documents that contain those words and phrases) and ranks them using heuristics such as automatic word weighting. As may be obvious, there are a few limits to this.

First, since WAIS is searching for matches of your keywords in its indexes, if the keywords aren't in the original documents or whatever the WAIS index is based on, WAIS can't find it. For example, if your articles are about or refer to "tiddlywinks," you simply use keywords like "tiddlywinks." If you know any tiddlywink jargon, you may also try keywords like "squidger" and "squopp." But you can't count on searches based on concepts, like "superhero" or "role-playing game" or "utopian fantasy" to match—unless WAIS is searching a description of the document and whoever added the document put the right terms in.

Second, WAIS can only search the documents it has access to, in the datasets you specify. If you search for "tiddlywinks" in the *Wall Street Journal,* you won't discover if there are any relevant articles in the *New York Times.* If an article is too new to have been added and indexed, WAIS can't find it for you. Even so, WAIS adds a powerful new way to munch through those haystacks of data to find those few matching needles.

### WAIS users report: They like it

The response at initial test case Peat Marwick, where WAIS was provided as a tool for $300 an hour, consultants were enthusiastic. "They loved it," reports Kahle. "They were using it all the time." As of mid-1992, developers at Thinking Machines and elsewhere in the Internet community had developed WAIS client software that can be run on a number of types of computers and operating systems, including Unix, VAX/VMS, Macintoshes, DOS, Microsoft Windows, and NeXt.

### WAIS and the Internet

What does all this have to do with the Internet? Lots. The Internet began as the way WAIS developers worked together. The Internet then provided WAIS developers with a worldwide testbed of users to "take WAIS out for a spin."

Today, many of the information bases of Internet resources and services, and Internet archives, have become WAIS-searchable; WAIS has also become the search tool used by people making both free-access and pay-for-view information available via the Internet.

**The Internet as developer's tool.** Initially, as with many new computer programs, developers at organizations which were connected to the Internet used the Internet as a way to work together.

**Providing a testbed.** Starting in January of 1990, WAIS developers took the next step; like archie, WAIS client and server software, along with a number of datasets, was put onto publicly available Internet-accessible computers. This gave WAIS developers a worldwide set of test users—and gave the Internet community the chance to experiment with another possible solution to our continually growing flood of information whose value is only as good as our ability to find things within it.

**WAIS access to Internet information.** By mid-1992, like archie, Gopher, and other tools, WAIS had established itself as one of the core new tools for using the Internet, for new and experienced users alike. Archives of many Internet mailing lists and Usenet Newsgroups have been indexed under WAIS, making it *much* easier to find things. One reason: instead of having to figure out where a given archive is stored, you simply access WAIS on the Internet. The first screen is the "directory of servers," a list of what WAISed servers and databases are available, which you can do a keyword search on. Once you've identified and selected one or more WAIS servers, you then can do the search.

For example, at one point I needed the electronic mail address of someone. It was too late at night to call and ask, and I wanted to send a message before I forgot—and at this time, there was no Internet-wide "people directory" available. But I knew this person had posted a message to the "com-priv" mailing list (a discussion about the commercialization and privatization of the Internet) at one point. And I knew that the full archives of this mailing list were available under WAIS. So I:

1. Dialed up to my account on World (a local call)
2. Established a remote login connection (using **telnet**) to the Thinking Machines' publicly accessible WAIS system
3. Selected the "com-priv" database by giving it as the keyword for WAIS to search in the database of servers (which is the first list offered)
4. Gave a unique string from the person's name that I knew appeared (e.g., if you were looking for me, you might try "Daniel" and "Dern" as keywords)
5. Requested to see one of the documents with a match—which in fact did have the person's e-mail address, as part of the message he had sent.

Elapsed time: a minute or two.

The "directory of WAIS servers" facility registers, lists, and describes the information available on each server, including any fees for their use. In terms of WAISed information for, about, and on the Internet, as of late 1992, Thinking Machines reported that about two new databases were being registered with the Directory of Servers at Thinking Machines every week. As of early 1993, the "Directory of Servers" databases included over 400 Internet-accessible WAIS servers at companies and universities in over 12 countries.

The WAIS server at Thinking Machines alone hosts over 60,000 documents including weather maps and forecasts, the CIA World Factbook, a collection of molecular biology abstracts, the Internet Info_Mac digests, and the Connection Machines Fortran manual. Other servers include a poetry server at M.I.T. with classical and modern poetry. The Library of Congress has plans to make their catalog available via the protocol. There are archives of e-mail discussions, documents, articles, images—mountains of network-accessible data waiting to be searched—from a single network point of contact.

The Internet community has given WAIS a rigorous test. Thinking Machines reports that during 1992, Thinking Machines' Internet-accessible public-access WAIS servers (including the directory of other WAIS servers) have received over 100,000 requests from users in over 200 companies and 28 countries. Plus there were about 100 downloads per day of the publicly available versions of WAIS software.

### Putting WAIS to work

Here's what some WAIS users have to say about "what a difference a WAIS makes."

**Massachusetts General Hospital (Boston, MA).** MGH, said to be the largest research hospital in the country, has been using WAIS (and Gopher) servers for a large variety of internal information since 1992. According to Dr. J. Michael Cherry, Director of Computing for the Department of Molecular Biology at MGH, "The vast majority of computers used in our research departments are Macintoshes. The WAIS and Gopher clients are easy to set up and allow researchers to quickly start exploring our internal WAIS servers and the wealth of WAIS servers available via the Internet."

Cherry's department at MGH is providing three WAIS databases to the world, about a small flowering plant and a nematode worm which are both used as model systems within biology. The WAIS-ed information bases contain either the complete information from a genome database or years' worth of newsgroup/mailing list archives. More use of WAIS for research and administrative information is underway at MGH. According to Cherry, "WAIS servers under development include a calendar of events, public memos, policy statements for many parts of the hospital, and a 'Frequently Asked Questions' database from the computer help desk." Other items under consideration include databases of information from a number of service departments within the hospital.

**M.I.T.: Student newspaper publication and archives.** And at M.I.T., where many WAIS developers studied, Reuven Lerner, System Administrator and former editor in chief of *The Tech,* the M.I.T. student newspaper, reports,

> We are about to launch a WAIS server for *The Tech,* with the last 12 years of its archives, and hope to soon begin publishing *The Tech* to WAIS at the same time as we print copies for distribution. Our WAIS server will serve both our readers (most, if not all, students and faculty at M.I.T. are on the Internet) as well as our reporters and editors, who will use it to give better background information when assigning stories.

**Thinking Machines.** Practicing what they preach, developers and technical support staff and others at Thinking Machines also use WAIS on a daily basis. "I use WAIS to index all the e-mail messages I've ever sent or received," said Kahle (before he left TMC for WAIS, Inc.). "I use this as my personal memory. This application alone can change your life."

Laird Popkin, multimedia specialist at Thinking Machines, uses WAIS regularly. "Quite frequently I need to locate a software tool to get my work done." Using WAIS, Popkin can search "all of the ReadMe files on the Internet," for example (also using archie), use that information to determine what programs to search for, and then retrieve the software—locating a single program from millions, across a thousand sites, in under an hour.

> I receive e-mail from someone who needs to know whether we can convert "CGM" image files to something we can use. Since I have no idea what CGM is, I do a WAIS search of all of the ReadMe files on the Internet (courtesy of archie and ftpable-readmes.src), locating a file that contains a long list of image formats. I retrieve and read this list, so now I know what CGM is. Then I do another WAIS search, this time of the database which has descriptions of the files on ftp sites (ftp-list.src) and locate a Macintosh program which can read CGM files, display them, and save them as PICT files. [The same information that archie servers are using to locate programs files.]
>
> Having found one or more sites that have this program, I transfer a copy of the file, using Xferit (since I'm working from a Macintosh running TCP/IP). I drop the CGM files in question onto the application, and everything works. Thanks to WAIS, this takes under an hour, and I didn't have to make any phone calls, send anyone e-mail, or post any queries. Without WAIS, I would probably have posted queries to one or more mailing lists and Usenet groups, not gotten responses for several days—if at all—and possibly then had to also query archie."

Art Medlar <medlar@adoc.xerox.com>, one of the original developers of WAIS and WAIStation, currently a consultant working at Xerox in Palo Alto, says,

> For me, the greatest value in WAIS is not in finding new information, but in refinding information that I have already seen. The projects I work on generally involve several people, inconveniently spread over time and space. As a result, I

### *WAIS—Not Just for Internet Users*

Don't make the mistake of seeing WAIS as only for Internet applications or for use by people who have access to the Internet. Like archie, Gopher, TechInfo, and other tools, WAIS can be run on a wide range of networked computing environments other than the Internet. "WAIS can be run over any digital network, including ISDN," says Kahle. "We've seen WAIS running in private corporate TCP/IP networks, over X.25, and even via modem connections."

A growing number of engineering, medical, government, academic, and other organizations are putting WAIS to use within their own network environments. Some of these organizations are on the Internet and make their WAISbases generally available. WAIS systems offer as great value for corporate and university networks as it has been for the Internet (which is, in some sense, "nothing more than" a very large enterprise network).

According to Michael L. Carroll, Manager, Advanced Computer & Software Applications at Lockheed Corporation (Calabasas, CA),

> At Lockheed, we have built a corporatewide information distribution system using NetNews and WAIS. This system, called the Technology Broker System, links together several different computing environments including VM, VAX/VMS, UNIX, DOS, MS-WINDOWS, and Macintoshes. It makes available within Lockheed information previously inaccessible on-line, such as proposals, research reports, management policies and procedures, the Lockheed employee phone list, corporate library catalogs, Commerce Business Daily, and Material Safety Data Sheets (MSDS).

According to Marc Fleischmann, in Lockheed's Information Integration area, their WAIS servers are managing over 2.5 Gbytes of data:

> The 50,000 MSDS sheets represent a Gbyte of data. Most of the other sources run from a couple of Mbytes to 100 Mbytes. Our server currently has two 1.3-Gbyte disks and they are almost full. We expect to have three more 1.3-Gbyte disks attached to the server by the end of October.
>
> WAIS is a storage "magnet" and becomes disk-intensive. Data that was located on lots of different systems gets put in WAIS and the aggregate gets larger and larger. No one saw the cost of storing it on the original system but it becomes very visible when put into WAIS.

On the other hand, he points out, "One year's worth of R&D research reports (about 150 three- to six-inch page reports) take up two 2-inch binders and weighs about 8 pounds. When put into WAIS they occupy 3 Mbytes of disk, about $1.50 worth of disk space at floppy prices."

Elsewhere, by now, Dow Jones & Co. should have a server available on their DowVision network that will contain several months of the *Wall Street Journal* and 450 business publications and will be a for-pay server.

use electronic mail as my primary communication medium. Prior to WAIS, one big problem with e-mail was with finding old messages. Often, I'd find myself facing a problem which I knew to be similar to one reported and solved some months ago, but had no easy way of digging up the relevant message.

For the past several years, I have archived every e-mail message I have sent or received, nearly 100 Mbytes worth. I keep it on-line and indexed. When I need to find an old message on a particular subject, I just type a few words or start a relevance-feedback search based on a similar note, and I have it within a couple of seconds. Previously, the search could have taken hours, or just been impossible.

Other types of on-line documentation and information have similar problems, and WAIS provides the same sort of solution. This means it's no longer necessary to spend lots of time cataloging and filing, and trying to remember some obscure taxonomy of files, subdirectories, and folders. Simply knowing roughly where a piece of information is, and generally what it's about, is almost always enough to find it.

## Using WAIS

The following is an overall discussion of how to use WAIS. As with discussions of other Internet tools, I'll focus on the essentials; once you master these, you should be able to pursue the more advanced and version-specific features on your own. (Also, like archie, Gopher, HYTELNET, and other Internet facilities, there are many different versions of WAIS software, for the different types of computers and access methods—and I am quite sure there have been major new updates released and features added since this book went to press.)

**Get access to WAIS.** To use WAIS, the first step is to access a WAIS *client*—the end-user side of the WAIS system which will forward your queries and commands to the selected WAIS server and display results. Remember, WAIS is a client-server application, like **telnet,** FTP, and Gopher. In other words, you need real-time Internet connections between your client and the selected WAIS server(s).

A WAIS client may be available on your computer or through one of the Internet front ends or navigators available to you. Otherwise, you'll have to locate and remote login to a WAIS client at a public-access WAIS client, using the TCP/IP **telnet** command (which is what the front end or navigator may be doing, anyway).

As with any Internet tool, start by seeing if a WAIS client is available on your local system by typing **wais<RETURN>.** If this doesn't work, try **swais<RETURN>** (for Simple WAIS); on a Unix system, try **xwais<RETURN>** (for X Window WAIS). (The **swais** program is somewhat slow; don't be surprised if it takes a minute or so before the first screen is ready for your commands.) For more information about finding local and remote clients for Internet tools, see "Where the Clients Are" at the beginning of Part 2, and "Think Globally, Look for Clients Locally" in Chap. 9. Figure 10.4 shows a screen for a WAIS client program that runs under X Windows.

If the above methods fail, open a remote login connection to one of the sites offering publicly accessible WAIS clients, such as by telnetting to quake.think.com. The WAIS client program you'll probably get this way is **swais**, the "Simple WAIS interface" for terminal emulator users. **swais** doesn't have all the features of the GUI-oriented WAIS client programs, but accessing and using it may be the easiest way to start. If at all possible, locate one of the GUI-oriented WAIS client programs, such as the ones for the Macintosh, Microsoft Windows, or X Windowing system, Kahle recommended. "These will have more features, and be far easier to use."

Login as "wais." Like most public-access guest accounts, you shouldn't need a password to access a public-access WAIS client, but—as the prompt will most likely remind you—Internet netiquette is to enter your Internet e-mail address here (e.g., alice@jabber.wock.com). For example:

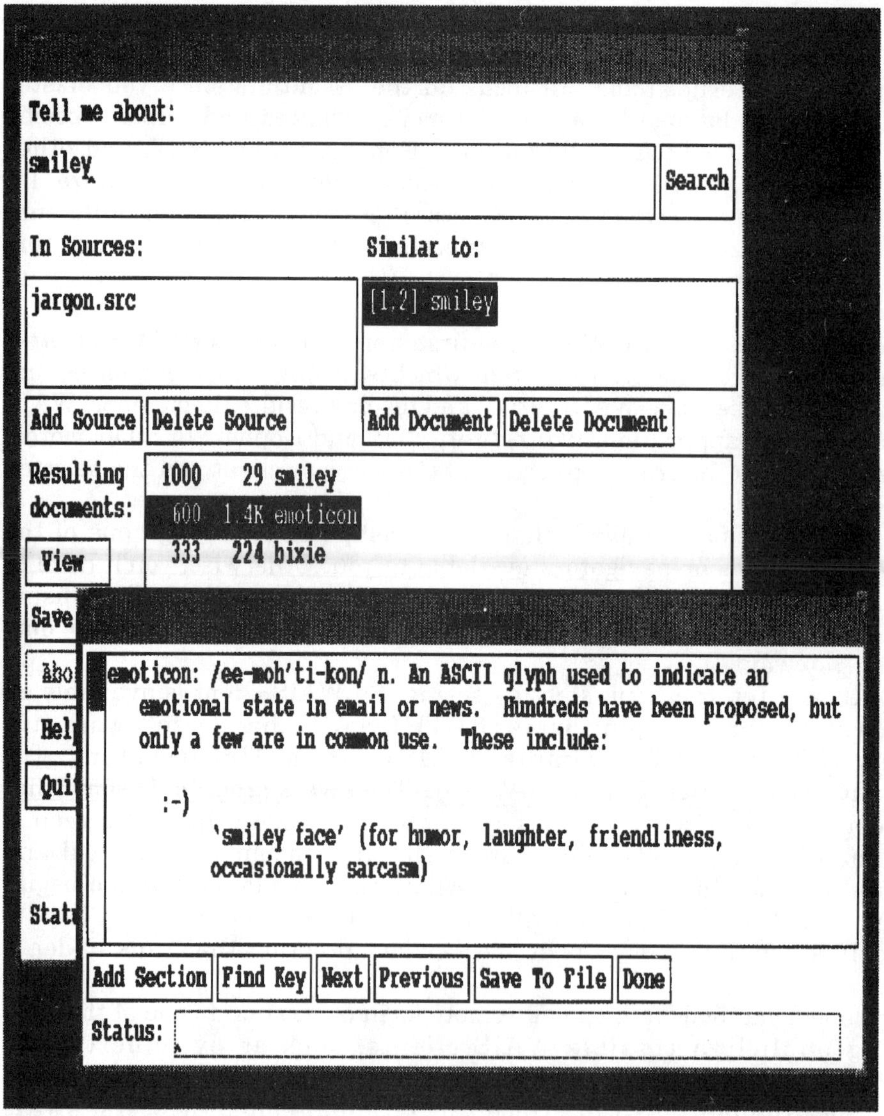

Tell me about:

smiley

Search

In Sources:

jargon.src

Similar to:

[1,2] smiley

Add Source | Delete Source | Add Document | Delete Document

Resulting documents:

1000 29 smiley
600 1.4K emoticon
333 224 bixie

View

Save

Abo

Hel

Qui

Stat

emoticon: /ee-moh'ti-kon/ n. An ASCII glyph used to indicate an emotional state in email or news. Hundreds have been proposed, but only a few are in common use. These include:

:-)
'smiley face' (for humor, laughter, friendliness, occasionally sarcasm)

Add Section | Find Key | Next | Previous | Save To File | Done

Status:

**Figure 10.4** An X Window WAIS client.

```
world% telnet quake.think.com
Trying 192.31.181.1...
Connected to quake.think.com.
Escape character is '^]'.

SunOS UNIX (quake)

login: wais
Welcome to swais.
Please type user identifier (optional, i.e. user@host) :
alice@jabber.wock.com
```

Here's a typical screen you might see when you login to Thinking Machines' public SWAIS:

```
SWAIS                          Source Selection          Sources: 316

001: [            archie.au] aarnet-resource-guide      Free
001: [            archie.au] aarnet-resource-guide      Free
003: [weedsmunin.ub2.lu.se] academic_email_conf         Free
004: [     archive.orst.edu] aeronautics                Free
005: [ bloat.media.mit.edu] Aesop-Fables                Free
006: [nostromo.oes.orst.ed] agricultural-market-news    Free
007: [     archive.orst.edu] alt.drugs                  Free
008: [     wais.oit.unc.edu] alt.gopher                 Free
009: [sun-wais.oit.unc.edu] alt.sys.sun                 Free
010: [     wais.oit.unc.edu] alt.wais                   Free
011: [      munin.ub2.lu.se] amiga_fish_contents        Free
012: [         150.203.76.2] ANU-Aboriginal-Studies     $0.00/minute
013: [    coombs.anu.edu.au] ANU-Asian-Religions        $0.00/minute
014: [         150.203.76.2] ANU-Pacific-Linguistics    $0.00/minute
015: [    coombs.anu.edu.au] ANU-Pacific-Manuscripts    Free
016: [    coombs.anu.edu.au] ANU-SocSci-Netlore         $0.00/minute
017: [         150.203.76.2] ANU-SSDA-Catalogues        $0.00/minute
018: [    coombs.anu.edu.au] ANU-Thai-Yunnan            Free

Keywords:
<space> selects, w for keywords, arrows move, <return> searches, q
quits, or ?
```

**Select dataset(s), or server(s).** Once you've accessed WAIS, the next step is to select the server(s) (i.e., datasets) you want to search. As with most Internet utilities, entering **?** or **h** gives you on-line help information.

At this point, you can:

- Use the arrow keys and <SPACE> to select sources.
- Enter **w** to indicate you want to give keyword search terms for search. Enter one or more keywords.

Using "new" as the keyword will always find some items in each of the databases. In response to your query, WAIS returns a list of documents that match your search criteria, listed in order of how closely they match (based on WAIS' search'n'match rules). At this point, you can tell WAIS to retrieve a document—display it—continue the search or begin a new search. (Not all of the freeware WAIS client software versions may support relevance-searching at this level (i.e., you may not be able to use the "find me more like this one" search technique).

To retrieve an item, for example, use the arrow keys and <RETURN>, or <SPACE>. To return to the "sources" screen, enter **s.** And to quit, enter **q.**

**WAIS netiquette.** As you use the public-access WAIS client sites and free-for-use WAIS servers, there may be times when the response time seems slow or the software doesn't work perfectly. So it's important to remember that many of the programs you are using are labors of love, done by people in their spare time, and that the services on many of the computers you're accessing are being made available on a voluntary basis. For example, some of the WAIS clients may seem to respond slowly or quit and break the connection unexpectedly. Trying not to "type-ahead" helps. And when WAIS does work well and gives you what you need, it's still worth remembering the voluntary, cooperative community that made it all possible, suggests Kahle. "You might even send a thank-you note to the maintainer of the database you like—the address will be in the database's source description entry."

### The Future of WAIS

Because WAIS can store and automatically resubmit queries, it can be the basis of your "personal window" to Internet information sources. For example, by having searches done every day or week on various Newsgroups, electronic mailing lists, or other periodically updated information bases, you can get a "weekly Internet WAIS gazette" that shows you what's new in your areas of interest, where you'd otherwise have to find and sort through large volumes of new data.

Also, many other Internet services have begun using WAIS as their search engine, even though you may never see a WAIS client or build a WAIS query. Many sites' Internet Gophers, for example, send their queries to a WAIS server. The archie servers are most likely using WAIS in some of their searching. Lastly, as commercial WAIS software and perhaps even pre-WAISed information becomes available, look for new WAIS-based free-for-use and pay-for-use information services over the coming year, available via the Internet or otherwise.

So when you're looking for information and you don't know where to look or how to look through it—call on WAIS.

### To learn more about and try WAIS

In early 1993, Brewster Kahle and others formed a new company, WAIS Inc. (Menlo Park, CA) to sell customized, fully supported commercial client and server software for information indexing and searching. In addition (like any self-respecting Internet application), there's a healthy supply of WAIS information, code, clients, and servers freely available. Software, specifications, and documentation are available for *freeWAIS,* a "freeware" version of WAIS, which includes support for boolean queries. CNIDR (see Chap. 12) is helping to coordinate distribution of freeWAIS code and information.

According to the freeWAIS FAQ document, "WAIS is available via anonymous-FTP from a variety of sources. The distributor of the original WAIS is quake.think.com, in the wais subdirectory. freeWAIS is distributed from ftp.cnidr.org." WAIS and freeWAIS clients are available for computer environments including the Macintosh (two versions), MS-DOS, Microsoft Windows, Unix (versions for command-line-oriented, screen-oriented, and X Windows systems), NeXtStep, and VAX/VMS. Software developers also discuss WAIS technology via e-mail and Usenet newsgroups.

WAIS information, code, clients, and servers are freely available in a range of ways:

- If you have e-mail access to the Internet, *subscribe* to the mailing list:
  - **wais-discussion,** a roughly weekly digest of messages from users and developers regarding electronic publishing issues, plus information on WAIS releases (includes wais-interest messages). To subscribe, send an e-mail message to wais-discussion-request@think.com (The message should be: "add <your-email-address> wais-discussion.")
  - **wais-talk,** unmoderated directly redistributed messages among developers (typically several messages per day); subscribe by sending e-mail to wais-talk-request@think.com ("add <your-email-address> wais-talk").
- If you have access to the Usenet, *read* the Usenet Netnews group comp.infosystems.wais. (All postings to the wais-discussion e-mail list also go here.)
- If you have Internet anonymous-FTP access (for file transfer), software and documents are available using anonymous-FTP file transfer from quake.think.com and ftp.cnidr.org.

In addition to software and documents, the archives at quake.think.com should include a Macintosh demonstration screen-recorder movie put together by Steve Cisler of Apple showing some of what WAIStation does (in /wais/WAIStation-Canned-Demo.sit.hqx) and e-mail list archives on host quake.think.com (in the directory /pub/wais/wais-discussion).

For more information on WAIS, contact:

Barbara Lincoln Brooks
WAIS Inc.
1040 Noel Drive
Menlo Park, CA 94025
415-327-WAIS
FAX: 415-327-6513
E-mail: barbara@wais.com

## A Few Closing Thoughts on Navigating the Internet

To date, no Internet navigator or front end has successfully addressed the complex questions of (1) finding new resources, (2) figuring out whether they're of interest to you, and (3) accumulating and maintaining a personalized menu for you. The Unix shellscript I cobbled together one evening (see App. D) is my admittedly low-end answer to (1). The overall problem remains and also begs the question, "What *is* available on the Internet that is relevant to [me]?"

But these are long-term philosophical, cultural, and business questions regarding the evolution of the Internet. For now, go find and try out one or more of the current crop of Internet navigators: go for a Gopher and burrow through GopherSpace, take a spin with TechInfo, hop onto HYTELNET, take a walk on the WorldWideWeb.

Part

# 4

# Help, Problems, Security, and Other Aspects of Being an Internet Citizen

Chapter

# 11

# Being an Internet Citizen

*"Don't mess with my blue suede shoes."*

CARL PERKINS

*"But...that would be wrong."*

*Caption to cartoon in text editor manual I wrote for Prime Computer in the late 1970s*

*"A robot may not injure a human being, or, through inaction, allow a human being to come to harm.*

*A robot must obey the orders given it by human beings except where such orders would conflict with the First Law."*

*The Three Laws of Robotics (Rules 1 and 2)*

ISAAC ASIMOV

In using the Internet, you are making use of a shared resource and participating in a worldwide environment whose community encompasses thousands of organizations and millions of other people. Because of the nature of computers and networks, it's possible for a single act to have an impact on some—or all—Internet resources and members. The Internet Worm, for example, a single program launched from a single computer, sent copies of itself over the Internet to other computers, where each copy in turn multiplied; before the Worm was "exterminated," hundreds of computers were put out of action from overload or security concerns.

Even something as simple as transferring large files during peak network usage times can interfere with other users. It also means that other people can affect you—possibly read, change, or delete your files—if your site and you have not taken appropriate security measures. Lastly, use of Internet resources and services costs money; it's important to know whose money you're causing to be spent.

## Rules for Being a "Good Internet Citizen"

In this chapter, we'll take a look at what it means to be a "Citizen of the Internet"—a good Internet citizen, that is. The Internet, like most resources, facilities, and utilities you use, and like most communities you participate in, has its own sets of rules, regulations, guidelines, and cultural traditions. Before you begin using the Internet, it's important—essential, in fact—that you be aware of these rules and the implicit or explicit agreements you're committing yourself to in making use of the Internet.

The intent of the various sets of rules and guidelines can be grouped into several categories:

- *Appropriate usage.* Does what you want to do fall within the boundaries of what each involved network party permits and are you allowed to do it?
- *Security.* Are you compromising the security of yourself or any other involved party?
- *Netiquette.* Are you doing something that is in conflict with Internet culture or community, in specific or general?
- *Cost.* Are you authorized to expend your organization's resources this way? Are you aware of possible other associated costs and resources you may consume?

As you may already have noticed, many other chapters, such as Chaps. 5 and 8 and the section about archie in Chap. 10, include specific discussions of netiquette usage as it applies to that chapter's topic. This section is more general and is about being a citizen of the Internet.

## Appropriate Usage, or Hey, You Can't or Can Do That on the Internet

*"I wouldn't want to belong to any club that would have me as a member."*

GROUCHO MARX

Just about everything in our lives has some form of rules, and the Internet is no exception. There are rules regarding our use of telephones. For example, most companies permit us to make occasional quick personal phone calls from work so we can check what to pick up for dinner, arrange for a doctor's appointment, see if our car is ready, etc. On the other hand, spending 3 hours daily making long-distance personal calls is not acceptable. Making a copy of a credit card application at work before mailing it is O.K.; making a thousand copies of your 5-year-old daughter's poem is not. Even the videotapes we rent come with rules. Many of the general resources we share have rules, too. You shouldn't park in spaces designated "Handicapped," drive in commuter lanes during rush hour, etc., unless appropriate. Don't commit murder, theft, or violence, drive on the wrong side of the road, etc. To complicate matters, the rules—and the punishments for breaking them—vary from company to company, state to state, country to country.

In terms of the rules and regulations regarding appropriate use of computers and networks, we're still learning what the full scope of questions are and how to determine limits. Few organizations will quibble if you save a few items of personal information on-line, like a list of birthdays and anniversaries. Filling up a gigabyte with digitized images of movie stars or running an after-hours betting ring, on the other hand, is most likely not going to meet with corporate approval. The addition of networking types of activity raises even trickier questions. Are you allowed to send a "Happy Birthday" message to a coworker or post a "For Sale" note to your company electronic bulletin board? Is the e-mail you create and send inviolate, or can any manager or system administrator read it? Are you responsible for preventing breaches of security if you have confidential information stored in your account? Answer: It depends on a number of factors.

In this section, we'll look at who's got rules regarding your use of the Internet and how to get a sense of what's O.K. and what's not. The rules regarding what's appropriate use of the Internet are complex and varying. Appropriate use is reflected and enforced in two major ways:

- Limiting or permitting which networks and sites a given organization or network can establish connections to
- Defining rules for permitted and unallowed activities

The first is done within the network routing software and defines whether, for example, you will be able to open a connection from your site to a given anonymous-FTP site. (See Box: Reach Out and Connect—Changing Times, Changing Rules; also see the discussion of "**telnet**-Through" in Chap. 10.) The second is a matter of setting, publicizing, and enforcing policies. To complicate matters:

- There is no single Internet authority to decide whether a given activity is O.K. or not.
- Rules change.
- Network connections and choice of service providers may change.

Ultimately, you as a user are responsible for being aware of, and obeying, all rules that apply to you. Always bear in mind that no set of rules can give you permission to do actions which are themselves illegal—and that you and your organization may be liable for the consequences of your actions.

In her document, "User Guidelines and Netiquette," Arlene H. Rinaldi <rinaldi@acc.fau.edu> in Academic/Institutional Support Services Education Training at Florida Atlantic University offers advice to her user community which is highly relevant to all Internet users:

> As a user of the network, you may be allowed to access other networks (and/or the computer systems attached to those networks). Each network or system has its own set of policies and procedures. Actions which are routinely allowed on one network/system may be controlled, or even forbidden, on other networks. It is the users' responsibility to abide by the policies and procedures of these other networks/systems. Remember, the fact that a user *can* perform a particular action does not imply that they *should* take that action.
>
> The use of the network is a privilege, not a right, which may temporarily be revoked at any time for abusive conduct. Such conduct would include the placing

**_Reach Out and Connect—Changing Times, Changing Rules_**

The many pieces of the Internet connect—but that doesn't always mean that user A can connect their computer to system B across networks C and D. Commercial customers considering joining the Internet have been increasingly baffled and frustrated by usage restrictions for the NSFnet backbone and many regional networks. "The Fortune 1000s, financial service companies, insurance and the like are used to being able to buy connectivity that doesn't have restrictions, whether for phone, data, or courier services," points out John Eldredge, Director of Sales at PSI. International users find rules deriving from the U.S.-centric R&D/DoD purpose of the original ARPAnet to be equally frustrating—and in some cases ethnocentric and offensive. "Fortunately, about 75 percent of the current U.S. Internet can be accessed today without confronting any 'acceptable usage' issues," says Eldredge.

From 1989 to 1992, the National Science Foundation's NSFnet acted as the primary backbone for the Internet within the United States, leading to a no-win situation for users needing connections via the NSFnet. Some users could; others couldn't. Several factors have changed this. Commercial network service providers such as Uunet and PSI have established their own national international network backbones. Many of the Internet member networks have established direct interconnections, such as between AlterNet and NEARnet. The Commercial Internet Exchanges (CIXes, a.k.a. "CIXen" in the computer community as in VAXen, the informal plural for a Digital Equipment VAX computer) have provided yet another method of interconnect that does not involve going across the NSFnet. (For more about this, see Chap. 1.)

Today, as PSI's Eldredge says above, most users within the United States can make connections freely and without having to restrict their activities to those falling within NSFnet Appropriate Use Policy (AUP) guidelines. Connectivity among the pieces of the Internet continues to improve at the same time that AUP restrictions are being relaxed or reexamined. But meanwhile, it's important to understand that, whether the reasons make sense or not, sometimes you "can't get there from here."

of unlawful information on a system, the use of abusive or otherwise objectionable language in either public or private messages, the sending of messages that are likely to result in the loss of recipients' work or systems, the sending of "chain letters," or "broadcast" messages to lists or individuals, and any other types of use which would cause congestion of the networks or otherwise interfere with the work of others.

## Appropriate use policies, procedures, and politics

The various organizations that comprise the Internet, in particular, whichever set of access, service, and resource providers you're currently using and whomever you're interacting with, each has explicit or implicit rules and guidelines regarding their appropriate use. The rules defining the types of traffic and activity a network or site is willing to support are generally in a document called an *Acceptable Use Policy*, or *AUP*. (Other common terms include Agreement, Terms & Conditions, or T&C.)

If you've ever signed up for an on-line service such as American On-Line, CompuServe, DELPHI, GEnie, or Prodigy, the on-line session undoubtedly displayed several screenfuls of "Agreement," followed by a question like, "To proceed and become an account-holder: Have you read and do you agree to the terms and conditions of the agreement just displayed (Enter YES/NO)?" Most of the public-access Internet sites have similar sign-up procedures. If your account is through an employer or academic institution, you may not have gone through such procedures—but you may be sure that some such policy exists. If nothing else, to obtain its connection through an Internet Service Provider, your organization has had to agree to abide by the provider's AUP, and, by extension, any other relevant AUPs.

Every organization that funds or acts as part of the Internet network should have an AUP; every site that connects to the Internet should have its own AUP. Site policies may be as simple as "We observe the NSFnet AUP" or may be extensive and often strongly different.

Who has rules you need to know about regarding use of the Internet? Answer: Lots of parties; for example:

- Your computer or system (e.g., hours for using certain facilities, how much storage you're allowed to consume)
- Your department, group, or project, regarding what resources you're entitled to access
- Your organization (which may be a public-access Internet site), regarding the appropriate use of the facility as a whole
- Your organization's Internet Service Provider (e.g., AlterNet, ANS, CERFnet, NEARnet, PSInet).
- Networks based on services from Internet Service Providers (e.g., NSFnet, NYSERNET).
- Other Internet and other member networks that you connect to (e.g., BITNET) and through, in particular, the NSFnet.
- Services and resources you connect to and make use of (e.g., archie and WAIS servers, Dow Jones, NASA databases, MUD sites)

This may seem like a lot of players. And it is; just as when you drive, you're subject to the driving rules for the local area, city, state, and country, plus the agreements that are part of your automobile insurance policy, rental car policy if you're renting the car, etc.

To complicate matters, it's largely up to you to figure out "what states you're driving through" and find the rules. When you're driving in your car, road signs tell you contextual information, such as when you're going from one city or state to another, what road and type (local, highway) you're on, changes in rules such as speed limits, and the like. On the Internet, however, there's no electronic signpost to remind you "Entering research and education area—no commercial messages for next six segments."

Before "hopping on the information highway," you should be sure you've read (and agreed to) the rules for all appropriate facilities. Many will be available on-line. The "What's O.K., what's not O.K." rules do change over time. Many organizations post a notice regarding major changes to the login banner you get when you log in to your system and/or e-mail bulletins. It is your responsibility to determine what they are, either agree to abide by them or decline to use them, and then follow these rules.

However, be warned: While the language of an AUP may apparently be clear, its meaning is not always as clear and can easily be subject to a range of interpretations. For example, is sending an invoice for commercial services or performing a commercial service (e.g., system administration) permissible on a noncommercial network in support of academic or research? Can I order textbooks with e-mail over the NSFnet? Can I send the text of a contract? How about an invoice? Is accessing a pay-for-use service over a "no commercial traffic" network for use in a noncommercial activity considered permissible or not?

To help you understand how Internet rules get interpreted, some examples and thoughts from several leading members of the Internet community follow.

Back when the ARPAnet was in existence, FTP Software (North Andover, MA) "listed providing technical support to our customers on the ARPAnet on our original application for ARPAnet connectivity," recalls Steve Knowles (stev@ftp.com), at FTP Software. FTP Software is a vendor of TCP/IP network products, which were used by many ARPAnet sites. During the transition of the ARPAnet into the NSFnet, says Knowles, "Steve Wolff [Director of the NSFnet] and I got into a conversation about the new [NSFnet] AUP, and its application to our company, in terms of our interest in continuing to provide technical support across the new NSFnet."

According to Knowles, Wolff said that FTP Software's request to connect to and use the NSFnet was granted, because:

> ...providing technical support activities on the NSFnet tends to enhance software used by the NSF, their grantees, and the U.S. government in general, by providing more robust, bug-free software. While selling is not allowed, supporting anyone, including people who are not government-sponsored users of the network, tended to allow for the quicker fixing of bugs, and the distribution of these fixes more quickly, and as such, was deemed to be an acceptable use.

John Curran of the NEARnet staff offers the following thoughts regarding commercial usage of the Internet and in particular the affect of the NEARnet and NSFnet AUPs:

> Within NEARnet (i.e., between NEARnet members), one may engage in any commercial activities desired, product support, software distribution, etc.—as long as they are legal and are not "unsolicited advertising." These policies also apply with respect to networks that we have direct connections with, such as AlterNet.
>
> By default, external traffic goes via the NSFnet network service, and the NSFnet AUP applies. Several of our sites select commercial routing, and then the ANS CO+RE AUP applies.
>
> The current NSFnet AUP specifically allows many types of traffic including: professional development, scholarly debate, standards activities, certain administrative traffic, and more. The two explicitly unacceptable uses for traffic that is going over the NSFnet are: extensive commercial usage, and use for for-profit activities. Note that an activity such as product support may or may not be acceptable under this policy depending on the circumstances. Your network provider can provide advice in this area, or you can contact NSF which is ultimately responsible for interpretation of the policy.
>
> Because of its AUP, the NSFnet does not meet the commercial networking needs of many of New England's high-technology firms, nor should it. The NSFnet AUP insures that federal funds are spent in accordance with the

enabling legislation, and in this case the purpose is support research and education. To meet the demand for commercial connectivity, NEARnet uses the commercial connectivity available via ANSnet to reach the Commercial Internet Exchange. In this manner, NEARnet members enjoy commercial connectivity to the largest possible community.

Erik E. Fair <fair@apple.com>, Postmaster & Internet Liaison in Engineering Computer Operations at Apple Computer, Inc. (Cupertino, CA) notes:

It is important to preface this with one central notion: the rules are not clear cut and they are in flux. Bear that in mind while reading what follows.

1. Offering a service on a network connected to NSFnet (e.g., BARRnet, NEARnet) does not necessarily put you ipso facto in violation of the NSFnet Acceptable Use Policy (AUP), regardless of what the service is, or who you are.

For example, we [Apple] offer an anonymous-FTP service with copies of Macintosh System Software, Technical Notes, etc., on it to help people who have bought our hardware. In my interpretation of the rules as I understand them, it is up to a person connecting to our service to determine if such a connection is within the acceptable use policies of the networks which are being used for transit (which may include, but is not limited to, the NSFnet).

2. The AUPs of specific networks [e.g., BARRnet, NEARnet] are not the same as NSFnet's. For example, of my last information, technical support activities are permitted WITHIN THE BOUNDS OF NEARnet, and so is just about anything else that's inherently legal. But you should check the policy statement from the appropriate network to be sure.

3. NSFnet's AUP doesn't even explicitly prohibit commercial activity, if it is in support of research and education. Once you include the NSFnet as a transit for some service, then the questions are: who are you talking to, and what is their purpose?

If it is a researcher or educator working toward the usual end of such professions (i.e., not doing commercial consulting—but we could still ask, "for whom" here too), then using the NSFnet is pretty much O.K.

If, for example, Apple and Pacer Software are collaborating on a new product soley for our own avaricious gain, then we can't use NSFnet for that. But there's lots of grey area in between the obviously prohibited, and the obviously allowed.

Ultimately, the real rules are: Watch the rules (they change), use your best judgment, and always strive to be a good "network citizen"—your peers in the network world will be much more willing to forgive a gaffe or lapse of judgment if you are a net contributor to the community.

The first step is to find and read the rules. To do that, you need to know what's got rules.

## Sample AUP excerpts

Let's take a look at some pieces of representative agreements and AUPs. (In terms of AUPs that apply to you, bear in mind that these policies may change over time—check locally for current copies of pertinent AUPs.)

**NSFnet AUP.** The most frequently cited statement relating to the use of the Internet is the NSFnet's AUP. Because the NSFnet is the backbone through which many regional networks currently interconnect, its policies often must be taken into consideration. At least two providers of United States-wide commercial Internet service include the NSFnet AUP by reference as part of their own service agreements. Many networks have also chosen to use the NSFnet AUP as the starting model for their own AUP.

The NSFnet charter is to support educational and research activity—and therefore only carry traffic relevant to such efforts. The occasional noneducational e-mail message or file transfer is unlikely to degrade service or otherwise interfere with chartered usage—but there clearly must be limits to the degree of commercial traffic finding its way onto the backbone. Here's the NSFnet Backbone Services Acceptable Use Policy, as of early 1993:

> GENERAL PRINCIPLE:
>
> (1) NSFnet Backbone services are provided to support open research and education in and among US research and instructional institutions, plus research arms of for-profit firms when engaged in open scholarly communication and research. Use for other purposes is not acceptable.
>
> SPECIFICALLY ACCEPTABLE USES:
>
> (2) Communication with foreign researchers and educators in connection with research or instruction, as long as any network that the foreign user employs for such communication provides reciprocal access to US researchers and educators.
>
> (3) Communication and exchange for professional development, to maintain currency, or to debate issues in a field or subfield of knowledge.
>
> (4) Use for disciplinary-society, university-association, government-advisory, or standards activities related to the user's research and instructional activities.
>
> (5) Use in applying for or administering grants or contracts for research or instruction, but not for other fundraising or public relations activities.
>
> (6) Any other administrative communications or activities in direct support of research and instruction.
>
> (7) Announcements of new products or services for use in research or instruction, but not advertising of any kind.
>
> (8) Any traffic originating from a network of another member agency of the Federal Networking Council if the traffic meets the acceptable use policy of that agency.
>
> (9) Communication incidental to otherwise acceptable use, except for illegal or specifically unacceptable use.
>
> UNACCEPTABLE USES:
>
> (10) Use for for-profit activities, unless covered by the General Principle or as a specifically acceptable use.
>
> (11) Extensive use for private or personal business.
>
> This statement applies to use of the NSFnet Backbone only. NSF expects that connecting networks will formulate their own use policies. The NSF Division of Networking and Communications Research and Infrastructure will resolve any questions about this Policy or its interpretation.

**Internet Service Provider AUPs.** Internet Service Providers are not necessarily the same thing as Internet member networks. Many provide services for specific networks. PSI, for example, provides the network for NYSERNET, but PSI's PSInet is itself national and international in scope. As of 1992, Advanced Network & Services provisions the network service for the NSFnet backbone, but also provides commercial Internet connectivity through its wholly owned subsidiary, ANS CO+RE. There are separate AUPs for ANS, the NSFnet, and ANS CO+RE—and there are significant differences among them. The ANS AUP, for example, states:

5. ANS networks shall not be used for commercial purposes. However, if a use is consistent with the purposes and objectives of ANS, then commercial activities in support of that use will be considered an acceptable use of the network.

while the ANS CO+RE states:

5. ANS CO+RE networks may be used for purposes consistent with the ANS and ANS CO+RE goals.

**ANS AUP.** Here's the ANS AUP, as of October 1992:

1. All use of ANS network services shall be intended to facilitate the exchange of information in furtherance of education and research, and otherwise be consistent with the broad objectives of ANS.
2. Users of ANS network services shall promote efficient use of the networks to minimize, and avoid if possible, congestion of the networks and interference with the work of other users of the networks.
3. Users of ANS network services shall not disrupt any of the ANS networks as a whole or any equipment or system forming part of its systems, or any services provided over, or in connection with, any of the ANS networks.
4. ANS networks shall not be used to transmit any communication where the meaning of the message, or its transmission or distribution, would violate any applicable law or regulation or would likely be highly offensive to the recipient or recipients thereof.
5. ANS networks shall not be used for commercial purposes. However, if a use is consistent with the purposes and objectives of ANS, then commercial activities in support of that use will be considered an acceptable use of the network.
6. Advertising of commercial offerings is forbidden. Discussion of a product's relative advantages and disadvantages by users of the product is encouraged. Vendors may respond to questions about their products as long as the responses are not in the nature of advertising.
7. Interpretation, application, and possible modification of this Acceptable Use Policy shall be within the sole discretion of ANS. Questions about any issue arising under this Policy should be directed to ANS by User Organizations when an issue first arises.

**NEARnet AUP (excerpt).** As you can see, the Acceptable Use Policy from the New England Academic and Research Network (NEARnet) is very explicit:

2.2 It is not acceptable to use NEARnet for illegal purposes.

2.3 It is not acceptable to use NEARnet to transmit threatening, obscene, or harassing materials.

2.4 It is not acceptable to use NEARnet so as to interfere with or disrupt network users, services, or equipment. Disruptions include, but are not limited to, distribution of unsolicited advertising, propagation of computer worms and viruses, and using the network to make unauthorized entry to any other machine accessible via the network.

2.5 It is assumed that information and resources accessible via NEARnet are private to the individuals and organizations which own or hold rights to those resources and information unless specifically stated otherwise by the owners or holders of rights. It is therefore not acceptable for an individual to use NEARnet to access information or resources unless permission to do so has been granted by the owners or holders of rights to those resources or information.

**Site policies.** *Sites* are where the computers and accounts of Internet users are. Your site—particularly if it's a corporation—probably has a strong statement of its own internal policies, in addition to those relating to Internet use. You are advised to be cautious in your use of Internet (and other) on-line computer and network resources that belong to your employer (or academic institution). Not only may inappropriate use cause problems for them, it can cause problems for you. There have been a number of major lawsuits between employees and employers over whether use of resources like e-mail was appropriate (and whether the organization had the right to read e-mail traffic and files to discover this). The cardinal rule of networking is as true for Internet use as elsewhere: When in doubt, don't do anything on-line you aren't willing to see in the morning newspaper or on your organization's bulletin board.

It is possible that there is little or no policy information available. Because many companies are still learning about the need for policies like this, and struggling to determine exactly what their policies are, there may be none. In their absence, use your discretion, and follow all other available guidelines. Here's examples of AUPs from several Internet sites.

**Software Tool & Die terms and conditions for World users.** Here's most of the Software Tool & Die's "Terms & Conditions" for users of The World, its public-access Internet site, as of October 1992:

**Terms & Conditions.** By accepting this account, customer agrees to the following:

1. Software Tool & Die, operators of The World, exercises no control whatsoever over the content of the information passing through its systems or stored on its systems.
2. Software Tool & Die makes no warranties of any kind, whether expressed or implied, for the service it is providing. Software Tool & Die disclaims any warranty of merchantability or fitness for a particular purpose. Software Tool & Die will not be responsible for any damage you suffer from use of its service including, but not limited to, loss of data, delays, misdeliveries or service interruptions caused by Software Tool & Die's negligence or your own errors or omissions.

3. The World may only be used for lawful purposes. Transmission of any material in violation of any US or state regulation is prohibited. This includes but is not limited to copyrighted material, threatening or obscene material, or material protected by trade secret. You agree to indemnify and hold harmless Software Tool & Die from any claims resulting from your use of the service which damages you or another party.
4. Any access to other networks through The World must comply with the rules appropriate for that network [i.e., if you connect to or through any other networks, you have to obey their rules as well].
5. Use of any information, programs, or data obtained from or via The World is at your own risk. Software Tool & Die specifically denies any responsibility for the accuracy or quality of information obtained through its services.
8. These Terms and Conditions supercede all previous representations, understandings or agreements and shall prevail notwithstanding any variance with terms and conditions of any order submitted.
9. Use of The World constitutes acceptance of these Terms and Conditions.

**Terms and conditions for IAT's HoloNet (excerpts).** Here, for comparison, are some of the terms and conditions from another public-access Internet site, HoloNet, as of February 1993:

1. Information Access Technologies, Inc. ("IAT") exercises no control whatsoever over the content of the information passing through HoloNet. IAT makes no warranties of any kind, whether expressed or implied, for the service it is providing. IAT also disclaims any warranty of merchantability or fitness for a particular purpose, and any obligation to maintain the confidentiality of information, although IAT's current practice is to utilize reasonable efforts to maintain such confidentiality. IAT will not be responsible for any damage you suffer from use of HoloNet. This includes loss of data resulting from delays, nondeliveries, misdeliveries, or service interruptions caused by its own negligence or your errors or omissions, or due to inadvertent release or disclosure of information sent by you. Use of any information obtained via HoloNet is at your own risk. IAT specifically denies any responsibility for the accuracy or quality of information obtained through its services.
3. The use of HoloNet to transmit certain kinds of information (including without limitation, computer software and other technical data) may violate export control laws and regulations of the United States, whether that information is received abroad or by foreign nationals within the United States. Since IAT exercises no control whatsoever over the content of information passing through HoloNet, the entire burden of complying with such laws and regulations rests with its customers. You agree to comply with such laws and regulations and to indemnify and hold IAT harmless from any damages it may suffer resulting from any violation of the export control laws of the United States.
8. These Terms and Conditions supersede all previous representations, understandings, or agreements and shall prevail notwithstanding any variance with terms and conditions of any order submitted. Use of HoloNet constitutes acceptance of these Terms and Conditions. These Terms and Conditions may be modified by IAT upon 30 days prior written notice to you. Continued use of HoloNet following such modifications constitutes acceptance of these Terms and Conditions, as modified.

**Other AUPs.** Beginning to get the idea? You could easily fill a book with nothing but AUPs and other related documents. We're going to stop here—but there's a few other AUP and usage documents you should be aware of and be prepared to get and read.

**Usenet AUP.** Usenet is, appropriately enough, a peculiar case. Usenet per se is a collective entity with no formal head. Usenet usage guidelines stem from a combination of:

- The AUP of the network service provider to a given site
- The policies of the site
- The policies of the specific Newsgroup.

In general, this means:

- No commercial advertising except in groups where this is explicitly permitted.
- Be careful in what you say that may be libel.

Usenet policies can be found in the periodic updating and repeated postings in Newsgroups including news.answers and news.announce.newusers. Many Newsgroups have their own FAQ (Frequently Asked Questions, and their answers) or other administrative "Welcome to..." posting. Read them carefully. For more information, see Chap. 6.

**CREN AUP for BITNET.** Although BITNET is technically not part of the Internet, the odds are good you may make use of BITNET services in one way or another. Many electronic mailing lists include BITNET users among their recipients, for example, although you may never be able to determine this short of seeing a BITNET return address on a message. Many of the electronic discussion groups you may be interested in may originate on BITNET, especially if you're involved in academic or library-related activities. BITNET also supports numerous automated document and information servers (see Chap. 17).

So it's important to be aware that BITNET, too, has its own AUP, called the CREN Acceptable Use Policy and to know what some of its key points are. For example, "CREN networks are for the use of persons legitimately affiliated with CREN Member or Affiliate organizations, to facilitate the exchange of information consistent with the academic, educational, and research purposes of its members." To get the CREN Acceptable Use Policy, send electronic mail to listserv@bitnic.educom.edu with **GET CREN NET-USE** in the message body. For more information, contact:

CREN
1112 Sixteenth Street, NW
Suite 600
Washington, DC 20036
202-872-4200
info@bitnic.educom.edu

**FARnet guidelines.** FARnet, the Federation of Academic & Research Networks, notes in its *Guidelines on Acceptable Use and Connection,* "Responsibility for the determination of whether a proposed use of the network is acceptable begins with the initiating user. If the user is uncertain, the associated connecting authority or mid-level should be contacted."

**Government and community guidelines.** Last, but not least, governments and communities may have legal control over some of what you do with the Internet (and other computers and networks, for that matter). For example:

*Business and legal aspects.* On-line networking opens up entire new worlds of potential business and legal misbehavior. Is it possible to commit mail fraud by e-mail? Is an electronic mail message legally binding? What is your liability if you send confidential company material by e-mail?

*International export laws.* The Internet allows you to communicate with over 40 countries. "Products" aren't always physical objects anymore; the information that represents a book, illustration, software program, or product design can easily be sent by e-mail or file transfer. There may be taxes, licenses—and legal restrictions—on what you do. Do your homework. Also, a number of countries have something called "trans-data border laws." Sending data or other types of traffic may incur taxes, penalties, or other unexpected surprises. For example, notes BBN's Cynd: Mills, "The German PTT [telephone company] prohibited sending X.25 traffic from one German site to another German site through a foreign country, considering it a circumvention of local tariffs."

*Secret stuff.* A surprising amount of the technology used in, or talked about, on the Internet isn't supposed to, for example, leave the U.S. borders (certain encryption technologies, for example). Don't send or discuss restricted technologies, programs, algorithms.

*Copyright, intellectual, and property rights.* Every new technology brings new questions and concerns regarding intellectual property rights, copyright, payment, and the like: copying machines, tape recorders, VCRs, and DAT tape, to name a few. Networks and on-line information, which can be copied, distributed, and modified in a few keystrokes, is an area still being explored. Much of the information on the Internet belongs to somebody—somebody else, not you. A lot of this owned information can be freely downloaded, forwarded, recirculated, and used, so long as the appropriate ownership information and any other guidelines in them are followed. However, a sizable percentage of the information and files accessible through the Internet are *not* there for your free, unrestrained reuse. For example, if you retrieve and use shareware, such as from the many anonymous-FTP archive sites, you are obligated to pay the indicated license fees, and respect the associated rules. In addition, you are not allowed to recirculate many of the postings from Usenet without permission (e.g., ClariNet's on-line versions of Dave Barry's and Miss Manners—which ClariNet pays for the right to redistribute, and sites subscribing to the ClariNet Newsgroups pay for the right to receive and make available to their users. You are not allowed to sell/resell them, incorporate them into your own work without attribution and permission.

The Internet works largely by expecting users to be aware of and respect the various rules and guidelines. Portions of *Matrix News,* for example, a newsletter put out by John S. Quarterman and Smoot Carl-Mitchell, Texas Internet Consulting <tic@tic.com> (Austin, TX), are distributed via the Internet; the full newsletter goes out as hardcopy. *Matrix News* includes this paragraph in appropriate places:

> We ask online subscribers not to redistribute the newsletter, or individual articles from it. Please do not remail them, and please do not put them up for anonymous-FTP, WAIS, etc. This is so that we and our contributors can continue to provide articles and we can continue to distribute them. We are, however, happy to discuss terms with organizations that wish to redistribute internally or to their customers.

According to Quarterman, "So far, it seems to work."

Don't put inappropriate information on-line. The same restrictions and courtesy applies to putting information, programs, images, etc., into electronic form onto the Internet (or to any other on-line computer network). Don't type in entire articles from newspapers or magazines without permission. Don't upload somebody else's program, whether it's a commercial product from a big-time vendor or something your cousin wrote, without permission. Most shareware packages include very clear instructions regarding what's allowed and what's not. To summarize:

- If you make inappropriate use of other people's intellectual property, you are depriving them of the right to earn a living—and potentially making yourself, your site, and your organization open to a lawsuit.
- If you do see something on the Internet you want to use or redistribute beyond acceptable uses, consider sending e-mail (or a letter or making a phone call) to the author, explaining what you want to do. As often as not, if your request is reasonable, you'll be granted permission. (If not, be a good sport, and take "no" for an answer.)

**Community guidelines.** Always keep in mind that you don't ever know for sure where things you put onto the Internet will be viewed—and in some of those places, some things you make available won't be viewed favorably. Legal and community actions against local BBSs and other on-line enterprises are becoming more prevalent. Services like CompuServe, DELPHI, and Prodigy are taking this very seriously. You should, too. Remember: Millions of people may see what you do, immediately or years later. And they may not all agree with you.

There are a lot of lawsuits and discussions regarding the free speech, censorship, and First Amendment aspects of this. It's possible that some information available via the Internet may be deemed by some parties to be inappropriate, based on objections by reason of religious or philosophical beliefs, age, etc. Be advised.

### *rot13: The Secret Decoder Ring of the Internet*

Within the Internet and Usenet communities, a common practice for potentially offensive messages is to scramble them so you can't read them without first going to some effort—the equivalent of sealing something in a letter versus writing it on a postcard. The most common method used is a technique called *encryption.* Encrypting your message before you send it means the reader has to make a deliberate effort in order to see a message, thus making it harder to be offended by something that just happens to be there.

The Internet community has developed a system called Privacy-Enhanced Mail (PEM), which uses a form of encryption called Public-Key technology, which lets its users "sign" letters in a way that lets a sender scramble it in a way that only the intended recipient can read it and lets the recipient verify that a message (1) is from who it says it is and (2) hasn't been altered. Another popular method is PGP (Pretty Good Protection).

One popular technique used in the Usenet and e-mail communities is "rotation" encryption. If you consider the alphabet as a wheel with the letters A through Z being 26 spokes, you "rotate" a message by shifting every letter in a message by a predesignated number of positions. This is what all those Little Orphan Annie and Captain Midnite Secret Decoder Rings did. The standard rotation used by the Usenet community is rotating 13 characters, a.k.a. **rot13** (pronounced "rot-thirteen"). Because the alphabet in the ASCII character set has 26 characters, doing a rot13 on text once will encrypt it, and doing it again effectively reverses the process, restoring the text to its original readable form. A rotated 13 becomes N, rotating N by 13 gives A, and so on. On a Unix system, you can create a one-line shellscript that will perform **rot13,** as shown in Chap. 4. Most Usenet News software includes a built-in **rot13** command.

### Finding AUPs and other agreements

If your Internet access is through an Internet Account Provider, check your system's on-line information. Look for "agreement," "AUP," "contract," "policy," or other appropriate-looking entries on your system's Help or other menu. Contact your system administrator or the staff of your network service provider.

Most of the Network Information Centers (NICs) maintain on-line-directories of current Appropriate-Usage Policies. The InterNIC should also have a collection of AUP statements in its on-line database.

Discussion of appropriate usage of the Internet can frequently be found in the RISKS moderated digest (available in the Usenet comp.risks group; to be added to the e-mail distribution list, send a message to risks-request@csl.sri.com), and in "com-priv," an unmoderated electronic mailing list concerning the commercialization and privatization of the Internet; to be added to the e-mail distribution list, send a message to com-priv-request@psi.com.

## Hackers, Crackers, Snoops, and Spies—Internet Security: Why You Care and What You Can Do

*"With great power comes great responsibility."*

STAN LEE
*Spiderman #1, Marvel Comics*

*"Don't leave your records in the sun /*
*They'll warp and they won't be good for anyone."*

JOHN HARTFORD

As a user of the Internet and member of the Internet community, you share in the common responsibility for the security of the computers and networks you are making use of.

Computer and network security is important—make no mistake about this. Connecting to the Internet is often compared to building a road that goes directly from your driveway to the interstate highway—suddenly a lot more people can have the potential to know about you and want to break into your computer and browse through your files. Another analogy: when you get a telephone, you're connected to the worldwide phone system. There are a lot of things for which having a telephone is useful to essential—but you are now susceptible to crank calls, telemarketing, phone "phreak" invasions, interruptions, etc.

If you have been using computers and networks, you should already have begun being security-conscious; connecting to and using the Internet "simply" brings additional dimensions. Just as you shouldn't leave your car parked with the window down and keys in it or leave home for a week with the doors open—or leave your wallet lying on your desk while you're away at lunch, exercising relatively common-sense precautions is part of being a responsible Internet user.

If you've followed headlines over the past few years, you've read about computer viruses, worms, computer "hackers,"* "trojan horses," "time bombs," software errors that have brought down a large portion of the U.S. phone system. It's not just science fiction any more. Don't feel so overwhelmed or paranoid that you avoid connecting to or using the Internet. But do learn and follow "safe nets" practices and procedures. Don't expect the vendors or service providers to have taken care of everything; become security-conscious and be ready to work with them.

### Internet security: Threats and sources

Internet security concerns can be categorized by the types of threats and by potential source. Major categories of security threat include:

- *Inadvertent or unauthorized access to data* (eavesdropping, snooping, unauthorized datanapping, system access, etc.) of e-mail, sessions, files being sent to the printer, stored files or programs (using, copying, deleting)
- *Spoofing.* Masquerading as another user or program (e.g., intruders, worms, and viruses) or falsifying e-mail names and contents
- *Repudiation.* Denying the transmission or content of a message
- *Denying service.* Preventing an authorized user from obtaining service (e.g., to an archive site, library catalog, or on-line service)
- *Deliberate alteration of messages in transit* (e.g., changing an e-mail message, or making a message unreadable)

How difficult—and prevalent—are these types of threats? According to

*The computer community prefers the term "crackers" for techno-malefactors; "hackers" has an older and well-respected positive meaning in the history of computer jargon.

### *Security Awareness at the Organizational Level*

While end users like you share the responsibility for maintaining security, it begins within the organization whose computer(s) and network(s) you are accessing the Internet from. Computer and network security are all too often bottom-of-the-list concerns at many organizations—until after some disaster strikes. While all organizations should be worrying about security, joining the Internet makes this concern all the more immediate and essential.

"Connecting to the Internet often forces organizations to implement the security they should already have," points out Peter Sevcik, a Principal at Northeast Consulting (Boston, MA). "Now you're literally hardwiring your entire network and computer systems up to the interoperable world, where anyone can try and break in. So you need security. You need 'firewalls' and barriers."

Internet-related security should be part of an overall set of security policy, procedures, and actions, Sevcik adds. "There's no point in 'putting a lock on your new front door and leaving the back windows open.' (i.e., only securing this new entry point).

"When an organization makes its initial attachment to the Internet is a good time to make sure you've been applying the common sense security precautions," suggests Jeff Ogden, Associate Director for MichNet at the Merit Network, Inc. (Ann Arbor, MI). "Examine your security needs. Depending on the systems involved, and the cost to secure them, you may decide it is appropriate to secure your Internet connection so intruders can't 'wander in.' For many sites, good passwords on the accounts are sufficient, and there is software available to put safe Internet-accessible applications up."

How much security is enough? After all, you don't want to "put a hundred-dollar lock on a fifty-dollar bicycle" (unless your business depends on that bicycle). "Analyze the technology available to you—and to potential network crackers—in relation to your applications," suggests Michael Baum, J.D., M.B.A., Principal of Independent Monitoring (Cambridge, MA). Some of the factors Baum cites as relevant include:

- What is (are) the specific application(s) involved and the inherent risk for information being lost, read, or misread?
- What is the current legal standing for the type of transaction involved (you may need different levels of security for different activities, for example, contracting versus government reporting versus soliciting versus casual communications)?
- What are the relevant industries doing?
- What controls are already in place or available internally?
- Who do the parties communicate with—and to what extent can or should you trust them?
- Who are the primary beneficiaries of the security?
- What is the cost of the technology to provide a given security feature?
- What is the extent of the control which can reasonably be exercised by management over the use of the communications mechanisms?

Craig Partridge, Research Scientist, at BBN Systems and Technologies, the first three are comparatively easy, denying service is hard, and the last, altering in-transit messages, is the hardest and very, very rare. "Outsiders are less likely to know what's important or how to break through your systems," says Cliff Stoll, the Berkeley astronomer and chocolate-chip cookie baker who found international spies prowling through the files of his organization's Unix systems (chronicled in his book, *The Cuckoo's Egg,* Doubleday). "Many of the crackers detected in the Internet are outsiders," observes Steve Kent, Chief Scientist at BBN Communications (Cambridge, MA), who has worked extensively in computer and network security areas. "However, a substantial amount of unauthorized activity is attributable to insiders as well."

Security breaches can come from a wide range of sources including:

- Disgruntled employees
- "Borrowed account" users unfamiliar with how to use facilities and with security concerns
- Students looking for test answers and to change their records
- Nosy "neighbors"
- Privacy invaders
- Crackers
- Software pirates
- Corporate and international spies
- Political activists
- Curious and careless computer programmers (many of whom are not intent on causing harm but misjudge the situation)
- Teenagers "cruising for data-burgers"

Lastly, don't overlook the security problems caused by mistakes and configuration errors in hardware and software. Many security penetrations, such as the Internet Worm, penetrate systems through easy-to-guess or nonexistent passwords or via software with debugging options left on. "Security breaches can arise from accidental problems, such as sending a sensitive message to the wrong person, as well as malicious efforts," points out BBN's Kent. "However, many of the techniques used to protect against these two classes of problems are different."

### Why is Internet security a special challenge?

The Internet poses a special security challenge because it almost always involves "other peoples' networks and computers" as well as your own. "Security for an individual computer often may be limited by the security of the other computers and networks with which it communicates," notes Steve Kent. In other words, you not only have to worry about your own computer and network but also any other computer or network involved—most of which neither you nor your organization control or own.

Paul Karger, Senior Technical Consultant, Computer Security, at the Open Software Foundation (Cambridge, MA) observes, "It's dangerous to ever assume you've secured something so well it can't be read or eavesdropped." The Internet has its roots in both highly secure and highly open computing. Much of the technology was developed to be usable by the U.S. Department of Defense, such as the MILNET network. On the other hand, the ARPAnet, and utilities like **telnet** and anonymous-FTP were created to help researchers, faculty, and students share resources easily. Today, these two motivations of security versus usability continue to shape the evolution of the Internet's growth.

To ensure that users are "who they say they are," most Internet resources and services require some form of *authentication,* such as a password. Many users and services often want *privacy*—some way to ensure that unauthorized parties can't read their traffic or files. Doing authentication across networks is one of the most important activities where such privacy is required. Yet, most protocols in use today rely on passwords for authentication, and passwords transmitted across a network in the clear (unencrypted) are highly vulnerable.

Encryption, where part or all of a message is encoded and subsequently decoded, using a *key,* is a security technique often used to provide authentication and confidentiality. Even sending encrypted passwords can be potentially a security hole if the key is obtained by the wrong person. One solution is *Kerberos,* developed by M.I.T.'s Project Athena. The Kerberos system uses separate keys and messages, called *Secrets,* exchanged through a Secrets server. Kerberos operates in such a way that users on the M.I.T. campuswide network (or any other network with Kerberos facilities) wouldn't have to send passwords, keys, or other compromising information across in "cleartext," thus making it impossible for eavesdroppers to get a key that would enable them to breach authentication or privacy security.

Privacy-Enhanced Mail, for example, uses a form of encryption called RSA public-key encryption to provide user authentication and message integrity via "digital signatures" and provides privacy via a DES key which in turn is conveyed under RSA encryption. "Privacy-Enhanced Mail is intended to address a growing dilemma many of us face, namely, working less effectively because we don't trust the network enough to transmit sensitive information, or taking risks by sending sensitive information over unsecure networks," observes BBN's Kent. "Neither alternative is acceptable."

Similarly, security measures are being developed for remote login and file transfer across the Internet so you won't have to send passwords in a way that they could be read and stolen. Meanwhile, if you think your system is already secure, and you haven't already read Cliff Stoll's *The Cuckoo's Egg,* go read it and then reask yourself if your computers and networks are secure.

Remember, network security is like a root canal. Prevention is less painful than the cure. And all the prevention in the world won't be a 100 percent guarantee that something bad won't happen. "Security is a continuous process, requiring careful attention to configuration management," adds Kent. "If you don't have the discipline to back up your disks, you probably don't have the discipline to maintain a secure system!"

## Qui Custodiat IPsos networks—Who guards the networks?

Security is a joint effort by many parties. This is particularly true for the Internet, where many people and organizations are involved in a given activity in some way. It starts with hardware and software vendors, creating products capable of working securely. Vendors to the Internet community continue to develop security products and services, such as Privacy-Enhanced Mail (PEM) for e-mail authentication and privacy, the Kerberos authentication system, Secure **telnet,** and security features for the SNMP Simple Network Management Protocol and the routing protocols.

The MIS and network planners in your organization, and the network service providers helping your organization connect to the Internet, have to work together to ensure security. Software must be installed with security in mind (for example, changing the often easy-to-guess default technical-support passwords) and routing tables, network ports, operating systems, and software such as e-mail and editor programs must be configured carefully, to "keep the bums out." Access permissions to directories and files and to executable programs must likewise be carefully set.

In the wake of an increasing level of security-breaching activity (See Box: Cuckoos and Worms), leading Internet security experts helped organize CERT, the Computer Emergency Response Team at the Software Engineering Institute at Carnegie Mellon University. CERT is a mostly volunteer effort whose main role is to act as central coordinator for Internet-related computer and network security emergencies. (Unfortunately, the nature of the Internet still means there is no real "center" to contact or alert.)

Within your organization, network operators and systems administrators typically have received at least some security training as well as advisories on who to contact when faced with potential security problems.

Lastly, security depends on you, the user, and your fellow users. In taking advantage of the Internet, you have an obligation as you use your computers and networks to always keep security considerations in mind. This ranges from not writing your passwords down on the bottom of your keyboard to not sending confidential information via unsecured e-mail. Just as you should

### *Securing Your Site's Systems*

Before going out and spending money, there are several basic steps any site can—and should—take to start the security process, according to Cliff Stoll:

> There are often lots of "holes," most of which can be fixed without buying any new hardware or software. It's a matter of putting in the necessary hours.
>
> Start with the obvious, zero-cost actions. Survey your networks, computers, and users, so you know what you've got.
>
> Kill inactive accounts; implement bug fixes for the known security holes in your operating systems. And make sure that your users and system administrators take the issue seriously.

Steve Kent advises:

> Install password-screening programs that test passwords when they are being chosen or changed, and also programs that search password files to detect guessable passwords. These programs ensure that the passwords selected are "good" ones, meaning not easily guessed by an attacker, relative to the standard password-guessing rules and to the lists of commonly-used passwords.

Once security systems have been set up, it's up to the systems managers to post and enforce the rules—and for users to follow them. All the cryptography and access managers won't keep the netcriminals out if you leave your password scrawled on the wall at the wrong place and time.

Some human traffic monitoring may also be in order, adds Stoll:

> Very few places actually monitor traffic into and out of a node of their LAN, whether it's dial-up modems, or internetwork traffic. Nobody actually watches the network traffic or computer activity for suspicious events, like too much traffic, messages from somebody known to be not there...or somebody trying to plant a trojan horse. It takes a human being to watch and decide this. Is it ethical? That's another question.

always be careful when you drive your car or use your bank card, you should "practice safe nets"—use the Internet carefully.

### Becoming a secure Internet user

Now that I've got you worried, what can you do, as an Internet user, to be security conscious? One way is to choose and use your passwords and other network IDs carefully:

- Choose a password that can't be easily guessed. Follow the rules for creating unguessable passwords. Don't use your name or that of any family member, any pet, or relating to any well-known hobby or interest.
- Don't write your password down in any easily findable place
- Don't share your password; don't loan your account.
- Change your password regularly.
- Don't send your password through unsecured e-mail or store it in unsecured on-line files.

Passwords are the most common security measure we use to assure computers "Yes, it's really me." Most of us use passwords in one form or another every day for everything from our bank cash cards, answering machines, voice mail, and telephone calling cards to home security systems, VCRs, and computers. Stolen and guessed passwords are responsible for many computer and network security breaches. Recent CERT evidence is that poor system management provides as common a vehicle for break-ins as poor passwords.

Knowledge of user-names, accompanied by verifying information such as passwords, is sought by computer crackers, enabling them to masquerade as legitimate users, or gain system operator privileges. The Morris Internet Worm (See Box: Cuckoos and Worms), for example, included a list of several hundred commonly used passwords—with which it "scored" a remarkably high success rate. In a security test at a public-access site in 1992, a relatively simple program was able to guess passwords for over a third of the several thousand account holders in under a week.

Increasingly, computer and network resources that require passwords are incorporating "password-checkers" that make sure you haven't selected an easily guessable password. In the process of doing research for this book, for example, I encountered the following response when I was applying on-line for an account:

```
Please select a secret password, it will not show on the
screen.
Password:
That's not a good password:
it is composed completely of lowercase letters
A UNIX system password should be at least 5 characters long
and include at least one upper case letter (A-Z), digit (0-
9) or punctuation character (such as . , or - ).
```

(Continued)

```
Passwords will NOT be accepted that:
    * Are less than 5 characters long.
    * Are composed entirely of uppercase or lowercase let-
      ters, numbers, or are simply capitalized.
    * Matches anything in your UNIX account information,
      such as your login name or an item from your "finger"
      data entry.
    * Are found in the hackers' dictionary of common pass-
      words.
    * Have less than 5 different characters.
    * Fail any of these tests when reversed, pluralized, or
      truncated.

Please select a secret password, it will not show on the
screen.
Password:
```

Other ways to be security conscious include:

1. Close out accounts you aren't using. Inactive accounts are popular prey for system crackers.
2. Make sure your read, write, and execute permissions are set properly on your files, directories, and programs.
3. Don't install software on a shared system without checking with your system administrator. Don't install software retrieved from untrusted sites without first scanning for viruses.
4. Know who to report potential security breaches to within your organization and/or your Internet Service Provider. If you're sending e-mail and you don't get a quick response, call. If it seems urgent, call immediately. Better an occasional false alarm then letting a major problem develop.
5. Familiarize yourself with your system's, site's, organization's, and Internet Service Provider's security arrangements, policies, and procedures.

### Legal aspects of security

Unauthorized use of government computers is a federal offense. Other laws vary by jurisdiction. "Export controls are rarely applied to individuals carrying software or hardware across borders for personal use; for the most part they apply to vendors," according to BBN's Kent. "Industrial espionage, perhaps carried out by a national intelligence agency, is an increasing concern. Think about all those eastern-bloc spies who are now freelancers!"

### Electronic privacy: The trail of virtual breadcrumbs, or the mother of all big brothers may watch you after the fact

Like Hansel and Gretl dropping breadcrumbs behind them as they tra-la through the woods, you and I are leaving an electronic trail behind us as we use the Internet. In fact, we're leaving trails as we use any computer or network resource, some of which we know about, many of which we don't. For example, you know when something gets logged to your phone bill, your credit card records, your checkbook.

As our daily transactions become managed by computer, they, too, become saved and stored somewhere—every videotape you rent, every book you take out from the library, perhaps every time you call your credit company. "Caller-ID" telephone services let people see and save the phone number you are calling from. Some new automobiles may be saving the most surprising data; while theoretically this is on behalf of service and repair records, your car may "know" where you've been and when. When you use Internet services and resources, your activities may similarly be monitored and logged, often without explicitly alerting you to the fact. For example, when you access a remote computer to use publicly available free-for-use services such as anonymous-FTP (file transfer), **telnet** (remote login), or WAIS, you are often asked to supply your e-mail address for resource tracking purposes. But even if you don't, the remote system can probably get this information from your computer. The term "anonymous" is highly misleading; the intent of the anonymous has been to enable you to access systems without having your own individual account and to provide a relatively standardized way to provide this across the Internet. But it's *not* really anonymous. According to Peter Deutsch of Bunyip Information Services, cocreater of archie:

> We still have a record of everyone who has ever queried the archie database server to look for an archived file. This includes every e-mail query, remote login, and client-server query. We originally started keeping them for debugging purposes and now use them for statistical analysis and load balancing.
>
> The same kind of information can easily exist for every Internet service, every time you "touch" the network. Who owns this information? How private is it? Can it be sold? Can it be subpoenaed? These are important questions, that have yet to be answered.

Your information and activities on your own account may similarly be less private than you think, in terms of being tracked and potentially subject to someone else looking at them:

- Every time you log on and off is most likely tracked for accounting purposes.
- It's possible there is a file listing every command you give within each session.
- Can someone else legally—or illegally—gain access to your stored files to search for information?
- Can someone monitor your e-mail and other activities without your knowledge?

### *Cuckoos and Worms*

It's quite possible that before you started reading this book you never heard of the Internet before. On the other hand, during the late 1980s, at least two Internet-related events happened which you just may have happened to hear about. For example, the case of the extra account:

Until August 1986, astronomer Cliff Stoll was, in his own words, "just another user on the net." Cliff was using the ARPAnet (precursor to the Internet) for his work in astronomy and was sending technical specifications and data back and forth. His responsibilities at the University of California at Berkeley included system administration. And one day that August, he noticed an accounting error in one of our computers.

"We discovered somebody had illegally added an account," Stoll recalls. "Instead of locking them out, we cleverly and quietly watched them. We found they were breaking into our computer, and from there systematically breaking into other ARPAnet and Internet sites, into military systems all over the country."

And by the time it was over, Stoll had been everywhere from the *New York Times* to the FBI, the CIA, and the Pentagon and had populated his office with up to several dozen borrowed printers, rigged a computer-driven Morse code beeper that more often than not caught him in the shower and had an adventure straight out of Robert Heinlein crossed with Len Deighton and Raymond Chandler.

"Over the next year, we watched the intruders, tracked them down—and finally caught them. Now I'm also a computer security expert."

Stoll's adventures made the national news—the *New York Times,* the *Wall Street Journal,* and others. Stoll subsequently chronicled his techno-escapades in an enthralling nonfiction book, *The Cuckoo's Egg,* was the focus of an episode of the television show, *NOVA*; and has spoken at conferences all around the world. (If you ever get the chance, see Cliff speak—he's great.)

Stoll's book is an instructive tale for our computer age of opportunity and of the pervasive carelessness by an industry and community of users regarding valuable resources. It's a who and howdunnit. It's an exciting "everyperson" story of a "civilian" getting caught up in international intrigue and leading the charge, and the vindication of the scientific method. If you don't think Internet security needs to be worried about, go read Stoll's book.

Two years later, something else happened—a more than 9-day wonder which permanently put the ARPAnet/Internet clearly into the public view and was the start of the media fascination with computer worms and viruses, the case I call "The Worm That Ate the Internet." "We are currently under attack from an Internet Virus." That was the beginning of an e-mail message from Peter Yee at NASA Ames Research Center to the ARPAnet's TCP-IP mailing list, at 11:28 p.m., Pacific Coast Time, Wednesday, November 1, 1988.

> It has hit UC Berkeley, UC San Diego, Lawrence Livermore, Stanford, and NASA Ames. The virus comes in via SMTP, and then is able to attack all 4.3BSD and SUN (3.X?) machines. It copies in a program, compiles and executes it. The program copies in VAX and SUN binaries that try to replicate the virus via connections to TELNETD, FTPD, FINGERED, RSHD, and SMTP. The programs also appear to have DES tables in them. They appear in /usr/tmp as files that start with the letter x. Removing them is not enough as they will come back in the next wave of attacks. For now turning off the above services seems to be the only help. The virus is able to take advantage of .rhosts files and hosts.equiv. We are not certain what the final result of the binaries is, hence the warning.

With this message began a bizarre series of days that felt like a cross between a computer detective novel and the War of the Worlds. A self-replicating worm*, unleashed either deliberately or accidentally, ran amuck across the ARPAnet and Internet. By the time it was done,

---

*A worm is a program that "infects" multitasking operating systems like Unix; it may masquerade as a legitimate program, such as by giving itself a misleading name, but does not conceal itself in other software. Worms were first created by John Shoch at XEROX PARC in Palo Alto in the late 1970s for measuring Ethernet loading; they self-replicated and spread to other computers using a network. John Brunner described computer worms in his science fiction book, *The Shockwave Rider.* A virus is a program that attaches itself to, and conceals itself in, other software, such as the Jerusalem Virus, Friday the 13th, Michaelangelo, etc.

thousands of host computers were infected, the connectivity of the Internet itself was disrupted—and the world was all too aware of networks and worms.

Within hours, the story was on national television and radio news and on the front page everywhere from the *Boston Globe* to the *New York Times* and *Wall Street Journal.* Within days, it not only reached all the computer trade publications but even local papers in upstate Vermont, *USA Today,* the Bloom County comic strip, and Erma Bombeck's column.

For weeks and months after, the story stayed news—the hunt for the alleged virus maker, the aftermath, editorials on "What have we learned and how do we prevent recurrences," and decreasingly sized stories on the various studies, committees, findings, and whatnot. My own clipping file about the Worm reached about 2 inches thick, before I stopped. (My personal favorite headline, from the November 21, 1988 issue of *MIS Week:* "Virus Suspect's Mom Stands by Her Son.")

Chuq Von Rospach <chuq@apple.com>, who was at Sun Microsystems when the Internet Worm struck, recalls:

> I was in charge of getting the worm under control for Sun—not isolating or fixing it, but making sure the customers knew about it and got it fixed. It was by far the worst week of my life. It brought into reality a point anyone involved with computers knows is a possibility—exactly how vulnerable anything that relies on computer technology is to outside forces. That's scary.

Donn Seeley, who was then at the University of Utah's Computer Science Department, noted the following in the concluding remarks of his technical report, "A Tour of the Worm":

> Our community has never been in the limelight in this way, and judging from the response, it's scared us. I won't offer any fancy platitudes about how the experience is going to change us, but I will say that I think these issues have been ignored for much longer than was safe, and I feel that a better understanding of the crisis just past will help us cope better with the next one. Let's just hope we're as lucky next time as we were this time.

Eugene H. Spafford of Purdue University's Department of Computer Sciences (W. Lafayette, IN), concluded, in his article "The Internet Worm Program: An Analysis," (*Computer Communication Review,* the newslettter of the ACM/SIGComm, vol. 19, no. 1, January 1989):

> It is important to note that the nature of both the Internet and UNIX helped to defeat the worm as well as spread it. The immediacy of communication, the ability to copy source and binary files from machine to machine, and the widespread availability of both source and expertise allowed personnel throughout the country to work together to solve the infection despite the widespread disconnection of parts of the network.
>
> Although the immediate reaction of some people might be to restrict communication or promote a diversity of incompatible software options to prevent a recurrence of a worm, that would be entirely the wrong reaction. Increasing the obstacles to open communication or decreasing the number of people with access to in-depth information will not prevent a determined attacker—it will only decrease the pool of expertise and resources available to fight such an attack.
>
> Further, such an attitude would be contrary to the whole purpose of having an open, research-oriented network. The Worm was caused by a breakdown of ethics as well as lapses in security—a purely technological attempt at prevention will not address the full problem, and may just cause new difficulties.

It's important to understand that the Internet Worm's "success" was *not* the fault of the network. The Worm wriggled through incorrectly configured electronic mail programs on hundreds of the computers reachable through the Internet and found or guessed passwords on hundreds more, using a few relatively simple techniques and lists.

The Internet Worm was the first, but not the last, to travel via the Internet. Would-be crackers working across the Internet have also grown more and more sophisticated (and often callous) than the gang caught by Stoll. The moral: It can happen. It may happen to you. Stay alert. (And know who to call.)

## Reading and resources

Books you can read include:

Crocker, Stephen D., "Operational Network Security," in the *Internet Systems Handbook,* Dan Lynch (ed.), Addison-Wesley.

Holbrook, J., and Reynolds, J., *RFC1244,* "Site Security Handbook," RFC 1244, July 1991.

Krol, Ed., Chap. 4, "What's Allowed on the Internet?" in *The Whole Internet User's Guide & Catalog,* O'Reilly & Associates, 1992, 375 pp.

Pethia, R., Crocker, S., and Fraser, B., *RFC1281,* "Guidelines for the Secure Operation of the Internet," RFC 1281, November 1991. This is intended to be a small set of guidelines that sites and networks can use to create their own security policies.

Spafford, Gene, and Garfinkel, Simson, *Practical UNIX Security,* O'Reilly & Associates, 1991, 482 pp.

Stoll, Cliff, *The Cuckoo's Egg,* Doubleday, 1989.

On-line sources include:

- The RISKS forum, one of the longest-running e-mail digests, edited by Peter Neumann, available in Usenet as comp.risks; as e-mail (subscribe by sending e-mail to risks-request@csl.sri.com and the Usenet comp.security Newsgroup).

Resources include CERT and products include Privacy-Enhanced Mail and COPS.

## Netiquette

*"Curtsey while you're thinking what to say. It saves time."*
*The Red Queen, "The Garden of Live Flowers,"*
*in Through the Looking Glass*
LEWIS CARROLL

*"Good manners are, to particular societies, what good morals are to society in general: their cement and their security."*
LORD CHESTERFIELD

*"As laws are necessary that good manners may be preserved, so good manners are necessary that laws may be maintained."*
NICCOLO MACHIAVELLI
*Discorsi, I*

*"This hallowed volume, composed, if I believe the title-page, by no less an authority than the wife of a Lord Mayor, has been, through life, my guide and monitor. By its solemn precepts I have learnt to test the moral worth of all who approach me. The man who bites his bread, or eats peas with a knife, I look upon as a lost creature, and he*

*who has not acquired the proper way of entering and leaving a room is the object of my pitying horror."*
*Rose Maybud in Ruddigore, Act I*
GILBERT & SULLIVAN

Etiquette (according to one of the many dictionaries above my desk) means "the forms, manners, and ceremonies established by convention as acceptable or required in social relations, in a profession, or in official life; or, the rules for such forms, manners, and ceremonies." In other words, the conventions, protocols, and behaviors that lubricate our interactions. Saying Thank You in response to a present, offering food and drink to guests before serving yourself, asking someone before changing their .login or Autoexec.bat file on their computer—none of these are part of any law, or even ever written down, but are as essential to a society as any set of written regulations.

Over the years, on-line computer and network communities, including the Internet, have evolved their own set of etiquette rules, known as *network etiquette,* or, more simply, *netiquette*. Internet netiquette complements the more formal rules and guidelines for Appropriate Usage, Security, and Cost by providing the social rules and guidelines to let the members of on-line electronic communities such as the Internet coexist peacefully and politely. Many other chapters, such as Chaps. 5, 8, and 10 include specific discussions of netiquette as they apply to that chapter's topic. You should read each before making use of the associated resource or service. This section addresses the general mindset of netiquette for being a good "Internet citizen."

"The network is like having hundreds of thousands of house guests (and being a house guest in hundreds of thousands of houses)," says Dave Schroeder, Ph.D. (<dlschroeder@exodus.valpo.edu>) Assistant Professor of Management Information Systems at the College of Business Administration at Valparaiso University (Valparaiso, IN). "We all want to know the house rules and to abide by them if we can. Sometimes we set the rules by example and sometimes we learn the rules by the example of others."

## Being a good user

Much of netiquette relates to being a good (i.e., responsible) user:

- Be aware of your organization's resources and budget. How much is available, what gets charged for what?
- Be considerate in your use of computer and network resources, such as CPU cycles, storage, bandwidth, and network ports. Avoid doing unnecessary activities during primary working hours that may slow down system response time, congest your organization's network, or cause system crashs.
- Observe "posted rules" (such as those displayed in login banners and in Appropriate Usage Policies, Terms & Conditions, etc.). For example, requests to limit dial-up or **telnet** session times.
- Obey any commercial restrictions and considerations.

- Learn and understand (and respect) your organization's policies regarding personal use of Internet (and other) resources and services, such as personal use, time-of-day restrictions, etc. If need be, seek out a private account on a Public-Access Internet Account Provider.
- Remember that the Internet is a very public shared resource. Be mindful of what you do in terms of not abusing resources or talking about private information.

Another aspect of netiquette relates to the interpersonal impact of your Internet activities—in particular, electronic mail and postings to Usenet Newsgroups:

- You're in public. Unless you are satisfied with the security surrounding your activities, never do or say anything you wouldn't be willing to see on the front page of tomorrow's newspaper or posted on the bulletin board in your cafeteria.
- Always bear in mind that you are representing your organization as you use the Internet.

In the preface to his "MacTCP and related Macintosh software" document, Eric Behr, Assistant Professor of Mathematics at the Math Department, Illinois State University (Normal, IL) says:

> For the sake of all of us, please be considerate! There are lots of things you can mess up if you don't know what you are doing. Connecting your computer to the [Internet] which spans continents and is used by millions of people in their work...is a serious act.
>
> Please follow this simple advice:
>
> - When in doubt, don't do anything without consulting manuals and/or a knowledgeable system administrator.
> - Before doing anything tricky, find out how to access the Internet documents (especially RFCs) and read the relevant ones.
> - Read [Usenet] Newsgroups such as comp.sys.protocols.tcp-ip...
> - Read the flaming manuals! and the FAQ lists, too!

In her document, "User Guidelines and Netiquette," Arlene H. Rinaldi <rinaldi@acc.fau.edu> states:

> The use of the network is a privilege which may be revoked at any time for abusive conduct.
>
> Such conduct would include, but not be limited to, the placing of unlawful information on a system, the use of obscene, abusive, or otherwise objectionable language in either public or private messages, the sending of messages that are likely to result in the loss of recipients' work or systems, the sending of "chain letters" or "broadcast" messages to lists or individuals, and any other types of use which would cause congestion of the networks or otherwise interfere with the work of others.

As you can probably see from the preceding quotes, the Internet has a very strong sense of what's appropriate. (Not everyone agrees on each specific, admittedly.) In the course of your Internet use, you are likely to encounter users who are inconsiderate, rude, consuming resources excessively, "not cleaning up after themselves," or simply less than helpful or polite. Try not to emulate their example.

For more information on netiquette, see:

Horton, Mark, and Spafford, Gene, "Rules of conduct on Usenet" (reposted monthly to the Usenet news.newusers Newsgroup).

Shapiro, Norman, et al., *Towards an Ethics and Etiquette for Electronic Mail,* Rand Corporation (publication R-3283-NSF/RC), 1985.

Von Rospach, Chuq, "A Primer on How to Work With the USENET Community" (reposted monthly to the Usenet news.newusers Newsgroup).

## Cost—Who Pays for What on the Internet?

*"I'm looking for free [accounts, dial-up* telnet *numbers, dial-up SLIP/PPP access]..."*
*Question frequently posted to Usenet Newsgroups*

*"TANSTAAFL—There Ain't No Such Thing as a Free Lunch"*
ROBERT HEINLEIN
*The Moon Is a Harsh Mistress*

Few things in this world are truly free, and your activities on the Internet are no exception. If you have ever used commercial on-line services like CompuServe, Dialogue, or Dow Jones, this probably isn't news to you. Many users still recall the shock of receiving their first bill for $200 or $300 before they understood how they were being charged. (Many of these organizations have since gone to a fixed monthly price for basic service.)

It costs money to run the computers and services you access, maintain the archive files, and so on. And it costs money to provide, operate, and maintain the many networks that comprise the Internet and the services needed to make the Internet work—the nameservers that convert network names into numeric identifiers, the routing tables, the administration of on-line mailing lists, the creation of RFC documents, and so on.

When you drive your car, no one sends you a bill for "use of highways," snow plowing, police, traffic lights, etc. The funding for these very necessary services comes through indirect sources: taxes, license fees, more taxes, highway concessions, state and federal funding derived from still more taxes, etc. Similarly, there's rarely a "meter" visibly ticking away at your workstation, any more than at most telephones, roads, televisions, or radios. But every second, keystroke, network bit, CPU cycle, and storage byte is costing someone, somewhere, some money—and someone is paying for it. Even where computers have been fully paid for, and "cycles" are now free, someone has to pay for electricity, the space being occupied, and a share of network connectivity. Consequently, it's important to understand how "big a bill" you can run up using the Internet, which you or your organization may be liable for in one way or another.

Charlotte Mooers, at User Services, BBN Systems & Technologies, explains:

> It is important to remain aware that when you access the Internet, you are connecting into a large global community, and to a vast network of resources. On a public utility like the telephone, you can only make one telephone call at a time, which limits "how much you can spend." You can't make a phone call that results in 50,000 people around the world picking up.
>
> The Internet allows you to contact thousands of systems and hundreds of thousands of users in a single act, deliberately or unintentionally. On a network like the Internet, you can reach out from your one computer and start up many connections and activities, at more or less the same time. You can even cause the systems you reach to invoke activities of other Internet systems in turn. The potential exists for an almost limitless liability.

"Newcomers to the Internet often fail to understand that you aren't always 'spending' money or consuming resources in a way directly related to the length of time you're on," cautions Cyndi Mills at Bolt Beranek & Newman (Cambridge, MA). "Your cost for using the phone is strongly tied to how long you use it. The Internet makes it possible to initiate activities which consume large amounts of resources in a short time. So it's important to be aware of who's paying for your use of Internet resources, and how much it costs."

Costs associated with using the Internet are outlined in the following:

#### Use of "Internet account"

If your account is provided by an organization, it's most likely covered as part of a departmental budget, and you may never see a bill—but you're still spending real or accounting dollars. If you pay for your own account (e.g., you have an account with one of the dial-up Public-Access Internet Account Providers such as PANIX in New York City, NetCom in California, or Halcyon in Seattle), you agreed to the pricing before signing on and get the bill every month—possibly about a dollar or two an hour for connect time and maybe other charges for long-distance access or excessive storage charges.

#### Your organization's local network and computing "infrastructure"

This includes fiber-optic and copper wiring, wiring hubs, bridges, routers, network management systems, network interface cards to desktop machines and to peripherals, printers, paper, tapes, and cartridges for doing backup, plus people-time for network management, installing software, training, answering user e-mail and phone calls, setting up new accounts, installing, maintaining and upgrading equipment, tracking down bugs, and a few hundred other tasks. Most of this is part of your organization's general MIS and network budget. For example, some portion of the dollar an hour I pay for time on The World is going to cover the salary of the system administrators (whom I periodically call with questions, or to request recovery of a file I accidentally deleted), the cost of their modems for us users to dial in to, and so on.

#### Your organization's connection to the Internet

Connections include routers and software at your site, "pipe" (telephone or other line) to your organization's Internet Service Provider, and associated management and administrative overhead. This is where much of the Internet funding occurs—from users. Some piece of my World fees are also going here, to pay for World's connection to AlterNet. Many research, academic, and government agencies get money from the government (e.g., as part of grants from the National Sciences Foundation, Department of Energy, etc.) which then goes for network service.

### Internet networks

The thousands of metropolitan, regional, national, and international networks that comprise the Internet include numerous telephone and other lines, routers, and all sorts of other equipment, personnel, siting, and the like—all of which cost money. A piece of my World hour-dollars goes up the line to these folks, as does some of your organization's Internet fees. The cost of networking varies widely—a fact which many users often lose track of.

"We in the USA have LOW cost access to [the Internet and BITNET] and assume that everyone else gets it 'free' as well," noted Jim Walters <walters@pc.maricopa.edu> of Phoenix College (Phoenix, AZ) in a message to the BITNET NETTRAIN mailing list. "This is NOT true."

Walters cited "e-mail friends" he visited in Eastern and Western Europe who pay for phone line service by the minute and in some cases by the kilobit:

> These people tend to sign off of [discussion] lists that are dominated by persons who ask simple questions that could be looked up in an ordinary dictionary or encyclopedia. When training new users, there needs to be a word of caution about sending messages. Messages should move the conversation forward and contribute to the understanding of the list members. [Messages with short content like "I agree with what was just said"] only create traffic and expense for a large population of people who make the net such a rich environment.

### Internet technology and infrastructure

The Internet is a complex, constantly evolving technological construct. Much of the underlying development is funded by government contracts—research into networking technologies, operation of certain support services, like the Internet Assigned Numbers Authority (IANA). Some of the Network Operations, Information and Service Centers (NOCs, NICs, and NISCs) are run by Internet Service Providers; others are run or funded by government agencies. (Even so, there's still no "one number to call.") Organizations like the Corporation for National Research Initiatives (CNRI) support a lot of Internet planning; they, too, in turn, get money from government funding and other sources.

Internet technology, and the surrounding research and decisions, comes largely from the members of the Internet Engineering Task Force (IETF) and Internet Research Task Force (IRTF). IETF and IRTF participation is a volunteer effort. Members belong to the hundreds of organizations that make, sell, and use computers and networks and to universities, all of whom recognize the value of participating in the Internet process. Somebody is paying for the salaries and other expenses of these people's Internet-related efforts. Much is recouped from sales of network products. But all this money has to come from somewhere—ultimately, that's you, the end user, taxpayer, and consumer.

### Use of Internet services and resources

What sets the Internet apart from many other network services is the ability to access the myriad universe of connected archives, services, and resources. It is here that the greatest potential exists to "run up a bill" and consume Internet services and resources, either deliberately or unintentionally. Some are part of the Internet's emerging user services infrastructure, such as the directories of user-names and e-mail addresses, the archive index locators provided by the archie system, and Yellow Pages for other Internet resources and services. In addition, like CompuServe, GEnie, and DELPHI, the Internet is host to thousands of special-interest electronic mailing lists, software and information archives, on-line services, special computers, etc.

### "Free" services and resources

The appellation "free" in terms of Internet resources, files, and services is dangerously misleading. Many Internet resources are "free" in that there is no charge to the user or user's organization for accessing the resource's computer (e.g., for retrieval of public-domain files from archives using anonymous-FTP file transfer, storing and getting of on-line documents from e-mail servers, etc.).

Much of the human effort, like managing archives, is volunteer work—a testimony to the value the Internet community places on these resources and services. (And many of these people and services evolve from volunteer to full-time jobs.) But someone's paying or has paid for the computers and storage, one way or another. Equally important, few of these "free" resources are unlimited in terms of how many users they can serve at a time or in total and how much service they can provide. If you're using a network port, that means someone else may not be able to.

For example, you can get any of a number of programs and other files "free" over the Internet, retrieved by file transfer or e-mail. This is true, in the sense that there is no transfer of money from you to the organization providing access to the file or to the file creator, unless you send them some money. But to get that file you have to use the network resources to move the data across and the computer resources to send and receive it.

Suppose, for example, you wanted a copy of a 100-page document which you knew was available in PostScript form "for free" on the Internet. You may have to first make a query or so to the archie resource locating service, perhaps by way of a full-text index search using a WAISed database. Then you establish a connection, bring a copy of the file across via anonymous-FTP to your computer, possibly then invest the CPU cycles to uncompress the file and do other manipulations, queue it to the laser printer, and so on. By the time you are done, you could have easily spent anywhere from 10 minutes to half an hour of your time finding, retrieving, and massaging the file, some indeterminate amount of network and computer service, plus the use of the laser printer.

If the book is available from a bookstore, it might be less expensive to buy a copy. The difference is, the movement of money is much more visible in the latter transaction. Admittedly, using the Internet is often more convenient—you don't have to leave your desk, use the phone, or go to a bookstore. Often, it will be more time- and cost-effective. But not always. Consider, for example, the availability of a number of popular "Internet archives" on CD-ROM (from Walnut Creek CD-ROM, Walnut Creek, CA). For between $25 to $50 you can get a CD-ROM with up to half a gigabyte's worth of popular public-domain and shareware programs. At that price (assuming you've already got a CD-ROM player), if you want more than a dozen or so programs, it may make more sense to buy the CD-ROM than keep pulling them across the Internet—if you can afford to wait.

Meanwhile, there is no "cost recovery" mechanism presently in effect for the "free" resources on the Internet. This is as much or more of a limit as a benefit; without funding related to use, the more popular services will get overextended but be unable to grow. Personally, I'd happily pay an "Internet service fee" of an extra nickel or so per hour to help fund archie, Gopher, WAIS, and the like.

### Pay-for-use resources and services

This is one of *the* hot growth areas in the Internet. It's not a new concept; there have been services and resources on the Internet whose use required having an account for years: supercomputers, special databases and library catalog services, and the like (see Chap. 14). Expect to see explosive growth in these services from on-line commercial databases to software "catalogs," perhaps even bookstores, financial services, and the like.

Here, it's clear who pays. You and me, the users. Part of the money goes to these organizations' Internet connections, plus their employees, computers, and so on. This is part of the Internet's future, an important one—because it will provide economic fuel for more growth. We may also see "paid-to-use" services, such as "advertisements" that generate some form of service or monetary credit to users, sites, or programs that access them. So, as you can see, there's a fair chunk of money moving around alongside all those data packets. Don't waste it.

Chapter

# 12

# Help!

*"The chief difficulty Alice found at first was in managing her flamingo."*
*"The Queen's Croquet Ground," Alice in Wonderland*

Sooner or later, occasionally or frequently, using, or trying to use, the Internet, you'll need help. Either you'll need information, or you'll have a problem—or both. It may be a simple question about something you don't understand or want to do but can't remember or find the command, like "how do I examine the beginning of a text file when using **ftp** without having to retrieve it all?" Or it may be a problem. Perhaps you've "lost" a file. Or your screen is frozen. Or you're positive that you're doing things exactly right—but you keep getting an error message. At times like these, we can all do with a little help. Maybe even a lot. Sometimes it's a matter of getting a piece of information. Sometimes you need a network or system operator to do something you aren't in a position to.

In this chapter, you'll learn:

- The various forms and sources that Internet help information comes in
- Where it's available
- How to find and get this information
- Which information resources are best for what types of questions
- Recommended "order of escalation" for using help resources
- Some common user problems and possible solutions

## Internet Help—Like the Internet, It's Abundant But Not Always Organized

When seeking help, it's important to remember to keep the multilevel, decentralized, and often disorganized nature of the Internet in mind, for example, the fact that there is no "person or organization in charge of the Internet"—so there is no individual, group, phone number, e-mail, or postal address you can contact for *all* your questions and problems.

The good news is that there is *lots* of helpful information scattered across the Internet and many people ready to be helpful when you've got a question or problem. The sources for Internet help will be equally varied, from the original developers of a program to groups of computer and network users who saw and tried to fill a need—and even from individual users just like you, who had a question and found that the answer was of interest to other users, too. (That's how books like this get started.)

The bad news is that none of this information or these people are necessarily organized the same way for each program, organization, site, or community. In fact, many of the older Internet resources and services assume that you know a fair amount of how the Internet and its facilities work and are familiar with any bugs or quirks. There's no single designated person, group, or company responsible for all Internet help or problem resolution. Also, many of the Internet services resources come from grass-roots volunteers, who are under no obligation to help, answer questions, or fix things. (That's the downside of "free" facilities.)

But there's lots of help—and the more you use the Internet, the more familiar you'll get with how to find help information and fix problems quickly and simply. Remember, the Internet, TCP/IP, and Unix have been in use for over a decade. Millions of people use these facilities in one way or another. They've all needed information and had problems. You won't be the first—and the questions and problems you encounter quite probably have been seen before—and solved, if solutions are possible. On the other hand, because the Internet continues to expand in terms of sites, services, new software, and new types of uses, you may be the first to ask a particular question or find a problem. So don't be surprised if your question or problem can't be resolved immediately.

### Internet help comes in many forms and sources

Help about and on the Internet comes in many forms, from a few lines of text built into the program you may be using to book-length documents accumulated over the course of a decade or more by people all over the world. The Internet community continues to work on the challenge of accumulating help information such as lists of resources, answers to questions, how to structure this information, and how to make it available, particularly when the user isn't sure what the question is or who to ask.

Here's a quick summary of the types of help information on the Internet. (Not everything you do or use will have all types of help available, of course.) Each information source tends to be most appropriate for different circumstances.

- *On-line help information.* This is information available when you're accessing your computer account, possibly requiring connection to other computers in your organization or to the Internet. Types of on-line information resources include:

- Help and error messages built-in to programs
- "Manpages" and other on-line standard program reference documentation; files and documents of reference and tutorial information, usually accompanying the program
- Local help facilities and information, often provided by your organization
- Internet documents and facilities, generated and distributed by members of the Internet community, available via file transfer, e-mail server, and Usenet
- Hypertext "Internet tours" and references

- *The "Internet bookshelf."* Printed information (manuals, articles, books, tutorials, workbooks, etc.).
- *Organizations and people who know about the Internet and answer questions.* Other users, system and network administrators, Help staffs, Network Information and Operations Centers, e-mail lists and Usenet Newsgroups, user groups, etc.
- Training, classes, tutorials, conferences, exhibitions, and other events.

### Think globally, seek locally—Getting help sensibly

In seeking Internet help, do your best to follow the "think globally, seek locally" approach stressed throughout this book for other efforts to find information through the Internet. First see if the information is already "in your own back yard"—available on-line, easily findable in a manual on your desk (check the index to this book), or covered by a posting in the Usenet. Don't post hastily to widely distributed Usenet Newsgroups or electronic mailing lists—save these resources until you've exhausted local ones.

## On-Line Internet Help

Let's take a look at the sources and types of help information available on-line.

### Help and error messages built-in to programs: Getting help from a program

A lot of "help" needs come when you're using a particular program, such as **telnet,** FTP, or Gopher. Most programs include at least some built-in help text and one or more ways to get to it. They are most useful for getting information about commands, syntax, etc. and least useful for examples, explanations, and problem resolution.

**Getting help from interactive programs.** *Interactive programs*—programs that present you with a prompt or screen—usually include a help facility that you can access without quitting. While there is no absolute standard for finding and accessing help information, here's a few tried-and-true commands used by many Internet developers that access help information. Most of them, if you don't include any parameters, offer a summary of help topics or entries.

There's no simple rule for determining which of them, if any, will work. You'll just have to try until you find the one that works.

**?<RETURN>.** Popular with line-oriented facilities (e.g., **telnet** and FTP) and screen-oriented facilities (e.g., Gopher, WAIS), and e-mail systems.

**h<RETURN>** (for "Help"). Popular with Internet navigators (Gopher, WAIS, etc.). Rarely used in e-mail programs, where "h" usually stands for "headers."

**help<RETURN>, help ?<RETURN>, help *<RETURN>.** Used in many TCP/IP utilities (e.g., **telnet** and FTP. Including **?** or * may generate a summary list of what help is available on.

**Control-H, Control-?.** Popular with many Unix utilities, such as **more** and **emacs.**

Also, if you're using a mouse and menu-driven program, check for a "Help" choice, of course.

**Getting help from noninteractive programs.** *Noninteractive programs*—programs that you invoke as a single command and receive results from—often have built-in help you can access by:

- Including the "help" parameter in the command. (Sorry, there's no single standard here.)
- Giving an invalid parameter in the command or leaving out required parameters. Many commands, if you give confusing or insufficient information, will respond by displaying their "syntax"—a summary of the required and permissible parameters, variables, switches, and other arguments. For example,

```
% telnet -h
telnet: illegal option — h
Usage: telnet [-8] [-E] [-L] [-a] [-d] [-e char] [-l user]
  [-n tracefile] [-r] [host-name [port]]
```

or even

```
% gopher -x
gopher: illegal option — x
Usage: gopher [-sb] [-p path] [-t title] [hostname port]
```

This is a somewhat clunky way to extract information, but if you're simply trying to remember a given keyword or switch, or other aspects of the syntax, this may be sufficient. It's also not a sure-fire information-generator. Some efforts will only give an error message, such as:

```
% telnet -?
no match.
```

```
% ftp -h
ftp: h: unknown option
% grep ?
No match.
```

**Other error messages.** Most programs include one or more *error messages*—relatively brief text messages displayed when the program can't perform a given command. In theory, these messages give you some combination of insight as to what the program "believes" you did wrong and how to correct it. In reality, as you may know by now, error messages may just as easily be misleading, incomprehensible, or both. However, an error message may be helpful. It has been known to happen. The Unix **awk** facility, for example, has one error message "Bailing out on line <number>." I don't know what "bailing out" means, but I've been told **awk** was doing this on line 47.

Many of the error messages you'll get may actually come from the operating system, such as the Unix shell or DOS command processor. You can usually tell because they begin with the name of the command that couldn't be processed, followed by the perceived problem. For example:

```
% gref dilithium *
gref: Command not found.
% maik lgulliver@laputa.org
maik: Command not found.
% telnet -h
telnet: illegal option — h
Usage: telnet  [-8] [-E] [-L] [-a] [-d] [-e char] [-l user]
[-n tracefile]
        [-r] [host-name [port]]
% www h
WWW Alert:  Can't access requested file.
WWW Alert:  Unable to access document.

WWW: Can't access `file://world/home/ie/ddern/h'
% grep
Usage: grep -blcnsviwh [ -e ] pattern file...
%
```

In these messages, the operating system is telling you it was unable to process your command line into a command that could be done, for any of a number of reasons such as:

- No command by this name could be found. (Possible reasons: typing error, using wrong name for command, command not installed, the directory the command's in isn't in your Path definition), for example:

  % **moer** (Typing error.)
  % **less** (Nonstandard command.)
  % **adventure** ("Games" directory not in your path, or it's called "advent" on your system.)

- Wrong switches, parameters, or other arguments used, such as **grep -T.**
- You've specified files or directories that don't exist.

- You're requesting too much of the system's resources.
- You're not authorized to use this command.

### Manpages and other on-line standard program reference documentation

As discussed in Chap. 4, most Unix systems include on-line versions of the Unix manual pages, called "man pages" or "manpages" (short for "manual pages"), which are a key part of the user reference documentation for Unix commands and associated facilities. This information in the manpages is reasonably comprehensive in many cases—a manpage can be anywhere from one to fifty pages long. Usually there are one or more commands for accessing and displaying this information to your screen so you can read it, as well as ways to save it to a file or send it to a printer.

The manpages are *most* useful for a full list of commands, switches, parameters, values, etc., and a comprehensive list of features and capabilities. They are *least* useful for entry-level learning and finding specific information or answers if you don't know what you're looking for, and for quick answers.

Depending on how much experience you've had with Unix and with Unix documentation, a manpage you consult may be somewhat cryptically written. (See "How to Read a Unix 'Manpage'" below.) But its information is most likely to correspond to what you're using—if whatever program you're looking up came through official sources, such as with the rest of the operating system or Internet application software, there is almost always an associated manpage, which should reflect the current version of the program you're using.

**How to read a Unix manpage.** Unix manual pages generally have a similar format; knowing what the different parts are, and where to look for what, will help you locate information you're looking for. (Knowing that something can be done or which command(s) to check out are the other—and harder—half of the process.) As an example, Fig. 12.1 shows parts of the manual page for the **archie** command. At the top of the manual page, the first section is labeled NAME. It contains the name(s) of the command and a brief description of what its function is. If the command was known by more than one name or if there were more commands with a similar function, they would be on the same manual page and listed in the NAME section.

Next is the SYNOPSIS section. It will briefly tell you what the command line for this command should be. In this case we see that archie has a variety of options.

The DESCRIPTION section explains the use and purpose of the command in some detail. It should explain each argument and tell you when to use switches and which ones to use. This is usually the longest section in the manpage. There may also be an ENVIRONMENT section, which lists environment variables used by the program, and a FILES section, which gives the name and use of any files used by the command.

SEE ALSO will give other commands which are related in some way. In this case it references seven other Unix commands.

```
ARCHIE(1)                 USER COMMANDS                 ARCHIE(1)

NAME
   archie—query the Archie anonymous-FTP databases using
   Prospero

SYNOPSIS
   archie [ -cers ] [ -a ] [ -l ] [ -t ] [ -m hits ]
          [ -N [ level ] ] [ -h hostname ] [ -o filename ]
          [ -L ] [ -V ] [ -v ] string

DESCRIPTION
   archie queries an archie anonymous-FTP database looking for
   the specified string using the Prospero protocol. This client is
   based on Prospero version Beta.4.2 and is provided
    .
    .
    .

OPTIONS
   The options currently available to this archie client are:
   -c     Search substrings paying attention to upper & lower case.
   -e     Exact string match. (This is the default.)
    .
    .
    .
ENVIRONMENT
   ARCHIEHOST
       This will change the host archie will consult when making queries.
       (The default value is what's been
    .
    .
    .
SEE ALSO
   For more information on regular expressions, see the manual pages on:
   regex(3), ed(1)
    .
    .
    .
AUTHORS
   The archie service was conceived and implemented by
   Alan Emtage, Peter Deutsch, and Bill Heelan. The entire Internet is in
   their debt.
BUGS
   There are none; only a few unexpected features.
```

**Figure 12.1** A sample Unix manual page.

BUGS will list some known problems. Other, optional sections include AUTHOR and ACKNOWLEDGMENT, give background information.

**Displaying and reading a manpage.** To get and read a manpage, you use the **man** (for manual page) command, followed by the name of the command you want information about. For example, to display the manual page for the

Unix **more** command you would type:

```
% man more
```

To see the manpage for FTP, at the system prompt, enter:

```
% man ftp
```

There are also manpages for a number of essential Unix concepts, including filenames and keywords. Also, each manpage includes a short description that includes all the keywords that are relevant, in its SYNOPSIS field.

The **man** command searches through the DESCRIPTION and SYNOPSIS fields of available manpages for potential matches. For example, the Unix Bourne shell, **sh,** includes an **if** internal command; the command **man if** will find the **sh** manpage.

**Identifying potentially relevant manpages.** Sometimes you'll want to see what manpages are relevant to a given command or keyword but not start reading them all. The **apropos** command (not available on all Unix systems) tells you which manpages have the specified keyword in their SYNOPSIS field.

The **apropos** command, like **man,** searches the DESCRIPTION and SYNOPSIS fields—but simply lists the name and description of the matching manpages. Apropos can be helpful if you don't know what command you're looking for; for example, to see what commands deal with passwords, enter

```
% apropos password
```

The **apropos** command will look for the string "password" in the index of the Unix manual and print out every line which contains that string. The output of the above command might look like this:

```
getpass (2)       - read a password
getpwent, getpwuid, getpwnam, setpwent, endpwent (2)
                  - get password file entry
passwd (1)        - change login password
passwd (5)        - password file
tpass (2)         - test supplied password against encrypted entry
%
```

(Please note that the output has been edited slightly to make it fit in the margins of this book.)

**Getting hardcopy of a manpage.** If you can't find a printed copy of the user command reference manual and want a hard copy, you may want to save a copy of this text into a file so you can edit or print it. One way to do this (for most versions of Unix) is:

```
% man command > filename
```

An example is:

```
% man ftp > ftp-manpage
% print ftp-manpage
```

Note that you may run into "reformatting delays." Many Unix systems store manpages in a different form from how they're displayed. If a display-format version isn't currently available, you may see a message like

```
Reformatting...wait...
```

for a few seconds until the displayable version has been regenerated.

### Local and other help facilities and information

Many organizations make their own local help facilities and information available, ranging from command explanations to usage policies, modem settings, and pointers to more information. The information may be a mix of writings by network and MIS staff—and users—at your site, plus information from other Internet sources. It is most useful for information specific to your site and answers to questions typical of your site's users. For example, here's the World's own "help" response during late 1992 (topics change over time):

```
% help
Listed below are help topics, just type the name of the topic, cho-
sen from the list, to the "Topic>" prompt on your screen. Many top-
ics have subtopics, just keep following it down. To return up a
level hit ENTER or RETURN on an empty line. To quit at any time
type quit<RETURN>. You might want to look at the HINTS file first.
  If you can't find the help you need, send e-mail to "help" or
call us at [World's voice number].
  Available help topics:
address          ftp            misc               sources
AGREEMENT        games          MUD                teach-emacs
AUP              General.Info   net-policies       terminal
BCS              headlines      newsgroups         unix
Books            help           obi                usenet
chatting         HINTS          online-libraries   uunet
compuserve       humor          password           vendor-info
DOS              internet       pc-pursuit         weather
Emacs            INTRO          Phone.Info         Welcome
FAQ              IRC            Primer             World.Info
file-transfer    Macintosh      rates
food             mail           software

Topic>
```

There may also be other on-line help and information facilities available, even interactive lessons—too many, varied, and unpredictable to cover here. By now, you should have identified some of the on-line help systems and commands on your system; try them and see what they have to offer. Increasingly, help and user information is also being organized through

Internet "navigator" tools like Gopher (see Chap. 11).

Here are some further suggestions:

- At the command line, try commands like **help, explain, nethelp, info, teach,** and **learn.**
- For topic keywords, try "ftp," "file transfer" (also file_transfer or file-transfer), "upload," and "download." For example:

```
% help ftp
% info file_transfer
```

### On-line help information via e-mail, file-transfer, and other methods

Over the years, the Internet community has generated a vast pile of information intended to document the Internet and/or help its users which is available in a variety of methods. This information includes documents and lists such as:

- Internet RFC (Request for Document) and FYI document series
- FAQ documents
- Lists (Internet Access Providers, services, topical resources, etc.)
- Help files for e-mail-oriented Internet services
- Readme and Help files and other Internet documents
- **Finger** information

**One User's Advice**

In the "Welcome to comp.unix.questions" monthly posting, Ted Timar <tmatimar@sunee.uwaterloo.ca> notes,

> You may save yourself a lot of time by reading [FAQ] articles before posting a question to the net.

Before you post a question to a Usenet Newsgroup, Timar recommends you should first try:

- Reading the manual for your system. Some day you may encounter the phrase "RTFM", which stands (more or less) for "Read the Fine Manual." If you ask someone a question and they tell you to RTFM, it's an indication that you haven't done your homework. For instance, if you are having trouble removing a file whose name begins with a "-", check the manpage for "rm". It might tell you what you need to know.
- Finding a knowledgeable user at your site. Many sites have at least a few Unix experts who will be happy to help you figure out how to remove a file whose name begins with "-". Many larger sites, particularly universities, may even have paid consultants whose job is to help you with Unix problems. Check with them first.
- Find a good introductory book on Unix. There are plenty of such books available, and you will save yourself a lot of trouble by having one handy and consulting it frequently. [The FAQ will usually list several.]

This information tends to reside on any or all of the following locations:

- At the site(s) it pertains to
- At archive sites run by Internet Access and Service Providers and other Network Information and Operations Centers
- Your site

and it may be available through some combination of:

- E-mail server, which automatically send you back requested document(s) as e-mail messages in response to e-mail from you
- File transfer, using anonymous-FTP
- Gopher, WAIS, archie, or other Internet navigator and resource-locating service
- Usenet Newsgroups
- Hardcopy print-out, pamphlets, brochures, and books
- CD-ROM.

For information on retrieving files via anonymous-FTP, see Chap. 15. For information on retrieving files via e-mail servers, see the section on "Internet Services Based on E-Mail" in Chap. 5. For information on retrieving files via Gopher and other Internet navigators, see Part 3. For information on obtaining Internet information in hard-copy and CD-ROM, see Chap. 18 and the Bibliography.

**Internet RFC and FYI document series.** RFCs are the official sets of documents defining standards and other aspects of the Internet, identified and often referred to by an RFC number (e.g., RFC 1822) as well as a title. Written by leading Internet developers, RFCs range from protocol specifications to proposals, analyses, specifications, and general reports—along with lighter items such as the occasional poem and humorous essay.

FYIs are a "series within a series" of RFC documents, intended to contain information for new users and developers; unlike non-FYI RFCs, FYIs may be updated from time to time. RFCs and FYIs are available via anonymous-FTP file transfer, e-mail server, Gopher, hardcopy, and even CD-ROM. For more information about RFCs and FYI RFCs, see the Bibliography.

**FAQ documents.** Like the name implies, FAQ documents are accumulations of the questions asked most frequently by users—or, in the judgment of the person(s) managing the document, questions *should* be asked—and their answers provided.

The Usenet community has created FAQs for most of the Newsgroups. As indicated in Chap. 6, the FAQs to the various groups are periodically revised and reposted to their corresponding Newsgroups and to one or more of the news.answers and other *.answers Newsgroups. If the one you want isn't currently available through your Usenet site or you don't have Usenet access, you can also get it by e-mail or anonymous-FTP from one of the Usenet FAQ archives, such as "pit-manager.mit.edu" maintained by Jonathan Kamens (jik@pit-manager.mit.edu). The convention "FAQ" is being increasingly used by other Internet groups for the "start here" document.

**Lists of Internet information.** There are lots of lists of Internet information—lists of Internet Access and Service Providers, lists of Public-Access Unix sites, lists of Internet services, lists of electronic mailing lists (group), lists of Usenet groups—there are even lists of these lists.

Like FAQs, different lists may be available via different means. Lists of Internet services and resources and Internet Service Provider lists tend to be available via anonymous-FTP file transfer and e-mail server; informally generated lists tend to be also available via Usenet Newsgroups—and some of these lists are available in book form.

**Help files for e-mail-oriented Internet services.** Many Internet services which can be queried by e-mail are set up to send you their standard help information document, in response to the appropriate help command; most will include "how to get help" information in their response, if your message doesn't include all necessary information, or includes errors. Any archie server, for example, should send you back its current help information, if you:

- Send a message containing "help" anywhere in the subject or body (and all other commands will be ignored)
- Send a blank message
- Send a message with one or more errors

For example:

```
% mail archie@sura.net
Subject: Help
Help, help!
<CONTROL-D>
% mail archie@rutgers.edu
Subject:
<CONTROL-D>
% mail archie@sura.net
ETAOIN SHRDLU
KLAATU VARADU NICHTU
<CONTROL-D>
```

Most other e-mail-servers, similarly, should have a "send help" command and a standard error message telling you how to get help. If you don't know the correct command, try any or all of the following in the body of a message:

help

send help

get help

You might also try:

info

index

with and without “send” or “get” in front.

**Readme and Help files, and other Internet documents.** Readme files are another popular convention for putting help information in a “well-known” place (i.e., a file with a reasonably predictable name). As a rule, you are sure to find these at any public-access file archive which you access via anonymous-FTP. Common variant names for Readme files include:

READ.ME

Read.Me

README

ReadMe

Remember that unlike DOS, Unix and many other operating systems consider upper- and lowercase letters as different letters. As explained in Chap. 8, using **|more** as the “filename to retrieve to” causes the retrieved Readme file to be displayed at your computer piped through **more** versus being put into a file.) Here’s an example of finding and retrieving a Readme file:

```
% ftp is.internic.net
Connected to is.internic.net.
220-**  Welcome to the Internic InfoSource Archive    **
...
220 is FTP server (Version 2.0WU(10) Thu Apr 8 17:52:08 PDT
1993) ready.
Name (is.internic.net:ddern): anonymous
331 Guest login ok, send your complete e-mail address as
password.
Password:
230-Logged Access from: jabber.wock.com
ftp> cd /infosource
250 CWD command successful.
ftp> ls
200 PORT command successful.
150 Opening ASCII mode data connection for /bin/ls.
total 87
-rw-rw-r—   1 refdesk  refdesk     25718 Apr  1 02:30 INDEX
drwxrwxr-x  8 refdesk  refdesk       512 May 26 23:29
about-information-services
drwxrwxr-x  3 refdesk  refdesk       512 May 26 23:25
about-infosource
drwxrwxr-x  8 refdesk  refdesk       512 May 26 23:12 get-
ting-started
```

*(Continued)*

```
-rw-rw-r-    1 refdesk  refdesk     52068 Apr 22 02:03
infosource-contents
drwxrwxr-x   8 refdesk  refdesk       512 Jun  2 19:42
internet-info-for-everybody
...
226 Transfer complete.
ftp> get infosource-contents |more
200 PORT command successful.
150 Opening BINARY mode data connection for infosource-con-
tents (52068 bytes).

InterNIC Info Source Gopher Road Map   Host:   is.inter-
nic.netLast Update: 3/31/93
Page:   1


Lev Name                                Type  Destination
-------------------------------------------------------------
 1 Information About the InterNIC       File  is.internic.net
 1 InterNIC Information Services
   (General Ato                         Dir   is.internic.net
 2  Welcome to the Info Source          Dir   is.internic.net
 3   What is the Info Source            File  is.internic.net
 3   Contributing to the Info Source    File  is.internic.net
   ...
```

Readme files are usually short—a few paragraphs to a few screens in length—and contain the most essential information, plus pointers to whether more information can be found.

As you can see, there's a lot of information available, in relatively easy-to-find, easy-to-retrieve facilities. Among the information available are:

- Documents and proceedings from the Internet Society and Internet Engineering Task Force
- Popular Internet documents such as "Mining the Internet," "Surfing the Internet," Internet resource guides, hyptertext "tours" (more about this shortly), etc.

### *finger* information

Many users and small organizations put key information in a file that enables other users to retrieve it using the TCP/IP **finger** command (explained in Chap. 5). This command retrieves and displays information about a specified user or computer on the Internet, including the contents of a specific file—for users, this would be one named .plan in their home directory. Unless otherwise specified, this file's contents are readable by **finger** commands issued by any and all Internet users. Examples are help information about a service you're offering, where to find special files you've put together, news about a project you're working on, etc.

By putting information you want to make available in this file, you can make it available to other Internet users without having to develop, install, or maintain a separate information-management facility (e.g., into anonymous-FTP space, an e-mail server, etc.).

## "Tours" and Other Hypertext Help Information

A number of Internet organizations have put together informational and tutorial tours of the Internet (including their own services) in the form of hypertext documents. A hypertext document is viewed using the appropriate computer and software (e.g., a Macintosh and HyperCard). The most well-known of these include the "Tour of the Internet" created by the NSFnet Network Services Center and "A Cruise of the Internet" created by MERIT Network, Inc.

In a hypertext document, selecting a highlighted item (with the mouse or keyboard) moves you directly to that item within the document—it's like reading a book but being able to jump to a cross-reference at the push of a button. These hypertext documents often include graphics, sounds, and even moving images. Internet hypertext documents are available via anonymous-FTP file retrieval; many are also distributed directly on floppy-disks at Internet events and via mail.

The "Internet bookshelf" is the collection of printed and other materials for Internet users, planners, developers, administrators, and others. The contents of this category keep getting bigger. It includes Internet-specific information, such as collections of RFCs, various Internet-related magazines and newsletters, and general and special-interest books for Internet users (such as this one), tutorials, and workbooks. It also includes reference books, manuals for developers, including Internet-specific works, as well as those for TCP/IP, Unix, and specific applications and protocols. For more information about these materials, see the Bibliography.

## Organizations and People Who Know About the Internet and Answer Questions

So far we've been talking about on-line and printed sources of information. Now let's move on to another major resource: organizations and people who know something about the Internet and are available and willing to answer your questions. One advantage of asking a person—particularly the right person—is that when they hear your question, they'll know what question you should be asking and perhaps the answer to that question (for example, when someone asks "How do I get to the Internet?", being able to determine that the asker wants e-mail and Usenet access).

Internet experts also can pull together on-line information scattered across local files, FAQs, RFCs, recent magazine articles—plus recent conferences and discussions, and, most valuable of all, their own experience from their years of being on the Internet—and asking and answering questions like yours. A person can also often provide basic definitions and relevant information, where most help documents assume some level of previous knowledge.

The downside of asking people is that they have to be available and willing to help you. The number of people in the Internet whose job includes answering questions is small, especially relative to the fast-growing population of novice, new-to-computer, new-to-networking users. People who answer the same question a few times often begin writing down the answers, which in turn often evolve into FAQs, FYIs, and entire books. One promising event happened in early 1993: the formation of the Internet Network Information Center, or InterNIC, whose charter includes some degree of helping end users (presumably after you've exhausted more local resources).

Internet experts, like on-line Internet information, are available for a variety of topics, from a variety of sources. The following discusses categories of people to consider asking.

### Office neighbor or classmate

Perhaps you've missed something obvious, so start locally. If you're in an organization that's on the Internet, you're probably not the only user, and many of these other folks will know more than you at this point. Often, especially in the beginning, your problems will be basic, common new-user misunderstandings. They are good for commands, files, local questions.

### System administrator

Your system administrator, also known as YFNSA (Your Friendly Neighborhood System Administrator), Network Operator, and other network or MIS help staff are the people whose job descriptions are most likely to include helping users—and who have the power to change or fix your computer account, check network settings, etc. Also, if you have been unable to answer your question or resolve your problem by consulting on-line resources, it's a good bet your problem is specific to your computer, site, or organization.

It's a good idea to learn who the appropriate people within your organization (or organization providing your account) are and the best ways and times to contact them (e-mail, voice-mail, talking in person, after lunch, etc.). This is good for accounts, local information, restoring local computer and network service, managing permissions and authorization for files and services, management of local mailing list distributions, etc.

### Local Internet, Unix, network, or whatever wizards

These are people who know a lot about Unix, TCP/IP, the Internet, your computers, etc.—and usually don't mind being helpful from time to time. Your "local wizard" may often be able to answer weird questions and resolve mystifying problems without thinking hard. On the other hand, the answers may often not make any sense to you—they may be stated poorly, or you may not know enough to understand them. And you may not be able to repeat whatever your local wizard did to fix things. They are good for Unix and TCP/IP questions that you can't figure out or get working from the manuals or on-line help and spotting subtle errors common to new users.

### Internet Service Provider Network Information Centers (NICs) and Network Operations Centers (NOCs) operations and support staff

These are the help staff's of organizations providing Internet connectivity (e.g., ANS, CERFnet, NEARnet, PSInet, Uunet). You're not too likely to call these people as an end user, nor should you; these are the people your organization's network and MIS management, help staff, and trainers liaise with. They are good for problems with connections, technical support, e-mail and Usenet not getting through, software configuration, poor service, etc.

### The InterNIC (NSFnet Network Information Center)

For many years, "who to call" for Internet help and information was a question with no easy answer—particularly if you were a commercial or public-access user. Although there were many involved in ARPAnet and Internet operations, there was no "one place to call" and no people whose official, paid jobs were to help many of the users.

In early 1993, for Internet users—and for organizations and individuals seeking to gain access to the Internet—this changed dramatically with the creation of the NSFnet Network Information Center, or InterNIC. The InterNIC was established April 1, 1993, through cooperative agreements between the U.S. National Science Foundation and three organizations, General Atomics (the organization that also runs CERFnet and the San Diego Supercomputer Center), for Information Services such as "user help desk" queries and "getting started" information and software; AT&T for directory and database services such as "who is, where is," user "phone books," and archive site listings; and Network Solutions Inc. (Herndon, VA) for registration services like issuing IP numbers and registering Domain Names.

Among other things, the InterNIC is the place to call for people seeking information about joining the Internet, provider lists, etc.—the long-awaited organization whose charter includes answering these calls and questions. (In the words of Kermit the Frog, "Yayyy!") Some of these activities were previously handled by organizations like the NSFnet Network Services Center (NNSC) run by Bolt Beranek and Newman in Cambridge, MA, and the Network Information Service Center (NISC) run by SRI International in Menlo Park, CA. Neither the NNSC nor the NISC are still in existence; there is now one collective entity responsible for these and other Internet management, operations, and user support activities: the InterNIC.

The overall result is that existing and prospective NSFnet and other Internet users now have a "place to call" with questions and problems. It's worth noting that the three organizations are physically located across the continental United States; this has been made viable largely thanks to the Internet and Internet technology. All will be reachable by e-mail as well as phone, mail, and fax; many of their resources and services will similarly be available via remote login and file transfer and through popular Internet tools like archie, Gopher, and WAIS.

"We view this as a consolidation of services being previously provided through a variety of organizations, plus new areas of activity like directory and database services," stated Don Mitchell of the U.S. National Science Foundation when I called him in January 1993, following the announcement of the InterNIC, to sort out what the news meant. "We are excited about using the network to permit collaborative cooperative agreements at geographically distributed sites as opposed to requiring that interdependent activities be physically co-located at one facility."

By the way, the InterNIC charter includes "using existing tools rather than 'reinventing the wheel.'" This includes archie, Gopher, WAIS, etc.

According to General Atomics' Susan Calcari, who will be a leading player in the InterNIC's Information Services group, "We will provide information to beginners on how to get connected, and a wide range of services for the entire community, such as seminars around the country, books and documentation, and pointers to resources."

Here's an overview of some of the services and information slated to be provided by the InterNIC. (These may change and expand over time, of course.) For specific information on how to access the branches of the InterNIC by e-mail, Internet tools, telephone, fax, and postal mail, see App. C.

**InterNIC—General information.** Information and on-line services provided by the new InterNIC groups will be accessible by methods that include popular Internet tools such as Gopher, WAIS, archie, anonymous-FTP file transfer, and electronic mail servers. The InterNIC will have client programs available for tools such as Gopher, WAIS, and archie which can be accessed by **telnet** remote login for users who don't have the appropriate clients available locally. The InterNIC will also be putting out a regular newsletter, the *InterNIC InterActive,* as well as a number of electronic mailing lists.

**InterNIC Information Services: Referral Desk, Info Source, and the Info Scout.** InterNIC Information Services includes the running the Referral Desk, maintaining on-line information such as the Info Source, and funding the Info Scout.

The InterNIC Information Services Referral Desk is responsible for responding to requests for information about the Internet by telephone, e-mail, fax, and hardcopy mailings. The Referral Desk can provide information including "listings of Internet Network Providers in the U.S. and abroad; books and documents to assist organizations and individuals in getting connected; and pointers to network tools and resources. When appropriate, contact information for local NIC and NOC organizations will be offered."

The Info Source, according to the InterNIC, is "a collection of information designed to make finding out about the Internet easier. There are sections for getting started, for NICs, and for general information which may be of interest to everyone. Also included is information on all the services offered by InterNIC Information Services. Browsing the 'Info Source Table of Contents' file will provide details on what is available." In some cases the Info Source will contain the documents themselves; in others, it will indicate where they can be obtained (e.g., elsewhere on the Internet).

The Info Scout, a role created as part of the InterNIC announcement, is a full-time position within the InterNIC Information Services group—a person who will be responsible for collecting and dissemination information about Internet tools and resources.

In addition, the InterNIC Information Services will run a number of electronic mailing lists concerning InterNIC updates and information of general interest to the Internet community.

**InterNIC Directory & Database Services.** This portion of the InterNIC will make a variety of directories, databases, and documents available to all Internet users through a variety of on-line and other means, as free-for-access services. *Free-for-access* means there is no charge for the information itself. Like any use of the Internet, you may have to pay for the activity in your own account in the process of accessing the information.

The Directory side of this group will provide a "Directory of Directories," which will contain *lists* of resources such as anonymous-FTP sites, white and yellow page directories, library catalogs, data archives, and other resources and services. According to information from AT&T as of April 1993, people and organizations can place short yellow pages listings—such as a short description and contact and address information—for resources or services they provide to the Internet community; there will be no charge for these short listings. Organizations may also have expanded listings stored for a monthly fee; these expanded listings will be part of the free-for-access on-line information available to users.

The Database side provides on-line access to a variety of documents and databases, such as:

- Materials recommended or contributed by the National Science Foundation such as introductory, tutorial, and policy documents.
- Communications documents that relate to the NSFnet and that are approved by the National Science Foundation (NSF), Internet Architecture Board (IAB), Internet Engineering Task Force (IETF) working groups, or other appropriate bodies, for example, RFCs (Request for Comments), FYIs (For Your Information), STDs (RFCs about standards), Internet Drafts, and other IETF documentation.
- Information from individuals, organizations, and other groups. There will be a monthly fee for storage and management of these databases; there is no charge to Internet users to access the information.

**InterNIC Registration Services.** Registration Services is responsible for tasks including registration of Internet site IDs, running a WHOIS service, and maintaining on-line archives of Internet information including network policy (AUP) documents and RFCs.

**Please note: InterNIC information and services may not be free.** You should be aware that the InterNIC may—legitimately—charge for some users for some of its services and information. The initial funding for the InterNIC comes from the U.S. National Science Foundation. As was the case with the old ARPAnet and the NSFnet backbone, the resulting services are therefore intended to be free ("prepaid" might be a better perspective) only to the appropriate communities, which does not necessarily include commercial or non-U.S. users.

Unlike prior U.S.-funded Internet information centers like the NNSC or NISC, however, the InterNIC charter does include providing services and support to other users. "User cost recovery" (i.e., some form of charging for certain services to certain users) is necessary to the operation of the InterNIC [and helps address legitimate concerns about U.S. tax dollars paying for services to non-NREN (National Research & Education Network) and non-domestic users].

"We will attempt to adhere to the Federal Networking Council's (FNC) principle of full cost recovery from users," NSF's Mitchell notes. The NSF has determined that the organizations handling InterNIC services "may charge users beyond the U.S. research and education community for any services provided," for example. To do this will require determining what the full cost of a given service is and what constitutes recovery, and defining who qualifies as research or education-related users—a nontrivial task in itself.

"From the user perspective, nothing will change," assures NSF's Mitchell. "Nothing that is 'free' today will not be 'free' this year; there will be new services available, however, that users beyond the NSF-supported community may have to pay for." Services likely to be free-for-use include on-line access via InterNIC-maintained archie, Gopher, and WAIS servers to databases such as anonymous-FTP archive listings, network "e-mail phone books," service provider lists, RFCs, resource directories, and some software.

Again: All this is good news. There is now a place to call for Internet information, whose charter lets them help anyone, for money; the U.S. NSF has "prepaid" for some support for its communities, and everyone else can simply "pay as you go."

## CNIDR Clearinghouse for Networked Information Discovery and Retrieval

There are a growing number of other Internet-related organizations around that are worth knowing about. Their charters don't tend to include user support as much as program and project activity, but they often collect and provide access to important Internet resources. The Clearinghouse for

Networked Information Discovery and Retrieval (CNIDR, pronounced "snyder") is one of the newer groups to help support Internet tool development and access as opposed to end-user support. Established in October 1992 at MCNC in Research Triangle Park, NC, with funds from the NSF and the MCNC Center for Communications, CNIDR has a core staff of three people—George Brett (Director and NSF Principal Investigator), Jim Fullton (Technical Director), and Jane Smith (Assistant).

According to Smith:

> CNIDR's role is one of advocacy for NIDR tools—not of adoption, control, or competition. We exist to promote the use of these and other emerging tools related to NIDR and to coordinate their further development and interoperability. CNIDR provides traditional clearinghouse functions of collecting, classifying, and disseminating the tools and information about them. We also work with users to answer their questions and gauge their needs. We coordinate with developers of NIDR software to create consensus and pool their talents to improve existing software, and to explore new approaches to NIDR.

For example, CNIDR offers software, documentation, and installation files for popular Internet tools like archie, Gopher, HYTELNET, WAIS, and WorldWideWeb; in early 1993, they began running a server for the VERONICA Gopher-indexer when the load on the original VERONICA server at the University of Nevada at Reno grew unsustainable (see Chap. 10 for information on all these exciting Internet tools).

Smith suggests:

> Internet users new to NIDR tools can **telnet** to demo.cnidr.org and enter "demo" at the Login: prompt for a menu of introductory information and on-line demonstrations. Users and system administrators can obtain current software releases and associated information through our Gopher server at gopher.cnidr.org. This server also contains searchable technical papers and general-information documents and bibliographies, information on past and upcoming workshops, and "news briefs" covering CNIDR activities.
>
> Internet NIDR software developers and information providers may contact CNIDR for information on protocols, interfaces, and current NDIR projects. We're always interested in hearing about, testing, and reporting on new projects. We'd also be glad to consult briefly with you about utilizing NIDR tools.

For information on how to access CNIDR files, services, and activities, contact them at:

Clearinghouse for Networked Information
Discovery and Retrieval
MCNC Center for Communications
P.O. Box 12889, 3021 Cornwallis Road
Research Triangle Park, NC 27709-2889
Phone: 919-248-1499
Fax: 919-248-1405
E-mail: info@cnidr.org

Sending a message to the above e-mail address will get you a general "How to access CNIDR" message automatically; no message Subject or body are required.

#### Other Network Information Centers (NICs) and Network Operations Centers (NOCs)

This includes information and administrative organizations such as the DDN NIC (Defense Data Network's Network Information Center). Like provider NICs and NOCs, these organizations work mostly with operations, administrative, and management-level people, rarely with end users. You're unlikely to need access to any of these groups, but you should be aware they exist.

### Other Internet Groups and Resources

Lastly, there are on-line and in-person ways to seek and get Internet information.

#### Electronic mailing lists and Usenet Newsgroups

It often makes sense to pose your question to a group rather than to one person. Internet mailing lists and Usenet Newsgroups can be excellent sources of information. However, these should *never* be your first recourse; send your questions here only after you've exhausted the obvious on-line and individual people resources, including FAQ files. If your organization has local "help" mailing lists or Usenet Newsgroups (or other BBS facilities, such as Lotus Notes), try these first. There are also a number of Usenet Newsgroups intended for exactly this purpose—to ask and answer questions.

#### User groups

User groups often offer help and support. Try your local computer society, etc.

#### Training, classes, tutorials, conferences, exhibitions, and other events

These are for general education rather than in response to a specific need or question. Ask your local support and operations staff about local classes either through your organization, user group, computer society, etc.

### Guidelines and Suggestions When Calling for Help

When calling for help, do your best to report the problem clearly. If you got error messages, save or write them down, if possible. Try to remember what you were doing, in terms of commands and results, the time, and anything else that seems relevant. If you need help quickly, and are on-line, try using a "talk" facility (such as **talk**), which can give you an "intercom"-type exchange of messages with your system administrator (only if they're on-line, of course). Otherwise, use the phone.

If you don't have an urgent need, consider sending e-mail. (Most organizations have a general e-mail account, such as "staff" or "help" for these messages.

## Problems—and Solutions: When Bad Things Happen to Good Networks

In the process of using the Internet (and in using computers and networks in general) you'll encounter problems and make mistakes. That's not a promise—but it's a prediction anyone who uses the Internet (and computers and networks in general) can make with great confidence. Some of these events will be the equivalent of taking the wrong exit off the highway or putting salt in your coffee—annoying but you can live with it. Others may be more frustrating—like forgetting your directions or not closing the windows all the way before you enter the carwash.

There's no way to predict what problems you'll encounter and what mistakes you'll make. It depends on what hardware and software you use, how you access the Internet, how your organization has set up your account and its Internet connection, what you are doing—and what any number of other Internet users are doing at the same time—and the conditions of all the myriad components, wires, and software that could affect your Internet use.

Perhaps you made a mistake while editing one of your configuration files—added or forgot a single- or double-quote character or made some other typo. Maybe you forgot to turn the power on to your modem or your network cable broke. Or maybe there's been some problem elsewhere on the Internet—the equivalent of the backhoe breaking the fiber-optic telephone cable or a flood in underground tunnels shorting out a city's worth of network connections. (These are real examples of telephone system problems.)

In other words, anything may happen. And sooner or later, something will. It won't always be your fault. And you won't always be able to fix it. But in any case, it's helpful to know:

- How things work, to some extent (see Chaps. 1 and 4).
- Where to look or who to call for help and information (see the previous portion of this chapter).
- Common places problems occur, typical symptoms and indications, and a few basic "kick here" tricks that may (or may not) resolve the problem; that's this section.
- Work-arounds (scattered throughout this book).

Part of the challenge in becoming your own Internet problem-solver and trouble-shooter is that you're not just dealing with a single computer anymore. In fact, you can't always be sure what you believe is a problem really is—as opposed to "the way things are." Equally, there may be big problems you don't see (but if they're interfering, they probably aren't problems—to you, anyway).

Over time, you'll learn enough to solve or avoid the easy problems—and how to report and describe them properly to the appropriate authorities (such as your system or network administrator) so they can fix 'em.

The advice in this section is at the same level as "Turn off the TV/car and try again," "Have you run out of gas?" and "Is it plugged in?" This is not the time or place to turn you into an "Internet repairperson." You won't see any advice that starts with "Take out your screwdriver" or "Using the following debugging program." These are jobs for professional experts. (Of course, if you find you enjoy doing this, and can do it successfully, consider a career—or at least summer job—as a system administrator, network operator, etc.) In many cases, you won't have the "system privileges" to tinker, anyway.

Learn your limits; if you can't resolve a problem within 5 or 10 minutes, call for help or go do something else. For now, your best bet is to pay attention, "RTFM"—"Read the(se) Fine Manual(s)"—and do your best. Let's start with some standard remedies.

### Quick things to try

Here's the starter list of quick, easy things you can do which may clear up the problem:

Enter Control-Q to make sure you haven't "frozen" the screen.

Enter Control-C to quit a program you're currently running if you don't have a prompt.

Enter Control-D to quit a program when you do have a prompt.

Exit and restart your program.

If you're logged in, logout and login again.

If you're connected via telephone, hang up and dial-in again.

If you're using a PC, reboot your computer or turn the power off and then on. (Careful: Make sure this won't cause more problems than it might solve.)

### Where problems can arise and things to try

Here's an overview of places that things can go awry and things you can try—actions you can take to try remedying them. This is by no means a complete list; it reflects problems and errors commonly encountered (including ones I've had myself or seen happen to other people).

**User errors.** That's you—or a mistake by another user. This category includes typing errors, mispositioning the mouse, misremembering or not knowing something, or other mistakes. For example, accidentally deleting all your files or misremembering someone's e-mail address or sending an e-mail reply to everyone on a mailing list instead of to just one person. (A common error.)

Take a look to see if there's anything obvious. Errors in this category also include forgetting what you changed your password to, generating enough static electricity to make your computer hiccup, spilling soda or coffee on the keyboard, etc. The general advice is, try again. If your computer is on, it's appropriate to reboot or power off and on again. As *Communications Week* editor Michael Dortch has observed, "If you can solve it by rebooting, it wasn't a problem." Similarly, be ready to restart the program, redial through your modem, etc. Many problems are transient, meaning they go away.

**Hardware problems.** This means your computer, keyboard, modem, etc. I'm not suggesting you should become a hardware repair expert. It's probably an ineffective use of your time, and unless you become very knowledgeable, you may instead know enough to be dangerous (i.e., create more problems than you fix). You should probably learn the equivalent of checking your oil level and tire pressure on your car—but the most important thing to learn is who (and when) to summon for help. With this in mind, here's a few of the more obvious symptoms and things you can try.

- *Power.* Are all switches on, all plugs in? Are any fuses blown? Things to try:
  - Turn power off; unplug and replug cables; turn power on. (Caution: Some computer equipment shouldn't be casually turned off or may need more effort to restart properly.)
  - Check *all* your equipment: computer, monitor, modem, surge/power protectors, etc.
- *Cables and connections.* Are all cables in correctly and securely? Remember, cable wiring and pins can break in ways you won't see. *Things to try*:
  - Tighten, or remove and reconnect, cable connections. If you have spare cables, try them.

**Other equipment failures.** Keyboards and mice break, hard disks fail, chips and boards wear out, internal batteries run down—anything with a moving part or a connection is a candidate for problems. *Things to try*: another keyboard, mouse, or computer; repower or reboot.

**Software problems.** Typical problems include input doesn't register on screen, output is "frozen," program is not getting your input correctly. Things to try:

- Check for mistakes or conflicts in your configuration files: AUTOEXEC.BAT and CONFIG.SYS (for DOS users), WIN.INI (for Windows users), "dot" files such as .login, .cshrc, .mailrc, .newsrc., and .telnetrc on the computer you're running your Internet applications from.
- Check your current computer "environment." What shell are you running? Check your PATH value. Do you have conflicting programs? Are programs unexpectedly still running?

- Make sure you haven't used "flow control" keys to "freeze" output [e.g., via Control-S ("pause output") or <PAUSE> key. Enter Control-Q ("unpause output"). Wait, then enter a <RETURN> or two. If you can now see text when you type it, the problem was you had hit this key by accident earlier.
- If your screen is full of funny-looking characters, like pieces of a maze or from other alphabets, see if you can reset the screen either at the software level (e.g., reexecute the command file with a "TERM = " statement, or disconnect and restart your telecom software) or hardware level (power off, wait 10 seconds, power on again).
- Exit the current program:
  - If you've got a prompt, try **q** (for quit) or Control-D, which should exit you from most programs. (Other "quit" commands to try include **bye, exit, ex,** and **quit.**)
  - If you don't have a prompt, try entering Control-C a few times to abort the program currently running (i.e., the process)
  - Escape to another "job." Your options here depend on what type of computer and operating system you're using. Try Control-Z; this may bring you to another "job." If you want to return to where you left, enter **fg** (for "foreground"). On a Unix computer, if you want to "kill" the process of the job you escaped from, first do a **ps** (show processes) command to see what processes you have running, then "kill" (terminate) the ones you no longer want, with the **kill** command.
  - Escape to a "subshell." Programs such as **telnet** have an *attention character*; entering this character gets you back to the program prompt. For example, entering the **telnet** escape character (on most computers, Control-]), gets you back to the "**telnet**>" prompt. Entering just a <RETURN> brings you back to where you were in the **telnet** session.
  - Interactive programs like FTP and e-mail programs often include a "shell" command or ways to run shell commands—usually **sh** to get to a subshell and **!<command>** to run some other command.
- Logout and login again: Enter **logout** or Control-D.

**Local network problems.** What if your computer seems to still be working—but nothing's there when you try to get files or make connection? Maybe your organization's network has a problem. Things to try:

- Disconnect and try again. (After that, consider calling for help.)
- Go out and take a break. Catch up on your paperwork. Try reading one of the manuals you never got around to yet.

If local "network services" aren't working—file server down, name server down or misconfigured, etc.—there won't be much you can do.

**Phone access problems.** If you're using the telephone, the problem might be at your end, within the phone company, or at the site you're accessing. Things to try:

- Hang up and listen for dial tone. Check your plugs and wiring to see if something came loose. Make sure the modem is connected to the computer and the phone line. Sometimes phone wiring to your office or home will break (it's happened to me). (And make sure you haven't had service turned off.) If you use a phone-line selector, make sure it's set correctly.
- Turn your modem off and then on again. Also consider restarting your computer.
- Try another phone number, if you have one. If you're making a 1-800 or long-distance toll call, consider dialing via a different long-distance carrier (e.g., dial 10288 to select AT&T or 10222 for MCI) before placing the call.
- If you have call-waiting, did you "disable" it (usually by dialing *70 at the dial tone) before placing the call? (Note: many older phone systems that offer call-waiting service don't support this feature.)
- Check the modem settings (in your software package). If you have another copy of your program or another telecom program, you may want to try it.
- Try another modem, if you've got one.
- Dial the number by hand and see if you get an answering modem signal.
- Try another on-line service, if you've got an account with one.
- Try plugging into a different phone jack. Try using a different telephone.
- Call the site's voice contact number; it's possible the system is down for service or due to problems.
- Call your telephone company if you think it's a problem with your telephone line or account.

**Internet access problems.** Here, you can use your computer, but you can't reach the Internet—can't establish a **telnet** or FTP connection, access Gopher or archie servers outside your organization, etc. This is often due to problems outside your control. For example, your name server may be overloaded and doesn't respond fast enough to let a connection be made. Maybe an entire piece of the Internet has crashed. Another possibility is that your site or network doesn't have permission to make this connection. Maybe there is something wrong with the routing tables in the network. Things to try:

- Try again.
- Try doing something else Internet-related.
- If you have other access—dial-up, etc.—try those.
- If you need access immediately, call your system or network administrator; otherwise, consider waiting 10 or 15 minutes and then trying again.

**Specific Internet resources unavailable.** For example, you can't reach a public client for WorldWideWeb or can't reach the WAIS list-of-servers. Things to try:

- Try an alternative server.
- If you can, **telnet** to another computer and try the tool from there.
- Wait a minute or two and then try again.
- Try a different tool.

### Typical problems, symptoms, and indications of problems

One way to identify and solve problems is by trying to figure out in which component the problem is. Another way to approach problem-resolution is by examining symptoms and other information, such as error messages. This is often a productive approach since Internet problems tend to manifest themselves in either of these two ways:

- *Symptoms.* Unexpected, strange things happening, or expected things not happening. Examples: slow response, no response, garbage on screen
- *Messages.* Error messages from programs, messages from programs or system administrators, etc.

Here's a quick look at common problems.

**Nothing happens when you type.** You may have done something that "freezes" output to your screen. Things to try:

- The best way to clear conditions of scrolling or flow control is to restart your terminal, log out and log back in again, or reboot your computer.
- Press Control-Q. Now type again. If your text is echoed, the problem was that you had hit a Control-S, which "freezes" output. (This relates to "flow control.")
- Hit the <NO-SCROLL> key. Try <RETURN>.

**Additional garbage characters on your screen.** The most likely cause of garbage is line noise, and it is most common on dial-up lines. Try hanging up and calling again. A short-term solution is to connect at a slower modem speed—2400 instead of 9600, 1200 instead of 2400, etc. Check your phone gear, talk with your system administrator, consider complaining to your telephone company.

**Funny-looking characters on your screen.** This may mean that your terminal has been set to a different character set. Reset the terminal or explicitly reset the character set (if possible).

**Other problems and possible things to do**

- *Echoing takes several seconds.* You don't see your input echoed for several seconds (or as long as a minute), but computer response to your commands seems reasonably prompt. This indicates a problem somewhere in the network. There isn't much you can do about it. Report the problem if it persists.
- *Response to your commands takes several seconds.* Here, the input echoing is reasonably prompt, but there is an unreasonable delay before your commands are executed. Your computer or a remote computer you're accessing may be overloaded. Wait and try again.
- *E-mail messages from somebody named "Damon" or "Daemon."* These aren't from a person. *Damon* or *Daemon* (also *demon,* from "daimon," a spirit) are common terms for a computer program running automatically to perform a service, such as a "mailer-demon" telling you why it couldn't deliver a message you sent or a system Damon warning you to clean out (remove) some of your files.

This in no way claims to be a complete list of what can go wrong or what to do. Over time, you'll develop a sense of what does go wrong and what to do when things happen—and most likely you'll also cultivate a "support network" of people to ask for help when you have done your best.

Part

# 5

# Commercial Services, Archives, Communities, and Miscellany

Chapter

# 13

# Communities of Interest: A Look at Who's Using the Internet

*"Beyond the obvious facts that he has at some time done manual labour, that he takes snuff, that he is a Freemason, that he has been in China, and that he has done a considerable amount of writing lately, I can deduce nothing else."*

*The Red-Headed League*
SIR ARTHUR CONAN DOYLE

The Internet user community unquestionably transcends every job description, reasons for use, age, ethnicity, and other demographics. It's with good reason that networking, whether you're talking about the Internet or a local electronic Bulletin Board System, is viewed as one of the most empowering technologies since the telephone and automobile. (Many consider Velcro and duct tape high on the list, admittedly.) For many discussions, however, several user communities tend to be called out, notably research (including industrial and commercial), business, education, and libraries. To this, I add "individuals."

The Internet has thus become home and facilitator for everything from teachers, students, and leading-edge researchers to librarians, marketing, and sales departments—people doing their jobs, people doing business, and people using the Internet as part of their social and personal lives. In most of the other chapters, we've been looking at what can be done on and with the Internet and how to do it. Let's take a short break and look at some of the communities the Internet serves and what they're doing.

## Research by Network: Reaching for Information

One of the driving motivations behind the development of the ARPAnet, grandpappy to today's Internet, was to help the research community by giving computer-using engineers and scientists real-time access to remote resources like supercomputers, radio telescopes, weather analysis programs, and special databases and to let them share information through electronic mail. Today, this is more true than ever, as people in every imaginable field, who once used typewriters, tape recorders, and word processors now use computers. It's been estimated that over 90 percent of the research sponsored by the U.S. government is conducted at institutions of higher education which are connected to the Internet.

All over the United States and around the world there are researchers, scientists, and engineers using the Internet to help them work by sharing information, accessing distant computers, and moving files. Seismologists are studying collecting earthquake data in one location, processing it on a supercomputer a thousand miles away, and looking at it still elsewhere. Weather research is being done jointly at distant universities. But thanks to the Internet, it's almost as if the people and computers are all in adjacent offices.

In Chap. 8, for example, you read about the Argonne National Laboratory (Argonne, IL) which is using the Internet to help teams of thousands of researchers, industrial and academic alike, around the country and world, share a major, one-of-a-kind—and very expensive—tool by using the Internet. Sharing these expensive, often unique computers and instruments replaces expensive travel and time-consuming shipment of tapes and makes key research and experiments possible.

Here's a few other examples:

- The Berkeley-Illinois-Maryland Millimeter Array (BIMA) telescope is located in Hat Creek, CA—yet can be controlled from College Park, MD, thanks to Internet connectivity. In some cases, remote utilization via the Internet tips the balance in justifying a project's economic viability.
- The Continuous Electron Beam Accelerator Facility (CEBAF) in Newport News, VA, is expected to be used by over 100 universities, connecting via the Internet—in fact, this expectation of network access played a major part in getting the CEBAF to happen.
- At Colorado State University's Natural Resource Ecology Laboratory (Fort Collins, CO) and at the University of Virginia's Department of Environmental Science, two groups of ecology researchers have been using the Internet to work together, enabling simulation modeling programs to work together. The programs are on computers half a continent apart—but because both institutions were already connected to the Internet, all that the researchers needed to do was include the Internet addresses for the participating computers.

Individual researchers as well as groups benefit from the Internet. Perhaps the most striking example is Philip Emeagwali, who won first place in the 1989 Gordon Bell Prize Competition for his research on underground petroleum recovery. Emeagwali used Thinking Machines Inc. Connection Machines and other supercomputers located in a dozen cities across the country, including Los Alamos, Nevada, and Argonne and Urbana-Champaign, both in

Illinois, and Cambridge, MA, all working from his workstation at the University of Michigan by connecting across the Internet.

And somewhere in Colorado, far from the beach, there's an oceanographer working away, doing research by connecting over the Internet to distant computers and instruments.

## Educational Networking: From Kindergarten through College, and Community, Too

The Internet began as a strongly research-oriented tool, but it wasn't long before it also got put to work for education. Today, the Internet plays a growing role in education and academia. According to Dr. Eric S. Hood, President, Federation of American Research Networks (FARNET), and Executive Director, NorthWestNet, in testimony submitted on March 12, 1992, in hearings to the U.S. House of Representatives Subcommittee on Science of the Committee on Science, Space, and Technology:

> The NSFNET now connects over 630 colleges and universities, or approximately 35 percent of our nation's four-year institutions of higher education. Approximately 70 percent of our nation's student population attending four-year colleges and universities have institutional access to the NSFNET. This communications and information infrastructure enables computer users at sites across the nation to share information and to work collaboratively on common tasks and projects. More than 1000 institutions, including colleges, universities, and not-for-profit, government, and corporate research facilities representing every state, are currently connected to the NSFNET. Today's NSFNET is also an important part of a larger communications network, the global Internet, which connects an estimated 750,000 computers and 5 million users worldwide.

Students are working over the Internet, in everything from international pen-pal correspondence and writing projects to collaborative role-playing studies. Faculty are developing courses, exchanging information and databases. And entire universities are becoming networked, enabling students to register, take classes, submit homework, and more, over networks.

The education community has also been swept away by the wave of networkmania. Not just for colleges and universities, but also community colleges, special education and kindergarten, primary, junior, and high schools (collectively referred to as "K through 12," or "K–12" for short).

Flowing through the Internet (and through BITNET ListServs, Usenet Newsgroups, and FidoNet) is a torrent of files, electronic mail messages, and discussions among teachers and students. Part of this initiative can be ascribed to the "E" in NREN, the "information superhighway" initiative within the United States, championed by Senator (and now, Vice President) Albert Gore of Tennessee.

But this is not all. Credit in equal portions also goes to EDUCOM (Princeton, NJ), to BITNET (see Chap. 17), to the many universities who have been on the Internet (and the ARPAnet before that), and to thousands of funded and volunteer people around the world involved through K12Net activities on FidoNet, through local BBSs, through Usenet, and numerous other places. Even so basic a tool as electronic mail has its role in academia. According to an article by David L. Wilson in *The Chronicle of Higher Education* [Sept. 30, 1992, pp. A17–19], "Huge Computer Network Quickens Pace of Academic Exchange and Collaboration":

> Paul D. Gottlieb, a doctoral candidate at Princeton University's Woodrow Wilson School of Public and International Affairs who is studying regional and urban development, says electronic messages make it much easier to carry on discussions with busy colleagues. "Trying to talk with people on the telephone is increasingly hopeless," he says. "E-mail is really the solution to this problem of not being able to reach anyone anymore."

But individual e-mail is only the smallest fraction of the role the Internet and other networks are playing in education. Aside from simply connecting more people, bringing the Internet into the picture has moved educational networking a step beyond just electronic mail and BBS communication. With the Internet, versus the store-and-forward, site-oriented information exchange, comes the ability to do real-time applications for users (i.e., students) in different, often distant places. Let's take a quick look at some of the students, teachers, and schools learning via the Internet.

## K–12 networking courtesy of Usenet and FidoNet

K–12 students and faculty with access to Usenet or FidoNet have a marvelous resource available: K12Net, which is a collection of more than 30 special interest conferences, or Newsgroups, devoted to curriculum and projects in K–12 education.

The K12 Network was established in September 1990 by a few FidoNet bulletin board system operators who were interested in developing an inexpensive telecommunications capability appropriate for use in an educational setting, according to Janet Murray <jmurray@psg.com>, one of its founders and a member of the K12Net Council of Coordinators. In 1991, the K12Net conferences became available as Usenet Newsgroups, enabling people with Usenet access to read and participate in the K–12 activity. Gateways between the FidoNet conferences and Usenet Newsgroups cause messages posted by users on FidoNet nodes to also go to Usenet sites, and vice versa.

"As of early 1993," Murray reports, "K12Net conferences were available on approximately 20 percent of Usenet sites, and more than 300 FidoNet-compatible nodes on five continents. An estimated several million students, teachers, and curriculum developers participate in K12Net."

Because sites with K12Net activity can usually be accessed as a local phone call for little or no user-account cost, students and faculty gain access to a wide range of curriculum-related information, educational files, classroom-to-classroom projects, and pools of people to ask and discuss questions with. K12Net activities include traditional curriculum areas, foreign language practice with native speakers, and structured classroom-to-classroom projects. Here's a few representative K12 groups:

| | |
|---|---|
| k12.ed.art | Art and Crafts education |
| k12.ed.business | Business education |
| k12.ed.math | Mathematics education |
| k12.lang.francais | Discussion in French only |
| k12.lang.deutsch-eng | Bilingual German/English |
| k12.sys.projects | Discussion of potential projects |

For more information, contact:

Janet Murray, Librarian
Wilson High School
1151 S.W. Vermont St.
Portland, OR 97219
(503) 280-5280 x450
janet.murray@f23.n105.z1.fidonet.org

**AskERIC—People to ask and piles of files**

It's no news that computers on the Internet are chockful of information. However, no matter how good the indexing and tools are, users—particularly new and infrequent users—can't always readily find what they're looking for. One solution is to add people to the loop, between the users and the information. One project that has taken this approach is AskERIC, one of the many activities done by the ERIC Clearinghouse on Information Resources program at Syracuse University (Syracuse, NY).

AskERIC, which began service in mid-November 1992, is an Internet-based Q&A, help and referral service for K–12 educators (teachers, librarians, administrators, etc.) run by the Syracuse ERIC Clearinghouse. ERIC is a national information system funded by the U.S. government that provides access to lots of education-related literature. ERIC stands for Educational Resources Information Center; the ERIC Clearinghouse Information Resources are collectively referred to as the ERIC System.

According to Andrew Abrahamson, AskERIC Coordinator, AskERIC is funded partially as part of the Smartline project, to test various approaches to meeting K–12 educators' information needs. AskERIC, Abrahamson states, is for "any type of question that an educator can ask, ranging from Internet-related questions to education-content related questions," says Abrahamson, who is completing his doctoral dissertation in educational technology. "If you have questions about K–12 education, learning, teaching, information technology, educational administration—AskERIC."

According to a message posted by Abrahamson to one of the Internet mailing lists, AskERIC has answered questions such as these:

- From a foreign language teacher—how to help students make e-mail penpals in Spain
- From an elementary school teacher—where to get information on multiage classrooms

- From a school principal—where to find samples of computer curricula for K–12 classes
- From a school board member—where to find information on school district restructuring

The underlying philosophy of AskERIC is that "Internet users need and prefer human intermediary contact when using the network," according to Abrahamson. "Internet resources are terrific—but complicated, and can easily be overwhelming. The AskERIC Network Information Specialists serve as 'electronic librarians,' helping users to define their needs and then assisting users to meet those needs." If the information to answer a question is not available at the Syracuse site, AskERIC can call on the full services of any and all ERIC sites to answer questions.

In addition to reading and replying personally to questions submitted by e-mail—which hit 300 questions per week within a few months of the start of the project—AskERIC is also making selected ERIC full-text and database information available via Gopher and anonymous-FTP. "We are putting up commonly asked questions and answers," says Abrahamson. "For example, someone interested in a 'mini-search' on elder abuse. That was already in the Mini-Search directory; citations on this topic were part of an answer to a question from a previous month." Abrahamson does his best to load in information generated by the other ERIC sites as well as his own. "We presently have hundreds of files, plus archives of the LM_NET School Librarian LISTSERV mailing list, and may add more."

While making information available via Internet tools, AskERIC will still include "access to people for help." "The original function of AskERIC will also remain: to provide a personalized question-answering, help and referral service for K–12 teachers, school librarians, and administrators," according to the message posted to the Internet.

"We provide the human contact that pure FTP and Gopher cannot: a human contact which can be essential for novice Internet users," Abrahamson points out. "And even experienced computer users find it can make a difference. We now have 'repeat customers' who know us by name."

The Internet address for the AskERIC site is askeric@ericir.syr.edu (e.g., for FTP or Gopher). For anonymous-FTP, look in the directory "pub"—or e-mail your questions to askeric@ericir.syr.edu. For more information, contact:

Andy Abrahamson, AskERIC Coordinator
ERIC Clearinghouse on Information Resources
030 Huntington Hall
Syracuse University
Syracuse, NY 13244-2340
Internet: askeric@ericir.syr.edu
Voice: (315) 443-9114
Fax: (315) 443-5448

### Networking schools on a shoestring

"Plugging a school into the Internet" needn't be prohibitively expensive. The National Science Foundation makes numerous "seed money" grants to help schools hop on the Internet. Internet consultants such as Brian Lloyd contribute *pro bono* time scavenging old PCs and modems, many of which can be surprisingly adequate network connectors.

Barry Shein, President of Software Tool & Die (Brookline, MA), which runs the Boston-area World public-access Internet site, recalls, "In mid-1992, someone in the Boston school system posted an e-mail message wanting to know how they could access the Internet—how much it would cost to begin with one login (account) per school district for 10 school districts?" According to Shein, "I thought about it for a few minutes and told him I'd provide him with 10 logins, one per district, with a total of 100 hours login time included for $100/month ($10/month/district), $1/hour thereafter." (At the time, this was half the World's regular rate.) For this price, the school system would be getting *full* Internet access including electronic mail, Usenet news, remote login (**telnet**), file transfer (FTP), and other services like Gopher, archie, and WAIS. Shein pointed out:

> All each given school would need to make contact, would be:
>
> - A telephone line
> - A personal computer—a PC, Mac, Amiga or even some old, obsolete, nonstandard system or dumb terminal (although I'd recommend a computer with a hard disk so they could download things like free books and other materials)
> - A modem (most any modem is fine, I'd recommend at least a 2400/MNP5; those are about $100)
> - Some sort of terminal emulator software would be more than adequate
>
> Since we're a local call from anywhere in Boston, that's essentially "lifeline" access to the Internet for the entire Boston school system (albeit a somewhat centralized subset) for $100/month, including some technical support. If they've already got computers and modems, they don't even need to buy anything.
>
> Admittedly, it's not the highest level of access, but this could be arranged for in 10 minutes with essentially no paperwork other than whatever it takes to approve a budget item of $100 per month. And this level of involvement might just be enough to help hone arguments about why they think someone should fund more activity, with or without my service.

### Examples of Internet educational activities—"on-line Olympics," talking with aliens, and pen-pals

As you can probably tell, the list of education-oriented resources and projects available through the Internet is incredibly diverse—yet set up to be accessible even to people with little or no equipment or money and perhaps only e-mail access to the Internet. Here are some examples of teachers and students using the Internet for education-related projects and some of the remarkable things they're doing.

During the 1991–1992 school year, the St. Julie Billiart K–8 school system

(Hamilton, OH) participated in a number of Internet-based K–12 projects. "We have had a grand year using telecommunications," said Mrs. Jean Stringer, a computer instructor in the school system, "and I think it helped the children to be more thoughtful and creative, on top of the knowledge they gained." Here's some excerpts from the activity log, with permission, courtesy of Stringer:

- An extensive electronic-mail pen-pal program had sixth graders corresponding with students in Cleveland, and seventh graders with students in Australia. "One 7th grader and one 6th grader have a pen pal in Moscow. They seem to have things to say to each other, and one 8th grader has maintained e-mail all year with a student in Norway."

  "I myself have been blessed with many pen pals, like Andry from Moscow, a physicist, who wrote a moving, poetic essay about the city of Moscow and the love her people have, and Delwynn from Australia who has become like a sister," adds Stringer. "I share most of this mail with the class, bringing new understanding of the world."
- World War II project (seventh grade). Students interviewed grandparents to find out information about what it was like living during World War II. The reports they wrote were sent on-line to a school in Virginia, which compiled a book from the best contributions from 12 participating schools.
- Space Simulation (sixth and eighth graders). "Space Shuttle tracking: information gathered about the shuttle. Did research on the Apollo 11 mission, each created reports regarding aspect of the mission. Created on-line graphics of replicas of parts of the mission. Learned about space junk! Created on-line weather format to send weather hourly to mission control. Participated in a global chat."
- Far Star Project (sixth and seventh grade). The students were contacted by aliens ("played" by a Ph.D. from St. John's University in New York) who asked many questions about earthlings. "The project at the present is continuing with the aliens asking us to prove we are real, and not made up by their teachers. The sixth are continuing, the seventh must move on. One seventh grader may become the alien for another school. This project has continued on a weekly basis and is developing into the alien leading the children through right brain/left brain thought processes."
- TeleOlympics: messages about an imaginary Olympics, with students participating from over 12 states in the United States and eight other countries including Argentina, Australia, Estonia, Finland, Spain, and Ukraine. Dr. Tom Grundner <tmg@nptn.org>, President of the National Public Telecomputing Network, did the honors and declared the TeleOlympics officially in progress, broadcasting ASCII graphics of doves, the torch, and a light for the torch. (Teams exchanged cheers and ASCII graphics throughout as well.) NPTN's Academy One program was responsible for the TeleOlympics, and the Space Simulations, Chatback, and Far Star activities which St. Julie students participated in.

***On Telecommunications I Have Written to Many Pen-Pals***

My Australian pen-pal and I have been writing for almost a year and we also write each other on paper. My Russian pen-pal and I have been exchanging a continuous story that we both have written. In Finland I am sponsoring a group that is participating in the worldwide TeleOlympics.

I think that writing on line with pen-pals is a good way to help bring different countries together. If everyone could have the experience of writing to people in other countries then I think that the world would be closer and more friendly.

Jenni Strickland
St. Julie School
Grade 7

## Role-playing educational games on the Internet

One way to use the Internet is to reach out from one school. Another is to "caucus" on e-mail and BBS forums. A third is to "come together" through real-time and e-mail connections, such as the following remarkable application of role-playing games and computer networks to education.

Through the magic of networking, for example, college, high school, and middle school students have been trying to resolve the Arab-Israeli conflict, following scientific expeditions and writing collaborative poetry anthologies. At the University of Michigan School of Education (Ann Arbor, MI), since 1982, the Interactive Communications and Simulations (ICS) Project has been giving students experiential learning experiences through participatory interactive role-playing simulations and other activities, through programs and scenarios run in their Confer computer-based conferencing facilities. The ICS effort grew out of simulations of the Arab-Israeli conflict done by a man named Edgar Taylor when he was a political science graduate student in the 1970s. In the late 1970s, says Taylor, "We ran role-playing simulations, using the computer as a means of communication, but with all the students physically gathered together. But by the 1980s, it became clear we could disperse the students, we saw how we could use computer conferencing systems to facilitate this."

ICS provides materials defining the roles, scenario, rules, and other essential information. "Our simulations all involve students playing 'real roles,' rather than making up their own character," Taylor notes. For example, characters in the Arab-Israeli exercise as of early 1993 include President Clinton, Egypt's President Mubarak, and Jordan's King Hussein as well as other current leaders involved in the conflict.

Other ICS projects are the International Poetry Guild, enabling students to write poetry and put journals together within the conferencing system and, ultimately, publish a collection of their work electronically and The Earth Odysseys, where students interact with travelers who respond to queries regarding social, environmental, and other information. In semesters when no expeditions are scheduled, previous "canned" trips are rerun over the semester. (E-mail links to live expeditions have also been contemplated for The Earth Odyssey, via packet radio—interested parties please note.)

What began as a project within Michigan now has participants from around the world—31 states, 5 Canadian provinces, and 25 countries overseas as of early 1993. Anywhere from 5 to 50 students make up a school's team; typically, teams from about 100 schools participate in each of the two terms per year. Taylor estimates that over 10,000 students from nearly 400 schools have been ICS "players."

"The Confer II conferencing system on the University of Michigan's mainframe acts as host, providing store-and-forwarding mediation of the activities," explains Clancy Wolf, Associate Director at ICS. Students must have an interactive connection to our system—such as through the Internet. The participation fee, which covers operating expenses and participant materials, is $275 per team per semester (which includes all communications time if using a non-Internet access mechanism). For information on ICS, call 313-763-6716 or send e-mail to info@ics.soe.umich.edu on the Internet.

### Big Mac prices, Global Village Newspaper, and antigravity

Rob Reilly <rreilly@Athena.mit.edu>, a computer education teacher in a K–6 school system in western Massachusetts (Lanesboro School System) and winner of the 1992 Mass. Dept of Education's 'Pathfinder Award,' offers the following:

> My students are heavily involved in several ongoing projects that are carried via Usenet and FidoNet technology. One project is one in which the participants discuss the price of Big Mac sandwiches around the world to gain an understanding of other monetary systems. They monitor the rise and fall of such costs and discuss the whys and wherefores of the process.
>
> Another project they are involved in is a "Global Village Newspaper" where they talk about what's going on in their locality. There is an outstanding project available that is called MathMagic; they do quite a bit there and each few days the leader of the project poses another "question" that needs to be solved. And in the foreign language areas, I have children here speaking German with actual children in Germany.

Reilly's students are also participating in the Cyberion City portion of the M.I.T.-based MicroMUSE role-playing project. (MicroMUSE is explained elsewhere in this chapter.) Cyberion City, the "base of operations," is a "tin can city"—-huge cylindrical satellite, 16 miles long and 8 miles across, orbiting the Earth (in virtual reality, that is). "My students are very active on the satellite city," Reilly reports. "Two of them are involved in developing antigravity products [such as] an AntiGravAttic which is a modular attic which can attach to your house or "anywhere"....The kids have also upscaled this "attic" to a warehouse and are commercially marketing it."

And I've heard another group has started a restaurant on the moon. The food's apparently great—but the place has no atmosphere. (Just kidding.)

### Big Sky Telegraph: In support of K–12 and community networking

Big Sky Telegraph, being run through Western Montana College, is acting as a Global K12 Telecurricular Clearinghouse for projects running on networks. According to Director Frank Odasz, "We're always looking for K12 resources, expertise, and innovative project ideas to collect and disseminate. We have 600 K12 lesson plans available for the taking, though we'd prefer to TRADE resources."

Big Sky also serves as a clearinghouse on Community Networking models (see the files in their "Class" area for information about low-cost school/community networks with Internet e-mail and distributed conferencing capabilities) and offers an on-line course "Microcomputer Telecommunications" covering the basics of telecomputing and modem use on a limited budget. To access Big Sky, **telnet** (login as "bbs") or Gopher to bigsky.bigsky.dillon.mt.us. For more information, contact:

Frank Odasz, Director
Big Sky Telegraph
Western Montana College of
The University of Montana
710 S. Atlantic
Dillon, MT 59725-3598
406/683-7870
Fax: 406-683-7493
E-Mail: franko@bigsky.dillon.mt.us
Modem: 406-683-7680

**MUSEs—Multi-User Simulation Environments.** The twenty-fourth-century simulation that Rob Reilly's students are exploring is part of MicroMUSE, one of a dozen or more MUSEs, or Multi-User Simulation Environments, operating across the United States. MicroMUSE is provided through the MicroMuse project, currently run by volunteers, using computer facilities provided by M.I.T. Barry Kort (barry@kudzu.cnidr.org), Consulting Scientist in Educational Technology Research at BBN Labs (Cambridge, MA) and a founding Director of MicroMuse, explains that "MicroMUSE offers students and other users a chance to participate in education-oriented multi-user role-playing and 'virtual reality' games. The system features explorations, adventures, and puzzles with an engaging mix of social, cultural, and educational content."

You work through facilities resembling a cross between the Internet Relay Chat and "Adventure" (a.k.a. "Colossal Cave"), which was one of the first interactive role-playing computer games ("You are in a maze of twisty little passages." "Plugh." "Axe troll." etc.). Unlike Adventure or many other games, however, MicroMUSE participants get to create their own virtual reality as well as participate in existing scenarios—and it's available to anyone via the Internet.

When you are connected to MicroMUSE, you are interacting with the Muse server, which has a database containing definitions of all the "objects" involved in MicroMUSE activities. As of early 1993, the database used by MicroMUSE contained nearly 50,000 "objects," including over 9000 Rooms, 17,000 Things, 21,000 Exits, plus the several thousand Players and Citizens. (Citizens, Kort explains, are "duly Registered Players who have read and agreed to abide by the 'Social Contract' which governs the MicroMuse Community." In particular, Citizens "understand that we are a nonviolent virtual community oriented toward informal science education and serving the K–12 community." Other Player categories besides Citizen include Guest, Visitor, Guide, Official, Administrator, Director, Robot, and Corporation.)

For example, according to information provided by Kort:

> The MicroMuse Science Center offers an Exploratorium and Mathematica Exhibit complete with interactive exhibits drawn from experience with Science Museums around the country. A highlight of the Mathematica Exhibit is "Professor Griffin's Logic Quest," based on Raymond Smullyan's classical puzzles about knights and knaves. The Narnia Adventure embeds challenging puzzles within a familiar children's classic. The Mission to Mars includes an elaborate tour of the red planet with accurate descriptions rivaling those found in *National Geographic.*
>
> Elsewhere, one can find a sailing cruise to the Virgin Islands which recreates the real-life adventure of the player who created it. Recently, an 8-year-old student designed and built an Oz adventure based on the movie version of that classic children's story, and a 9-year-old contributor created a working model of Yellowstone National Park, complete with erupting geysers and a wandering moose.
>
> For younger players, "text-based virtual realities foster literacy skills: reading, writing, and composition, and technical skills such as keyboarding and spelling. For adolescent players, social interaction skills, interpersonal skills, and personality development emerge as primary activities. College students who are not computer science majors enjoy the opportunity to gain some computer literacy and try their hand at creating their own contributions to the cyberspace worlds, usually with the helpful guidance of friendly players with more experience. The more ingenious and inventive players design and build elaborate and powerful artifacts such as electronic newspapers, voice-mail recorders, and self-activated transit systems.

According to Kort, MicroMUSE is one of the largest MUSEs, and the first MUSE site fully dedicated to educational purposes. "We have had about 3000 registered users since MicroMUSE began in late 1990. Currently we have 1600 active Citizens of Cyberion City, and we typically get between 600 and 800 logins a day. Our users come from USA, Canada, South America, United Kingdom, France, Germany, Spain, Italy, Sweden, Denmark, Netherlands, Australia, South Africa, Russia, and Israel." To try MicroMUSE:

telnet to: michael.ai.mit.edu [18.43.0.177]

login as: guest [no password required]

and enter: **connect guest** [Connect to MicroMuse]

(You'll want to get a copy of the MicroMUSE client software if you become a "frequent MUSEr.") You will then be shuttled to the Cyberion City Transport Receiving Station, where you will be given further information to assist you in your exploration. Some useful commands:

**news** General news command
**help** On-line help command
**/quit** Exit MicroMuse

Information about the MicroMUSE project is also available via anonymous-FTP file retrieval from michael.ai.mit.edu or chezmoto.ai.mit.edu in the muse/info directory and other nearby directories.

For more information:

Barry Kort
BBN Labs
Mail Stop 6/4a
10 Moulton Street
Cambridge, MA 01230
bkort@bbn.com
(617) 873-2358 (Office)

Nils McCarthy
1831 Tatum Street
Falcon Heights, MN 55113
nils@geom.umn.edu

So if you're a student somewhere between kindergarten and twelfth grade and want to get educationally networked, don't feel you have to wait until college. There's lots of Internet scholastic activity for you right now (and for K–12 teachers, too, of course).

## Libraries: Catalogs and Contents Go On-Line

In Part 3, we talked some about how Internet navigators like Gopher and HYTELNET were helping users access the growing number of on-line library catalogs that can be reached via the Internet. Chapter 14 looks at organizations like OCLC and RLIN that are helping provide free or pay-for-use searching and access to library information. Now let's take a brief look at a librarian's eye view of the Internet.

You may have noticed a few changes involving computers taking place in libraries during the past few years. When you check out and return books, many libraries scan your books like a bag of groceries, automatically updating their "what's available, what's out" inventory. (And telling you whether you have any outstanding fines for overdue books.) The change is even more dramatic, however, when you decide to look for a book or for a magazine article. Instead of going to the card catalog, you've probably found yourself in front of a computer terminal. Information about what's in the library is a natural for computerizing. How better to store, manage, and search through lists of hundreds of thousands, perhaps millions, of books by author, title, subject, or descriptive summary?

And once that information is in the computer, why not make it possible to see if your library has the latest book by Stephen King or something on home repair without having to be at the library. Why not plug the library's computer into the Internet? In fact, why not plug lots of library catalogs in—city, state, university, specialty archives, maybe even the Library of Congress? Especially since many libraries have already moved to on-line catalogs and many colleges, universities, and other schools and institutions are themselves already on the Internet.

Why not, indeed? Hundreds of libraries in dozens of countries around the world have plugged into the Internet, accessible to anyone who can do a remote login (**telnet**). In addition to catalogs of holdings, many libraries also offer access to on-line and indexing, which is helpful for checking references and citations. For example, the University of Colorado, Colorado Springs (arlo.colorado.edu; login as ARLO) lists over 200,000 titles, emphasizing business, electrical engineering, and psychology. Here are a few examples of special library collections whose catalogs are available via the Internet:

- The Robert M. Stecher Collection of Charles Darwin Books & Manuscripts at Case Western Reserve University
- Over 2500 items related to chess, in the Cleveland Public Library's John G. White Collection of Folklore, Orientalia, and Chess
- The Elizabeth Ball Collection of Children's Literature at Indiana University (8500+ items)
- The A. W. Kuchler Vegetation Map Collection and McGuffey Collection of School Textbooks at Miami University in Ohio
- The Batchelder-McPharlin Puppetry Collection at the University of New Mexico
- The William B. Carins Collection (300 works by American women before 1900) at the University of Wisconsin-Madison

The number of library catalogs accessible through the Internet is growing as quickly as the Internet itself. In July of 1991, over 270 on-line library catalogs and collections, 120 of them international, including libraries in Germany, Mexico, New Zealand, Australia, Israel, Switzerland, Sweden, and the United Kingdom, were reachable through the Internet. By early 1993, this had climbed to over 600 libraries in more than two dozen countries.

Can't find a book in your local university? Logon, **telnet** over, and search through a few other catalogs. Once you've located the book you want, your local library can probably request it through Interlibrary Loan. Libraries on the Internet range within the United States from Alabama's Auburn

**A Librarian's Eye View of the Internet**

"For librarians and library users, the Internet has accelerated changes in our concepts of information resources and ways to get to them," states Marian Bremer (mbremer@bbn.com), Manager, BBN Libraries, at Bolt Beranek & Newman, Inc., (Cambridge, MA). A former public librarian, Bremer uses the Internet to query on-line databases, libraries, and other info-resources.

"The Internet is (among other things) a GIANT library, rapidly becoming a viable information delivery system for all its users. For information which is on-line, all libraries are rapidly becoming your local library," she notes. "Already, many once-separate resources can be explored as one large distributed resource, with a single keystroke or click of a mouse."

But, the Internet does *not* do away with the need for librarians, Bremer cautions. "We all need saving from a world with too much information. The Internet's geometrically growing seas of data need [librarians] more than ever, to help guide the organization and labelling of the 'virtual stacks,' and to develop sensible strategies for incorporating its resources into those already proven. Otherwise you can wander for hours without finding what you're looking for."

University to Washington State University, along with Harvard and M.I.T. and globally, from Australia and Canada to Germany, Israel, the United Kingdom, and New Zealand, and Oxford in England. And parts of the Library of Congress catalog reachable this way, too (telnet dra.com or locis.loc.gov).

Not sure what libraries are on the Internet or what their electronic addresses are? The new breed of Internet navigators, such as Gopher and HYTELNET, can help (see Chap. 10). Not sure which library to try first or how many libraries you've got the stamina to access? If you (or your organization) have accounts with the appropriate organizations, the library and information services community has an answer to that. Organizations such as the Research Libraries Information Network (RLIN) and the On-Line Computer Library Center (OCLC) have merged the information from hundreds of individual catalogs into large databases, allowing you to search legions of library catalogs in a single command (see Chap. 14).

Just don't talk loud while you're connected and be sure to return any catalog records you have read. (Just kidding, on both counts.) To learn more:

- Explore the menus in Gopher, HYTELNET, LIBS, and other Internet navigators for library catalogs.
- Read the LIBS-L BITNET ListServ mailing list (subscribe by sending a message to LISTSERV@bitnic.educom.edu with "Subscribe LIBS-L Your-firstname Your-last-name" as the message text).

Also look for the following books:

*Public Libraries and the Internet/NREN: New Challenges, New Opportunities,* by Dr. Charles R. McClure, Joe Ryan, Diana Lauterbach, and William Moen, July 1, 1992 (40 pages); available at $15.00 from:

Publications Office
School of Information Studies
Syracuse University
Syracuse, NY 13244-4100
(315) 443-2911

"Surfing the Internet," by Jean Armour Polly <polly@LPL.ORG>, *Wilson Library Bulletin,* June 1992; describes the Liverpool NY public library's use of the Internet and lists sources of information

## Business, Government Stuff, Free-Nets, and Just Plain End Users

This only scratches the surface of who's using the Internet and the reasons. Governments and government agencies use the Internet, too. The Smithsonian Institution is connected to the Internet. (So is the Internal Revenue Service, as least for e-mail.)

### Business solutions via the Internet

Thousands of businesses also use the Internet in one way or another. Almost every major computer and network company is, you can bet. The same goes for every company in the aerospace industry. (Many of these companies and agencies connect for e-mail but have "firewall" gateways or other preventatives to keep out unwanted, unauthorized users.) And thousands more businesses large and small are coming "hopping on the Internet" as an essential business tool, for activities such as:

- E-mail with suppliers and customers
- Access to on-line database services such as Dialog and Dow Jones and to information such as the Business Wire and Federal Register (see Chap. 14)
- Distributing sales information and software updates—and making them available for users to retrieve
- Collaborative program and product development
- Remote network and system management and software installation
- Connecting remote offices for file access.

Here are some examples from some Internet users:

Midnight Networks (Waltham, MA), a small startup company that creates smart tools for TCP/IP network administrators, considers its 10-Mbit Internet connection "vital to our strategy and operations," according to Peter Schmidt, President of the company:

> For example, to do alpha-testing of our first product, we used anonymous-FTP to distribute copies to six sites in the U.S. and Canada, taking feedback via e-mail. As another big example: we routinely use archie to locate public-domain software tools that would represent as much as a week's worth of development each. The savings we realize from finding and getting even one such program more than

pays for the cost of our Internet connection for the month! And we do that sort of thing all the time.

Andrew Karp, Program Manager for the Quality of Service Evaluation System at Pacific Gas & Electric Company (San Francisco, CA), says:

> I participate in the Statistics and SAS Users bulletin boards extensively. Membership on both lists gives me instant access to thousands of other statisticians and/or users of the SAS software product around the world, and there is a phenomenal amount of sharing of ideas among list participants. It's like having immediate access to a wide array of programming and methodological experts without having to leave my office in San Francisco.
>
> For example, I needed some input about a particular type of measurement scaling system to present at a meeting here at Pacific Gas & Electric Company a few months ago. I posted my question to the STAT-L board, and within two days had a dozen responses from around the world. Needless to say, my co-workers were very impressed with the quality and diversity of viewpoints I was able to share with them on this topic.

For Michael Stein Associates (Washington, D.C.) who develop custom LAN applications, the Internet provides an easy, affordable way to exchange program files with the company's one-person "field office" in Germany. "I'm a big CompuServe fan for a lot of my U.S.-oriented needs, but Internet service seemed better for this," says Stein.

Rohm and Haas Company, a multinational specialty chemicals company headquartered in Philadelphia, PA, first connected to the Internet in 1988. At the time, their use consisted mostly of a few people sending occasional e-mail and connecting to the Minnesota Supercomputer Center to run molecular modeling codes. Today, according to Scientific Programmer/Analyst Thomas J. Cozzolino, R&H is also using archie, Gopher (including local VERONICA searches), WAIS, and WorldWideWeb with the XMosaic client, for internal information as well as to access archives and databases on the Internet. He said:

> Nearly all of the internal customers who have seen these Internet Discovery Tools have been interested in learning more. Everyone is intrigued by the idea of WAN-based information services that provide cost-effective and reliable access to internal and external information.
>
> I am especially excited about XMosaic, one of the X Windows clients for WorldWideWeb, since it allows smooth access to Gopher, WAIS, NNTP, X.500, archie, and other servers, and includes a built-in hook to display PostScript documents via GhostScript.

Adam Gaffin, a reporter at the *Middlesex News* (Framingham, MA) is one of a growing number of reporters who use the Internet for stories or sources:

> It lets reporters at small newspapers cover things they could never do otherwise. Through the Internet, we've been able to provide first-person accounts of everything from the Gulf War to the San Francisco earthquake. It's also a great place to ask the sort of oddball questions reporters sometimes have to answer, such as whether Passover wine was kosher during Prohibition—it was.

### The Internet as marketplace and "delivery tool"

Dozens, perhaps hundreds, of businesses are springing up based largely on use of the Internet. These range from organizations like Dialog and MEAD Data who use the Internet to provide an alternative access method to electronic information publishers and deliverers like American Cybercast, ClariNet, and Counterpoint who use the Internet to provide sophisticated new delivery and access to on-line information (see Chaps. 10 and 14).

### Individuals on the Internet

Through public-access sites such as Access Express (in D.C.), DELPHI, Halcyon (Seattle), NetCom (California), the WELL (San Francisco), and of course, The World (Boston) and the thousands of public-access Unix sites and other BBSs, there are tens of thousands of individuals like me (and maybe you), forming a new Internet community demographic—people who want to be on the Internet as individuals rather than as members of a company or an academic institution (for more information about public-access accounts, see Chap. 16).

For Ken Greenberg (kgreenb@panix.com), a neon artist and commercial neon designer at Krypton Neon (Long Island City, NY):

> I've found the Internet to be much more comprehensive than the on-line consumer services as a source of useful freeware and shareware programs. There are more programs, a lot more esoteric ones, and more "context" in terms of people who are using and debugging them. For example, at the time that the new PKUnzip (2.04c) was first coming out, it seemed that PANIX had the bug reports and fixes already in the works months before the commercial services did.
>
> Also, the on-line "unzip" facilities let me check out the documentation after I've FTP'ed a file to PANIX—which only takes a few seconds—but before I spend a quarter-hour downloading a megabyte or so to my PC by modem, which takes a while at 2400 bps.
>
> The Internet means that I'll be able to make contact with entire groups, organizations, and resources that relate to arts and technology—which I find more valuable than just participating in a discussion group.
>
> Lastly, now that I've gotten familiar with Unix shells like **bash,** I find the shell prompt much easier and more useful than a low-end proprietary menu. My account on PANIX is like an extension of my computer—I can create subdirectories, work directly with files, etc.
>
> And it's a lot of fun.

City-like communities are emerging, as well. Free-Nets, such as the Cleveland Free-Net pioneered by Tom Grunder through his National Public Telecomputing Network, are a public-access combination of a city or regional BBS and an Internet site. A dozen or more Free-Nets have sprung up around the United States (check your local Gopher, HYTELNET, or other Internet navigator menu).

As you can see, it's not possible to pigeonhole a given Internet user into a single category, any more than they have a single way or reason to use the Internet. A lot of research is happening within universities. Libraries and corporations alike are into on-line catalog and database searching. The only fact we can be sure of: The number of people using the Internet, and the ways we are finding to use it, keep growing daily.

Chapter

# 14

# Commercial and Other Information Services on the Internet: Databases, Libraries, and Other Info-mongers

*"I've information vegetable, animal, and mineral."*
*The Pirates of Penzance*
GILBERT AND SULLIVAN

For many companies, the most immediate motivator for joining and making use of the Internet is the continually growing number of information services available on a pay-for-use or other basis. Cost savings in terms of access costs to traditional commercial services can strongly justify the monthly costs of an Internet connection; other Internet services "follow along for free."

Services such as e-mail, file transfer, Usenet News, and archives access may be valuable—but these are often harder to explain or justify to the bean counters in the decision loop. Access to on-line databases like DIALOG and NEXIS/LEXIS, on the other hand, is something they are familiar with and used to spending money on; saying you've found a better, less expensive way to get to them is an easy "business case" to make, and the other aspects of Internet service can follow as a side-effect. For example:

- Established big database and full-text providers like DIALOG, Dow Jones, and Mead Data are plugging their systems into the Internet.
- Library services like the On-Line Computer Library Center (OCLC) and Research Libraries Information Network (RLIN) have been "on the net" for years; now many are adding full-text retrieval to their catalog searching,

and major library institutions like the Columbia Law Library and U.S. Library of Congress have started to become Internet-accessible.

- Daily-generated information such as UPI (from ClariNet Communications) and Reuters (from MSEN Inc.) news feeds, stock quotes, on-line airline guides (from DELPHI), and the U.S. government's *Federal Register* and *Commerce Business Daily* (from Counterpoint Publishing) are available via the Internet. Many, notably those from ClariNet, MSEN, and Counterpoint, can be used via popular, familiar Internet tools such as Usenet newsreaders, Gopher, and WAIS. (Some information services may be only available to subscribers in the United States.)
- Book publisher catalogs, journal tables of contents, press releases, newsletters, and other information are available for browsing.
- Reference books, journals, fiction, and multimedia works are becoming available for searching, browsing, and downloading (OnLine BookStore).

Trend-wise, this is a big—although not surprising—additional direction for the Internet. "The Internet has historically been populated by programs and services that were largely 'homebrewed' and did not charge for their access or use, such as anonymous-FTP archive sites, Internet Relay Chat (IRC), and Gopher," notes John Quarterman, author of the best-selling *The Matrix,* editor of the *Matrix News* newsletter, and Secretary of Matrix Information & Directory Services (Austin, Texas). "Now, these are being joined by commercially developed, pay-for-use services."

The concept itself is not new. Remote login to most facilities has always required users to have an account; many services, including the Supercomputer Centers, have sold accounts, along with or instead of availability based on work requirements (e.g., research projects, being associated with an appropriate government effort, etc.). What is new is the "coming on board" as an additional or alternative way to access pay-for-use services. Also, many of these info-purveyors may not otherwise be Internet users (i.e., they're plugging in so *you* can access what they sell, not so they can also access other services or exchange e-mail with you and me).

In this chapter, we'll take a look at:

- What an on-line information service is
- The advantages of information being available via the Internet
- Information access "Internet-style"
- Example of available services

## Background on On-Line Information Services

### What's an on-line information service?

On-line information services, which include on-line databases, on-line search and retrieval, and information brokers, specialize in some combination of putting data into computer-readable format and making it accessible to use from our terminals and computers. Some are reselling information from other sources (adding value through indexing, searching, etc.); others are offering information originating internally.

According to Howard Karten, a technology writer and consultant in Randolph, MA (and one of the first people I knew to use on-line services as a research tool), there are roughly a dozen major players in this industry, including ABI/Inform, BRS, Data Courier, Dialog Information Services Inc., H.H. Wilson, Information Access Corp., Maxwell Orbit, Mead Data, and LEXIS/NEXIS. This dozen-odd represents the big "information supermarket" players—but there are hundreds of other specialized and smaller info-mongers also out there.

There are topically focused services, such as LEGI-SLATE and MED-LINE, as well as specialists in library collection indexes, abstracts, citations, and documents and organizations such as the RLIN, from the Research Libraries Group; CARL, the Colorado Association of Research Libraries; OCLC, the On-Line Computer Library Center; and Faxon (Westwood, MA).

Prime-time use of many of these services isn't necessarily cheap. Rates of $100 and up an hour are common—and presumably the results are worth it. (Many of these services offer off-hours or restricted services at rates affordable to nonbusiness users such as home-based investors.) It's not uncommon for requests within a company to flow through corporate librarians who have taken courses in how to use a specific system and how to do effective database searches. Equally, there are a number of organizations that buy access to multiple databases—"bundle" them and then resell access—and individuals who specialize in doing searches, for a price.

Barbara Quint, editor of *Database Searcher,* a magazine from Meckler Corporation for professional database and on-line information searchers, estimated that as of mid-1992 there were 2000+ database producers and 700+ on-line services. There are also thousands of BBSs (on-line Bulletin Board Systems), many dedicated to specific topics, organizations, products, or issues, accessible either for-pay or free. Plus, on-line conferencing systems like CompuServe, DELPHI, GEnie, and ZIFFnet have accumulated substantial information bases, such as topically grouped postings and discussion summaries from their members.

## What information is available?

What's in these mountains of on-line data? Lots. That's one of the reasons these organizations exist (and make a living). They provide better access to the information and better management (i.e., searching, evaluating, and delivering it).

By mid-1992 there were over 5500 commercial databases, according to Quint. DIALOG alone has 400+ databases, containing over 2 Tbytes (that's 1,000,000 Mbytes!) of data. According to Ruth Orenstein, publisher of *Full-Text Sources On-Line* and of *Newspapers On-Line* by Susan Bjorner, "The full text of over 3600 newspapers, magazines, journals, newswires, newsletters, and other types of regularly issued periodicals is available on-line." She estimates that abstract-only information is available several times for this many publications. (Don't forget that you may already have access to fresh and recent text feeds for many newspapers, journals, and columns through Campus-Wide Information Systems [CWISs] or in Usenet if your site subscribes to the ClariNet groups, which may include everything from Dave Barry and Ms. Manners' columns to selected stock quotes and business wires.)

Through one service alone, Dow Jones News/Retrieval, users can access over 1300 publications, including 35 of the largest 50 newspapers, 22 of the major business publications, and about 70 databases. The library and archive catalogs searchable via organizations like RLIN and OCLC contain tens of millions of individual items owned by hundreds to thousands of institutions. This information may be general reference information such as the contents of encyclopedias, dictionaries, and atlases or corporate 10K forms filed with the Securities and Exchange Commission. It may be freshly generated information, such as the morning editions of the *New York Times* or from an edition 20 or more years ago. Or it may be real-time information, such as weather readings, stock quotes, and currency exchange rates.

Noncommercial information databases may be one-of-a-kind documents, like the Dead Sea Scrolls or arts and literature, such as Sir Arthur Conan Doyle's adventures of Sherlock Holmes, the lyrics of the Grateful Dead, or images from the National Art Gallery in Washington, D.C. The biggest commercial on-line information services offer access to massive databases of partial and full text materials, taken from the tens of thousands of newspapers, periodicals, journals, magazines, newsletters, research reports, and other "data chunks" that appear daily. As you can see, the types and quantity of information available on-line is vast, and growing daily. The rapid growth is due to a combination of cheaper storage (CD-ROM, optical discs, etc.), more powerful scanning and search software, and more networking. (Plus, there's money to be made, the ultimate persuader.)

Here's one categorization of the types of information available via the Internet:

- *Indexes and abstracts versus full-text.* Indexes and abstracts provide pointers to information (e.g., tables of contents for journals and books, newspaper headlines, and article summaries). "Full-text" means the entire item is available for searching and retrieving—although if it isn't in ASCII, but something like fonted text, graphics, or audio, your computer may not be capable of displaying or receiving it.
- *Periodically generated cumulative information.* A lot of information is generated on an hourly, daily, or other basis, such as newspaper articles, weather maps, stock quotes, magazine contents, and more. You may want current information, or to search across a period of time, such as the *Wall Street Journal* from 1980 to 1990.
- *Periodically revised information.* Airline schedules and prices, product information, etc.

- *Reference information.* Dictionaries, encyclopedia, legal references, and business directories such as company profiles.
- *Miscellaneous fact and fiction.* Textbooks, novels, poetry, music, etc.
- *Databases.* Economic indices, scientific data, etc.
- *"Holdings."* Lists of items available from institutions, such as book collections, recordings, maps, etc., not (yet) available in on-line digitized format.

### Who uses commercial on-line information services?

The range of people and organizations that use these commercial on-line services is as wide as the types of services themselves. For example:

- Individual home users, to check the On-line Airline Guide schedules
- Investors, to get current stock prices from Dow Jones
- Students, to search and download encyclopedia articles
- Writers (like yours truly), to search library catalogs and publications indexes for articles on something we're writing about.
- Researchers at universities, engineering firms, and *Fortune* 1000 companies, to look for legal, business, scientific, patent, and other information. DIALOG, for example, reports that their customers include all (or nearly all) the *Fortune* 1000 companies. DIALOG has 100,000 to 150,000 customer accounts; each of these accounts potentially represents hundreds of users, even tens of thousands of users. (That is, there are a lot of folks using on-line information services out there.)

## Accessing On-Line Services: The Internet Way

### Pre-Internet access methods

Historically, on-line information services have made themselves available to their users by a variety of methods, all more or less providing a direct terminal connection between your terminal—or terminal-emulating computer—and the service's computers. (None of these access methods is free, of course; you'd see their cost either as a separate bill—from your phone company—or reflected as a higher rate.) For example:

- Direct dial-up—often a long-distance call or to a 1-800 number
- Dial-up access to a Public Data Net (PDN) or Value-Added Network (VAN), such as TymNet or SprintNet, which in turn connected to the service
- Gatewayed through an on-line service, such as CompuServe or MCI Mail, as a value-added service
- Building their own private computer network (e.g., CompuServe Packet Network for CompuServe), providing local access phone numbers for user dial-up.

However, each of these approaches had several negatives:

- *Expensive.* Charges often reflected the time a user kept a connection going—even though the traffic going to and fro only occupied a small fraction of the total time and bandwidth.
- *Noise-prone.* Particularly for the dial-up part, the connection was prone to line noise, which often garbled your commands and what you got back.
- *Slow connections.* Dial-up modems limited users to 2400-, 1200-, or even 300-bps connections—painfully slow if you wanted to download more than a screen or two of output. (Things have gotten somewhat better; most services do support 9600-bps modem connections—although they charge commensurately, which makes "dead time" even more costly.)
- *Often not integrated in with other on-line activities.* In the extreme case, commercial on-line services required you to use a special terminal, such as a slow, thermal-printing machine. To use such a service meant leaving your workstation and desk, and it resulted in output that could not easily be merged with your main base of data and files.

For users within an organization, modem-oriented connections also meant either you had to have a modem or there had to be modems somewhere within your organization's network that you could connect to. If there was any problem with the modems—or they were tied up—there went your access.

Telecommunications managers often found two other concerns in helping their users obtain and manage access to these services: lack of economies of scale and lack of budget control. In other words, there were no savings in contracting for several services. Worst, the communications costs were often based on usage and therefore were unpredictable. (Versus a fixed, known in advance cost, which can thereby be budgeted for.)

### Plugging into the Internet

Many of these info-mongers have begun plugging into the Internet, enabling anyone on the Internet to connect and query simply by entering something like

```
% telnet dialog.com
```

from their computer (assuming that they have an account on the appropriate commercial service, of course). For Internet users, access to these services via the Internet means:

- You can access these services from your computer at your desk (or from wherever you are logged into your Internet account from).
- If your computer can multitask (do several things at the same time), you can open a window, start a query, and continue other tasks while waiting for results, including querying several different information services at the same time.
- You don't have to worry as much about the costs to connect. (You may still

be paying for connection time, as well as by the query or result "hits"—so be sure you understand how and why you get charged.)

- If your computer connects to the Internet through your organization's internal networks, you don't need a modem or don't have to wait until a network modem is available.
- You can have a higher-speed connection.
- You can request session results be saved to a file and forwarded to your coworkers (e.g., from librarians performing information requests and retrievals being delivered to whoever made the actual request) without having to see and capture information as a screen dump or download.
- Depending on the service, you may be able to create automated queries, invoked periodically or from other programs. (Some commercial services currently allow this.)
- Depending on the service, you may be able to submit and receive queries as e-mail, rather than asking and waiting for replies in real-time. Having queries processed during off-peak hours may often be much less expensive.

Marian Bremer, Corporate Librarian at Bolt Beranek & Newman (Cambridge, MA), who has been using the Internet since the mid-1980s, reports:

> It was immediately obvious how we could take advantage of remote login (using the TCP/IP **telnet** facility) to the traditional (commercial) sources of information with which we were already familiar. The Internet now serves as an alternative conduit to resources once only available via modem and often-noisy, slow (1200 to 9600 bps), relatively expensive phone networks.
>
> The result: From my Internet-attached workstation, I can open a session or window to these information providers, ask a question, and capture the results directly to my file system—without getting up from my desk, or requiring a modem or an extra phone line. Depending on the workstation I'm using, I can continue working in another window, read e-mail—even access other services at the same time.
>
> The cost of full-text information delivery via the Internet is VERY competitive: a typical article from a newspaper or a trade publication can cost under $2.00; versus typical $9.00 to $12.00 per article charges for paper copies. (The network-delivered document is not pretty, though.)

For organizations who use these services, Internet-based access can simplify telecom provisioning. Joel Maloff, Vice President-Client Services, at Advanced Networks & Services (Elmsford, NY), points out:

> An organization can easily be spending five to ten thousand dollars annually in telephone access costs to just one of these on-line vendors. For the same amount of money, it's possible to get a full-time, higher bandwidth connection to the Internet, capable of supporting not only the access to this service, but all the other Internet activities as well—such as access to other on-line commercial information services.

For individuals and small organizations whose Internet access may be through a dial-up terminal-type shell account (e.g., NYC's PANIX system) or network connection (e.g., PPP from a PowerBook to CERFnet's Dial'n'CERF service), connectivity costs anywhere from $1 to $5 per hour—a clear savings. And for the vendors, the Internet offers marketing and operations benefits; for example:

- One link to an "outsourced" global access network already serving current and potential customers.
- A way to provide use-for-free limited access as a marketing tool. Recordings for the Blind (Princeton, NJ), for example, is making access to its catalog listings freely available via the Internet; their paying users can also place orders.

To be fair, Internet-based access does have potential down-sides:

- Availability, response time, and reliability may not always be adequate for production requirements (i.e., doing business). Because you're sharing the network, you can be affected by congestion from other traffic (e.g., big image files being transferred). Also, you may be traversing several networks, possibly with differing bandwidth levels and service quality.
- Internet connections require care, feeding, and management. As mentioned elsewhere, plugging your organization directly into the Internet requires some overhead of planning, administration, equipment, costs, and security management (i.e., keep service's X.25 and dial-up numbers and accounts on hand for back-up access methods).
- Many of the existing user interfaces will need some changes. For example, the <BREAK> key used by many interfaces won't work over Internet connections.

### The advantages of offering access via the Internet

For many organizations, the ability to access one or more of these information services via the Internet is by itself sufficient reason to plug in. Taylor Walsh, President of Washington Information Services (Washington, D.C.) and author of the report *New Commerce: A Report on Trends and Opportunities in the Emerging National Public Network* (GT Communications, Sacramento, CA, Oct. 1992), states: "The information providers that are connecting to the Internet are trying to reach their existing clientele through less expensive methods."

Equally, in at least several cases, commercial on-line information providers report having been literally "forced" to join the Internet—to get desired organizations as customers, that is. Many academic institutions specify "Internet access" as the preferred, even only, access mechanism they will accept. In turn, many customers are finding that by using the Internet as an alternative way to get to these pay-for-use services, the savings in overall telecommunications expenditures (i.e., long-distance phone calls and other charges) help pay for the cost of their Internet connection and thereby subsidize or otherwise justify their other Internet-related activity.

## Access, Internet style

Plugging into the Internet is bringing changes to how information providers can provide "new ways of accessing" their information instead of just using the Internet purely as a replacement method to access the service. These changes, not surprisingly, echo the past few years' evolution in the "home-grown Internet utilities" such as archie, Gopher, HYTELNET, WAIS, and WorldWideWeb. (Traditional commercial services such as CompuServe are showing signs of following suit.) Internet-style service methods include:

- Graphic interfaces that make use of menus, mice, icons, color, etc., for the access programs run by users on their DOS, Windows, Macintosh, X Window system/Motif, and other systems (different programs for each type of system, of course). An example is the TurboGopher client program for the Macintosh.
- Using "client" programs to access these services versus purely terminal-emulator style access. The client program handles a lot of the work of formulating queries, presenting the results, capturing them, and often some of the subsequent processing.
- Offering information either (1) delivered to your site, such as the UPI newswire service, offered by ClariNet, or newspapers and journals, via American Cybercast, or (2) by accessing a server run by the organization (e.g., many of the WAISed databases). Some organizations, such as Counterpoint Publishing, offer both options, plus CD-ROM delivery of accumulated information for historical searching.
- Using popular, familiar Internet tools which are widely and inexpensively or freely available and many users are already familiar with, such as Gopher and WAIS clients and Usenet newsreader. For example, the UPI newswire feed from ClariNet and the Reuters newswire feed from MSEN Inc. arrives as articles organized into hierarchies of Usenet Newsgroups. You can browse and read articles with your favorite newsreader program. And if your site has set up the appropriate facilities, articles get indexed via WAIS several times daily, letting you do keyword searches to locate articles containing a match for "Clinton/Gore electronic highway." Similarly, Counterpoint Publishing offers the *Federal Register* and *Commerce Business Daily,* two key daily publications from the U.S. government via the Internet; you can browse, search, and read (you'll need an account for some of this) using a newsreader, Gopher, and/or WAIS. (They have a Gopher/WAIS client available via **telnet**, in case you don't have or want to run your own locally.)

If you have and already know how to use these tools, becoming a user of such services is as simple as knowing about it and where to find it—adding a few Newsgroups to your Usenet subscription profile and finding the appropriate Gopher menu and adding it to your "Gopher profile" as a *bookmark*. Many tools even let you define and save a search query, which then is reexecuted automatically the next time you select it.

- Ability to save, forward, and print results. Gopher, WAIS, and Usenet newsreaders typically include options that let you easily save and share what you find. Common options (not every tool offers every one, though) include:
  - Save results as a file in your account
  - E-mail results to yourself or someone else
  - Queue results to a printer
- Most Usenet newsreader programs also include the ability to "pipe" results through another Unix command.

## Sample Information Services Available on the Internet

Let's take a look at some of the commercial and related information services that were Internet-accessible as of early 1993 (Fig. 14.1 gives a partial list.) More pop up every week; one job for the anticipated "Internet Yellow Pages" will be ways to list and locate such services.

### Commercial services offering Internet access

By early 1993, most of the leading business-oriented on-line information and database services had connected to the Internet, allowing users to access their accounts via remote login (**telnet**) as an alternative to other telephone or network methods.

**DIALOG information services.** "DIALOG is a repository of 'industrial grade' information, intended for use in the corporate or professional environment," says DIALOG engineering marketing manager Mike Yuen. At the other end of the spectrum, services like Prodigy are more for home, entertainment, and consumer services; CompuServe is in the middle. DIALOG's information is used by researchers, according to Yuen. "Our best customers are librarians."

BRS (Bibliographic Retrieval Service) brs.com
CompuServe hermes.merit.edu
Data-Star reserve.rs.ch
DELPHI delphi.com
Dialog / Knowledge Index dialog.com
Dow Jones News/Retrieval djnr.dowjones.com
EPIC/FirstSearch epic.prod.oclc.org
Medlars medlars.nlm.nih.gov
LEXIS/NEXIS (Mead Data General) lexis.meaddata.com
OnLine BookStore world.std.com
ORBIT orbit.com
RLIN (Research Libraries Information Network)
 rlg.stanford.edu or rlin.stanford.edu

**Figure 14.1** Internet-accessible information services and addresses.

DIALOG has been making its services reachable via the Internet since 1992. "We want to be available on a medium that researchers are familiar with," Yuen states. "Additionally, the Internet represents a facility for features that you cannot get on some of the public packet nets (e.g., file transfer, e-mail)."

As of early 1993, DIALOG users are charged based on a combination of session time and "hits," or records retrieved. DIALOG can be accessed via methods such as TymNet, SprintNet, a 1-800 number, their own 1500-node network, and via the Internet. A low-end user might run up a monthly bill of a few hundred dollars—but high-end user tabs can easily be in the tens of thousands of dollars. As of early 1993, DIALOG was charging its users $3 per hour access via the Internet, versus roughly $11 per hour via an X.25 network (plus usage, in either case—and this doesn't include the cost of *your* access to the Internet).

**Dow Jones News/Retrieval.** Although there is some overlap, each information service has tended to select and focus on a specific market and specific set of databases and publications. Owned by the same folks who do the *Wall Street Journal*, Dow Jones (Princeton, NJ) is a leading provider of on-line business financial news and information, with over 1300 publications and 70 databases. Dow Jones targets business information; their customers include businesses, universities, and folks involved in the stock market.

According to Maggie Landis, Public Relations Liaison at Dow Jones, Dow Jones/News Retrieval's data repositories include over 150 Gbytes of raw data (article and publication text) in text files and 100 Gbytes of financial corporate and other databases. Additionally, on a daily basis, DJ/NR typically adds 15,000 new documents and 5000 articles from the newswires and updates several hundred thousand stock quotes and other datums. "We found our academic customers all had access to the Internet," reports Landis. "For them to disconnect, and then dial into our News Retrieval service was harder. If we were on the Internet, they could get to us easier. And users see faster connections, making retrieval less time-consuming."

**DELPHI, CompuServe, etc.—stock quotes, On-line Airline Guides, encyclopedia, and other consumer information.** One of the reasons many people sign up for on-line consumer services such as DELPHI and CompuServe is quick on-line access to stock quotes, the On-Line Airline Guide, encyclopedias, and other information. Are these resources available through the Internet? Yes—for a price, of course. Both DELPHI and CompuServe—and possibly others by now—can be accessed via **telnet** remote login; both these services offer these types of resources. You'll need an account with CompuServe, DELPHI, etc., of course, in addition to your Internet account.

As of early 1993, for example, DELPHI had connected its systems directly to the Internet, joining the ranks of the public-access Internet site. Users can access their DELPHI accounts by telnetting to "delphi.com" (e.g., from an account at a company on the Internet or from another public-access site, via

PSI's Global Dial-Up Service). Because DELPHI has connected its systems fully to the Internet, DELPHI users (who have paid the additional monthly charge for access to Internet services) can use Internet facilities such as **telnet,** Gopher, and Internet Chat Relay that connect to sites and services elsewhere on the Internet.

CompuServe's case is more complicated—and worth understanding, since "Can I access my CompuServe account via **telnet**?" is one of the more frequently asked questions by new Internet users. The answer is Yes, but this may not be the least expensive method.

As of early 1993, it was *possible* to access CompuServe by remote login over the Internet, by telnetting to hermes.merit.edu and from this point selecting CompuServe as the service to connect to. However, CompuServe adds a communications surcharge, billed to the user's CompuServe account, for access done in this fashion. According to a Usenet posting by someone who contacted CompuServe, the surcharge is equivalent to that of 2400-bps calls made using SprintNet—$11.70 per hour during prime SprintNet hours, $1.70 per hour off-prime (prices as of March 1993). (And remember that these charges are in addition to the cost of your account—and the surcharge "meter" keeps ticking even when you're in CompuServe areas labeled "FREE.") For users within the United States who have modems, calling one of CompuServe's own access numbers is likely to be a less expensive approach. For many users outside the United States, however, using the Internet-based connection may prove the less expensive access method.

Remember that in any of these cases, you'd need an account, with a minimum monthly charge of $5 to $10—more than some people care to spend for a few look-ups per month.

In early 1993, General VideoTex, the company that owns DELPHI, was exploring the possibility of an interesting alternative: offering access to specific information services such as stock quotes, the OAG, or encyclopedias as a pay-for-use service on a per-organization basis. Here, your organization (company, public-access site, etc.) would pay a fixed price, permitting all its users to access these services. For individual users, the costs might be either incorporated as part of your basic service or added to your monthly bill for your Internet account. If and when such services become available, they may provide an adequate solution—not free, naturally, but affordable and easy to use.

### Library catalog, reference, and related services

Libraries have been bringing their card catalogs and other resources on-line for years. However, searching library holdings is like searching anonymous-FTP sites—you really want to be able to search as many sites as possible in a single query rather than to access one, search, access the next, search that, and so on.

The archie Internet resource location system began as an effort to catalog and search anonymous-FTP holdings. Efforts such as OCLC (which predates archie by four decades) and RLIN do the same for library holdings. Of necessity, most of these are pay-for-use services. (Unlike many commercial ones, where monthly bills can hit $50,000 and over, however, the library-oriented services are often comparatively less expensive.)

**Research Libraries Information Network (RLIN).** RLIN is an on-line database service from the Research Libraries Group (RLG), a nonprofit organization. RLIN has an on-line bibliographic database containing descriptions of the cataloged holdings of over a hundred special collections, research libraries, and archives. The RLIN database comprises over 20 million unique titles (the database actually totals over 55 million bibliographic entries, reflecting users' ability to enter their own records for the same title), representing not only books but also music scores, sound recordings, serials, maps, visual materials, manuscripts, government records, and computer files.

RLIN is noted for its access to research-oriented materials not available on-line elsewhere—such as U.N. library holdings, the contents of the Vatican Archives, and the Rigler-Deutsch index to pre-1950 commercial sound recordings. RLIN services include a large bibliographic, abstracting, and indexing database service, drawn from catalogs of its members. RLG also offers CitaDel, its citations-access and document-delivery service, via the Internet, using RLG's Ariel document transmission software. (They also "deliver" via fax and hardcopy.)

According to RLG, CitaDel's popular and scholarly databases contain information about articles, dissertations, and books in fields ranging from art and architecture to business, engineering, law, and public and social policy, indexed by such agencies as University Microfilms, Engineering Information, Library of Congress, and Public Affairs Information Service. To search and retrieve from RLIN and CitaDel, you'll need an account. If your organization or local library doesn't have one, you can arrange for a direct account. (For information, e-mail bl.ric@rlg.stanford.edu or call 1-800-537-RLIN.)

**On-Line Computer Library Center (OCLC).** Considered by many to be the de facto information base for archival information, OCLC has 25 databases, which includes over 26 million card catalog descriptions representing holdings in member libraries. The OCLC databases include one-third of a million archival and manuscript records from many state, museum, and society archives which are themselves unique resources (that is, found at only one site).

OCLC databases are available through EPIC, a command-driven interface intended for use by librarians and experienced searchers, and FIRST-SEARCH, a menu-driven interface for general library patrons. Over 4500 individuals or organizations have EPIC accounts.

OCLC's reference services are available through the Internet; as of early 1993 they were exploring making the cataloging services (card catalog information) Internet-available as well. By using the Internet as a carrier, and connecting to library systems and CWISs, OCLC's "catalog of catalogs" may become a readily available secondary resource for millions of people at universities, libraries, and other places, needing only a VT100-compatible terminal (or emulator) and the knowledge of how to use a card catalog.

**Library of Congress.** Information from the U.S. Library of Congress is available via the Internet in at least two ways. LOCIS, the Library of Congress Information System, became available in May 1993 for remote login (**telnet**) access. (You may want to also check for access via Gopher, anonymous-FTP, WAIS, and other Internet navigation tools in case they have been added.) According to the announcement, LOCIS "includes over 15 million catalog records and over 10 million records for other types of information: federal legislation, copyright registrations, Braille and audio, organizations, and selected foreign legal materials." Keyword searching is provided.

LOCIS is available during the following hours (Eastern Standard Time), except on U.S. national holidays:

| | |
|---|---|
| Monday–Friday | 6:30 a.m.–9:30 p.m. |
| Saturday | 8:00 a.m.–5:00 p.m. |
| Sunday | 1:00 p.m.–5:00 p.m. |

The address for LOCIS is locis.loc.gov (140.147.254.3). LOCIS remote login supports both line mode and 3270 mode. On-line manuals should be available by anonymous-FTP from seq1.loc.gov in directory /pub/LC.Online; you should also be able to buy printed manuals.

The "card catalog" for the U.S. Library of Congress is also available for searching by remote login via the Internet through Data Research Associates (St. Louis, MO), as a public service, with the restriction that access to this database may not be used for "cataloging or competitive purposes." According to Carl Grant, Vice-President of Sales & Marketing, the DRA Library of Congress database contains over 3.5 million cataloging records, representing the "Books All, Maps, Music, Serials, and Visual Materials services as distributed by the Cataloging Distribution Service (CDS) of the Library of Congress." Internet users may search this database by author, title, author/title, ISBN, ISSN, and LCCN as well as qualifying searches by language, date, or format. As of early 1993, these searches can be done without charge; DRA was also investigating offering keyword and subject search features as a pay-for-use option.

While the DRA database represents only a subset of the full Library of Congress database offered through LOCIS, the DRA one is available 24 hours a day, and its search tools are more geared for use by the public. For additional information, contact:

Data Research Associates, Inc.
Sales Department
1276 North Warson Road
St. Louis, MO 63105
(314) 432-1100
1-800-325-0888
E-Mail: sales@dranet.dra.com

**Other libraries.** As indicated earlier, the on-line catalogs for over 600 libraries in two dozen countries are accessible via the Internet.

### Internet-style information services: New information and Internet methods

Another exciting development in the 1992 to 1993 time frame has been the surge of Internet-based, Internet-style information services, making use of tools like Gopher, WAIS, and Usenet newsreaders (which you've probably begun to try by now). By early 1993, new types of information and new organizations offering them were appearing at the rate of one a week. Here's a look at a few of these.

**ClariNet: News and then some.** As also mentioned in the Usenet section, ClariNet Communications provides information delivered to Internet sites (and dial-up BBSs) and users in the form of Usenet Newsgroup articles, in over 200 Newsgroups, for a regular fixed-price subscription fee.

According to ClariNet founder Brad Templeton (brad@clarinet.com):

> Like many printed newspapers—not to mention much of the radio and television electronic media—we generate only a small portion of our reporting ourselves. We gather news from newswires, news and feature syndicates, computer industry reporters and other sources and put it in a form that network users can easily read.
>
> Our niche is to sell valuable, copyrighted news directly to people's networks. We publish UPI wire service news including international, national, and local news, sports, business, stock market and technology news, along with radio headline news summaries for Canada, the USA, and 35 local regions. We add to this daily computer industry news, syndicated features and a rather unusual product called the Street Price Report, which is a database of direct buyer prices on over 4000 items of computer equipment, gathered from the ads in magazines like *PC* and *Computer Shopper*.
>
> For most of our current customers, ClariNet is available as Usenet-like groups, under the clari.* hierarchy. This means users at a subscribing site can access and read a group with software they're probably already using.

You may be able to apply other Internet tools to this information, making it accessible to even more users, including novice and nonexpert users. At Software Tool & Die's World where I have my primary Internet account, the ClariNet UPI feed can be viewed via WAIS, enabling me to do a search against keywords and phrases, displaying all matches and giving me the option to view the full articles. As of late 1992, ClariNet was sending about two Mbytes per day to an estimated 25,000 readers at subscribing universities and companies.

Costs for ClariNet range from $9.95 per year for something as simple as an individual e-mail subscription to the Dave Barry column to a price to organizations based on the number of users and number of sources made available.

For medium-to-large organizations, it would cost about $1 per month per reader for all the material published by ClariNet. For more information, contact ClariNet at:

ClariNet
Box 1479
Cupertino, CA 95015
1-800-USE-NETS, 408-296-0366
E-Mail: info@clarinet.com

**MSEN Inc.—Reuters.** MSEN Inc., in addition to user accounts and "anonymous-FTP space for rent," offers the Reuters news service, delivered as a hierarchy of Usenet Newsgroups.

**Counterpoint Publishing: U.S. government daily information.** The U.S. government emits an astonishing amount of information available to anyone free or for a price. Two daily publications closely followed by many companies and universities, both within the United States and internationally, who work with the U.S. government or are affected by its regulations, are the *Federal Register* (*FR*) and the *Commerce Business Daily* (*CBD*).

The *Federal Register* is an official U.S. government daily publication containing all proposed and final rules and notices from more than 130 government agencies, from the Department of Defense and Environmental Protection Agency to dozens of smaller ones. Articles in the *FR* contain, for example, new EPA regulations, grant and funding opportunities, Presidential documents, and hundreds of other proposals, rules, and meeting notices each day.

"If you're in a regulated industry, university, etc., you have to read the *Register* every day, because it's the only place these new regulations and information about meetings about them can be found," according to Sandy Friedman, President of Counterpoint Publishing (Cambridge, MA). Other organizations who follow the *FR,* according to Friedman, include universities, especially contract and grant administrators looking for funding opportunities, as well as government agencies, corporations, and libraries.

The *Commerce Business Daily* is a daily listing of all U.S. government procurement invitations, research opportunities, contract awards, subcontracting leads, sales of surplus property, and foreign business opportunities. The readership encompasses anyone who's a government contractor, which can include universities and service organizations, who may be interested in bidding or otherwise being aware of activity.

The U.S. Government Printing Office (GPO) publishes these two publications daily—in 8-point type (tiny stuff) on thin paper. The *Commerce Business Daily* is typically 50 to 75 pages long—a lot of reading each day to find those items you need to know about! The GPO also sells *FR* and *CDB* information in electronic format. Database services such as DIALOG have carried the *Federal Register* for years. Organizations such as Counterpoint have offered the information in CD-ROM format. In early 1993, Counterpoint Publishing began offering both the *Federal Register* and *Commerce Business Daily* via the Internet in a format usable by popular Internet user tools including Usenet, Gopher, and WAIS.

"Anyone with a direct connection to the Internet can now browse, search, and retrieve the full text of any article printed in the *Federal Register,*" says Sandy Friedman. "Articles appear the same day that the GPO makes them available in electronic format." (Often almost a day before the printed version is available.) Organizations can either receive the information locally in bulk via a Usenet News-style feed and browse it via Usenet newsreader programs, or they can access the information over the Internet on Gopher or WAIS servers run by Counterpoint. In the latter case, users may either run local Gopher or WAIS client programs or use **telnet** to do a remote login to Gopher or WAIS client programs at Counterpoint.

The various options have different pricing structures; which one makes sense for you will depend on how many concurrent and/or total users you have and how many of the *Federal Register* Newsgroups you want to access, etc. Counterpoint intends to make the Table of Contents and some information categories available without charge. Expect other categories of government information to follow (and also expect other organizations besides Counterpoint to offer some of the same information). For more information, contact:

Counterpoint Publishing
Cambridge, MA
800-998-4515
617-547-4515
fedreg@internet.com

**The OnLine BookStore.** Want books—or a part of a book? How about finding a bed-and-breakfast by searching a book about it on-line or listening to poets read their work as you see the text or hearing an author's commentary on their stories or search and retrieve encyclopedia and reference articles or download sample chapters of new books? Welcome to the OnLine Bookstore (OBS), a joint venture between The World (Brookline, MA) and literary agency/book packager Editorial Inc. (Rockport, MA) that opened for business in early 1993.

Users may browse through the title catalog free; there are additional charges associated with "opening" a title (e.g., to read, search, or download from it). Charges vary based on the book and type of activity; for example, requesting a download of the entire book incurs a fixed cost—less than the cost of buying the book in printed form, estimates Barry Shein, President of The World and co-founder of the OBS—while reading and searching will have time-based charges. (According to Shein, authors will receive royalties based on access to their works. For example, on a full download, they receive amounts comparable to the royalty for a book sale.)

The OnLine Bookstore will be making a variety of works of fiction and nonfiction available for reading and viewing and downloading via the Internet, many including audio, scanned-in photos, and possibly other data types. Initial OBS offerings included prose and poetry by John Ashbery, Robert Coover, and Gregory Stock. OBS nonfiction guidebooks scheduled for Spring 1993 included: *The Vintage Guide to Classical Music, Bed and Breakfast of New England,* and *Maya: The Riddle and Rediscovery of a Lost Civilization.*

As of early 1993, you would need an account at The World to access and use the OBS. To reach The World, **telnet** to world.std.com or dial 617-739-WRLD (set your modem to 8 bits, 1 stop bit, Parity none, up to 9.6 kbps) and login as "new." (For more information, send e-mail to obs@world.std.com or call 1-617-739-0202.)

Again, these are only a sampling of commercial services available to you as an Internet user—and the list will only keep getting longer.

## Things to Think About: Service and Reachability

Remember that the Internet, like the phone system, is not a single entity but a network of connected networks. Where you, and services you access, connect can have strong consequences on the quality of service. The more "hops" your traffic has to go through, the greater the possibility of delay and the greater the likely delay. For example, if you're both on the same network provider, response is likely to be best. The more network nodes, and the more networks and gateways, that your traffic has to go through, the more opportunities for delay. Another common source of service slowness, often forgotten, is the load on whatever system you're accessing the Internet from. If your terminal server or computer is heavily loaded, it may respond slower. Don't always blame the network.

In choosing an Internet access provider, either as a user or vendor of commercial on-line services, be sure that your access provider does in fact have "permission" to establish connections to those networks and sites you intend to connect to and can in fact do so. For example, before the CIX (Commercial Internet Exchange) was started in 1991, you couldn't **telnet** or **ftp** from a site on Alternet to one PSInet (although you could send e-mail). Until mid-1992, as a user on The World, I was unable to **telnet** or **ftp** to systems reachable only via the NSFnet. (Remember the "**telnet**-through" technique discussed in the chapter on FTP?) So, although the constraints of AUP (Appropriate Usage Policy) restrictions are going away slowly but surely, and Internet providers increasingly ensuring full connectivity, be sure you "can get there from here."

And lastly, be sure you understand what and how any commercial information services you are accessing charge. Even though the cost of Internet access may be itself low, it's still all too easy to run up a big bill in a short time.

Chapter

# 15

# Anonymous-FTP and Other Archives on the Internet: Gigabytes for the Taking

*I've treacle and toffee, I've tea and I've coffee,*
*soft tommy and succulent chops.*
*I've chickens and conies, and pretty polonies,*
*and excellent peppermint drops.*

*H.M.S. Pinafore*
GILBERT AND SULLIVAN

For many who seek Internet access, the Internet means info-booty—virtual oceans of software and information free for the taking. Electronic mail and Usenet news may be the most popular uses of the Internet. But access to the Internet's archives is the primary motivation of many users.

As an Internet user, you have access to on-line treasure houses—vast repositories, or *archives,* containing gigabytes of programs, text, documents, databases, images, and other materials, available by file transfer downloads and e-mail servers. The contents of these archives represent a mind-boggling variety and volume of software and other files. There are collections of highly specialized software, like mathematical modeling algorithms. And there are general-purpose programs, ranging from public-domain editors and e-mail programs to client software for popular Internet tools like Gopher, WAIS, the Internet Relay Chat, plus educational software, home-computer programs, games, and much, much more.

Not surprisingly, a lot of this software is for Unix systems. But there's also many, many programs for use on DOS, Macintosh, Microsoft Windows, Amiga, VAX/VMS, and other systems, written in everything from ADA and C to FORTRAN, LISP, and CP/M. The amount and variety of files in Internet archives are likely greater than what's available on any given BBS or on-line service.* (I'll give some comparative numbers in a minute.) Not only that, but the majority of these archives are available to you at no additional cost, beyond the use of your Internet account. (Such programs are often referred to as *public-domain* or *freeware.* There will also be a lot of *shareware* programs, which request that users send in a registration fee if they decide after trying it that they want to continue using such programs. There are also bound to be a number of pay-for-use services, requiring an account or fees to access.)

Unlike a given BBS which may be a long-distance call, you reach out to Internet archive sites via the Internet itself. Over the years, also, the Internet community has evolved a set of programs and conventions to make it easier for you to locate and retrieve the files you want. Extensive access to Internet archives can require, and certainly is easier with, a real-time Internet connection (e.g., the ability to access sites via FTP or Gopher). (You'd still be using FTP to do the file transfer, but Gopher will act as the front end to FTP for you.)

However, as you'll see, you don't even need full Internet access to retrieve files from many of these sites. As a rule, if a file is available via anonymous-FTP file transfer, you can retrieve it using electronic mail. Popular files are usually available within Usenet Newsgroups; most public-access Internet and Unix sites maintain archives locally as well, as these are a popular reason to have an account. The more popular collections of files are even available on CD-ROM, as well as magtape or direct downloading by modem from 1-900 numbers.

## What's an Archive Site?

The Internet's archives are actually files stored on computers scattered across the Internet. The term *archive* is used to refer equally to a collection of files, the computer whose storage devices the files are kept on, or the site where the computer is (see "Don't Be Misled by the Term *Archives*" elsewhere in this chapter). Because these archive sites' files are typically accessible via anonymous-FTP, they are also often called *anonymous-FTP sites, FTP archives, anonymous-FTP archives,* and *IAFAs* (for Internet Anonymous-FTP Archives). (FTP, the Internet's file transfer facility, is discussed in Chap. 8; it includes a discussion of anonymous-FTP.) They're also often called *public archives* because their files are set up so they can be accessed via any Internet user connecting to the site.

The access permissions on these files and directories are usually set so that users have "read-only" access—you'll be able to examine, read, and retrieve them, but you won't be able to change or delete them. (Some archive sites will also have places you can "deposit" files.) According to John Granrose (odin@pilot.njin.net), Mike Jones (mjones@ux1.cso.uiuc.edu), and Tom

---

*On the other hand, the core set of popular programs, such as compression utilities, shareware editors, and telecomm packages are bound to be available everywhere and anywhere.

**Internet Archive Space for Rent**

In December 1992, MSEN Inc. (Ann Arbor, MI) announced its new MSEN Archive Service, a simple and easy way for people to publish materials on the Internet without having to have their own site or system, or even their own Internet access or account. According to Ed Vielmetti, MSEN's vice president for research, "We offer space on our archive, which you can manage for yourself, so that you can publish your materials on a well-run Internet FTP site." Typical uses, Vielmetti suggests, could include new products, service, information guides, (encrypted) beta test or product upgrades, or firmware. Space on MSEN's archive server is available for $0.50 per megabyte per month (minimum $10 per month). You can upload and manage your archive files either via the Internet or via dial-up for those who don't have or want their own Internet account. (Other organizations, such as UUNET, also provide archive space for rent.)

Czarnik (profile@netcom.com) in the anonymous-FTP FAQ document, "Typically, a directory called 'pub' is where the interesting things are stored. Some sites will have a file with a name like ls-lR, that contains a complete list of the files on that site. Otherwise, you can type ls -lR and get such a listing—for some sites, this can take a LONG time."

Some of the Internet archive sites have been in existence for close to 2 decades, in fact. Others are fairly new. The responsibility for some collections of software have been passed from site to site. Many of the sites have arranged to carry copies of the same collections. This is often done using a facility called *mirror* that handles the duplication and synchronizing among sites automatically. These sites are often called *mirror sites.*

Some archive sites are relatively well known. For example, the system ftp.uu.net, run by UUNET Technologies, Inc. (Falls Church, VA), has several gigabytes worth of popular Usenet and Internet file archives; so does Software Tool & Die's World (Brookline, MA). The PANIX public-access Internet site in New York City specializes in Macintosh-oriented files. Some of the files are obscure—but thanks to Internet indexing and search tools like archie, Gopher, VERONICA, and WAIS, you'll be able to ferret (or gopher) them out.

Many of these archive sites are run by organizations or individuals as a free-for-use service to the rest of the Internet community. Some are maintained by educational institutions, others by Internet Service Providers, and still others by individuals and small companies. In fact, it's even possible to "rent" space—by the megabyte-month—to make files available, without having to maintain your own anonymous-FTP server. (See Box: Internet Archive Space for Rent.)

### Don't be misled by the term *archives*

The term *archives,* commonly used to refer to repositories of publicly accessible software and other files, is somewhat misleading, as Peter Deutsch, President, Bunyip Information Systems, an internetworking applications developer in Dorval, Quebec, and coinventor of the archie resource tracking system, and other Internet experts periodically point out:

- *Archives may not be permanent.* There is no guarantee that any particular file—or indeed, an entire repository or site—will be available to the Internet from one moment to the next. Many of the free-for-use public-access sites are provided by individuals or organizations as public service to Internet users, without explicit funding or support. An archive site may "disappear" suddenly if a key person moves to another organization, the organization's policies change, or the use of computer resources or the network connection becomes unacceptable. Similarly, new archive sites may "appear" spontaneously, and existing archive sites may acquire additional "collections." (See Box: Archives Come and Go—The Tale of SIMTEL20.)
- *Archives aren't necessarily coordinated.* There is no guarantee that a given file available on one archive will be available on others. Although many leading archives sites make an effort to obtain and offer popular files, they are under no obligation to do so.
- *Archives may not retain files.* Don't count on archive sites retaining old files and older versions. Every file takes up space. Archive site administrators may easily decide to delete older, less-in-demand files in favor of new ones.

Increasingly, however, Internet service providers and public-access Internet sites are including popular Internet archive collections among their offerings to help ensure that they'll "have a home" and be more readily available to Internet users.

## Archive Sites and Files—Lots and Lots of Them

How many archive sites are on the Internet? How many files and how much information is available? It's difficult to give exact numbers, for several reasons. One, the fact that an archive is available to Internet users doesn't automatically mean anyone knows about it. Two, more archive sites continue to become connected, and more organizations keep making archives available. Three, increasingly cheap storage makes it possible for even a small, low-budget to put more information on-line. A few gigabytes' capacity at a site is common these days.

According to Bunyip's Deutsch, as of early 1993, archie servers track over 230 Gbytes worth of 2.1 million files, housed on 1500+ anonymous-FTP sites

### Archives Come and Go—The Tale of SIMTEL20

During the late 1980s, the SIMTEL20 computer at White Sands Missile Range housed what was perhaps for its time the world's largest repository of public-domain shareware and other freely distributable programs—nearly a gigabyte. Managed by Frank Wancho, the 14 or so collections at SIMTEL20 included software written for ADA, CP/M, Unix, Macintosh, and MS-DOS (their own MS-DOS collection, plus the "PC Blue" collection). Then one day, resources to house and access the SIMTEL20 became unavailable. Within a year, however, the bulk of the SIMTEL20 archives found new homes at other archive sites across the Internet. Much of the SIMTEL20 archives are also available via CD-ROM.

in companies, universities, government agencies, BBSs, and other organizations around the world, all connected to the Internet. Even allowing for duplicates, versions for different platforms, and updates, that's still a *lot* of files—enough to fill over 100 million floppy disks or 250 CD-ROM disks—and the true number is likely far more.

## O.K., So What's in Internet Archives?

These millions of files include programs for use in MS-DOS, Unix, C, ADA, Apple, Mac, Amiga, VAX, CP/M, and other types of systems. In addition to software, Internet file archives also include text, documents, abstracts, graphic images, databases, many types of scanned images, and prerecorded sounds. Much of the code is shareware, freeware, or public-domain software. Many companies are also using the Internet as part of their distribution channel; Apple, for example, makes some software for the Macintosh available for downloading via the Internet.

By comparison, Rosalind Resnick reported in her article, "Exploring the Online World," in *Home Office Computing* (Feb. 1993, p. 72) that GEnie offers 100,000+ files; America On-Line, 70,000+; CompuServe, 50,000; and DELPHI and Prodigy, through ZiffNet, 2500. On a basis of purely comparing numbers, that is maybe 10 percent of what's on the Internet.

### A sampling of popular Internet archive sites

Here are some of the popular Internet archive sites, based on information in the Anonymous-FTP Sites list and other sources:

- If you're a Mac user, check out:

  ftp.apple.com

  sumex-aim.stanford.edu

  mac.archive.umich.edu

- Microsoft Windows users may want to cruise oak.oakland.edu for applications running under Microsoft Windows 3.1.
- For public-domain TCP/IP tools for microcomputers such as packet drivers and mailers, there are Grape and Sun servers at Potsdam, NY.

Other sites to consider exploring:

- wuarchive.wustl.edu. For MS/DOS, Mac, Atari, Amiga, Unix, etc., look at Mirrors Simtel20.
- oak.oakland.edu. For MS/DOS, Mac, CP/M, Unix, others. Mirrors Simtel20 collection.
- titan.cs.rice.edu. For the official SunSpots (Sun Microsystems) archives, mailing list archives, sources, sounds, etc.
- software.watson.ibm.com. The IBM official OS/2 anonymous-FTP site.

- aixpdslib.seas.ucla.edu. The official AIX (RS/6000) source server.
- schizo.samsung.com. Has archives of the Usenet groups alt.sources, comp.sources.games, comp.sources.sun, comp.sources.unix, and comp.sources.x, various networking software, and GIF archives.
- export.lcs.mit.edu. X11R4; official repository of contributed X Windows System software.
- mars.ee.msstate.edu. Amiga, Atari, and IBM/PC files.
- oswego.oswego.edu. Macintosh, IBM/PC, Commodore (C128/C64, not Amiga).

Some other recommended sites:

archive.umich.edu

ftp.funet.fi

ftp.uu.net

src.doc.ic.ac.uk

### A taste of archives—samples of what's in the Internet archives

Here's a sampling of what you can find in Internet public-access archives:

- Apple Computer has made available via the Internet everything from System 7.0 for the Macintosh and new software updates to public-domain code programs and documents (from ftp.apple.com).
- Looking for CP/M programs? MS-DOS, Macintosh, or Unix? See the SIMTEL20 Software Archives, available from numerous sites (and via CD-ROM).
- Popular user programs for TCP/IP users, including: the Eudora mailreader program for Mac and Window users; TCP/IP and UUCP code; clients and some servers for Internet tools such as archie, Gopher, and WAIS.
- The Dante Project. Attention, Dante scholars—over 600 years of commentary on Dante Alighieri's *Divine Comedy* (and the Petrocchi version of the poem) can be accessed by **telnet** at lib.dartmouth.edu. (For information send e-mail to dante@dartmouth.edu.; *Note:* Texts are in their original languages, without translations.)
- Gene-Server (gene-server@bchs.uh.edu) offers e-mail-based database searching and software distribution. You can request an entry from GenBank, from the Protein Information Resource protein sequence database, query the Matrix of Biological Knowledge, and get molecular biology software for your Macintosh, DOS, Unix, and VAX/VMS computers. (For a starter help file, send a message containing "HELP".)
- The Medieval and Early Modern Data Bank, a project at Rutgers University cosponsored by the Resource Libraries Group, Inc., gives paid subscribers of RLIN (the Research Libraries Information Network) access

to scholarly data on the medieval and early modern periods (A.D. 800 to 1800, roughly), such as paleopathology studies, wills and inventories, and records of taxation, parishes, companies, records, etc.

- Want mathematical software? Send the on-line e-mail message "send index" to netlib@ornl.gov. Software collections include approximation algorithms, gaussian elimination, univariate quadrature, and lots more.

## Who Uses Archives?

Who uses the Internet archives? *Lots* of people. Software developers, home computer users, Amiga hackers, engineers, physicists, mathematicians, literature professors, amateur radio operators, bicyclists, music lovers, science fiction fans, cooks—there's something there for almost everyone. To give you a sense of how strongly Internet archives are used: According to Christinger Tomer in the November/December 1992 issue of *Academic and Library Computing,* during 1991, from one site alone, St. Louis' Washington University (which includes a copy of the SIMTEL archives in its holdings), copies of files representing over $7^1/_2$ million files and 800 Gbytes were retrieved via anonymous-FTP file transfer—an average of 20,000 files and 2 Gbytes a day. These requests originated from over 70,000 systems across the Internet.

### Is what you want available?

As you can see, there are literally millions of programs and documents of potential interest available through the Internet. But just like you should check your own bookshelves and local library before requesting an interlibrary loan for a book, follow common-sense procedures before consuming Internet bandwidth and system resources unnecessarily. The first step is to determine whether what you want is available and if so, where from. With thousands of sites to choose from, this could easily be a daunting, impossible task. Fortunately, in the past year or so, Internet tools such as archie, Gopher, VERONICA, HYTELNET, and WAIS have turned this step into one any user can do (see Chap. 10 for information about these, WAIS, and other Internet front ends, navigators, and services).

To discover and locate files:

- See if your site already has it. Start by looking locally, on your system, and elsewhere within your organization. Is the program already available on your system, LAN, or site? Check the public directories. Ask your systems administrator. For documents, check with your librarian, etc. Consider posting a message to your local message board. There's no point in downloading and installing additional copies.

- Query the archie name and description indexes of Internet archive holdings to find the "network-closest" site. This is especially important information for users at the far end of expensive, low-bandwidth international links or whose sites or networks are restricted from connecting to primary FTP sites for desired code.

- Work through the menu(s) of your favorite Internet navigator(s), such as Gopher, HYTELNET, TechInfo, WAIS, or COMPASS, to connect to or get Internet addresses for popular Internet archive sites.
- Query the VERONICA index of "GopherSpace" entries.
- Read, and post queries to, the appropriate Usenet Newsgroups—after checking the associated FAQ documents. Good places to start include:

  comp.archives

  news.answers

  comp.sources

  news.newusers.questions

  Be sure to read through the FAQs "periodic" messages before posting a query; they contain answers to a surprising range of questions.
- And if all else fails, ask your local system administrator for advice.

As you may discover, many files are available from more than one location. The leading networks and public-access sites make a concerted effort to "mirror," or replicate, the most popular archive files and collections. (They have programs to do this automatically, of course.) For example, at one point I did an archie query for the Eudora mail reader program for the Macintosh and learned that the file was available from close to four dozen sites. Distributing copies to a dozen or more locations across the Internet spreads the load of supporting file retrieval requests among more of the Internet community. Additionally, it helps minimize the use of more expensive and lower-bandwidth network connections by bringing popular collections "closer" to local user communities.

## Accessing the Archives: By File Transfer, E-Mail, and More

Once you've found a site with a copy of the file(s) you are interested in, if it isn't already available on your local system, the next step is to retrieve it. The archives on the Internet are available by a wide variety of mechanisms and tools to suit almost everyone's needs. The anonymous-FTP site FAQ provides an excellent up-to-date overview of current methods and tools; I strongly advise you read this FAQ before trying to find and retrieve files from Internet archives.

### Locally available archives

In searching for files, follow the rule "Think globally, start locally." "The first thing you should do is exhaust the local resources that are available to you," points out Czarnik in the anonymous-FTP site FAQ. "Often, a program that you are looking for will already be accessible somewhere on your system." Good places to look locally include in directories with names like /sources or /pub and for likely looking topics in local on-line "help" information.

"Since each site has different local resources, it's impossible to give details here about the resources at any specific site," according to Czarnik's FAQ. "All that can be said is, 'Find someone at your site to ask.' Nearly every site has someone whose job it is to answer questions from other users, and the sites that don't have someone doing it officially often have someone doing it unofficially."

### Anonymous-FTP file transfer

Anonymous-FTP is probably the best known and most frequently used way to retrieve files from Internet archives. This means using the TCP/IP **ftp** command to copy the desired file(s) from the remote site to your system. As explained in Chap. 8, anonymous-FTP is a feature built into FTP server software to let a group of users access and retrieve files without each needing their own account on the remote system. The most commonly used user IDs on anonymous-FTP sites are "anonymous" and "ftp." If asked for a password, standard Internet practice is to give your e-mail address. Remember, "anonymous-FTP" is *not* "anonymous"—the computer you're contacting knows the account-name, computer, and site you are connecting from, and can capture that information. So even if there's no "Password" prompt, or you don't give any response to one, your identity is still known. "Public-access-FTP" or "anyone-FTP" would be more accurate.

Gopher and many new versions of FTP include features for using anonymous-FTP that will automatically supply the user-ID and give your e-mail address (or whatever else you've configured to be provided) in response to the Password: prompt.

---

*Tip:* For anonymous-FTP, use Gopher and other navigators or front ends such as **ncftp**. Using Gopher and other Internet tools can make using archie and anonymous-FTP much, much easier, as you'll rapidly discover.

---

## Usenet *.sources Newsgroups

In addition to the Internet anonymous-FTP archives, many programs and other files are distributed via Usenet *.sources Newsgroups, such as comp.sources.* The comp.archives Newsgroup, for example, moderated by Ed Vielmetti, contains:

> Announcements of archive sites and their contents. If you cannot find what you're looking for in the comp.archives postings available at your site at any given time, then you can read the Newsgroup for a while and watch for new postings that are of interest to you, or you can try to find an archive site that archives the postings in comp.archives (e.g., wuarchive.wustl.edu, cs.dal.ca).

Before "trolling the Internet" for source code or other files, you should read the "anon-FTP FAQ"—the document of Frequently Asked Questions (and their answers) for anonymous-FTP. As it says in this FAQ, "This posting discusses the resources available to people who are looking for source code.

Please read it before posting source code requests to comp.sources.wanted, alt.sources.wanted or any other Newsgroup."

### Via e-mail

If you can't use FTP because you don't have a real-time connection to the Internet (or any other reason), don't despair. You can still search, request, and receive files—by e-mail. As explained in Chap. 10, you can query the archie indexes via e-mail to locate files of interest. It may take you several rounds of queries to identify the files and sites you feel are the best prospects. Once you've located the file(s) of interest, you can submit a request to one of the many "ftp-by-email" servers located across the Internet. If you are accessing the Internet through a service such as PSI's PSILink, it may include a "batch request for anonymous-FTP" service.

As discussed in Chap. 5, these facilities:

- Accept e-mail messages containing your commands for an anonymous-FTP session.
- Perform the anonymous-FTP commands to connect from the ftp-by-email server to the designated archive site(s) and retrieve the designated file(s) back to the ftp-by-email server.
- Send the retrieved file(s) back to you in e-mail message(s). Many ftp-by-email servers will let you request various types of encoding and compression, and split long files into several messages short enough for the intervening mail systems to handle. Because of the number of requests these servers get, don't expect necessarily instant response. There may easily be a thousand or more unfilled requests ahead of you. Most of these servers will acknowledge your request messages, including an estimate of when your request will be handled.

### Other ways to get Internet archives

In addition to file transfer, Usenet, and e-mail, there are a number of other options that may be appropriate:

- *CD-ROM and magtape.* Many files and collections are available on physical storage media, which you can order by phone, e-mail (if you don't mind including a credit card number in an unsecured message), fax, or regular mail. At about $25 to $50 per disk, if you've got a CD-ROM drive; this may be easier than downloading all those megabytes. Some files are available for the cost of the media reproduction, shipping, and handling.
- *FTP server.* Internet account providers such as PSILink and WorldLink offer anonymous-FTP service similar to that of ftp-by-email. You enter a request which is submitted for processing; in a subsequent session, if the file has been retrieved, you download it.
- *UUCP retrieval.* Explaining how to use UUCP is outside the scope of this book, but it's worth mentioning it as an option. Many Internet and Usenet

archive sites permit files to be retrieved over dial-up phone connections, from your computer and modem, connecting via UUCP. UUCP stands for Unix-to-Unix Copy Protocol; however, versions are available for DOS, Windows, Macintosh, and many other types of computers. UUNET Technologies, Inc., for example, offers 1-900 access (1-900-GET-SRCS) via interactive file transfer to several gigabytes of popular Internet/Usenet sources, using UUCP. (Don't forget that you will be billed for use of the 1-900 number.) In addition to UUNET Technologies' 1-900 access, there are hundreds of anonymous-UUCP archive sites around the world you can access if you have UUCP and know how to use it. (See information about obtaining the "nixpub" list in Chap. 2.)

- *Dial-up retrieval via KERMIT, X-Modem, Y-Modem, or Z-Modem protocols.* UUNET Technologies' 1-900-GET-SRCS number also supports access and file transfer using popular file transfer protocols: KERMIT, X-Modem, Y-Modem, and Z-Modem. One or more of these are included in most of today's telecom and terminal emulation packages; you should therefore be able to retrieve files with almost any PC and modem combination.

## Before You Install or Use Retrieved Software

It is imperative that you practice "safe nets" in regard to software retrieved from the Internet (or any other source, for that matter):

- Check with your systems and/or network administrator before installing anything that will involve Internet use.
- Check incoming code for viruses, and scan your system regularly.

If you are getting into the habit of anonymously FTPing files for your Mac, you should get in the habit of scanning for viruses, just as you would for programs downloaded from BBSs, suggests Jeff Schiller, Network Manager at M.I.T.'s Network Center. "If you are going to execute code you got from somewhere, you better have a way to believe it is safe." Be very suspicious of code for games, Schiller adds—this is one of the favorite places for putting viruses.

## Compressing, Decompressing, etc.: Packing Files for Storage and Transfer

Storing, transferring, and downloading files across networks can involve a number of challenges. Maintaining on-line archives takes up storage space. Transferring files across the Internet consumes network resources. Downloading them by modem, even at the speeds of 14.4 to 56 kbps achieved by many of today's modems and transfer protocols, takes time when you're retrieving megabytes' worth of binary goodies.

Over the years, the Internet community, along with other network and BBS developers, have devised a variety of schemes, technologies, and conventions to help (1) minimize the storage, transfer, and downloading requirements, (2) simplify the process of retrieving multifile items, and (3) ensure binary files are transferred accurately. Many of these Internet's retrievable files are stored in *archival* format for easy and optimum access by users. This typically includes:

- Packing multiple files and subdirectories into a single master file
- Compressing files, via compression algorithms, to minimize storage and network transfer overhead
- Encoding binary files to permit them to be sent in 7-bit format

Tools to retrieve and uncompress archive files are readily available as well; usually, any site having archived files will also have the software tools to turn archive files into usable ones. (You may have to retrieve the software tools, of course.) PC, Mac, Unix, and other developers have, over time, come up with a well-defined, readily available set of programs and procedures. The main compression program used on most archives is compress. Programs for compressing and packaging include ZIP- and UNZIP-type programs for DOS, BinHex, and StuffIt for Macs, and tar for Unix; for encoding and decoding binary files into highly portable formats, there are programs like Uuencode.

There are too many variations in downloading programs and procedures to cover here. In brief: as a rule, you can expect every archive site to include copies of the appropriate utilities and Readme documentation to let you retrieve and "unwrap" program sources.

### Retrieval tips from the anonymous-FTP FAQ

Here's some advice from the anonymous-FTP FAQ:

> Usually, files are grouped in archive files, so you don't have to get many small files separately. The most common archival file format for the Internet is tar. Occasionally, people use shell archives (shar) instead. Tar archives can be unpacked by running the 'tar' command—you may want to first do a 'tar t' on the file to see what it contains before unpacking it. Be careful when unpacking shell-archives since they have to be run through the Bourne shell to unpack them. (The simplest way is to use the **unshar** command.)

Grouping doesn't necessarily compress files. Files are often stored compressed—for Unix, the most common scheme is the compress program, indicated by a .Z suffix on the file name. Sometimes, people use programs like Arc or Zoo, which are combined archival and compression formats. (There are probably other archival formats as well—talk to the systems staff if you encounter them and don't know how to deal with them.) On Unix systems, the following conventions are usually used as the end of the filename to indicate the type of file:

| Filename suffix | Type of file | Tool to use after retrieving |
|---|---|---|
| .Z | Binary | compress |
| .arc | Binary | ARChive |
| .shar | ASCII | SHell ARchive |
| .tar | Binary | Tape ARchive |
| .uu | ASCII | uuencode/uudecode |
| .zip | Binary | Zip |
| .zoo | Binary | Zoo |
| .z | Binary | GNU zip |

For a chart that will tell you how to decompress files, look for a copy of the file maintained by David Lemson (lemson@uiuc.edu).

Files listing file compression and archiving methods and the programs to uncompress and unarchive (on the PC, Mac, Unix, VM/CMS, AtariST, and Amiga systems) are available via anonymous-FTP, including:

ftp.cso.uiuc.edu /doc/pcnet/compression

gator.netcom.com /pub/profile/compression.Z

Many products include their own programs to convert their files to "7-bit transfer format." For example, WordPerfect includes convert.exe to convert documents between WordPerfect format (which includes all the non-ASCII formatting, fonts, and other codes) into a format that can be included in e-mail messages.

### Mac archiving

For Macintosh users, the Binhex program converts (1) binary files into ASCII (i.e., encoded for 7-bit transmission), usually giving them .hqx suffixes, and (2) restores "binhex"ed files back from ASCII into their original binary format. Programs like StuffIt compress and decompress the file. Figure 15.1 shows how Mac files get prepared for and retrieved from Internet archives.

Jeff Shaevel (shaevel@guest.apple.com) cautions novices that "Sometimes the binhexed files have additional text at the beginning (e.g., mail headers, instructions, disclaimers, and licensing agreements) and this will usually have to be edited out before running the file through the BinHex program."

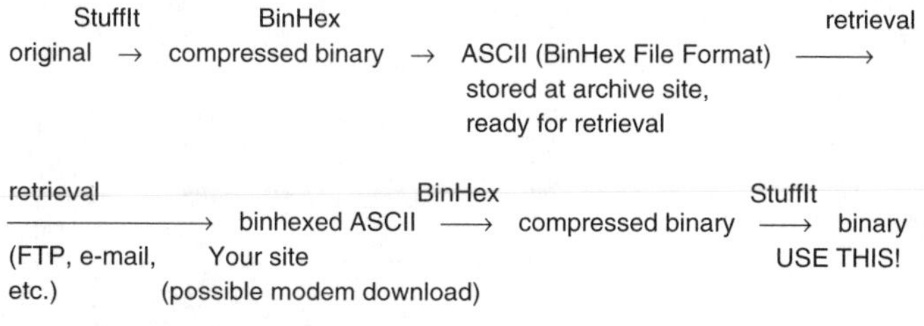


**Figure 15.1** The distribution of Macintosh archive files.

## One user's learning experiences accessing Internet archives

In response to one e-mail query I posted to the Internet while writing this book, Dave Robinson (drobinson@tuxedo.enet.dec.com) offers his "two pennies worth" regarding use of the Internet's archives:

> My first real introduction to the Internet involved retrieving some PD software and text files for an Amiga. Since then I have explored sites that contain PC, MAC, Unix and VMS anonymous ftp sites. Each platform seems to have its own traditional or favorite archive packing methods. Unfortunately, it isn't always easy to figure them out, and the rules seem to change every six months or so.
>
> Even if you want to retrieve PostScript text from somewhere, it often will be "packed" in the format preferred by the provider. I didn't really feel comfortable with ftp, ftpmail services or email transmission of files until I found many de-archiving tools for my three primary platforms, Amiga, Unix & VMS. By searching the net and asking the net wizards, I found executables that run on the Amiga for common MAC, PC, Unix and VMS systems. Then I found the same set including common Amiga de-archiving tools that run on Unix and VMS.

The overview messages for many programs, such as archie and HYTELNET, include summary information on how to retrieve, download, and install program files. Lastly, some communications and TCP/IP packages include these facilities, and may even invoke them automatically for you. For more information:

For procedures involved in FTPing Macintosh files, retrieve and read: ftp-primer.txt on sumex-aim.stanford.edu in the directory /info-mac/reports

The anonymous-FTP FAQ and lists of Files and Sites, posted monthly to the Usenet news.answers and other Newsgroups.

Usenet Newsgroups to read:

| | |
|---|---|
| comp.archives | Descriptions of public access archives (moderated) |
| comp.archives.admin | Issues relating to computer archive administration |
| comp.archives.* | Other announcements about specific archives |
| comp.binaries.* | Source code |
| comp.sources.* | Source code, reviews, bug reports and fixes, etc. |

Chapter

# 16

# Electronic Mailing Lists: How to Join, Read, and Participate in Them

*"I know, my dear Watson, that you share my love of all that is bizarre and outside the conventions and hum-drum routine of everyday life."*

*The Red-Headed League*
SIR ARTHUR CONAN DOYLE

One of the most powerful outgrowths of electronic mail has been the development of *mailing lists,* a.k.a. *electronic mailing lists* or *e-mail lists.* In this chapter, you'll learn how to participate in electronic mail lists, including how to locate, join, contribute to—and leave—them. As you probably know by now, e-mail lists overlap very strongly with Usenet Newsgroups; if you haven't already, you should consider reading Chap. 6. You may also want to see Chap. 17 for its e-mail list aspects.

## E-Mail Lists: Groups of Interested Parties

As you saw in Chap. 5, an electronic mail message can be sent to just one person—or to hundreds, even thousands. The electronic mail software can just as easily make large numbers of copies of your message; the limit is really how many names you're willing and able to type in. Suppose you didn't have to type all those names in each and every time? Suppose you could enter, store, and reuse that list? In fact, you can.

An e-mail name can represent an individual, such as alice@jabber.wock.com—or it can be a *mail alias*, representing a list of e-mail names, stored in a file. An electronic mailing list is single electronic mail name and address, or *mail alias,* that refers to "a list of e-mail addresses to send copies of a message to." Any message sent to this mail alias is copied and sent to every name on this list. It can be stored in a file that you create, own, and manage or in a database managed by your organization's systems and network administrators.

One simple use for this feature is to save typing. For example, to distributed departmental memos, announcements, and reports, create a list with everyone in the department's e-mail address, and then simply do something like

```
% mail my-dept
```

You can even have a number of such lists, perhaps "direct-reports" and "indirect-reports"—and "all-reports," which could simply contain the entries:

direct-reports

indirect-reports

Another use is by topic or interest, say, for example:

| | |
|---|---|
| mac-developers | People interested in Macintosh development |
| info-cdrom | People interested in CD-ROM |

or even:

| | |
|---|---|
| swing-dance | People interested in swing dancing |
| gopher-discuss | People who want to talk about the Internet Gopher |
| dimsum | People who like to eat *dim sum* |

Within a given organization, there can easily be dozens, even hundreds of such lists. Equally well, a given person might be on, and receive mail from, any number of lists, limited only by how much e-mail they're willing to get and read. There's no reason this type of topical mail-sharing has to be limited to a single organization or site. The Internet, after all, can carry e-mail among thousands of organizations. Why not, then, let groups of Internet users who may be at different organizations exchange e-mail in this manner—via mailing lists? Why not indeed? And in fact, we do.

## The Internet's Got Lots of Mailing Lists

Within the Internet community, there are lots of topical mailing lists. How many? It's impossible to know how many total because many are internal to their organizations, or not publicized. Many of these lists are "publicly known"—their existence is not private, and anyone (usually) is welcome to join—meaning, have their name added to the list of people receiving copies of messages. Over time, various people began collecting key administrative information about these lists, put into a "list of mailing lists," commonly called the *List of Lists*.

As of early 1993, the Internet List of Lists listed about 3000 electronic mailing lists. For various reasons, it's impossible to know exactly how many people read each list, or all lists. Some have perhaps a few hundred or even few dozen readers. Some are undoubtedly read by tens, even hundreds of thousands of Internet users.

The topics of the Internet mailing lists are as diverse as the community itself. There's dozens of lists concerning computer science and other aspects of research, science, and engineering. There are also electronic mailing lists for science fiction, dog owners, the commercialization of the Internet, for journalists, ham-radio, techno-nomads, for recipes, for discussions of cultures and theories, amateur magicians—literally almost everything under the sun (and a lot of outer space stuff too).

"Sf-lovers," the most well-known of these, has been in existence since 1979, and was given a special award by the science fiction fan community in 1989, according to TomGalloway. Similarly, the RISKS mailing list, started up in August 1985, has been providing the Internet community with a "Forum on risks to the public in computers and related systems."

Since the Internet can exchange electronic mail with other networks, participation in Internet mailing lists also spills over outside the Internet as fast as a given network can establish the ability to exchange e-mail. Users on ATT Mail, BITNET, CompuServe, and MCI Mail as well as UUCP and FidoNet users—and countless others—participate in Internet mailing lists. These mailing lists, along with Usenet Newsgroups, constitute a global community in excess of 10 million, from every country and continent.

## How Mailing Lists Work: Unmoderated, Moderated, Digest

Like any form of group communication, electronic mailing lists have evolved their own sets of operating methods. An *unmoderated* list means that when you send a message to this list, it is "redistributed"—copies are sent—to all other users automatically. No administrator looks at it or makes any decisions; it simply gets copied and forwarded. In a *moderated* list, all messages go to a person (or group) acting as the *moderator,* who inspects each message and decides whether or not it should be passed along to the list. As a rule, the moderator is acting as a filter for inappropriate messages. This includes messages sent by accident "to the list" that are really intended:

- For the attention of an administrative person, such as "Please add my name to this list"
- As a reply to a specific individual, such as "Let's meet for lunch but don't tell so-and-so."

It may also include messages that aren't relevant to the purpose of the mailing list. The moderator may also decide to not pass along a message because they are concerned that it may be libelous, illegal, or otherwise inappropriate.

Depending on circumstances such as how many messages are sent "to the list" and how important it is for them to be seen quickly, the moderator may pass along each message as quickly as possible. Alternatively, the moderator may let messages accumulate, put them all into a file, and send them as a single message, called a *digest.* The moderator may simply collect messages without comment or may include some overall comments and even include notes within messages (CLEARLY IDENTIFIED BY SOME TYPOGRAPHIC SYMBOLS, AND USUALLY WITH THE EDITOR'S INITIALS, LIKE SO—-DPD). Digests usually include a summary at the beginning of the subjects and authors of the main contents.

There is a standard "digest format" that is understood by many e-mail programs, enabling you to examine and read through a digest message as a series of separate messages. (FAQ documents often follow similar conventions.) Electronic mailing lists thus can be—and have become—electronic newspapers and magazines. Some, in fact, like Sf-lovers and RISKS, have readerships rivaling those of printed publications and often have an influence as great or greater. References to "postings" from these mailing lists are common in Internet documents and in research and academic papers. Within the past few years, trade press articles and even occasionally newspapers and magazines like the *New York Times* have quoted from these mailing lists (with attribution) as sources.

## E-Mail Distribution Methods for Efficient Use of Network and Computer Resources

Mailing lists get distributed in any of a number of ways, including:

- *Mailing from a central point.* Newer versions of e-mail programs let multiple copies to a given site be sent as the list of names followed by a single copy of the actual message. When there are a lot of copies and long messages, this makes a big difference in minimizing network traffic.
- *Local redistribution.* Here, your organization maintains a list locally of people who want to receive a given list. One address for your organization is put on the master central list; for example, jabber-risks@jabber.wock.com. This allows the system administrators at your site to handle mailing list additions and deletions locally.

Usenet Newsgroups are another distribution mechanism for Internet mailing lists and a convenient, powerful way to distribute e-mail lists. E-mail, after all, offers a powerful tool to get messages to lots of individuals. However, for messages that may have many readers at a site, it is harder to make e-mail an efficient distribution mechanism. And for "highly active" mailing lists, which might have anywhere from 10 to 50 messages per day, you might well prefer to have access to lists without them cluttering up your electronic mailbox and forcing you to sort through them to get to work-related messages.

Creating a Usenet Newsgroup for an e-mail list provides an easy solution to the concerns of minimizing the use of network and site resources, enabling users to subscribe and unsubscribe locally and flexibly, even on a per-day basis. It also means that these mailing list messages don't overwhelm interpersonal mail messages and lets you examine, read, and filter messages using the features of Usenet Newsreader programs.

Often, as a mailing list passes a certain threshhold in terms of the number of people interested in it, a corresponding Usenet Newsgroup becomes created, and the e-mail list "gatewayed" to it, such that messages sent as e-mail also appear in the Usenet Newsgroup version and vice versa.

For information on how to read mailing lists which are available as Usenet Newsgroups, see Chap. 6.

### Keep track of your e-mail subscriptions

If possible, you should keep track of "how you subscribe" since you will probably need to know this to "unsubscribe." A common suggestion is to save a copy of your original message in which you request to be added, as well as the acknowledgment message (if there is one) since this often summarizes the "how to unsubscribe" information.

## Using Mailing Lists: Finding, Joining, Contributing to, Leaving

The basic types of activities you do involving Internet electronic mailing list are:

- Finding out about the list
- Joining ("subscribing") and leaving ("unsubscribing")
- Receiving current messages
- Saving, filing, and retrieving previous messages and "back issues"
- Contributing ("posting") messages to a mailing list—new messages, follow-ups
- Replying to an individual regarding a mailing list posting

Most of these tasks can be accomplished solely via e-mail. However, it's possible to also involve some combination of other tools you will learn to use elsewhere in this book, from standard Unix commands and FTP to archie, Gopher, VERONICA, and WAIS.

Moderated lists, especially digest-format moderated lists, typically include most essential information at the beginning or end of each digest message. Figure 16.1 shows the header to a typical "issue" of RISKS, one of the Internet's more long-running and popular e-mail digests (also available as the Usenet Newsgroup comp.risks). This header is taken from a real example, but some changes have been made.

### Finding out about a list

Common ways to learn about relevant lists is for someone to tell you or to see mentions of them in other publications or messages. The List-of-Lists for Internet and BITNET mailing lists is accessible in a number of ways. It's periodically reposted to Usenet in the news.answers and news.announce.newusers Newsgroups and is also available by e-mail and anonymous-FTP file retrieval (e.g., from the Usenet FAQ archives maintained at pit-manager.mit.edu) and in the book *Internet: Mailing Lists* by Edward Hardie and Vivian Neou (Prentice-Hall). (The book obviously won't

**Figure 16.1** RISKS digest header.

From risks@csl.sri.com Mon May 3 10:09:57 1993
Return-Path: <risks@csl.sri.com>
Received: from chiron.csl.sri.com by world.std.com (5.65c/Spike-2.0) id AA26661; Mon, 3 May 1993 10:09:51 -0400
Received: by chiron.csl.sri.com id AA07091
(5.65b/IDA-1.4.3.12 for ddern@world.std.com);
Mon, 3 May 93 07:09:49 -0700
From: RISKS Forum <risks@csl.sri.com>
Sender: RISKS Forum <risks@csl.sri.com>
Date: Mon, 3 May 93 7:09:49 PDT
Subject: RISKS DIGEST 14.57
Reply-To: risks@csl.sri.com
To: ddern@world.std.com
Message-Id: <CMM.0.90.1.736438189.risks@chiron.csl.sri.com>
Status: R

RISKS-LIST: RISKS-FORUM Digest Monday 3 May 1993 Volume 14 : Issue 57

FORUM ON RISKS TO THE PUBLIC IN COMPUTERS AND RELATED SYSTEMS
ACM Committee on Computers and Public Policy, Peter G. Neumann, moderator

Contents:
The risks of non-24-hour days (Debora Weber-Wulff)
Flaws in government computer bond auction (Mark Seecof)
Evading 1-900 blocking (John Carr)
New Computer Virus Reported in Japan (David Fowler)
Stunning vending machines (Edward N Kittlitz)
Junk mail reduction request can add to your junk mail, too (Rich Rosenbaum)
.
.
.
Re: Human vs. computer in space (Craig Partridge, Espen Andersen, Scott Alexander, R. Mehlman)
Re: Worries over the Clipper Chip (Brinton Cooper)
Re: Too much electricity (DonB)

The RISKS Forum is a moderated digest discussing risks; comp.risks is its Usenet counterpart. Undigestifiers are available throughout the Internet, but not from RISKS. Contributions should be relevant, sound, in good taste, objective, cogent, coherent, concise, and nonrepetitious. Diversity is welcome. CONTRIBUTIONS to RISKS@CSL.SRI.COM, with appropriate, substantive "Subject:" line. Others may be ignored! Contributions will not be ACKed. The load is too great. **PLEASE** INCLUDE YOUR NAME & INTERNET FROM: ADDRESS, especially .UUCP folks. REQUESTS please to RISKS-Request@CSL.SRI.COM.

Vol i issue j, type "FTP CRVAX.SRI.COM<CR>login anonymous<CR>AnyNonNullPW<CR> CD RISKS:<CR>GET RISKS-i.j<CR>" (where i=1 to 14, j always TWO digits). Vol i summaries in j=00; "dir risks-*.*<CR>" gives directory; "bye<CR>" logs out. The COLON in "CD RISKS:" is essential. "CRVAX.SRI.COM" = "128.18.10.1". <CR>=CarriageReturn; FTPs may differ; UNIX prompts for username, password.

For information regarding delivery of RISKS by FAX, phone 310-455-9300 (or send FAX to RISKS at 310-455-2364, or EMail to risks-fax@vortex.com).

ALL CONTRIBUTIONS CONSIDERED AS PERSONAL COMMENTS; USUAL DISCLAIMERS APPLY. Relevant contributions may appear in the RISKS section of regular issues of ACM SIGSOFT's SOFTWARE ENGINEERING NOTES, unless you state otherwise.

........................................................................................................

Date: Sun, 2 May 1993 12:26:02 GMT
From: dww@math.fu-berlin.de (Debora Weber-Wulff)
Subject: The risks of non-24-hour days

A student told this quite believable tale about a German steel-producer last week:

The steel production line is completely automated, with the molten ingots having to cool a certain number of minutes/hours before force is applied to flatten them out. It appears the programmers of the system didn't want to construct their own clock, and so from a security point of view they used the

.

.

.

be the completely up-to-date list, but it has other useful information, and may be easier to browse.)

The full lists are on the long side, so look for local copies before retrieving them (and don't post copies of the entire lists to e-mail lists or Usenet Newsgroups). By the time you read this, I predict one or more parties will have made the lists of mailing lists (and Usenet Newsgroups) available by some combination of archie, Gopher, and WAIS keyword searches; there may also be tools to help manage, locate, and subscribe to mailing lists.

**Joining ("subscribing") and leaving ("unsubscribing").** There are a number of ways to join and leave a mailing list. If a list is available as a Usenet Newsgroup, to join, add the appropriate entry to the "dot" file used by the Usenet reader software you use (e.g., if you use **rn** (ReadNews) or **trn** (Threaded ReadNews), add to your ".newsrc" file:

comp.risks:

comp.infosystems.gopher:

alt.internet.services:

etc.

If you have access to the Usenet Newsgroups, this is the most resource-sparing approach and will help reduce the amount of new messages to your electronic mailbox.

To leave a Newsgroup, simply use the appropriate command in your Usenet reader program to "unsubscribe," or edit out the line in your .newsrc file manually, using your text editor.

If you want to receive and contribute to the mailing list as e-mail messages, you want to send e-mail to the appropriate person or computer program that administers the list of recipients. Joining a mailing list in this fashion is also referred to as "subscribing" and "being added." Leaving a mailing list is also referred to as "unsubscribing," "being removed from the list," and "being dropped from the list." As a rule, each mailing list has a separate e-mail name and account for "administrative" messages, such as being added ("subscribing") and removed ("unsubscribing"). To complicate matters, for some lists, these messages are read and processed by a person; others are handled by computer programs. To complicate matters even further, there is more than one type of "mailing list management" computer program and more than one corresponding syntax to send messages to these automated subscription managers.

Notwithstanding, there are relatively established conventions for the administrative e-mail names and addresses and the messages sent to them:

- If your organization supports "local redistribution" administered by humans, send a message to your system administrator (e.g., "staff") indicating the name of the list you'd like to be added to, for example:

```
% mail staff
Subject: Please add me to the RISKS mailing list
Thanks.
Control-D
%
```

- If your organization supports "local redistribution" administered by computers, find out what the appropriate name and address is and the appropriate message format.

> *Tip:* If you aren't sure whether your organization supports local mailing list redistribution, consider calling or sending e-mail to your system administrator to find out.

- If there is a master distribution list, send a message to the list administrator.

The convention for Internet mailing lists is to add "-request" to the list name, before the network address portion. For example:

| Administrative address | Contributions (Postings) address |
|---|---|
| risks-request@csl.sri.com | risks@csl.sri.com |
| com-priv-request@psi.com | com-priv@psi.com |
| archie-people-request@bunyip.com | archie-people@bunyip.com |

As indicated in Chap. 17, there are about 3000 mailing lists that originate from and are administered from BITNET. Most of these mailing lists are administered by a software program named ListServ. Administrative messages go to the address of a ListServ program running on BITNET; contributions go directly to the list's address. See Chap. 17 for more about this.

Traditionally, administrative messages for Internet mailing lists are going to someplace that is by definition specific to that list and are read by a human. Therefore, almost any message, with the information either in the message subject or body text, suffices, as long as it's clear whether you want to be added or removed. Your user-name and e-mail address should be available from the message header itself, unless you want to have messages sent to a different address. Here are four examples:

```
% mail risks-request@csl.sri.com
Subject: Please add me to RISKs
Thanks,
Lem Gulliver
Control-D

% mail risks-request@csl.sri.com
Subject: Please add me to RISKs
Please add me as
lemg@flack.laputa.com
Rather than to this account.
Thanks,
Lem
Control-D

% mail com-priv-request@psi.com
Subject: add
Control-D

% mail com-priv-request@psi.com
Subject:
Remove me from this list.
Thanks
Control-D
```

To locally redistributed list, send something like:

```
% mail staff
Subject: Please add me to the local redistribution of the RISKS
mailing list
Thanks.
Control-D
%
```

Similarly, to stop getting messages, send something like:

```
% mail com-priv-request@psi.com
Subject: Please remove me from com-priv.
Thanks!
alice@jabber.wock.com
Control-D
%
```

**Subscribing via ListServ.** Programs like ListServ, by contrast, require a more rigid format. Since ListServ is handling lots of lists, it also needs to know what list you're requesting service for. The BITNET version of ListServ, for example, requires:

Command list-name your-full-name

For example:

```
subscribe nettrain Alice Lidell
unsub nettrain Lemuel Gulliver
```

For more information about joining and participating in BITNET electronic mailing lists via ListServ, see Chap. 17. (Remember, hundreds of the BITNET ListServ lists are also available as Usenet Newsgroups.)

### The e-mail subscriber's challenge: Keeping track of what you get and remembering who, where, and how to contact

As mentioned above, there's more than one version of ListServ across the Internet and BITNET. Plus there are other e-mail-administrator programs besides ListServ, running out there in the Internet and elsewhere. Some use different formats or want the information in a different order. And many of the Internet mailing lists administered via "listname-request" addresses are now using ListServ or other programs rather than directly by a person.

Users who forget or aren't aware of the differences in who and where to send these messages periodically account for a substantial percentage of messages in a mailing list. You'll get used to it and to skipping past these. (You may decide to send some of these people a short polite message explaining to, or reminding them, how this particular list works. Don't send them angry messages, and don't reply to the list with your answer.)

The odds are high that there will never be one single mailing list program or "administrative command language." It is hoped that, over time, new e-mail list management tools will become available for users which can "automagically" determine who and how to do these tasks so that you as a user simply select a list name and have a menu of action choices such as "Join" and "Leave."

### The move to moderation and Newsgroups

As a mailing list grows, "storms" of inappropriate messages can quickly lead to a group's "voting" to become moderated. The effort of moderation involves more work for one person—the moderator-to-be, usually the "owner" of the list. This process of voting and opinion-slinging typically takes about 2 to 4 weeks and is probably the subject for a doctoral thesis somewhere out there in academia-land.

Similarly, sufficient demand for a mailing list can cause it to also become available as a Usenet Newsgroup (unmoderated, moderated, or moderated/digest).

### Receiving current messages

This is easy. They arrive like any other electronic mail messages, to your designated electronic mail address. (Usually, this is the address associated with your account, but it may be possible to arrange for messages to go to a different file, or you may have set up your e-mail program to automatically sort these messages to another file.)

You read, file, or delete these like any other e-mail messages. Most mailing lists, particularly the technical and other nonrecreational lists, are "archived" somewhere—there's a file with copies of all messages accumulating somewhere, which you may be able to access, via anonymous-FTP or Gopher. Several dozen of these archives have been "WAISed"—put into a database that can be queried via a WAIS Wide-Area Information Server, which can do keyword-matching against full-text searches (see Chap. 10).

As shown in the sample RISKS digest header in Fig. 16.1, the RISKS Internet mailing list, for example, has archives available via file transfer using anonymous-FTP; each digest issue contains summary instructions on how to get it. Archives for messages to "com-priv," the Internet commercialization and privatization mailing list, are accessible as a WAIS database. If the mailing list is also available as a Usenet Newsgroup at your organization, relatively recent postings (within the past 2 to 4 weeks) may still be available here.

## Contributing (posting) to a mailing list

Messages to mailing lists, like any other type of e-mail or Usenet postings, can either be:

- About a new topic
- A follow-up to one or more previous messages on an existing topic

(It's possible to post a message to a mailing list you don't currently subscribe to—but unless you get the list, you can't count on seeing other people's comments.)

**Sending a message on a new topic.** To send a message about a new topic to a mailing list, you compose your message and send it to the mailing list's address (or post it to the corresponding Usenet Newsgroup).

**Sending a message following up to previous one.** If your message is a follow-up to a previous message topic, there are standard procedures and conventions for the message contents, and for sending the message.

**Addressing.** To address the message, you may simply use your e-mail program's "reply" command. However, *be sure to check the To: field of the header of your message before you send it.* Depending on how other e-mail programs have been configured, including the one used by the person who sent the message you're replying to, and the program that handles the mailing list, you may be inadvertently sending your reply to the wrong person or list. If need be, edit the To: and/or Cc: fields until you have the correct addresses in and incorrect ones out.

**Subject lines for follow-ups.** The Internet and Usenet convention to indicate a message as a follow-up is to start the subject of your message with "Re:" followed by the subject line of the message yours is a follow-up to. Most e-mail programs will do this automatically when you use the **reply** (a.k.a. "answer") command.

```
& r 15
To: info-cobol@cobol.com
Subject: Re: Object oriented standards
```

Remember to change the To: line if the sender's name is used instead of the name/address of the mailing list itself.

If you're changing the subject somewhat, you may want to start with your new subject; a popular convention is to first enter your new subject text, then put "(Was: Re <old-subject> )" at the end of the subject line. For example:

```
% mail traditions@ships.nav.uk
Subject: Berth on ship (Was: Relative stations)
```

**Contents for follow-ups.** In addition to indicating which message yours is a follow-up to, you may wish to include some or all of one or more messages along with your comments. The convention in Internet mailing lists and Usenet Newsgroups is to include text from this message:

- Starting with a line identifying who you are quoting
- Indicating the included text by indenting it one or more spaces to the right and inserting a character, such as > or a <TAB> character in the left-hand column of each line.

Most Internet e-mail and Usenet reader programs will include a feature to include messages, with or without the "indent and flag" feature. For example, in the **mail** program's default message editor, it is the **~m** command; in the **trn** Threaded ReadNews program, it is the **M** command. For example:

```
> From lbutterc@bumboat.com.uk Wed Apr 21 11:01:22 1993
> Date: Wed, 21 Apr 93 10:01:18 -0500
> From: lbutterc@bumboat.com.uk (Mrs. Cripps)
> Based on what I've seen from visiting a lot of the fleet
> recently I'd say that things aren't always what they seem
That still doesn't mean that love can level all ranks. I'd
rather have that from a higher authority. -RR
```

Whenever possible, edit out all but those portions of the included message you're responding to.

### Replying to an individual regarding a mailing list posting

Lastly, you may want to send a message to the person who originally sent the message. Some e-mail programs will have commands that can do this correctly—depending on how the sender and mailing-list's e-mail programs handled matters. For example, if the message arrives as "From" the "mailing-list," or if the Reply-To: field is set to the name of the mailing-list, using your e-mail program's "reply" command will cause the reply message to be addressed to the mailing-list itself (i.e., to everyone who read this list). So it's important to pay attention. You may find it easiest—or necessary—to put the person's address in manually.

### Mailing list netiquette

"Netiquette"—network etiquette—for belonging to and participating in electronic mailing lists begins with the same advice given to all users of electronic mail and the Usenet. (See the netiquette discussions in Chaps. 5, 6, and 11.)

In addition, netiquette for electronic mailing lists includes:

- Be careful when replying to individuals that you aren't inadvertently sending your reply to everyone on the list.
- If you use a program to automatically answer e-mail messages, be sure it doesn't respond to mailing list messages (which can be tricky, as they may appear to be from an individual).

Lastly, one reminder worth repeating: Treat everything you send or plan to send as if it might appear on your organization's public bulletin board or on the front page of tomorrow's newspaper—and remember that it may be saved and found years later for similar purposes.

### Mailing list tips

- As mentioned earlier, you should save a copy of the "please-subscribe" message and response (if any) for each mailing list you join (e.g., include yourself in the Cc: field and save all these messages to one file). This will make it much easier to unsubscribe or to tell other people how to subscribe.
- If you are going to be away from your account for an extended period of time, such as spring break or summer vacation, consider "signing off" for this period. Otherwise, you may come back to a thousand or more total messages in your e-mail box.

### *Create Your Own Mailing List*

All Internet users can manage their own mailing lists. Mary Reindeau and Elizabeth Newman, who are, respectively, Manager and Tech Support of Software Tool & Die's World public-access Internet site, offer the following advice:

1. First, you need to select a name for your list. You can use anything you like, though we recommend you use as descriptive a name as possible. For example: "storytellers," "musicals," "netthink."

   The mailing list name must be a unique name [within your organization's set of names] (i.e., it cannot be the same as any user login, nor the same as an existing mailing alias). If the name of your list conflicts with an existing name, we will inform you and you can select another name. If you need assistance selecting a name, our staff is ready to help.

   Mailing list aliases can be as long as you like, so take a moment to think carefully about your name. The name of the list is not limited to a certain number of characters, but don't get carried away. The Sinead O'Connor list, "jump-in-the-river," ended up being aliased to 'jitr.' Remember that your members are going to see this name frequently and type it frequently so you want something unique yet not too complex.

2. In addition to the mailing list name, two additional aliases are created for each mailing list. For example, the mailing list, "storytellers" also has the aliases:

   storytellers-request
   owner-storytellers

   The name of the list is "storytellers" and that's where the primary discussion takes place.

   "storytellers-request" is the name for members to send to when making requests to add or delete members of the list. A common problem on mailing lists is that all additions and deletions are announced on the main list thereby distracting the members from the topic at hand.

   The second alias, "owner-storytellers" is sent to the owner of the list and any undeliverable mail that results in error returns will be sent to the owner and not to the entire membership of the mailing list. We will set up both these auxiliary aliases for any mailing list alias.

3. In addition, you need to designate and name the file which will hold the addresses for your mailing list. This file is just an ordinary file where each line is the address of a member. You can include comments and comment lines (just be careful about the use of characters like the exclamation point (!) which have special meanings to the Unix shells).

   Here's a sample address file:

```
# Cat-lovers mailing list
# Owner: Russ Blue
# Started: May 1989
alice@jabber.wock.com
pirates@mabel.penzance.nav.uk
venice!roma!parma!kmkate
juliet@mcimail.com
123456.7890@compuserve.com  # Felicity O'Neill
                              katt@spencer.rover.com
```

   Usually, the name of a mailing list's address file consists of the mailing list name plus "-addresses" at the end. For example, the "storytellers" address file would be called

   **storytellers-addresses**

   You designate where the file will be kept within your directory structure, and tell the appropriate system administrator. For example, you might create a subdirectory ".MAIL.LISTS" under your home directory, e.g.,

   **alice/.MAIL.LISTS/portmanteau-addresses**

You will also need to set the permissions on these files and the directory(s) they are in correctly—check with your system administrator about this. (It's possible to create a major security hole if you do this wrong—so be sure you work with your system administrator on this. You'll need to contact them anyway to get the appropriate mail aliases set up.)

Whether or not you'll be charged for setting up or running a mailing list depends on your organization's policies. (Probably you won't be.)

Some Hints for Successful Mailing List Management:

- It's nice to have a short welcome message to send to new subscribers, telling them what addresses to use, what the list is used for (yes, people will join a list without knowing what it's about), and any related rules.
- If you want Internet users in general to know about your list, you should send a brief description of the list along with your name and the contact address (usually "listname-request@your-site-address") to the "List of Lists"—check the contact name given. You should also announce it in any appropriate Usenet Newsgroups.

Keep add requests in a file after processing for a while, in case someone's address "bounces" (is returned to you as undeliverable) and you need to try to work out a valid address.

Also, learn to read the header of a "bounce" message (failed mail) to see if it was a temporary problem, or something requiring you to take action. These messages may appear cryptic but read carefully and you really will find an "English" explanation of the error. When in doubt, ask "staff" for advice.

As a mailing list manager, you are responsible for errors generated by your list and are expected to resolve problems in a quick and effective manner.

If you want to keep an archive of the messages, you may need additional disk space. See "help rates" for info on disk quotas.

The archive does not have to be on the same site as the mailing list. You may find someone else who owns disk space directly and is willing to let some be used for the list archives.

Chapter

# 17

# BITNET: Another Network Worth Knowing About

As you begin using the Internet, you'll keep running into references to other computer networks. One of these is Usenet, which is covered in Chap. 6. Another is BITNET, an international network for education and research. There is a strong overlap and interaction between the Internet and BITNET communities—enough to merit this chapter on BITNET and how to work with it as an Internet user. BITNET's potential importance to you as an Internet user—the main ways you may "use" BITNET are:

- To exchange e-mail with BITNET users. BITNET has a large population of users, representing significant academic, research, and international communities.
- To participate in electronic mailing lists and receive "on-line journals." BITNET supports over three thousand topical electronic mailing lists and discussion groups, managed by a facility named ListServ, which you may want to join and participate in. (Many of these may also be available to you as local Usenet Newsgroups—see the section "BITNET, K12, DDN and other 'gatewayed' and relayed groups" in Chap. 6 for more information.)
- BITNET sites are home to major archives of files containing documents, programs, and databases which you can query and retrieve, also via e-mail messages to ListServ facilities.

## BITNET: Origins and Today

According to Ira Fuchs, Vice President for Computing and Information Technology at Princeton University, he and Greydon Freeman created BITNET in 1981 as a small store-and-forward network of IBM computers based at the City University of New York (CUNY) and at Yale University in New Haven, CT. "I then wrote to 60 or so academic institutions in the United States and Canada which were running compatible software, and invited them to join the network, which we dubbed BITNET, the 'Because It's Time' Network."

The reason it started with IBM software was to make use of existing, installed software, Fuchs recalls—but "versions of the software that ran on the Unix and Digital Equipment VMS operating systems started popping up within another six months, until Digital VMS-based computers soon outnumbered the IBM ones." The intent of BITNET was to create a network for "all universities and all disciplines," Fuchs says. At the time, connections to the ARPAnet were restricted to the research and government communities, and CSNET was only for the computer science and engineering parts of academia. "BITNET was for everyone in the research and education communities, long before the Internet opened up and became widely accessible."

Today, BITNET is a worldwide network for the electronic exchange of information in support of research and education. BITNET links over 1400 organizations and 3000+ nodes in over 50 countries on 6 continents around the world, from Argentina and Austria through Uruguay and Yugoslavia. In the United States alone, BITNET member organizations include over 550 universities, colleges, schools (including some kindergarten through twelfth grade schools and school districts), industrial research centers, and government agencies. In the January 1993 issue of *Matrix Times,* John Quarterman and Smoot Carl-Mitchell estimated the BITNET population at nearly a quarter million users.

Like the Internet, BITNET comprises both computers, often referred to as *nodes,* and the network that connect them. Unlike the Internet, which uses the TCP/IP protocol suite and provides real-time connections, BITNET uses the IBM NJE communications protocol and provides *store-and-forward* service. This makes BITNET suitable for activities like e-mail and file retrieval but not for remote login or other interactive tasks other than interactive messages (similar to the Internet *talk* and Internet Relay Chat facilities described in Chap. 18).

Also, like the Internet, BITNET actually consists of a number of administratively distinct networks, termed *Cooperating Networks*—although unlike the Internet, these networks are operationally a single network. The Cooperating Network serving the United States and Mexico is itself called BITNET. (Yes, the name *BITNET* is being used for both a part and the whole.) Within the United States, BITNET is operated and administered by the Corporation for Research and Education Networking, a.k.a. CREN, (Washington, DC), a nonprofit membership corporation.

Users—that's you—see BITNET as a single network. In fact, BITNET will appear to Internet users as part of Matrix—one of the "other networks" that Internet users can interact with via e-mail but not with direct real-time applications such as remote login, file transfer, or Gopher. (Increasing numbers of BITNET sites are also becoming full Internet sites, allowing real-time interaction with other sites—although at this point they're arguably Internet, not BITNET, users.) Equally, BITNET users can interact with Internet users and services only via e-mail.

In terms of size, locations, communities, and activities it supports, BITNET is a major part of the global "WorldNet." For many purposes, BITNET is often considered part of the Internet. In particular, hundreds of the on-line electronic mailing lists and discussion groups from the Internet and BITNET are read and contributed to by members of both communities.

### The BITNET-Internet connection: By gateways

BITNET connects to the Internet via *gateways* that let the two networks exchange electronic mail messages. Many sites are connected to both the Internet and BITNET. Many mailing lists from one network also go to users on the other; hundreds of BITNET mailing lists have also become available as Usenet Newsgroups. According to Jim Conklin, Director of the BITNET Network Information Center (BITNIC) in Washington, D.C., there are currently about a dozen Internet/BITNET e-mail gateways within the United States, plus others in Europe and Asia.

There are several documents available on how to use BITNET resources and services; many, in fact, you can obtain via e-mail (and by the end of this chapter, you should know how). Let's take a summary look at what you need to know to interact with BITNET users and services.

## Addressing E-Mail to BITNET

BITNET and the Internet connect via gateways—network devices that, among other activities, relay electronic mail messages between the two networks. Depending on various factors such as the e-mail program you use, how things are set up at your site, and information available to your network's nameservers, you may be able to send e-mail to BITNET using ".bitnet" as if it were the top-level Domain Name.* Otherwise, you will have to use "gateway" format addressing (see "'Gateway Syntax' for Sending E-Mail to Other Networks" and "E-Mail Addressing Conventions and Formats for Other Networks" in Chap. 5).

### If you use .bitnet instead of a top-level Domain Name

The electronic mail programs at some—but not all—Internet sites will be "smart" enough to use .bitnet instead of a top-level Domain Name, letting you simply address Internet-to-BITNET messages using the format:

```
NAME@bithost.bitnet
```

where "name" is the e-mail ID of the person or program you are trying to reach, and "bithost" is the name of their site or system; for example:

```
quertyvm3@uiop.bitnet
```

To determine whether your mail system can handle this, you can ask your system or network administrator—or test it by sending a message addressed using this shorter format.

---

*Which it isn't. But the mail software, if it can handle it, will treat ".bitnet" as a top-level Domain and take care of supplying the gateway address and other tasks for you.

### Addressing via a BITNET gateway

If using .bitnet as the top-level Domain Name doesn't work—to send an e-mail message from the Internet to BITNET—you must send the message to one of the BITNET gateways. The e-mail program in the gateway will automatically translate this into a full Internet-to-BITNET address, complete with a gateway name, and forward the message to the BITNET addressee.

There are a number of Internet/BITNET e-mail gateways located across the United States and elsewhere around the world; each system has an Internet and a BITNET address. For example:

| | |
|---|---|
| cunyvm.cuny.edu | CUNY, New York |
| cornellc.cit.cornell.edu | Cornell University, New York |
| pucc.princeton.edu | Princeton University, New Jersey |

You do this by addressing a message as follows:

**BITNET-user-ID%bitnet_node**.bitnet**@bitnet-gateway-address**

For example, if you want to send a message to NAME, whose BITNET address is NAME@BITHOST on BITNET, as an Internet user, you would address it to:

```
NAME%BITHOST.bitnet@cunyvm.cuny.edu
```

According to Conklin, you can use *any* of the BITNET/Internet gateways for this purpose; for example:

```
quert67%yuiop.bitnet@cunyvm.cuny.edu
quert67%yuiop.bitnet@pucc.princeton.edu
```

If the "@bithost.bitnet" method doesn't work, Conklin advises new Internet users to simply use the cunyvm.cuny.edu gateway for addressing Internet-to-BITNET e-mail—but again, *any* BITNET-Internet gateway should work.

## BITNET ListServ E-Mail Discussion Lists

As mentioned earlier, like the Internet and Usenet, BITNET is home to thousands of topical unmoderated and moderated electronic mail discussion lists. As of late 1992, there were over 3000 "public" lists (i.e., lists that are publicly listed and whose membership is open to anyone). See Table 17.1 for some representative BITNET ListServ mailing lists. BITNET mailing list groups are handled by a program called ListServ (which stands for List Server). ListServ lets a BITNET user create a topical list, such as "QUARKS-L."

List names must be no more than eight characters, and the first character must be a letter. Some names end in "-L" (for "-list"); in case you're creating a new list, you should be aware that it isn't necessary to follow this convention.

**TABLE 17.1 Sample BITNET ListServs**

| List | Topic |
|---|---|
| ACADV | Academic Advising Forum |
| APPL-L | Computer Applications in Science and Education |
| ARTCRIT | Art Criticism Discussion Forum |
| BLINDNWS | Blind News List |
| CHEMED-L | Chemistry Education Discussion List |
| CHINA | Chinese Studies List |
| DANCE-L | International Folk Dance, etc. |
| ENVST-L | Environmental Studies Discussion List |
| PACS-L | Public-Access Computer Systems |

Once a BITNET list has been set up on one of the ListServ nodes, e-mail users on BITNET—or anywhere else across the Internet or Matrix—can add their names to this list (if it's an "open" list, meaning permitting users to be added). Then, for example, whenever you or someone else sends a message to the ListServ program handling QUARKS-L, the ListServ will send a copy of each message to each "subscriber" to the QUARKS-L list. The ListServ program also provides a number of other services for e-mail and file distribution, as you'll see soon.

As an Internet user, you can join ("subscribe" to) BITNET ListServ lists. Once you have done this, you can receive copies of messages to these lists in your electronic mailbox and also contribute to these lists. (Before you do, however, you may want to see if the mailing list in question is available to you locally as a Usenet Newsgroup. This will help minimize how much e-mail you get and also simplify the process of subscribing and unsubscribing. For more information, see the discussion of the Usenet bit.* Newsgroup hierarchy in Chap. 6.

### Sending messages to a ListServ facility

There are copies of ListServ running at many different computers within BITNET; they are referred to as ListServ nodes. (Some people may call them *ListServers.*) Each ListServ node is responsible for one or more ListServ lists. Fortunately, notes Jim Conklin, you don't need to know which ListServer is responsible for which lists to subscribe. (Just as you don't have to send e-mail to BITNET via a particular Internet/BITNET gateway.)

You can send *many* ListServ-related messages to *many* of the computers running a copy of the ListServ program. If the ListServ program you've sent your message to isn't the one that handles the list or services you want, it will automatically forward your message to the right one. (If your message is forwarded, the first ListServ may send you a message indicating this has been done.)

Conklin advises Internet users to begin by sending all BITNET ListServ commands (i.e., messages with ListServ commands) to:

```
ListServ@bitnic.educom.edu
```

### Sending messages to a ListServ-based mailing list

The ListServ facilities handle your e-mail requests for joining, leaving, and searching BITNET lists. To send messages to the participants in a given BITNET ListServ list, you send the message to the list address itself, just as you would with an Internet-based mailing list. The address for the list should be included in the message you receive as part of the automatic "you have been added to the following list" acknowledgment message from ListServ—and will be in the message header of the postings you will get as a participant in this list. For example:

```
carr-l@ulkyvm.bitnet
carr-l%ulkyvm.bitnet@cunyvm.vm.edu
```

## Using ListServ

ListServ is an e-mail-based facility. You interact with it by sending messages to a ListServ program; it responds by sending messages back to you containing the requested information and confirmation (or error) messages.

### Basic rules for ListServ

Here are the basic rules for messages you send to ListServ:

1. Put ListServ commands in the body of the mail message.
2. ListServ will ignore anything in the Subject line. You can leave it blank. (If you want to "cc:" yourself to keep track of what you've done, you may want to put a Subject that makes sense to you.)
3. Don't include any text in the message body other than the ListServ commands (e.g., "Please," "Thank you," your name and "signature"), as it will confuse the ListServ program.
4. Don't put any punctuation marks in your message. This includes not using quotation marks.
5. In commands that require your name, use your "real name" (e.g., Alice Lidell) not your computer address (e.g., alice@jabber.wock.com).

### Essential ListServ commands

BITNET ListServs act as home to a wide range of documents, lists, and databases, as well as archives of messages and documents pertaining to the ListServ mailing lists. ListServ commands let you perform searches on these and get the results, ask for lists of what's available, and get entire documents e-mailed back to you. Here's a summary of essential ListServ commands and information you can request via e-mail to ListServ:

**help.** To get a brief list of ListServ commands.

**info.** To get information about ListServ. For example:

**info refcard.** Gets you a Command Reference Card—an expanded list of ListServ commands

**info ?** Gets you a list of ListServ information guides.

**info pr.** Gets you the document "Presentation of ListServ for New Users"

**info gen.** Gets you the "General Information about Revised ListServ"

**LIST.** To get lists; examples follow.

**list global.** Gets you a copy of the file "ListServ Lists," which contains summary information (usually one line) about all current public ListServ lists (roughly 3000 as of late 1992), including:

- The *list_name* of the list
- The *node(s)* of the ListServer from which the list is distributed (there may be more than one)
- A brief description of the list's intended function

For example:

```
HELP-NET HELP-NET@TEMPLEVM Bitnet/Internet Help Resource
```

At 3000+ lines, the response to "Global" may be longer than you want to plough through—and more than you need. To get only a subset of the full Global list, send the command:

```
list global /keyword
```

ListServ will only send those lines from the file that include a match to *keyword*. Matching is case-insensitive, and you can only use one keyword per request. You can include more than one request per message. For example:

```
list global /pacs
list global /REPORTING
```

**get, send, sendme.** Causes the specified file(s) or list archives to be sent to you. ("info" is only for information about ListServ.) Generally, a filename will consist of two or three words separated by a space:

```
get filename-1 filename-2
```

or

```
get filename-1 filename-2 filelist-name
```

For example:

**get bitnet userhelp.** Gets you a BITNET guide, including the popular "Bitnet for the Compleat Idiot."

**get netinfo filelist.** The "netinfo Filelist" contains a list of all the files on the ListServer you send to. (Each ListServ node will have a different set of files available.)

The Box: "Useful BITNET Files You Can Retrieve from ListServ" gives you a list of some of the more useful BITNET information files you can get via the ListServ "get" command.

***Useful BITNET Files You Can Retrieve from ListServ***

Useful files and documents you can retrieve from BITNET nodes, using the ListServ GET command, include:

NETINFO FILELIST. Lists names and short descriptions of documentation about the network. Available from ListServ@bitnic.educom.edu

LISTSERV FILELIST. Lists all FILELISTs on the ListServ

CREN NET_USE. The CREN Acceptable Use Policy for BITNET and CSNET

BITNET INTRO. An introduction to using BITNET

BITNET USERHELP. "The BITNET Guide for the Compleat Idiot," a good introductory manual by Chris Condon

BITNET OVERVIEW. A brief description of BITNET

BITNET TOPICS. A list of topics covered by BITNET discussion lists

BITNET SERVERS. A list of ListServ and other servers on BITNET, with information on the services they provide and on how to access those services

### Subscribing and unsubscribing to BITNET ListServ mailing lists

To join, leave, or obtain information relating to a specific BITNET ListServ list, send e-mail messages to any BITNET ListServ node.

To *subscribe* to a list (join and have copies of messages sent to you):

```
SUBSCRIBE list_name your-full-name
```

For example:

```
subscribe nettrain Alice Lidell
```

To *unsubscribe* from a list (stop getting it):*

```
UNSUBSCRIBE list_name
```

*Notice that this subscribe and unsubscribe method is very different from how you join and leave Internet mailing lists, where you send a message to a person care of the address *list-name*-request@*list-address*. With ListServ, you are sending messages to a program; with Internet mailing lists, you are sending messages to a human administrator. Failing to understand (or remember) this major difference in methods accounts for why you see (so) many messages in Internet mailing lists containing nothing but "sub (or unsub) listname user-name," and in BITNET lists, "Please add/drop me from this list."

CREN's Conklin reminds subscribing and unsubscribing users: "Your messages must be sent to ListServ, not to the "list_name".

Also, he cautions:

> Your "unsubscribe" message for a list must be sent from the same e-mail address (user-ID and host) which you used to subscribe to the list. If you have difficulty in unsubscribing, you may wish to use the ListServ REVIEW command to check the list for you, in order to see what user-name and node ListServ shows for your subscription.

To get more information about a given list—its description, characteristics, and current subscribers:

```
REVIEW list_name
```

in which "list_name" is the name of the ListServ list as shown in the file. For example:

```
REVIEW NETTRAIN
```

### Posting to ListServ lists

To send messages to a ListServ list, send e-mail to the address of the list, just as if it were a person's mail address. For example, to send a message to the readers of NETTRAIN, which is ListServed on the node UBVM, as an Internet user, you send your message to nettrain@ubvm.bitnet or nettrain%ubvm.bitnet@bitnet-gateway. (If you are not already on the list, and you want a copy of the message, be sure to include your own e-mail name in the message's To: or cc: field.)

Conklin reminds Internet (and all other) users that any message sent to a BITNET ListServ list "should be consistent with the intended purpose of the list and with the CREN Acceptable Use Policy." (See Chap. 11 for a summary of the CREN/BITNET AUP; to get a current copy of the CREN/BITNET AUP, send e-mail to listserv@bitnic.educom.edu with "get cren net_use" in the message body.)

### Other ways to get ListServ lists and information about them

Like Internet mailing lists, many of the BITNET ListServ mailing lists are also available as Usenet Newsgroups—CREN's Conklin estimates that as many as two-thirds or more of the ListServ discussions may be available through Usenet Newsgroups. If you have access to the Usenet, you can read and reply to these ListServ lists without needing to have them added to your incoming e-mail. (Remember, to subscribe to a Usenet group, you *don't* send a message to the ListServ; you either give the appropriate command to the Usenet program you use, or [if you're confident about what you're doing] you can add the appropriate entry line to your .newsrc file manually.) If you access the ListServ list via Usenet, remember you'll have to invoke your Usenet-reading program to read the messages—if you don't want to have to remember to check Usenet News for this group, subscribe via the ListServ mechanism and have them sent to your electronic mailbox.

### Where and how to get lists of BITNET ListServ discussions

In addition to requesting a summary of ListServ discussion via the ListServ Send Global command, there are several other ways you may be able to read or query the current list of public ListServs:

- Read the periodically updated BITNET FAQ posting in Usenet Newsgroups such as news.answers.
- Check the ListServ index by sending a message to listserv@bitnic.educom.edu (e.g., list global /amiga).
- Read (or check the index) in the book, *INTERNET: Mailing Lists,* which is listed in the Bibliography.

By early 1993, this information may have been made available for query via some combination of archie and WAIS queries, from an archie, Gopher, or other Internet front end. This should let you do keyword searches of the list without having to locate or download the entire file.

### For more information

For more information about CREN and BITNET (in addition to the information files indicated earlier in this chapter):

CREN
1112 Sixteenth Street, NW
Suite 600
Washington, DC 20036
202-872-4200
info@bitnic.educom.edu

Chapter

# 18

# And Away You Go—Some Closing Tips, Tools, Toys, Pointers, and Suggestions

*Will you, won't you, will you, won't you,*
*Will you join the dance?*
*Will you, won't you, will you, won't you,*
*Won't you join the dance?*
*"The Lobster Quadrille," Alice in Wonderland*

*"Then let the throng Our joy advance,*
*With laughing song, and merry dance,*
*With joyous shout and ringing cheer,*
*Inaugurate our new career."*
*The Mikado*
GILBERT AND SULLIVAN

Welcome to the last chapter (not counting the appendixes and other back matter, of course). In this chapter, we'll take a quick tour of some of the other services and resources available to you as a member of the Internet community, including some tools that weren't covered elsewhere, some of the "toys"—the fun parts of the Internet (it isn't all serious and work-related, as you've probably figured out by now), and some good starting points to continue your use and exploration of the Internet.

As you'll see, I've given very brief summaries plus suggestions on where to look for more information, software, and the like, rather than the more comprehensive information in previous chapters. One reason is that these are comparatively ancillary aspects of the Internet, not relevant to as many users, or they are simple to master and use. But the most important reason is that at this point, you may be a beginning user, but you're no longer a "new user." Armed with only the information that something exists and its name or an Internet address, you should be able to locate the appropriate on-line man-pages, FAQs, mailing lists, and Usenet Newsgroups, archive sites, etc.

As a reminder, in general, for more information and Internet addresses, check through:

- FAQs in the Usenet news.answers Newsgroup
- Scott Yanoff's "Special Internet Connections" list (discussed later in this chapter) and other Internet resource directories and lists

Good luck—and have fun.

## nslookup, ping, and other Useful Tools

### nslookup

The **nslookup** program is one of the TCP/IP utilities that is useful for determining information about computers and sites on the Internet. For example, you can use **nslookup** to:

- Determine a system's IP address, if you know its Domain Name, and vice versa
- Determine what kind of hardware and operating system a specific computer is using
- Get information about computers in a particular Domain

**nslookup** is an interactive command; to use it, enter **nslookup<RETURN>** at the command prompt. If all you want to do is a name and address lookup, you can give the Domain Name on the command line; for example:

```
world% nslookup panix.com
Server: world.std.com
Address: 192.74.137.5

Non-authoritative answer:
Name: panix.com
Address: 198.7.0.1
```

### ping

The TCP/IP **ping** command* is basically a tool to "ping" another computer across the Internet to see if it's there and there's some path between your computer and it. **ping** is mostly used by network operators and software developers; "ping" is also used conversationally as jargon (e.g., "I'll ping their office and see if they're in").

## Conversational Facilities: talk, and the Internet Relay Chat (IRC)

If you belong to any Bulletin Board Systems or on-line consumer services, you may have heard about or participated in the on-line "CB" activities, where

---

*Like **grep, ping** may have begun as an acronym; one popular definition is "Packet Internet Groper."

users exchange messages in real time, like a telephone party line or CB radio channel. For most Internet users, e-mail and Usenet discussion groups are a more than adequate way to exchange messages. Messages often get there within seconds to minutes. However, the direct connections among Internet sites also makes possible direct real-time electronic conversations, similar to telephone or CB radio; over the years, Internet developers have done a number of interesting things with these facilities.

For convenience (e.g., to minimize keystrokes), on-line chatting tends to make use of a variety of abbreviations, jargon, and other conventions from sources such as CB radio, ham radio, Morse code, plus what's evolved on BBSs and the Usenet. Here's a few examples:

**GA** Go Ahead (you're done with your current thought and it's the other person's turn to "talk").

**BB** Bye Bye.

**TTFN** "Ta ta for now" (Goodbye).

**:-)** Humorous smiley face

See the Glossary for some popular Internet and Usenet jargon, abbreviations, and emoticons.

### talk—Talking with another user

If e-mail is like trading phone messages, the **talk** facility is the equivalent of a direct phone connection; it is the basic real-time communication facility between two users. When you give the command, **talk username,** for example, **talk lgulliver** or **talk alicel@jabber.wock.com**, the operating system checks to see if this user is currently logged in. If the user you want to talk with is on the same system as you, "username" should be sufficient.

If the indicated user is logged in (which you may be able to determine by using the **finger, who,** or **ps**—"display process status"—command), the operating system displays a message on this user's screen, indicating someone (giving your user name) wants to "talk" with them and what they should do if interested.

The message you see when you give the talk command:

```
% talk lbutterc@bumboat.com.uk
[Waiting for your party to respond]
```

Here's what the other party sees:

```
Message from Talk_Daemon@pinafore at 16:00...
talk: connection requested by captain@pinafore.nav.uk.
talk: respond with:  talk captain@pinafore.nav.uk.
```

The "request to talk" message goes to your screen but not to any files you're working on. For example, if you're in the middle of editing a file, the talk request doesn't get inserted into your document (it shouldn't, anyway). If you

```
Captain, you seem sad. GA
Why? GA—You cn talk to me.
So...
Ah. I understand. GA
Whoops, here comes J—TTFN
--------------------------------------------------------
Yes, Mrs C.
Sir Jos. P wants to marry my daughter Jo
She does not tackle kindly to it :-(
Any advice? GA
Bye <CONTROL-C>
```

**Figure 18.1** Sample talk session.

don't want to be "interrupted" by "request to talk" messages, on Unix systems you can set your session to refuse these requests and not even display them, with the command **mesg no** in your login file or at the command prompt.

On most systems, when a "talk" session has been mutually established, **talk** typically splits the screen, as illustrated in Fig. 18.1. As you type, the other user sees it (including mistakes and corrections as you <BACK-SPACE>). You can both type at the same time.

One common use for **talk** is when you have a brief question or problem for your system administrator and don't want to wait for them to check and respond to e-mail—but don't know their phone number. It's also good for terse conversations when you're both on-line, versus swapping e-mail, and brief idle chit-chat. If you can establish a connection but **talk** doesn't seem to work, try the **ntalk** command, a version of **talk** designed to work on a wider range of types of computers.

## IRC (the Internet Relay Chat)—Real-time "CB radio" conferencing

One popular feature of on-line consumer services like CompuServe and DELPHI and of many BBSs is real-time conferencing à la CB radio. On **talk**-like facilities, two users exchange messages; here, dozens or hundreds may be seeing and entering message lines simultaneously. As with topical forums, the systems often separate these real-time conversations into "channels." On many consumer services, scheduled interviews and "call-in" sessions with noted personalities are also a regular feature.

On CompuServe or DELPHI, the users may be scattered across the country or world, but they are all accessing the same common computer system. On the Internet, however, users seeking to chat may easily be on computers at dozens or hundreds of locations around the world.

Over the years, programmers in the Internet community have developed the IRC, a real-time "chat" system, where each user's input is replicated on the screens of other users who are "tuned" to the same topical "channel."*

*There's also a multiuser facility called *forumnet*, similar to IRC in purpose but not used that much these days.

IRC is a client-server program; IRC client programs include **irc** and **ircii** (IRC II), a more powerful version of the initial IRC program.

According to the manual page for IRC, "The screen is split into two parts, separated by an inverse-video status line (if supported). The upper (larger) part of the screen displays responses from the IRC server. The lower part of the screen (a single line) accepts keyboard input." The IRC lets users form different "channels," so you don't have to "hear" everyone, just people on the topic you want to participate in.

During the Persian Gulf War in 1991, for example, I "listened" briefly, as dozens of users from all over the world, from Germany to Finland, Israel, and Australia, made comments and discussed events, with an occasional pause as certain users had to put on gas masks. Months later, as Hurricane Bob swept the East Coast, while the electric power where I was living went out, I logged into the World with my battery-powered portable computer and chatted briefly on the "hurricane" channel (mostly people discussing where pizza was available, admittedly).

There are commands to let you set a nickname, let "automatons" (programs) participate, and much more. Many of the Internet's multiuser games are based on IRC. If your site has the appropriate IRC programs available, you can run it directly; there are also a number of public-access IRC sites you can do a remote login (**telnet**) to. IRC code is available from Internet archive sites. (You may want to try it via a public-access client first, and check with your system administrator before trying to bring up IRC on your system.) For more information, also see the Usenet alt.irc.* Newsgroups.

## Multiuser Games—Go, Chess, MUDs, and More

The on-line gaming community is quite active on the Internet. The same technology that supports multiuser conversations can—and does—also support real-time multiuser games, from chess, Go, and backgammon to role-playing games, with ASCII or graphic-based screens. (There are also "non-real-time" games which you can play by e-mail, just like there are people who play chess by mail.)

Is it O.K. to use the Internet to play games? Sure, why not—if you're within the Appropriate Use Policies of your site and its network provider (see the section on Appropriate Usage in Chap. 11). Playing games on the network or on a computer that belongs to your school or organization is not an inherent right. As the MUD FAQ notes, "When you paid money to your school's computer department for an account, you entered into a contract with that department. Most schools have a well-written Computer Policy document, that will detail exactly what you have rights to. Most schools classify MUD as a game, and games as nonessentials." If you're not sure, check with your system administrator.

For more information, in addition to postings in the Usenet news.answers Newsgroup and Scott Yanoff's list, look for appropriate Newsgroups and articles in the rec.games and alt.games Usenet hierarchies; for information specific to your type of computer, also check in the appropriate comp.sys.*.games Newsgroup (e.g., comp.sys.mac.games).

### Go, chess, backgammon, and other board games

You can play board games via the Internet. Depending on what game you're interested in, you can either participate by remote login to a public-access client or by installing the appropriate client (and possibly server) program(s) on your system.

For Go players, the Internet Go Server (IGS) lets Internet users **telnet** in and play Go any time of the day or night, according to Go fan Jeff Shaevel <shaevel@guest.apple.com>. "It's always a reasonable hour *somewhere,*" Shaevel points out. In addition to the standard 19 by 19 squares board, IGS also supports smaller sizes such as 9 by 9 and 13 by 13, often used by beginners.

The ASCII version, which uses standard ASCII characters to represent the Go board, is generally considered not the easiest to read—and can get a little unwieldy when filled with pieces, notes Shaevel. However, "People have written graphic versions of Internet Go Server clients which make viewing easier and allow for 'point-and-click' playing." IGS GUI clients are available for environments including X Windowing systems, the Macintosh, DOS, and Microsoft Windows.

A client IGS program that sets up multiple windows on the Mac for observation, talk, and playing is available from John Bate (bate@cs.umanitoba.ca). The program uses the Apple Terminal Tool to provide full terminal emulation and includes basic modem communication. The Mac Go client is semi-freeware, according to Shaevel. (You have to play two games with Bate in "payment.") A variety of Go clients, including GoServant, are available from ftp.u.washington.edu (in /pub/go/igs/prog).

According to Shaevel, there have now been two IGS Go tournaments that had an excellent turnout. The second tournament had almost 150 participants from 20 countries. Half, says Shaevel, were from the United States; the others, in descending order of participants, came from Canada, Germany, China, Finland, Sweden, France, Great Britain, Korea, Hungary, Netherlands, Taiwan, Austria, Australia, Switzerland, Denmark, Italy, Israel, Norway, and New Zealand. "These international tournaments are very exciting and, I think, one of the greatest uses of the IGS," Shaevel says. "There will be more of them in the future—we hope that a tournament among Go professionals can be arranged sometime."

Chess, Backgammon, and Bridge servers are also available (what, no euchre?). For more information, also see Usenet Newsgroups including rec.games.go, and rec.games.video.

The OKbridge program allows you to play in real-time or by e-mail and supports duplicate bridge. For more information, see the FAQ in the Usenet rec.games.bridge Newsgroup or do an archie search for OKbridge. There's even an "OKscreen" TSR program for IBM PCs that adds color.

### MUDs—Multiuser role-playing games

Role-playing games have an ancient and honorable tradition. Over the past two decades, computers have continued to add new dimensions to how we can play them. Some, like MicroMUSE (in Chap. 13) are being put to use for education—but there's a sizable population of on-line game players.

The general term for multiuser interactive role-playing games on the Internet is *MUD*; participating in a MUD is called *MUDding* or *mudding*. According to the MUD FAQ:

> A MUD (Multiple User Dimension, Multiple User Dungeon, or Multiple User Dialogue) is a computer program which users can log into and explore. Each user takes control of a computerized persona/avatar/incarnation/ character. You can walk around, chat with other characters, explore dangerous monster-infested areas, solve puzzles, and even create your very own rooms, descriptions, and items.

There are many, many MUDs out there. Some MUDs have been running continuously (the site or game, not individual users) for several years, offering everything from cities to "on-line karaoke" and frisbee-playing. (I don't know how they do this, but that's what the message said.) Some of these have as many as 2000 players and 10,000 rooms. For more information, see the MUD FAQ, plus any Newsgroups and documents for specific MUDs you are interested in. It's recommended that you spend some time reading through the FAQs and related information before actually beginning to participate in a MUD.

## Other Interesting Unix Facilities

Over the years, the Unix community has developed a variety of games and whimsical commands. Some are included with most versions of Unix; others are readily available. By the way, many of these commands have nothing to do with networking or the Internet but are part of the Unix and Usenet cultures.

### The *fortune* command

The **fortune** command prints a "random, hopefully interesting, adage." For example:

```
% fortune
Q: What's a light-year?
A: One-third less calories than a regular year.

% fortune
Real programmers don't draw flowcharts. Flowcharts are, after
all, the illiterate's form of documentation. Cavemen drew flow-
charts; look how much good it did them.
```

One common practice is to put the **fortune** command at the end of your .login file. For more information, see the **fortune** manual page.

### Cookie servers

A cookie server is a program that gives you an amusing saying when you do a remote login (**telnet**) to it and then disconnects. You may be accessing a copy of the **fortune** program.

### Adventure—Exploring the Colossal Caves

For many of us computer-users over the age of 35, Adventure was the first interactive line-oriented computer game ("You are standing at the end of a road before a small brick building.") we encountered. According to the manual page, "The object of the game is to locate and explore Colossal Cave, find the treasures hidden there, and bring them back to the building with you. The program is self-describing to a point, but part of the game is to discover its rules." Adventure is available on most Unix systems, as well as for downloading in versions that should run on most computers, such as any IBM-compatible PC. It's still fun—and the current version appears to include some extensions to the original game.

### NetHack—Exploring the Mazes of Menace

"Display-oriented" computer games bear the same relation to games like Adventure that graphic-oriented user interfaces (GUIs) like MacOs and X Windows do to command-line interfaces such as DOS. Many can be played on any computer and display. NetHack is "a display-oriented Dungeons & Dragons-like game" whose display and command structure resemble *rogue,* another popular computer game. According to the NetHack manual page, "To win the game (as opposed to merely playing to beat other people's high scores) you must locate the Amulet of Yendor which is somewhere below the 20th level of the dungeon and get it out."

A lot of dedicated people have worked on NetHack; it is a complex and often very frustrating game. NetHack and Adventure are games you play on your local system, so they don't consume Internet resources; if you enjoy these, and pay for your account or have to tie up a phone connection to use your account, consider downloading copies of the programs to your computer.

## Other Miscellaneous Internet Services

Here's a few sample services you can access via the Internet, courtesy of Scott Yanoff's "Special Internet Connections" list:

- Geographic name server (gives information such as longitude and latitude of town, based on information you enter), **telnet** to martini.eecs.umich.edu 3000
- National Bureau of Standards Time (exact time and other time information), **telnet** to india.colorado.edu 13
- Earthquakes—finger quake@geophys.washington.edu; contains information about recent earthquakes

## Lists of Resources and Services

Interestingly, some of the most useful and popular "start here" lists of resources and contacts in the Internet seem to come from private individuals. For example, for people seeking "Internet accounts," Peter Kaminski's PDIAL list of Public Dial-up Internet Access providers has been the best place to start. Similarly, the "official" Internet resources list is being put together by the InterNIC Directory & Database Services group, but you may find it easier to start with a locally available, shorter list. These lists assume you know enough about using the Internet to recognize and use Domain or IP addresses and can do remote login (**telnet**), anonymous file transfer (anonymous-FTP), locate Usenet Newsgroups, and use e-mail (although the lists often include reminders of key points).

### Scott Yanoff's "Special Internet Connections" list

Scott Yanoff maintains a list of Internet-accessible services, called "Special Internet Connections." Yanoff's list is an excellent starting point if you're looking, say, for a public Gopher client, Go, or chess—or curious what else the Internet has to offer. This list is periodically posted to Usenet Newsgroups including alt.internet.services and alt.bbs.internet, under the title "Updated Internet Services List"; other ways to get this list include from the site csd4.csd.uwm.edu, by anonymous-FTP file transfer from /pub/inet.services.txt or by Gopher or by sending e-mail to bbslist@aug3.augsburg.edu (you'll get the list back automatically, no subject or message body needed).

### "Zamfield's Internet BBS List"

If you're looking for Bulletin Board Systems to access via the Internet, check out "Zamfield's Internet BBS List," which is maintained by Thomas A. Kreeger <zamfield@Dune.EE.MsState.Edu>. The list is irregularly posted to the Usenet alt.bbs.internet Newsgroup.

### The MaasInfo Files

The MaasInfo Files from Robert E. Maas (rem@btr.com) comprise a "top-level index to the Internet." For example, his file MaasInfo.TopIndex is the "Index of Indexes," an InterNet on-line file pointing at all the major indexes that are posted on Internet or BITNET. These indexes then point at all the known interest groups, archive sites, special services such as library catalogs file-finding and FTP-via-email, and some major tutorial documentation that are located on Internet BITNET or Usenet. MaasInfo.TopIndex also points at the other attempts at meta-indexes, namely the Internet Resource Guide, the "Catalog of Catalogs" (TopNode), and the AARnet Resource guide.

As of April 1993, a set of the MaasInfo files is available by anonymous-FTP file transfer from niord.shsu.edu (192.92.115.8) in the directory maasinfo/ and by e-mail fileserver from fileserv@shsu.edu (for help and general information, put "directory maasinfo" in the message body). A message concerning other archive locations for the MaasInfo files is reposted periodically to a variety of mailing lists and Newsgroups. However, there is no archived location presently for the current version of this message; if you can't find a current message at your site, get the information from the above-named site.

The files are available as "trivial shareware" according to the message from Maas, "If they are worth more than a dollar to you, please do some nice favor of comparable value in return, such as supplying answers to SQWAs. See MaasInfo.TopIndex for details of "trivial shareware" policy."

As you've also seen in Chap. 12, the Internet is full of lists and listings and of people creating more. If you can't find what you're looking for, and posting questions in the obvious places doesn't turn up anything, you may have found a niche you can fill.

## Where You Can Go from Here—Some Final Comments from the Author

So we're finally at the end—of the beginning. If you've made it this far, you should know enough about the Internet to join in, plug in, hop on, and check it out.

You've probably done the equivalent of "passing your Internet driver's test." By now, you probably have an account somewhere, either within your organization or through a public-access provider and have mastered the basics of creating, sending, and reading e-mail; reading and posting to Usenet Newsgroups; doing remote login and file transfer; and using Internet navigators. I presume you've sent and received a few dozen e-mail messages, joined (and unjoined) a few Usenet Newsgroups and a mailing list or two, probably tried Gopher or some other navigator, and gotten at least one file sent to you by e-mail. You may have decided you like using Unix (or not). You've probably concocted a "signature" file, and I suspect you find yourself occasionally using smiley-face emoticons without thinking it's the least bit strange :-) to do so.

You may also have begun to get a sense of what you want to do here and where to go to do it. I hope you've begun to find communities and resources of interest to you—or begun to help create them.

As you've seen, the Internet is a "Wonder of the World" in itself, representing years of work by thousands of people all around the world. You have the opportunity, even as an individual new user, to make a major contribution, if you so choose—invent the next "archie" or "publish" the next popular list of resources. You may be the person instrumental in getting schools and libraries in your town hooked up to the Internet and become their first Internet trainer. Or, you may choose to simply be "just a user."

Again, the Internet can easily become a way of working, a career, a community, and a home (not to mention an "infinite time sink"). But don't forget that there are a lot of other folks out there who aren't on the Internet (yet); there will always be times when it makes more sense to "use the phone, Luke," send a fax, put hardcopy in the mail, or even pay a visit in person. On the other hand, there will be many other times—more, as you become experienced in using them, and start to "think Internet"—when using e-mail, a Usenet Newsgroup, or other Internet services will be the right way to go.

I hope this book has helped you make sense of the Internet and learn to begin to use it and its myriad services. When I began using the Internet in 1983, there were no books like this available—and no navigator tools like archie or Gopher to make its use easier. For users like you in the 1990s, the Internet offers immeasurably more riches and has become much easier to use. Check out a few more Newsgroups, see what new directories of services and resources have become available, try a new navigator tool—welcome to the Internet.

Appendix

# Third-Party TCP/IP Software for Your Computer

TCP/IP software, including the protocol stack and popular applications, is readily available for most types of computers. If you have a Unix workstation, TCP/IP is probably already included. Apple, Banyan, Digital Equipment, IBM, Microsoft, Novell, Sun, and other companies offer versions of TCP/IP for use with their microcomputer and LAN-oriented products. Third-party commercial, shareware, and freeware TCP/IP software is also available for most of these platforms. Software available includes the TCP/IP networking software, either individually or bundled in with the TCP/IP networking software:

- Applications such as **telnet,** FTP, **finger,** etc.
- "On-line" and "off-line" programs for reading e-mail and Usenet News
- Serial protocols such as PPP, SLIP, and XRemote, for connecting via phone lines

Here's information on selected third-party TCP/IP products for leading personal computer environments. This list in no way claims to be complete or an endorsement of the products and companies mentioned. You may want to contact a local Internet public-access site or user group for your type of computer and see what they recommend; also check the advertisements in the appropriate trade magazines.

### For DOS and Windows systems

PC/TCP
FTP Software, Inc.
2 High Street
North Andover, MA 01845-2620
(508) 685-4000
Fax: 508-794-4477
E-mail: sales@ftp.com

BW/TCP
Beame & Whiteside Software Ltd.
P.O. Box 8130
Dundas, Ontario L9H 5E7
CANADA
(416) 765-0822
Fax: 416-765-0815
E-mail: sales@bws.com

## For the Apple Macintosh

TCP/ConnectII
InterCon Systems Corporation
950 Herndon Parkway
Herndon, VA 22070
1-800-638-2968
703-709-9890
Fax: 703-709-9896
E-mail: sales@intercon.com

## For Amigas

AmigaTcp package (KA9Q for Amigas)
Fish disk 225 from the FISH collection

(Available from popular Internet Amiga archives,
or try your local Amiga users group)

Appendix

# B

# Common Editors on Unix Systems and How to Exit Them

As a computer user, one of the types of programs you'll be using frequently is a text editor. Teaching you how to use a text editor is beyond the scope of this book—I don't know which ones you have available or which one you'll decide you like best. Several are standard, included as part of most versions of Unix or installed by system administrators—for example, **ed**, **ex**, **emacs**, and **vi**. Some e-mail systems include their own text-entry editors. What is worth covering in this book is how to *exit* (quit, leave, get out of) some of the more common (I hesitate to say "popular") text editors found on Unix systems. You can easily find yourself "trapped" in an unfamiliar editor by typing "ed" instead of "emacs" or making other mistakes. Here's how to figure out which one you've invoked and how to get out.

## ed

**ed** ("ed" or "ee-dee") is an old line-oriented editor. This means you don't see the file, or even any part of it, except when you give commands to print (display) lines. When you invoke **ed,** it tells you how many characters are in the file. For example:

```
% ed resume
3362
```

Being in **ed** can feel like being in the Twilight Zone if you're not used to it, as there's no way to tell what's going on. To exit **ed,** type **q<RETURN>** at the beginning of a line. (Hit <RETURN> first, if you aren't at the beginning of a line.)

```
% ed myfile
329
q<RETURN>
%
```

### emacs

**emacs** (pronounced "ee-macs") is a visual screen-oriented text editor and one of the more popular editors among programmers. Look for the word "emacs" on the screen as the program starts up. To exit emacs, type **Control-X Control-C.** If you have made any changes to the file during the session, **emacs** will ask you whether or not you want to save these changes; for example:

```
Save file /users/lgulliver/triplog? (y or n)
```

To save these changes, answer **y<RETURN>.**

### ex

**ex** ("ee-ex"), also known under the name **edit,** is another old line editor. **ex** gives you a little more information when you start it: the number of lines and characters in the file. To exit from **ex,** at the colon enter **q<RETURN>** as follows:

```
% ex myfile
"mfile" 6 lines, 391 characters
:q<RETURN>
%
```

### vi

**vi** (Visual Interactive editor, usually pronounced "vee-eye," although some say "veye") is a version of **ex** that displays the current file on the screen. A ~ character at the beginning of a line indicates you're between the end of the file and the bottom of the screen. To exit **vi,** type **:q<RETURN> vi** lets you invoke **ex**; to exit from this mode, type **<ESCAPE>:q** a few times, then try **:q<RETURN>** again.

### Mail Default Dumb Text-Entry Editor

Many e-mail systems include a "default" text-entry editor, which lets you enter text and make corrections only to the current line of text. To exit, try either **.<RETURN>** or **Control-D** at the beginning of a line. If none of these work, try one or more of these:

**Control-Z.** If you are working within a Unix shell that supports *job control,* this will pause your current activity and get you to a Unix shell prompt. You haven't quit the editor, but from here you may be able to determine what it was you escaped from. (Try examining your current processes with the **ps** command.)

**Control-C.** Good for getting out of noninteractive programs.

**Control-D.** The definitive "End of File" signal (this may log you out in the process).

**Control-Q** If you "paused" things by entering **Control-S** or the <PAUSE> key, this should "unfreeze" things. Now go try **Control-Z, Control-C,** or **Control-D** again.

**Control-]** or other **telnet** escape character. If you've connected via **telnet,** escape back to the **telnet** prompt and give the **telnet close** command.

If you're connected via dial-up, and none of this works, end the telecommunications session, unplug the phone line, or turn off the modem. If none of these work, call your systems administrator.

Appendix

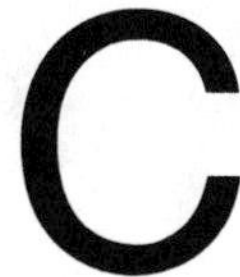

# InterNIC Access Information

Here's information on how to access the information and services provided by the NSFnet Internet Network Information Center (InterNIC) as of April 1993.

## InterNIC—General Information

The "top-level" information sources for the InterNIC are:

*1-800-444-4345.* (voice response "phone tree" which will direct your call to appropriate part of InterNIC).

*Gopher.* gopher.internic.net (top-level menu pointers to all InterNIC gopher servers).

*E-mail.* info@internic.net (queries sent to this mailbox will be read and answered/forwarded by the InterNIC Referral Desk staff).

*InterNIC InterActive newsletter.* To subscribe, send a message to interactive-request@internic.net (or call). Your message should indicate which format(s) you want: e-mail and/or hardcopy. (You may want to see if your site can receive it as a Usenet Newsgroup.)

## InterNIC Information Services

General Atomics
P.O. Box 85608
San Diego, CA
619-455-4600
Fax: 619-455-3900

E-mail: info@is.internic.net (general address)
scout@internic.net (regarding tools, resources, and services)

*Referral desk hours.* Monday through Friday, 5:00 a.m. to 7:00 p.m. (Pacific Daylight time)

*Gopher server.* gopher.internic.net

*Anonymous-FTP server.* is.internic.net (see directory "infosource")

*WAIS server.* internic-infosource (selected from list of WAIS servers)

*Local clients available via remote login (**telnet** remote login to is.internic.net).* gopher (login as "gopher")

*E-mail server(s).* mailserv@is.internic.net

To use the Information Services mailserver, put commands in message body. Command words are case-insensitive; filenames are case-sensitive. Commands include:

| | |
|---|---|
| **send help** | To get general "how to use" information |
| **index** | To get list of filenames of documents available |

### Mailing lists

To join, send mail to listserv@is.internic.net; put commands in the message body:

```
subscribe mailing-listname your name
```

for example:

```
subscribe nis Alice Liddell
```

Mailing lists include:

*announce@is.internic.net.* Moderated announcements only mailing list of information about the InterNIC and its services.

*net-happenings@is.internic.net.* Moderated announcements of new Internet "Network Information Services," such as tools and resources; will include forwardings and summaries from other mailing lists and Newsgroups, for Internet users and service providers who want to minimize how many lists and Newsgroups they follow.

### InterNIC Directory & Database Services

AT&T
5000 Hadley Road, Room 1B13
South Plainfield, NJ 07080
908-668-6587
Fax: 908-668-3763

admin@ds.internic.net

*Gopher server.* gopher.internic.net

*Anonymous-FTP server.* ds.internic.net

*WAIS server.* ds.internic.net

*X.500 QUIPU Directory Service Agent (DSA).* Access DSA from any remote Directory User Agent (DUA)

*E-mail server(s).* mailserv@ds.internic.net; archie@ds.internic.net

*Local clients available via remote login (**telnet** to ds.internic.net):*

general client (offers menu of all available client service; log in as "guest" or "newuser")

Gopher (log in as "gopher")

WAIS (log in as "wais")

archie (log in as "archie")

X.500 QUIPU Directory User Agent (DUA) (log in as "x500"); Access DUA from **telnet** to ds.internic.net, login as "x500"

Netfind (log in as "netfind")

Tutorial Login (log in as "guest" or "newuser")

*E-mail server.* mailserv@ds.internic.net

The Directory Services mailserver lets you do:

- White and yellow pages queries
- "ls" directory searches of anonymous-FTP holdings and retrieve files, specifying encoding
- Name and keyword searches of documents and resources

To use the Database & Directories mailserver, put commands in the message body. The contents of the Subject: field will be ignored. Command words are case-insensitive, command parameters are case-sensitive. Each request message must be limited to a maximum number of queries or files, up to 500K per file transfer; requests will be given only up to 15-seconds processing time. For information on how to use this mailserver, including its commands and their syntax, send a message with "help" in the body.

## InterNIC Registration Services

Network Solutions, Inc. (NSI)
505 Huntmar Park Drive
Herndon, VA
703-742-4757

*E-mail:*

hostmaster@rs.internic.net (host, domain, network changes, and updates)

action@rs.internic.net (computer operations)

mailserv@rs.internic.net (automatic mail service)

*Gopher server.* gopher.internic.net

*Anonymous-FTP server.* rs.internic.net

*Local clients available via remote login (**telnet** to rs.internic.net):*

gopher (log in as "gopher")

wais (log in as "wais")

whois (log in as "whois")

*E-mail server.* mailserv@rs.internic.net

To use the Registration Services mailserver, put request in message header. Commands include:

| | |
|---|---|
| HELP | To get help information and a list of current services |
| INDEX | To get the master list of available index files |
| NETINFO filename | To get a designated file (use "index" for a list of files) |
| RFC nnn | To get RFC #nnn (use "index" for a list of RFCs) |
| SEND filename | To get a fully specified filename. |
| WHOIS name | To get **whois** information about name (use "help" for information on how to use **whois**) |

Appendix

# Free! A Simple Internet Front-End Unix ShellScript

No matter how many Internet navigators, front ends, and other tools you get, none is likely to keep track of the commands and utilities you care about. Here's an easy way to make a note of them once and then be reminded when you forget—all you have to do is remember to type **ho.**

Once you're comfortable working with your text editor, you can enter and alter this script to suit you. (Pay attention to the placement and matching of the punctuation marks, or you'll get errors. Be sure to include the **;;** at the end of each choice.) You can even add a line in your login file such as:

```
echo "Remember - type 'ho' for a reminder Internet list"

#!/bin/sh
: ho - Internet front end alias-like batch file
: Created by Daniel P. Dern, October 1992
: syntax ho service args—give list if no params

: test for presence of parameters, display list if none.
case ${1:-MENU} in

mail )
 echo "ho: Invoking e-mail program..."
 pine ${2} ;;

usenet )
 echo "ho: Invoking Usenet newsreader..."
 trn ${2} ;;

ftp )
 echo "ho: Invoking FTP file transfer program..."
```

```
 ftp ${2} ;;

telnet )
echo "ho:Invoking telnet remote-login program..."
telnet ${2} ;;

finger )
echo "ho: Finger-ing status of specified user..."
finger ${2?"Um, like, for who, dude? (No username specified)"} ;;

pink )
echo "ho: Grep (substring match) for someone in my .mailrc
file..."
 grep ${2:?"Hey, ya gotta gimme a name!"} ${HOME}/.mailrc ;;

archie)
 shift
 echo "ho: Invoke archie, do case-insensitive substring match"
 echo " 10 maxhits, piped through more"
 archie -s -m10 ${1} | more ;;

gopher )
 echo "ho: Entering GopherSpace ('b' to view bookmarks)"
 gopher ${2} ;;

hytel )
 echo "ho: Invoking HYTELNET hypercard telnet to Internet services"
 hytelnet ;;

netfind)
 echo "ho: Invoking netfind: login as netfind, no password..."
 telnet bruno.cs.colorado.edu ;;

nic )
 echo "ho: Opening Gopher connection to InterNIC Gopher server..."
 gopher gopher.internic.net ;;

wais)
 echo "ho: Connecting to TMC WAIS Server; login as 'wais'"
 telnet quake.think.com ;;

web)
 echo "ho: Connecting to WorldWideWeb in Switzerland..."
 telnet info.cern.ch ;;

MENU )
 echo "ho services currently defined:

BASIC SERVICES:
mail      - read or send e-mail
usenet    - read Usenet Newsgroups
ftp       - Do file-transfers (use 'anonymous' or 'ftp' for
            anonymous-FTP logins)
telnet    - Do remote-login
finger    - Check status of specified user
pink      - Grep to see if someone's in your .mailrc file
```

```
NAVIGATOR, FRONT-ENDS AND OTHER SERVICES:
archie    - invoke archie (give program-name)(substring match)
gopher    - enter Gopherspace (give '-b' to view your bookmarks)
hytel     - hypercard telnet (libraries and other services)
nic       - connect to InterNIC Gopher
netfind   - Internet e-mail name searcher
wais      - telnet to public-access WAIS client (login as 'wais')
web       - telnet to public-access WorldWideWeb client
MENU      - Display this message (default if no choice given)

Other things to try: irc (Internet Relay Chat), talk, fortune " ;;

*)     echo "No such service listed with ho" ;;

esac
```

Appendix

# Internet-Related Organizations Worth Knowing About

Coalition for Networked Information (CNI)
1527 New Hampshire St. NW
Washington, D.C. 20036
1-202-232-2466
Fax: 202-462-7842
Paul Evan Peters
paul@cni.org

Coalition for School Networking (CoSN)
(focuses on K–12 networking)
1112 Sixteenth Street NW, Suite 600
Washington, D.C. 20036
1-202-872-4200
Fax: 202-872-4318
John Clement, Director
clemtn@educom.edu

Coalition for Research & Education Networking (CREN)
1112 Sixteenth Street NW, Suite 600
Washington, D.C. 20036
202-872-4200
Fax: 202-872-4318
E-mail: postmaster@cren.net.edu

EDUCOM (a nonprofit consortium of universities, colleges, and other institutions)
1112 Sixteenth Street NW, Suite 600
Washington, D.C. 20036
202-872-4200
Fax: 202-872-4318
E-mail: info@bitnic.educom.edu

Federation of American Research Networks (FARNET)
Laura Breeden, Executive Director
114 Waltham Street, Suite 12
Lexington, MA 02173
800-723-2763
617-860-9445
Fax: 617-860-9345
breeden@farnet.org

Internet CERT (Computer Emergency Response Team)
(Clearinghouse for Internet security concerns, including 24-hour hot-line)
Software Engineering Institute
Carnegie Mellon University
Pittsburgh, PA 15213-3890
1-412-268-7090
cert@cert.org

Internet Society
1985 Preston White Drive, Suite 100
Reston, VA 22091
1-703-648-9888
Fax: 1-703-620-0913
E-mail: isoc@nri.reston.va.us

The Interop Company (runs the INTEROP Conferences)
480 San Antonio Road, Suite 100
Mountain View, CA 94040
1-800-INTEROP (voice)
Fax: 415-949-1779
E-mail: info@interop.com

# Bibliography

Depending on your definition, the "Internet bookshelf" threatens to fill a room of its own. Here's some suggested places to go for more on specific topics and the Internet in general, including information about books referred to in chapters of this book. (For more information, see RFC 1432, "Recent Internet Books," March 1993.)

## Jargon and Smiley-Faces Dictionaries


Godin, Seth, *The Smiley Dictionary: Cool Things to Do with Your Key Board,* Peachpit Press, Berkeley, CA, 77 pp.

Raymond, Eric S., and Guy Steele (eds.), *The New Hacker's Dictionary,* M.I.T. Press, Cambridge, MA, 1991, 453 pp.

Sanderson, David, *Smileys,* O'Reilly & Associates, Sebastopol, CA, 1993, 96 pp.


## Internet Resource Guides and Directories

The number of general and special-interest Internet guides and directories seems to grow almost weekly. Here's some to consider:


Hardie, Edward, and Vivian Neou, *Internet: Mailing Lists* (SRI Internet Information Series), PTR Prentice-Hall, Englewood Cliffs, NJ, 1993, 311 pp. Information about the major Internet and BITNET electronic mailing lists, including how to join, where they're archived, etc.

Kehoe, Brendan P., *Zen and the Art of the Internet—A Beginner's Guide,* PTR Prentice-Hall, Englewood Cliffs, NJ, 1993, 112 pp.

Krol, Ed, *The Whole Internet User's Guide and Catalog,* O'Reilly & Associates, Inc., Sebastopol, CA, 1992, 376 pp.

Lane, Elizabeth S., and Craig A. Summerhill, *An Internet Primer for Information Professionals: A Basic Guide to Networking Technology,* Meckler Corp., Westport, CT, 1992, 200 pp.

LaQuey, Tracy, and Jeanne C. Ryer, *The Internet Companion: A Beginner's Guide to Global Networking,* Addison-Wesley, Reading, MA, October 1992, 208 pp.

Marine, April, with Susan Kirkpatrick, Vivian Neou, and Carol Ward, *Internet: Getting Started,* (SRI Internet Information Series), PTR Prentice-Hall, Englewood Cliffs, NJ, 1993, 360 pp. For more in-depth information about hooking up to the Internet and about Internet Service Providers.

*The New User's Guide to Useful and Unique Resources on the Internet,* NYSERNET, Syracuse, NY 13244.

Polly, Jean Armour, "Surfing the INTERNET: An Introduction," Version 2.0.2, December 16, 1992. Available via anonymous-FTP from nysernet.org, directory /pub/guides, file surfing.2.0.2.txt.

Tennant, Roy, John Ober, and Anne G. Lipow, *Crossing the Internet Threshold: An Instructional Handbook,* Library Solutions Press, Berkeley, CA, 1993, 142 pp. Includes helpful fact sheets on various Internet tools from FTP and **telnet** to archie, gopher, WAIS, and WorldWideWeb.

## Other Books about the Internet


Malamud, Carl, *Exploring the Internet—A Technical Travelogue,* PTR Prentice-Hall, Englewood Cliffs, NJ, 1992, 379 pp.

Stoll, Clifford, *The Cuckoo's Egg: Tracking a Spy through the Maze of Computer Espionage,* Doubleday, New York, 1989, 332 pp. The definitive "Internet adventure book."


## Essential Internet Reference Books


Frey, Donnalyn, and Rick Adams, *!%@:: A Dictionary of Electronic Mail Addressing and Networks,* O'Reilly & Associates, Sebastopol, CA, 1993.

Hunt, Craig: *TCP/IP Network Administration,* Sebastopol, CA, O'Reilly & Associates, 1992, 471 pp. For system administrators.

LaQuey, Tracey L. (ed.), *A User's Directory of Computer Networks,* Digital Press, Bedford, MA, 1990, 630 pp.

Quarterman, John S., *The Matrix: Computer Networks and Conferencing Systems Worldwide,* Digital Press, Bedford, MA, 1990, 746 pp.


## Further Readings on Selected Topics

### For more about IP naming and addressing:


Carl-Mitchell, Smoot, and John S. Quarterman, Texas Internet Consulting, "Naming," *RS/Magazine,* March 1992.

Gerber, Barry, "IP Routing: Learn to Follow the Yellow Brick Road," *Network Computing,* April 1992, pp. 98–104. About IP addresses (ABCDE, binary<->dotted decimal notation, subnet masking).


### To learn more about Unix:


Birns, Peter M., Patrick Brown, and John C. C. Muster, *UNIX for People,* Prentice-Hall, Englewood Cliffs, NJ, 1985.

O'Reilly, Tim (ed.), *UNIX Power Tools,* O'Reilly & Associates and Bantam Books, 1993, 1119 pp. Unix wizards offer their best Unix shellscripts, tips, hints, administration gotchas, and lots more.

Quarterman, John S., *Etiquette and Ethics,* ConneXions (Interop Company), vol. 3, no. 4 (1989), pp. 12–16.

"The UNIX System," AT&T Bell Laboratories Technical Journal, October 1984, vol. 63, no. 9, Part 2. An excellent collection of mildly technical articles about Unix.


### To learn more about security:


Denning, Peter J., (ed.), *Computers Under Attack: Intruders, Worms, and Viruses,* ACM Press/Addison-Wesley, Reading, MA, 1990; 574 pp. A definitive collection of essays and articles about computer and network security.


## Magazines and Newsletters


*Boardwatch Magazine: Guide to Online Information Services and Electronic Bulletin Boards*
7586 West Jewell Ave., Suite 200
Lakewood, CO 80232
1-800-933-6038 (subscriptions)
Monthly, $36/year

*ConneXions, The Interoperability Report*
The Interop Company
480 San Antonio Road, Suite 100
Mountain View, CA 94040
1-800-INTEROP
E-mail: connexions@interop.com
Monthly newsletter, $150/year

*Internet World*
Meckler Corporation
11 Ferry Lane West
Westport, CT 06880
1-800-MECKLER
1-203-226-6967
Fax: 1-203-454-5840
E-mail: meckler@jvnc.net
6X/year magazine, $29/year (individual, K–12), $49/year (institutional)

*Matrix News*
1106 Clayton Lane, Suite 500W
Austin, TX 78723
E-mail: mids@tic.com
Phone: 1-512-451-7602
Fax: 1-512-450-1436
Monthly newsletter, $30/year

*Sun Expert* (especially the "Ask Mr. Protocol" column)
Computer Publishing Group
1330 Beacon Street
Brookline, MA 02146
617-739-7002
Fax: 617-739-7003
Monthly, free to qualified subscribers; else $60/year in the United States

# Glossary

This glossary contains short definitions of key Internet, Unix, and Usenet words, phrases, abbreviations, acronyms, usually not defined elsewhere in this book—including some that don't occur in this book but which you're likely to encounter on your Internet voyages. (Many have been taken from RFC 1392, "Internet Users' Glossary," with attribution.) If you don't see a definition here, check the index. Other good resources to check include your local on-line system help, the Unix manual pages, on-line glossaries and dictionaries available via the Internet, and printed Internet, Unix, Usenet, and computer and networking glossaries and dictionaries. In particular:

- *The Hacker's Dictionary* (a.k.a. the Jargon file), available on-line in WAISed form and in book form
- RFC 1392 (a.k.a. FYI 18), "Internet Users' Glossary," Tracy LaQuey Parker and Gary Malkin
- RFC 1325 (a.k.a. FYI 4) "Q/A—for New Internet Users"

**Acceptable Use Policy (AUP)** The official policy statement regarding use of a network (e.g., the NSFnet), or a computer system (e.g., World).

**address resolution** "Conversion of an Internet address into the corresponding physical address." (*Source:* RFC 1392)

**aTdHvAaNnKcSe, AtDhVaAnNkCsE** "Thanks in advance," usually used in a message asking for something. Also seen as TIA.

**article** A posting in a Usenet Newsgroup. Each article is usually held in a separate file.

**ASCII** American Standard Code for Information Interchange. A standard numeric encoding of characters widely used in the computer industry.

**AUP** *See* Acceptable Use Policy.

**authentication** Verifying the identity of a person (e.g., you) or computer process (e.g., a command from a network management system).

**BCNU** Be seein' you.

**Berkeley Internet Name Domain (BIND)** "Implementation of a DNS server developed and distributed by the University of California at Berkeley. Many Internet hosts run

BIND, and it is the ancestor of many commercial BIND implementations." (*Source:* RFC 1392)

**Birds of a Feather (BOF, also BoF)** Informal discussion group, usually for a specific topic. Often a mechanism for informal and/or unofficial meetings at conferences.

**BOF** *See* Birds of a Feather.

**bounce, bounced** E-mail being returned because it couldn't be delivered, with diagnostic error messages from the e-mail software showing that it tried. On long messages, only the beginning of the actual message is returned after the first bounce.

**bozo filter** *See* kill file.

**BTW** By the way.

**cyberspace** Meanings include: the universe of computers, programs, and data; perceiving and inhabiting this universe as a virtual reality; or society from this perspective. Cyberspace inhabitants include cybernauts, cyberpunks, etc. First popular usage: William Gibson in his novel *Neuromancer.*

**/dev/null** A pseudo-file in the Unix file system which can be written to but not read. The computer equivalent of the military "tell it to the chaplain."

**dot address (dotted decimal notation)** "The common notation for IP addresses, in the form A.B.C.D, where each letter represents, in decimal, one byte of a four byte IP address." (*Source:* RFC 1392)

**EFF** *See* Electronic Frontier Foundation. "A foundation established to address social and legal issues arising from the impact on society of the increasingly pervasive use of computers as a means of communication and information distribution." (*Source:* RFC 1392)

**FAQ** Frequently Asked Question; in general, FAQ refers to a document (on-line or printed) containing Frequently Asked Questions and their answers.

**feed** *See* Newsfeed.

**flame** "A strong opinion and/or criticism of something, usually as a frank inflammatory statement, in an electronic mail message. It is common to precede a flame with an indication of pending fire (i.e., FLAME ON!). Flame Wars occur when people start flaming other people for flaming when they shouldn't have." (*Source:* RFC 1392)

**For Your Information (FYI)** "A subseries of RFCs that are not technical standards or descriptions of protocols. FYIs convey general information about topics related to TCP/IP or the Internet. See also: Request For Comments, STD." (*Source:* RFC 1392)

**foo, foo bar** Common "placeholder terms" or generic names, as in "Appends file foo," or "Grep for the string foo in file bar."

**FWIW** For what it's worth.

**FYI** *See* For Your Information.

**<grin>** Presmiley emoticon; similarly <snicker>, <SIGH>, etc.

**header** "The portion of a packet, preceding the actual data, containing source and destination addresses, and error checking and other fields. A header is also the part of an electronic mail message that precedes the body of a message and contains, among other things, the message originator, date and time." (*Source:* RFC 1392)

**IAB** *See* Internet Architecture Board.

**IANAL** I am not a lawyer.

**IESG** *See* Internet Engineering Steering Group.

**IETF** *See* Internet Engineering Task Force.

**IMHO** In my humble opinion.

**IMO** In my opinion.

**IMNSHO** In my not so humble opinion.

**Internaut** Someone who uses the Internet.

**Internet Architecture Board (IAB)** "The technical body that oversees the development of the Internet suite of protocols. It has two task forces: the IETF and the IRTF. 'IAB' previously stood for Internet Activities Board. See also: Internet Engineering Task Force, Internet Research Task Force." (*Source:* RFC 1392)

**Internet Engineering Steering Group (IESG)** "The IESG is composed of the IETF Area Directors and the IETF Chair. It provides the first technical review of Internet standards and is responsible for day-to-day "management" of the IETF. See also: Internet Engineering Task Force." (*Source:* RFC 1392)

**Internet Engineering Task Force (IETF)** "The IETF is a large, open community of network designers, operators, vendors, and researchers whose purpose is to coordinate the operation, management and evolution of the Internet, and to resolve short-range and mid-range protocol and architectural issues. It is a major source of proposals for protocol standards which are submitted to the IAB for final approval. The IETF meets three times a year and extensive minutes are included in the IETF Proceedings. See also: Internet Architecture Board." (*Source:* RFC 1392)

**Internet Protocol (IP)** "The Internet Protocol, defined in STD 5, RFC 791, is the network layer for the TCP/IP Protocol Suite. It is a connectionless, best-effort packet switching protocol." (*Source:* RFC 1392)

**Internet Research Steering Group (IRSG)** "The 'governing body' of the IRTF. See also: Internet Research Task Force." (*Source:* RFC 1392)

**Internet Research Task Force (IRTF)** "The IRTF is chartered by the IAB to consider long-term Internet issues from a theoretical point of view. It has Research Groups, similar to IETF Working Groups, which are each tasked to discuss different research topics. Multicast audio/video conferencing and privacy enhanced mail are samples of IRTF output. See also: Internet Architecture Board, Internet Engineering Task Force, Privacy Enhanced Mail." (*Source:* RFC 1392)

**IRSG** *See* Internet Research Steering Group.

**IRTF** *See* Internet Research Task Force.

**ISOC** The Internet Society.

**kill file** The file(s) defining people, topics, and threads you don't want to see Usenet articles from; more generally, "the list of people/topics you intend to ignore."

**LBJ** Light bulb joke. There is a canonical list of LBJs, indeed, canonical lists of many jokes, available via Usenet or the Internet. *See also* YA.

**line eater** Some old versions of Usenet software would "eat" the first line or two or users' postings. For some years after this was fixed, posters would include "food for the line eater" at the start of messages not essential to their posting, just in case.

**lurker** Someone who participates in a mailing list, Usenet Newsgroup, etc., by reading but not posting. Encouraged for beginners as a way to become familiar with a given community or group (before posting a basic or foolish question, for example). The term is not intended as a pejorative, although it is occasionally used that way.

**Mail Exchange Record (MX Record)** "A DNS resource record type indicating which host can handle mail for a particular domain." (*Source:* RFC 1392)

**mail exploder** "Part of an electronic mail delivery system which allows a message to be delivered to a list of addresses. Mail exploders are used to implement mailing lists. Users send messages to a single address and the mail exploder takes care of delivery to the individual mailboxes in the list." (*Source:* RFC 1392, from RFC 1208)

**martian, martian packet** "A humorous term applied to packets that turn up unexpectedly on the wrong network because of bogus routing entries. Also used as a name for a packet which has an altogether bogus (nonregistered or ill-formed) internet address." (*Source:* RFC 1392, from RFC 1208)

**MX Record** *See* Mail Exchange Record.

**name resolution** "The process of mapping a name into its corresponding address." (*Source:* RFC 1392, from RFC 1208) An example is from a Fully Qualified Domain Name to its IP address, or vice-versa.

**net.gods** People who have been involved in the Internet/Usenet long enough to have strong opinions about some aspect of the Usenet or Internet—and are often in a position to do something about them, if provoked. Don't mess with them casually.

**net.police** The mysterious, quasi-mythological enforcers of site, AUP, and Internet policies. Do they exist? Who are they? Are they reading every e-mail and Usenet message, watching your every move? You may find out.

**netiquette** "A pun on 'etiquette' referring to proper behavior on a network." (*Source:* RFC 1392)

**Netnews** Another name for Usenet, often refers to Usenet News when being received via the Internet, via NNTP.

**Network News Transfer Protocol (NNTP)** "A protocol, defined in RFC 977, for the distribution, inquiry, retrieval, and posting of news articles." (*Source:* RFC 1392)

**newsfeed** A source to obtain a regular "feed" of Usenet Newsgroups from.

**NNTP** *See* Network News Transfer Protocol.

**OB, OBJ** Obligatory joke (in addition to serious content of a message). *See* recursive.

**plugh** A magical word in the Adventure game. *See also* xyzzy.

**Point Of Presence (POP), Point of Presence (PoP)** "A site where there exists a collection of telecommunications equipment, usually digital leased lines and multi-protocol routers." (*Source:* RFC 1392)

**Post Office Protocol (POP)** "A protocol designed to allow single user hosts to read mail from a server. There are three versions: POP, POP2, and POP3. Latter versions are NOT compatible with earlier versions." (*Source:* RFC 1392)

**recursive** Something that refers to itself, as in "recursive program." *See* recursive.

**Request For Comments (RFC)** "The document series, begun in 1969, which describes the Internet suite of protocols and related experiments. Not all (in fact, very few) RFCs describe Internet standards, but all Internet standards are written up as

RFCs. The RFC series of documents is unusual in that the proposed protocols are forwarded by the Internet research and development community, acting on their own behalf, as opposed to the formally reviewed and standardized protocols that are promoted by organizations such as CCITT and ANSI. See also: For Your Information, STD." (*Source:* RFC 1392)

**RFC 822** The RFC that describes the format of the "envelopes" and message body for electronic mail messages.

**ROFL** Rolling on (the) floor laughing.

**RSN** Real Soon Now.

**RTFM** Read the manual (the "F" is silent); also, Read this fine manual.

**SIG** Special Interest Group.

**Simple Mail Transfer Protocol (SMTP)** A protocol, defined in STD 10, RFC 821, used to transfer electronic mail between computers. It is a server to server protocol, so other protocols are used to access the messages. (*Source:* RFC 1392); also, the protocol used by e-mail systems and gateways that support SMTP to deliver electronic mail.

**Simple Network Management Protocol (SNMP)** "The Internet standard protocol, defined in STD 15, RFC 1157, developed to manage nodes on an IP network. It is currently possible to manage wiring hubs, toasters, jukeboxes, etc." (*Source:* RFC 1392)

**smileys, smiley faces, emoticons** Combinations of alphanumeric and punctuation characters to represent facial expressions and figures, typically used to indicate tone of voice, emotion, or state of mind. To view a smiley face, tilt your head to the left, or the image to the right, until the left-hand side is at the top. See how :-) suddenly looks like a smiling face? There you go. Now go call your chiropractor, and next time tilt the monitor instead. There are hundreds of smiley faces; for example:

| | |
|---|---|
| [:] | User is a robot. |
| 8-) | User is wearing sunglasses. |
| E-:-) | User is a Ham radio operator. |

Many have multiple definitions; in general, there are no "official, absolute" definitions. Printed and on-line smiley dictionaries are available; as are programs to look them up or randomly display them.

**SMTP** *See* Simple Mail Transfer Protocol.

**snail mail** The postal service, used for sending hardcopy, books, etc. Pejorative when implying slowness relative to e-mail.

**SNMP** *See* Simple Network Management Protocol.

**spoilers, spoiler warnings** For messages about books, movies, comic books, etc., it's considered bad form to give away the ending or other important plot twists without warning, as it often *spoils* the potential enjoyment of the reader. Usually, something like "SPOILER WARNING" or "SPOILER AHEAD" is put several lines before the spoiler itself. If you can insert a Control-L character into your posting—interpreted by most Usenet reader software as a "break to new text page" character—do that.

**STD** "A subseries of RFCs that specify Internet standards. The official list of Internet standards is in STD 1. See also: For Your Information, Request For Comments." (*Source:* RFC 1392)

**string** A series of characters (e.g., a text string). No more string jokes please.

**summarize to the list, please (or will)** Replies to a query directed to one individual, who collects and hopefully organizes them and then posts this summary.

**TANSTAAFL** "There ain't no such thing as a free lunch" (origin, Robert Heinlein's book *The Moon Is a Harsh Mistress*).

**TLA** Three-Letter Acronym (sic).

**TN3270** "A variant of the **Telnet** program that allows one to attach to IBM mainframes and use the mainframe as if you had a 3270 or similar terminal." (*Source:* RFC 1392)

**Trojan Horse** "A computer program which carries within itself a means to allow the creator of the program access to the system using it. *See also* virus, worm. See RFC 1135." (*Source:* RFC 1392)

**TTFN** Ta-Ta for now.

**vanilla** The standard version, with no extra features.

**virus** "A program which replicates itself on computer systems by incorporating itself into other programs which are shared among computer systems. *See also* Trojan Horse, worm." (*Source:* RFC 1392)

**worm** "A computer program which replicates itself and is self-propagating. Worms, as opposed to viruses, are meant to spawn in network environments. Network worms were first defined by Shoch & Hupp of Xerox in ACM Communications (March 1982). The Internet worm of November 1988 is perhaps the most famous; it successfully propagated itself on over 6000 systems across the Internet. *See also* Trojan Horse, virus." (*Source:* RFC 1392)

**WRT** With regard to.

**X** "X is the name for TCP/IP based network-oriented window systems. Network window systems allow a program to use a display on a different computer. The most widely-implemented window system is X11—a component of MIT's Project Athena." (*Source:* RFC 1392)

**xyzzy** A magical word from the Adventure game. *See also* plugh.

**YA** Yet Another (e.g., yet another light bulb joke).

# Index

*Note*: The *f.* after a page number refers to a figure; the *n.* to a note; and the *t.* to a table.

## ABOUT THE AUTHOR

Daniel P. Dern (ddern@world.std.com) has been using and writing about the Internet for over a decade. A free-lance writer and editor of *Internet World* magazine, his articles have appeared in computer and network publications including *Byte*, *Datamation*, *Home Office Computing*, *InfoWorld*, *LAN Times*, and *Mac WEEK*. He also writes computer humor, science fiction, and musical comedy; has spoken at INTEROP conferences; and is a very amateur magician.

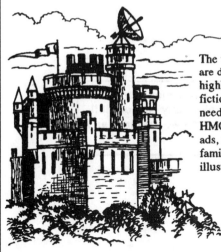

**This coupon is solely the offering of the manufacturer. Neither McGraw-Hill nor the author takes any responsibility for the fulfillment of this order nor do we endorse any of these products or services.**

**This coupon is solely the offering of the manufacturer. Neither McGraw-Hill nor the author takes any responsibility for the fulfillment of this order nor do we endorse any of these products or services.**

This coupon is solely the offering of the manufacturer. Neither McGraw-Hill nor the author takes any responsibility for the fulfillment of this order nor do we endorse any of these products or services.

This coupon is solely the offering of the manufacturer. Neither McGraw-Hill nor the author takes any responsibility for the fulfillment of this order nor do we endorse any of these products or services.

This coupon is solely the offering of the manufacturer. Neither McGraw-Hill nor the author takes any responsibility for the fulfillment of this order nor do we endorse any of these products or services.